THE AGE OF TITIAN

THE AGE OF TITIAN

VENETIAN RENAISSANCE ART FROM SCOTTISH COLLECTIONS

PETER HUMFREY · TIMOTHY CLIFFORD

AIDAN WESTON-LEWIS · MICHAEL BURY

NATIONAL GALLERIES OF SCOTLAND · 2004

Published by the Trustees of the National Galleries
of Scotland on the occasion of the exhibition *The Age of
Titian: Venetian Renaissance Art from Scottish Collections*
held at the Royal Scottish Academy Building, Edinburgh,
from 5 August to 5 December 2004.

© Trustees of the National Galleries of Scotland,
Edinburgh 2004

ISBN 1 903278 54 6 *paperback*

ISBN 1 903278 53 8 *hardback*

Catalogue edited by Aidan Weston-Lewis
Designed by Dalrymple
Typeset in Indigo by Brian Young
Printed in Belgium by Snoeck-Ducaju & Zoon

Front cover: Titian *Diana and Actaeon* (detail)
National Gallery of Scotland, Edinburgh on loan
from the Duke of Sutherland (cat.no.54)

Back cover: *Portrait Medallion of Titian and his Son Orazio*
National Museums of Scotland, Edinburgh (cat.no.202)

Frontispiece: Titian *Venus Anadyomene* (detail)
National Gallery of Scotland, Edinburgh
(cat.no.19)

CONTENTS

Lloyds TSB
Scotland

Lloyds TSB Scotland is especially pleased to support *The Age of Titian*, an exhibition which marks the completion of the Playfair Project and provides Scotland with a world-class venue for the arts.

We have forged a highly successful partnership with the National Galleries of Scotland over recent years; a partnership which has assisted in bringing major works, classic and modern, to Scotland and encouraged ever more visitors through the doors of our wonderful galleries.

The exhibition *The Age of Titian* brings together a stunning collection of Venetian Renaissance art from public and private collections. It's certain to be a major attraction throughout its four month run in this, Scotland's newest exhibition complex.

SUSAN RICE
Chief Executive, Lloyds TSB Scotland

FOREWORD

This exhibition follows hard on the heels of last year's huge success *Monet: The Seine and The Sea*, a show that attracted not only wide critical acclaim but also 173,000 visitors. The Monet show illumined a relatively little-known era in the artist's life and it was especially appropriate because its nucleus was formed around a Monet masterpiece in the National Gallery of Scotland's collection. Monet was one of the central figures in Impressionism, the breakaway movement that rebelled against French academic art and established entirely new critical criteria for artists in the western world. The show was mounted to mark the completion of the first phase of the Playfair Project – the opening of the modernised and radically refurbished Royal Scottish Academy building.

This exhibition, *The Age of Titian*, is a show about an age and not an individual artist, about grand, and perhaps at first sight, conventional old master paintings. But art in Venice during the age of Titian went through just as momentous a change as was engendered by Impressionism in France. The catalyst may have been that shadowy figure Giorgione, a creature still more of legend than of paint, but the real and sustained revolution happened with Titian. Titian's artistic persona was extraordinary and exceptional, with his rich painterly art developing in an utterly different direction from his immediate predecessors Bellini, Cima, Vivarini, and Catena. Here was *the* artist who taught his own, and subsequent generations, how to relish the range and opportunities for oil paint on canvas, and used his eye and mind to conjure up images using raw colour and texture in a way hardly dreamt of in contemporary central Italian painting, where other sorts of dramatic developments were taking place centred on the personalities of Leonardo, Michelangelo and Raphael. Their art, of course, had its effects on Venice, but Titian and his contemporaries and followers developed their own remarkable art that can convey intense religious emotion, provide magisterial portrait images, conjure up poetic idylls of Arcady or bring us up short with the most sharply observed naturalism. However, this exhibition is not just about a protean period of painting but about Venice and her all embracing artistic achievement over a century and a half. The exhibition covers paintings, drawings, prints, sculpture, glass, rock crystal, enamels, metalwork, maiolica, 'sgraffito' decorated earthenware, books and manuscripts. Perforce it overlooks architecture, music, and the arts of maritime warfare, all of which were equally crucial to the period. All of the exhibits either are, or historically were, in Scottish collections so this show provides us with an opportunity to assess the cultural impact of the city of Venice, the *Serenissima*, an ancient maritime republic, admittedly in decline but still opulent, vigorous and inspirational. The flowering of sixteenth-century Venice never fails to astonish and is on a par with fifth-century Athens, and fifteenth century Florence, or early twentieth-century Paris. The paradox of Venice at this time was why it flourished pictorially as it had never done before, when militarily it had been humiliated by the defeat of Agnadello in 1509 by the combined forces of France, Spain and the papacy. It was ravaged by famine in 1527 and 1528, and visited by plague in 1528 and 1575–7 and frequent epidemics of typhus.

Lord Norwich in his *History of Venice* (1982) goes some way to answer this question: *Whenever the law of the jungle prevails - and certainly no other law prevailed in Renaissance Europe – weakness must be concealed and full use must be made of any special gifts that providence has been pleased to bestow. If Venice had allowed any obvious signs of her economic or moral sickness to become evident to the outside world, her chances of survival would have been dangerously reduced: she took care not to do so. As for her special gifts, she possessed three. The first, her birthright was her unrivalled position in her lagoon, isolated and impregnable. The second, to some extent a corollary, was her innate knowledge and understanding of the sea and all that pertained to it. The third was her genius for splendour and parade.*

The flourishing of Scottish culture during the Age of Enlightenment drew inspiration from the rational architecture of Palladio, the enquiring ideas of free thinkers like Paolo Sarpi, and the political structure of a Republic that had lasted a thousand years. Venice provided an exemplar of a maritime nation, tolerant of religion, that had operated a sophisticated civil service and, after many years, an adroit diplomatic corps. Her special love in art for colour and the range of possibilities for oil paint exerted, admittedly through French followers, a powerful influence on Scottish artists in the nineteenth and twentieth centuries. The existence of the Venetian artefacts exhibited here in accessible collections both public and private exerted, and will continue to exert, a positive and lively impact on the cultural life in Scotland.

This exhibition could not have taken place were it not for the enthusiastic support of all the institutions and private individuals, both within Scotland and beyond its borders, who have kindly agreed to lend works. We are particularly indebted to our colleagues at the National Museums of Scotland, the National Library of Scotland, Glasgow Museums, and the Hunterian Art Gallery for the generosity of their loans. At the core of the exhibition are the great Titians that through the enlightened generosity of the previous and present Dukes of Sutherland have been on public view at the National Gallery of Scotland for almost sixty years.

Having myself been closely involved with this

project from the outset, I am well aware of the huge team effort that has gone into the realisation of the exhibition and the production of its catalogue. Professor Peter Humfrey, our guest curator for the paintings section of this exhibition, has not only researched and written the lion's share of the catalogue, but has also been closely involved in the selection of exhibits and in many other aspects of the show. We are extremely grateful to him for his unstinting commitment and enthusiasm for the project. Michael Bury kindly agreed to help select and to catalogue prints in the exhibition. Godfrey Evans at the National Museums of Scotland, and Helen Vincent, Iain Gordon Brown and Diana Webster at the National Library of Scotland, have all provided invaluable advice and catalogue entries relating to works in their collections. Anne Varick Lauder kindly contributed an entry on one of the Battista Franco drawings about which she has made important new discoveries (cat.no.99). The challenging task of organising and co-ordinating the exhibition has fallen to my colleague Aidan Weston-Lewis, who has also edited the catalogue. The publication of this substantial volume has been expertly overseen by Janis Adams and her colleagues Christine Thompson and David Simpson, and its elegant design is due to Robert Dalrymple. A great deal of conservation work has been undertaken for the exhibition – notably the full restoration of one of the Paris Bordon paintings from Glasgow and the Schiavone from Gosford (cat.nos.30 and 56). I am particularly grateful to Michael Gallagher, Lesley Stevenson, Donald Forbes, Graeme Gollan and Keith Morrison for their efforts. Also published here for the first time are the findings of the conservation of four of the Sutherland Titians undertaken some years ago by the former Keeper of Conservation, John Dick, and we are most grateful to him for his contributions. Anne Buddle, Agnes Valencak-Kruger and Alastair Patten have overseen the transport and installation arrangements with their customary efficiency. Charlotte Chessell has provided invaluable administrative support, and the task of typing up my indecipherable handwriting has fallen to my personal secretary Christine Bates, to whom I am particularly grateful.

A host of other people who have assisted in one way or another with the preparation of the exhibition appear in the list of acknowledgements and we are grateful to them all.

This has been, above all, a Scottish team effort and a fine operation of co-operation and partnership. By bringing these collections together to provide a clearer idea of the cultural achievements of the *Serenissima* in *The Age of Titian*, we hope to give delight to a very wide public and provide scholars with material, some of which may be little known to them.

Finally, I should like to say that this exhibition marks the opening, a year before time and on budget, of our Playfair Project, providing the people of Scotland with one of the finest exhibition complexes in Europe. Much credit for this goes to my Chairman, Brian Ivory, to his Trustees and to Michael Clarke, Director of the National Gallery of Scotland, ably assisted by Scott Robertson, Playfair Project Advisor. Had it not been for Michael Clarke attending to so much of the detail of this ambitious enterprise, I would not have had the time to devote to this exhibition.

Exhibitions such as this are very costly and cannot go forward without considerable sponsorship. This year we are yet again most grateful to Susan Rice, Chief Executive of Lloyds TSB Scotland, for her company's enthusiastic and most generous support. We would also like to thank the Samuel H. Kress Foundation who have supported the interpretative material connected with the exhibition, which we hope will take this important show to the widest possible audience.

SIR TIMOTHY CLIFFORD
Director-General, National Galleries of Scotland

ACKNOWLEDGEMENTS

The organisers of the exhibition and authors of the catalogue would like to thank the following people for their help: Fiona Anderson, Tony Axe, Alessandro Ballarin, Davide Banzato, Herbert Beck, Andrea Bellieni, Suzanne Benfield, Caroline Best, Peter Black, Piero Boccardo, Julian Brooks, Beverly Louise Brown, Christopher Brown, David Alan Brown, Iain Gordon Brown, John Brown, David Bryant, Polly Buston, Johnny Bute, Caroline Campbell, Ilay Campbell, Mungo Campbell, Jane Carmichael, Hugo Chapman, Keith Christiansen, Rosalyn Clancey, Martin Clayton, Patricia Collins, Roberto Contini, David Cranstoun, Pat Crichton, Anthony Crichton-Stuart, Alastair Cunningham, Steve Dale, Glenys Davies, Jim Devenport, Elsa DeZuanni, Simon Dickinson, Jill Dunkerton, Jeff Dunn, David Ekserdjian, Susan Elliot, Donato Esposito, Godfrey Evans, Miguel Falomir, Gabriele Finaldi, Donald Forbes, Duncan Forbes, David Franklin, Michael Gallagher, Olive Geddes, Catherine Goguel, Emilie Gordenker, Ian Gow, Deborah Gribbon, Alexander Hamilton, Vivien Hamilton, David Hemsoll, Lee Hendrix, James Holloway, Allan Hood , Charles Hope, Deborah Howard, Deborah Hunter, Valerie Hunter, David Jaffé, Paul Joannides, Nicola Kalinsky, Laurence B. Kanter, Jan Kelch, Luigi Koelliker, David Landau, James Laurenson, Bruce Lenman, Eckart Lingenauber, Emilio Lippi, Christopher Lloyd, Stephen Lloyd, Julia Lloyd Williams, Mauro Lucco, Jack Mackenzie, J. Patrice Marandel, Giorgio Marini, Ellen McAdam, Bridget McConnell, Brenda McGoff, Elizabeth McGrath, Andrew McLean, Kate Mitchell, Philippe de Montebello, Minna Moore-Ede, Stanley Moss, Peta Motture, Giovanna Nepi Scirè, Arnold Nesselrath, Mark O'Neill, Helen Nicoll, William O'Reilly, Linda Padgett, Giuseppe Pavanello, Nando Peretti, Francesca Pivirotto, Carol Plazzotta, Earl A. Powell III, Roger Rearick, Antonia Reeve, Andrea L. Rich, Gordon Rintoul, Kate Robertson, Francesco Rossi, Francis Russell, Jochen Sander, Charles Saumarez-Smith, Scott Schaefer, Charlotte Schreiter, Mhairi Scott, Sheila Scott, Helen Smailes, Polly Smith, Daniela Sogliani, Paul Spencer-Longhurst, Anna Maria Spiazzi, Michael Tavuzzi, Jacqueline Thalmann, Katrina Thomson, Ken Thorburn, Ennio Troili, Winnie Tyrrell, Richard Verdi, Giovanni C. F. Villa, Martyn Wade, David M. Walker, Robert Wenley, Catherine Whistler, Lucy Whitaker, Timothy Wilson, Jeremy Wood, Clara Young and Yvonne Zafran.

Peter Humfrey would also like to acknowledge his gratitude for the Research Leave Award he received from the AHRB (Arts and Humanities Research Board) and the Research Grant he received from the British Academy.

LENDERS TO THE EXHIBITION

The Barber Institute of Fine Arts,
University of Birmingham

Berlin, Staatliche Museen zu Berlin, Gemäldegalerie

The Duke of Buccleuch and Queensberry KT

Sir Robert Clerk Bt

The Dominican Friars in Scotland

Dundee City Council, McManus Galleries

The National Library of Scotland, Edinburgh

The National Museums of Scotland, Edinburgh

Glasgow Museums

Glasgow University, The Hunterian Art Gallery

The Collection of Hopetoun House, South Queensferry

The Koelliker Collection, Milan

The National Gallery, London

Los Angeles County Museum of Art

The J. Paul Getty Museum, Los Angeles

Private Collection at Mount Stuart, Isle of Bute

The National Trust for Scotland

The Metropolitan Museum of Art, New York

The Southesk Collection

The Duke of Sutherland

The National Gallery of Art, Washington DC

The Earl of Wemyss and March KT

and private collectors who prefer
to remain anonymous

VENETIAN PAINTING IN THE AGE OF TITIAN

Peter Humfrey

In the long history of Venetian painting – stretching from the twelfth-century mosaics of Torcello and San Marco to the end of the eighteenth century – the age of Titian has always been regarded as the most glorious. Loosely defined for the purposes of the present exhibition as the long sixteenth century (about 1460 to 1620), the period was one extraordinarily rich in artistic talent. Titian was merely the greatest in a constellation of pictorial geniuses working in Venice and the Venetian territories on the mainland (known as the *terraferma*). These included Giovanni Bellini, Giorgione, Lorenzo Lotto, Jacopo Bassano, Jacopo Tintoretto and Paolo Veronese, as well as numerous other, only slightly lesser, figures. As it happens, virtually all of these are represented in the present exhibition, often with works of superlative quality. Although the purpose of the exhibition is in part to illuminate an important episode in the history of British collecting, it also presents a reasonably balanced survey of Venetian Renaissance painting in microcosm.[1]

THE HISTORICAL CONTEXT

The city of Venice in the age of Titian was one of the wealthiest and most populous in all Christendom.[2] The Venetian Republic was a world power and, alone among the Italian Renaissance city states, it not only ruled over an extensive neighbouring territory, but also possessed a chain of overseas colonies, stretching from Istria and Dalmatia in the Adriatic to Cyprus in the eastern Mediterranean. A perfect image of this wealthy, powerful and culturally sophisticated state on parade is provided by the *Procession in the Piazza San Marco* (fig.1), painted by Gentile Bellini (elder brother of Giovanni) in 1496, just before Titian arrived in Venice as a boy to learn the art of painting. Despite a degree of subtle idealisation, Gentile's piazza looks much as it does today (fig.2), with the east side dominated by the

venerable basilica of San Marco, with the Doge's Palace beside it and the campanile (bell-tower) opposite.

Venice's wealth was based on centuries of trade with the eastern Mediterranean, and on its ability to exploit its geographical position to import goods from oriental markets into northern and western Europe. The resulting contacts with the cultures both of Christian Constantinople and of Islam exerted a profound and permanent influence on the character of Venetian art and on the appearance of the city. In Gentile's painting this is above all evident in San Marco itself, with its Byzantine-style domes, and its gorgeously exotic display of coloured marbles and shimmering mosaics. In front of the basilica, turbaned orientals mingle with the Venetian bystanders. On a deeper level, Gentile's palette, with its warm reds and rich golds, reflects an age-old Venetian taste for luxurious materials and artefacts imported from the east.

Venice's maritime empire was developed for purely commercial reasons, to protect and expand the Republic's trading interests. The same was true – at least initially – of its second empire, the *terraferma*. In the first thirty years of the fifteenth century the Republic's toe-hold on the mainland was greatly expanded to include the cities of Padua, Vicenza and Verona, and then also Brescia and Bergamo in Lombardy, close to the borders of Milan. These cities, situated along the northern margin of the Po valley at the foot of the Alps, provided essential access to overland trade routes to southern Germany. By the beginning of the sixteenth century, however, Venice's extensive mainland territories provided a valuable alternative source of wealth for Venetians as their maritime empire began to crumble with the westward advance of the Ottoman Turks. Constantinople had fallen to the Turks in 1453; in 1470 the Venetians lost their strategically important colony of Negroponte in

Fig.1 | Gentile Bellini, *A Procession in the Piazza San Marco*
Venice, Galleria dell'Accademia

opposite | Detail of fig.1

the Aegean; and a succession of further disastrous losses culminated in the capture by the Turks of Cyprus in 1571. In compensation for the dwindling Mediterranean trade, Venetian patrician families began to invest more heavily in land, transforming themselves in the process from merchants into landed aristocrats, and constructing elegant country villas. Striking images of this new role are provided by Francesco Beccaruzzi's *Hunting Scene* of about 1540 (cat.no.39) and Bonifacio de' Pitati's *The Return of the Prodigal Son* of about a decade later (cat.no.49). At the same time, Venetian rule on the *terraferma* also brought new prosperity to the cities of the Veneto and to the provincial nobility, and with it positive effects for local culture. Thus while some artists from these cities – Paolo Veronese, for example – chose to gravitate towards the metropolis, others, such as Moretto, from Brescia, and Moroni, from Bergamo, succeeded in finding or creating plenty of custom at home, and in developing distinctive local artistic traditions.

Venice's success in establishing itself as a power on the Italian mainland was bound to arouse the enmity of its neighbours, and in particular of Milan and the papacy. The Republic was embroiled in a number of mainland wars in the fifteenth century, but none was so serious as the War of the League of Cambrai (1509–17), at the beginning of which an alliance of Italian and European powers succeeded in capturing Venice's entire mainland empire, and even threatened the Republic with extinction. Almost miraculously, it managed both to survive and to win back its former territories; but from this time onwards – right down to the final fall of the Republic to Napoleonic troops in 1798 – Venice's foreign policy was no longer one of expansion but of damage limitation. For most of Titian's career the Republic deliberately sought to present itself to its own citizens and to the outside world as a haven of peace and prosperity,

liberty and justice. Gentile's *Procession in the Piazza San Marco* already provides a utopian view of the wealth and civic orderliness of the Venetian state, but the use of art as propaganda became more pronounced over the course of the sixteenth century. A more explicitly idealised image of the magnificent serenity of the Venetian political and judicial system, set in a classicising but still materially gorgeous version of the Piazza San Marco, is provided by Titian's former pupil Paris Bordon, in *The Fisherman Delivering the Ring*, 1534–5 (fig.4).

The Venetian constitution remained largely identical with that crystallised at the end of the thirteenth century. The Republic was ruled by a patrician oligarchy, with the doge as head of state. The fact that this office was elective and not hereditary was designed to ensure that no individual or family became too powerful. In Paris Bordon's picture the doge, with his luxurious brocaded mantle and characteristic horned cap, sits on an appropriately dignified throne, but is assisted in his deliberations by his ten counsellors. An important task for all official painters to the Venetian state, from Giovanni Bellini (fig.5) to Titian (cat.nos.37–8) and Palma Giovane (cat.no.81), was to paint a portrait of the doge in his robes of office. As the living embodiment of the power and sanctity of the Most Serene Republic (the *Serenissima*), Titian's Doge Francesco Donà (cat.no.38) is appropriately accompanied by a view of the Piazza San Marco, representing the combined civic and religious heart of the Venetian state.

It is not just the piazza that has remained essentially unchanged down to the present day. The configuration of the astonishing, waterborne city itself, with its innumerable islands and canals bisected by the great inverted 'S' of the Grand Canal, had already reached its present form in medieval times (fig.3). As has often been observed, the extraordinary site of Venice, in the middle of the sea, has made its own contribution

Fig.2 | View of Piazza San Marco looking towards the Façade of the Basilica

Fig.3 | Attributed to Jacopo de' Barbari, *Bird's Eye View of Venice* London, British Museum

left to right

Fig.4 | Paris Bordon, *The Fisherman Delivering the Ring* Venice, Galleria dell'Accademia

Fig.5 | Giovanni Bellini, *Doge Leonardo Loredan* London, National Gallery

Fig.6 | Giovanni Bellini, *The Madonna of the Meadow*, London, National Gallery

to the peculiar character of Venetian art. This is obviously particularly true of architecture, but Venetian painters were hardly less responsive to the phenomenological aspect of their physical environment: its characteristically moisture-laden air, its ever-changing lighting, and the constant play of watery reflections. Already in the late landscapes of Giovanni Bellini (fig.6), the hard contours of his early work are blurred and softened, and hills and meadows, instead of receding with clear spatial logic into the distance, hover weightlessly and resolve themselves into patterns of repeating colour. This process reaches a climax in the late work of Titian, as illustrated by his two great works *Diana and Actaeon* and *Diana and Callisto*, 1556–9 (cat.nos.54–5), where nature is perceived as an incessant flux of dissolving forms and shifting lights.

THE AGE OF GIOVANNI BELLINI

Just as Titian dominated Venetian painting for much of the sixteenth century, so his probable master, the equally long-lived Giovanni Bellini, dominated it during the second half of the fifteenth century. Bellini's career is characterised by a tireless inventiveness of style and technique. At its beginning, around 1460, the prevailing artistic style in painting, as well as in architecture and sculpture, was still an opulent late Gothic, and Venetian artists had scarcely begun to respond to the dramatic developments that had taken place at the beginning of the century in Florence. Under Bellini's leadership, Venetian painters gradually absorbed the intellectual logic of Renaissance realism, but, at the same time, invested it with a new sensuousness and luminos-ity made possible by the Flemish technique of oil painting. In his earlier career, up to about the mid-1470s, Bellini still employed the traditional Italian technique of egg tempera, which by its very nature tended to promote sharp contours, hard modelling and matt surfaces. But stimulated by the arrival in Venice of Flemish panel paint-ings in the tradition of Jan van Eyck, and also by a visit to the city in 1475–6 by the Flemish-trained Sicilian painter Antonello da Messina, Bellini began to experiment with oils. These allowed the painter to achieve much softer tonal transitions, and a much greater depth and transparency of colour. Well before his death in 1516, Bellini had created a local school of painting that was not only generally recognised to be as advanced as that of Florence and Rome, but which remained distinctively Venetian in its exploitation of sensuous effects of light, colour and texture.

Although towards the end of his career Bellini painted a magnificent scene from pagan mythol-ogy, *The Feast of the Gods*, 1514 (see cat.no.17), he was active above all as a painter of sacred subjects. His achievement in this field may be illustrated by his masterly triptych of 1488, which still occupies its original altar in the sacristy of Santa Maria Gloriosa dei Frari (fig.7), the principal Franciscan church in Venice. Although in fact painted on three separate panels, Bellini created the illusion that the richly carved and gilded Renaissance-style frame is a sort of proscenium, behind which light and air flow freely between the spaces occupied by the enthroned Virgin and Child, and the standing saints at the sides. He created, in other words, a

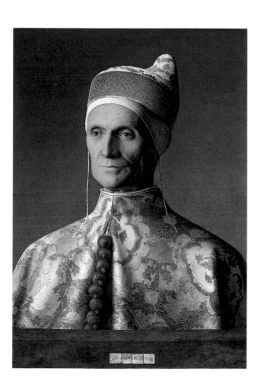

Fig.7 | Giovanni Bellini, *The Virgin and Child Enthroned with Saints*
Venice, Church of Santa Maria Gloriosa dei Frari

spatial and spiritual unity that did not exist in earlier polyptychs, such as that of about 1465 by his slightly older contemporary Bartolomeo Vivarini (cat.no.1). While adopting certain devices of Renaissance realism, including geometric perspective and three-dimensional modelling, Vivarini did not subordinate these to a traditional taste for material luxury, and in the three figures of the central panel he cheerfully preserved an archaic inconsistency of scale. Yet Bellini's triptych is remarkable not merely for its much greater modernity, but for its much more sophisticated combination of innovation and tradition. More directly than Vivarini, Bellini referred back to the Venetian tradition represented by the basilica of San Marco, in the steps of coloured marble, in the hanging of sumptuous red brocade, and in the half-dome of golden mosaic. At the same time, thanks to his new mastery of the oil technique, he was able to evoke the shimmer of light on their surface in a way

that is both naturalistically plausible and suggestive of the presence of the divine.

Bellini's favourite subject on a more intimate scale was that of the Virgin and Child, represented in half-length and close-up, alone (cat.nos.3, 4) or accompanied by flanking saints (fig.80). His example in this area was widely imitated, not only by younger Venetian painters such as Cima da Conegliano (fig.8), Catena (cat.no.8) and Lotto (cat.no.11), but also by distinguished foreigners such as the German Albrecht Dürer. Although much busier than Bellini's Madonnas, both in its wealth of detail and in the activity of its figures, Dürer's *The Madonna of the Siskin* (fig.9), painted in Venice in 1506, was clearly intended as a homage to the revered patriarch of Venetian painting.

Although the Frari triptych (fig.7) includes only narrow slivers of landscape at its outermost edges, Bellini had a particular genius for landscape painting. In a late Virgin and Child

left to right

Fig.8 | Cima da Conegliano, *The Virgin and Child*
Detroit Institute of Arts, Gift of James E. Scripps
Formerly in the collection of James Dennistoun

Fig.9 | Albrecht Dürer, *The Madonna of the Siskin*
Berlin, Staatliche Museen zu Berlin, Gemäldegalerie
Formerly in the collection of the Marquesses of Lothian

Fig.10 | Vincenzo Catena, *The Rest on the Flight into Egypt*
Pasadena, The Norton Simon Museum
Formerly in the Forbes of Pitsligo collection

Fig.11 | Vittore Carpaccio,
The Return of the English Ambassadors
Venice, Galleria dell' Accademia

composition such as the *Madonna of the Meadow* of about 1505 (fig.6; see also cat.no.5), the background is wonderfully evocative of the countryside of the Veneto north of Venice, where the plain begins to rise into the Alpine foothills. The cool sunlight and bare tree on the left suggest that the season is early spring. Although the bucolic activity in the background, together with the various plants and birds, add further verisimilitude to the scene, such details were certainly meant by Bellini to carry an additional symbolic significance, in keeping with the deep religious seriousness of his temperament. In every respect, in fact – structure, colour, mood – the landscape is tightly bound to the foreground Madonna group, in which the sleeping pose of the Child serves as a premonition of his future self-sacrifice and death.

A similarly close spiritual unity between holy figures and landscape may be discerned in Bellini's many and much-imitated representa-

tions of *St Jerome in the Desert* (see cat.nos.2, 44). The association between this very popular saint and landscape may account for Cima's introduction of a purely natural setting into his *Madonna of the Orange Tree* (fig.81), in place of the architectural setting until then standard in Venetian altarpieces. Some of the wealth of scintillating detail represented by Cima is probably, as in Bellini's subjects of this kind, meant to be symbolic. Yet it is probably also true that much of it reflects a growing taste among painters and patrons for landscape in its own right. In Catena's *Rest on the Flight into Egypt* (fig.10), in which the holy figures have become almost genre-like, it is even more evident that the subject was chosen largely as a pretext for the representation of a delightfully serene, idealised version of the Venetian *terraferma*.

In the last three decades of his life, Giovanni Bellini was heavily involved in the cycle of history paintings commissioned for the principal council chamber of the Doge's Palace. This cycle was destroyed by fire in 1577, and today the fifteenth-century tradition of large-scale narrative painting is best represented by the work of Giovanni's elder brother Gentile, as exemplified by his *Procession in the Piazza San Marco* (fig.1), and especially by that of Gentile's pupil Vittore Carpaccio. The typical ingredients of a painting by Carpaccio such as *The Return of the English Ambassadors* of about 1496–8 (fig.11) – with its crowds of finely dressed, processing figures, its diplomatic comings and goings, its marble-clad loggias and palaces, and its richness of anecdotal detail – were to continue to resonate in the sixteenth century in the work of Paris Bordon (fig.4) and Bonifacio Veronese (cat.no.49). Painted on canvas rather than wood, this kind of picture was also important in establishing canvas as a standard support for Venetian painting in general. Virtually all of Giovanni Bellini's devotional pictures, large and small, were painted

on the smooth surface of wooden panels, and his handling is correspondingly smooth, leaving little evidence of the brush. From the beginning of the sixteenth century, however, Venetian painters were increasingly to explore the expressive effects achieved by combining the more textured surface of canvas with a more varied and visible brushstroke.

As is evident from his magisterial *Doge Leonardo Loredan* of about 1501 (fig.5), Bellini also dominated the art of portraiture in early Renaissance Venice. But a particularly important contribution to this field was also made by Antonello da Messina, who, as well as painting a number of astonishingly vivid portraits during his brief stay in the city in 1475–6, probably shipped several others to Venice from his home in Sicily. Antonello's characteristic formula, which completely superceded the older profile type, is well illustrated by his *Portrait of a Man* dated 1474 (fig.12), in which the face is represented in three-quarter view, and the figure is seen in bust length behind a marble ledge. In keeping with Antonello's Flemish artistic education are the sharp precision of detail and the strong illumination from the left. Bellini clearly owed much to Antonello's example, but in the case of *Doge Leonardo Loredan* he succeeded in transforming the effect of everyday immediacy into one of timeless majesty.

THE GIORGIONESQUE REVOLUTION

The life of Giorgione, the first great Venetian painter of the sixteenth century, was so short that he predeceased Giovanni Bellini, who was old enough to have been his grandfather. Partly for this reason, but partly also because of the intrinsically elusive nature of his art, his career and personality remain shrouded in mystery. Even today, after more than a century of intense art historical debate, there exists little critical consensus about what his pictures represent or,

indeed, which pictures are actually by him. There is general agreement, however, that he was a revolutionary who profoundly influenced the course of Venetian painting, both by transforming existing pictorial types and by inventing completely new ones.

All Giorgione's qualities are evident in one of his few universally accepted works, *The Three Philosophers*, painted around 1504–8 (fig.13). The picture is indebted to Bellini and the Venetian tradition in a number of ways: in the figure types, in the glowing warmth and depth of the colour, in the importance of the landscape. But the surfaces are physically more sensuous than those of Bellini; the poetic mood is heightened by the glamorous effects of the setting sun and the thickening twilight; and the composition, with the figures grouped emphatically in the right half, is unprecedentedly informal. Technical investigation has revealed a much freer underdrawing than was habitually employed by Bellini, and paint is applied to the canvas support with a greater variety of brushstroke. But probably the greatest novelty is the subject, which obstinately resists clarification. One attractive suggestion is that the three figures should be identified with the three Magi on their way to Bethlehem; but if so, they have lost their traditional retinue, and the Christian story has become entirely secularised. Another line of interpretation is that the picture is an allegory: of the three ages of man; of contrasting philosophical systems; of contrasting religions. Or perhaps it simply represents what its popular name implies: three anonymous sages gathered in a poetic landscape – much as sages or shepherds gather in the landscapes drawn or engraved by Giorgione's close follower Giulio Campagnola.

Another work universally accepted as by Giorgione, the so-called *Laura* (fig.14), bears the date 1506. The evocation of surfaces, such as the velvet of the deep-red jacket and the fur lining

left to right

Fig.12 | Antonello da Messina, *Portrait of a Man*
Berlin, Staatliche Museen zu Berlin, Gemäldegalerie
Formerly in the collection of the Dukes of Hamilton

Fig.13 | Giorgione, *The Three Philosophers*
Vienna, Kunsthistorisches Museum

Fig.14 | Giorgione, *Laura*
Vienna, Kunsthistorisches Museum

Fig.15 | Titian, *Concert Champêtre*
Paris, Musée du Louvre

that brushes the figure's exposed breast, is even more sensuous than in the *Three Philosophers*, and again the forms melt suggestively into shadow. The picture clearly resembles a portrait, but does it portray a particular woman? Or should it be read as an allegory, perhaps contributing to the current debate on the differing capacities of the arts of poetry and painting to evoke female beauty?[3] Whatever Giorgione's intentions were in this picture, he completely transformed the fifteenth-century tradition of portraiture received from Bellini and Antonello. His male portraits are presented not objectively, in terms of their sitters' external appearance and of their place in the social hierarchy, but as persons of inner thought and feeling (cat.no.12). The *Laura* was to the first in a long line of Venetian images of beautiful women, a category that was all the more potent for being fluid and adaptable. Thus Titian could develop the type to portray a man's ideal of the beloved (fig.131), Giovanni Cariani to portray a female saint (cat.no.22), Bernardino Licinio to present an allegory of love (cat.no.23), and Paris Bordon to portray a seductive courtesan (cat.no.47).

The novelty of Giorgione's art is usually interpreted as a reflection of contemporary fashions in poetry, and in particular for the pastoral genre made popular by Jacopo Sannazaro's *Arcadia*, published in 1504. Expressing the longing of a sophisticated city dweller for the simple rustic life, Sannazaro's romance evokes an ideally beautiful never-never land, where shepherds tend their flocks and sing of love. The Venetian picture that most perfectly captures the spirit of this arcadian dream world is the so-called *Concert Champêtre* in the Louvre (fig.15), in which a well-dressed youth in a red velvet doublet strums his lute in the company of a shepherd and two nymphs in a luxuriant pastoral landscape. As the figures play music and exchange glances, their conversation is surely of the sweetness and sorrow of love, and of the transience of human life and happiness.[4] A problem with giving full credit to Giorgione for introducing the pastoral mode into Venetian painting is that the *Concert Champêtre*, long regarded as a key late picture by him, is now widely regarded as the work of the young Titian. To judge from the figure types, the treatment of the foliage, and the energy of the brushwork, the current attribution is the correct one and the picture was probably painted by Titian soon after the premature death of Giorgione in 1510. The *Concert Champêtre* remains, nevertheless, profoundly and probably deliberately Giorgionesque, above all in the use of landscape to evoke a pervasive mood of nostalgic poetry. Its strongly escapist character becomes particularly evident when one recalls that the picture must have been painted during the worst phase of the War of the League of Cambrai, when the very survival of Venice was hanging in the balance.

Not more than two or three years later, Titian painted another masterpiece in the pastoral genre, *The Three Ages of Man* (cat.no.15). Many of the same intertwined themes recur: shepherds and sheep, music, love, intimations of mortality. Both the *Concert Champêtre* and *The Three Ages of Man* are probably meant as allegories, albeit of a general and accessible rather than of a complicated or erudite kind. The extraordinary success, however, of the pastoral mode in Venetian painting resulted in the creation of numerous pictures in which the figures – whether poets, musicians, shepherds or lovers – seem to be no more than the picturesque inhabitants of a picturesque landscape. Examples include a *Pastoral Concert* (fig.16) usually attributed to Palma Vecchio,[5] in which the pose of the male figure closely repeats that in *The Three Ages of Man*; another picture of musicians (cat.no.16), here attributed to Giovanni da Asola; and Girolamo da Santacroce's *Four Poets in a Landscape* (cat.no.20). Giorgionesque landscapes also provided appropriate settings for small-scale mythological scenes, as exemplified by a picture in the National Gallery, London, which is possibly by Bonifacio Veronese (fig.17).[6]

It was also natural that the pastoral mode should impose itself on the existing Venetian taste for landscape as an accompaniment to religious subjects. The second decade of the sixteenth century saw the emergence of the highly popular type in which the Virgin and Child are seated in a landscape in intimate communion with an informal gathering of saints (cat.nos.25, 26, 29, 30, 31; fig.18). A shady grove in the foreground, and rolling pastures beyond, dotted with sheep, shepherds and rustic buildings, are standard ingredients of the Venetian vision of Arcadia. Frequently, too, the type retains reminiscences of those stories from Christ's infancy with strong pastoral associations, such as the adoration of the shepherds or the rest on the flight into Egypt. It is a measure of the potency of the spell cast by Giorgione over Venetian painting that the Giorgionesque themes of music-making shepherds and rustic idylls continue to appear in the 1530s and beyond, in the works of painters such as Savoldo (cat.no.41), Paris Bordon and Bonifacio.

TITIAN: THE HEROIC PHASE

Within a very few years of painting *The Three Ages of Man*, however, Titian himself moved from the lyrical mode of Giorgione to one that was altogether more heroic. Probably in 1515, even before the death of Giovanni Bellini, Titian undertook the commission for *The Assumption of the Virgin* (fig.19), a gigantic panel for the high altar of Santa Maria Gloriosa dei Frari, the church for which Bellini had painted his triptych thirty years earlier (fig.7). Fully realising the dramatic potential of the subject, Titian portrayed the tightly-knit group of apostles in energetic movement, gesticulating with amazement as they gaze up towards the ascending Virgin and the jubilant throng of child angels. The figures possess the heroic, classicising proportions of the contemporary work of Michelangelo in Florence and Raphael in Rome, but the powerful contrasts of light and shade, and the characteristically Venetian richness and resonance of colour, lend the miraculous event an overwhelming effect of sensuous immediacy. At one stroke Titian established himself as Bellini's heir as the undisputed leader of Venetian painting, a position that he was to retain for the next half century.

Titian followed up the *Assumption of the Virgin* with a series of further grandiose, scarcely less dramatic altarpieces for Venetian churches, all of which transformed existing conventions of altarpiece design and provided inspirational models for the later sixteenth century and the Baroque era. In the *Madonna of Ca' Pesaro* of 1519–26, for example (fig.20), painted for a side altar in the same huge church of the Frari, he revolutionised the traditional symmetrical and static design of altarpieces by shifting the enthroned Madonna well to the right of the

above Fig.16 | Circle of Palma Vecchio, *Pastoral Concert*
Private Collection
Formerly in the collection of Lady Colum Crichton-Stuart, Ardencraig, Bute

below left Fig.17 | Attributed to Bonifacio Veronese, *Mythological Scene*
London, National Gallery
Formerly in the collection of the Dukes of Hamilton

below right Fig.18 | Bonifacio Veronese, *The Holy Family with St Elizabeth, the Infant St John the Baptist and Two Shepherds*.
Los Angeles County Museum of Art,
William Randolph Hearst Collection
Formerly in the collection of Robert Napier

opposite Fig.19 | Titian, *The Assumption of the Virgin*
Venice, Church of Santa Maria Gloriosa dei Frari

central axis, and by introducing a much more dynamic interplay between the holy figures. Even more revolutionary in concept was the *Death of St Peter Martyr*, painted in 1526–9 for a side altar in the rival church of the Dominicans, Santi Giovanni e Paolo. This great work was destroyed by fire in 1867, but as is evident from numerous copies and reproductive prints (cat.nos.147, 159), it showed the brutal assassination of the charismatic Dominican preacher at the edge of a windswept forest, while angels swooped down from heaven with the victorious palm of martyrdom. Numerous descriptions attest to the painting's communicative power, and to the tragic emotions of pity and terror that it aroused in its viewers.

At the same time that Titian was consolidating his leading position in Venice with large-scale public works such as these, he was also forging for himself a parallel career as an international court painter. Already by the time the *Assumption of the Virgin* was in progress, he had attracted the attention of Alfonso d'Este, duke of the neighbouring state of Ferrara. Bellini had painted his *Feast of the Gods* (fig.91) for Alfonso in 1514, and between 1517 and 1523 Titian complemented it with a series of three further large-scale canvases with bacchanalian themes. The third of these, the magnificent *Bacchus and Ariadne* (fig.21; see cat.no.18), illustrates his ability to extend the physical energy and joyous exhilaration of the *Assumption of the Virgin* to an amorous subject from pagan myth. As with his religious paintings of this period, the Ferrara Bacchanals were to become constant sources of inspiration for all mythological painting in the subsequent history of European art.

Titian's enormous success at the court of Ferrara in the 1520s led to competing demands for his services from the courts of Mantua and Urbino in the 1530s. No further commissions for mythological narratives were forthcoming for the time being, but Titian's work for Alfonso d'Este had established him as the supreme master of the sensuous female nude, and in 1538 Guidobaldo della Rovere, son and heir of the Duke of Urbino, had to fight off stiff competition to secure the acquisition of the picture subsequently known as *The Venus of Urbino* (fig.22). Giorgione had already painted a full-length reclining Venus (Dresden, Gemäldegalerie), but asleep in a landscape. By showing her on a couch in her bedroom, awake and fully aware of the gaze of the spectator, Titian greatly heightened the figure's erotic suggestiveness. His example was immediately imitated by the Venetian painters Paris Bordon (cat.no.47) and Lambert Sustris (fig.130), and Titian himself was later to develop a number of variations on his work.

Titian's success at the north Italian courts was also due in large part to his unrivalled skills as a

portrait painter. Although he moved away from Giorgione's concentration on the private, inner personality of his sitters, Titian nevertheless adopted and extended the range of formal devices introduced by Giorgione into portraiture to convey the dignity and public persona of sitters that were often of the highest social rank. In his portrait of the Duke of Urbino of 1536, for example (fig.23), the painter portrays the sitter in a glittering suit of parade armour, the hard, metallic sheen of which is offset by the hanging of soft crimson velvet behind him. Giorgione had

Fig.20 | Titian, *The Madonna of Ca' Pesaro*
Venice, Church of Santa Maria Gloriosa dei Frari

Fig.21 | Titian, *Bacchus and Ariadne*
London, National Gallery
Imported into Britain by James Irvine and William
Buchanan and subsequently in the collection of the
8th Baron Kinnaird

Fig.22 | Titian, *The Venus of Urbino*
Florence, Galleria degli Uffizi

already been interested in the play of reflected light on armour, as is evident from the painting *Portrait of an Archer* in the present exhibition (cat.no.12). But Titian, as well as going far beyond Giorgione in the virtuoso display of reflections, invests the duke's facial expression and pose with the decisiveness and vigour appropriate to a heroic leader accustomed to command. Further direct references to his military prowess are provided by the plumed and crested helmet and by the batons of command on the shelf.

It was indeed primarily as a portrait painter that Titian gained the patronage of two of the most powerful European leaders of the 1530s and 1540s: the Emperor Charles V and Pope Paul III. Following an initial meeting at the court of Mantua in 1529, Titian painted two portraits of the emperor in Bologna in 1533: one three-quarter length, in armour, in a format very similar to that of the *Duke of Urbino* (lost);[7] and the other in the even grander format of a life-size, full-length standing pose (Madrid, Museo Nacional del Prado). Fifteen years later in 1548, at the imperial court in Augsburg, Titian created three more highly influential prototypes for grandiose state portraiture with three more images of the emperor: a double portrait seated at a table with the Empress Isabella (lost); a full-length seated portrait (Munich, Alte Pinakothek); and a huge equestrian portrait, painted to celebrate Charles's recent victory over the German Protestant princes at the Battle of Mühlberg (Madrid, Museo Nacional del Prado).

Titian adopted different formats again, in both cases appropriately adapted from the papal portraits of Raphael, for his two principal portraits of Paul III. The first, painted in Bologna in 1543, shows the aged pontiff enthroned, in three-quarter length, mesmerising the spectator with his sharp outward glance (fig.24). The second (also Naples, Museo Nazionale di Capodimonte), painted during an extended trip made to Rome in 1545–6, shows Paul in a full-length group portrait, in an apparently tense conversation with two of his adult grandsons. In these, as well as in his later portraits of the emperor, Titian succeeded in combining highly inventive, imposing compositions with an extraordinarily acute insight into two of the central personalities on the contemporary world stage.

While pursuing his career as an international court painter, earning considerable financial rewards and collecting honours that included an imperial knighthood, Titian remained a resident of Venice, and continued to dominate artistic life at home. Throughout the 1530s and 1540s he undertook further large-scale commissions for Venetian churches (see cat.no.126), confraternities and state buildings, and to paint the portraits of doges (cat.nos.37, 38), admirals

(cat.no.35), senators, and men of letters. His fellow Venetian painters could hardly ignore the force of his example; yet for the more talented of them this was more stimulating than inhibiting. In the late 1520s, for example, his older contemporary Lorenzo Lotto, whose style at the outset of his career was close to that of Bellini (see cat.no.11), returned to Venice after a long absence, and began producing a series of portraits that were highly innovative and expressive, and yet utterly different from those of Titian (cat.nos.32–3). Around the same time, the Friulian painter Pordenone (see cat.no.87) settled in Venice and began to present serious competition for Titian in the field of large-scale public commissions. Then, between 1539 and 1542, two leading members of the younger generation of Florentine painters, Francesco Salviati and Giorgio Vasari, visited Venice and excited considerable interest among their Venetian colleagues for their particular brand of central Italian Mannerism. Titian himself remained fairly immune to this fashion for gracefully elongated proportions, convoluted poses, and hard, sculptural surfaces. But during the 1540s and earlier 1550s many of his younger Venetian contemporaries – including Andrea Schiavone (cat.nos.56, 95), Lambert Sustris (fig.130), Jacopo Bassano, Jacopo Tintoretto, and even the already well-established Paris Bordon (cat.nos.46–8, 50) – flirted with Mannerism, experimentally synthesising it in different ways with the Venetian tradition. Creative blends of Tusco-Roman and Venetian styles were also provided by Salviati's pupil Giuseppe Salviati (cat.no.96), who stayed on in the city after his master's departure in 1540, and by Battista Franco (cat.nos.97–100), who returned to his native Venice around 1552 after an earlier career in central Italy.

Fig.23 | Titian, *Portrait of Francesco Maria della Rovere, Duke of Urbino*
Florence, Galleria degli Uffizi

Fig.24 | Titian, *Portrait of Pope Paul III*
Naples, Museo Nazionale di Capodimonte

MYTHOLOGICAL PAINTING

On his visit to Rome in 1545–6, Titian brought with him a picture commissioned by the pope's eldest grandson, Cardinal Alessandro Farnese, depicting the mythological tale of Danaë and the shower of golden rain (fig.25). The cardinal had seen and admired the *Venus of Urbino*, and was inspired by it to commission an equally seductive reclining nude for himself. Titian would have been perfectly aware of the Roman destination of his work, and of the fact that it would be scrutinised closely by artists and cognoscenti at the papal court. He made certain concessions to the local taste for ancient and modern sculpture in the poses of both Danaë and Cupid. But on the whole, the picture emphatically asserts its Venetian-ness, in the way in which the figures are enveloped in a warm, luminous haze, and in the sensuous evocation of surface texture, above all of soft, female skin.

Twenty years later, in his biography of Titian in the second edition of the *Lives of the Artists* (1568), Vasari recounted how he had inspected the newly completed *Danaë* in the company of

Michelangelo.[8] The great sculptor admired the picture's colouring and naturalness, but deplored the undisciplined character of the drawing and the figure's lack of ideal beauty. Vasari then expanded on these remarks to draw an unfavourable comparison between the Tusco-Roman and the Venetian schools in general, and implicitly between their respective standard-bearers, Michelangelo and Titian. In doing so he was contributing to a critical debate on the relative aesthetic merits of *disegno* (drawing and design) and *colorito* (colour and pictorial handling) that had been developing since the 1530s. Titian, however, had acquired his own literary champions in this debate, notably Pietro Aretino and Lodovico Dolce; and already by the time he painted the *Danaë*, he would have been aware that his own instinctive practice as a painter was eloquently underpinned by a body of art theory and criticism. As Dolce was later to explain, Titian's power of *colorito* made him superior to both of the great central Italians, Michelangelo and Raphael, because it gave his work the pulse of life:

Fig.25 | Titian, *Danaë*
Naples, Museo Nazionale di Capodimonte

Titian moves in step with nature, so that every one of his figures has life, movement and flesh which palpitates. He has shown in his work no empty gracefulness, but a palette which is properly appropriate; no artificiality of ornamentation, but the mellowness and softness of nature. And the highlights and shadows in his creations always contend and interplay with one another, and fade out and decrease in the very same way as nature itself has them do.[9]

These words were written in about 1554–5, very soon after Titian had painted a second, even more explicitly erotic version of the *Danaë* (fig.26) for the future Philip II of Spain. In 1551, during a second trip to Augsburg, Titian seems to have come to an agreement with the crown prince to send him a regular series of large-scale mythological paintings during the course of the following ten years. This series, of which the *Danaë*, the *Venus and Adonis* (fig.27), the *Diana and Actaeon* and the *Diana and Callisto* (cat.nos.54–5) all formed part, represents a coming to fruition of Titian's late style, and one of the greatest achievements of his entire career. Partly because patron and painter lived at such a distance apart – with Philip in the Netherlands, England and Spain, and Titian in Venice – the commission afforded the painter a freedom accorded to few other Italian Renaissance artists, in matters both of content and of style and technique. The subjects of the six mythologies – or *poesie*, as Titian called them – were not dictated by a court humanist, as had been the case thirty years earlier in Ferrara, but were chosen by the painter himself. Most of the stories were based on the highly popular and frequently reprinted and translated *Metamorphoses* of Ovid (see cat.no.165). In selecting them, Titian seems to have been guided in the first place by their erotic potential,

by the possibilities they afforded for displays of the female nude. This is clear from a letter he wrote in September 1554, in which the painter pointed out to Philip that the attraction of the *Venus and Adonis* was that it showed the figure of Venus from the back, whereas the *Danaë* had shown the nude protagonist from the front.[10] Yet much more than in the Ferrara mythologies, the elderly painter was also interested in exploring the human and tragic implications of Ovid's stories; in contrast to the joyful exuberance of the *Bacchus and Ariadne*, the *Diana and Actaeon*, in particular, represents a profound and moving meditation on the arbitrariness and cruelty of fate.

Even at the beginning of his career, in such pictures as *The Three Ages of Man* (cat.no.15), Titian had departed radically from the pictorial techniques developed by Giovanni Bellini. Although Bellini was primarily responsible for establishing oil painting in Venice, he retained the habits of a panel painter, making his forms adhere closely to their contours, and employing a smooth, meticulous finish. Titian's habitual support was the rougher surface of canvas, which he primed rather thinly, so that the weave contributed to the unevenness of the painted surface. Although he was to continue to employ underdrawings throughout his career, from the beginning these were no longer based on carefully prepared drawings on paper, but were executed in a sketchy freehand that allowed him to make constant changes (pentimenti) as the painting progressed. *The Three Ages of Man* already shows him exploiting the flexibility of the oil medium to the full, using paint that is sometimes thin and dilute, and sometimes thick and impasted, and applying it with a great variety of brushstroke.

In the mythologies for Philip II, beginning

above left Fig.26 | Titian, *Danaë*
Madrid, Museo Nacional del Prado

above right Fig.27 | Titian, *Venus and Adonis*
Madrid, Museo Nacional del Prado

below Fig.28 | Titian, *Nymph and Shepherd*
Vienna, Kunsthistorisches Museum

below left Fig.29 | Paolo Veronese, *An Allegory of Navigation with an Astrolabe: Ptolemy.*
Los Angeles County Museum of Art, Gift of the Ahmanson Foundation
Formerly in the collections of the Marquess of Breadalbane and of the Hon. Mrs Robert Baillie-Hamilton

below right Fig.30 | Paolo Veronese, *An Allegory of Navigation with a Cross-staff: Averroës.*
Los Angeles County Museum of Art, Gift of the Ahmanson Foundation
Formerly in the collections of the Marquess of Breadalbane and of the Hon. Mrs Robert Baillie-Hamilton

with the second *Danaë*, Titian pushed these tendencies towards improvisation and pictorialism much further. His basic procedures remained essentially the same, and his pentimenti did not necessarily become more radical. But he adopted increasingly loose and broken brushwork, so that the solid forms of the figures now appear to melt and fuse with their surroundings to form a continuous vibrating web of light and colour. In the *Danaë* and *Diana and Actaeon* and *Diana and Callisto*, individual colours remain saturated and intense, and selective details are brought into relatively sharp focus. But in certain very late works such as the *Nymph and Shepherd* (fig.28) – in which the aged painter returned to the lyrical, pastoral theme of *The Three Ages of Man*, painted some sixty years previously – the restriction of the palette, and the overall submersion of the figures, landscape, and

sky into a flickering atmospheric haze, have given rise to uncertainty as to whether or not the picture is actually finished. Perhaps the most satisfactory explanation is that while Titian in his late career was prepared to bring some pictures to a higher state of finish than others, depending on the tastes of particular patrons, he would still have felt that the poetic magic of a painting such as the *Nymph and Shepherd* would have had little to gain from further labour.

Titian's activity as a painter of mythological subjects was the direct consequence of his career as an international court painter, and Venetian patrons showed little interest in large-scale mythological painting before the middle of the century. But from the 1550s onwards most Venetian painters, including the most prominent of Titian's younger contemporaries, Tintoretto and Veronese, were commissioned to paint

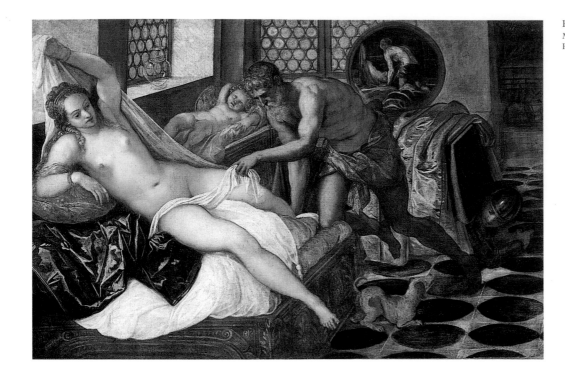

Fig.31 | Jacopo Tintoretto, *Venus, Mars and Vulcan*
Munich, Alte Pinakothek, Bayerische Staatsgemäldesammlungen
Formerly in the collection of H. A. J. Munro of Novar

mythologies and allegories for Venetian public buildings or private palaces (figs.29–30). An important early response to the Diana pictures was provided by Andrea Schiavone's *The Infancy of Jupiter* (cat.no.56), and it is significant that several of Veronese's most ambitious mythologies, including *The Rape of Europa* of about 1575 (Venice, Palazzo Ducale) and *Venus and Adonis* of about 1580 (fig.27), repeat subjects that Titian had already painted for Philip II. Both Veronese, for example in his *Venus, Cupid and Mars* (cat.no.69), and Tintoretto, as in his *Venus, Mars and Vulcan* of about 1555 (fig.31), tended to treat mythological and erotic subjects with lighthearted humour, and avoid the dramatic and tragic dimension explored by Titian. In some of Veronese's later works, however, including the *Venus and Adonis* (fig.32), the dazzling pictorial beauty is complemented by a touching humanity and by a mood of elegiac wistfulness.

RELIGIOUS PAINTING AND THE COUNTER-REFORMATION

Venice considered herself to be a holy city, especially favoured by God. Venetian churches, beginning with San Marco itself, were packed with the relics as well as the images of saints, and Gentile Bellini's *Procession in the Piazza San Marco* (fig.1) records just one of the many annual religious ceremonies observed by Venetians of every social class. In spite of the importance of religion in the daily life of the city – or rather, in large part because of it – relations between the *Serenissima* and the papacy were traditionally tense. The Venetian government reserved for

itself the right of all ecclesiastical jurisdiction within the boundaries of the Republic, and resented any attempt by the Roman Curia – which it saw as a political rival – to interfere in Venetian religious affairs. This remained the case in the early phase of the Reformation crisis, in the first two or three decades after Luther's rebellion of 1517, when the Venetian government reacted with relative tolerance towards signs of religious heterodoxy among its citizens.

By the mid-1540s, however, the government had begun to accept that the suppression of religious dissent was in its own political interest. After the conclusion of the Council of Trent in 1563 it sought systematically to promote conformity to orthodox Catholic belief and to implement the Tridentine decrees within its dominions. The decrees included a reaffirmation of the church's traditional defence of sacred art as a potent means of instructing the faithful in the articles of their faith, and of inspiring them with greater religious devotion.

The overwhelming majority of subjects represented by Venetian painters, as elsewhere in medieval and Renaissance Europe, had never ceased to be religious. But from the 1550s onwards there was a marked increase in the type of subject favoured by the Counter-Reformation church, such as scenes from Christ's Passion and the martyrdom of saints. An inspirational model for Venetian martyrdom altarpieces of the period was provided by Titian's *Death of St Peter Martyr*, 1526–9 (see cat.nos.147, 159), and Titian himself followed this up in the early 1550s with the equally influential *The Martyrdom of St Lawrence*

above left Fig.32 | Paolo Veronese,
Venus and Adonis
Madrid, Museo Nacional del Prado

below Fig.34 | Titian, *The Entombment*
Madrid, Museo Nacional del Prado

above right Fig.33 | Titian,
The Martyrdom of St Lawrence
Venice, Church of the Gesuiti

for the church of the Crociferi (now the Gesuiti, Venice, fig.33). There are clear signs, too, that these as well as traditional subjects were represented with a new spiritual intensity. Very often these developments may be interpreted less as the result of instructions from bishops and the clergy than as a spontaneous response by artists and their lay patrons to a generally diffused mood of religious revival. This is probably true, for example, of the late religious works of Titian such as *The Entombment* (fig.34), which he sent to Philip II together with *Diana and Actaeon* and *Diana and Callisto* and which presumably, like them, was his own choice of subject. In contrast to the extrovert drama of the much earlier *Assumption of the Virgin* (fig.19), the expression of religious emotion in *The Entombment* is all the deeper for being internalised.

Tintoretto, who by the 1550s had become the most prolific painter of large-scale canvases for Venice's churches and lay confraternities, dedicated himself and his art even more spontaneously and wholeheartedly to the communal piety of his age. This is above all evident in the three cycles he painted for the Scuola di San Rocco between 1564 and 1587, all three comprising vast cosmic dramas on human suffering and divine redemption. The same shadowy, tormented world, illumined and transfigured by divine intervention, recurs in his *Christ Carried to the Tomb* of about 1565 (cat.no.66) and the *Christ Washing the Disciples' Feet* (fig.35), painted at about the same date for the chapel of the Holy

Sacrament in the church of San Trovaso. Occasionally Tintoretto's handling of form is conspicuously more refined and sensuous, as in *The Temptation of St Anthony* of about 1577 (fig.36; see also cat.no.152). This was painted for another chapel in the same church, for the top civil servant Antonio Milledonne, who had been a member of the Venetian delegation to the Council of Trent in 1562–3. But the sensuousness here, especially of the half-nude female demons who seek to ensnare the saint with their jewels and their comely flesh, only serves to heighten the glory of St Anthony's moral victory, as he gazes ecstatically upwards at the dramatically descending figure of Christ.[11]

Initially less sensitive than Titian or Tintoretto to the changing religious climate, Veronese was shocked into conformity with the spirit and letter of Counter-Reformation religion by a brush with the Inquisition in 1571. In that year he was summoned to a tribunal to explain why he had painted a Last Supper for the friars' refectory of Santi Giovanni e Paolo in a spirit of apparent levity, with an abundance of figures unsanctioned by the gospel text. The painter famously escaped both punishment and damage to his painting by simply giving it a new title, *Feast in the House of Levi* (Venice, Galleria dell'Accademia), so that the subject no longer possessed the deep sacramental significance of the last supper. But Veronese's experience with the Inquisition clearly affected his subsequent approach to religious subject matter, as is evident

from the contrast between the bright and joyous *Mystic Marriage of St Catherine* of the mid-1550s (cat.no.57) and the dusky, tragic and explicitly counter-reformatory *Martyrdom and Last Communion of St Lucy* of the mid-1580s (cat.no.71).

Following the example of the late Titian and especially Tintoretto, much of Venetian religious painting passed during the course of the 1560s, 1570s and 1580s from daylight to twilight, to an encircling gloom. A contrast in the work of the Bassano family that parallels that in Veronese may be illustrated by the splendid and colourful *The Adoration of the Kings* of 1542 (cat.no.40) and the much more austere and muted *The Israelites Drinking the Miraculous Water* of the mid-1560s (cat.no.72). Then, from the mid-1570s, the works of Jacopo and his busy workshop become increasingly nocturnal. The many Old Testament scenes painted by the Bassano workshop, including several versions of the Israelites, were painted for the private spaces of houses or palaces, and so were probably less subject to counter-reformatory pressures than altarpieces and other pictures destined for churches. Even so, it is likely that underlying the genre-like emphasis on farm animals and children, and pots and pans, some sort of moralising message was intended. In the case of the *Israelites Drinking the Miraculous Water*, the water in the foreground clearly refers to God's attention to both the bodily and spiritual needs of mankind, and the journey to the Promised Land in the background to the hope for salvation.

above Fig.35 | Jacopo Tintoretto, *Christ Washing the Disciples' Feet* London, National Gallery Formerly in the collection of the Dukes of Hamilton

LATER SIXTEENTH-CENTURY PORTRAITURE

The portraits painted by the generation of Tintoretto and Veronese were inevitably deeply indebted to the example set by Titian in the 1530s and 1540s. Some of the prototypes he created for his princely patrons – the equestrian portrait, for example – were obviously inappropriate for republican Venice. Despite the sometimes enormous disparities of wealth within the governing class, Venetian patricians liked to maintain the fiction of equality within the oligarchy, in a way that was underlined by a strict dress code. The doge naturally wore robes that would compare in luxury with those worn by other heads of state, but custom dictated that his peers wore the official uniform of a simple crimson toga, or gown. The painter who best captured this ethos of dignified uniformity was Tintoretto, who characteristically adopted a relatively modest and conservative format for his many portraits of Venetian senators and patricians. This is not to deny that he occasionally borrowed more ambitious poses and compositions from Titian, for example for the *Portrait of Jacopo Soranzo* of *c*.1550 (fig.37), which is based on Titian's *Portrait of Doge Francesco Donà* (cat.no.38), or in the late, three-quarter-length seated *Procurator of St Mark's* (cat.no.68).

Other Venetian painters were more open to the new range of formats introduced by Titian. This was especially true of those working on the *terraferma* for the provincial nobility. Veronese,

for example, prior to his move from Verona to Venice around 1555, painted his *Portrait of Livia da Porto Thiene* (fig.38), a painting that is remarkable on a number of counts: in representing the sitter in a grand, full-length, standing pose (a format reserved by Titian for the very grandest of his patrons); in the very fact that the sitter is a woman (female portraits, as opposed to images of anonymous beauties, were still rare in Venice itself); and also for introducing the touching subsidiary figure of the sitter's young daughter. After his move to the metropolis, Veronese continued to expand the range of Venetian portraiture, especially by popularising Titian's designs. His *Portrait of Admiral Girolamo Contarini* of *c*.1560 (fig.40), for example, is clearly based on Titian's *Portrait of Vincenzo Cappello* (cat.no.35), and ultimately on his portrait of the Duke of Urbino (fig.23).

Similarly Moroni, who spent almost his entire career in the rather remote provincial capital of Bergamo, painted his local sitters, male and female, in full length as well as three-quarter length, and in both standing and seated poses. Compositions and accoutrements were characteristically chosen to reflect the sitter's social status. Thus, male aristocrats tended to be shown standing, perhaps surrounded by fragments of classical architecture, with great attention paid to sleeves and breeches of coloured silk (cat.no.60). Professional men and scholars, on the other

opposite Fig.36 | Jacopo Tintoretto, *The Temptation of St Anthony*
Venice, Church of San Trovaso

right Fig.37 | Jacopo Tintoretto, *Portrait of Jacopo Soranzo*
Venice, Galleria dell'Accademia

far right Fig.38 | Paolo Veronese, *Portrait of Livia da Porto Thiene*
Baltimore, The Walters Art Museum

29

hand, tended to be shown dressed in sober black and seated, as in the *Portrait of a Magistrate*, 1560 (fig.41; see also cat.no.62). Whatever their rank, Moroni's sitters characteristically turn their heads sideways to engage the eye of the spectator, in a way that created a vivid sense of spontaneity and psychological immediacy otherwise rarely found in Venetian portraiture.

Moroni's portraits, even the most ambitious, also have a soberly factual quality that has been linked to the moral regeneration of the Counter-Reformation. This connection is particularly

plausible in the case of the *Portrait of Abbess Lucrezia Agliardi Vertova*, 1557 (fig.39), in which the pious noblewoman is represented in meditation over a book of devotion. Despite her high social rank, the painter has made no attempt to beautify her wrinkled and flabby features, but the very truthfulness of the representation serves to underline the moral and spiritual force of the sitter. Something of the same equation between honest realism and religious seriousness may be seen in Leandro Bassano's *Portrait of a Widow at her Devotions*

Fig.39 | Giovanni Battista Moroni,
Portrait of Abbess Lucrezia Agliardi Vertova
New York, The Metropolitan Museum of Art, Theodore M. Davis Collection, Bequest of Theodore M. Davis (1915. 30.95.255)

above left Fig.40 | Paolo Veronese, *Portrait of Admiral Girolamo Contarini*
Philadelphia Museum of Art, John G. Johnson Collection, 1917
Formerly in the collection of the Dukes of Hamilton

above right Fig.41| Giovanni Battista Moroni,
Portrait of a Magistrate
Brescia, Pinacoteca Tosio Martinengo

(cat.no.75), in which another elderly female sitter is shown intent on her prayers.

The literal realism of much of late sixteenth- and early seventeenth-century portraiture could sometimes co-exist, not necessarily comfortably, with the high idealisation demanded of religious and allegorical painting. Such a combination – as well as the general state of Venetian painting at the end of our period – may be illustrated by the grand *Votive Picture of Doge Marcantonio Memmo* (fig.42), painted for the Doge's Palace in 1615 by Palma Giovane, the leading painter in Venice after the deaths of Veronese and Tintoretto. Even more explicit as a piece of patriotic propaganda than Gentile Bellini's

Procession in the Piazza San Marco of more than a century earlier, Palma's vast canvas shows the doge kneeling in a noble architectural setting before a cloud-borne Virgin and Child, surrounded by his patron saints. These include Mark, with his winged lion, who was both patron of the *Serenissima* and Memmo's name-saint. In the central background, as in Titian's earlier portrait of *Doge Francesco Donà* (cat.no.38), is a view of the piazza from across the lagoon. To the right, in a landscape setting, are allegorical representations of the *terraferma* cities of which Memmo had been provincial governor before his election as doge, including Padua, Vicenza, Verona, Treviso and Brescia. Palma's eclectic style self-consciously sought to synthesise those of all three of the great Venetian painters of the later sixteenth century – Titian, Tintoretto and Veronese –with the added ingredient of *disegno* derived from his direct experience of the Tusco-Roman tradition. The resulting academic compromise unfortunately falls short of its ambition to infuse new life into a flagging local tradition; and the picture may be seen as marking the end of Venice's great age of painting. It was to be followed by eight decades of largely undistinguished achievement, until the spectacular revival of Venetian painting at the beginning of the eighteenth century.

Fig.42 | Palma Giovane,
Votive Picture of Doge Marcantonio Memmo
Venice, Palazzo Ducale

THE AGE OF TITIAN: THE PAINTINGS IN CONTEXT

Timothy Clifford

One of the delights of visiting Venice – apart from its spectacular setting with the marble encrusted churches and palaces reflected in a myriad of canals – is experiencing pictures in their original setting, still as living, and meaningful images. It is exhilarating to cross over the Grand Canal glistening in the sun to follow a maze of dark, narrow *calli* with their little humpback bridges bounded by ancient, picturesquely crumbling houses, to open out, dramatically into the Campo dei Frari.

That Campo is dominated by the Franciscan basilica of Santa Maria Gloriosa dei Frari. Entering this large medieval brick building we experience the cool expanse of the nave, its height, length, and breadth. It was built by a mendicant preaching order to accommodate massive congregations. As you walk further in and centre yourself beneath the gabled roof, flanked by ranks of side chapels, each with their painted altarpieces and tombs recording dead doges, the mortal remains of patricians, admirals and artists, you are faced by a richly carved marble rood screen that portions off the monks' choir from the nave. The tiled floor of pink Verona marble offsets white Istrian limestone and, high up ahead above the high altar table, neatly framed by the round headed arch of the choir screen, is one of the greatest masterpieces of the world: Titian's *Assumption of the Virgin* (fig.19). This colossal painting, with its three tiers of images, is still contained within its original, richly carved and gilded, tabernacle frame (fig.43). Titian's picture was painted for a sacred function and, in situ, it admirably fulfils that function.[1] But how can other such works of art divorced from their original, intended destinations – and even parted from Venice – ever exert such potent magic? At the Frari that magic is heightened and contained by the surrounding context, the monks' choir with its intricately carved images of saints and scenes of Venice worked in intarsia, the sweet aroma of incense clinging in the air, the crucifix and candles standing on the altar table beneath, the plethora and palimpsest of artistic masterpieces – stained glass, marbles, mosaics, bronzes, wood carvings, textiles, church furnishings – that, together, constitute an unforgettable ensemble.

We have intentionally tried in this exhibition to provide some of these sensations by showing not only paintings, drawings and prints but also sculpture, furniture, textiles, ceramics, glass, and enamels. Some were made in Venice, or on the islands of the lagoon, but others were made on the *terraferma* of the Veneto, for the delectation of Titian's Venetian contemporaries. These works of art have been selected from historic or contemporary Scottish collections to represent what Venetians used in the late fifteenth and throughout the sixteenth century.

When looking at a picture in this exhibition I suggest that we might ask ourselves a few questions. Who was it painted for? Why? Are the family introduced into the picture? If so, what do we know about that family? What was the original purpose of the picture? How was it originally framed, lit, and hung? How high was it supposed to be? Was it indeed built into furniture like a *cassone* or the frieze or wainscoting of a room? Was it originally placed in juxtaposition with free-standing sculpture? Do similar pieces of marble, bronze, textiles, maiolica or glass seen in this exhibition re-appear in the picture? Was a dialogue originally intended between the painting, the sculpture and the spectator? Questions of condition and attribution are of course crucial but pictures live on so many other planes.

In the Frari, San Marco, Santi Giovanni e Paolo (known in local dialect as San Zanipolo) and indeed other more modest Venetian churches, we admire sacred pictures by the artists represented in this exhibition; but, unlike those in the Edinburgh show, many are still contained within their original marble or wooden frames, sometimes with magnificent cut velvet or damask altar-frontals suspended beneath and, on the raised altar tables, still stand bronze crucifixes and candlesticks. Bronze statuettes commonly appear mounted as terminals to holy water stoups, and supporting candle branches, while full-length statues, in painted wood or marble, either serve as altarpieces themselves or flank painted altarpieces. High up in the lancets or rose windows may be stained glass designed by some of the greatest artists – Giovanni Bellini, Vivarini, Cima da Conegliano, or Mansueti (fig.44).[2] Because of the unavoidable presence of rising and penetrating damp, fresco, so familiar all over other parts of Italy, was quite often avoided in Venice itself, with the painted images by artists like Titian, Palma Vecchio and Tintoretto here being transposed into mosaics.[3]

Frames in fifteenth-century Italy, the Low Countries and Germany, were usually designed. This was probably the case for Giovanni Bellini's *Virgin and Child Enthroned with Saints* (1488) in the sacristy of the Frari (fig.7), the frame of which is signed by the frame-maker Jacopo da Faenza, an independent craftsman presumably working to Bellini's designs. Here a *Sacra conversazione* is divided into three vertical sections, with in the centre the Virgin and Child enthroned within an apse, flanked by two standing saints to the left and to the right. The concept is a triumphal arch motif, with elaborately carved and gilded Corinthian pilasters, which are then quoted in Bellini's own picture space; the spiky cresting, with its pairs of winged sirens supporting flaming candelabra, provides a delightful reflection of typical early fifteenth-

Fig.43 | View of the interior of the Church of Santa Maria Gloriosa dei Frari, Venice, looking towards the high altar and showing Titian's *The Assumption of the Virgin*

opposite | Detail from cat.no.193

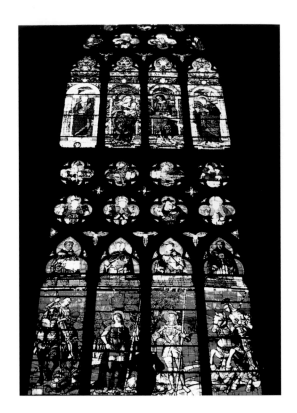

century Venetian triptychs with their crocketed and pinnacled gables. Such frames, not usually as complex as the Frari altarpiece, continued to be integral to the pictures. Exceptions appear more commonly as the sixteenth century unfolded. For example, Jacopo Tintoretto's *Christ Carried to the Tomb* (cat.no.66) was originally framed in stone and en suite in San Francesco della Vigna with the other altars designed by the architect Jacopo Sansovino.

To view easel pictures in Edinburgh by Jacopo Tintoretto but not to experience his luxuriant canvases in situ in the Scuola di San Rocco, just two minutes walk away from the Frari, may be something of a disappointment. At the Scuola, in the Sala Superiore, Tintoretto's oil paintings are contained by the massive carpentry of a richly carved and gilded walnut ceiling, writhing with flutes, volutes, and strapwork of complex geometry (fig.45).[4] The ceiling carpentry was begun in 1574 and substantially completed by the following year; Tintoretto's cycle of twenty-one oil paintings was finished by February 1578. Tintoretto's San Rocco paintings, in particular his enormous *Crucifixion,* are nothing short of breathtaking, the closest equivalent in Venice to Michelangelo's Sistine frescoes.

The framing of ceiling paintings was commonly the responsibility of the architect and not the painter, but that architect often performed roles other than pure architecture. The concept of the distinct specialist architect was, however, hardly recognisable in fifteenth-century Italy, but with the likes of Sanmicheli, Scamozzi, and

Palladio in the following century, it was to become a profession. Today we think of a familiar type of Venetian sixteenth-century mannerist frame with its symmetrical arrangement of strapwork as a 'Sansovino' frame (fig.46); Jacopo Sansovino may have designed the first, but we have no firm evidence for this. After the terrible fires in the Palazzo Ducale of 1574 and 1577, there was an immediate demand for new ceilings and these illusionistic ceilings, complete with extended Sansovino-type mouldings, became most fashionable. One of the chief designers of such ceilings was Cristoforo Sorte (1506/10–after 1594), the Veronese architect, engineer and cartographer who had worked, in his youth, for Giulio Romano at Palazzo Tè in Mantua. It was Sorte who was responsible for the enormous ceiling of the Sala del Maggior Consiglio (1578–83) and the Sala del Senato, or Pregadi (1578–87) which incorporated, respectively thirty-five and thirteen inset paintings (fig.48).[5]

Context cannot be confined just to churches and religious confraternities. One cannot overlook the multitude of state buildings, and private houses belonging to Venetian patricians, that contained ceilings painted with allegories, glories and family apotheoses, along with ranks of portraits. Snaking down the Grand Canal are these characteristic glittering palaces (or 'Cà' in Venice, the abbreviation of 'Casa'). Their tiled roofs are articulated by a variety of curious funnel-like chimney-stacks, built to lift smoke well above the city, and studded with obelisks to record the domain of a distinguished naval family

above left Fig.44 | Giovanni Antonio Licinio and others after designs by Bartolomeo Vivarini, Cima da Conegliano and Giromano Mocetto, stained-glass windows
Venice, Church of Santi Giovanni e Paolo

above Fig.45 | The Chapter Room of the Scuola Grande di San Rocco, Venice, showing the cycle of canvases executed by Jacopo Tintoretto

below Fig.46 | Jacopo Sansovino, *The Virgin and Child,* polychromed and parcel-gilt cartapesta, in a carved wooden 'Sansovino' frame
Fort Worth, Kimbell Art Museum

Fig.49 | Carlo Naya, *View taken from the Traghetto di San Tomà showing the Palazzi Rezzonico, Giustiniani and Foscari, Venice*
England, Private Collection

below left Fig.47 | Cristoforo Sorte, *Design for the Ceiling of the Sala dei Pregadi in the Palazzo Ducale, Venice*
London, Victoria and Albert Museum

below right Fig. 48 | Cristoforo Sorte and others, *The Ceiling of the Sala dei Pregadi*
Venice, Palazzo Ducale

that boasted a 'capitano da mar' (or Venetian admiral).[6] These buildings are marked off by painted posts, like barbers' poles, sunk into the mud of the canal for mooring boats (see fig.49). They are invariably painted with the heraldic colours and metals of the family livery.

Venetian palaces follow a common pattern forced upon them by being built on rafts supported on oak piles driven into the mud. They are attached by their sides to their neighbouring palaces, allowing windows only onto the canal in front and onto a courtyard behind. Inside the

basamenti, which open onto the canal, are boat houses, store rooms, and a dock for the family gondola. Up the first flight of steps is a hall or *portego* with a symmetrical, formal arrangement of seats and benches, where family heraldry was often introduced. There may also have been a painted family pedigree, flags from captured Turkish ships, and a carved wooden lanthorn from the poop of a Venetian admiral's galley. Rising another flight there is usually a long narrow *gran salone*, lit at one end by a generous window looking onto the Grand Canal and at the other end by lesser windows lit from a subsidiary canal, courtyard, or *calle*. These buildings usually form a set pattern, the *gran salone* having a timber ceiling with a range of painted and gilded beams running parallel to the canal. Further floors above culminate in an attic storey, hot in the summer and cold in the winter, retained for the servants' quarters.

Within these fine buildings with their offices, studies, private chapels and bedrooms were originally hung pictures – portraits, devotional pictures, classical mythologies – and sometimes Flemish tapestries, while Turkey carpets covered tables or were hung out of windows on high days and holidays. Then there were rare pieces of Chinese porcelain, sets of *sgabelli* (hall chairs or stands for busts, with solid wooden platforms), pairs of *cassoni* (chests for storing textiles, forming part of a marriage dowry), all most sophisticated in design and carved in walnut, often partly gilt (see cat.nos.216, 219 and 220). Precious vessel glass would have been much in evidence, being a speciality manufacture of the Venetian island of Murano, and there also might have been a *credenza* (set of tiered shelves) of Venetian maiolica (tin-glazed earthenware). These *istoriato* (literally decorated with painted

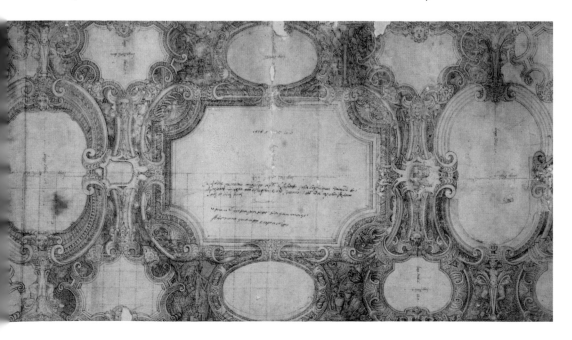

histories) maiolica dishes would come in sets often painted with moralising historical and mythological subjects. Probably most of the maiolica Venetians owned would have been made at Castel Durante or Urbino – away south in the Marches – but they might also have bought pieces locally, for example from Domenico da Venezia, who was an active and prolific potter and painter during the mid-century (see cat.nos.238–42, 248). Maiolica was never really a speciality of Venice, for they had their own magnificent glass manufacture and, moreover, much easier access to oriental porcelain than most of the other Italian city states. Noticeably, in his *Feast of the Gods* now in Washington (see cat.no.17 and fig.91), Bellini provided Parnassus with a fine show of Chinese, Ming dynasty, blue and white porcelain vessels. Such Chinese (and Islamic) exemplars were often copied by potters painting in blue on a white ground ('alla porcellana'), or sometimes in blue and white on a greyish blue glaze ('al berettino'). Artists were clearly aware of their native potters' ability and it was Titian himself that Alfonso I, Duke of Ferrara contacted in Venice in 1520 to commission a set of maiolica jars. By the mid-1550s Venice seems to have specialised in pottery distinctively decorated with fruit. The potter Cipriano Piccolpasso of Castel Durante in his *I Tre libri del Arte del Vassaio* mentions specifically 'fruit … a Venetian style of painting, very pretty things'. (see cat.nos.238, 239).[7]

We still know far too little about the designers of maiolica in Venice and the Veneto. Certainly, the Venetian painter Battista Franco made a large number of drawings for maiolica produced in the Marche factories of Castel Durante, Urbino, and Pesaro – the so-called 'Scuola Metaurensis'; one of Franco's designs of the *History of Joseph*, although much debased, almost certainly appears on a Pesaro dish exhibited here (cat.no.244).[8] Textiles were also designed by some of the major artists, with tapestries invented by Andrea Schiavone and liturgical vestments and hangings by Jacopo and Domenico Tintoretto and Palma Giovane (see cat.no.118).[9]

Out of Venice in the countryside of the *terraferma*, Venetian patricians passed their lives in classical villas often frescoed with mythologies, bucolic and hunting scenes appropriate to their rural environment. These villas – farms, for the most part on reclaimed land – many by Andrea Palladio (see cat.no.167), were self-conscious re-creations of ancient Roman architecture and the sixteenth-century Venetian owners, luxuriating in benefits culled from their Venetian maritime empire, were to live out their lives engrossed in reading the works of Virgil, Julius Caesar, Cicero, and Pliny, as much ancient Romans as cinquecento Venetians – in remarkably the same way as British patricians, enjoying the benefits of an even larger maritime empire, lived out their lives in Palladian country houses two hundred years later.

Sculpture, such a permanent memorial of antiquity, was one of the great providers of aesthetic delights of this golden age. The *paragone,* or argument over the rival claims to superiority between sculpture and painting, became a burning issue in Renaissance Italy, especially in Venice. Although the Venetians conspicuously lacked a great Roman history of their own, curiously enough it was they and not the Florentines who were to commission the most faithful recreations of classical sculpture. More than was the case with the painters, many of the sculptors working in Venice were technically not Venetians. We think, for example, of Nicolò di Giovanni Fiorentino, Riccio, Moderno, the Lombardo family, Mosca, Jacopo Sansovino, Alessandro Vittoria; none of them were born in Venice.

The progress of Venetian sculpture in the fifteenth and early sixteenth centuries is not in synchrony with Venetian painting and, as in Tuscany, developments in reproducing and simulating classical sculpture preceded the same movement in painting. The prolific Antonio Rizzo (1430–1499), not represented in this exhibition, produced massive tombs of doges inhabited by tiers of sculpted figures, resembling something not unlike a triumphal arch but ornamented by ranges of standing figures like the west end of a Gothic cathedral. These sumptuous old-fashioned edifices differed from the controlled classicism of the architect and sculptor Pietro Lombardo (1435–1515, see fig.50) and his sons Tullio (1455–1532) and Antonio (1458–1516). Not only were Lombardo statues in the antique manner, but they were soundly realised anatomically. The chiselling, drilling and polishing was superb. So too were a series of rectangular marble high reliefs, full of recondite scholarly classical allusions that Antonio Lombardo pioneered, the majority carved for the so-called *camerino di marmo* (or *d'alabastro*) of Alfonso d'Este in the castle of Ferrara. Other small portable reliefs from the Lombardo circle, some bearing Latin inscriptions carefully cut into the backs, seem to have been made specifically for a small group of Paduan humanists and have their closest parallels with the prints of Giulio Campagnola and certain Paduan bronze plaquettes. Clearly trained in Antonio Lombardo's shop, Giovanni Maria Mosca made similar reliefs, and was responsible for a handsome image of *Mucius Scaevola* (cat.no.191).

The sculptural influence of those two great Florentines, Donatello and Verrocchio, through their great equestrian bronze images of the celebrated *condottieri* (mercenary commanders), Gattamelata and Colleone, impacted notably on

Fig.50 | Pietro Lombardo,
Funerary Monument of Doge Pietro Mocenigo
Venice, Church of Santi Giovanni e Paolo

their studies. Foremost amongst the Paduan medallists and providers of plaquettes was Andrea del Briosco called 'il Riccio' (literally 'curly head'). He was a lively and original sculptor who shared with Andrea Mantegna a love of antiquity and, when not modelling sacred subjects, rejoiced in portraying mythological beasts and half humans like sphinxes, satyrs, tritons and nereids indulging in lascivious acts.

One of Riccio's most celebrated works was a massive paschal candlestick made for the basilica of Sant'Antonio (the 'Santo'), Padua. Sections of the model for this great work he then re-used, incorporating elements in his small bronzes. His large output of plaquettes is represented here by three examples (cat.nos.185–7). But Riccio and his contemporaries we know for their lamps, inkstands, sandboxes, bells, mortars, andirons, candlesticks, and doorknockers. Some of the small bronzes to be seen in this exhibition were cast in Padua and Verona, but others were cast in Venice where foundries proliferated mainly to service the large naval Arsenal.

The major sculptor to take up residence in Renaissance Venice was Jacopo Tatti, called Sansovino, who adopted the surname of his master Andrea Sansovino, no relation.[10] Jacopo Sansovino by birth and training was Florentine. He was invited to Venice after the Sack of Rome in 1527 to operate as *proto* or architectural majordomo for the Procurators of St Mark's. His mellifluous early style, influenced by Andrea del Sarto (with whom he had shared a studio) and classical antiquity, probably influenced his friend Titian. Certainly Sansovino and Titian appear to have shared something of a common language in their Madonnas and mythologies. Jacopo modelled a series of statuettes and reliefs (see fig.187) that were cast in bronze for the sacristy door and two pulpits in the basilica of St Mark's. He also modelled and cast four much larger figures of gods in niches for the Loggetta beneath the Campanile in St Mark's Square (see fig.51). His relief style continued to betray his Florentine training and even a nostalgic admiration for Donatello and Ghiberti, while some of his visual vocabulary was even nurtured on the poetic imagery of Dante. We know that Sansovino, as a youth in Florence, had supplied clay or wax models to assist the painters Perugino and Sarto and he may perhaps have done the same later for Titian and Lotto.[11]

In his role as *proto*, Sansovino must have spent much of his time not in sculpting but in designing. His great architectural achievements, like the Zecca (Mint), the Libreria Marciana (Library), the Logetta and the Procuratie Nuove (new offices of the Procurators) – the latter first conceived by Sansovino but built after his death by Scamozzi – required a great deal of free-standing and relief sculpture. Considering these

sculptors and foundries working within the Veneto as, of course, did Donatello's superb bronzes for the high altar of church of Sant'Antonio Padua. Bartolomeo Bellano's art depended heavily on Donatello's influence, as is manifested here by Severo's bronze of *David* (cat.no.180). Many small bronze plaquettes with reliefs in imitation, or even as counterfeits, of classical prototypes were produced in Padua, as well as counterfeit Roman coins and medals. These coins, mostly struck or cast by Giovanni da Cavino (1500–1570), known as 'Paduans', were also manufactured for classical scholars to furnish

Fig.51 | Jacopo Sansovino, *The Loggetta*
Venice, Piazza San Marco

Fig.52 | Alessandro Vittoria, Palazzo Balbi
on the Grand Canal, Venice

opposite | Detail from cat.no.216

major schemes, it is remarkable how few of Sansovino's models and drawings survive. He certainly depended on a talented band of pupils and assistants to carry out these sculptural programmes. None of them became more of an alter ego for him than the sculptor Alessandro Vittoria, who had been summoned to Venice from his native Trento by Cardinal (Prince) Cristoforo Madruzzo in 1543 and remained working as Sansovino's apprentice and assistant for twelve years (cat.nos.203–6). As a decorative sculptor providing stucco reliefs for the vaulted ceiling of the Scala d'Oro in the Ducal Palace, marble figures in the spandrels of the Marciana Library, figures of caryatids, slaves, fantastic chimney pieces and decorative window surrounds, Vittoria was without equal in Venice and the Veneto. Vittoria, however, fell out with his master in 1551–3 and he left Venice for Vicenza, only returning when his quarrel with Sansovino was patched up, through the good offices of Pietro Aretino. Above all it was Vittoria who produced a magnificent series of portrait busts of contemporary Venetian worthies which are the nearest equivalent we have in sculpture to Titian's great portraits. These busts were all modelled in clay and then transferred to marble, with the draped and / or armoured torsos and socles often following a standard formula. This exhibition contains a little known terracotta *Head of an Elderly Warrior* probably by Vittoria (cat.no.207).

Vittoria also worked as an architect designing, the Scuola di San Girolamo (now the Ateneo Veneto) and the Palazzo Balbi (fig.52), and assisting Sansovino with the church of San

Zulian. Indeed, after the death of Sansovino in 1570 and Titian in 1576, Vittoria became the dominant Venetian artist until his own death in 1608. The painter most closely akin to Vittoria was Veronese and, with Veronese's fictive architecture and sculpture, one cannot but ask oneself are these designs by Vittoria or might Vittoria sometimes have been working to the designs of Veronese?

The biographies of many talented sculptors in Venice during the mid- to late sixteenth century follow similar patterns. They were trained under Sansovino, commissioned to carve, in marble or Istrian stone, parapet statues and other enrichments on Sansovino's buildings and sometimes those of his rivals. They sculpted monuments in churches for members of the Venetian oligarchy, and competed for prestigious commissions for the marble shrine of St Anthony in his eponymous basilica at Padua. They also produced a few small signed bronzes. These were often prominently placed, surmounting holy water stoups in churches. At other times they produced little objects 'all'antica', to gratify the tastes of a later generation of humanist scholar-collectors.[12] This applies to such artists as Danese Cattaneo (*c*.1509–1572), his pupil Girolamo Campagna, Tiziano Aspetti, who sometimes operated as Campagna's assistant, and Nicolò Roccatagliata (cat.nos.213–5), who according to his earliest biographer, Raffaello Soprani, was employed by Jacopo Tintoretto as a 'maker of models'.

Nearly all the works of art in this exhibition were acquired for, or even specifically designed for, buildings in Venice and its dominions. Some were probably displayed in palaces and churches in the Venetian gothic style, characteristic of the lagoon, with Latin cross plans, often in brick with Istrian stone enrichments to ogee gables, windows with reticulated tracery and trefoil or quatrefoil heads, merlon parapets regimented with pinnacles. Roofs were timber framed; stone vaults were usually avoided as they were very liable to crack from subsidence. The façades in brick with Istrian stone were usually clad in a veneer of rich marbles and porphyry, displaying a marked Eastern, Byzantine influence. At its richest this style is manifested in the Ducal Palace. It is these types of buildings that John Ruskin lauded in *The Stones of Venice* (1851–3) and it was these buildings that were so much copied in nineteenth-century Britain, especially in Glasgow in such buildings as the Ca'd'Oro, Gordon Street by John Honeyman (1872), the Stock Exchange, Buchannan Street by John Burnet (1875–7) and Templeton's Factory, Glasgow Green by William Leiper (1888). In Edinburgh we boast a Venetian palace in Robert Rowand Anderson's Scottish National Portrait Gallery, Queen Street, of 1885–90.

Sixteenth-century Venice and the Veneto were dominated architecturally by three supreme classical architects. Jacopo Sansovino, the multi-talented Florentine who had arrived in Venice after the Sack of Rome to become architect and surveyor of St Mark's, has already been discussed. There were then his rivals Michele Sanmicheli of Verona (1484–1559), the great fortifications expert who built the magnificent gates of Verona and the fort of Sant'Andrea al Lido guarding the sea approach to the *Serenissima*, and Andrea Palladio, who had first worked in his native Vicenza (see fig.54).

It was above all Palladio who was to make much later the biggest impact on Scottish domestic architecture and this is indeed a continuing legacy.[13] Palladio developed on the *terraferma,* and especially along the banks of the Brenta canal, a type of courtly house, often of modest dimensions. He largely adhered to the purity of the Vitruvian architectural orders and proportions, often with rusticated ground floors, imposing outside staircases to the *piano nobile*, triangular headed pedimented porticoes, like temple fronts, and pairs of independent pavilions to accommodate mundane functions like farm barns, kitchens and offices that were linked to the nucleus by elegant colonnades. Two hundred years later these houses, known from Palladio's celebrated book *I Quattro libri dell'architettura di Andrea Palladio*, first published in Venice in 1570 (see cat.no.167), became the most favoured models for Scottish architects. One wonders how architects like William Adam, William Chambers, Robert Mylne, and Robert Adam and his brothers would have developed without Palladio

as their lode star. Indeed such familiar houses in Scotland as Arniston, Duddingston, Duff House, the House of Dun, Pollock, and Paxton are such credible Palladian revivals that they would not look out of place on the Brenta.

In Venice itself, by the 1560s, Palladio was getting commissions to build churches like San Giorgio Maggiore (begun in 1566 but completed only in 1611, long after the architect's death), the votive church of the Redentore (the Redeemer, 1577–92) and the façade of San Francesco della Vigna, added to a building already built by Sansovino. When discussing context we should be aware that this exhibition provides us with the special opportunity not only to see the foundation medal of the church of San Francesco, with on the reverse a portrait of its very distinguished patron Doge Andrea Gritti (cat.no.197), but also to see a book dedicated to Gritti (cat.no.163) and two drawings by Battista Franco for the Barbaro chapel inside (cat.nos.97, 98), and also Jacopo Tintoretto's altarpiece of *Christ Carried to the Tomb*, painted for the Dal Basso chapel (cat.no.66).

It is often stated that Venice by the late fifteenth century was already in decline and that the battle of Agnadello in 1509, when Venice lost its entire *terraferma* empire to a powerful coalition of the Papacy, the French, and the Holy Roman Empire, was confirmation of this situation. However, by 1517 all the *terraferma* had been recovered. Venice was increasingly under pressure from the sea route discovered by Vasco da Gama around the Cape of Good Hope in 1498, which was to undermine their own maritime trade routes with the near east connected by land to India and China. They were also pressured by the Turkish menace, only halted dramatically in 1571 by the great sea battle of Lepanto, a victory that was never properly followed up. The message that Venetians wished to proclaim in all their artistic manifestations was that the *Serenissima* was still a great and energetic power to be reckoned with, and, moreover, it was still fabulously wealthy. This was demonstrated by their luxurious paintings, with the *dramatis personae* habited in the richest velvets, spotted furs, silks and satins, publicising their authority and majesty. Prestige or *bella figura* is, and was, everything in Italy and so the Venetians continued to build on a sumptuous scale and cultivated their native industries, particularly of glass and mosaic.

As Venice had always traded with the Levant, Persian carpets, Islamic brass utensils and Syrian glass were particularly familiar in the grander Venetian homes.[14] Indeed, Eastern carpets and rugs often appear in the paintings of artists like Lotto, Moroni, and the Bassano, sometimes at the foot of the Virgin's throne in a *Sacra conversazione*, or draped over trestle tables. Syrian

Fig.53 | Carlo Ponti, *Libreria Marciana and the Columns with Statues of the Lion of St Mark and St Theodore* Edinburgh, Scottish National Photography Collection, Scottish National Portrait Gallery

Fig.54 | Andrea Palladio, a doorway at San Giorgio Maggiore, Venice

style glass lamps appear suspended in the fictive apses painted in altarpieces or lighting the study of St Jerome. The turbaned Turk was clearly a familiar sight in Venice. Near-eastern metalworkers may have lived in Venice and cast, turned, chased and inlaid candlesticks, dishes and boxes in brass with elaborately engraved geometric arabesques – so called Veneto-Saracenic work (see cat.nos. 221–3). Judging from the frequent incorporation of Venetian heraldry, these were made as luxury items for Venetian oligarchs. Also in Venice flourished a native production of enamels. These largely consisted of show dishes (*piatti di pompa*), chalices, candlesticks, flasks, and salts that were enamelled in smalt blue and white, lightly gilded. The repoussé forms, often with whirls of bulbous fluting, and pricket candlesticks of squat spreading forms, following contemporary patterns of brass and silver, were clearly produced in large quantities.[15]

Sumptuous textiles were imported from Turkey and Syria, and these rich patterns of luxuriant blooms, fruit, and foliage were copied in Venice. Unfortunately, it is virtually impossible to differentiate velvets, silks, and satins made in Venice from those made by their rivals in say Genoa, Florence, or Lucca. But contemporary Venetians would not have confined themselves to Venetian fabrics. These rich stuffs were hung as 'cloths of honour' behind the throne of the Blessed Virgin, worn by the doge and procurators, and as liturgical vestments by the clergy. Venetian ladies, and particularly Venetian

courtesans (a speciality of the city), were sumptuously attired but it seems that some of the grander ladies' and men's habits were hired out for functions.

Venice still survives, plundered by Napoleon and by generations of rapacious collectors but with a good many of her treasures still intact, providing a context for her art. In Venice one is always aware of water and the wide variety of boats – in particular that most elegant historic conveyance, the gondola (fig.55). Sadly, no great Venetian galley of the era of Lepanto survives intact. Such sleek vessels magnificently decorated by a plethora of craftsmen, equipped with armoured soldiers, bronze cannon and tiers of galley slaves, must have been unforgettable images of power and beauty, effortlessly unifying the arts of war with the fine and decorative arts. Such galleys were the pride of the *Serenissima*, built to defend a vision of Utopia. That Utopia, as conceived by the Venetian Senate, was articulated by one of them in 1535:
[Venice] has grown, been ornamented and constructed so as to become the most beautiful and illustrious city which at present exists in the world.[16]

Fig.55 | Carlo Naya, *View of St Mark's Square from the Bacino*
Edinburgh, Scottish National Photography Collection,
Scottish National Portrait Gallery

COLLECTING VENETIAN PAINTING IN SCOTLAND

Peter Humfrey

Some months after the outbreak of the Civil War in 1642, the magnificent private collection assembled by James, 3rd Marquess and later 1st Duke of Hamilton (1606–1649, fig.56), was packed into forty-four crates. The plan was to send his pictures, numbering a staggering 600, from the dangers surrounding his London home of Chelsea Place to his ancestral seat in Scotland. Of this 600, a very high proportion consisted of masterpieces by the great names of Venetian Renaissance painting: Giovanni Bellini, Giorgione, Titian, Jacopo Bassano, Tintoretto and Veronese.

The pictures never reached their intended destination. The arrangements for their evacuation were made too late, and the crates were confiscated by parliament. After Hamilton had followed his royal master, Charles I, to the scaffold in 1649, many of the finest of the pictures were sold to Archduke Leopold Wilhelm, the Austrian governor of the southern Netherlands. Some idea both of the quality of the former Hamilton collection and of its predominantly Venetian character may be judged from the various depictions of the archducal gallery in Brussels made immediately afterwards by Leopold Wilhelm's court painter David Teniers. Clearly discernible in Teniers's picture (fig.57), are Giorgione's *Three Philosophers* (fig.13) and *Laura* (fig.14); Titian's *Nymph and Shepherd* (fig.28) and versions of his *Doge Francesco Donà* (cat.no.38), *Diana and Callisto* (cat.no.55), *Woman at her Toilet* (fig.131), and *Danaë* (fig.26); together

with pictures by Schiavone, Bassano, Tintoretto and Veronese, most of them likewise now in the Kunsthistorisches Museum in Vienna.[1]

It is an intriguing thought that if the catastrophic events of the 1640s had played out differently, Scotland might by the middle of the seventeenth century have possessed one of the richest collections of Venetian Renaissance paintings in the world. It would be unwise, however, to dwell for too long on this thought. At this early date in the history of British collecting, the medieval stronghold of Hamilton Palace, in the wilds of Lanarkshire, would have been regarded by no one, least of all by Hamilton himself, as an appropriate permanent home for a gallery of great Italian pictures. One can only guess why he nearly wrecked his family's fortune by the extravagance of his spending on art, but a central motive would certainly have been to win prestige and influence with the king. Charles I had created his own magnificent collection at Whitehall, again with a strongly Venetian character, and showing a particular predilection for Titian (see cat.no.65). Venetian pictures also featured prominently in the collections of other leading members of Charles's court, notably those of the Earl of Arundel and the Duke of Buckingham; Hamilton's own father, the 2nd Marquess, had owned works by, or attributed to, Palma Vecchio, Schiavone, Bassano, Tintoretto, Veronese and Palma Giovane.[2] Hamilton was provided with the perfect opportunity to imitate the king and to compete with his political rivals

Fig.56 | Daniel Mytens, *Portrait of James Hamilton, 1st Duke of Hamilton*
Edinburgh, Scottish National Portrait Gallery

Fig.57 | David Teniers, *The Picture Gallery of Archduke Leopold Wilhelm*
Madrid, Museo Nacional del Prado

opposite | Detail from cat.no.40

when in 1634 his brother-in-law Basil, Lord Feilding, became English ambassador to the Republic of Venice. During the course of the next three or four years, Hamilton acquired, through Feilding, three entire Venetian collections of exceptional quality and by having these shipped to London, he would have been well aware of the potential value of his pictures as strategic gifts to the king. Hamilton was not primarily an aesthete but a highly ambitious courtier, and his flamboyance as a collector may indeed have contributed indirectly to his elevation to a dukedom in 1643.

Most of Hamilton's fellow Scots would have agreed that the only proper place for his collection was near the court in London, but their perspective would have been a very different one. In mid-seventeenth-century Scotland, probably even more than in England, the collecting of Italian pictures would have seemed an entirely frivolous pursuit. Giorgione's *Laura* and Titian's *Diana and Callisto* would have been deemed scandalously lascivious, and Tintoretto's *Christ Carried to the Tomb* and Veronese's *Adoration of the Kings* deplorably popish. Their presence, in short, would not have been welcome. It was to be another century and a half before the aesthetic tastes of the much resented Charles I and his Scottish deputy began to be fully shared by Scottish collectors.

THE FIRST VENETIAN PAINTINGS IN SCOTLAND

In the seventeenth and eighteenth centuries the paintings that furnished even the grandest of Scottish houses would have consisted above all of family portraits. To these might have been added topographical views, likewise painted by local artists; but here, too, the main purpose of art was the strictly utilitarian one of stressing the owner's status and lineage, and perhaps also his political loyalties. Any taste for continental art naturally focused on Dutch rather than Italian painting, as a result of long-established commercial and cultural ties with the northern Netherlands, and a shared Calvinist religion. Already by 1700, in fact, some quite important collections of Dutch pictures had been formed in Scotland by members of the nobility and landed gentry such as the Earls of Lothian and the Earls of Balcarres, and the Clerks, baronets of Penicuik. Their example was followed in the eighteenth century by the Dukes of Argyll, the Earls of Wemyss, and many others.[3]

It was, however, William Kerr, 3rd Earl of Lothian (*c*.1605–1675), working with John Clerk, a Scottish merchant based in Paris, who may be given credit for taking the first modest step towards importing Venetian pictures into Scotland.[4] In many ways characteristic of its time and place, the collection formed by Lothian from the 1640s onwards at his seat of Newbattle

Abbey, near Dalkeith, consisted almost exclusively of portraits by Netherlandish, English and Scottish painters. But its much more ambitious scope was unusual, numbering as it did some 300 works, among which – in a spirit of Renaissance humanism – were the images of men and women from all lands and periods, some famous but some anonymous. Also unusual was the breadth of Lothian's cultural horizons. In 1624–5, as a young man, he had undertaken a Grand Tour of the Continent, including Venice, and immediately following a visit to Paris in 1643, where he met Clerk, he engaged him to buy two portraits attributed to Tintoretto from the Portuguese dealer Alfonso López, which had been intended for the recently deceased Cardinal Richelieu.[5] One of these portraits, described simply as a 'pourtraict off a woman' [sic], is now lost or unrecognised. The other, however, described as 'victor Capello large to the knee', is probably identical with a rather damaged portrait still at Newbattle Abbey, seemingly painted by the workshop of Veronese, which may well originally have been a three-quarter length (fig.58).[6] Two other Venetian portraits recorded in a Newbattle inventory of *c*.1726 – a 'Turkish Bashaw' attributed to Tintoretto and a 'Gentleman' by Veronese, are likely similarly to have been acquired by the 3rd Earl of Lothian.

Lothian's agent John Clerk (1611–1674) also imported pictures from the Netherlands and France to Scotland on his own account, including, apparently, the first Rembrandt in 1665,[7] as well as an identified Palma Vecchio and a copy after Titian.[8] Clerk's success as a merchant enabled him to buy the estate of Penicuik, and to launch the careers of his descendants as lairds and baronets. His grandson Sir John, 2nd baronet (1676–1755), and great-grandson Sir James, 3rd baronet (1709–1782), also undertook the Grand Tour of Italy; even if they could not afford to become great collectors, they certainly became cultural leaders in their respective generations, and trusted advisers to British travellers on the sights of Rome, Naples and Venice. Both were enthusiasts for sixteenth- and seventeenth-century Italian painting, including Venetian, and may be credited with helping to stimulate a greater receptiveness for it among their fellow Scots.[9]

Exceedingly expensive as the Grand Tour was, several of the wealthier Scottish noblemen undertook one- or two-year trips to Italy in the eighteenth century. Sometimes, as in the case of the 2nd Marquess of Annandale in 1718–21, the tour was treated in part as a shopping expedition, and the traveller sent quantities of paintings and sculptures back home as trophies to adorn his family seat.[10] In the first half of the century most Scots, including Annandale, gravitated more naturally to Rome than to Venice, prompted in

Fig.58 | School of Paolo Veronese, *Portrait of Agostino Barbarigo*
Newbattle Abbey, Dalkeith, Midlothian
From the collection of the Earls and Marquesses of Lothian

part by their predominantly classical education, and in part by the presence in Rome of the exiled Stuart court.[11] In 1770–1, however, George III's former prime minister, John Stuart, 3rd Earl of Bute (fig.59), stayed in Venice for six months and bought a number of Venetian cinquecento pictures, which besides those in the present exhibition (cat.nos.38, 42, 44, 50, 57), included two Tintorettesque ceiling paintings (fig.61). Yet Bute was somewhat atypical in undertaking his Italian tour comparatively late in life. As a rule, grand tourists were young noblemen sent by their fathers, under the guidance of a tutor, to complete their education and to broaden their minds, but without significant resources to buy art, although many sat to the fashionable portrait painter Pompeo Batoni.[12] During the ancien régime, in any case, Venetian pictures had not yet come onto the market in any quantity, and the patrician owners of important collections in Genoa, as well as in Venice itself, were not yet under any serious pressure to sell.

Like other Scottish noblemen prominent in the affairs of the United Kingdom, Lord Bute's principal residence was in the south of England, at Luton Park not far from London, and it was only in the middle of the twentieth century that the bulk of his collection finally reached his native Scotland. Since the number of Venetian pictures to arrive north of the border before the beginning of the nineteenth century was to remain tiny, it is important to note two exceptional instances. The first of these was at Hamilton Palace, where in 1723 John Macky recorded in the long gallery 'The Marriage of Cana, by Tentoret, which contains more figures than that celebrated one by Paul Veronese in St George's at Venice, also a masterly Piece'. This picture, which Thomas Pennant later in the century described as by Veronese himself, is now unfortunately lost or unrecognised.[13] Surviving in situ at Dumfries House, Ayrshire, by contrast, is a version of Jacopo Bassano's *Jacob's Journey* (the original is in the Royal Collection at Hampton Court), set into an elaborate rococo frame of 1759 by the carver William Mathie of London (fig.60). Nothing is known of the circumstances of the picture's acquisition, but presumably it was bought immediately beforehand by William Dalrymple, 4th Earl of Dumfries, on the fledgling London art market.[14]

For Lord Dumfries, a Venetian picture with a bucolic subject such as the Bassano may have seemed the perfect complement to the Palladian

top Fig.59 | Allan Ramsay,
Portrait of John Stuart, 3rd Earl of Bute
National Trust for Scotland, Bute House

above Fig.60 | Jacopo Bassano, *Jacob's Journey*
Private Collection at Dumfries House

right Fig.61 | School of Tintoretto,
An Allegorical Scene
Private Collection at Mount Stuart

dignity of the house recently built for him by John and Robert Adam in 1754–9. More generally, by the middle of the eighteenth century the Scottish nobility was becoming more responsive to Italian art and culture as an appropriate backdrop to civilised living. But pictures by, or attributed to, the great names of Italian painting were accepted as essential to another important activity: the training of contemporary artists. It was for this reason, rather than for social prestige, that the Glasgow bookseller and publisher Robert Foulis (1707–1776) travelled to Paris and the Netherlands in 1751–2 on an expedition to buy paintings and prints. He had long planned to create an art academy on the continental model, and he accepted that a central part of the students' training was to make copies of religious and mythological subjects by the most admired old masters of the sixteenth and seventeenth centuries.[15]

Unfortunately, Foulis's enterprise turned into a financial disaster. He failed to win any royal or noble patronage for his academy, which was forced to close in 1775, and his collection was sold immediately after his death the following year for a pitifully small sum. According to the three-volume catalogue compiled by Foulis himself, the enormous number of 550 items included thirty-nine optimistically attributed to Raphael, while of the attributions to Venetian cinquecento masters, no fewer than twenty-two were given to Titian, nine to Jacopo Bassano, and eight to Veronese. One of only two paintings from the collection of the Foulis Academy to have been recognised is the copy after Raphael's Borghese *Entombment*, now in the Hunterian Art Gallery, which was bought at the Foulis sale by the University of Glasgow. It seems that the vast majority of Foulis's pictures consisted of seventeenth- and early eighteenth-century copies after old masters, rather than originals. This impression is confirmed by the poor quality engraving of 1764 by one of Foulis's students, James Mitchell (fig.62), after a version then in the academy's collection of Titian's *The Three Ages of Man* (cat.no.15). Although Foulis rashly claimed that some considered his version compared well with Titian's original, then in the celebrated Orléans collection in Paris, Foulis's picture is more likely to have been a copy by the same French painter from whose daughter he bought it.[16] For all his high-minded ambition and idealism, Robert Foulis added little in the end to the still meagre stock of Venetian pictures in eighteenth-century Scotland.

THE ORLÉANS EFFECT AND THREE SCOTTISH DEALERS

Twenty-two years after the spectacularly unsuccessful Foulis sale, the Orléans collection itself – including the original of Titian's *The*

Three Ages of Man – was put up for sale in London.[17] By contrast, this was the most spectacular art sale staged in London since the dispersal of Charles I's pictures in 1649. The collection had been formed principally by Philippe, 2nd Duc d'Orléans (1674–1723), nephew of Louis XIV and regent to Louis XV, and was the greatest private collection in eighteenth-century Europe. While the French royal collection was confiscated by the revolutionary government after 1789, the Orléans collection was allowed to escape to the London art market. Although the cream of the Italian pictures – including eight shown in the present exhibition (cat.nos.11, 15, 19, 25, 54, 55, 66, 81) – had been reserved in advance by a syndicate of three English noblemen, they were exhibited to an astonished public for six months in rooms at Pall Mall and the Strand between December 1798 and July 1799.

The exhibition made a profound impact on British artists and art lovers. Until the foundation of the National Gallery, London in 1824, the opportunities for seeing continental old masters in the original, as opposed to copies or reproductive engravings, were rare. The critic William Hazlitt wrote in rhapsodic terms of the revelatory experience of seeing pictures by Titian, Raphael and the Bolognese masters for the very first time: 'A new sense came upon me, a new heaven and a new earth stood before me …' Hazlitt was particularly responsive to the colouristic tradition of Titian and the Venetians, as opposed to the classicising tradition of Rome and Bologna advocated (although not in practice followed) in the previous generation by Sir Joshua Reynolds. And first-hand acquaintance with the Orléans pictures made artists, too, realise that the British tradition of painting owed more to the Venetians, by way of Rubens and Van Dyck, than to the academic concept of the grand manner.[18]

More directly relevant in the present context, however, is the impact made by the Orléans exhibition on at least two generations of British collectors. In their case the distinction between the Venetian and the Roman-Bolognese tradition was less important than the realisation that huge artistic spoils were to be won from the political and social upheavals taking place in post-revolutionary France and southern Europe. The Orléans collection was just the tip of an iceberg that extended into Italy and Spain, where a suddenly impoverished nobility was being forced to sell artistic treasures accumulated by their ancestors over centuries.[19] The Republic of Venice had finally fallen in 1797, when the last of its 120 doges was deposed and the patriciate lost its hereditary right to govern. In the previous year Napoleon had also taken Genoa, the rich collections of which included a large number of

Fig.62 | James Mitchell, *The Three Ages of Man*
Glasgow, The Mitchell Library

Venetian pictures. The situation of the British nobility was in absolute contrast to the continental ancien régime. Political power, international trade and colonisation, and the Industrial Revolution had made Britain the wealthiest country in the world and this wealth, in Scotland as well as England, belonged almost exclusively to the landed aristocracy. This élite was perfectly placed to give external expression to its power and wealth by acquiring the works of art that were now flooding onto the market from Italy in unprecedented quantity and quality.

But to avail themselves of the continental treasures, most aspiring collectors required the services of middlemen such as dealers or advisers. Of the many such figures operating in the immediate aftermath of the Orléans exhibition and sale, three of the most important happened to be Scots: James Irvine (1759–1831), William Buchanan (1777–1864), and Andrew Wilson (1780–1848).[20] Irvine and Wilson were painters who spent long periods in Italy buying pictures and collections for export to Britain; Buchanan was a trained lawyer who, from his base in Edinburgh and then London, identified and wooed suitable buyers. Although all three spent most of their careers away from their native Scotland, they all naturally had particularly close contacts with the Scottish market. Buchanan was also responsible for writing the most comprehensive contemporary account of the dramatic influx of old master paintings from the Continent in his two-volume *Memoirs of Painting, with a Chronological History of the Importation of Pictures by the Great Masters into England since the French Revolution*, published in 1824.

Irvine, the eldest of the three, was already active as a dealer in Rome in the 1780s, but his most successful period began in the year of the Orléans exhibition, when he met Buchanan in Edinburgh and persuaded him of the opportunities that had been opened up for speculation in old master paintings. For a period of five or six years the two were in partnership, with Irvine travelling to the main cities of Italy to identify suitable pictures, and Buchanan informing him from Edinburgh and London on what to buy, creating the necessary publicity at home and advertising: 'The great object at present is to make a Noise about these pictures, and to let all the Dilettanti know of them.'[21] In a series of letters to Irvine, Buchanan provides a vivid sketch of the current state of the market in London. He wrote scornfully of the collectors' motives: 'It must likewise be taken into consideration that Vanity principally prompts the English to buy – and that Vanity leads purchasers to please the prevailing taste and fashion of their friends, or be governed by the whim and voice of the artists.'[22] Yet Buchanan had no intention of attempting to resist these fashions, and he went

on to name the artists most in demand: 'Of the popular masters at present, Titian and Rubens take the lead', followed by Raphael, Correggio, the Carracci, Van Dyck, Domenichino, Guido Reni, Claude and Murillo. Even when by these great masters, 'disagreeable subjects' and 'brown dark pictures of the Saints and the like' were to be avoided, and the works selected should be of their respective artists' 'best period'.

Here and elsewhere in Buchanan's letters it is noticeable that in the first two or three decades of the nineteenth century, taste attached itself to the big names of the sixteenth and seventeenth centuries rather than to particular schools or traditions. Since Titian was the most sought-after painter of all, a Titianesque subject such as a Danaë by a follower such as Paris Bordon or Schiavone would be an acceptable second best.[23] But of the other great Venetians, Buchanan notes that Veronese was not particularly in demand;[24] he mentions Tintoretto only once and Giorgione not at all. He does refer several times to Bellini's *The Feast of the Gods* (fig.91), but as a picture with which Titian is known to have been involved, and as a pendant to the *Bacchus and Ariadne* (fig.21), rather than as a masterpiece in its own right. The importation of the *Bacchus and Ariadne* in 1806–7 from Rome to London was regarded by both Buchanan and Irvine as the greatest achievement of their partnership. It was immediately bought by the Scottish nobleman Charles, 8th Baron Kinnaird, but never came to Scotland.

Although naturally taking advantage of the British market as a whole, Buchanan and Irvine had many Scottish clients, even if like Lord Kinnaird they were often buying primarily with their London homes in mind. In his line of business, Buchanan was keenly aware of the importance of personal networks. In 1804, in connection with Van Dyck's *Portrait of Charles I in Three Positions* (Windsor Castle, Royal Collection), and with the recent arrival of Lord Breadalbane in Edinburgh, he hoped that 'it may occur to some of the Scotch folks to prompt their great friends to secure this interesting picture'.[25] Years later, in 1827, he corresponded with James Skene of Rubislaw, secretary of the Royal Institution in Edinburgh, about the prospect of founding a National Gallery of Scotland, and offered five pictures for sale – three of which were Venetian, including two supposed Titians – as a basis for a national collection.

Around the same time the now elderly Irvine, still in Italy, put together an art collection of exceptional quality, including several Venetian pictures (cat.nos.33, 36, 37, 60, 71), for Sir William Forbes of Pitsligo, a governor of the Royal Institution, and a neighbour of Irvine's brother, the laird of Drum in Aberdeenshire. It is again indicative of his good connections with

Scottish collectors that when Forbes died in 1828 without ever seeing his collection, Irvine immediately offered one of the pictures, a *Portrait of Pietro Aretino in Profile* attributed to Titian, first to Thomas Erskine of Linlathen, near Dundee, and then to Erskine's brother-in-law, Charles Stirling of Cawder.[26] And in the previous year, 1827, Irvine's one-time business rival, Andrew Wilson, wrote to Skene recommending that Irvine be elected a member of the institution, saying 'he is not a distinguished Artist, but his life has been one of singular benefit to this country for the number of valuable Works of Art which by his exertions have been sent to Britain'.[27]

Wilson had competed with Irvine and Buchanan for the acquisition of the Balbi collection in Genoa in 1805, the biggest prize of which was Jacopo Bassano's *The Adoration of the Kings* (cat.no.40; then attributed to Titian), and on that occasion he had won. In 1818, however, he returned to his native Edinburgh, where among other responsibilities he organised the annual exhibitions of the Royal Institution, and advised the 4th Earl of Hopetoun on picture buying. Back in Genoa in 1826–32 he bought a number of paintings, including several Venetian ones, both for the Royal Institution (cat.nos.48, 67) and for the 5th Earl (cat.no.80).

One of the pictures that Wilson bought for the 4th Earl, the huge *Hunting Scene* here attributed to Francesco Beccaruzzi (cat.no.39), but at that time given to Titian, was acquired from a 'Mr Martin of Edinburgh'. This was almost certainly the dealer Thompson Martin, who in 1822–3 also supplied Sir James Carnegie with Moretto's *King David with a Donor* (cat.no.43), then attributed to Domenichino, and who in 1825 transported a number of pictures from London to Edinburgh for sale by the auctioneer Francis Wright.[28] The local art market had naturally been slower to respond than London to the opportunities created by the Napoleonic wars, and until about 1820 the field was dominated by prints, mainly Netherlandish and English. But thanks to the activities of men such as Martin and Wright, and of other dealers and auctioneers such as Francis Cameron, Charles Galli, and later C.B. Tait, continental old masters began to be sold in Edinburgh,[29] making Venetian pictures available to a Scottish clientele that was no longer limited to grandees with houses in London.

THE GOLDEN AGE OF SCOTTISH COLLECTING

In Scotland, as in England, the first half of the nineteenth century may be regarded as the golden age of the private collecting of old master paintings, including Venetian. It is true that some major Anglo-Scottish collectors kept their

collections in London. That of the 4th Earl of Aberdeen (1784–1860), for example, which included works by Titian (cat.no.64) and Veronese (cat.no.58), seems not to have been transferred to his Scottish seat of Haddo House in his lifetime; that of the 1st Duke of Sutherland (1758–1833) – alias the 2nd Marquess of Stafford – remained at Stafford House in St James's, and never came to Scotland at all. Another distinguished Scottish collection with Venetian pictures, including Titian's early *Rest on the Flight into Egypt* (fig.63) and Tintoretto's *Venus, Mars and Vulcan* (fig.31), was that of Professor H.A.J. Munro of Novar (1819–1878); but it, too, remained in London before being sold after the owner's death.[30] Mention should also be made in this context of the outstanding collection of drawings formed by John Malcolm of Poltalloch (1803–1893), again including important works by Venetian masters such as Giovanni Bellini, Cima, Carpaccio, Titian and Lotto. Although Laird of Poltalloch in Argyllshire from 1857, and often resident at the mansion built by his brother near Lochgilphead, Malcolm kept his collection at his home in London, and his drawings entered the British Museum in 1895 without ever travelling north of the border.[31]

Yet as may be judged from the summaries of individual collections provided in the appendix, the number and quality of those that were based in Scotland in the nineteenth century are truly impressive. As in England, it was now increasingly usual for families belonging to the propertied élite to keep their art collections at their

Fig.63 | Titian, *The Rest on the Flight into Egypt*
Longleat House, Wiltshire, Marquess of Bath
Formerly in the collection of H. A. J. Munro of Novar

country seats rather than in their town houses. In the case of Scotland, this tendency was encouraged by a growing sense of national pride, boosted by the visit to Edinburgh of George IV in 1822, and later by the long love affair between Queen Victoria and Scotland. The rediscovery of the Scottish landscape as an object of romantic beauty further inclined the great landowners to spend more of their time on their estates. The advent of the railways, too, made their seats more accessible from London and Edinburgh. In this same period a large number of the ancestral homes of the Scottish nobility were remodelled or rebuilt, variously in the pompous neoclassical style of the Duke of Hamilton's Hamilton Palace, in the extravagant neo-gothic of the Marquess of Breadalbane's Taymouth Castle or of Lord Kinnaird's Rossie Priory, and in the neo-Tudor of the Earl of Dunmore's Dunmore Park. It is certainly no accident that the same noble re-builders of their seats (or their immediate heirs) were also largely responsible for furnishing them with appropriately splendid collections of old master paintings.

The majority of collectors listed in the appendix were just such aristocratic landowners. Sometimes, as in the cases of the Dukes of Hamilton, the Earls of Crawford and the Earls of Wemyss, these noble families also benefited from the discovery of minerals on their land, and were made newly wealthy by the Industrial Revolution. But agriculture and rents still provided sufficient revenues for the owners of vast Scottish estates such as the Marquess of Breadalbane to fund ambitious building projects and art collections. The same is true of men slightly lower down the social hierarchy, such as those belong-

ing to the baronetage of landed gentry, many of whom, in any case, drew further substantial income from commerce. Charles Stirling of Cawder, for example, was both a local laird and a partner in a Glasgow company trading in the West Indies; Sir William Forbes of Pitsligo had inherited a fortune in banking, as well as his Kincardineshire estate, from his father; and the painter John Graham-Gilbert could similarly afford to be a collector thanks to commercial fortunes inherited from his father and from his wife. Apart from commerce, one of the most lucrative and socially prestigious professions for Scots who preferred not to emigrate south was the law; among the judges (or their sons) whose collections included important Venetian pictures were John Clerk, Lord Eldin, and Sir Archibald Campbell of Succoth. Virtually all the collectors listed here, in fact, even Archibald McLellan, whose father had been a highly successful Glasgow coach-builder, were from a prosperous, if not an aristocratic, social background. The case of Robert Napier, who rose from being the son of a blacksmith to become one of the great ship-building magnates of his day, represents an exception to the rule that was still rare before the middle of the nineteenth century.

For all Scottish collectors of the period, the pace was set by the premier peer of Scotland, Alexander Hamilton, 10th Duke of Hamilton (fig.64). He was the earliest in the field, having begun collecting in Italy as Marquess of Douglas soon after the Orléans sale in London, and the collection with which he furnished his grandiose seat of Hamilton Palace, which was largely rebuilt from the 1820s, remained unsurpassed in Scotland in size, if not always in quality. This and

Fig.64 | Henry Raeburn, *Portrait of Alexander Hamilton, 10th Duke of Hamilton*
Lord Cowdray

Fig.65 | Jacopo Tintoretto, *Moses Striking the Rock*
Frankfurt, Städelsches Kunstinstitut
Formerly in the collection of the Dukes of Hamilton

the other main collections formed before about 1850 continue to reflect a taste that essentially corresponds to that of the Orléans collection: that is to say, of the eighteenth century. Predictably well represented at Hamilton Palace were seventeenth-century masters such as Annibale and Lodovico Carracci, Domenichino, Poussin, Rubens, Van Dyck and Salvator Rosa; and of the sixteenth-century masters, the Venetians predominated, with works by Titian (cat.no.35), Bonifacio, Schiavone, Moroni (cat.no.61), Tintoretto (fig.65) and Veronese (fig.40).

The Hamilton collection also reflects the beginnings of a new interest in the so-called Italian Primitives, the masters of the fifteenth century and earlier. As early as 1800–1, when in Italy, the future duke had bought Antonello da Messina's *Portrait of a Man*, 1474 (fig.12) and a huge, Bellinesque altarpiece by Girolamo dai Libri (fig.66).[32] These acquisitions may in part reflect the influence of William Beckford, an early enthusiast for the Primitives, whom Hamilton had known since he was a boy, and whose daughter, Susan, he married in 1810.[33] In the case of two other fifteenth-century pictures, however, by Catena and Cima (cat.nos.7, 10), the novelty was disguised by wildly inaccurate attributions, respectively to Leonardo da Vinci

and Herri met de Bles. But from about the 1840s two Scottish collectors, James Dennistoun and Lord Lindsay, were playing a major pioneering role in establishing a more widespread taste for pre-sixteenth-century painting. While Lindsay clearly preferred the Florentines and the Umbrians, Dennistoun owned not only a Madonna by Cima (fig.8), but also a gold-ground polyptych by the mid-fifteenth-century Paduan painter Giorgio Schiavone (fig.67).

Other collections to reflect this novel taste were those of Lord Elcho, who owned a triptych by Bartolomeo Vivarini (cat.no.1); Archibald McLellan, whose Catena was then attributed to Cima (cat.no.8); and John Graham-Gilbert, who owned probably the first authentic Giovanni Bellini to come to Scotland (cat.no.3). But none of these collectors, not even Dennistoun and Lindsay, attempted to be rigidly purist in their interest in the fifteenth century and, not surprisingly, among their Venetian pictures the sixteenth century continued to predominate. Indeed, the new interest in the Primitives was a manifestation of a broadening concept of the history of art, whereby whole schools and periods became objects of study and appreciation, and attention was no longer focused, as in Buchanan's day, on a limited number of great

Fig.66 | Girolamo dai Libri, *The Virgin and Child with Saints*
New York, The Metropolitan Museum of Art, Fletcher Fund, 1920 (20.92)
Formerly in the collection of the Dukes of Hamilton

Fig.67 | Giorgio Schiavone, *Polyptych with the Virgin and Child Enthroned, the Pietà, and Eight Saints*
London, National Gallery
Formerly in the collections of James Johnston of Straiton and James Dennistoun

Fig.68 | A. J. Woolmer, *A View of British Institution Showing the 1832 Exhibition*
New Haven, Yale Center for British Art, Paul Mellon Collection

Fig.69 | William Donaldson Clark, *Princes Street with the Scott Monument and the Royal Institution*
Edinburgh, Scottish National Photography Collection, Scottish National Portrait Gallery

names. Thus, even within the Venetian cinquecento, it was no longer simply pictures by Titian – or supposedly by Titian – that were regarded as collectable, but also those of his predecessors, contemporaries and successors. And even within the work of Titian, interest was no longer restricted to his central or 'best period', but was expanded to include the previously less highly regarded late works.[34]

The circumstances under which the principal Scottish collectors of the nineteenth century acquired their pictures are often far from clear. Sometimes, as in the previous century, they were bought on tours of Italy. In the case of noblemen such as the future Lord Elcho, such tours might continue to be undertaken when the traveller was still a young man, to round off an expensive education. But equally, the newly wealthy such as John Waldie of Hendersyde Park, near Kelso, or the Glasgow merchant James Ewing, might undertake continental tours later in life, to reap the rewards of their labours. Transporting their acquisitions back to Scotland was not without its hazards, as is illustrated by the unfortunate experience of Waldie, whose cargo of twenty pictures bought in Venice in 1827, together with some classical antiquities, was shipwrecked off the coast of Brittany.[35]

More often, however, and more conveniently, collectors could take advantage of the burgeoning art market in London, which comprised not just the eighteenth-century auction houses of Christie's and Sotheby's, but specialist dealers in old masters such as William Buchanan, Samuel Woodburn and John Smith. It is known, for example, that both Archibald McLellan and John Graham-Gilbert of Glasgow bought on occasion from John Smith, although much research remains to be done on the sources of their

acquisitions. It is similarly not always clear how far collectors acted according to their own taste and initiative, and how far they were dependent on the expert advice of painters and dealers. Thus, during his long collecting career the 10th Duke of Hamilton made use of many such experts, including the artist-collector Richard Cosway and the dealer Woodburn.[36] Similarly, McLellan regularly employed the services of Andrew Wilson's son, Charles Heath Wilson. On the other hand, scholars and aesthetes such as Dennistoun and Lindsay clearly had no need of professional advice. Lord Elcho, too, spent a picture-buying career trusting his own taste.

THE FIRST PUBLIC COLLECTIONS

Throughout the first half of the nineteenth century all of the most important Scottish collections were in private hands and were difficult to access for the general public. But the display of the Orléans collection in London in 1798–9 had stimulated an appetite for looking at pictures, and in 1805 the British Institution was founded, with the primary function of mounting annual old master exhibitions in its rooms in Pall Mall (fig.68). The enormous success of these London exhibitions led to the foundation in 1819, four years after Waterloo, of the similarly conceived Institution for the Encouragement of the Fine Arts in Scotland. As with its London counterpart, the principal brief of the institution in Edinburgh – later known as the Royal Institution – was to organise exhibitions of old masters lent for the season by its aristocratic governors.[37] But shortly before receiving its royal charter in 1827, the institution began forming a permanent collection, and this was later to form the nucleus of the National Gallery of Scotland.

In the same year, the Royal Institution moved

into its handsome new Grecian temple on the Mound, built by William Henry Playfair (fig.69). Also in 1827, William Buchanan wrote to the secretary, James Skene, proposing the foundation of a Scottish National Gallery:

It has long appeared to many of those who desire to see the Fine Arts flourish and brought to perfection in Scotland – a Country which has of late years produced so many eminent Artists – that a Gallery of Art should be formed of the Works of the Great Masters of the various schools of painting, for the purpose of aiding the efforts of the Student, of diffusing a general knowledge of the Art of painting, and of forming one of those agreeable Sources of Public Amusement, which in modern times is to be found in every Capital of Europe.[38]

The most obvious model was the National Gallery in London, which had opened its doors in 1824, and the foundation of which Buchanan himself had advocated as early as 1803.[39] His motives in contacting Skene were in part self-interested, since in the same letter he invited the institution to buy five pictures, two of which were 'by Titian, formerly in the Borghese Palace of Rome', and one was 'a finely coloured picture by Paul Veronese'. One of the supposed Titians is identifiable as the *Venus* now in the Rijks-museum, Amsterdam (fig.130), which is closely modelled on Titian's *Venus of Urbino* (fig.22), but in fact is by his Dutch follower Lambert Sustris.[40]

Although Skene did not take up Buchanan's offer, already in the previous year the institution had begun to buy old masters. One of its earliest acquisitions was Jacopo Bassano's *Christ Driving the Moneychangers from the Temple* (fig.70; now considered to be largely the work of the painter's assistants), which Andrew Wilson had bought in Italy in 1805, but had subsequently sold.[41] Wilson, who had been employed by the Royal Institution to organise its annual exhibitions of old masters since its foundation in 1819, recommended the purchase of the picture from a

Mr Berry of Glasgow shortly before his return to Italy in 1826; there, from a distance, he was commissioned to buy a core collection of old masters. Between 1829 and 1831 he purchased some thirty-eight pictures for the Royal Institution, among them works of the calibre of Van Dyck's great *Lomellini Family* (Edinburgh, National Gallery of Scotland).[42] As on his previous Italian sojourn in 1803–6, Wilson's principal base was Genoa, and among the Venetian pictures he bought from the indigent Genoese noble families at this time were the Tintorettesque *Portrait of a Gentleman* (cat.no.67) and Paris Bordon's *Venetian Women at their Toilet* (cat.no.48) both formerly in the Grimaldi collection. Other Venetian purchases by Wilson are less impressive. These include a supposed self-portrait by Giorgione, in reality a late copy after Sebastiano del Piombo's *Shepherd with a Flute* at Wilton House and three weak Tintorettesque representations of the *Seasons*.[43]

By the time that the Royal Institution acquired its next Venetian paintings, the project to house its rapidly expanding collections in a National Gallery of Scotland was well advanced. Thus, between the laying of the foundation stone of Playfair's new building in 1850 and the opening of the National Gallery of Scotland in 1859, the Royal Institution bought a *Holy Family* attributed to Titian (but more likely by his brother Francesco) from the dealer Schiavone in Venice (cat.no.27), and Veronese's *Venus, Cupid and Mars* from Belvedere House in Kent (cat.no.69). Meanwhile in 1856 the Royal Institution's sister-organisation and frequent rival, the Royal Scottish Academy, had purchased a true masterpiece of Venetian cinquecento painting in Bassano's *The Adoration of the Kings*, albeit with an erroneous attribution to Titian (cat.no.40). The Academy did not normally buy old masters, although its commitment to the pictorial tradition of Venetian painting is

below left Fig.70 | Studio of Jacopo Bassano, *Christ Driving the Moneychangers from the Temple* Edinburgh, National Gallery of Scotland

below right Fig.71 | William Etty, *The Venus of Urbino* (after Titian) Edinburgh, Royal Scottish Academy

Fig.72 | Follower of Giovanni Bellini, *The Virgin and Child Enthroned with Saints and Musician Angels*
Glasgow Museums: Kelvingrove Art Gallery and Museum

Fig.73 | After Ludwig Knaus,
Portrait of Gustav Friedrich Waagen
London, British Museum

illustrated by its acquisition in 1853 of a splendid full-size copy of Titian's *Venus of Urbino* by William Etty (fig.71), and of an anonymous copy of Titian's *Bacchanal of the Andrians*, likewise from Etty's estate.[44] The Bassano *Adoration of the Kings* was presumably a special case, because it had belonged to both Andrew Wilson and Lord Eldin, and the Edinburgh public would have remembered it as the outstanding item in the Eldin sale twenty years earlier.[45]

Another important event to take place in the 1850s was the foundation in Glasgow of Scotland's first municipal art gallery. The driving force behind this was Archibald McLellan, a man with a weighty sense of civic responsibility and a conviction in the importance of art for public education and welfare. This is spelt out in his 1853 deed of bequest of his collection to 'the citizens of Glasgow in all time coming':

I, Archibald M'Lellan, coachbuilder in Glasgow, considering that I have, for thirty years, spent much of my spare time in making a Collection of Pictures illustrative of the characteristics and progress of the various schools of painting in Italy, Germany, Spain, the Low Countries, and France … and believing that … such a collection … may be of some use to those desirous of studying the progress of Art; and also believing that it may be made to form the foundation for a more extensive and complete Collection …; and being impressed with the belief that the study of what are called the 'Fine Arts' is eminently conducive to the elevation and refinement of all classes, as well as intimately connected with the manufacturing and mercantile prosperity of this community – from these various motives … I have resolved to devote my said Collection to public use and exhibition …[46]

Although the bequest created severe financial problems for the Corporation of Glasgow when McLellan died suddenly in the following year leaving large debts, he had already built a gallery of three rooms in Sauchiehall Street to house the collection; and this is where his 437 pictures were first put on public display in 1855.

As has already been mentioned, McLellan seems to have used his trusted adviser Charles Heath Wilson when building up his collection. In keeping with his educational ideal, he aimed to buy examples of different periods and schools rather than simply pictures by the canonical big names. Thus, his interesting and important group of Venetian paintings included works attributed to Cima (cat.no.8; actually by Catena), Giorgione (fig.72; a huge Bellinesque composition still awaiting a satisfactory attribution),[47] Paris Bordon (cat.no.30), and Schiavone (cat.no.51; actually closer to Tintoretto). There is a happy irony, therefore, in the fact that the *Christ and the Adulteress* (cat.no.13), which McLellan bought with an unassuming attribution to Bonifacio, became famous during much of the twentieth century as a major work by Giorgione, and is now equally highly prized by many as a key early work by Titian.

THE VISITS TO SCOTLAND OF G.F. WAAGEN

The attribution of the *Christ and the Adulteress* to Giorgione was first made by the eminent German art historian Gustav Friedrich Waagen (1794–1868, fig.73), Director of the Berlin Museum, on a visit to the McLellan Gallery in 1856, the year of its opening. This was the second of two trips made by Waagen to Scotland, as part of several tours of public and private art collections all over Britain. The lists and descriptions of Scottish collections made by Waagen in 1856 and on the previous visit of 1851 provide the most important single source for our knowledge of old master paintings accumulated during the golden age of the first half of the nineteenth century.[48] Waagen's visits were undertaken, moreover, at what turned out to have been a climactic moment in the history of private collecting in Scotland, a moment of amazing richness, just before the onset of an inexorable decline.

Waagen declared that the 'chief object of my visit to Scotland' in 1851 was Hamilton Palace, and he devotes more pages to its contents than to any other Scottish collection. There were probably also correspondingly more Venetian pictures at Hamilton Palace than elsewhere in Scotland, although exact numbers are difficult to calculate since Waagen made no attempt to provide a complete inventory of the collections he visited, but merely noted the works that he considered to be the most significant. Other collections with Venetian pictures described on the first visit include those of the Royal Institution and of James Dennistoun in Edinburgh; Hopetoun House, near Edinburgh; the collection of Archibald McLellan in Glasgow, then still at the owner's house; and Garscube House outside Glasgow, the home of Sir Archibald Campbell of Succoth. Waagen was keenly aware that on his whistle-stop tour of central Scotland he was neglecting other collections worthy of note, and he accordingly listed several of these that he knew only from hearsay. These include the collections of: Charles Stirling of Cawder, near Glasgow; Lord Corehouse, near Lanark; the Dukes of Buccleuch at Dalkeith Palace; the Earls of Dunmore at Dunmore Park; the marine engineer Robert Napier at West Shandon, Gareloch; James Stirling of Glentyan; William Stirling at Keir, near Dunblane; Lord Gray at Kinfauns Castle, near Perth; and Thomas Erskine of Linlathen, near Dundee.

On his second visit Waagen noted with pleasure some of the developments that had been taking place in the five years since his first tour: the advancing construction of the National Gallery of Scotland; the acquisition by the Royal Scottish Academy of *The Adoration of the Kings* (which he promptly reattributed, wrongly, to Pordenone); and the housing of the collection of the recently deceased Archibald McLellan in the 'three noble and well-lighted apartments' of the Corporation Gallery in Glasgow. Although Waagen clearly much enjoyed being wined and dined by his aristocratic hosts in the grandest houses in the land, he was also a museum director with a visionary concept of the educational value of art galleries accessible to the general public; indeed, he may have been in part responsible for inspiring the sentiments expressed by McLellan in his deed of bequest quoted above.

Waagen similarly approved of the loan by Lord Elgin of his pictures to the Glasgow gallery 'so that they might be generally seen', and took the opportunity of reattributing the owner's *Portrait of a Blacksmith* (fig.74) from Moroni to Moretto.[49] Among the country seats with Venetian pictures that Waagen visited in 1856 were two that he had previously mentioned, but not yet seen (Dunmore and Keir), and also Gosford (which, however, had few Italian pictures at that date) and Rossie Priory near Dundee, the home of Lord Kinnaird. Waagen did not have the time or the information to venture further north, where there would have been much of interest in Kincardineshire and Aberdeenshire, and neither did he visit any houses in the Borders. Nor, more surprisingly, did he visit Newbattle Abbey near Dalkeith, the seat of the Marquesses of Lothian, which housed a collection of more than 500 pictures, albeit most of them British portraits.

Waagen's taste in pictures was rather traditional. That is to say, he would probably have been in close agreement with Buchanan about which of the old masters were universally the greatest. Titian was a member of this select band (although Waagen still thought that his late works showed a regrettable decline); Giovanni Bellini was of interest as a forerunner of a greater age; and Tintoretto represented the Venetian school in a state of decadence. But besides having a much keener historical sense than the British experts of a previous generation, Waagen was much more experienced and impartial as a connoisseur. His laconic comment on a now unidentified *Adoration of the Shepherds* attributed to Titian at Dunmore Park – 'Of the SCHOOL OF TITIAN. For the master himself not clever enough'[50] – is characteristic of a new and more sceptical approach to attributions, anticipating the even more refined connoisseurship of critics such as Bernard Berenson later in the century. Waagen was similarly frank in his scorn for some of Andrew Wilson's less felicitous purchases for the Royal Institution, such as the Tintorettesque *Seasons*.

DECLINE AND RETRENCHMENT

At least two important Scottish aristocratic collections with Venetian pictures were still in the early process of formation when Waagen was in Scotland in the 1850s: that of the 8th Marquess of Lothian, and that of the 9th Earl of Southesk. Compared with collections formed a generation earlier, these now show a definite shift of taste towards the Primitives, as is clearly reflected in the purchase by Southesk of Bellini's very early *St Jerome in the Desert* (cat.no.2) from the Davenport Bromley sale in 1863. Lothian even owned Dürer's *Madonna of the Siskin* (fig.9), an early German painting with strong Venetian associations.

A proud reaffirmation of the splendour of Scottish collections was provided in 1883 by Lord Elcho, who on becoming 10th Earl of Wemyss decided to remove his distinguished picture collection from London, and to rehouse it in the magnificent new wing that he added for the purpose to his ancestral seat of Gosford in East Lothian. In the same year, another celebration of the glories of Scottish aristocratic collecting took place in the Royal Institution building, with an exhibition of 550 paintings and 100 drawings lent by a range of private collectors.[51] Several of the paintings shown on that occasion, including Lord Lothian's Bonifacio (cat.no.49), Lord Aberdeen's Titian (cat.no.64), and two more Titians belonging to Lord Clinton (cat.nos.36, 37), have been reunited in the same building for the present exhibition.

Fig.74 | Attributed to Paolo Farinati, *Portrait of a Blacksmith* The Earl of Elgin and Kincardine, KT

Fig.75 | Palma Vecchio, *The Virgin and Child with Saints*
Glasgow Museums: Kelvingrove Art Gallery and Museum

Fig.76 | Photograph of the picture gallery at Bridgewater
House, London, *c*.1900

In reality, however, the situation was far from healthy, as was dramatically illustrated in the previous year with the sale at Christie's of virtually the entire contents of Hamilton Palace. At one blow the greatest art collection ever to have been formed in Scotland was dispersed. The land-owning classes were beginning to feel the chill winds of agricultural depression, increased income tax and death duties, and movements for democratic reform. With the gradual decline of their power and wealth inevitably came a parallel decline in their activity as art collectors, and a growing pressure to start selling their accumulated treasures. Although few sales were as dramatic as that of Hamilton Palace, and most dispersals were piecemeal, they were none the less relentless. During the course of the twentieth century virtually all the private collections formed in Scotland in the earlier nineteenth century and listed in the appendix were severely thinned, if not entirely dissolved, with the majority of their pictures going abroad, in particular to the United States. One great collection arose to take their place, that of the Glasgow shipping magnate Sir William Burrell. But in part, perhaps, as a deliberate reaction against the prevailing tastes of the nineteenth century, Burrell had little interest in Venetian painting; and his purchase in 1936 of a beautiful *Virgin and Child* by Bellini (cat.no.4) represented a rare exception to his usual tastes as a collector.

In the seven or eight decades up to the Second World War, the decline in private collecting was only in part compensated for by a corresponding growth in the number of Venetian paintings in Scottish public collections. In Glasgow the nucleus represented by the McLellan collection was valuably augmented by the bequest made in 1877 by John Graham-Gilbert's widow, which included pictures by Bellini (cat.no.3), Giovanni da Asola (cat.no.16; then attributed to Giorgione), Palma Vecchio (fig.75), and Paris Bordon (cat.no.29). Indeed, when the museum's new building at Kelvingrove opened in 1902, its collection of Venetian Renaissance painting was rather more distinguished than that of the National Gallery of Scotland. But the latter also attracted bequests, notably that of Lady Ruthven in 1885, which included *An Archer*, often attributed to Giorgione (cat.no.12), and a good, if fragmentary, portrait by Tintoretto (cat.no.52). Following the reorganisation of the Edinburgh institutions and their buildings in 1910, Bassano's *The Adoration of the Kings* (cat.no.40) was transferred from the Royal Scottish Academy to the National Gallery of Scotland. In 1913 the Gallery bought a fragment of a great Veronese altarpiece, previously in the collection of the Duke of Sutherland in London (cat.no.59). The bequest in 1941 by the 11th Marquess of Lothian to the Gallery of eighteen pictures included a painting bought by the 8th Marquess as a Titian, but which is by a follower (cat.no.28).

On the whole, however, the acquisitions up to 1945 by both Edinburgh and Glasgow were few in relation to the overall losses, and disappointingly few of the Venetian pictures sold from the disintegrating private collections remained in Scotland. Of the great Hamilton collection, only Titian's *Portrait of Admiral Vincenzo Cappello* (cat.no.35) returned north of the border for a few decades after 1893, when it was bought by the 5th Earl of Rosebery for his seat at Dalmeny. But even this was sold to the United States in 1939.

Immediately after the Second World War, the quality of the National Gallery of Scotland's holdings of Venetian painting was transformed in quite spectacular fashion with the arrival on loan of a large group of pictures belonging to the 5th Earl of Ellesmere. The majority of these, and the greatest, had previously belonged to the famous Orléans collection, and since 1799 had hung in the Stafford Gallery, later renamed the Bridgewater Gallery, in London (fig.76). But after Bridgewater House was badly damaged by bombardment during the Second World War, Lord Ellesmere – who in 1963 succeeded as 6th Duke of Sutherland – offered a group of thirty pictures on long-term loan to Edinburgh. In addition to masterpieces by Raphael and Poussin, the group included eight Venetian pictures, five of which are by Titian (cat.nos.15, 19, 25, 54, 55), two by Tintoretto (cat.nos.53, 66), and one by Lotto (cat.no.11). At least three of the Titians – the early *Three Ages of Man* (cat.no.15) and the late *Diana and Actaeon* and *Diana and Callisto* (cat.nos.54, 55) – may be counted among his supreme achievements.

The consequent rise in the Gallery's profile as a site of outstanding importance for viewing Venetian cinquecento painting has been consolidated in the last two or three decades by the acquisition of further pictures of exceptionally high quality. In 1977 the Gallery purchased Moroni's *Portrait of Giovanni Bressani*, formerly in the collection of Lord Rosebery (cat.no.62). In 1984 it acquired two of the Orléans-Sutherland pictures previously on loan, Lotto's *Virgin and Child with Saints* (cat.no.11) and Tintoretto's *Christ Carried to the Tomb* (cat.no.66). Cariani's *St Agatha* (cat.no.22) was purchased in 1989 and in 1996 the Gallery acquired Paris Bordon's *The Rest on the Flight into Egypt*, formerly in the Stirling of Keir collection (cat.no.46). Finally, at the opening of the new millennium, the Gallery acquired a third Orléans-Sutherland picture, the august provenance of which goes back to the seventeenth-century collection of Queen Christina of Sweden: Titian's sensuously beautiful *Venus Anadyomene* (cat.no.19).

I PAINTINGS

CATALOGUE NOTE

Dimensions given are maximum dimensions, with height followed by width (followed by depth, where applicable).

The footnotes to the essays and catalogue entries are on pages 427–47

To avoid over-burdening the catalogue entries, biographical information about the principal artists and collectors represented in the exhibition is included in the two appendices on pages 407–20.

The following abbreviations have been used:

Bartsch = A. von Bartsch, *Le peintre-graveur*, 21 vols, Vienna, 1803–21.

Hollstein = F. W. H. Hollstein, *Dutch and Flemish Etchings, Engravings and Woodcuts*, 64 volumes, Amsterdam and Rotterdam, 1949–2004 (ongoing series).

Lugt = F. Lugt, *Les marques de collections de dessins et d'estampes*, Amsterdam, 1921; *Supplément*, The Hague, 1956.

The catalogue entries on paintings have been written by Peter Humfrey; drawings by Aidan Weston-Lewis; prints by Michael Bury; and those on sculpture and decorative arts by Timothy Clifford.

Additional contributors to the catalogue are denoted by their initials at the end of the entry, as follows:

IGB Iain Gordon Brown

JD John Dick

GE Godfrey Evans

MG Michael Gallagher

AVL Anne Varick Lauder

LS Lesley Stevenson

HV Helen Vincent

DW Diana Webster

opposite | Detail from cat.no.71

Bartolomeo Vivarini   VENICE (MURANO) c.1430–AFTER 1491 VENICE (?)

1 ❧ *A Triptych*

CENTRAL PANEL

The Virgin and Child with a Nun as Donor

LEFT PANEL

The Angel of the Annunciation;
The Nativity

RIGHT PANEL

The Virgin Annunciate; The Pietà

Tempera on panel | 53.8 × 44.1cm (centre);
24.9 × 21.6cm (upper left); 24.8 × 21.7cm
(lower left); 24.8 × 21.3cm (upper right);
24.9 × 21.6cm (lower right). Measurements are
those of the painted surfaces; the frame is not
original | c.1460–70

Provenance: Francis, Lord Elcho, later 10th Earl
of Wemyss, Gosford House, Longniddry;
purchased through the dealer R. Langton
Douglas by Philip Lehman, 1916
(acc.no.1975.1.82)

NEW YORK, METROPOLITAN MUSEUM OF
ART, ROBERT LEHMAN COLLECTION

Fig.77 | Bartolomeo Vivarini, *The Virgin and Child*
Enthroned with Saints
Naples, Museo Nazionale di Capodimonte

This intimately scaled triptych was presumably
commissioned for private devotion by the nun
represented at the left of the central panel, who is
dressed in the white robe and black cloak of the
Dominican order.[1] The various scenes represented serve to glorify the Virgin Mary by
showing a selection of her Joys and Sorrows. In
the central panel the Virgin is shown both as the
Madonna of Humility, seated on the ground in a
landscape, and as Queen of Heaven, attired in
luxurious brocade and crowned by flying angels.
The fruit trees in the background, abundantly
laden with pears, presumably allude to her role as
the New Eve. Close iconographic links are
created between the centre and side panels, for
instance by echoing the joyous central motif of
the Christ Child seated in his mother's lap in the
tragic Pietà group at the lower right.

The work illustrates well Vivarini's transi-
tional position between the Gothic and Renaissance styles of painting. More specifically, it
reflects both his training in the workshop of his
elder brother and occasional collaborator
Antonio Vivarini, and his interest in the revolutionary style of the great Paduan master Andrea
Mantegna. Modern features include the ostenta-
tious use of geometric perspective in the four
lateral scenes, and the sculptural representation
of form, using hard, linear creases for the drapery
folds. But these are combined with a more
traditional taste for flat pattern and material
richness (especially evident in the lavish use of
gold leaf), and with the striking inconsistency of
figure scale in the central panel. Repeating areas
of red and blue, the principal colours of the
Virgin's draperies, help to integrate the five
picture fields. Although the present frame is
modern, the original is likely to have been of a
similarly Gothic design. There is general
agreement among scholars that the triptych
must, on stylistic grounds, date from around the
same time as the *Virgin and Child with Saints* in
Naples, which is signed and dated 1465 (fig.77).[2]

Bought in London by Lord Elcho some time
before 1883, when he became 10th Earl of
Wemyss, and subsequently brought to Gosford,
this is one of the very few Venetian pictures
dating from before 1480 known to have been
acquired by a Scottish collector.

Giovanni Bellini VENICE c.1438–1516 VENICE

2 ❧ St Jerome in the Desert

Tempera on panel | 44 × 22.9cm | c.1460

Inscribed at the lower centre on a *cartellino*: 'IHOVANES BELINVS'

Provenance: D. Goodyear, Barton House, Gloucester; his sale, Christie's, 6 June 1856 (lot 537; bought in); Davenport Bromley sale, Christie's, 12 June 1863 (lot 59), bought by the 6th Earl of Southesk; by descent in the Southesk collection, Kinnaird Castle, Brechin; Southesk sale, Christie's, 3 July 1948 (lot 42); bought by Lady Barber from Agnew's, 1949

BIRMINGHAM, THE TRUSTEES OF THE BARBER INSTITUTE OF FINE ARTS

Bellini shows Jerome as a semi-naked hermit in the Syrian desert, seated on a rock in front of his cave, with only his faithful lion for company. The saint raises his hand in blessing as the poor beast, whose paw had been wounded by a huge thorn, howls in pain. With his other hand Jerome holds open a book, an allusion to his scholarly activity as translator of the bible into Latin. Several of the details of the landscape, while apparently included simply for verisimilitude, are probably likewise intended to allude to his moral and spiritual achievements. The rabbit in its burrow, for example, probably refers to the hermit in his cave; the grazing ass to Jerome's poverty and humility; and the withered tree in the central middle ground, which sprouts fresh shoots, to the new life that his translation will bring to the scriptures.[1]

The panel is among the earliest treatments of a subject that was to become one of the most popular in Venetian Renaissance painting. Influenced by the several variations on the theme painted by Bellini at different stages of his career, the subject's popularity reached a climax in the decades around 1500 in the work of such painters as Cima (cat.no.10), Catena, Lotto and Paris Bordon; as late as 1575 Titian painted an important example for Philip II of Spain (now in the Escorial, Madrid). Bellini had in turn been inspired by the various representations of St Jerome by his father and teacher Jacopo, whose panel now in the Museo di Castelvecchio, Verona, dates from about 1440, and who included no fewer than five versions of the subject in his two albums of drawings, in the British Museum and the Louvre (fig.78).[2] The saint owed his popularity among his devotees in large part to the variety of his roles – as cardinal of the church, as a scholar, and as a penitent – and the emphasis in the present instance on learning rather than on the more usual acts of self-mortifying penance may imply that the picture was painted for some Venetian humanist.[3] But

another major attraction of the subject for patrons and painters was unquestionably to be found in the opportunities it provided for landscape painting, and for surrounding the saint with the beauties of nature.

Especially since it became more widely known after being exhibited in the great Giovanni Bellini exhibition held in Venice in 1949, this little panel has been widely accepted as the painter's earliest surviving work.[4] It is deeply indebted to the example of Jacopo Bellini, not only in its general concept, but also in particular motifs and in pictorial style. The lion, for example, is borrowed literally from one of seven drawings of lions on a sheet in Jacopo's Louvre album (folio 72v);[5] while the saint's slender proportions, and the linear undulations of his white beard, closely resemble those of Jacopo's figure of Anthony in his *Saints Anthony Abbot and Bernardino of Siena* (Washington, National Gallery of Art). By contrast, the panel shows relatively little response as yet to the work of Bellini's famous brother-in-law, Andrea Mantegna – although the geological patterns on the left do already clearly reflect similar rocks and crags by Mantegna, such as those that appear at the left of the *Calling of James and John* fresco in the Ovetari chapel in the Eremitani, Padua.[6]

Yet these comparisons also confirm the extent of the young Giovanni's independence of his elders, and reveal the deeply poetic sensibility that was to characterise his work throughout his long career. He drastically reduced the wealth of incident that Jacopo packs into his landscapes; spatial recession is more gradual and more convincing; and the contours of the distant hills are softer, as if immersed in atmosphere. Similarly, the thin veils of cloud do not at all resemble the stony cumulus formations of Mantegna. It has often plausibly been suggested that Giovanni's use of delicate strokes of silver and gold on the rocks at the left and highlighting some of the details in the middle ground might reflect an early experience as an illuminator of manuscripts. Yet the effect even of these is not of artificial richness of ornament, but of a natural illumination that bathes the landscape in a mood of divinely-inspired serenity.[7]

The picture has traditionally been dated to around 1450, on the assumption that Giovanni was born in the early 1430s. More recently, however, it has been argued that his birth date should be placed several years later, and that a more likely date for the *St Jerome in the Desert* is about 1459–60.[8] This argument rests on the identification of Jacopo's *Saints Anthony Abbot and Bernardino of Siena* and three predella panels (Venice, Museo Correr; Padua, Museo Civico; Ferrara, Pinacoteca Nazionale) as components of the altarpiece that he is known to have painted in 1460, in collaboration with his sons Gentile and

Giovanni, for the Gattamelata chapel in the church of the Santo in Padua. The *St Jerome in the Desert* is stylistically so close to that of the predella panels, and in particular to the *Adoration of the Kings* in Ferrara, that it seems likely not only that they date from around the same time, but also that the predella was the part of the ensemble on which the young Giovanni chiefly collaborated.

For a few years in the mid-nineteenth century, the present painting belonged to one of the most important Victorian collectors of early Italian painting, the Revd Walter Davenport Bromley of Wootton Hall in Staffordshire. It was one of three Venetian St Jeromes bought from his sale in 1863 by the 9th Earl of Southesk, the others being attributed to Jacopo Bellini's contemporary Jacobello del Fiore (destroyed by fire in 1921) and to the Paduan Francesco Squarcione (untraced).[9] Lord Southesk's genuine admiration for Giovanni Bellini's work is evident from his comments on the Naples *Transfiguration* in his essay *Britain's Art Paradise*: 'Bellini has brooded over it with all his mind and heart, and filled it with a life born of his meditation on the superhuman scene'.[10]

Fig.78 | Jacopo Bellini, *St Jerome in the Desert*
Paris, Musée du Louvre

IHOVANES BELINVS

61

Giovanni Bellini VENICE c.1438–1516 VENICE

3 ✥ The Virgin and Child

Oil on panel | 61 × 47cm | c.1480–5

Provenance: John Graham-Gilbert, Glasgow; bequeathed by his widow to the Glasgow Museum, 1877 (acc.no.575)

GLASGOW MUSEUMS: KELVINGROVE ART GALLERY AND MUSEUM

The theme of the Virgin and Child was favoured by Giovanni Bellini above all others, and he painted innumerable variations on it during the course of his long career. Characteristically, the figure of the Virgin in this version is portrayed in half length behind a marble parapet, which serves both as a firm base for the triangular figure composition, and as a way of separating the sacred space of the figures from the real world of the viewer. Unusual in this instance is the fact that the figures focus their attention beyond the picture to the lower left, almost as if the Child was blessing an unseen kneeling donor. Relatively unusual, too, is Bellini's use of a dark, neutral background, instead of a curtain, landscape or sky. But X-radiography has shown the dark background to be original; in fact, Bellini employs it in several of his other devotional half-lengths, including the probably closely contemporary *Virgin and Child with Two Female Saints* in the Galleria dell'Accademia, Venice.

This picture has not been widely discussed in the art-historical literature, a neglect that perhaps reflects doubts on its autograph status,[1] and probably also the fact that it has not been seen outside Glasgow since it was acquired by John Graham-Gilbert in the mid-nineteenth century. It is true that the Virgin's robe (in which red glazes were painted over a layer of gold) and blue cloak have been extensively over-painted, presumably to compensate for damage to the original paint layers. The flesh areas are also a little thin in places, making the painter's hatched underdrawing visible to the naked eye. But the quality of these relatively undamaged areas is high, and the tender expressiveness of the faces of both figures can only be attributed to Bellini himself.

Suggested dates for the picture range between about 1475 and 1490,[2] and the picture clearly does reflect an interest in the volumetric style of Antonello da Messina, who visited Venice in 1475–6. Perhaps the date can be narrowed down most plausibly to the early 1480s,[3] to a phase immediately following Bellini's great San Giobbe altarpiece (Venice, Galleria dell'Accademia), datable to about 1478–80. As in the altarpiece, the physiognomies are more spherical and less elongated than in Bellini's works of the earlier 1470s; and while the painter was by this date experimenting with the new medium of oil, he retained a taste for silhouetted, rhythmically undulating outlines. By contrast, although the pose of the standing Child is very similar to that of his counterpart in the Frari triptych of 1488 (fig.7), by that date Bellini's forms had become much more softly rounded.

Giovanni Bellini VENICE c.1438–1516 VENICE

4 ❧ The Virgin and Child

Oil on panel | 62 × 47.6cm | c.1485–8

Provenance: Cardinal Francesco Barberini, Rome, by 1649 (as Perino del Vaga); by descent in the Barberini collection until *c*.1935; with the dealer Arnold Seligmann, Paris (as by Nicolò Rondinelli); from whom purchased by Sir William Burrell, Hutton Castle, Berwickshire, 1936; by whom presented to the City of Glasgow, 1944

GLASGOW MUSEUMS: THE BURRELL COLLECTION

Like the Graham-Gilbert picture (cat.no.3), the Burrell painting shows Bellini tackling his favourite theme of the half-length Virgin and Child. In this case the figures are set in front of a green curtain and the Child dangles a sprig, perhaps of myrtle, on the end of a string. Yet the mood is not at all playful, and the Child's gesture is invested with a precocious deliberation and solemnity. Similarly, the expression of the Virgin is characteristically introspective and melancholy, implying that she can already foresee her son's future Passion and death.

In the nineteenth century the picture was attributed to followers of Bellini such as Pasqualino Veneto or Rondinelli,[1] and more recently it has often been seen as a work of collaboration.[2] But despite the damaged condition of the Virgin's blue cloak, the picture is of high quality and shows passages of exceptional originality and subtlety, as in the shadows cast by the figures on the curtain, and in the choice of violet for the cloak's lining. The widely accepted dating to the mid- or late 1480s is well justified: the sculpturally rounded forms and the pose of the Child closely resemble those of Bellini's Frari triptych of 1488 (see fig.7); and the painter pays less attention to rhythmical outlines than in the slightly earlier Graham-Gilbert painting. The picture must in any case have been painted by 1489, the date inscribed on a workshop variant recorded in 1916 in the collection of Countess Brentani in Bergamo.[3] There exist at least seventeen other versions of this composition by Bellini's assistants or followers, but all are of mediocre quality.[4] The motif of the decorative border on the Virgin's veil, apparently employed here by Bellini for the first time, was to be taken up with enthusiasm by followers such as Previtali and Rondinelli in succeeding decades.

Overcoming his usual lack of interest in the art of the Italian Renaissance, Sir William Burrell bought the picture in 1936 following its sale from Palazzo Barberini, with the encouragement of Kenneth Clark,[5] then director of the National Gallery, London, where it was exhibited until the outbreak of war in 1939. Although initially reluctant, Burrell quickly became convinced of the high quality of his purchase, and staunchly defended it against those who doubted its autograph status.[6] From the unusual motif of the plant on a string, the picture may be identified – despite a bizarre attribution to Perino del Vaga – with one recorded in the 1649 inventory of the collection of Cardinal Francesco Barberini (1597–1679), nephew of Pope Urban VIII.[7] Cardinal Barberini is known to have used his position to acquire pictures from Venetian collections through members of the papal nunciature in Venice, including the distinguished connoisseur Monsignor Giovanni Battista Agucchi, who was nuncio from 1624 to 1631, and the nuncio's secretary Giovanni Antonio Massani, in 1632.[8]

Follower of Giovanni Bellini VENICE *c.1438–1516* VENICE

5 ❦ *The Virgin and Child*

Tempera and oil on panel | 34 × 27.7cm | *c.*1510

Provenance: Acquired in Venice *c.*1770 by the British Resident, John Strange, from the collection of the papal nuncio to Verona; Strange sale, European Museum, London, 17 May 1799 (lot 179, as Cima da Conegliano); William Beckford, Bath, by 1822; by inheritance to his daughter Susan, Duchess of Hamilton, 1844; Hamilton Palace sale, Christie's, 17 June 1882 (lot 395, as Cima); acquired from Agnew's by Sir Michael Shaw-Stewart (1826–1903), Ardgowan, near Greenock, by 1894; by descent to Walter Shaw-Stewart (1861–1934), Fonthill Abbey, Wiltshire; his sale, Sotheby's, 7 December 1927 (lot 44, as Cima); with Duveen Bros., New York; from whom acquired by Jules S. Bache, New York, 1928; by whom bequeathed to the Museum, 1949 (acc.no.49.7.2)

NEW YORK, THE METROPOLITAN MUSEUM OF ART

From as early as the 1460s, as an alternative to the more neutral settings adopted for the two Virgin and Child pictures from Glasgow collections (cat.nos.3, 4), Bellini regularly placed his half-length Madonna compositions against backgrounds of radiant landscape. Although smaller in scale than most of Bellini's Madonnas, the present work is characteristic of the type of composition he popularised. Specific motifs were borrowed from autograph paintings by Bellini: for example, the shepherd leaning on his staff from the *Resurrection* of about 1478 (Berlin, Staatliche Museen, Gemäldegalerie); and the hilltop castle from *The Madonna of the Meadow*, *c.*1505 (fig.6; this motif also recurs in Girolamo da Santacroce's *Four Poets in a Landscape*, cat.no.20). Although Bellini, and especially the members of his large workshop, did habitually repeat his compositions and motifs, the present work appears not to have been executed under his direct supervision, and may be attributed rather to a follower, probably a former pupil. Apart from the fact that the holy figures lack the spiritual depth characteristic of Bellini's own work, the handling of the paint is smoother, and the treatment of detail more precise than is found in his late style after about 1500.[1] As in the probably slightly later pictures by Capriolo (cat.no.21) and Paris Bordon (cat.no.30), the traditional motif of the small bird held by the Child – in this case a swallow – alludes to his future Passion.

For over a century, from about 1770 to 1882, this painting was paired with Cima's *St Jerome in the Desert* (cat.no.10), a picture closely similar in dimensions, and likewise showing a luminous distant landscape. Together they passed from the collection of John Strange, British Resident in Venice, to that of William Beckford in Bath, where Waagen perceptively proposed changing the traditional attribution of *The Virgin and Child* from Cima to Andrea Previtali,[2] a follower of Giovanni Bellini whose style indeed has much in common with that of the present work. When inherited by Beckford's daughter, the Duchess of Hamilton, the two pictures appear to have been hung at Hamilton House in London before being taken to Hamilton Palace in Scotland in 1863.[3] After the Hamilton Palace sale in 1882, the painting was acquired (still as by Cima) by Sir Michael Shaw-Stewart of Ardgowan, near Greenock, and thus became one of the very few Hamilton pictures to make at least a brief return to Scotland. It was then inherited by Sir Michael's younger son Walter, who lived – by a remarkable coincidence – on the site of Beckford's famous house of Fonthill Abbey in Wiltshire.

Jacometto Veneziano ACTIVE IN VENICE 1472–1497

6 ❧ *Portrait of Alvise Contarini* [FRONT]; *A Seated Hart* [BACK]

Oil on panel | 10.3 × 7.3cm | *c*.1485–95

Inscribed on the back: 'AIEI' (Forever)

Provenance: Walter Francis, 5th Duke of Buccleuch; by descent to the present owner

THE DUKE OF BUCCLEUCH AND
QUEENSBERRY KT

This highly refined miniature portrait and its reverse are almost exact but slightly smaller replicas of Jacometto's *Portrait of Alvise Contarini* and its reverse in the Lehman collection at the Metropolitan Museum of Art, New York (fig.79).[1] The Lehman panel and its female pendant are the only certain works by the mysterious Jacometto, since they are clearly identifiable with a work recorded by the Venetian connoisseur Marcantonio Michiel in 1543, who described it as 'a little portrait of messer Alvise Contarini, who died some years ago; and on the same panel there is a portrait of a nun of San Secondo. On the cover of these portraits is a small deer in a landscape; and their leather case is decorated with foliage stamped with gold. This most perfect work is by the hand of Jacometto'.[2] Michiel's description is not quite exact: the portrait of the nun is on a separate panel, and was presumably originally framed with the *Portrait of Alvise Contarini* as a hinged diptych; and the deer on the reverse is not seated in a landscape, but on a rocky ledge in front of a porphyry wall, to which it is chained.

The present, high-quality replica shows only slight divergences from the Lehman version, most notably in the landscape on the right. As in the original, however, the area between the middle-ground trees and the distant buildings, with their characteristically Venetian, funnel-shaped chimneys, is certainly meant to represent a stretch of blue water, and only appears green because of the discoloured varnish. The sitter is shown wearing the official dress of a Venetian patrician, consisting of a black toga and stole over the shoulder, and a black cap. Nothing more is known of him, and nor, therefore, of the reason why he was paired, in the Lehman version, with the portrait of a nun. It is natural to suppose that the present version, too, once had a pendant; and indeed, a close variant of the Lehman *Nun of San Secondo* exists in the Cleveland Museum of Art. That panel, however, is more than twice the size of the Buccleuch Contarini portrait (24 × 17.5cm), and therefore could not have been paired with it.[3]

The deer and inscription on the reverse may record the sitter's personal emblem and motto as a symbol of fidelity and submission. However, the chained animal may signify rather that the work was commissioned as a token of love.[4] Another inscription on the present version, above the words 'AIEI', is too abraded to be legible.

None of the various other works by Jacometto recorded by Michiel in Venetian collections has survived, but it is clear from his descriptions that most of them similarly represented small-scale portraits of Venetian patricians. Michiel also states that he thought that the face of Antonello da Messina's *St Jerome in his Study* (London, National Gallery) had been painted, and the whole figure repainted, by Jacometto.[5] This association between Jacometto and Antonello is borne out by the resemblance of the present portrait to the type of portraiture introduced into Venice by Antonello in the 1470s (see fig.12), in which a soberly-dressed male sitter is shown in bust length, and his features are represented with a precision and delicacy reminiscent of Flemish portraiture of this period.

The present work forms part of the exceptionally distinguished group of miniature portraits collected by Walter Francis, 5th Duke of Buccleuch (1806–1884). In the nineteenth century it understandably bore an attribution to Antonello.[6] The frame, which is not original, incorporates a sliding panel, which serves as a protective cover for the seated deer. The cover bears an abraded inscription in gold lettering, the only legible word of which is reads 'MEMORIA'; this appears not to be contemporary with the painting, but may record an original inscription.

Fig.79 | Jacometto Veneziano,
Portrait of Alvise Contarini and, on the back, *A Seated Hart*;
Portrait of a Lady, possibly a Nun of San Secondo
New York, Metropolitan Museum of Art,
Robert Lehman Collection

Vincenzo Catena VENICE (?) c.1470/80–1531 VENICE

7 ❧ Portrait of a Young Man

Oil on panel | 30.5 × 23.5cm | c.1505–10

Provenance: Alexander, 10th Duke of Hamilton, Hamilton Palace, Lanarkshire; Hamilton Palace sale, Christie's, 24 June 1882 (lot 344, as Leonardo da Vinci), bought by the National Gallery (acc.no.1121)

LONDON, NATIONAL GALLERY

The unknown sitter of this highly refined portrait wears the austere formal dress common to Venetians of the patrician and citizen classes, with just a hint of luxury provided by the fur lining that peeps out from under his black robe. Characteristic of the tradition of portraiture established by Catena's master Giovanni Bellini is the bust-length format and the background of blue sky, although Bellini himself preferred to place his sitters in three-quarters view, with a marble parapet at the base of the composition. Although the panel is cut at the top, there is no evidence that the present picture ever included such a parapet.[1] There is general consensus that it is an early work by Catena, probably dating from about 1505–10,[2] and is thus close in date to his Glasgow *Virgin and Child with St Mary Magdalene and another Female Saint* (cat.no.8).

It has been suggested that this portrait may be identical with one by Catena acquired by the 1st Duke of Hamilton before 1643,[3] but it is much more likely that it was in fact purchased in the nineteenth century by the 10th Duke for the newly refurbished Hamilton Palace. At the palace sale in 1882 it carried an absurd attribution to Leonardo da Vinci, but was already more plausibly described as Bellini by Christie's in their bill for its purchase by the National Gallery.[4]

Fig.80 | Giovanni Bellini, *The Virgin and Child with Saints John the Baptist and Elisabeth*
Frankfurt, Städelsches Kunstinstitut

Vincenzo Catena VENICE (?) c.1470/80–1531 VENICE

8 ❧ *The Virgin and Child with St Mary Magdalene and another Female Saint*

Oil on panel | 61.6 × 83.5cm | *c*.1500–5

Inscribed with a now fragmentary signature on the ledge: 'VINZENZIVS·CA[T]ENA'

Provenance: Archibald McLellan; by whom bequeathed to the Glasgow Museum, 1854 (acc.no.199)

GLASGOW MUSEUMS: KELVINGROVE ART GALLERY AND MUSEUM

The compositional type, showing the Virgin and Child in half length flanked by saints, was invented by Giovanni Bellini in the 1480s, and by the end of the century had become one of the most popular in Venetian painting. By setting the figures against a dark, neutral background rather than against the more usual sky, Catena follows one of his master's earliest examples of the type, *The Virgin and Child with St Mary Magdalene and another Female Saint* in the Accademia Gallery, Venice. Catena's Magdalene is identified by her attribute of an ointment jar, but as in the

prototype by Bellini the identity of the saint on the left (whose face has suffered damage) is unclear. It has been suggested – perhaps on the basis of a black and white photograph, which makes her right breast appear bare – that she is St Agatha,[1] who was tortured by having her breasts cut off (see cat.no.22). But in common with many female saints in Venetian painting of the period, this figure is in fact shown wearing a tight-fitting bodice over her chemise. A more promising key to her identity may be provided by her crown of olive leaves.

The central Madonna group derives very literally from a composition by Bellini of the *Virgin and Child with Saints John the Baptist and Elizabeth*, which exists in two versions (Urbino, Galleria Nazionale delle Marche and Frankfurt, fig.80). The latter picture shows a number of slight adjustments (pentimenti) between the underdrawing and the final painting, notably in the Virgin's right hand; from these it may be inferred that although the execution may be in large part by the workshop, the master is likely to have played a close supervisory role. Catena's design, which follows exactly that of the com-

pleted painting rather than the underdrawing, was probably based on a tracing of Bellini's original but it is also considerably smaller in scale,[2] suggesting that he employed some mechanical device for reducing it. The same figure group reappears in signed works by other pupils of Bellini, such as Nicolò Rondinelli (Rome, Galleria Doria Pamphili) and Lattanzio da Rimini (formerly Berlin, Schlossmuseum), as well as in numerous other workshop variants.[3] The close dependence on Bellini, as well as the hard surfaces, incisive contours and enamel-like colours, suggest that this is one of Catena's earliest works, probably dating from soon after 1500. By about 1510 his forms were becoming softer, more ample and more luminous.

The damaged inscription on the foreground parapet was uncovered only relatively recently, and when in the McLellan collection the picture bore an attribution to Cima da Conegliano.[5] In 1857 Waagen rightly corrected this to 'School of Bellini',[6] but it was not until the picture was exhibited at the New Gallery in London in 1894–5 that Bernard Berenson recognised its true author.[7]

Follower of Cima da Conegliano CONEGLIANO (TREVISO) 1459/60–1517/18 CONEGLIANO *or* VENICE

9 ❧ *The Virgin and Child with Saints Andrew and Peter*

Oil on panel | 47.7 × 39.7cm | *c.*1505–15

Provenance: Counts (later Princes) of Collalto, Castello di San Salvatore, Susegana (near Treviso); Ottavio Ellero, Perugia, *c.*1830; from whom purchased by his son Alessandro Ellero; from whom purchased by Margaret Peter Dove, 1887; by whom presented to the Gallery, 1915 (ACC.NO.NG 1190)

EDINBURGH, NATIONAL GALLERY OF SCOTLAND

Despite its poor physical condition and mediocre artistic quality, the picture is of exceptional interest as a rare surviving example of a Venetian panel painting that was abandoned in mid-execution. In composition it resembles a small-scale version of altarpieces by Cima such as *The Madonna of the Orange Tree* of around 1496–8 (fig.81), which likewise includes a view of a fortified hill-town in the left background. The figure types are also close to Cima, and the figure of Andrew is apparently based on his counterpart in Cima's *Virgin and Child with Saints Michael and Andrew*, again datable to about 1496–8 (Parma, Galleria Nazionale). But comparison with these autograph works rather suggests that the present panel was executed by an assistant or close follower. The Virgin's pose is rigidly frontal, without the gentle inclination characteristic of the master; the saints are similarly unresponsive to the central figure group; and the composition as a whole lacks any sense of organic unity, as if the painter simply adapted piecemeal a number of Cima's motifs.[1] Drapery folds very similar to those of St Andrew, and staring, button-like eyes like those of the Virgin, appear in a *Coronation of the Virgin* (Udine, Museo Civico) signed by Cima's follower Girolamo da Udine, suggesting that he may well be the author of the present work.[2]

In accordance with general Venetian practice in the last two decades of the fifteenth century,[3] the painting is executed on a plank of poplar wood covered with a thick ground of smooth white gesso. The artist began with a relatively detailed underdrawing, made with the tip of the brush in iron gall ink, mapping the outlines of the principal forms, and indicating modelling by means of diagonal parallel hatchings. These are particularly evident in the draperies of Peter, and in the castle in the background. Although several of the forms were based on existing designs by Cima, the painter here apparently copied them freehand, without employing a mechanical device of a type evidently used by Catena in his *The Virgin and Child with St Mary Magdalene and another Female Saint* (cat.no.8). He then began to apply the colour in thin, regular layers of oil paint to discrete areas, carefully respecting the contours established by the underdrawing. The flesh tones of the Virgin's face and of the Child's body were achieved by lightly tinted glazes, with the thinnest layers corresponding to the highlights. The darker colours of Andrew's draperies are the result of a thicker build up of paint layers, but even these are probably not quite finished, and the painter would have intended to modify them further with surface glazes. The bare tree would certainly have been covered in foliage, as in Cima's *The Madonna of the Orange Tree*. The area of grey-blue at the top left probably represents a crude attempt by some later painter to complete the picture, which was then fortunately abandoned.

Fig.81 | Cima da Conegliano, *The Madonna of the Orange Tree* Venice, Galleria dell'Accademia

10 ✠ *St Jerome in the Desert*

Oil on panel | 32 × 25.5cm | *c.*1505–10

Provenance: Acquired in Venice by the British Resident, John Strange, from the collection of the papal nuncio to Verona, 1770; Strange sale, European Museum, London, 17 May 1799 (lot 146); William Beckford, Bath, by 1822; by inheritance to his daughter Susan, Duchess of Hamilton, 1844; Hamilton Palace sale, Christie's, 17 June 1882 (lot 26), bought by the National Gallery (acc.no.1120)

LONDON, NATIONAL GALLERY

Following the tradition established by Jacopo (fig.78) and Giovanni Bellini (cat.no.2), Cima painted several versions of *St Jerome in the Desert*,[1] in which the 'desert' consists of a verdant landscape full of picturesque flora and fauna, and extends back to distant blue mountains on the horizon. Unlike Giovanni Bellini, Cima tended, as in the present instance, to portray the saint as an active penitent, holding a stone with which to mortify his flesh, while gazing in rapture at a cross or crucifix. As in Bellini's renditions, several of the details, while naturalistically plausible, clearly also carry a symbolic significance. Thus, the serpent crawling from under the rock on the left signifies evil, while the bird of prey perched on the dead branch at the centre signifies death – both of which will be overcome through the saint's faith in Christ. The turbaned orientals strolling down the path in the middle ground are perhaps meant to locate the scene in Syria, and also to convey the hope that Christianity will eventually prevail over Islam.

The picture probably dates from *c.*1505–10,[2] nearly half a century later than Bellini's early picture in Birmingham. In the intervening period Venetian painters, following the example of their Flemish counterparts, had abandoned the traditional tempera technique for oil, as is evident in the much greater tonal range of Cima's painting, and the richer glow of the colours. The combination of the luministic effects of oil painting with a detailed and extensive landscape panorama executed on a tiny scale, suggests in fact that the painter was here deliberately setting out to emulate the much-admired devotional panels imported into Venice from the Netherlands. If so, he was almost too successful, for his picture later acquired an attribution to the mid-sixteenth-century Flemish painter Herri met de Bles, known in Italy as 'Il Civetta'.

For about a century, from 1770 to 1882, this painting was paired with *The Virgin and Child* now attributed to a close follower of Giovanni Bellini (cat.no.5), but which at that time – confusingly – was attributed to Cima. Both pictures were previously in the collection of the papal nuncio to Verona, and after belonging to John Strange, British Resident of Venice, they were sold in London in 1799.[3] By 1822 they belonged to the wealthy eccentric William Beckford, and at the time of his death in 1844 they hung in the oratory of his home at Lansdown Tower, Bath.[4] Although in 1835 Waagen had suggested a much more plausible attribution for *St Jerome in the Desert* to Marco Basaiti,[5] the picture was still listed as by Civetta in the 1844 Beckford inventory, and subsequently when in the Hamilton collection. In 1844 both pictures were probably sent to Hamilton House in Arlington Street, London, when Beckford's

daughter Susan, Duchess of Hamilton, inherited his collection; certainly, Waagen did not record them at Hamilton Palace on his visit of 1851, and they are known to have been removed from London to Scotland on the death of the 11th Duke in 1863. Only when the painting was acquired by the National Gallery at the Hamilton Palace sale of 1882 was the attribution to Civetta finally discarded in favour of Cima.

11 🦋 *The Virgin and Child with Saints Jerome(?), Peter, Francis and an Unidentified Female Saint*

Oil on canvas, transferred from panel
80.5 × 102.5cm | c.1504–6

Inscribed on the *banderole*: 'L. LOTVS. F.'

Provenance: Probably Philippe, Duc d'Orléans, by 1723; Louis, Duc d'Orléans, by 1727; by descent at the Palais Royal, Paris, to Louis-Philippe-Joseph, Duc d'Orléans (Philippe Égalité); by whom sold in 1791 to Viscount Walchiers; François de Laborde de Méréville; exhibited for sale at Bryan's Gallery, London, 1798–9 (no.234), but reserved for the 3rd Duke of Bridgewater; by inheritance to the 2nd Marquess of Stafford (later 1st Duke of Sutherland), Stafford House, London; by inheritance to Lord Francis Egerton, later 1st Earl of Ellesmere, Bridgewater House, London; by descent to the 5th Earl of Ellesmere (later 6th Duke of Sutherland) by whom placed on loan to the Gallery in 1945; purchased from the Ellesmere Trustees by private treaty with the aid of the National Heritage Memorial Fund, 1984 (acc.no.NG 2418)

EDINBURGH, NATIONAL GALLERY OF SCOTLAND

Like Catena's probably closely contemporary *The Virgin and Child with St Mary Magdalene and another Female Saint* (cat.no.8), Lotto's picture belongs to a pictorial type made popular by Giovanni Bellini in the final decades of the fifteenth century (fig.80). Of Lotto's four saints, Peter and Francis are clearly identified by their types and attributes, but the identity of the other two is less certain. The female saint is usually identified as Clare, founder of the second order of Franciscans, but in that case the colour of her habit should really match that of her companion Francis. With his bald head and long white beard, the figure on the left corresponds in type to St Jerome, and he is half naked under his red cloak; but he lacks the usual attributes of Jerome, and holds instead a scroll, an attribute usually associated with Old Testament prophets.

Lotto's composition is much more inventive than that of Catena, in that he introduces a strong element of physical animation and psychological interaction into the figure group, and provides an evocative glimpse of landscape background at the top. The idea of making the Virgin and Child turn in different directions to engage more actively with the flanking saints had already been explored by Cima in the 1490s (fig.81), but Lotto here invests it with a greater emotional intensity. The Christ Child leans over rather awkwardly to study the prophecy on Jerome's scroll, which carries the painter's signature on the back. This lends charm and even a note of humour to the scene; yet the attentive viewer will also sense that the prophecy tells of Christ's future Passion and death. This message

is reinforced on the left by Francis, who actively displays to the Virgin the wounds in his hands and side, mystically imprinted from the wounds of Christ.[1] Similarly at the top, the distant figures of the woodcutters provide a premonition of the Crucifixion by felling an upright, green tree, an allusion to the wood of the cross.[2] In another compositional novelty, the vertical cloth-of-honour that represents such a standard feature of Bellinesque Madonnas (cat.no.4; fig.72) is replaced by a horizontally slung curtain, which creates a sort of sacred precinct for the holy figures, separating them from the ordinary world beyond.[3]

The picture has always rightly been regarded as one of Lotto's earliest works, close in style and date to his documented altarpiece for the parish church of Santa Cristina al Tiverone, near Treviso, of 1504–6 (fig.82).[4] While already clearly expressing the painter's own, highly distinctive artistic personality, the present picture still reveals a clear stylistic debt to his probable master Giovanni Bellini, not only in the compositional type, but in the treatment of the Virgin's draperies, which fall into patterns of angular planes. The motif of the woodcutters in the background was apparently also drawn from Bellini's recent *Death of St Peter Martyr* (London, National Gallery). But the picture also reflects the young Lotto's interest in the work of two much more modern artists, neither of them Venetian: Leonardo da Vinci and Albrecht Dürer. The influence of the first is the more limited, but the head of the female saint to the right appears to be adapted from Leonardo's *Madonna Litta* (St Petersburg, State Hermitage Museum), a version of which is known to have been in Venice in the first half of the sixteeenth century.[5] Much more pervasive is the influence of Dürer, who was present in Venice for about twelve months from the autumn of 1505. Lotto would certainly have known the principal public work that Dürer painted during his visit, the *Feast of the Rosegarlands* (Prague, National Gallery); but he may also have known the *Christ Among the Doctors*, painted in 1506 – or at least, the artist's preparatory drawings for it (fig.83).[6] Common to both that picture and to Lotto's are the closely packed, idiosyncratic heads, and the equally expressive, oversized hands. No less indebted to Dürer – though probably in this case less to his paintings than to his many engravings imported into Venice – is Lotto's landscape vignette, in which the vegetation has a bristling

dynamism quite unlike the placid landscapes of Bellini and Cima.

During the years 1503–6, Lotto was based not in his native Venice, but in the nearby mainland city of Treviso, where he enjoyed the patronage of the local bishop, Bernardo de' Rossi. It is possible that this picture was painted for Rossi, although as with the Santa Cristina altarpiece, it is equally likely that it was commissioned by some member of his immediate circle, and perhaps by a member of the Franciscan order. In either case, it is relevant to note that the female saint was borrowed and repeated in a number of pictures by a follower of Bellini and Cima named Lucantonio Buscatti, whose altarpiece of the *Incredulity of Thomas* in San Nicolò, Treviso, contains a portrait of Bishop Rossi.[7] There is no actual record of Lotto's picture, however, until 1727, when it is listed in the collection of the Duc d'Orléans in Paris.[8]

An X-radiograph of the painting reveals a number of changes that took place during the course of execution. Originally, for example, the Child's proper left leg was placed slightly to the left of its present position; the folds of the Virgin's draperies were arranged more vertically; and most significantly, the saints' heads were placed directly against a more extensive landscape backdrop, and the green curtain was introduced as an afterthought.

Fig.82 | Lorenzo Lotto, *The Virgin and Child Enthroned with Saints*
Santa Cristina al Tiverone (Treviso), Parish Church

Fig.83 | Albrecht Dürer, *Christ among the Doctors*
Madrid, Museo Thyssen-Bornemisza

Attributed to Giorgione or a close follower CASTELFRANCO VENETO 1477/8–1510 VENICE

12 ✤ *Portrait of An Archer*

Oil on panel | 53.5 × 41.5cm | *c.*1500–10

Provenance: Mary Hamilton Campbell, Lady Ruthven; by whom bequeathed to the Gallery, 1885 (acc.no.NG 690)

EDINBURGH, NATIONAL GALLERY OF SCOTLAND

This unfortunately badly rubbed, but, nevertheless, poetically suggestive image typifies many of the innovations introduced by Giorgione into Venetian portraiture. Presumably – although not unambiguously – a portrait of a particular individual, the picture does not provide any clear indication of the sitter's social or professional status, as does Catena's probably closely contemporary, but much more traditional *Portrait of a Young Man* (cat.no.7). Instead, the painter sets out to evoke the figure's state of mind and inner personality by means of the transitory nature of the facial expression, of the placing of his hand to his breast, and of the oblique presentation of the sitter. Although the figure's fashionably long hair is now so worn as to be virtually illegible, it must always have blended softly with the background, enhancing the effect of the figure emerging from the surrounding darkness. The particular form of the glove, which affords protection for the hand and forefinger but mobility for the other fingers, appears to confirm the traditional assumption that the sitter is indeed an archer.[1] By contrast, it would be unwise to deduce anything from the style of the hat, which has been entirely re-painted, and which possibly once represented a metal helmet. It seems clear, nevertheless, that as so often with Giorgione and his immediate followers, the costume always had the appearance of fancy dress, as if the sitter were presenting himself in a romantic guise.

Equally Giorgionesque is the way in which the gleaming breastplate does not merely catch reflections of light, but serves as a mirror for the hand. This recalls the celebrated passage in Paolo Pino's *Dialogue on Painting* of 1548, in which the author describes a painting by Giorgione of an armoured St George in a landscape, in which the figure was reflected in mirrors to either side and in a foreground stream.[2] Pino makes it clear that the picture was conceived as a contribution to the *paragone* debate, stemming from Leonardo da Vinci, on the relative merits of the arts of poetry, painting and sculpture. Although it has often been assumed that Pino's description was an invention, designed as a neat demonstration of the superiority of Giorgione's art to that of sculpture, it has recently been argued that the picture did indeed once exist, and that the 'mirrors' in the landscape were discarded pieces of the saint's shining armour.[3]

It is tempting to agree with those recent authorities who have reaffirmed the traditional attribution of the *Portrait of an Archer* to Giorgione himself,[4] especially given the high quality of the best-preserved parts of the hand and breastplate. It should also be said that none of the various attributions to other painters that have been put forward have won any critical support.[5] On the other hand, the notorious problems attending any attribution to Giorgione

are here further compounded by the picture's poor condition, and in the end it is best to be cautious. If the *St George* described by Pino did indeed exist, the *Portrait of an Archer* may constitute rather a response to it, as well as to Giorgione's innovative portraiture, by a close and highly talented follower. In that case it might date from *c.*1510–15, shortly after Giorgione's early death, rather than from within the brief period of his artistic maturity (*c.*1500–10). The X-radiograph of the painting (fig.84) offers intriguing evidence that there was originally a landscape background behind the figure, at least at the left.

The picture has no certain history before it was bequeathed to the Gallery by Lady Ruthven in 1885. It may well, however, be identical with one recorded in the collection of Johannes and Jacob 'Van Voert' (Van Veerle) in Antwerp by Carlo Ridolfi in 1648, who described it as the portrait of 'a young man with a soft mane of hair, wearing armour in which his hand is reflected; a picture of exquisite beauty (by Giorgione)'.[6] It may also be identical with a picture attributed to Giorgione listed in the inventory of the Portuguese collector Diego Duarte in Amsterdam in 1682, where it is described as 'A half life-size portrait of a man wearing a breastplate, on which his gloved hand is placed.'[7] Finally, the picture may correspond to one sold at Christie's on 30 June 1827 (lot 53) as 'Giorgione. Himself as an Officer of the Archers.'[8] If so, it is likely to have been bought on that occasion by Lord and Lady Ruthven of Winton Castle, Pencaitland.

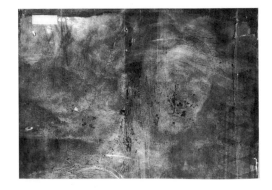

Fig.84 | X-radiograph (detail)

Titian PIEVE DI CADORE *c.*1485/90–1576 VENICE

13 & 14 ✢ *Christ and the Adulteress* and *Head of a Man*

Christ and the Adulteress

Oil on canvas | 139.2 × 181.7cm | *c.*1508–10

Provenance: Archibald McLellan; by whom bequeathed to the Glasgow Museum, 1854 (acc.no.181)

Head of a Man

Oil on canvas | 47 × 40.5cm | *c.*1508–10

Provenance: Private collection, Dumfriesshire; with Max Rothschild, London, 1927; with Agnew's, London, 1927; from whom acquired by Arthur Sachs, New York, 1927; with Agnew's, London; from whom purchased by Major Alfred Alinatt, 1962; sold Sotheby's, 30 June 1971 (lot 21), bought by Glasgow Museums (acc.no.3283)

GLASGOW MUSEUMS: KELVINGROVE ART GALLERY AND MUSEUM

The famous and controversial *Christ and the Adulteress* has been cut down by some thirty to fifty centimetres at the right, and the *Head of a Man* represents a fragment of the amputated section. A fairly accurate impression of the appearance of the original composition is provided by a full-size, fairly literal early copy in the Accademia Carrara, Bergamo (fig.85). Restoration of the principal fragment of the original in 1952–3 revealed the projecting knee at the right edge, overlapping the woman's skirt, which had been overpainted some time after the painting was cut down.[1]

The story of Christ and the adulteress is recounted in John 8: 2–11. Seeking to trap Jesus into refusing to support Mosaic law, the Pharisees brought before him a woman who had been discovered in the act of adultery, and demanded that she be stoned to death; besides showing compassion towards the woman, Jesus disarmed her accusers by saying 'He that is without sin among you, let him first cast a stone at her.' In the painting the scene is set in the open air, not in the temple, as is described in the gospel; and of the various bystanders, only the robed figure on the far left has the appearance of a pharisee. Partly for these reasons, the subject has often been identified instead as *Daniel and Susanna*.[2] This story is described in an apocryphal addition to the Old Testament Book of Daniel, in which the virtuous Susanna was falsely accused of adultery by two corrupt elders, but was saved from death by Daniel, who established the guilt of her accusers. Leaving aside the fact that this subject was very rare in art – unlike the quite common one of Christ and the adulteress – the visual evidence in the Glasgow picture simply does not support such an identification: Susanna was not brought before Daniel, who was still a young man without any position of authority, and who had uncovered the truth on his own initiative. Further confirmation that the subject is indeed Christ and the adulteress is provided by the following: Christ's leaning pose, as if he has just risen from stooping to write on the ground, as the gospel describes; by the medallion of a Roman emperor – presumably Tiberius – set into the wall above him; and above all by the traces of a cruciform halo around Christ's head, uncovered during the cleaning of 1952–3, and represented prominently in the Bergamo copy.

More problematic is the matter of the picture's attribution. For about a century after it was bequeathed to the Glasgow Museum, most scholars regarded it as an important late work by Giorgione.[3] But this was an expansionist phase of attributions to Giorgione, and it is now widely accepted that the physical vehemence of the figures, the range and intensity of the colours, and the lightness of the shadows have little in common with the small group of works universally agreed to be by him. Furthermore, if by Giorgione, it would have to be a late work, close to his lost frescoes of 1508 for the Fondaco dei Tedeschi in Venice; yet it is hard to credit a major master at the height of his powers with such awkwardness of spatial construction and anatomical articulation. A minority of scholars has always been unhappy with the attribution to Giorgione, and in the decades around 1900 some alternative names were suggested, including those of Sebastiano del Piombo, Domenico Campagnola, Cariani, Romanino, and Titian. Of these, only the last has persisted, and is now prevalent.[4] One or two critics, however, remain unconvinced by the attribution to Titian, presumably because of the picture's admittedly uneven quality, and have proposed instead that it might be by Domenico Mancini, a minor painter who is known exclusively from a single signed work, a *Virgin and Child with an Angel* in the cathedral of Lendinara, in which the main figure group is borrowed directly from Giovanni Bellini's San Zaccaria altarpiece of 1505.[5]

The manifest faults of the *Christ and the Adulteress*, as well as its even more striking qualities, may be attributed rather to the fact that it represents one of the earliest large-scale works by a highly ambitious young painter who had not yet fully mastered his art. Although the movements of the figures lack proper co-ordination, they act out their parts with an impulsive energy. The complicated pose of the soldier on the left, seen from the rear, appears to be based on that of an antique statue.[6] The colours, which include expensive orpiment and realgar in the orange doublet of the central youth, and ultramarine in

Fig.85 | After Titian, *Christ and the Adulteress*
Bergamo, Accademia Carrara

Fig.86 | Titian, *The Miracle of the Speaking Babe* (detail)
Padua, Scuola del Santo

the robe of Christ, are almost too rich and varied; yet they endow the work with great chromatic vitality. Similarly, the painter's delight in evoking the lustrous surfaces of armour and silk, while somewhat detracting from the dramatic unity, contribute a powerful and sensuous effect of immediacy. He displays no less virtuosity in the contrast between the detailed treatment of the plants in the foreground, reminiscent of Dürer, and the boldness of the brushwork in the right background, in which the pastoral vignette of the shepherd with his sheep is evoked with rapid touches of unblended paint.

Assuming, on the one hand, that Titian was born around 1490, and on the other that this is a youthful work painted before he was twenty, it would date from about 1508–10, that is, roughly contemporaneous with his frescoes for the Fondaco de' Tedeschi. As far as can be judged from prints after Titian's *Judith*, his principal fresco for the Fondaco which is now a scarcely-legible ruin, the dominant figure resembled those in the *Christ and the Adulteress* in its active pose and volumetric drapery from which fleshy but organically unconvincing limbs protruded. The background similarly comprises bright and dark contrasting planes that served more as a foil for the figures than to evoke rational space. In terms of both its composition and its style, *Christ and the Adulteress* has frequently and convincingly been compared with the largest of Titian's frescoes in the Scuola del Santo in Padua, *The Miracle of the Speaking Babe* (fig.86), although the latter is in some respects already more orderly and restrained.

X-radiographs made during the restoration of 1952–3 reveal that the painter made a number of adjustments to the placing of his forms during the process of execution, in a way that was to become characteristic of his mature practice. The woman's head, for example, was originally placed about five centimetres to the left of its present position; the position of Christ's head was shifted several times; and his knee was originally placed higher.[7]

Nothing is known of the painting's history before it was bequeathed by Archibald McLellan to the city of Glasgow in 1854. Presumably it was painted for a public setting – conceivably, given its theme of justice and mercy, for a judicial chamber – and since there is no early mention of its presence in Venice, it may have been painted for a town on the Venetian mainland. It has been plausibly suggested that the copy in Bergamo may have been commissioned to replace it when it was removed from its original setting, but nothing is known of the provenance of that picture either. There have been various attempts to identify the *Christ and the Adulteress* with one recorded in the collection of Queen Christina of Sweden in 1689, with an attribution to Giorgione.[8] But this picture was almost certainly identical with a half-length version of the subject later in the Orléans collection, at which time it was engraved with an attribution to Pordenone.[9] Earlier, to judge from the recorded dimensions (which were about one third smaller than those of the Glasgow painting in its uncut state), Queen Christina's picture had been in the collections of Gian Vincenzo Imperiale (1648) and Francesco Maria Balbi (1665) in Genoa, as by Giorgione.[10] It is worth emphasising in this connection that when owned by McLellan the picture bore an attribution to Bonifacio de' Pitati, and that it was first attributed to Giorgione by Waagen when he saw it in 1856.[11] Any mention of it, therefore, in seventeeth- and eighteenth-century inventories is more likely to be under the name of Bonifacio than of Giorgione. There is no information about when and under what circumstances the picture was cut down, but since the *Head of a Man* also has a Scottish provenance, it may be that this took place as late as the early nineteenth century in Scotland.

15 ❧ *The Three Ages of Man*

Oil on canvas | 90 × 151.7cm | *c.*1513

Provenance: Probably Emiliano Targone, Venice; by inheritance to Giovanni Bernardi da Castel Bolognese (1496–1553), Faenza, by 1548/9; Cardinal Otto Truchsess von Waldburg (1514–73), Augsburg and Dillingen; Matthäus Hopfer, Augsburg (died 1623); Queen Christina of Sweden (1626–1689), Palazzo Riario, Rome, by *c.*1662; by whom bequeathed to Cardinal Decio Azzolino (died 1689); by inheritance to his nephew, Marchese Pomponio Azzolino; from whom purchased in 1692 by Prince Livio Odescalchi (died 1713); by inheritance to Prince Odescalchi-Erba; from whom purchased in 1720 by Philippe, 2nd Duc d'Orléans (1674–1723); by descent in the Orléans collection at the Palais Royal, Paris, to Louis-Philippe-Joseph, 5th Duc d'Orléans (Philippe Égalité); by whom sold in 1791 to Viscount Walchiers; François de Laborde de Méréville; exhibited for sale at Bryan's Gallery, London, 1798–9 (no.278), but reserved for the 3rd Duke of Bridgewater; by inheritance to the 2nd Marquess of Stafford (later 1st Duke of Sutherland), Stafford House, London; by inheritance to Lord Francis Egerton, later 1st Earl of Ellesmere, Bridgewater

House, London; by descent to the 7th Duke of Sutherland. On long-term loan to the Gallery since 1945.

EDINBURGH, NATIONAL GALLERY OF SCOTLAND (DUKE OF SUTHERLAND LOAN)

This masterpiece of Titian's early career is almost certainly identical with one described by Vasari in his *Life* of Titian (1568):
After he had returned to Venice, for the father-in-law of Giovanni da Castel Bolognese, Titian did a painting in oils on canvas of a naked shepherd and a country girl who is offering some pipes for him to play, with an extremely beautiful landscape. This picture is to be found today in Faenza, in Giovanni's house.[1]
Giovanni Bernardi da Castel Bolognese was one of the most celebrated gem-engravers of the sixteenth century, and his handsome house in Faenza was a gift from the papal nephew Cardinal Alessandro Farnese, who was also a patron of Titian. Vasari must have seen *The Three Ages of Man*, together with a portrait of Giovanni's father-in-law by Giorgione, when he was a guest at the house in 1548/9.[2] This father-

in-law, who according to Vasari commissioned both pictures, was a goldsmith named Emiliano Targone (or Targhetta).[3] In 1536 Benvenuto Cellini, who regarded himself as a rival of both Bernardi and Targone, called the latter 'the finest jeweller in the world'.[4]

Vasari's account of the subject of Titian's picture is purely descriptive, and gives no hint of what he thought it meant. The current title, *The Three Ages of Man*, first recorded by Joachim von Sandrart in 1675,[5] implies that the picture is an allegory of the different phases of human life, from infancy – symbolised by the two sleeping babies on the right, watched over by a winged cupid – to young adulthood, and to old age and death. But as is notoriously the case with paintings by Giorgione such as *The Three Philosophers* (fig.13), or with Titian's own *Concert Champêtre* (fig.15), the question of interpretation remains controversial, and it has recently been suggested that the picture is not primarily an allegory but an illustration of the pastoral romance *Daphnis and Chloe* by the third-century Greek writer Longus.[6] According to this reading, the two lovers appear on the right as infants, as soon after their birth they were abandoned by their respective parents and grew up separately in

the woods and fields. The old man at the centre would then represent Daphnis's father Dionysophanes, mourning the death of his two other children. Such an interpretation of the subject would explain the unusual fact that it is the young man who is naked, just as Longus describes Daphnis as he was first seen by Chloe.

Yet as so often in the works of Giorgione, the painting does not ultimately correspond sufficiently closely with the text to prove that Titian intended to represent specific characters; although Sandrart's interpretation is now generally regarded as too limited and schematic, a majority of critics continue to read the picture as some sort of allegory on the transience of human life.[7] Perhaps it also reflects the kinds of debate on different aspects of love articulated by Pietro Bembo in his widely-read *Gli asolani* (cat.no.162): thus the infants would represent the instinctive, innocent love of childhood; the young adults sexual passion; and the old man a higher, spiritual love, achieved when all passion is spent. Symbols consistent with this message are the young woman's crown of myrtle, a plant sacred to Venus, and the rustic church or chapel, significantly placed directly above the old man. The choice of a pastoral setting, with sheep grazing in the lush pastures and the lovers represented as shepherds, reflects (without illustrating) another highly popular literary work of the period, Jacopo Sannazaro's *Arcadia*. Central to the pastoral as a poetic genre is the concept of 'Et in Arcadia ego': the poignant realisation that all human beauty and happiness will inevitably die. Both the *Asolani* and the *Arcadia* were written in the vernacular rather than in Latin, and the ideas and mood they communicate would have been perfectly accessible to a prosperous, but probably hardly scholarly craftsman such as Titian's patron Emiliano Targone. Significantly, too, in the earliest recorded reference to *The Three Ages of Man* – in an inventory of Giovanni Bernardi's property compiled after his death in 1553 – it is called 'a picture of love and death'.[8]

Another much-discussed aspect of the content is that of music, and the implications of the fact that the woman holds a recorder in each hand, while the shepherd holds a third by his side.[9] While Vasari thought that she is offering her pipes for him to play, more recent critics have variously suggested rather that she has just

finished playing them herself, or that the lovers are about to play a duet, or that they have just played one. In any case, the pipes are entirely appropriate both as the customary instruments of Arcadian shepherds, and as providing the food of love for the passionately involved couple. The art of music, which exists in time rather than space, and dies away into silence when it has been performed, may also be seen as a potent metaphor for the underlying theme of transience.

The *Three Ages of Man* is usually dated on stylistic evidence to about 1512–14, and in style and pictorial handling it does indeed appear contemporary with other works traditionally dated to this phase, such as the *Noli me Tangere* (London, National Gallery) and the *Baptism* (Rome, Pinacoteca Capitolina), and slightly earlier than the *Sacred and Profane Love* (Rome, Galleria Borghese), which is datable on external evidence to about 1514–15. But Titian's early chronology continues to be a matter of debate, and it has recently been argued that the *Three Ages of Man* dates from 1516.[10] It is true that Vasari's phrase 'after he had returned to Venice' follows on from his discussion of Titian's work for the court of Ferrara, which he first visited in 1516. But this may simply be a rhetorical continuity device on the part of Vasari, and evidence that the *Three Ages of Man* was at least well under way by early 1514 is provided by the *Holy Innocents* roundel in the predella of Romanino's documented Santa Giustina altarpiece (Padua, Museo Civico, fig.87), in which the infants are loosely, but clearly adapted from Titian's group on the right.[11]

This is not, however, to exclude the possibility that the execution of the picture may have extended over two or three years; that although Titian had established his composition by 1513, he made extensive revisions before completing it. Evidence for this supposition is provided by the X-radiograph of the picture (fig.88), which even by the standards of Titian's characteristically spontaneous and experimental technique, shows an unusually large number of pentimenti, or changes of mind.[12] The most obvious of these include: the deletion of Cupid's quiver, originally suspended from the top of the tree on the right; the deletion of a tower in the central background; and the reduction of the number of skulls surrounding the old man from four to two. But of exceptional interest is the fact that several of

these deleted elements appear in two variant copies of Titian's composition, both probably dating from the seventeenth century, and in an etching by Valentin Lefebvre (cat.no.158). It seems that these must record two additional, lost versions of the *Three Ages of Man* produced in Titian's studio, and possibly by Titian himself, before the present, original version had reached its final form. Besides implying that the *Three Ages of Man* evolved slowly, as did so many of Titian's works later in his career, the existence of contemporaneous variants for different customers lends further weight to the supposition that the allegorical message of the picture was of a general – rather than a particularly personal or erudite – nature.

Giovanni Bernardi died in 1553, a few years after Vasari's visit to his house. The next recorded owner of the *Three Ages of Man* was the Cardinal of Augsburg, Otto Truchsess von Waldburg, a keen collector and patron of art, who was in close personal contact with Titian at the time of the imperial diets at Augsburg in 1548 and 1551, and perhaps on other occasions in Venice.[13] In 1628, or perhaps a few years later, it was seen in the former house of Matthäus Hopfer in Augsburg by Joachim von Sandrart, who recorded that it was sold from there by 'Walberg' to Queen Christina of Sweden – probably in October 1655 as she travelled through Augsburg on her journey south to take up residence in Rome.[14] From the early 1660s onwards the picture shared its history with the *Venus Anadyomene* (cat.no.19), and passed through the same series of celebrated aristocratic collections.[15]

Nearly two centuries before the arrival of the painting in Scotland from Bridgewater House in London, immediately after the Second World War, another, now lost version was acquired by Robert Foulis for his Academy in Glasgow. Comparing his version to the present picture, at that time in the Orléans collection in Paris, Foulis wrote: 'There is another in the Palais Royal, which some think, who have seen both, is neither so highly finished nor so well preserved.'[16] He does not, however, go so far as to claim his own version as superior in quality; indeed, to judge from the rather poor engraving of it by James Mitchell of 1764 (fig.62) – into which a highland cottage has been inserted – it was merely a copy, probably executed in the early eighteenth century in Paris.

Fig.87 | Girolamo Romanino, *The Holy Innocents* Padua, Museo Civico

Fig.88 | X-radiograph mosaic

Attributed to Giovanni da Asola ASOLA ACTIVE 1512–1531 VENICE

16 ❧ *Musicians in a Landscape*

Oil on panel | 56.4 × 43.2cm | *c*.1516

Provenance: John Graham-Gilbert, Glasgow; bequeathed by his widow to the Glasgow Museum, 1877 (acc.no.579)

GLASGOW MUSEUMS: KELVINGROVE ART GALLERY AND MUSEUM

The subject of figures playing music in a pastoral landscape was a highly popular one in Venice in the second and third decades of the sixteenth century. Unlike Titian's *Concert Champêtre* (fig.15) or *The Three Ages of Man* (cat.no.15), however, the present picture does not appear to convey any deeper allegorical or philosophical message, but simply represents two picturesquely dressed players of viols (a viola da gamba and a viola da braccio) whose music accords sweetly with their rustic surroundings. As a small-scale, Giorgionesque genre picture, the work may be compared with engravings by Giulio Campagnola such as *The Young Shepherd* (fig.89) and the *Shepherds and Musicians* (the latter completed by Domenico Campagnola).

An X-radiograph of the picture shows that the right arm of the figure on the left has been lowered from its original position, possibly implying that he was not actually bowing his instrument as he is in the final version.

When in the collection of John Graham-Gilbert the picture was attributed to Giorgione, and it was exhibited as such in the New Gallery, London, in 1894–5. Exposure there prompted new attributions to Domenico Campagnola and to Romanino by expert visitors to the exhibition,[1] but neither of these suggestions has won general acceptance. The most convincing attribution to be advanced in recent years has been to the still mysterious painter Giovanni da Asola, who was active in Venice by 1512, and who died there in 1531.[2] Stylistically comparable works by Giovanni include a painting of St Jerome in the Rijksmuseum, Amsterdam; two versions of the *Adoration of the Shepherds* in the National Gallery, London and Nelson-Atkins Museum, Kansas City; and especially *The Resurrection* in San Francesco della Vigna, Venice (fig.90). This last picture, which is inscribed with the date 1516, also provides an approximate date for the *Musicians in a Landscape*.

Fig.89 | Giulio Campagnola, *The Young Shepherd*
London, British Museum

Fig.90 | Attributed to Giovanni da Asola, *The Resurrection*
Venice, Church of San Francesco della Vigna

After Giovanni Bellini VENICE c.1438–1516 VENICE

17 ❦ The Feast of the Gods

Oil on canvas | 174 × 192.4cm

Inscribed on the *cartellino*: 'Johannes bellinus venetus / No. 204. MDXIIII'

Provenance: William Coningham; his sale, Christie's, London, 9 June 1849 (lot 4, as by Poussin), bought by Sir Charles Eastlake; by whom presented to the National Gallery of Scotland, 1862 (acc.no.NG458)

EDINBURGH, NATIONAL GALLERY OF SCOTLAND

This is a full-size, precise copy of one of the great achievements of Bellini's last years, *The Feast of the Gods* of 1514 (fig.91).[1] After a long career devoted almost exclusively to painting sacred subjects, Bellini was finally persuaded by Alfonso d'Este, Duke of Ferrara, to contribute a large-scale mythology to his *camerino* or private study in the palace complex at Ferrara. As conceived around 1511, the *camerino* was to be decorated with a series of bacchanalian subjects by the leading painters of central and northern Italy. However, for various reasons, the planned contributions by Fra Bartolomeo, Michelangelo and Raphael never materialised, and the project was eventually brought to completion with three major mythologies by Titian and other pictures by the local court artist Dosso Dossi. By the time that Titian had painted the *Bacchus and Ariadne* in 1523 (fig.21), *The Feast of the Gods* would have looked incongruously old-fashioned; soon afterwards Alfonso commissioned the younger painter to harmonise Bellini's picture with his own three by completely repainting the background with a dramatic landscape.

Bellini's subject, which was almost certainly devised by the court humanist Mario Equicola, was based on a number of classical literary sources, the principal of which was Ovid's *Fasti* (I: 391–440; VI: 319–48). The story concerns a feast thrown by Cybele, goddess of nature and fertility, for her fellow Olympians. While the gods were drowsy with the abundant wine provided by Bacchus, the libidinous Priapus attempted to rape the sleeping Lotis (on the extreme right), but before he could succeed, the braying of Silenus's ass (towards the left) aroused the gods, who chased away the transgressor with their laughter. Most of the gods are clearly identifiable by their attributes: thus, the four male figures seated in the front row are Mercury (with his helmet and caduceus), Jupiter (with his eagle), Neptune (with his trident) and Apollo (with his laurel wreath). With them in the foreground are Ceres, with the garland of wheat in her hair, and Cybele herself. Bacchus – the tutelary deity of the feast – is shown in the unusual form of a child, with vine leaves in his hair, filling a jug from the substantial wine barrel.

When the state of Ferrara devolved to the papacy in 1598 the series of bacchanals, including Bellini's *The Feast of the Gods*, were appropriated by the papal nephew Cardinal Pietro Aldobrandini and taken to Rome. The painting remained in Rome until 1855, when it was acquired by the 4th Duke of Northumberland and brought to Alnwick Castle. Soon after the First World War it was sold to the United States, and it entered the National Gallery of Art in Washington in 1942.

The present copy evidently dates from the early seventeenth century, when Bellini's original was in the Aldobrandini collection. The number 204 inscribed by the copyist on the slip of paper at the lower right corresponds to the number assigned to the original in an inventory of the Aldobrandini pictures compiled in 1603 by Giovanni Battista Agucchi.[3] It is not known on what evidence the copy was attributed to Nicolas Poussin when it was owned by William Coningham in the mid-nineteenth century, and some modern scholars have rejected the attribution.[2] But Coningham bought a number of his pictures in Rome,[4] and it may well be that the attribution is based on a reliable local tradition. Furthermore, the copy is of high artistic quality, and it shares with most of Poussin's earlier works the technical peculiarity of having been painted over a warm reddish-brown ground that has become more visible over the centuries than can have been intended, especially in the flesh areas. Although no copy by Poussin after *The Feast of the Gods* is recorded in the early sources, he is known to have made a close study of the Ferrara Bacchanals. His own *Bacchanal with the Guitar Player* of about 1627–8 (Paris, Louvre), for example, is manifestly inspired as much by Bellini's *The Feast of the Gods* as by Titian's three bacchanals, and the figure of the river god on the left is directly borrowed from Bellini's Mercury.[5] This would provide a plausible approximate date for the present picture.

Fig.91 | Giovanni Bellini, *The Feast of the Gods*
Washington, National Gallery of Art, Widner Collection
(1942.9.1(PA) 597)

After Titian PIEVE DI CADORE *c.*1485/90–1576 VENICE

18 ❦ *Bacchus*

Oil on canvas | 92.5 × 74.5cm

Provenance: Probably Borghese collection, Rome, by 1700; John Rushout, 2nd Baron Northwick, Thirlestane House, Cheltenham; his sale, Philips, Cheltenham, 11 August 1859 (lot 1095, as Agostino Carracci), bought by Alexander William, Lord Lindsay, later 25th Earl of Crawford and 8th Earl of Balcarres

PRIVATE COLLECTION

This is a copy of the central figure in Titian's *Bacchus and Ariadne* of 1520–3 (fig.21), one of the three great mythologies he painted for the *camerino* of Alfonso, Duke of Ferrara. Although Titian's celebrated original never came to Scotland, it is worth recording in the present context that it was imported from Rome to Britain in 1806/7 by two Scottish dealers, James Irvine and William Buchanan, and once it had arrived in London it was immediately bought by a Scottish nobleman, the profligate Charles, 8th Baron Kinnaird of Rossie Priory.[1] A few years earlier, in 1799–1800, when the picture was still in Rome, the future 10th Duke of Hamilton had attempted to buy it for Hamilton Palace, but had failed to meet the asking price.[2]

Titian depicted the god of wine, his head garlanded with vine leaves, leaping from his cheetah-drawn chariot to embrace Ariadne as she wandered disconsolately on the seashore. In making his figure of Bacchus into a self-sufficient picture, the copyist was forced to invent a new foreground, consisting of a cloud and some plants, and to shift the background city, with its huge obelisk, closer to the figure. In 1854 Waagen identified the copyist as Agostino Carracci,[3] a painter who would indeed have known Titian's picture before its removal from Ferrara to Rome in 1598. There is no good stylistic reason for this attribution, however, and more plausible is a recent suggestion that the copy was made by the Ferrarese court painter Dosso Dossi (*c.*1486–1542), another contributor to Alfonso's *camerino*.[4] It is true that Dosso is not known to have made copies after other artists' works, and any borrowings are customarily transformed into his own highly personal idiom. Yet a number of parallels of handling with Dosso's work of the mid-1520s are evident: the foreground plants and the firmly modelled musculature of the torso, for example, resemble those of the *Apollo* of about 1524 (Rome, Galleria Borghese); while the background landscape is endowed with a sultriness foreign to Titian, but which is close to that of Dosso's *St Sebastian* of about 1526 (Milan, Pinacoteca di Brera).[5]

Recently an alternative attribution of the present painting to the Cavaliere d'Arpino (1568–1640) has been proposed, with the suggestion that it is to be identified with one of the partial copies of the *Bacchus and Ariadne* attributed to the Cavaliere in seventeenth- and eighteenth-century descriptions and inventories of the Borghese collection in Rome.[6] One of these copies is known to have shown the figure of Bacchus, as here, leaping from a cloud ('in atto di scendere precipitoso da una nuvola') but the style of the present picture has little in common with that of the Cavaliere.[7] On balance it seems likely that the present picture is indeed identical with the one recorded in the Borghese collection, but

that the attribution given in the early sources to the Cavaliere d'Arpino was erroneous. An old photograph of the painting shows the inventory number '41' painted in the lower right corner, removed in a subsequent restoration; this may provide a useful lead for further research into its provenance.

It remains surprising that this picture should have been purchased at the Northwick sale of 1859 by Lord Lindsay. The author of the *Sketches of the History of Christian Art* is known to have had no particular admiration for either Titian or Agostino Carracci, or for erotic mythological painting in general.[7]

Fig.92 | Titian, *Bacchus and Ariadne* (detail) London, National Gallery

Titian PIEVE DI CADORE *c.*1485/90–1576 VENICE

19 ❧ *Venus Anadyomene (Venus Rising from the Sea)*

Oil on canvas | 74 × 56.2cm | *c.*1520

Inscribed on the back of the original canvas: '41' and 'RAffe Raggio'

Provenance: Queen Christina of Sweden, Palazzo Riario, Rome, by *c.*1662; by whom bequeathed to Cardinal Dezio Azzolino (died 1689); by inheritance to his nephew Marchese Pomponio Azzolino; from whom purchased in 1692 by Prince Livio Odescalchi (died 1713); by inheritance to Prince Odescalchi-Erba; from whom purchased in 1720 by Philippe, 2nd Duc d'Orléans (1674–1723); by descent in the Orléans collection at the Palais Royal, Paris, to Louis-Philippe-Joseph, 5th Duc d'Orléans (Philippe Égalité); by whom sold in 1791 to Viscount Walchiers; François de Laborde de Méréville; exhibited for sale at Bryan's Gallery, London, 1798–9 (no.49), but reserved for the 3rd Duke of Bridgewater; by inheritance to the 2nd Marquess of Stafford (later 1st Duke of Sutherland), Stafford House, London; by inheritance to Lord Francis Egerton, later 1st Earl of Ellesmere, Bridgewater House, London; by descent to the 5th Earl of Ellesmere (later 6th Duke of Sutherland) by whom placed on loan to the Gallery in 1945; acquired by the Gallery by private treaty sale, partially in lieu of inheritance tax, from the Trustees of the 7th Duke of Sutherland, with the aid of the Hertiage Lottery Fund, the Scottish Executive, and the National Art Collections Fund, 2003 (acc.no.NG 2751)

EDINBURGH, NATIONAL GALLERY OF SCOTLAND

This apparently simple representation of the goddess of love emerging from the sea is actually an image exceptionally rich in cultural resonance, as well as one that is warmly and vividly sensuous. According to classical mythology, Venus was created when the genitals of Uranus, cut off by his son Chronos, were cast into the sea; and already fully grown, she was wafted by the Zephyrs on a scallop shell to Paphos in Cyprus, where she was greeted by the three Horae. Here she is seen gently moving forwards from her shell towards the shore, wringing the water from her long golden-brown hair. But unlike Botticelli in his famous *Birth of Venus* (Florence, Galleria degli Uffizi), painted about forty years earlier, Titian does not include the Zephyrs and the Horae; and the curiously small and unfunctional shell serves more as an identifying attribute of the goddess – who might otherwise be mistaken for a mere bathing woman – than as an element in the narrative.[1]

Titian's concept was certainly inspired by a well-known passage in Pliny the Elder's *Natural History*, in which the writer described a *Venus Anadyomene* by the most famous painter of classical antiquity, Apelles, which had been brought from the Greek island of Kos on the orders of the Emperor Augustus and installed in the Temple of Caesar in Rome.[2] By Pliny's time in the first century AD, the lower part of Apelles's painting had been damaged; accordingly, Titian shows Venus in thigh length, but includes a naturalistic explanation for the truncation in the form of the foaming sea water that laps around her knees. Pliny also records a tradition that Apelles used his mistress Campaspe as his model; and it may be that Titian, too – who was rumoured to be enjoying sexual relations with his female models around this very time – purposefully employed his current mistress as a model for the *Venus Anadyomene*.[3]

There is broad critical agreement that for stylistic reasons the *Venus Anadyomene* dates from Titian's early maturity, and is contemporary with the three bacchanals that he painted for Alfonso d'Este, Duke of Ferrara, in the years around 1520. The Venus is indeed particularly close in type to the female figures in *The Bacchanal of the Andrians* (Madrid, Museo Nacional del Prado), a picture that is nowadays usually seen as the third in the series, datable to about 1524–5, but which was probably actually the second, painted in 1519–20.[4] During the period of his active involvement with the Ferrarese court Titian certainly painted a number of other smaller pictures for the duke, possibly including the *Venus Anadyomene*; but his base remained Venice, and he continued to work for a range of other patrons. There are, in fact, a number of reasons why the subject of *Venus Anadyomene* might have been favoured by a Venetian patron. In the mythography of the city,

Fig.93 | Antonio Lombardo, *Venus Anadyomene*
London, Victoria and Albert Museum

which itself seems to emerge miraculously from the sea, Venice was often compared with Venus – indeed, its very name was supposed to have derived from that of the goddess.[5] Furthermore, Cyprus, the locus of her antique cult, was a Venetian colony and the Republic's most important possession in the eastern Mediterranean. Contemporary images clearly inspired by such considerations include the reverse of a medal of about 1523 of the Venetian patrician Sebastiano Venier, which shows a female nude riding on the waves and an inscription referring to the mythical origins of Venice.[6] Similarly, an engraving of 1506 by Marcantonio Raimondi, made during his period of residence in the city, and perhaps based on a lost drawing by Giorgione, shows Venus standing on the sea-shore, wringing out her hair.

Yet there are equally compelling reasons to suggest that Titian's *Venus Anadyomene* may have been commissioned by the Duke of Ferrara.[7] All three of the bacchanals were based on *ekphrases* – that is to say, on literary evocations of works of art – and the humanist culture of courtly Ferrara is probably more likely than that of Venice to have provided the stimulus for Titian's similarly *ekphrastic* painting, in which the artist self-consciously seeks to recreate a famous lost work of art from classical antiquity. In so doing, he would have been implicitly comparing himself with Apelles, perhaps for the first time in his long career, but certainly not for the last.[8] By the 1530s it had become commonplace for Titian to be hailed as the greatest painter of modern times, and therefore as a new Apelles; it is possible that he may have been prompted to claim this title by the unexpected death in April 1520 of Raphael, who had also been commissioned to paint an *ekphrastic* bacchanal for Alfonso. The recreation of the lost masterpiece would in any case have flatteringly compared Titian's patron both with Alexander the Great, patron of Apelles, and with the Emperor Augustus, who had the original *Venus Anadyomene* brought to Rome. Such a comparison already lay behind Alfonso's probable commission of an earlier representation of this subject, the *Venus Anadyomene* in marble relief by the Venetian sculptor Antonio Lombardo (fig.93).[9] Indeed, even if Alfonso did not commission the picture, Titian is likely to have known Antonio's relief from his various visits to Ferrara, and it may well have inspired him to tackle the subject himself.

While probably alluding to Antonio's relief, Titian would also have intended to challenge it, and to express the superiority of his own art of painting. The *paragone*, or debate on the respective merits of the different arts, was already widespread in the first half of the sixteenth century, and it is clearly reflected in several of Titian's early works,[10] as well as in those of his elder contemporary Giorgione (see cat.no.12). The obvious advantage of painting over sculpture was its far greater power of verisimilitude, achieved through effects of colour, light and texture; in exploiting these qualities in his painting, Titian was ambitiously setting out to challenge not just the relatively minor Antonio Lombardo, but also the various surviving antique statues of the *Venus Anadyomene*. Without adopting the pose of a particular classical model,[11] the ample form and swivelling contrapposto of Titian's figure create no less convincing an effect of movement in space; yet no statue could compare with the painting in its evocation of the plump softness of the goddess's flesh, of the fall of light on her left shoulder and breasts, or of the amorphous surrounding elements of air and water. Equally unlike his sculptural prototypes, Titian endows his ideal figure with an inner life that transcends mere physical beauty. Her face as she emerges from the sea is less the flawless mask of a goddess than the expressive face of a real woman, lost in thought.

The recently discovered inscription on the reverse, apparently in a sixteenth- or seventeenth-century hand, presumably refers to an owner named Raffaelle Raggi or Raggio. An early sixteenth-century Genoese nobleman named Raffaelle Raggi was portrayed a century later by Van Dyck (Washington, National Gallery of Art), and it is possible that a later member of the family with the same name owned the picture before it is first definitely recorded in about 1662. Thereafter, together with the slightly earlier *The Three Ages of Man* (cat.no.15), it passed through three of the most famous collections of the seventeenth, eighteenth and nineteenth centuries: those of Queen Christina of Sweden, of the Ducs d'Orléans (to which the inventory number 41 on the back refers) and of the Earls of Ellesmere.[12] Like *The Three Ages of Man*, it is one of the pictures that helped establish Titian as one of the most avidly sought-after old masters among collectors in Regency and Victorian Britain.

The X-radiograph mosaic (fig.94) shows a number of minor shifts in the figure's contours, and it is possible that the head was originally turned more to the left. Contrary, however, to what has been implied,[13] the position of the head did not follow Antonio Lombardo's relief in being tilted upwards.

Fig.94 | X-radiograph mosaic

Technical Note

Painted on medium weight normal weave canvas, *Venus Anadyomene* was relined by Kennedy North in 1931.[14] This was an early instance of the use of wax as a lining adhesive and Kennedy North, with his strong belief in the virtues of wax as a preservative, also liberally coated the surface of the painting with the material. Among the drawbacks of wax is its tendency to blanch and become opaque with age, and its attraction of grime. Prior to its most recent restoration, the very grimy surface coating of the painting obscured both the surface texture of the canvas and the liveliness of the brushwork (fig.95).

The relined canvas support was severely deformed due mainly to the thick layer of adhesive between the canvases and to the effect of an old paste lining discovered during relining. On removal of this lining an old inscription 'RAffe Raggio' was found on the reverse of the original canvas (fig.96). The original canvas proved to be in such good condition that it was possible to leave it unlined, with only a dry canvas to provide additional support. The X-radiograph shows deformation marks in the weave caused by the original stretching of the canvas which prove there has been little or no reduction in its size. It also reveals that the angle of Venus' head had been quite radically altered during the course of execution (fig.94). Freed from the wax coating, the paint appeared in excellent condition with only minor cracking and paint losses in the thicker passages of paint (fig.97). An apparent prominent damage in Venus's upper arm proved to be an indentation in the paint filled with tinted wax. Cleaning also revealed Titian's final touches in a translucent brown paint used to define the forms of the contours such as elbows and shoulders and to accent the darker shadows. This paint has an unusual characteristic: it has separated into little globules as if it had been partly rejected by the underlying oil paint (fig.98).

Paint sample cross sections show that the painting has a red-brown ground (fig.99). This use of a coloured ground is unusual for the period, although it has been reported that Titian's rather earlier *Holy Family with a Shepherd* (London, National Gallery) is painted on a grey-tinted ground.[15] JD

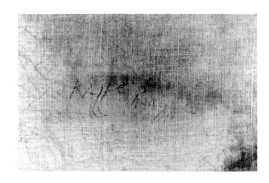

Fig.96 | Detail of the back of the original canvas, showing inscription

Fig.97 | Detail of Venus' right hand, after cleaning, before retouching

Fig.98 | Detail of Venus' breast and hair, after cleaning

Fig.95 | Detail of Venus' face, during cleaning

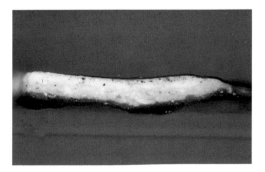

Fig.99 | Paint sample cross section showing red-brown ground

Girolamo da Santacroce SANTACROCE (BERGAMO) *c.*1480/5–*c.*1556 VENICE
20 ❧ *Four Poets in a Landscape*

Oil on panel | 30 × 72.4cm | *c.*1515–20

Provenance: Francis, Lord Elcho (later 10th Earl of Wemyss); by descent to the present owner

THE EARL OF WEMYSS AND MARCH KT

Fig.100 | Marcantonio Raimondi, *Parnassus*
(after Raphael)
London, British Museum

Girolamo's unashamedly derivative approach to composition is evident in this nostalgic vision of the Venetian *terraferma*. The fortified city on the left is a literal transcription of its counterpart in Giovanni Bellini's *The Madonna of the Meadow* of about 1505 (fig.6; see also cat.no.5) – or more probably, given Girolamo's access to the Bellini workshop, on a preparatory drawing that Bellini may have made for this detail. The group of poets with laurel wreaths at the right, by contrast, is copied with equal literalness from the far left of Marcantonio Riamondi's well-circulated engraving after Raphael's *Parnassus* of about 1509–11 in the Stanza della Segnatura of the Vatican Palace (fig.100). There is much argument about the identity of Raphael's poets, but in any case Girolamo made no attempt to give them individual features or attributes. It is likely, in fact, that in common with a number of other small-scale landscape pictures produced by Venetian painters of the generation of Giorgione, Girolamo's panel has no particular subject. Rather, it simply sets out to evoke a mood of pastoral serenity by means of a landscape bathed in summer sunlight and picturesquely peopled with anonymous poets and rustics.

A date in the second decade of the sixteenth century, in the wake of Marcantonio's engraving, is probably the most likely for this panel,[1] but given Girolamo's habit of repeating himself and his progressive archaism as a painter, a date in the 1520s or even later cannot be excluded. The picture was already attributed to Girolamo when it was acquired by Lord Elcho in the later nineteenth century, and this has been accepted by the few writers to mention it.[2]

Attributed to Domenico Capriolo VENICE *c*.1494–1528 TREVISO

21 ❧ *The Virgin and Child*

Oil on panel | 33 × 22.9cm | *c*.1515

Provenance: Mrs John G. Coats; by whom presented to the Glasgow Museum, 1948 (acc.no.3182)

GLASGOW MUSEUMS: KELVINGROVE ART
GALLERY AND MUSEUM

In this little devotional panel the theme of the Virgin and Child as popularised in the late fifteenth century by Giovanni Bellini (cat.nos.3, 4), is updated in accordance with early sixteenth-century taste. The foreground parapet is now stepped, as in a number of works by Giorgione and the young Titian. The pose of the Child is more self-consciously classicising, as if imitating that of an antique statue. And the sunset landscape, with its picturesquely rustic buildings and its mood of romantic nostalgia, corresponds to the ideal prevalent in the second decade of the new century (see cat.nos.15, 16). As in Paris Bordon's *The Virgin and Child with Saints John the Baptist, Mary Magdalene and George* (cat.no.30), the traditional motif of the small bird held by the Christ Child alludes to his future Passion.

Generically attributed to a 'Follower of Palma Vecchio' when given to the Gallery, the picture has more recently been reassigned both to the young Pordenone, *c*.1512,[1] and to Domenico Capriolo, *c*.1515.[2] The close similarities of the facial types and the background landscape to the latter's signed and dated *The Adoration of the Shepherds* of 1518 (fig.101) make the attribution to Capriolo the more plausible; but in either case, the present work represents an attractive, although somewhat provincial response to the artistic revolution created in Venice by Giorgione in the first decade of the century.

Fig.101 | Domenico Capriolo, *The Adoration of the Shepherds,* Treviso, Museo Civico 'Luigi Bailo'

Giovanni Busi, called Cariani VAL BREMBANA (BERGAMO) c.1485–AFTER 1547 VENICE (?)

22 ❧ St Agatha

Oil on canvas | 69 × 58cm | c.1516–17

Provenance: Sale, Sotheby's, London, 10 December 1986 (lot 22), bought Colnaghi, London and New York; from whom purchased by the Gallery, 1989 (acc.no.NG2494)

EDINBURGH, NATIONAL GALLERY OF SCOTLAND

The figure is clearly identifiable as St Agatha from her martyr's palm and from the pair of amputated breasts that she displays in the glass dish. Agatha lived in Catania in Sicily in the reign of the Emperor Decius in the third century, and one of the many cruel tortures she suffered for her steadfast Christian faith was to have her breasts cut off with shears. The simulated relief in the lower left corner is not perfectly legible, partly because of abrasion of the paint surface in this area, but it appears to show a battle between nude warriors and a man on horseback, of a type found on classical sarcophagi. The message is presumably that through her faith in Christ, Agatha was ultimately victorious over pagan violence and brutality.

The picture belongs to a type of image that enjoyed a particular popularity in Venice in the second decade of the sixteenth century, in which a beautiful woman is represented in half length. The type, of which important examples exist by Sebastiano del Piombo, Titian and Palma Vecchio, contains formal and expressive elements variously associated with portraiture, allegory, erotic genre and images of devotion, but in fluctuating proportions, so that its meaning is often, and perhaps deliberately, ambivalent. It is a matter of debate whether the present picture is intended as an image of the saint, which nevertheless draws on conventions of portraiture, or whether it actually constitutes a portrait of a real woman presented in the guise of St Agatha, presumably in honour of her name saint.[1] In favour of the latter interpretation are the portrait-like features; the elements of modern dress; the absence of a halo; and, perhaps above all, the provocative sensuality with which the figure fingers the breast and base of the palm, and which might seem indecorous for an image of devotion. Examples of other Venetian pictures in which the sitter is shown in the guise of his or her name saint include Sebastiano's *Portrait of a Lady as St Agatha* (London, National Gallery), Savoldo's *Portrait of a Man as St George* (Washington, National Gallery of Art),[2] and the same painter's *Portrait of a Lady as St Margaret* (Rome, Pinacoteca Capitolina); while Lotto's *Portrait of a Lady as Lucretia* in the present exhibition (cat.no.32) shows a similar invocation of the example of a secular heroine.

Against these considerations, however, it may be noted that Cariani is not an artist who shared Sebastiano's or Titian's powers of idealisation, and that the saints in his religious pictures routinely retain a portrait-like character. Further, the fashionable elements of costume – the dress, with its slashing of the fabric on the upper arm, and the arrangement of the hair in a snood – co-exist with elements that are clearly meant to appear timeless, such as the pink shawl and the yellow cloak. Furthermore, portraits of particular women were still uncommon in Venice in the second decade and examples of the kind mentioned above, in which the sitter was shown in a particular guise, were at this early date rarer still. All this is to conclude that the picture is probably not, after all, intended as a portrait, but rather as an image of the saint that catered simultaneously for the needs of pious contemplation and of sensuous and aesthetic pleasure. Evidence that contemporaries found it possible to reconcile such apparently contradictory functions in the privacy of their homes is provided by Titian's highly voluptuous *St Mary Magdalene* (Florence, Palazzo Pitti) of the mid-1530s.

In the short time since it first came to public attention, the *St Agatha* has generally been dated to the beginning of Cariani's career, about 1510–14.[3] This is chiefly because it was clearly influenced by two important 'beautiful woman' pictures painted in Venice by Sebastiano del Piombo: the *Salome* (or *Judith*) 1510 (London, National Gallery); and the *Wise Virgin* of 1511 (Washington, National Gallery of Art). According to this view of Cariani's very uncertain stylistic development, his art reached an early peak in quality under the direct inspiration of Giorgione and Sebastiano, and thereafter went into a long and gradual decline. But the two pictures by Sebastiano, like the earliest portraits of Titian, show the figure in waist length, and it is hard to give Cariani credit here, and in another supposedly early work, a *Judith* (private collection), for anticipating Titian in extending the format to thigh length. Other elements in the *St Agatha* – the incorporation of the narrative relief, the juxtaposition of a dark foil for the figure and arched opening to the sky, and the sensuous trails of loose hair and of the silken fringe of the shawl – similarly appear to be dependant on the example of Titian's works of around 1515–16, such as the *Salome-Judith* (Rome, Galleria Doria Pamphili)[4] and the *Sacred and Profane Love* (Rome, Galleria Borghese). Cariani was clearly, in fact, an artist who developed in fits and starts, depending on the inspiration of the moment; while sometimes achieving works of high quality, as here, he equally often appears oddly inept and provincial. Confirmation that the *St Agatha* is likely to have been painted about 1516–17 rather than five years or so earlier is provided by the major documented work of his early maturity, the splendid *St Gottard* altarpiece of 1518–19 (Milan, Pinacoteca di Brera).[5] The two works appear stylistically perfectly compatible in their choice colour combinations, warmly chromatic shadows and treatment of the landscape background; and none of these features are particularly close to the style of Sebastiano.

Bernardino Licinio VENICE *c.*1490–*c.*1549 VENICE

23 ❧ *An Allegory of Love*

Oil on canvas | 106 × 91cm | *c.*1520

Provenance: George, 9th Baron Kinnaird, Rossie Priory, Perthshire, by 1856; Kinnaird sale, Christie's, London, 21 June 1946 (lot 45), bought by Rosendaal; Walpole Gallery, London, by 1995; from whom purchased by the present owner

MILAN, KOELLIKER COLLECTION

This picture shows a type of composition highly popular in Venice in the first three decades of the sixteenth century, in which a group of two or three half-length figures are shown engaged in amorous conversation and / or music making. An early example of the type is Giorgione's so-called *Three Ages of Man*, of about 1500–5 (Florence, Palazzo Pitti, Galleria Palatina); relatively late examples include Paris Bordon's *Lovers* of about 1525 (Milan, Brera), and Licinio's own *Concert* of about the same date (Hampton Court, Royal Collection). The prominence of the young woman in the latter two examples, as well as in the present picture, also relates them closely to another popular type invented by Giorgione, that of the 'beautiful woman', represented by his *Laura* of 1506 (fig.14), or in this exhibition by Cariani's *St Agatha* (cat.no.22). The compositional device of the foreground ledge, which was frequently adopted for both Giorgionesque types, as well as for portraits and devotional pictures of the period, serves both as a barrier between the real world of the spectator and the illusionistic world of the painting, and as a means of transition from one to the other. Thus, while the ledge appears to coincide with the surface plane of the picture, the woman's right sleeve, the sprigs of roses and the musical part-book all appear to project forward beyond the limits of the plane.

Part of the attraction of both Giorgionesque types was that they could easily be adapted to suggest different meanings. In the present case, the use of contemporary dress and particular-ised physiognomies makes the picture resemble a triple portrait, yet the compositional subordi-nation of the two male figures to the woman makes it unlikely that they were meant to be recognised as three real people.[1] Nor can this be a simple scene of everyday music making, in which the older man invites silence so that the recital can begin. Although the open part-book displays real, playable music, the part is for an instrument, not the voice;[2] the three figures are represented neither as instrumentalists nor as singers. More probably, therefore, music has an allegorical significance, and refers, as in so many Venetian paintings with musical themes of the first two or three decades of the sixteenth century, to the sweetness and poignancy of love, and to the transience of beauty and happiness (see cat.no.15). Such a meaning is certainly conveyed by the roses on the ledge and inserted into the woman's belt. More specifically, it has been suggested that the older man is a tutor, who seeks to instruct his pupil in the need to restrain youthful passion in his approach to love and beauty, and to focus on the more elevated thoughts that the woman and her music may inspire.[3] It remains doubtful, however, whether the painter would have intended to convey so heavily moralising a message.

Although the picture is unsigned, it was already recognised as a characteristic work by Licinio by G.F. Waagen when he visited Rossie Priory in 1856.[4] Modern critics have concurred in seeing it as a relatively early work, in which the not entirely successful Giorgionesque introspec-tion of the *Young Man with a Skull* of about 1510–15 (Oxford, Ashmolean Museum) has given way to a more opulent manner, inspired by Titian's works of the second decade.[5] The style of the costumes is consistent with a date around 1520.

Girolamo Romanino BRESCIA 1484/7–c.1560 BRESCIA

24 ❧ The Adoration of the Shepherds

Oil on panel | 64.1 × 51.2cm (with an addition of 1.5cm at the lower edge) | c.1524–5

Inscribed to the right of the Virgin's head: 'GIORGIVS BARBARELLI'

Provenance: Litta collection, Milan; Roverselli collection, Milan; from whom purchased by Francis, Lord Elcho (later 10th Earl of Wemyss), 1842; by descent to the present owner

THE EARL OF WEMYSS AND MARCH KT

The false signature testifies to an old attribution to Giorgione, which was maintained by G.F. Waagen when he saw the picture in the collection of Lord Elcho in 1851.[1] Crowe and Cavalcaselle later reattributed it to the Lombard painter Callisto Piazza,[2] before the now generally accepted attribution to Romanino was advanced by Bernard Berenson.[3] In its engagingly eccentric figure style, the picture also recalls the work of the Cremonese painter Altobello Melone, and probably for this reason it has usually been dated to early in Romanino's career, when his style was closest to Altobello.[4] A comparable expressionism, inspired by German prints, is evident in Romanino's Passion frescoes in Cremona Cathedral of 1519; and in the present panel, too, the picturesquely ramshackle stable, silhouetted against the sky in dramatic foreshortening, is generally reminiscent of prints by Dürer such as the *Nativity* engraving of 1504, or the corresponding woodcut from the *Life of the Virgin* series of about the same date. The landscape on the right is unfortunately rather damaged and repainted, but the warmly Venetian palette nevertheless reflects Romanino's admiration for Titian, and in particular for his *Resurrection* polyptych, painted for the church of Santi Nazzaro e Celso in Romanino's home town of Brescia in 1522.

Although Lord Elcho bought most of his collection on the London art market, he acquired this picture in Milan on his first trip to Italy in 1842 at the age of twenty-four, 'from a café-holder named Roverselli who had purchased many pictures out of Palazzo Litta opposite his café'.[5] Later he considered the acquistion to have been 'one of the best I ever made'.

Titian PIEVE DI CADORE c.1485/90–1576 VENICE

25 ❧ *The Virgin and Child with St John the Baptist and an Unidentified Male Saint*

Oil on canvas, transferred from wood
62.7 × 93cm | *c.*1517–20

Provenance: Probably Alfonso Lopez, Amsterdam (died 1641); probably Everhard Jabach, Paris; his posthumous sale, 17 July 1696 (lot 118); Prince de Condé; from whom acquired by Philippe, 2nd Duc d'Orléans, by 1723 (as by Palma Vecchio); by descent in the Orléans collection at the Palais Royal, Paris, to Louis-Philippe-Joseph, 5th Duc d'Orléans (Philippe Égalité); by whom sold in 1791 to Viscount Walchiers; François de Laborde de Méréville; exhibited for sale at Bryan's Gallery, London, 1798–9 (no.112), but reserved for the 3rd Duke of Bridgewater; by inheritance to the 2nd Marquess of Stafford (later 1st Duke of Sutherland), Stafford House, London; by inheritance to Lord Francis Egerton (later 1st Earl of Ellesmere), Bridgewater House, London; by descent to the 7th Duke of Sutherland. On loan to the Gallery since 1945

EDINBURGH, NATIONAL GALLERY OF SCOTLAND (DUKE OF SUTHERLAND LOAN)

This beautiful but damaged picture has not always been recognised as by Titian. While in the Orléans collection in the eighteenth century, and at Bridgewater House in the nineteenth, it bore an attribution to Palma Vecchio. However, during the course of the twentieth century Titian's authorship has gradually come to be universally accepted, and its high quality became especially evident when it was cleaned in 1993.[1]

The work remains problematic, however, both in terms of its iconography and its dating. The identity of St John the Baptist, pointing to his customary attribute of a sacrificial lamb, is perfectly clear (see cat.no.30). But the figure on the right lacks attributes, and has variously been interpreted as St James (whose colour iconography was variable), or as a donor portrait, or as a donor in the guise of his name-saint. He is most plausibly identified, however, as Joseph, largely because of the closeness of his physical and emotional contact with the Virgin and Child. It is true that the Virgin's spouse was more usually shown wearing an orange or yellow cloak over a

blue or purple robe (see cat.no.40), and traditionally he was also represented as an elderly man, with grey hair and beard. But Joseph's colour iconography was not rigidly fixed either, and as the focus of a growing cult in the early sixteenth century, he was increasingly shown with more youthful features, and as a more active protagonist in representations of the Virgin and Child with other figures. It is also true that after about 1520 the motif of an adult male reaching out to hold the Child became highly popular, and could be transferred from Joseph to other saints (see cat.nos.26, 30); yet it still seems likely that the early representations, including the present work, are meant to portray Christ's earthly father.[2]

Despite the consensus now reached on the attribution, current datings range from the very beginning of Titian's career, around 1507–8, to the period of the Ferrara mythologies and the *Venus Anadyomene* (cat.no.19) of about a decade later.[3] The question of the dating is closely bound up with that of the painter's early

chronology in general. Obvious differences of style make it impossible, for example, that Titian should have painted the *Virgin and Child with St John the Baptist and an Unidentified Male Saint* contemporaneously with the Glasgow *Christ and the Adulteress* (cat.no.13); for those critics who favour an early date for the present picture, *Christ and the Adulteress* cannot be by Titian. But the treatment of the draperies is also unlike that in a picture universally accepted as very early, the *Gypsy Madonna* of about 1510 (Vienna, Kunsthistorisches Museum). A more usual solution is to place the present picture some three or four years later than *Christ and the Adulteress*, close to *The Three Ages of Man* (cat.no.15). Yet the rather tighter compositional structure of the painting and the more calculatedly precise treatment of certain areas (including the Virgin's robe, with its play of highlights comparable to those in *The Bacchanal of the Andrians*), and especially the physiognomy of the Virgin, all point to an even later date of about 1517–20, contemporaneous with the first two Ferrara bacchanals.

This relatively late dating carries implications for understanding the early development of the popular Venetian theme of the Virgin and Child seated with saints in a pastoral landscape, but the arguments are complicated and lie beyond the scope of the present entry. Suffice it to say that Titian played a seminal role in this development, and that the present work, although probably not the earliest example of the genre, seems to have served as an important prototype for later

painters such as Paris Bordon (cat.nos.29, 30) and Bonifacio Veronese (fig.18).

Until recently, the earliest recorded owner of the picture was the Prince de Condé, from whom Philippe, Duc d'Orléans, acquired it, probably shortly before his death in 1723.[4] But it has been pointed out that a drawing after Titian's *Man with a Blue Sleeve* (London, National Gallery) by the Dutch artist Theodor Matham, apparently made when the portrait was in the collection of Alfonso Lopez in Amsterdam in 1639–41, also includes, on the same sheet, a quick sketch of the *Virgin and Child with St John the Baptist and an Unidentified Male Saint* (fig.102).[5] This implies that the picture likewise belonged to Lopez, and may have been sold with the portrait in Paris in December 1641. It was probably acquired either then, or at some point subsequently, by the banker Everhard Jabach, for a picture exactly matching it is described in the sale of Jabach's possessions of 1696.[6] The attribution is described as 'Après Titien', perhaps reflecting an uncertainty about its status that by the 1720s was to lead it to be re-baptised as Palma.

Technical Note

Apart from the usual consequences of ageing, the main influence on the condition of this painting lies in its transfer from the original wood support to canvas, a process probably carried out in France in the latter part of the eighteenth century, when it was in the Orléans collection. This radical and risky procedure, with its typical associated damages, combined with the inherent problems of wood as a support – the weakness of a join in the panel and the losses along the grain of the wood caused by changing environmental conditions – had given rise to an unpleasant, leathery surface accompanied by a disturbing undulation far removed from the original planar quality of a wood support.

The painting was conserved again in the early 1930s by Martin de Wild, who also later conserved *The Three Ages of Man* (cat.no.15). De Wild

relined the painting using a wax-resin adhesive – an early instance of the use of this material – and carried out extensive restoration of paint losses. These subsequently darkened with age, particularly in the modelling of the Baptist's flesh, in the Virgin's blue robe and in the folds of her sleeve. De Wild's varnish contained a high proportion of oil, which originally gave a high gloss finish, but also developed a minute wrinkling which produced a progressively patchy appearance. This had become so disturbing it was decided to replace it.

Removal of the varnish and repaints uncovered numerous small fillings which, when seen in an exploratory X-radiograph, were thought to be paint losses. However, most of these proved to be small indentations caused by shrinkage of the paint layer during the transfer process. To correct this it was decided to reline the painting. During removal of the De Wild wax lining it was found that he had left in place an old paste lining dating from the time of the transfer. Typically, the original gesso ground had been almost entirely removed in the procedure. Treatment fortunately corrected most of the indentations, recovered the original paint and avoided the need for the extensive filling that had been present previously.

The surface of the paint now bears a foreign canvas weave imprint probably introduced by the transfer process, but other areas, previously heavily restored, such as the vermilion cloak of the male saint, with its modifying crimson glaze (fig.102a), his purple tunic – a mixture of ultramarine and a crimson lake (fig.102b) – the crimson glazed sleeve of the Virgin's robe and the modelling of the Baptist's flesh, are all in reasonably good condition. Surprisingly, layers of grime and discoloured varnish had been left during the previous restoration at both bottom corners, obscuring the crisp, precise and well preserved foliage now visible. It is also now more apparent that the medium-rich paint of the Virgin's head and the sky contrasts with the thinner, drier appearance of the rest of the paint, particularly the Baptist's flesh, and may represent a later reworking by the painter.

Fig.102 | Theodor Matham, Drawn copies of the *'Portrait of a Man with a Blue Sleeve'* and *'The Virgin and Child with St John the Baptist and an Unidentified Male Saint'* (after Titian) Brunswick, Herzog Anton Ulrich-Museum

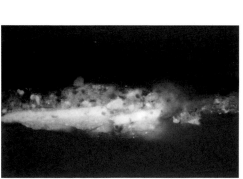

Fig.102a | Cross section of a paint sample taken from the cloak of the male saint

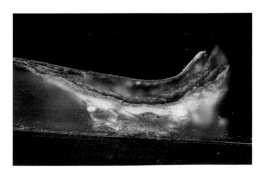

Fig.102b | Cross section of a paint sample taken from the tunic of the male saint

Attributed to Francesco Vecellio PIEVE DI CADORE c.1485/95–1559/60 PIEVE DI CADORE

26 ❧ The Virgin and Child with Saints Dorothy and Jerome

Oil on canvas, transferred from panel
58.5 × 86.5cm | c.1520

Provenance: Archibald McLellan; by whom bequeathed to the Museum, 1854 (acc.no.192)

GLASGOW MUSEUMS: KELVINGROVE ART GALLERY AND MUSEUM

Like the probably closely contemporary pair of pictures by Paris Bordon (cat.nos.29, 30), this represents a variation on the theme of the Virgin and Child seated with saints in a landscape which was popularised by Titian in the second decade of the sixteenth century. The saints here are clearly identified by their attributes: Dorothy with her basket of red and white flowers and Jerome by the tame lion sitting behind him.

The composition is obviously very closely related to Titian's *Virgin and Child with St John the Baptist and an Unidentified Male Saint* of about 1517–20 (cat.no.25) and may be assumed to derive from it. Indeed, the X-radiograph of the painting (fig.103) shows that the position of the Virgin's head originally corresponded exactly to that in Titian's picture, and that there was a glimpse of sky through the foliage above the head of the kneeling saint, again as in the Titian. The radiograph also shows radical changes to the pose of Jerome, who was originally represented crouching on one knee, and supporting himself on his left arm. In this last respect his former pose resembles that of the principal figure in a drawing usually attributed to the young Titian, *Two Satyrs with an Astrological Disc* (New York, Metropolitan Museum of Art).[1] Ribbons originally fluttered from the escutcheon, and the foliage was extended further to the right.

In the earliest catalogues of the McLellan

left to right

Fig.103 | X-radiograph mosaic

Fig.104 | Attributed to Francesco Vecellio, *The Holy Family* Bergamo, Accademia Carrara

Fig.105 | Infrared reflectogram mosaic

collection, the Glasgow picture is described as a copy after Titian,[2] but soon afterwards it was claimed to be autograph, and an attribution to Titian himself has been maintained by a number of leading scholars up to the present day.[3] As early as 1894, however, when it was exhibited at the New Gallery in London, Bernard Berenson again downgraded it;[4] his re-attribution of it to Titian's follower Polidoro da Lanciano was accepted by a number of subsequent critics.[5] This latter attribution cannot, however, be sustained: Polidoro, who was born in the Abruzzi in about 1515, did not reach Venice until the mid-1530s at the earliest and his borrowings from Titian were from pictures from a much later stage of the master's career.

The question of attribution is much complicated by the picture's poor state of preservation, which was presumably the reason for its transfer at an unknown date from its original panel to canvas. Cleaning in preparation for the present exhibition has placed in sharper contrast the difference of quality between the rather fine figure of St Jerome and the much cruder figure of St Dorothy. Yet even the figure of Jerome does not seem to be worthy of Titian himself, and it is proposed here that the greater part of the picture is the work of Titian's elder brother Francesco Vecellio,[6] who was active in Venice, and in close contact with Titian, throughout the second and third decades of the century. Francesco's oeuvre remains ill-defined for want of certain works and dates, but among the most plausible candidates for the phase around 1520 are the *Adoration of the Shepherds* from San Giuseppe, Belluno (now Houston, Museum of Fine Arts) and a *Holy Family* in Bergamo (fig.104).[7] The style and handling of these – flatter, harder and more schematic than the work of Titian – closely resemble those of the present picture. Possibly also by Francesco, at least in part, is another picture traditionally associated with Titian, but of less than autograph quality, the *Virgin and Child with Saints* in the Gemäldegalerie, Dresden, also datable to the early 1520s.[8]

The present painting was etched as by Titian in the later seventeenth century by Valentin Lefèvre in his *Opera Selectiora* published posthu-

mously in 1680.[9] Although there are a number of differences between the painting and the print – most notably the somewhat taller format of the latter – these may be interpreted as slight variations introduced by the etcher and there is no need to infer that he was following another version of the painting. Virtually all the etchings in Lefèvre's album were made after paintings at that time in Venice and it may be assumed that the *Virgin and Child with Saints Dorothy and Jerome* was likewise in a collection in Venice or the Veneto in the 1670s. The escutcheon suspended at the top of the composition above the Child's head, consisting of red and white quarterings, has not been identified, but given that Francesco seems to have worked chiefly for mainland rather than Venetian patrons, it may be that of one of the *terraferma* families.[10]

Technical Note

The painting has been transferred from its original wooden panel support to a multiple canvas support. It is very rigid but otherwise its present surface bears little relationship to the qualities of a panel painting. The date of the transfer is unknown, but it could have been carried out as early as the eighteenth century. Old filling obscures the edges of the painting and the composition itself has been crudely overpainted in many areas making an accurate assessment of its condition extremely difficult. It is clear that there was a split in the original wooden support corresponding to a thin line of horizontal paint loss across the lower third of the composition. There are other smaller lacunae scattered throughout and it may be assumed that the painting had a history of flaking that precipitated its transfer. In preparation for the current exhibition, it was decided to undertake a limited conservation intervention, removing an extremely discoloured varnish as well as the most disturbing overpainting, in order to make the picture more legible and thereby assist in resolving the vexing question of its authorship. The painting was examined with X-radiography and infrared reflectography and comparisons were made with Titian's *Virgin and Child with St John the*

Baptist and an Unidentified Male Saint (see cat.no.25), from which it is clearly derived. A tracing was also made of this painting and compared to the X-radiograph (fig.103) of the Glasgow picture. Many elements correspond almost exactly to those in Titian's composition, particularly the original position of the Virgin's head, as well as the Christ Child and the glimpse of foliage above the head of St Jerome. This suggests the transfer of a pre-existing design. A comparison of the X-radiographs of the two paintings, however, reveals quite different image quality. The *Virgin and Child with St John the Baptist and an Unidentified Male Saint* is contrast-rich, with freely brushed, layered paintwork. The Glasgow painting appears softer and the forms and brushwork seem more fused and blended. It should be noted that much of this reduced contrast may be attributed to the present multiple fabric support and to the fact that the

painting has been radically overpainted. For example, the Virgin's red robe, originally executed with deep crimson glazes over a pale pink under layer, has been completely covered with a much cruder opaque rendering of the same pattern of folds. At the time of writing, a decision is still pending as to whether this should be removed, since the re-painting implies that the original is in a compromised condition. St Dorothy's drapery has also been overpainted. However, despite this interference there is no doubt that she was always an infinitely weaker figure. Examination with infrared reflectography has revealed that there is a careful brush under-drawing for this figure that is quite at odds with the rest of the picture (fig.105). Stylistically, its laboured outlining suggests that a different and possibly much later hand added St Dorothy to the composition. Clumsily inserted into the corner space, she is a little out of proportion with

the Virgin and St Jerome and the handling of the detail is wooden and awkward with no evidence of the type of painterly execution that can be seen in the head of the male saint. Possibly an existing figure was removed and replaced by the female saint, although the physical evidence for this is inconclusive. Curiously, although the figure of St Dorothy appears much later in style, and her presence is certainly visually jarring, her flesh tones, pale draperies and flowers, none of which have been overpainted, all share the same mixture of fine, vertical age craquelure and minute drying cracks that are a surface feature of the rest of the composition. None the less, although some of the physical evidence is inconclusive, and although we can only surmise why the figure of St Dorothy was added, the naked eye tells us unequivocally that she is indeed an ill thought out and poorly executed addition. MG

Attributed to Francesco Vecellio PIEVE DI CADORE *c.*1485/95–1559/60 PIEVE DI CADORE

27 ❧ *The Holy Family*

Oil on panel | 42.6 × 52cm | *c.*1520–5

Provenance: Count Cornian degli Algarotti, Venice (according to an inscription on the back); with the dealer Felice Schiavone, Venice; from whom purchased by Lord Wood on behalf of the Royal Institution, Edinburgh, 1852 (acc.no.NG 105)

EDINBURGH, NATIONAL GALLERY OF SCOTLAND

The principal figure group, with the Virgin praying over the Christ Child who reclines on her lap, recurs in a number of pictures associated with Titian's workshop and followers.[1] Probably the earliest and best of these, which were apparently executed by a number of different hands over a period of about two decades, is a full length *Virgin and Child with Saints Francis, Jerome and Anthony Abbot* of about 1520 in the Bayerische Staatsgemäldesammlungen, Ansbach. Although often in the past accepted as an autograph Titian, even this is now rightly regarded as a work painted with extensive workshop assistance. The present *Holy Family*, while harder and more laborious in execution, shows a close dependence on Titian's figure style of the same period: thus, the head of the Virgin closely resembles its couterparts in such autograph works as the Treviso *Annunciation*, the *Virgin and Child with Two Saints* (Madrid, Prado),

and the Ca' Pesaro Madonna (fig.20). If, as seems probable, *The Holy Family* likewise dates from the early 1520s, it cannot be by Polidoro da Lanciano, to whom it is currently attributed in the Gallery catalogue,[2] since this painter was born in 1515. A more plausible candidate is Titian's elder brother Francesco Vecellio, to whom the Glasgow *Virgin and Child with Saints Dorothy and Jerome* is also attributed here (cat.no.26).[3] This attribution seems consistent with one of the few certain works by Francesco of this phase, the *Adoration of the Shepherds* in the Museum of Fine Arts in Houston, Texas. Already generally accepted as by Francesco is another of the versions of the present composition, *The Holy Family* in the Accademia Carrara, Bergamo (fig.104).[4]

X-radiography has revealed that the picture was painted over a quite different composition, placed at right angles to the present one, showing a female figure in bust length.

28 ❧ *The Virgin and Sleeping Christ Child*

Oil on canvas | 53 × 67.3cm | *c.*1525–30

Provenance: Acquired in Rome by the 8th Marquess of Lothian, 1861 (as by Titian); by descent to the 11th Marquess of Lothian; by whom bequeathed to the Gallery, 1941 (acc.no.1931)

EDINBURGH, NATIONAL GALLERY OF SCOTLAND

The figure group appears in at least two other pictures: a *Virgin and Child* in a private collection in Sweden,[1] and a *Virgin and Child with St Joseph*, formerly in the collection of the Archduke Leopold Wilhelm in Brussels, and recorded in a copy by David Teniers (London, Kenwood House, Iveagh Bequest).[2] The latter work was attributed to Titian's follower Polidoro da Lanciano, and partly on that basis the present work has been catalogued as by Polidoro since its

acquisition by the Gallery.[3] But Polidoro did not arrive in Venice from his native Abruzzi until the mid-1530s, and the present *Virgin and Sleeping Christ Child* is not particularly close stylistically to his only documented work, *The Descent of the Holy Spirit* of 1545 (fig.106).[4] The *Virgin and Sleeping Christ Child* is closer rather to Titian's paintings of the Virgin and saints in pastoral landscapes of the second decade (see cat.no.25), as well as to similar compositions by Paris Bordon of the early 1520s (see cat.nos.29, 30).

The picture was one of a number of purchases – including a Madonna attributed to Giovanni Bellini – made by the 8th Marquess of Lothian (1832–1870) on a tour of Italy in 1860–1.[5]

Fig.106 | Polidoro da Lanciano,
The Descent of the Holy Spirit
Venice, Galleria dell'Accademia

Paris Bordon TREVISO 1500–1571 VENICE

29 ✣ *The Virgin and Child with Saints Jerome and Anthony Abbot and a Donor*

Oil on panel | 61 × 82.9cm | *c*.1522

Inscribed on the scroll: 'Pariss. Bor / donus. Taruisi / nus. /.f.'

Provenance: Paolo del Sera, Venice, before 1654; Cardinal Giovan Carlo de' Medici, Florence; his sale, 1663–4; John Graham-Gilbert, Glasgow; his widow's bequest to the Glasgow Museum, 1877 (acc.no.570)

GLASGOW MUSEUMS: KELVINGROVE ART GALLERY AND MUSEUM

Fig.107 | Paris Bordon, *The Virgin and Child with St Anthony Abbot and a Donor*
London, Simon Dickinson Ltd. Formerly in the collection of Sir George Warrender, Lochend, Dunbar.

Fig.108 | Paris Bordon, *The Holy Family with St Ambrose*
Milan, Pinacoteca di Brera

This is one of the earliest of Paris Bordon's many contributions to the theme, highly popular in Venice in the second and third decades of the sixteenth century, of the Virgin and Child informally seated with a group of saints in an idyllic pastoral landscape. In this case a kneeling donor is being encouraged to approach the group by his patron saint, Anthony Abbot, while St Jerome, who spent many years as a penitent in the wilderness (see cat.nos.2, 10, 44), draws the donor's attention to his attribute of a crucifix. Although the subject is timeless, the compositional type is naturally reminiscent of stories from Christ's infancy such as the Adoration of the Kings, and especially the Rest on the Flight into Egypt, which likewise calls for a landscape setting. The Rest on the Flight was, in fact, another of Bordon's favourite subjects, as is illustrated by another early work that reached Scotland in the nineteenth century,[1] as well as the later example by him in this exhibition (cat.no.46). In the present case, an association with the Rest on the Flight into Egypt may also account for the motif of the curtain on the right, slung over a rustic pole as if to create a makeshift tent.

Bordon was a pupil in Titian's workshop between about 1514 and 1518, and his treatment of the subject closely reflects examples by Titian such as the *Virgin and Child with St John the Baptist and an Unidentified Male Saint* of about 1517–20 (cat.no.25). More generally, details such as the reclining shepherds with their sheep in the left background, and the rustic building in the centre, are deeply indebted to the type of pastoral landscape evolved by Titian in this decade for subjects both sacred and secular (cat.no.15). At the same time, Bordon's pictorial handling diverges from that of Titian in combining passages of breadth and freedom with a graphic precision that recalls rather the work of Giorgione, as in the delicate brushstrokes that describe Jerome's beard and the rhythmical stippling of the foliage. The figures are also slighter of build than those by Titian of this date, and are less infused with physical energy. This evidence of Bordon deliberately imitating the style of Giorgione, who had died in 1510, conforms with the later report by Vasari that the young Paris was dissatisfied with Titian as a teacher, and 'grieved much that Giorgione was then dead, for that master's style pleased him exceedingly, and he thought much more of Giorgione's reputation of being a willing and careful teacher of what he knew. Not being able to do better, Paris resolved to adopt Giorgione's style.'[2]

The present picture is usually and convincingly dated to the early 1520s.[3] In other words, it is very close in style, composition and date both to *The Virgin and Child with St Anthony Abbot and a Donor* of *c*.1520 formerly in the Warrender collection at Lochend House, Dunbar (fig.107),[4] in which the figure of Anthony is almost identical, and to *The Holy Family with St Ambrose and a Donor* of about 1524 in the Brera Gallery, Milan (fig.108), in which the pose of the Virgin is repeated. It may also be noted that the head of the Virgin in the present picture closely resembles that in Titian's *Annunciation* painted for the cathedral of Paris's home town of Treviso in about 1520–2.

The earliest record of the picture dates from 1648, when Carlo Ridolfi recorded it in the collection of Paolo del Sera in Venice, and noted the delicacy of its execution.[5] In 1660 Marco Boschini expanded on this information by identifying the donor as one Dr Genova, a physician who also came from Treviso,[6] and who presumably for this reason commissioned the picture from his young compatriot. Genova's first name is not known, and Anthony Abbot may have been included as his name saint (see cat.no.59), although it is equally likely that Genova chose him because of his medical associations, as a protector against disease and the plague. Surprisingly for a physician, but presumably indicating that he had chivalric pretensions besides considerable wealth, the donor wears spurs as part of his luxurious costume.

Paolo del Sera was a Florentine who was resident in Venice between 1640 and 1672 and was particularly active in the purchase of works of art for the collections of various members of the Medici family.[7] Among the Venetian pictures he sent back to Florence were others by Paris Bordon, including a Rest on the Flight for Cardinal Leopoldo de' Medici which also later came to Scotland, to the collection of Lord Gray at Kinfauns Castle, Perthshire (fig.129).[8] The *Virgin and Child with Saints Jerome and Anthony Abbot and a Donor* was acquired in 1654 by another brother of the Grand-Duke Ferdinand, Cardinal Giovan Carlo de' Medici (1611–1663), for his splendid collection housed in the Via della Scala in Florence.[9] But Giovan Carlo owned the picture for no more than nine years, and after his early death all trace of it was lost until it reappeared in the Graham-Gilbert collection in Glasgow in the later nineteenth century.[10]

In the inventory of 1663 the two figures on the right are described as 'two friars', and it seems that it was the cardinal who decided that Dr Genova, with his portrait-like features and rich costume, should be overpainted to become an anonymous cleric. This overpaint remained until the picture was restored in 1981–5. The same restoration revealed a left foot placed immediately in front of the donor. As in the ex-Warrender picture (fig.107), this was clearly intended to belong to Anthony Abbot; but shifted for some reason to the left, it renders his pose inexplicable.

111

Paris Bordon Treviso 1500–1571 Venice

30 ❧ The Virgin and Child with Saints John the Baptist, Mary Magdalene and George (?)

Oil on panel | 85.4 × 117.5cm | c.1524

Provenance: Archibald McLellan; his bequest to the Glasgow Museum, 1854 (acc.no.191)

Glasgow Museums: Kelvingrove Art Gallery and Museum

Like the slightly earlier *Virgin and Child with Saints Jerome and Anthony Abbot and a Donor*, also from Glasgow (cat.no.29), this picture represents an early example of one of Paris Bordon's favourite and most characteristic subjects, with the saints grouped informally against a serene pastoral landscape. The Baptist and Mary Magdalene are clearly identified by their respective attributes, in his case a lamb and a reed cross, in hers an ointment jar. But the armoured saint does not carry the banner that would definitely identify him either as St George, the object of a lively cult in Venice, or as St Liberale, patron saint of Paris's native city of Treviso. Symbolic allusions to Christ's future Passion are provided by the sacrificial lamb, to which the Baptist draws the spectator's attention, and by the goldfinch that the infant Jesus clutches in his left hand.

The composition is rather grander than that of the *Virgin and Child and Saints Jerome and Anthony Abbot and a Donor*, with the Virgin elevated on a rustic throne, and the landscape vista blocked on the right by stately classicising architecture. The compositional rhythms are also rather more complex, and the dynamic, spatially conceived pose of the Virgin reflects the painter's knowledge of her counterpart in a major contemporary work by Titian, the Ca' Pesaro Madonna in the church of the Frari, Venice of about 1519–26 (fig.20). But while probably slightly later than Bordon's other picture in Glasgow, the protagonists in the *Virgin and Child with Saints John the Baptist, Mary Magdalene and George* is not yet as physically assertive as those in the Manfron altarpiece of 1525–6 (Lovere, Accademia Tadini),[1] and the picture retains much in common with works by Titian and his followers from the previous decade. The detail of the boy fishing in the left background, for example, recalls a drawing of c.1517–20 by Domenico Campagnola (Washington, National Gallery of Art),[2] while a dog similarly chases a rabbit in the background of Titian's *Sacred and Profane Love* of about 1514–16 (Rome, Galleria Borghese). Similarly, the motif, much beloved by Paris, of a saint reaching forwards to receive the Christ Child from his mother derives from Titian's recent *Virgin and Child with St John the Baptist and an Unidentified Male Saint* (cat.no.25). From all this it may be concluded that a likely date for the picture is about 1524.[3]

The picture was described as an early work by Paris Bordon by Waagen in 1854, an attribution that was followed in the earliest catalogues of the McLellan collection.[4] It is odd, therefore, that subsequent gallery catalogues, until as late as 1931, attributed it Bonifacio Veronese. The information given by these later catalogues that it was once in the Riccardi (formerly Medici) palace in Florence may be equally suspect.[5]

Fig.109 | X-radiograph mosaic

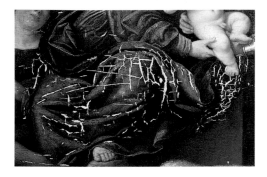

Fig.110 | Detail of the Virgin's mantle during restoration showing drying cracks

Fig.111 | Infrared reflectogram (detail)

Technical Note

The National Galleries of Scotland undertook full conservation treatment of this panel painting in preparation for this exhibition. As discoloured layers of varnish and overpaint were removed and the painting was fully restored, a unique opportunity arose to examine more closely the materials and techniques used in the painting.

The original support appears to be poplar wood. Although there is evidence of several structural interventions in the past, the painting is not physically constrained by a conventional cradle, unlike many other panels of this age.[6] Despite the consequent pronounced convex warp, the paint layers are secure.

Prior to the recent conservation treatment, a disfiguring feature of the paint surface was large-scale, wide-mouthed so-called 'drying' or contraction craquelure, which affected many differently pigmented areas, for example the figure of St John the Baptist and the Virgin's blue and red drapery (fig. 110).[7] This phenomenon is likely to have occurred within the artist's lifetime and it is directly related to how the artist used his materials, rather than the result of damage or ageing. It is difficult to ascertain conclusively why this has developed to such a dramatic extent with this particular painting and not in other panels produced at this early stage in Bordon's career (see cat.no.29).[8] At the time the panel was painted, the technique of painting in an oil medium had only relatively recently been introduced into Venice, and it is possible that Bordon had difficulty with the varying propor-tions of oil, pigment and diluent. Another possible explanation for the cracking may be the adulteration of the materials used or some inter-layer antipathy between either the ground preparation and paint layers or indeed between the paint layers themselves. Certainly, there are no such drying defects visible in the few later works by Bordon that have been examined (see cat. nos. 46, 48), and for which a more absorbent canvas support was usually selected in place of the rigid wooden panels typical of his earliest works.

Both X-radiography and infrared reflectography offer valuable insight into an artist's working method and in particular highlight any compositional changes (pentimenti) that were made during the early stages. The X-radiograph mosaic (fig.109) reveals the extent to which Bordon laboured over this composition, with numerous alterations visible.[9] Notable changes include the entire alignment of the saint in armour at the right, whose head and shoulders have subtly shifted and whose left leg was moved to the right. The sword was originally more upright and the standard now rests on his right rather than his left shoulder. The Child's left arm originally stretched across towards a mysterious and now invisible cupped hand. The

Magdalene may have worn a more elaborate headdress which was replaced by the present simple band. In the landscape background, both a house with a deep combed roof and what appears to be a church steeple were painted out just behind the Magdalene's head. In addition, trees have replaced what was earlier conceived as a rolling skyline of hills and near the tall, central tree a man on horseback can just be discerned in the distance. This latter detail is particularly evident in the infrared reflectogram (fig.111).

Once identified in the X-radiograph many of these alterations can be detected on the surface as incongruous strokes of impasto that do not correspond to the present design. It is worth noting that the difficulty encountered with the composition is likely to account significantly for the development of the aforementioned drying craquelure. This is especially true of St John, who is so scarred by cracks that he is barely legible in the X-radiograph. LS

Bonifacio Veronese and workshop VERONA 1487–1553 VENICE

31 ❧ *The Holy Family with the Young St John the Baptist and St Catherine of Alexandria*

Oil on canvas | 116.8 × 167.7cm | *c*.1528–30

Provenance: Thomas Erskine of Linlathen; bequeathed to the museum by his nephew James E. Erskine (died 1897), per life-rent of his daughter, Mrs K.E. Frost of Crieff (died 1945)

DUNDEE CITY COUNCIL LEISURE & ARTS, MCMANUS GALLERIES

Like his master Palma Vecchio, as well as his younger contemporary Paris Bordon (see cats.29, 30), Bonifacio was prolific as a painter of Holy Families with saints seated in extensive landscapes. In style and composition the present picture remains closely dependent on Palma, as is evident from a characteristic example by him such as the damaged picture in Glasgow (fig.75).[1] Indeed, the closeness of the present picture to Palma suggests that it was painted soon after the latter's premature death in 1528, when Bonifacio inherited his workshop and with it the market for this genre of domestic devotional painting. His somewhat staid composition lacks Palma's rhythmical fluency, and a certain clumsiness of execution suggests that the picture was painted with workshop assistance. Even so, in the sunset landscape, with its picturesque travellers and shepherds, castles and distant mountains, the painter is notably successful in evoking a mood of sensuous warmth and poetic serenity.

In 1854 Waagen reported that the collection of Mr Erskine of Linlathen contained 'good Italian pictures purchased in Rome by the advice of M. Colombo'.[3] This Colombo, who is perhaps identical with the Nazarene painter Giovanni Colombo (*c*.1784–1853), also advised Thomas Erskine's cousin and close friend James Stirling of Glentyan, and is known to have bought actively at the sale of Cardinal Fesch in Rome in 1845. Since Erskine was in Rome early in the following year, it is possible that he acquired the present picture on that occasion. Equally, however, he may have bought it in Venice in 1827, when he was certainly attempting to by a painting by, or attributed to, Titian.[4] In 1907 Berenson listed the picture as by Francesco Beccaruzzi, but had dropped that attribution by 1957.[5]

Lorenzo Lotto VENICE *c*.1480–1556/7 LORETO

32 ❧ *Portrait of a Lady as Lucretia*

Oil on canvas | 95.9 × 110.5cm | *c*.1533

Inscribed on the *cartellino*: 'NEC VLLA
IMPVDICA LVCRETIAE EXEMPLO VIVET'
(Nor shall any unchaste woman live through the
example of Lucretia)

Provenance: Ca' Pesaro, Venice, until at least
1797; Abate Celotti, Venice; acquired from him
by James Irvine for Sir William Forbes of
Pitsligo, 1828; by descent to Sir John Forbes; Sir
James Carnegie (later 9th Earl of Southesk),
Kinnaird Castle, Brechin, by 1854; by whom
sold to R.S. Holford, London, 1855; Holford
sale, Christie's, London, 15 July 1927 (lot 68),
bought by the National Gallery (acc.no.4256)

LONDON, NATIONAL GALLERY

Lotto's achievement in this visually sumptuous
and highly expressive portrait is all the more
astonishing considering that female portraits
were comparatively rare in Venetian painting
before the later sixteenth century. In Venice most
close-up images of young women showed them
in an ideal or erotic guise, and on a smaller scale,
as in Giorgione's *Laura* (fig.14), Titian's *Woman
at her Toilet* (fig.131) and Cariani's *St Agatha*
(cat.no.22). In this respect Lotto benefited from
his long absence from Venice, and in particular
from the twelve years that he spent in Bergamo
in Venetian Lombardy (1513–25), where female
portraiture was much more common. At the
same time, the present portrait is not a simple,
factual description of the sitter, but is rich in a
symbolism that alludes to the sitter's moral
aspirations, and probably also to her name.[1]

Apparently having just risen from her chair,
the young woman urgently draws the spectator's
attention to three items on the right of the
composition: the sprig of wallflowers on the dark
red tablecloth; the piece of unfolded paper with
its inscription; and the drawing she holds in her
left hand. This represents the Roman heroine
Lucretia, about to commit virtuous suicide with
a dagger. Lucretia, wife of Collantinus, had been
forced to submit to a sexual assault by Sextus
Tarquinius, the brutal son of the tyrannical king
Tarquin, because the rapist threatened that if she
did not, he would kill her and claim that he had
discovered her committing adultery with her
servant. To save her own posthumous reputation
and that of her husband, Lucretia chose the lesser
of two evils, which was to survive long enough to
accuse her violator, but then to kill herself, so
that she would not have to live with her shame.
Although the story was well known in the Italian

Renaissance, and Lucretia was widely recognised
as an exemplar of female virtue,[1] Lotto provides
the viewer with a quotation from the principal
literary source, Livy's *History of Rome* (1. 58). The
wallflowers provide a further reference to the all-
important female virtue of chastity.

Although the Roman heroine would represent
a commendable model for any Renaissance wife,
it is reasonable to assume that the comparison is
made explicit in the present portrait because the
sitter's name was Lucrezia. On the further
plausible assumption that since the picture
belonged to the patrician Pesaro family in the
late eighteenth century, the sitter might represent a Pesaro wife, she has been identified as one
Lucrezia Valier, who married Benedetto di
Girolamo Pesaro in January 1533.[3] (The two sons
born to the couple are probably the two boys
later painted by Titian; cat.no.36). The Pesaro-
Valier wedding would provide a likely occasion
for the commission of the portrait, and this date
is consistent both with the style of the fashionable dress and with Lotto's pictorial style. In his
Holy Family with St Catherine of Alexandria dated
1533 (Bergamo, Accademia Carrara), the
pointing gesture of Joseph is very similar to that
in the portrait. An association with a wedding, or
at least with a betrothal, is confirmed by the
prominent inclusion of the large jewelled
pendant. Consisting of a large ruby framed by
pairs of putti and cornucopias (symbols of
fertility and abundance), the pendant is of a type
closely associated in the sixteenth century with
marriage and procreation.[4]

In several of the other portraits he painted in
Venice during his seven-year stay from 1526 to
1533, Lotto adopted a similar horizontal format.
This is unusual for portraiture, which more
naturally lends itself to a vertical format, but it
provides additional scope for the symbolic still-
life accessories, and in this case, too, for the
sitter's expansive and expressively unstable pose.
The treatment of the costume represents a
compromise between the display of bridal
splendour and the allusion to her historical
prototype. Her magnificent dress of orange and
green striped silk, trimmed with squirrel fur, is
complemented by an elaborately curled and
ribboned bonnet and the gold necklace made up
of multiple strands with its exceedingly luxurious
pendant. But the sitter's costume is in evident
disarray: the necklace is suspended from her
bodice rather than from her neck, and the veil
that should cover her chest has come untucked
and is trailing loosely behind her right shoulder.
It is as if she has exposed her snowy bosom to
demonstrate her readiness to imitate her heroic
Roman namesake.

When he returned to work in Venice at the
end of 1525, Lotto was entering a competitive
field dominated by the city's leading painter,

Titian. A portrait such as this may be seen as both highly ambitious and deliberately different from the type of portraiture practised by Titian. As well as preferring expressive urgency to elegant naturalness, Lotto lends his forms a much sharper definition than those of Titian, with more precisely described textures and a more striking brilliance of colour. X-radiographs (fig.112) and paint samples have revealed that at one stage in the design Lotto planned to paint both the tablecloth and the background with a pattern of light blue and pink stripes – an effect that would perhaps have been too bold even for him.[5]

When in the possession of the Pesaro family in the late eighteenth century the portrait bore an attribution to Giorgione, and this was retained by its Scottish owners, Sir John Forbes and Sir James Carnegie. It is not clear under what circumstances the picture passed from Forbes to the Carnegie family, but they were close neighbours and Forbes may have sold it to Sir James's father, the 5th Baronet, soon after acquiring it in 1829. Sir James lent it to the British Institution in 1854 with an attribution to Giorgione,[6] and only in 1871 was Lotto recognised as its true author.[7]

Fig.112 | X-radiograph mosaic

119

Lorenzo Lotto VENICE *c*.1480–1556/7 LORETO

33 ❧ *Portrait of an Architect*

Oil on canvas | 86 × 120cm | *c*.1540

Provenance: Antonio Fidanza, Milan; from whom purchased by James Irvine for Sir William Forbes of Pitsligo, 1827; by descent to the present owner

PRIVATE COLLECTION

This compelling and previously unpublished portrait represents a major addition to the catalogue of Lorenzo Lotto's paintings. Although the picture is unsigned, the haunting melancholy of the expression is completely characteristic of Lotto as, too, is the effect of disquiet created by the unstable diagonal of the pose. Lotto made frequent use of this horizontal format, otherwise rare in Renaissance portraiture, during his principal period of residence in Venice between 1525 and 1533. Examples include the *Andrea Odoni* (Hampton Court, Royal Collection), the *Portrait of a Lady as Lucretia* (cat.no.32), and the *Young Man in his Study* (Venice, Galleria dell'Accademia), in which the figure is similarly shown leaning against a table. In these examples, however, the display of accessories, many of them clearly symbolic, is much richer than in the present picture, which is sparer in detail, thereby focusing greater attention on the face. This suggests that the picture is unlikely to date from before about 1540, when Lotto began a whole series of portraits of darkly-dressed, gloomily introspective sitters, including the *Febo da Brescia* of 1543 (Milan, Pinacoteca di Brera), the *Portrait of a Man* (Rome, Galleria Doria Pamphili), and the *Portrait of an Architect* in Berlin (fig.113). None of these portraits is horizontal in format, but it may be that Lotto re-adopted it for the present portrait during his residence in Venice between 1540, when he returned from the Marche, and 1543, when he departed for Treviso.[1]

As with Titian's contemporary *Portrait of Giulio Romano* (fig.114), the sitter's attributes – in this case a set-square and a compass – identify him as an architect.[2] Lotto was friendly with a number of architects living in Venice, including Sebastiano Serlio (1475–1553/5), Jacopo

Sansovino (1486–1570), and Giovanni dal Coro, a master builder from Ancona.[3] By 1540, Serlio was famous as an architectural theorist and writer, and it is unlikely that Lotto would have portrayed him without a book. The features of Sansovino as they are recorded in the admittedly much later portrait by Tintoretto (Florence, Galleria degli Uffizi) do not closely resemble those of the present sitter,[4] and the fact that the sitter does not look older than fifty would again exclude both Serlio and Sansovino. Much less is known of Giovanni dal Coro, but it is evident from the frequent mention of him in Lotto's account book during the 1540s, as well as in his will of 1546, that the two men were close friends and colleagues.[5] Giovanni designed the architectural frames for at least two of the altarpieces that Lotto painted for churches in the Marche, and lent him money to travel to Ancona in 1549. He has sometimes been identified as the sitter in the Berlin *Portrait of an Architect*, represented holding a compass;[6] indeed, it is just possible that the Berlin portrait represents the same sitter as in the present one, perhaps painted some years later. In the absence, however, of any certain portrait of Giovanni dal Coro, or of any evidence that Lotto actually portrayed him, the identification of him as the sitter in either portrait must remain very conjectural.

The present picture was acquired in June 1827 for Sir William Forbes by James Irvine from his business associate and friend Antonio Fidanza, a dealer in Milan, as a 'Portrait of Sansovino by Titian'.[7] Two other Venetian portraits were acquired at the same time from the same source: a half-length 'Portrait of Count Anguisciolo', also attributed to Titian (subsequently sold at Rainy, London, 2 June, 1842, lot 27); and a bust-length 'Portrait of a Woman' attributed to Veronese (untraced).

Fig.113 | Lorenzo Lotto, *Portrait of an Architect*
Berlin, Staatliche Museen zu Berlin, Gemäldegalerie

Fig.114 | Titian, *Portrait of Giulio Romano*
Mantua, Collezioni Provinciali. Formerly in the collection of the Barons Kinnaird at Rossie Priory, Perthshire

34 ❧ Portrait of Jacopo Dolfin

Oil on canvas | 105 × 91cm | c.1530–5

Inscribed on the letter: 'Al Cl[arissi]mo S[ignor] iacomo dolfin / [the rest illegible]'

Provenance: Probably Jacopo di Alvise Dolfin, Venice; Antonio Canova, Rome; acquired in Venice by James Ewing, Stathleven, Dumbartonshire, 1845; by descent to Mrs Ian Hamilton (née Crum-Ewing); sale Christie's London, 2 December 1977 (lot 41), bought Agnew's; from whom purchased for the Museum as a gift of the Ahmanson Foundation, 1981

LOS ANGELES COUNTY MUSEUM OF ART

Rediscovered as recently as the late 1970s, this imposing portrait has not yet taken its proper place in the scholarly literature on Titian.[1] It is clear from the first line of the inscription on the letter that the sitter is one Jacopo (or Giacomo) Dolfin, but since the rest of the inscription is badly abraded, it does not indicate clearly which of two possible Venetian noblemen of that name the portrait represents. Nor is there any sign of a date. For stylistic reasons, however, it has been convincingly argued that it was painted in the early 1530s.[2] Thus, the pyramidal design, including both hands, is a variant of Titian's *Portrait of Alfonso d'Este* of the late 1520s (lost; copy in the Metropolitan Museum of Art, New York), and the gesture of holding out a letter towards the spectator, as well as the pictorial handling of the crimson official robes, echoes his *Portrait of Andrea de' Franceschi* (Detroit Institute of Arts), datable on circumstantial evidence to soon after 1529. The still relatively precise modelling of the head resembles that of the *Supper at Emmaus* (Paris, Musée du Louvre), which is generally dated to the mid-1530s.

Compared with the Alfonso d'Este painting and Titian's other courtly portraits of the late 1520s and early 1530s, the Jacopo Dolfin portrait is restrained in its colour-range and in its use of costume and accessories, in keeping with the republican ethos of the ruling Venetian oligarchy. Yet compared with the official portraiture of an earlier generation, it is endowed with a new effect of physical presence and with a new grandeur of scale. In these respects it was the kind of Titian portrait that served as a model for later sixteenth-century portraits of Venetian noblemen and office-holders, especially those of Tintoretto (cat.no.68).[3]

The portrait is presumably identical with one described by Vasari in 1568 as of 'a gentleman of the Delfini family' by Titian, which he says was in the house of the sculptor Danese Cattaneo in Venice.[4] It remains a matter of debate, however, whether the sitter is to be identified as Jacopo di Alvise Dolfin (1489–1552), or as his distant cousin Jacopo di Andrea Dolfin (1469–1544), both of whom had distinguished careers in government service and held a string of public offices. Thus in the early 1530s, while Jacopo di Alvise served successively as Savio di Terraferma, as Provvedidore sopra le Mariegole, and Podestà and Capitano of Treviso, Jacopo di Andrea served as Provvedidore of the Venetian fortress of Orzinuovi, near Brescia.[5] In favour of the latter, it has been argued that the damaged part of the inscription can most plausibly be interpreted as referring the last appointment; the fact that he died without direct heirs has been advanced as a reason why the portrait had apparently come into the hands of Cattaneo before 1568.[6] But against this identification, and in favour of Jacopo di Alvise, is the fact that Jacopo di Andrea had reached his sixties by the 1530s, whereas Titian's sitter, although bald, has the thick black beard and unwrinkled face of a man in his forties. The abraded part of the inscription could just as easily have referred to Venice as to Orzinuovi. Nor is it necessary to infer from Vasari's reference that Cattaneo was the actual owner of the portrait. From the later 1540s Cattaneo was a leading Venetian practitioner of the portrait bust, and in an important example such as his *Pietro Bembo* of about 1549 (Padua, Basilica del Santo) he owes an obvious debt to the painted portraiture of Titian.[7] It may well be, therefore, that he was commissioned by Jacopo di Alvise's sons to sculpt a posthumous bust of their father, and was lent Titian's portrait by them as a model. If so, Cattaneo – who was one of Vasari's principal informants on Venetian art – may simply have mentioned the portrait in a letter while it happened to be temporarily in his possession.

If indeed Titian's portrait represents Jacopo di Alvise Dolfin, it is likely to have been commissioned to commemorate the most important appointment of his career, as Podestà (provincial governor) of the mainland city of Treviso in 1532.[8] A little more of his biography emerges from his will, made fourteen months before his death in October 1552.[9] He was a member of the Sant'Angelo branch of the family, and requested to be buried in his local parish church. As was customary, he left numerous pious donations to Venetian monasteries, confraternities and hospitals, and made provision for masses to be said for his soul at Sant'Angelo and elsewhere. A portrait bust commissioned by his sons from Cattaneo may have been intended to be placed in the church, close to his tomb. Finally, it may be noted that Jacopo di Alvise's mother was a member of the Donà family, and that he was one of the electors of Doge Francesco Donà in 1545.[10] He may, therefore, have been closely related to the doge, who sat to Titian in 1546–7 (see cat.no.38).

By the beginning of the nineteenth century Titian's portrait belonged to another distinguished sculptor, Antonio Canova (1757–1822), whose collection of Venetian pictures was largely acquired for him by his agent Ferdinando Tonioli. The collection was then sold in Venice after his death in 1822 by his half-brother Monsignor Giambattista Sartori.[11] Canova's ownership of the portrait is attested by a label on the back, and by the information given to the Glasgow merchant James Ewing when he acquired it in Venice in 1845. Oddly, Ewing wrote to his friend Mathieson that the portrait represented 'Morosini, conqueror of the Morea' – in other words, Doge Francesco Morosini, who reigned more than a century after Titian's death (1688–94).[12] Perhaps Ewing had been told that in the eighteenth century the picture had belonged to the family of that doge, but had misunderstood this information.

Before the picture was cleaned in 1980 it showed a curtain hanging behind the sitter's head. The curtain is included in an old copy of identical dimensions now in the Norton Simon Museum, Pasadena.[13]

35 ❧ Titian *Portrait of Admiral Vincenzo Cappello*

Oil on canvas | 141 × 118cm | 1540

Provenance: Probably William Beckford (1760–1844), Bath (as Tintoretto); by inheritance to his daughter Susan, Duchess of Hamilton; Hamilton Palace sale, Christie's, 24 June 1882 (lot 410, as Tintoretto), purchased by Colnaghi's; H.B. Mildmay; his sale, Christie's, 24 June 1893 (lot 73, as Tintoretto), purchased by Agnew's; from whom purchased by the 5th Earl of Rosebery (1847–1929), Dalmeny House, 1893; Rosebery sale, Christie's, 5 May 1939 (lot 45, as Giorgione); Wildenstein and Co., New York; from whom purchased by the Samuel H. Kress Foundation, 1954 (as by Titian); by whom presented to the Gallery, 1957 (acc.no.1957.14.3)

WASHINGTON, NATIONAL GALLERY OF ART, SAMUEL H. KRESS COLLECTION

Although a nineteenth-century attribution to Tintoretto still finds occasional adherents,[1] the portrait is almost certainly identifiable with the one of Cappello known to have been painted by Titian in 1540. This date is provided by a letter and a sonnet in praise of both the portrait and the sitter sent by the painter's friend Pietro Aretino to Cappello's nephew on Christmas Day of that year.[2]

Vincenzo di Nicolò Cappello (1469–1541) was a Venetian patrician who had an exceptionally distinguished naval career in the service of the Republic.[3] The display of batons of command in his right hand and on the shelf to his left refer to the fact that he held office as Capitano Generale da Mar no fewer than five times. Other honours bestowed on him included a knighthood from Henry VII during his embassy to England in 1504, and his appointment as a procurator of St Mark's in 1539. A full-length statue of him in antique costume, carved after his death in 1541 by the sculptor Domenico di Pietro Grazioli da Salò, is still to be seen above the main portal of his parish church of Santa Maria Formosa in Venice.

By 1540 Titian's services as a portrait painter were in heavy demand by an international circle of princely patrons, and his portraits of his fellow-Venetians were becoming increasingly rare. Even in the case of so distinguished a sitter as Cappello, Titian adapted his composition from that of an earlier portrait of a military commander, the Duke of Urbino, of 1536 (fig.23). The Cappello portrait nevertheless enjoyed a great public success in Venice, as is

evident both from the number of early replicas and copies,[4] and from the inspiration it provided for the military portraits of Tintoretto and Veronese. One of the early copies, now in the Chrysler Museum (fig.115), may, in fact, be by Tintoretto; the comparison helps to confirm the attribution of the present portrait to Titian, while also in part accounting for its mistaken association with the name of Tintoretto.[5] Entirely characteristic of Tintoretto's treatment of highlights are the rapid slashes of unblended white paint in the Chrysler portrait, as, for example, in his *A Procurator of St Mark's* (cat.no.68); whereas the more calculated and highly worked quality of the brushwork in the present portrait is equally characteristic of Titian. It would similarly be typical of Tintoretto's modification of Titian's style to have raised the dome of the sitter's balding head, and to enhance the linear rhythms of the beard. Another version, formerly in the collection of the Earls of Dunmore at Dunmore Park, near Falkirk, is probably attributable to Titian's workshop (fig.116).[6]

Although the first definite modern reference to the present picture does not occur until the Hamilton Palace sale catalogue of 1882, it is almost certainly identical with one described as a 'Portrait of a Spanish Admiral in armour holding a baton, Tintoretto', listed in the posthumous inventory of the 10th Duke of Hamilton's father-in-law, William Beckford, in 1844.[7] After the Hamilton sale the portrait left Scotland for a decade, but was bought by the Earl of Rosebery for Dalmeny in 1893, before finally crossing the Atlantic in 1939.

Fig.115 | Attributed to Jacopo Tintoretto, *Portrait of Admiral Vincenzo Cappello* (after Titian) Norfolk, Va., Chrysler Museum

Fig.116 | Workshop of Titian, *Portrait of Admiral Vincenzo Cappello* Milan, Koelliker Collection. Formerly in the collection of the Earls of Dunmore at Dunmore Park, Falkirk

Titian and workshop PIEVE DI CADORE c.1485/90–1576 VENICE

36 ❧ Two Boys of the Pesaro Family

Oil on canvas | 91.5 × 77cm | c.1540–5

Provenance: Ca' Pesaro, Venice, by 1797; Abate Luigi Celotti, Venice, by 1828; from whom purchased by James Irvine on behalf of Sir William Forbes of Pitsligo, Fettercairn, Kincardineshire; by descent to Sir John Forbes; by inheritance to his son-in-law, 20th Baron Clinton, by 1883

PRIVATE COLLECTION

First published in 1971 and lent to *The Genius of Venice* exhibition at the Royal Academy in London in 1983,[1] this charming double portrait of two brothers is an important recent addition to the small group that represents Titian's portraits of children, of which the *Ranuccio Farnese* of 1542 (Washington, National Gallery of Art), the *Clarissa Strozzi* of the same year (Berlin, Gemäldegalerie), and the children in the *Vendramin Family* of about 1542–7 (London, National Gallery) are the most celebrated examples. To judge from the costumes, with the high frilled white collars and sleeves that follow the contours of the arms, the picture was painted at around the same time as these other child portraits. Indeed, the success of the first two, representing children of non-Venetian patrons, may have led directly to the commission for the present work, which almost certainly represents members of the Venetian patrician Pesaro family. The two boys are each shown with a musical instrument: the elder with a lute, which he holds by the neck, and the younger with a recorder, which he has laid on the table in front of him. The open musical score does not apparently correspond to any known composition.

The identity of the sitters has been deduced from the fact that the portrait was in the possession of the Pesaro family at the time of the fall of the Venetian Republic in 1797. They have been identified more specifically as the brothers Gerolamo Melchiorre and Francesco Santo Pesaro, born respectively in June 1536 and November 1537.[2] Their father was Benedetto Pesaro, grandson of the famous Generalissimo da Mar of the same name, whose grandiose monument surrounds the doorway to the sacristy in the church of the Frari; there are good reasons for identifying their mother Lucrezia as the sitter for Lotto's *Portrait of a Lady as Lucretia* (see cat.no.32). This branch of the Pesaro family, called 'di San Benetto', were the cousins of the Pesaro dal Carro branch, for whom Titian painted his great Ca' Pesaro altarpiece in 1519–26, also in the church of the Frari, and also including an engaging portrait of a child (fig.20).[3]

The traditional attribution of the present portrait to Titian himself has not been universally accepted, and it has been suggested that it might in fact be by his faithful assistant Gerolamo Dente.[4] It is true that there are weaknesses of draughtsmanship and pictorial handling that are not worthy of Titian at his best, for example in both of the foremost hands and in the perspective of the foreground table. But the marvellously expressive heads, touching in their combination of aristocratic pride and childlike diffidence, go far beyond the capacities of Gerolamo or of any of Titian's other assistants, and are certainly the work of the master. It may be reasonably inferred, therefore, that Titian was responsible for sketch-ing in the composition, and for painting the heads in the presence of the sitters, but that he left the execution of the rest to an assistant. The 1540s were an extremely busy decade for Titian, especially in the phase leading up to his journey to Rome late in 1545, and even the most favoured of his Venetian patrons had to be content with the work of assistants. The pendant to his portrait of his friend Pietro Aretino of 1545 (Florence, Palazzo Pitti), for example, a portrait of Giovanni dalle Bande Nere, was commissioned by Aretino as a diplomatic gift for Duke Cosimo de' Medici, but was delegated by Titian to his assistant Gian Paolo Pace.[5]

The X-radiograph of the painting (fig.117) reveals a number of alterations made during the process of execution, including a simplification of the part-book and the elimination of what seems to be a patterned Turkey carpet that originally covered the foreground table. The presence of this object lends further support to the conclusion that much of the picture is the work of an assistant, since unlike Lotto and other contemporaries, Titian seems never to have included carpets in his own autograph portraits.

Together with several other pictures in the present exhibition (cat.nos.32, 33, 37, 60, 71), this portrait was acquired by James Irvine in Italy for Sir William Forbes of Pitsligo. As he wrote to Forbes in November 1828, Irvine had already assumed that the sitters were members of the Pesaro family: 'This picture came from the Palazzo Pesaro and probably represents two boys of that family for which Titian painted his famous picture at the Pesaro altar at the Mada dei Frari so much admired by Reynolds, and where many of the portraits of that family are introduced'.[6] Together with the *Portrait of Doge Andrea Gritti* (cat.no.37), the picture was lent by Lord Clinton, the widower of Forbes's grand-daughter, to the exhibition at the Royal Scottish Academy in Edinburgh in 1883.[7]

Fig.117 | X-radiograph mosaic

37 ❧ *Portrait of Doge Andrea Gritti*

Oil on canvas | 84 × 66cm | *c.*1540–50

Numbered in oil paint on the back of the canvas: '360'

Provenance: Giuseppe Longhi, Milan; from whom purchased by James Irvine for Sir William Forbes of Pitsligo, 1827; by descent to Sir John Forbes; by inheritance to his son-in-law, 20th Baron Clinton, by 1883

PRIVATE COLLECTION

This previously unpublished portrait represents the greatest Venetian doge of the sixteenth century, who was a major patron of Titian. Andrea Gritti (1455–1538) had held a series of important diplomatic and military posts before being elected doge in 1523, and during his relatively long reign he demonstrated highly effective leadership, both in international politics and in promoting the visual arts as an instrument of political ideology. It was Gritti who was chiefly responsible for persuading the eminent Florentine architect and sculptor Jacopo Sansovino to settle in Venice, and who was the driving force behind Sansovino's classicising reconstruction of the Piazza San Marco. Gritti also commissioned Sansovino to rebuild the church of San Francesco della Vigna, in commemoration of which a medal was struck with the doge's portrait on the obverse (cat.no.197).

Titian painted at least three portraits of Gritti.[2] Unquestionably the finest is the magnificently vital picture once in the collection of Charles I, and now in the National Gallery of Art, Washington. That portrait, which was probably painted posthumously in about 1545, is unique of its type, and is likely to have been painted for a member of the doge's family, or on some other unofficial commission. Earlier, in 1531, Titian portrayed Gritti in full length and in profile, kneeling before the Virgin and Child and saints, in a votive picture for the Sala del Collegio in the Doge's Palace. That picture was destroyed by fire in 1574, but the portrait included in the replacement painted by Tintoretto (in situ) is based on Titian's prototype.

The most widely diffused image of Gritti, of which the present work represents an example, was that commissioned from Titian in 1540 for the Sala del Maggior Consiglio (Hall of the Greater Council) in the Doge's Palace.[3] It belonged to a cycle portraying every Venetian doge since the early ninth century, placed in a frieze above the main narrative cycle in the chamber. The doges were represented in pairs, in waist length and three-quarter view, facing towards one another.[4] In 1577 the hall went up in flames, and Titian's portraits of Gritti and various other doges (including Francesco Donà; see cat.no.38) were destroyed with the rest of the pictorial decoration. Immediately after the fire, however, the narrative and portrait cycles were both replaced, where possible on the basis of surviving visual evidence. Thus the replacement of the portrait of Gritti, paired with that of Antonio Grimani, and perhaps painted by Domenico Tintoretto (fig.118), was clearly based on a surviving version of Titian's lost original.

Until now, the most faithful replica of Titian's official image of Gritti has been thought to be a picture in the Metropolitan Museum of Art, New York (fig.119). But in that painting, and in a closely related version in Kenosha, Wisconsin, the doge looks slightly upwards,[5] whereas in the present portrait he looks slightly downwards, and his expression is more animated. The portrait corresponds more closely, in other words, to the late sixteenth-century copy in the Doge's Palace, in which Gritti gestures towards his companion, and the two are engaged in conversation. Since in design it more directly meets the needs of a pendant than do the more self-sufficient New York and Kenosha versions, it probably also corresponds more closely to Titian's lost original.

The present picture also appears to be of much higher quality than the New York and Kenosha pictures. Both of these are generally accepted as products of Titian's workshop, and even the lost original – which was placed high and was not accessible to close inspection – may not have been fully autograph. Although the present work cannot be regarded as entirely from Titian's own hand, some direct participation by the master is possible.

The picture was bought as Titian's portrait of Gritti by James Irvine from the dealer Giuseppe Longhi in Milan in July 1827.[6] By 1842 the identity of the sitter had become confused, since it is described in the catalogue of the Forbes sale of that year as 'Portrait of the Doge Grimani'.[7] The picture failed to sell, however, and in 1883 it was lent by Forbes's heir Lord Clinton, together with Titian's *Two Boys of the Pesaro Family* (cat.no.36), to the old masters exhibition at the Royal Institution building in Edinburgh.[8]

Fig.118 | Attributed to Domenico Tintoretto, *Portrait of Doges Antonio Grimani and Andrea Gritti* Venice, Palazzo Ducale

Fig.119 | Workshop of Titian, *Portrait of Doge Andrea Gritti* New York, The Metropolitan Museum of Art

38 ❧ *Portrait of Doge Francesco Donà*

Oil on canvas | 104 × 91.4cm | *c.*1555–65

Provenance: Probably acquired by John, 3rd Earl of Bute, in Venice, 1770–1; by descent to the present owner

PRIVATE COLLECTION AT MOUNT STUART, ISLE OF BUTE

In this unpublished portrait Titian shows Francesco Donà (or Donato, 1468–1552) enthroned in the full ducal regalia of brocaded gown and cloak, ermine cape, and embroidered cap (*corno*), with a view over the lagoon to Venice in the background. Clearly discernible are the Doge's Palace, Sansovino's Marciana Library, the twin columns at the entrance to the Piazzetta San Marco, and the bell-tower (*campanile*) beyond.

As the holder of an annual stipend from the Salt Office, Titian was required to paint the portrait of every new doge for the cycle that ran round the frieze of the Sala del Maggior Consiglio in the Doge's Palace (see also cat.no.37). In 1547, two years after the election of Doge Donà, Titian was paid for painting his official portrait for the cycle, together with that of his predecessor, Doge Pietro Lando.[1] This double portrait was destroyed by fire in 1577, but in keeping with the standard formula, the two doges would have been shown in three-quarter view, obliquely facing one another (compare fig.118). The present composition, which must have originated from a separate, unofficial commission, shows the doge in a much more mobile pose, with his head turned at right angles to his body, as if to receive or bestow counsel. Donà was a thoughtful, cultivated man and, unlike Doge Gritti, before being elected he was active not in arms but in government administration.[2] His demeanour and expression are accordingly venerable and sagacious, in contrast to the energy, even ferocity with which Titian invested Gritti in the portrait now in Washington.

At the time of Donà's election in 1545 Titian was in Rome, and the composition of his portrait owes much to his recent direct experience of papal portraiture. The basic arrangement, with the sitter shown enthroned in three-quarter view, adheres to that established by Raphael in his *Portrait of Julius II* (London, National Gallery) and followed by Titian himself in his *Portrait of Pope Paul III* of 1543 (fig.24). The introduction of the twist of the head, however, also reflects knowledge of Sebastiano del Piombo's *Portrait of Clement VII* of *c.*1526 (Naples, Museo Nazionale di Capodimonte).[3] Titian's example was in turn to be hugely influential on later ducal portraiture in Venice, as is evident in the two portraits of

Doge Marcantonio Memmo in the present exhibition (cat.nos.80, 81).

Another version of the present portrait (Vienna, Kunsthistorisches Museum), formerly in the collection of the 1st Duke of Hamilton, appears in one of Teniers's views of the gallery of the Archduke Leopold Wilhelm in Brussels (fig.57).[4] As is generally recognised, however, the prosaic and mechanical rendering of the Vienna picture suggests that it is simply a copy after Titian. Although the present picture is definitely finer in quality, it is unlikely to represent Titian's original of about 1550 either, because it is executed with a breadth of handling more characteristic of his later career. For this reason it is perhaps best regarded as a replica made in Titian's workshop, but possibly with some intervention by the master himself.

Probably acquired in Venice with an attribu-

tion to 'Palma' by the 3rd Earl of Bute in 1770–1,[5] the painting is listed in the 1799 inventory of Luton Park as a portrait of Doge Antonio Grimani by Titian.[6] In 1838 Waagen reattributed it to Tintoretto, an attribution that was retained when it was shown together with the rest of the Bute collection at Bethnal Green, Glasgow and Manchester in 1882–5.[7]

Attributed to Francesco Beccaruzzi CONEGLIANO(?) (TREVISO) c.1500–c.1550 TREVISO(?)

39 ❧ A Hunting Scene

Oil on canvas | 231.4 × 396.2cm | c.1540

Provenance: Probably Borghese collection, Rome (by 1693); probably with Thompson Martin, Edinburgh, from whom purchased by the 4th Earl of Hopetoun, 1819

FROM THE COLLECTION OF HOPETOUN HOUSE, SOUTH QUEENSFERRY

It is difficult to think of any other north Italian painting of the mid-sixteenth century, let alone one of this enormous scale, in which the subject appears to consist simply of a scene from everyday life, without any religious, allegorical or mythological pretext. The central figure is presumably a portrait, and the idea of depicting a contemporary personage in full length with dogs may have been inspired by Titian's *Portrait of the Emperor Charles V with a Hound* of 1533 (Madrid, Museo Nacional del Prado). However, Titian's portrait is quite different in concept, being limited to the single figure of the emperor, and the present work may equally well have been inspired by genre-like representations of parables by Bonifacio, such as his *Dives and Lazarus* of c.1535–40 (fig.132), or indeed *The Return of the Prodigal Son* (cat.no.49), both of which include subsidiary scenes from mid-sixteenth-century villa life, including hunting and field sports. Yet in Bonifacio's pictures these have a moralising justification apparently entirely absent from the *Hunting Scene*. Since large-scale paintings in villas themselves tended to be painted in fresco rather than on canvas, the present work is perhaps most likely to have been painted for one of the main reception rooms of a Venetian palace.

The question of the picture's attribution is problematic. It was included in the Andrea

Palladio exhibition in London in 1975 with a tentative attribution to Bernardino Licinio and has retained that attribution ever since.[1] But the stylistic resemblance to the work of Licinio is not close, and a much better candidate is the Trevigian painter Francesco Beccaruzzi. The latter's *Portrait of a Ball-player*, for example (fig.120), shows a noble sportsman with a page in a similarly genre-like situation, with a topo-

Fig.120 | Attributed to Francesco Beccaruzzi, *Portrait of a Ball-player*
Berlin, Staatliche Museen zu Berlin, Gemäldegalerie

graphical vignette (in this case showing the Piazza dei Signori in Treviso) in the background. Similar, too, is the somewhat stiff anatomy and thickly padded doublet, and the literal approach to details of costume and physiognomy.[2] To judge from the style of the costumes, both pictures probably date from around 1540. The pose of the groom on the right, doffing his cap, is derived from Giovanni Britto's woodcut of about 1535–40 after Titian's *Adoration of the Shepherds*, while the hunting dogs were clearly inspired by Dürer's famous *St Eustace* engraving.

Given its unusual subject and large size, the picture is probably identical with one recorded in 1693 with an attribution to Giorgione in the Palazzo Borghese, Rome, as 'a large hunting picture with dogs and figures'.[3] It is likely to have been imported into Britain at the beginning of the nineteenth century, and documents at Hopetoun record that it was acquired in 1819 by the 4th Earl from 'Mr Martin of Edinburgh' – probably the dealer Thompson Martin – through the agency of Andrew Wilson.[4] It is described in the printed catalogue as 'A Prince of the States of Venice going out to sport' by Titian. This attribution was maintained by Waagen, who visited Hopetoun in 1851.[5]

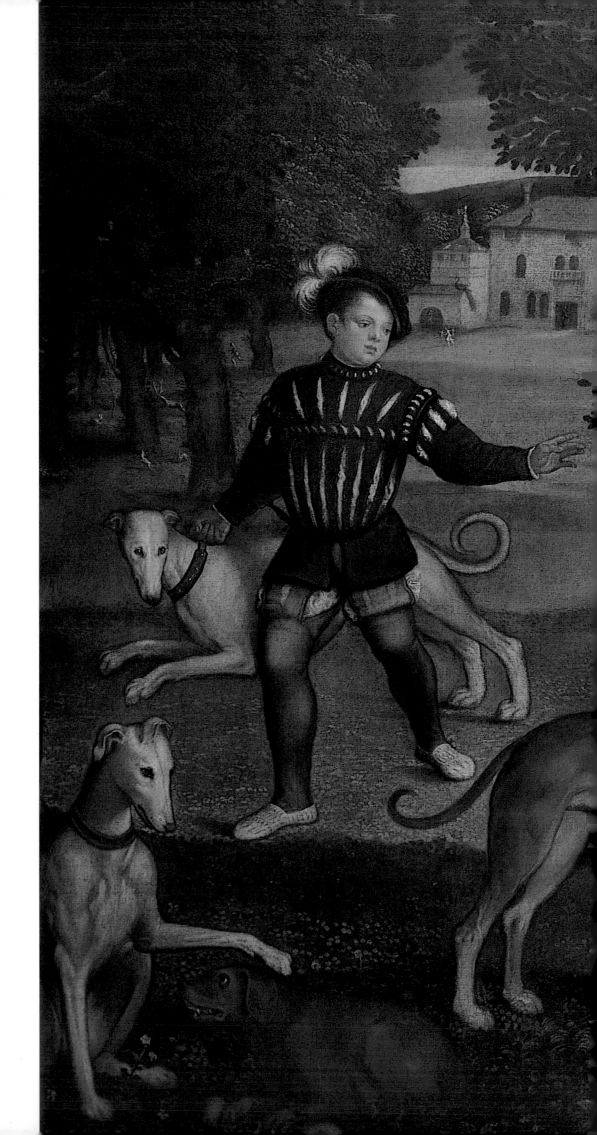

40 ❧ *The Adoration of the Kings*

Oil on canvas | 183 × 235cm | 1542

Provenance: Possibly Juan Alfonso Enríquez de Cabrera, Admiral of Castile, Madrid, by 1647; Francesco Maria Balbi, Genoa, by 1677 (as by Titian); by descent to Giacomo Balbi, by 1758; acquired by Andrew Wilson from Palazzo Balbi, 1805; his sale, Peter Coxe, London, 6 May 1807 (lot 28), probably bought by Lord Eldin; his sale, Winstanley, Edinburgh, 15 March 1833 (lot 13), bought by Mr Neil; acquired from him by the Royal Scottish Academy, 1856; transferred to the National Gallery of Scotland, 1910 (acc.no.NG 100)

EDINBURGH, NATIONAL GALLERY OF
SCOTLAND

As shown by the recently published account book of the Bassano family workshop, this magnificent work of Jacopo's early maturity was commissioned on 29 April 1542 by one Jacopo Ghisi.[1] This was almost certainly the Venetian patrician Jacopo di Jacopo Ghisi of the parish of San Zulian, who was born in 1515, married in 1534, and made wills in 1559 and 1564.[2] Ghisi seems, however, never to have taken possession of his commission, since Jacopo's account book records that an advance made by the patron in July 1542 was subsequently returned to him by the painter. The bearded king in green and gold stripes whose head marks the centre of the picture looks like a portrait, as do the two boys behind him, but in view of the uncertainty over who actually paid for the picture, their identification as Jacopo Ghisi and two putative sons is problematic.[3]

Even before information on the commission came to light, the painting was generally dated to about 1540 on stylistic grounds.[4] Trained in his father's workshop in Bassano, Jacopo completed his artistic education in Venice under Bonifacio Veronese around 1533–4, and *The Adoration of the Kings* retains a strong flavour of Bonifacio's artistic vocabulary and decorative use of colour (compare cat.no.31, fig.18). But Bonifacio's own style was essentially placid and undramatic, and

by the late 1530s Jacopo's contact with a wider range of artistic styles, notably that of the Friulian painter Pordenone (see cat.no.87), stimulated him to introduce a greater sense of movement and energy. In composing this painting he evidently paid particular attention to Pordenone's frescoed version of the same subject in the Malchiostro chapel in Treviso Cathedral of 1520 (fig.121), since he took over not just its dynamic compositional rhythms, but also, in reverse, a particular figure – that of the bulgingly muscular, somewhat indecorously posed servant at the lower left. Jacopo was also clearly intent on widening his artistic horizons through the study of prints. The curving sweep of men and horses on the right, for example, owes much to Raphael's *Way to Calvary*, as transmitted by Agostino Veneziano's engraving, while part of the ruined building at the upper right is derived fairly literally from Dürer's *Holy Family in Egypt* woodcut of about 1502, from his *Life of the Virgin* series (fig.122).[5]

At the same time, these various borrowings are successfully fused into an idiom that is already entirely Jacopo's own. Few of his Venetian contemporaries could match his attention to still-life detail, and none could approach him as a painter of animals. However, engaging as they are, the details are integrated into a clear compositional structure, and do not detract from the whole. Similarly, the planes of intense, decoratively repeating colour, and the sensuously evoked surface textures, are offset against broader, cooler and more neutral areas, allowing the eye some rest as it scans the busy scene. Seen from a distance, the picture retains both its legibility and its chromatic splendour.

The richness of colour and detail are obviously entirely appropriate to the festive subject, in which the three kings present to the new born Christ Child their gifts of gold, frankincense and myrrh. Traditional features of adoration iconography include the ox and the ass, and the classical ruins. While the ox, symbolising the Gentiles, raises its head in recognition of its master, the ass, symbolising the Jews, notably fails to do so.

The crumbling of a classical building traditionally refers to the passing of the pagan order with the coming of Christ (see cat.no.45). Other likely symbols include the tree-stump close to the infant Christ (referring to the wood of the Cross), and the columbine nearby (which is presumably a punning reference to the Holy Spirit). It has also been suggested that the picture was intended to present a didactic contrast between the worshippers to the left, who recognise Christ and are admitted to the sacred precinct created by the ruined wall at the centre, and the coarse and ignorant figures on the right, who show no awareness of the miracle they are witnessing and turn their backs on their Saviour.[6] Such an interpretation of the kings' retinue remains speculative, however, and it is by no means clear that Jacopo meant his picture to be read as a moralising sermon.

When acquired by Andrew Wilson from Palazzo Balbi in Genoa in 1805 *The Adoration of the Kings* bore an attribution to Titian; it is under this name that it can be traced back to the collection of Francesco Maria Balbi (1619–1704) in the late seventeenth century.[7] Previously it may have belonged to Juan Alfonso Enríquez, Duke of Medina de Ríoseco and Admiral of Castile.[8] Hearing that the Balbi collection was up for sale in 1803, and given the huge demand for pictures by Titian in London, William Buchanan strenuously urged his partner in Italy, James Irvine, to acquire it, but they were out-manoeuvred by Wilson.[9] The picture retained the attribution to Titian when subsequently in the collection of Lord Eldin, who in 1826 lent it to the old masters exhibition at the Royal Institution in Edinburgh, and at whose sale in 1833 it was the star item.[10] Commenting on it shortly after it had been acquired by the Royal Scottish Academy in 1856, Waagen recognised the implausibility of the Titian attribution, and suggested the name of Pordenone instead.[11] Only in 1871 was Jacopo Bassano correctly recognised as the picture's true author.[12]

Fig.121 | Pordenone, *The Adoration of the Kings*
Treviso, Cathedral

Fig.122 | Albrecht Dürer, *The Holy Family in Egypt*
Edinburgh, National Gallery of Scotland

Giovanni Girolamo Savoldo BRESCIA(?) ACTIVE 1506–c.1548 VENICE

41 ❧ *A Shepherd with a Flute*

Oil on canvas | 103 × 78cm | *c*.1540

Provenance: Acquired by the 8th Earl of Wemyss, *c*.1838–40; by descent to the present owner

THE EARL OF WEMYSS AND MARCH KT

This beautiful but severely abraded painting poses problems of status as well as of dating and interpretation. In composition it is very similar to Savoldo's much better preserved picture now in the Getty Museum (fig.123), and because the comparison is unfavourable to the present picture, this has often been regarded as a later copy. However, it was characteristic of Savoldo to paint different versions of the same composition, apparently within a relatively short period, as was the case with his series of at least four subtly differentiated renderings of *St Mary Magdalene*. Similarly, the differences between this and the Getty version of the picture (the background on the right, the cloud formations, the position of the figure's right hand in relation to the flute, the position of his left leg) are most unlikely to have been introduced by a copyist. Indeed, in some respects the expression of the present figure may be seen as more suggestively poetic.

Savoldo's chronology is notoriously difficult to establish, partly because of the scarcity of certain dates, but especially because his style did not develop consistently in any particular direction. Thus, the Getty painting has been dated both to around 1525, close to the documented *Virgin and Child in Glory with Saints* (Milan, Pinacoteca di Brera), and to about 1535–40, close to the *Nativity* (Brescia, Pinacoteca Tosio Martinengo) from the Bargnani chapel in San Barnaba.[2] This latter work includes a shepherd wearing an identical broad-brimmed felt hat, but more tellingly, the treatment of the draperies, with similar thick, deeply excavated folds, and the magical light effects that appear in both pictures, helps to confirm that the *Nativity* and both versions of the *Shepherd with a Flute* are more or less contemporaneous. Furthermore, a comparable mixture of rustic buildings and classicising ruins in the background is to be found in the background of other works generally accepted as dating from Savoldo's late career, such as the *Rest on the Flight into Egypt* in the Episcopal Gallery, Dubrovnik, and the half-length *Nativity* formerly in the Crespi Morbio collection.

The pastoral subject harks back to the period around 1510 when musical shepherds were popular in Venetian painting, as in Titian's *The Three Ages of Man* (cat.no.15). More directly relevant to the present picture were Giorgionesque figures shown close-up, in a

portrait-like format, as in the *Shepherd* variously attributed to Giorgione or Titian at Hampton Court, or Sebastiano del Piombo's *Shepherd* at Wilton House.[3] As was the case with the parallel type of the half-length female beauty (see cat.no.22), this category of image is perhaps deliberately ambivalent, and it is not always clear whether the figure is meant to constitute a portrait of a recognisable person, or whether it represents an anonymous ideal. In support of the former interpretation, it has been suggested that the Getty picture portrays a gentleman in rustic guise – since according to the early sixteenth-century authority on good breeding, Baldassare Castiglione, a man's true nobility remains evident even when he is dressed as a shepherd.[4] Yet this interpretation appears to be contradicted by the very existence of the Wemyss version,

since while the features are not exactly replicated, it is difficult to see them as those of a different sitter. Probably, therefore, the picture is best interpreted in terms of poetic genre, as representing a typical inhabitant of an ideal arcadian or bucolic world. Either way, Savoldo's characteristic contribution to the type is to reinforce the effect of a psychological rapport with the spectator by making the figure appear to react and respond to an outside presence.

This picture was acquired by the 8th Earl of Wemyss on the advice of his undergraduate grandson, the future Lord Elcho and 10th Earl, apparently with an attribution to Giorgione.[5] Waagen expressed some scepticism about this attribution when he visited Gosford House in 1856,[6] and Savoldo was correctly recognised as the author in 1871.[7]

School of the Veneto
42 ❧ *Portrait of a Lady*

Oil on canvas | 110 × 89cm | *c.*1540–5

Provenance: Probably purchased in Venice by John, 3rd Earl of Bute, 1770–1; by descent to the present owner

PRIVATE COLLECTION AT MOUNT STUART, ISLE OF BUTE

Neither the sitter nor the author of this striking, high-quality portrait is known. It is datable on the basis of the fashionable costume to about 1540–5, but it does not appear to be by any of the leading portrait painters working in Venice or the eastern Veneto at this period, such as Paris Bordon, Lorenzo Lotto or Bernardino Licinio. The high sheen on the pinkish-red sleeves and skirt recalls more strongly the work of Moretto da Brescia and of his pupil Moroni, but the portrait does not appear to be by either of these masters either. It is nevertheless most likely to originate from this western, Lombard part of the Venetian *terraferma*. The costume is similar in style to those in Licinio's *Lady in a Red Dress*, dated 1540, in the Pinacoteca Malaspina, Pavia, and to Lotto's *Laura da Pola* of 1543 (Milan, Pinacoteca di Brera). It is also close to those in the female portraits by Paris Bordon in the National Gallery, London, and the Kisters Collection, Kreuzlingen.[1]

Like his other Venetian pictures (cat.nos.38, 44, 50, 57; fig.60), this portrait was probably acquired by the 3rd Earl of Bute in Venice in 1770–1. It was recorded by Waagen in 1854 with an attribution to Paris Bordon.[2]

Fig.123 | Giovanni Girolamo Savoldo, *A Shepherd with a Flute* Los Angeles, J. Paul Getty Museum

Moretto da Brescia BRESCIA *c.*1498–1554 BRESCIA

43 ✢ *King David with a Donor*

Oil on canvas | 74 × 85.5cm | *c.*1550–4

Provenance: Probably Cardinal Pietro Aldobrandini, by 1603; Alexander Day, London, by 1800; Sir James Carnegie, Kinnaird Castle, 1822–3; by inheritance to the Earls of Southesk

THE SOUTHESK COLLECTION

King David, who holds a Renaissance *lira da braccio* with mother-of-pearl inlays on its neck rather than his more traditional harp,[1] directs the attention of the kneeling cleric upwards to a source of heavenly radiance. Presumably the unknown donor had a particular devotion to David, perhaps as his name-saint, or because of his association with music and psalmody. The unadorned realism with which not just the donor but also the holy figure are portrayed, and the directness and intimacy of their relationship, are characteristic of Lombard, and in particular of Brescian, as opposed to Venetian painting. Although the canvas may have been trimmed at the edges, there is no good reason to accept the suggestion that it is a fragment of a much larger composition.[2]

With its dusky, almost Rembrandtesque naturalism, the picture was long considered to be a work of the seventeenth century; the correct attribution to Moretto dates from as recently as 1986.[3] Since then it has been accepted as a relatively early work of about 1525–30, close to the series of Old Testament prophets that Moretto painted in 1521–4 for the chapel of the Holy Sacrament in the church of San Giovanni Evangelista in Brescia (in situ).[4] But comparison with these, including with the figure of David (fig.124), shows that in the 1520s Moretto's style was crisper and more chiselled, his palette was lighter and more silvery, and he favoured pronounced effects of contre-jour, with figures silhouetted against a luminous sky. The *King David with a Donor*, with its warmer, more brownish tone and its much greater degree of atmospheric fusion, resembles rather the *Lamentation* of 1554 (New York, Metropolitan Museum of Art) and other works of the painter's later period.

Because of its unusual subject the picture may be identified with one recorded in the 1603 inventory of the collection of Cardinal Pietro Aldobrandini (nephew of Pope Clement VIII) with an attribution to Giorgione: 'A picture with David playing the lyre (*lira*), with someone kneeling in front of him with clasped hands, by Giorgione.'[5] Further inventories record its continued presence in the Aldobrandini collection in Rome throughout the seventeenth century, and it probably remained there until the end of the eighteenth.[6] Then in 1800–1 it was exhibited in London, together with other pictures from the 'Aldobrandini Villa', by the dealer Alexander Day as 'Giorgione – King David instructing a pious man in his devotions.'[7] Two decades later, in 1822–3 (by which time it had been given an altogether less plausible attribution to the Bolognese seventeenth-century artist Domenichino) it was acquired by Sir James Carnegie from the Edinburgh dealer, Thompson Martin.[8] At some point subsequently it was reattributed, equally implausibly, to another seventeenth-century artist from Emilia, Guercino.

Fig.124 | Moretto da Brescia, *King David*
Brescia, Church of San Giovanni Evangelista

Attributed to Bonifacio Veronese VERONA 1487–1553 VENICE

44 ❦ *St Jerome in the Desert*

Oil on canvas | 98 × 188cm | *c*.1530–5

Inscribed with initials on the stump beside the saint: 'B. F.'

Provenance: Probably purchased in Venice by the 3rd Earl of Bute, 1770–1; by descent to the present owner

PRIVATE COLLECTION AT MOUNT STUART, ISLE OF BUTE

As in Cima's painting of a generation earlier (cat.10), the half-naked saint is shown mortifying himself with a stone before a crucifix. Represented in the right middle ground are the saint's cell, lion, and cardinal's hat, and beyond, the monastery founded by Jerome in Bethlehem. To the left is a magnificent panoramic vista, clearly influenced by the so-called world landscapes of Netherlandish painters such as Joachim Patinir and particularly Jan van Scorel.

When bought by Lord Bute in Venice, the picture was presumably attributed to Paris Bordon, since it appears under his name in the Luton Park inventory of 1799.[1] It was apparently Waagen in 1838 who introduced the name of Bonifacio, perhaps on the basis of the initials 'B.F.' ('Bonifacius Fecit'?) inscribed on the stump in the centre foreground.[2] Although the picture is hardly typical of Bonifacio, and the landscape differs markedly from many of his landscape backgrounds, Waagen's suggestion still has much to recommend it. The figure is compatible with his types, and the landscape may have been painted by an assistant. Bonifacio ran a large workshop, and the very northern character of the landscape background in a picture such as his *Adoration of the Kings* in the Palazzo Rosso, Genoa (fig.125) suggests that he may occasionally have made use of Netherlandish collaborators. The landscape is also comparable to that in his *St Michael overcoming Satan* of *c*.1530 in Santi Giovanni e Paolo, Venice.[3]

Fig.125 | Bonifacio Veronese, *The Adoration of the Kings*
Genoa, Galleria di Palazzo Rosso

Bonifacio Veronese VERONA 1487–1553 VENICE

45 ❧ *The Rest on the Flight into Egypt*

Oil on canvas | 96 × 113cm | *c.*1540–5

Provenance: 2nd Marquess of Stafford, Cleveland House, London, by 1808; by inheritance to Francis Egerton, later 1st Earl of Ellesmere, Bridgewater House, London, 1833; by descent to the present owner

EDINBURGH, NATIONAL GALLERY OF SCOTLAND (DUKE OF SUTHERLAND LOAN)

Like Paris Bordon's probably closely contemporary *The Rest on the Flight into Egypt* (cat.no.46), the subject represents a narrative version of Bonifacio's favourite theme of the Holy Family seated in a landscape (see cat.no.31). While resting on their journey into exile in Egypt, the Holy Family encountered the young St John the Baptist, who had already precociously embarked on his career as a hermit. Bonifacio, like Paris, shows the children embracing under the benign supervision of the Virgin; in this case, however, a servant takes charge of the donkey in the background while Joseph rests. The ruins of an antique temple at the right, while reflecting a fashionable taste for picturesque decay, are probably intended to signify the collapse of the pagan order with the coming of Christ, as in Jacopo Bassano's *The Adoration of the Kings* (cat.no.40). The pair of rabbits in the foreground might likewise have been susceptible to symbolic interpretation by contemporaries, but in this instance Bonifacio's motive for including them was probably purely decorative.[1] Entirely characteristic of the painter is the comfortable placidity of his rendering, in contrast to the tortuousness and tension of Bordon's version.

Although Bonifacio's chronology remains problematic, there is general critical agreement that the picture dates from relatively late in his career, probably the early 1540s.[2] The figures are not as robust, and the compositional structure is not as stable as in his Virgin and Child with saints pictures of the late 1520s: his masterpiece in the Louvre; which is now in Los Angeles, but formerly in the collection of Robert Napier at West Shandon, Gareloch (fig.18);[3] or the picture from Dundee in the present exhibition (cat.no.31). In the present painting the figures

have become slimmer and more flaccid, and are subordinated to an undulating compositional rhythm – features that one also finds in Bonifacio's documented *Annunciation* of 1543–4 for the Palazzo dei Camerlenghi (Venice, Galleria dell'Accademia), and in a three-quarter-length version of *The Rest on the Flight into Egypt* now in Adelaide, but formerly in the Campbell of Succoth collection at Garscube (fig.126).[4]

A little-known compositional variant of *The Rest on the Flight into Egypt* from the Lanckoronsky collection in Vienna is now in the Royal Castle in Cracow (fig.127). Although in the past it has been suggested that the Lanckoronsky picture is a later replica,[5] space and form are more clearly articulated than in the present version, which indicates that it is in fact probably the earlier of the two. It remains a matter of debate whether Bonifacio's stylistic tendencies in the 1540s represent an attempt to update his work in response to the spread of central Italian and Emilian Mannerism, or whether they merely correspond to a decline in creative energy in his later years.

When in the Stafford and Bridgewater Galleries in the nineteenth century, the picture was attributed to Bonifacio's master Palma Vecchio.[6] It is almost certainly identical, therefore, with a picture exhibited in 1801–2 at Bryan's Gallery in London, described as a 'Madonna, Infant Christ and St John' by Palma, and as one of a number of 'capital pictures, bought from Paris, principally from Mr Robit's famous collection, and other distinguished cabinets'.[7] Already in 1838, however, Waagen had rejected the attribution to Palma,[8] and by 1903 Bonifacio had been recognised as the work's true author.[9]

Fig.126 | Bonifacio Veronese, *The Rest on the Flight into Egypt*
Adelaide, Art Gallery of South Australia. Formerly in the Campbell of Garscube collection.

Fig.127 | Bonifacio Veronese, *The Rest on the Flight into Egypt*
Cracow, Wawel Castle

Paris Bordon treviso 1500–1571 venice

46 ✻ *The Rest on the Flight into Egypt*

Oil on canvas | 104 × 140.8cm | *c.*1540–50

Provenance: Casa Venier, Venice; Sir Philip Stephens; his sale, Christie's, 17 May 1810 (lot 77, as by Bonifacio Veronese; bought in); by inheritance to Viscount Ranelagh; his sale, Christie's, 16 May 1829 (lot 23, as by Bonifacio), bought by Charles Stirling of Cawder; by descent to Col. W.J. Stirling of Keir; his sale, Sotheby's, 3 July 1963 (lot 44, bought in); acquired from his estate, largely in lieu of inheritance tax, 1996 (acc.no.NG 2561)

EDINBURGH, NATIONAL GALLERY OF SCOTLAND

This painting depicts a variation on the popular theme of the Rest on the Flight into Egypt (see also cat.no.45). According to a legend recounted by late medieval devotional writers such as the Franciscan Pseudo-Bonaventure and the Dominican Domenico Cavalca, St John the Baptist began his career as a hermit in the wilderness while still a child. There he encountered the Holy Family as they travelled to Egypt to escape persecution by Herod.[1] The scene therefore portrays the first affectionate meeting between the infant St John and his cousin Jesus, while the resting Virgin supports herself on a travelling basket, and in the middle-distance Joseph waters his donkey. Part of the attraction of the subject for Venetian painters and patrons was the opportunity it gave for the representation of landscape, and Bordon sets the holy figures against a lushly verdant panorama, full of flowers, streams, woods and meadows, and stretching back to distant mountains on the horizon. To the right, in keeping with the pastoral taste popular since the first decade of the century, a shepherd tends his sheep. Certain elements in the landscape may also have been meant to carry a religious symbolism: just as the sacrificial lamb in the left foreground prefigures Christ's future self-sacrifice on the cross, so the river in the middle-ground may allude to his Baptism by John in the waters of the Jordan.

Stylistically the picture is very different from Bordon's two smaller Virgin and Child with saints pictures of the early 1520s (cat.nos.29, 30), and it probably dates from the 1540s.[2] The heroically-scaled figure of the Virgin has acquired an almost Michelangelesque grandeur, and Bordon's style in general has become less naturalistic and more self-consciously artificial. There is evidence that in 1538 he paid a brief visit to the French court at Fontainebleau, where he would have become acquainted with the courtly mannerist style then in vogue; immediately afterwards, between 1539 and 1541, two leading Florentine mannerist painters, Francesco Salviati and Giorgio Vasari, visited Venice. The adoption here of a high viewpoint and a high horizon, allowing a vista of vast distances, also suggests that Bordon had been studying examples of the so-called world landscapes by Netherlandish painters such as Joachim Patinir, Jan van Scorel and Herri met de Bles, all of whom were well known in Venice.[3]

Bordon's response to these experiences has resulted in a somewhat uncomfortable combination of stylistic elements. The poses of the foreground figures are arranged in a deliberately planar manner, as if to evoke relief sculpture, and despite the extensiveness of the landscape, they are not really integrated with it, but are compressed into a shallow plane in the immediate foreground. Surface pattern is further empha-

sised by the restless wrigglings of the Baptist's scroll and the draperies. The foreground plants have a metallic, ornamental quality that contrasts with the glistening radiance of the background. The preciosity of the Virgin's classical sandal and the golden embroidery of her robe sit uneasily both with her plump sensuousness and the supposed informality of the scene. The lack of documentation for Paris's work in the 1540s makes it difficult to pinpoint the date of the painting more precisely but it certainly precedes the *Baptism* of *c*.1551 (Milan, Pinacoteca di Brera), which marks his return to a softer style, in which figures and landscape are atmospherically more fused.[4]

In 1660 *The Rest on the Flight into Egypt* is recorded with fulsome praise by Marco Boschini in 'Casa Venier',[5] probably the Palazzo Venier at Santi Apostoli, owned by the Venetian nobleman Nicolò di Girolamo Venier (1592–1689).[6] Despite his distinguished political and adminis-

trative career as Procurator of San Marco and Podestà of Bergamo, Venier was apparently not particularly active as a collector, and it is likely that he inherited the picture from a sixteenth-century ancestor.

The pose of the Virgin is repeated exactly, but on a somewhat smaller scale, in a roughly contemporary picture representing *The Holy Family with St John the Baptist* (fig.128).[7] For three hundred years this latter picture shared the same history as Titian's *The Three Ages of Man* (cat.no.15) and *Venus Anadyomene* (cat.no.19), passing through the collections of Queen Christina of Sweden, the Dukes of Orléans and the Earls of Ellesmere, but it was only briefly in Scotland between 1945 and 1961, before being sold abroad in 1976. Another picture by Paris of a very similar subject, style and date, also with a Scottish provenance, is *The Holy Family with St Jerome* (fig.129), formerly in the collection of Lord Gray at Kinfauns Castle, near Perth.[8]

above left Fig.128 | Paris Bordon,
The Holy Family with St John the Baptist
Private Collection. Formerly in the collection of the Earls of Ellesmere.

above right Fig.129 | Paris Bordon,
The Holy Family with St Jerome
London, Simon Dickinson Ltd.
Formerly in the collection of the Barons Gray at Kinfauns Castle, Perthshire

left Fig.130 | Lambert Sustris,
Reclining Venus
Amsterdam, Rijksmuseum

Paris Bordon TREVISO 1500–1571 VENICE

47 ❧ *Reclining Nude*

Oil on canvas | 81 × 67cm | *c*.1537–8

Provenance: Acquired from Foster's, London, by
Francis, Lord Elcho, later 10th Earl of Wemyss;
by descent to the present owner

THE EARL OF WEMYSS AND MARCH KT

Paris Bordon made a lifelong speciality of
painting voluptuously provocative women in
varying states of undress (see also cat.no.48). The
present picture is a fragment, and presumably the
figure was originally represented in full length,
reclining on a couch. From about 1510, following
the example of Giorgione and Titian's *Sleeping
Venus* (Dresden, Gemäldegalerie), reclining nudes
were customarily represented by Venetian
painters in a landscape setting. However, in
1536-8 Titian created a new prototype with his
Venus of Urbino (fig.22), in which the figure was
shown in the more intimate and erotically
suggestive surroundings of a bedroom. Like
Lambert Sustris's *Venus* now in Amsterdam
(fig.130) – a picture that was unsuccessfully
offered for sale by William Buchanan to the Royal
Institution in Edinburgh in 1827[1] – the present
fragment clearly reflects the direct inspiration of
the *Venus of Urbino*. It remains a matter of
controversy whether Titian's picture and its
progeny were meant to represent the goddess of
love herself, or merely an ideally beautiful and
anonymous nude. Another, more prosaic
explanation is that they represent the portraits of
particular courtesans. In the present case, the
sexually explicit way in which the figure fondles
her breast while gazing out at the viewer has
tended to encourage the last interpretation.[2] It
may simply be, however, that Bordon lacked
Titian's power to combine sensuous immediacy
with ideal, poetic beauty.

To judge from its style and pictorial handling,
this *Reclining Nude* was painted very soon after
the *Venus of Urbino*, perhaps as early as 1537–8.[3]
Thus, the Titianesque warmth of the palette and
the simplicity of the pose remain close to
Bordon's key work of the mid-1530s, *The Fisherman Delivering the Ring* (fig.4), and, unlike the
Venetian Women at their Toilet (cat.no.48), do not
yet reflect his adoption of some aspects of
mannerist art, probably prompted by a trip to
Fontainebleau in 1538–9.

The picture was lent by Lord Elcho to the
British Institution in 1855, and a year later
Waagen listed it as one of several acquired by the
owner since 1851.[4] Waagen commented that 'the
head was furnished by a model of uncommon
beauty, which is somewhat marred by an undue
space between the right eye and the nose'.[4] Lord
Elcho, by then 10th Earl of Wemyss, brought the
picture to Scotland, together with the rest of his
collection, in 1890.

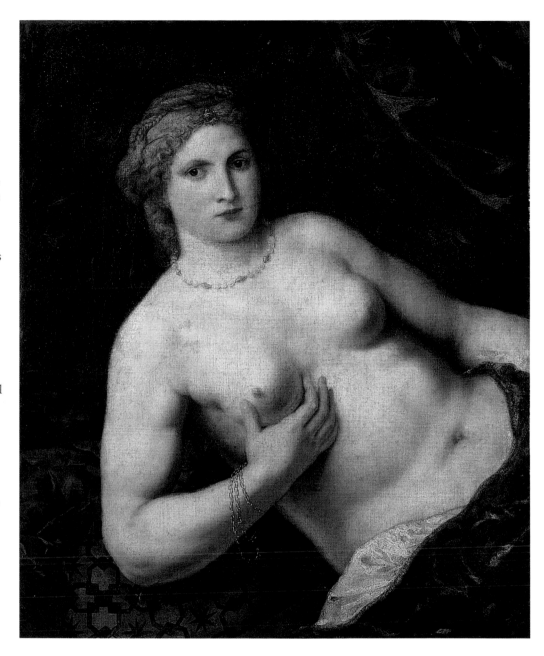

Paris Bordon TREVISO 1500–1571 VENICE

48 ❧ *Venetian Women at their Toilet*

Oil on canvas | 94 × 141cm | *c*.1540–50

Inscribed with a fragmentary signature at the lower left: '[PA]RIS B.'

Provenance: Palazzo Widmann at San Canciano, Venice, by 1648; Cardinal Cristoforo Widmann (died 1660); probably acquired from his estate by Giuseppe Maria Durazzo, Genoa, in 1661; Giovanni Battista Grimaldi, Genoa, by 1788; by inheritance to Marchesa Teresa Grimaldi Pallavicini; from whom purchased by Andrew Wilson on behalf of the Royal Institution, Edinburgh, 1830 (acc.no.NG 10)

EDINBURGH, NATIONAL GALLERY OF SCOTLAND

The two young women in a state of undress are accompanied by an older maidservant, whose swarthy skin, marked with facial tattoos, serves as a foil for their own fair, pink and white complexions. Despite the unrealistic elaborateness of the background architecture, which resembles the façade of a building in the tradition of Pietro Lombardo rather than a domestic interior, the scene is suggestive of the intimacy of a bedchamber. The accessories of feminine toilet – a mirror, an ointment jar and a comb – are spread out in the foreground. Yet the young women are not entirely absorbed in what should be a private activity, and both are clearly conscious of being watched and admired. Only half-covering her nakedness with a silken drapery, the beauty on the right looks archly over her shoulder to meet the gaze of the implicitly male spectator, while her companion in the middle displays herself with even less pretence of modesty.

The picture belongs in the tradition of the half-length 'beautiful woman' (*bella donna*), a type that was made popular in Venice in the second and third decades of the sixteenth century by such painters as Sebastiano del Piombo, Titian and Palma Vecchio (see cat.no.22). The most relevant prototype for Bordon's picture is Titian's *Woman at her Toilet* of *c*.1514 (fig.131), in which a mirror is held up for the central figure by a male admirer while she dresses her hair. However, Titian's eroticism is much more subtle than that of Bordon, and the more blatantly provocative aspects of the *Venetian Women at their Toilet* owe more to the example of Palma Vecchio in the early 1520s: the *Woman in Profile* (Vienna, Kunsthistorisches Museum), who looks coquettishly over her shoulder like Paris's woman;[1] or the so-called *Cortigiana* (Milan, Museo Poldi Pezzoli), who although wearing a fashionable dress, has her chemise open to reveal her naked breasts. Palma also anticipated Bordon in widening the format to include three figures, as in his so-called *Three Sisters* (Dresden, Gemäldegalerie). Palma did not, however, go as far as Bordon in emphasising the genre-like aspect of the 'beautiful woman' type; the younger artist here transformed it into what appears to be a scene from everyday life, set in the boudoir of a pair of Venetian courtesans with their procuress.[2] A type of image that in the art of Titian had provided a focus for male romantic and poetic longings thus became in Paris Bordon's work a source of more straightforward sexual titillation.

In this context it is not easy to decide how far the accessories of toilet are also meant to be read allegorically. The ointment jar, for example, was a standard attribute of Mary Magdalene, the patron saint of courtesans, but its presence here may simply be functional. The mirror may be a vanitas motif, alluding to the transience of

female beauty, but this point could have been made more tellingly if the maidservant, or procuress, had been portrayed as a wrinkled hag instead of as an only slightly older woman. Yet in favour of an allegorical interpretation of the jar and mirror is the consideration that the picture's patron, while doubtless attracted chiefly by the eroticism of the subject, may nevertheless have preferred to retain some sort of moralising message by way of justification.[3] Similarly, the understated allusion to the mythological theme of the toilet of Venus would have provided a welcome dimension of classical erudition.

Usually and convincingly dated to the 1540s,[4] the picture is probably approximately contemporary with Paris's *The Rest on the Flight into Egypt* (cat.no.46), as well as with the *Perseus armed by Mercury and Minerva* (Birmingham, Alabama, Museum of Art)[5] and a number of other mythological-allegorical subjects showing a trio of figures three-quarter length in a broad format. By the 1540s Bordon's style had become much harder and more contortedly linear than in his earlier, more Titianesque period (compare cat.nos.29, 30), partly in response to an exposure to central Italian Mannerism. The frozen rigidity of the pose of the central woman and the Michelangelesque muscularity of her arms continue nevertheless to co-exist with a characteristically Venetian evocation of the softness of her thick-piled, red velvet gown.

The *Venetian Women at their Toilet* is first recorded by Carlo Ridolfi in 1648,[6] in the ornate palace of the nouveau riche Widmann family at San Canciano in Venice, which had recently been rebuilt by Baldassare Longhena. It is again recorded there in an inventory of 1649,[7] but after the death in the following year of Cardinal Cristoforo Widmann, it was apparently sold to the Genoese nobleman, Giuseppe Maria Durazzo.[8] It then reappears in the palace of Giovanni Battista Grimaldi in Genoa at the end of the eighteenth century,[9] before being sold by the Marchesa Grimaldi Pallavicini to Andrew Wilson, acting on behalf of the Royal Institution in Edinburgh.[10] Visiting the Royal Institution in 1851, G.F. Waagen admired 'the animation and luminous flesh tones' typical of Bordon, but judged it to belong 'to his somewhat gaudy works'.[11]

Fig.131 | Titian,
A Woman at her Toilet
Paris, Musée du Louvre

Bonifacio Veronese and workshop VERONA 1487–1553 VENICE
49 🎕 *The Return of the Prodigal Son*

Oil on canvas | 188 × 457cm | *c*.1550

Provenance: Possibly Vincenzo Zen, Venice (by 1648); John Talbot, 16th Earl of Shrewsbury, Alton Towers, Staffordshire (by 1838); Bertram Arthur Talbot, 17th Earl of Shrewsbury; his posthumous sale, Christie's (at Alton Towers), 6 July to 8 August 1857, bought by William, 8th Marquess of Lothian, Newbattle Abbey, Dalkeith; by descent to the present owner

PRIVATE COLLECTION

Christ's parable of the prodigal son (Luke 15: 11–32) describes how the younger son of a rich landowner, having gone abroad and 'wasted his substance with riotous living', was reduced to becoming a swineherd before returning to his father to beg his forgiveness. The landowner is here seen welcoming his abjectly penitent son in the right foreground, while in response to his instructions one fashionably-dressed servant brings the son a ring, and another brings a fresh robe. In the right background more servants kill a fatted calf and make other preparations for the celebratory feast, and musicians gather on the balcony. The figure on horseback in the left background is presumably the elder son, who on returning from work on the estate 'called one of the servants and asked what these things meant'. His reaction was one of natural indignation until he was enjoined by his father likewise to forgive his younger brother and to rejoice in his safe return home. One of the vignettes in the left background, representing a banquet, may refer to the time spent by the prodigal son feasting in the company of harlots.

While the painting is obviously meant to convey a lesson in the Christian virtues of repentance and forgiveness, Bonifacio does not insist on the moral message too sternly. As in another illustration of a parable, the *Dives and Lazarus* of *c*.1535–40 (fig.132), or in another representation of *The Return of the Prodigal Son* by Bonifacio's follower Antonio Palma (Rome, Galleria Borghese),[1] the painter here is equally concerned with celebrating the pleasures of country life on the Venetian *terraferma*. The rich man of the parable is clearly the owner of a magnificent villa, equipped with porticos, loggias, and an extensive terrace with a well-stocked dovecote, and his estate is the setting more for recreational field sports than for serious agriculture. As a decorative tableau full of picturesque accessories and subordinate incident, the painting belongs firmly in the tradition of narrative painting represented in the fifteenth century by Gentile Bellini (fig.1), Carpaccio (fig.11), and more recently by Paris Bordon's

The Fisherman Delivering the Ring of 1534–5 (fig.4).

All of these earlier examples, however, were painted for the meeting-houses of Venice's devotional confraternities, whereas *The Return of the Prodigal Son* was probably painted for the principal reception room on the piano nobile of a Venetian palace. In 1648 Carlo Ridolfi recorded two representations of the subject attributed to Bonifacio in Venetian palaces: 'In the house of the heirs of the Most Serene Doge Erizzo there is the story of the Prodigal Son, and Signor Vincenzo Zen also has a large picture of the same subject, showing all the relevant episodes, and how he was reconciled with his father.'[2] The present picture may well be the version belonging to Zen, probably identifiable as Vincenzo di Zuanne Zen (1614–1659),[3] in which case the smaller picture in the Borghese Gallery now attributed to Antonio Palma may correspond to the Erizzo version.

Bonifacio's works are not always easy to date, but the fashion of the men's costumes suggests that the picture was painted around 1550. At this date, and up to his death in 1553, Bonifacio employed extensive workshop assistance in virtually all of his work; indeed, the quality of the execution here is not on the level of autograph works of a similar kind, such as the *Dives and Lazarus*, or of the *Finding of Moses* of about 1538–40 (Milan, Pinacoteca di Brera). On the other hand, the picture does not closely resemble the independent work of Bonifacio's principal assistant Antonio Palma, who inherited his studio after his death. In Antonio's signed *Resurrection* (Stuttgart, Staatsgalerie), or in his own version of *The Return of the Prodigal Son*, datable to about 1560, the figures adopt more obviously rhetorical gestures, whereas in the present work the poses remain restrained and somewhat stilted. The attribution to

Domenico Capriolo proposed by Bernard
Berenson in 1907 is completely unconvincing.[5]

The picture is first definitely recorded in 1838,
with an attribution to Titian, in the collection of
John, 16th Earl of Shrewsbury, at Alton Towers,
when Waagen recognised it as a 'chef-d'oeuvre'
by Bonifacio.[6] Most of the paintings in the
collection had been acquired by the earl in Rome
in 1829 from the mother of Napoleon, having
previously belonged to his brother Lucien
Bonaparte,[7] and it is possible that this, too, came
from that source. After the death in 1856 of
Bertram, 17th Earl of Shrewsbury, it was
acquired with a group of other Italian pictures by
the 8th Marquess of Lothian, whose wife was a
distant cousin of the Shrewsburys.[8] In 1883
Lothian lent it, together with his *Madonna of the
Siskin* by Dürer (fig.9), to the old master
exhibition at the Royal Institution in
Edinburgh.[9]

Fig.132 | Bonifacio Veronese, *The Parable of Dives and Lazarus*
Venice, Galleria dell'Accademia

Paris Bordon TREVISO 1500–1571 VENICE

50 ❧ *Christ and the Centurion*

Oil on canvas | 194.5 × 305cm | *c*.1555

Provenance: Probably purchased in Venice, 1770–1, by John, 3rd Earl of Bute, for Luton House, Bedfordshire; by descent to the present owner

PRIVATE COLLECTION AT MOUNT STUART, ISLE OF BUTE

Like Schiavone's *The Infancy of Jupiter* (cat.no.56), this large and imposing canvas has never previously been published, and its rediscovery is of exceptional interest, not least because of its unusual subject. This portrays a miracle performed by Christ in Capernaum, as recounted in two of the gospels (Matthew 8: 5–13; Luke 7: 1–10). A Roman centurion, who despite being accustomed to command absolute obedience from his soldiers, humbly begged Christ to heal his sick servant with the words 'Lord, I am not worthy that thou shouldst come under my roof: but speak the word only, and my servant shall be healed.' The painting accordingly shows the centurion at the forefront of his soldiers, kneeling in faith and humility before Christ with his disciples, while the actual miracle of healing takes place off stage. Presumably the classical building in the right background is meant to represent the centurion's house, which he declares is unworthy of the honour of Christ's presence.

One of the very few other large-scale renderings of this subject in Venetian Renaissance painting, that by Paolo Veronese of about 1573 (fig.133), bears a striking compositional resemblance to Bordon's picture, suggesting that the younger artist must have known it. It is all the more surprising, therefore, that the Mount Stuart picture does not appear to be recorded in any early Venetian source, and that nothing is known of its early provenance. Like Veronese's version, which is almost identical in its dimensions and is first recorded in the house of the noble Contarini family in Padua,[1] Bordon's picture was probably painted not for a church, but for the grand, first-floor reception room of a Venetian palace.

Although the dearth of certain dates makes Bordon's chronology problematic, on stylistic grounds the *Christ and the Centurion* seems to fit best with his work of the 1550s. It appears to post-date the self-consciously mannerist works of the 1540s such as *The Rest on the Flight into Egypt* (cat.no.46) and the *Venetian Women at their Toilet* (cat.no.48), but certainly precedes the decadently flaccid style that he practised in the last decade before his death in 1570. The picture is close in style to works of the mid-1550s such as the *Virgin and Child with Four Saints* in the Brera, Milan, or the *St Andrew* altarpiece in the church of San Giobbe, Venice, which share the elongated but still robust proportions of the figures, and the tilting foreground, which makes the figures appear as if dancing on tiptoe. Another painting very close in style is the *Adoration of the Shepherds* of around 1559 in Treviso Cathedral, in which the kneeling pose of the shepherd in the right foreground repeats that of the centurion.[2]

Like the other Venetian pictures from Mount Stuart in the present exhibition (cat.nos.38, 42, 44, 57), the *Christ and the Centurion* was probably acquired by the 3rd Earl of Bute during his visit to Venice of 1770–1.[3] It is listed in the Luton House inventory of 1799,[4] and was later recorded there by Waagen in 1838 and 1854.[5] In 1883 it was lent by the 3rd Marquess to exhibitions of the Bute collection at Bethnal Green and Glasgow.[6]

Fig.133 | Paolo Veronese, *Christ and the Centurion*
Madrid, Museo Nacional del Prado

Workshop of Jacopo Tintoretto VENICE 1519–1594 VENICE

51 ❧ *The Ordeal of Tuccia*

Oil on canvas | 47.6 × 103.2cm | *c*.1555

Provenance: Possibly the Countess of Arundel, before 1654; Archibald McLellan; by whom bequeathed to the museum, 1854 (acc.no.189)

GLASGOW MUSEUMS: KELVINGROVE ART GALLERY AND MUSEUM

Previously interpreted as Salome carrying the head of St John the Baptist, the subject was correctly identified as the story of the Vestal Tuccia at the time of the famous exhibition of Italian Art at the Royal Academy in 1930.[1] As a priestess of the temple of Vesta in ancient Rome, Tuccia was sworn to chastity. When unjustly accused of adultery, she undertook to prove her innocence by miraculously carrying a sieve full of water from the river Tiber back to her temple. Although recounted by several classical authors, the story was probably most familiar to sixteenth-century readers from the version in Petrarch's *Trionfi*, where Tuccia is described as running to the Tiber.[2] In this painting the artist sets the scene in Rome not only by depicting a classical ruin on the right, complete with a statue in a niche and a columned doorway, but by including the celebrated landmark of the Castel Sant'Angelo at the left.

The picture belongs to a sizeable group of small-scale pictures of horizontal format associated with the early career of Tintoretto and representing scenes from biblical or classical history. At the core of the group is a series of Old Testament scenes in the Kunsthistorisches Museum, Vienna, datable to the 1540s, and usually described as *cassone* panels – in other words, as paintings set into dowry chests or other items of domestic furniture. The edifying theme of the present picture would obviously have been appropriate for such a purpose; on the other hand, the fact that it is executed on canvas rather than wood suggests that it is more likely to have

been intended as a wall painting – perhaps as part of a frieze – than set into furniture. In either case, it is likely to have been paired with a representation of the story of Claudia, another Vestal who was forced by her accusers to provide dramatic evidence of her chastity. The format of the painting was originally even longer and narrower, but at some later date the composition was heightened at the top by about a third.[3]

Until the 1920s the Vienna group of panels was attributed to Andrea Schiavone, as was the present picture.[4] Since the Royal Academy exhibition of 1930, however, it has been generally accepted either as an autograph Tintoretto, datable to *c*.1545,[5] or else by a close follower, in which case it might date from up to a decade later. In favour of the latter supposition are the slack draughtsmanship and poorly articulated anatomies, as well as the apparent influence of Veronese in the use of blue draperies with yellow highlights. A possible candidate for this follower is Giovanni Galizzi, to whom a stylistically very similar *Solomon and the Queen of Sheba* (Greenville, SC, Bob Jones University) has recently been attributed.[6] Less convincing is an alternative recent attribution of the present picture to Lambert Sustris.[7]

Although there is no certain record of the picture before it was recorded in the McLellan bequest in 1855,[8] it is possibly identical with one described as showing a 'Roman woman carrying water to the Tiber' by Tintoretto in the inventory of the Countess of Arundel in Amsterdam in 1654.[9]

Jacopo Tintoretto VENICE 1519–1594 VENICE

52 ❧ Portrait of a Bearded Man

Oil on canvas | 36 × 27.2cm | *c.*1550–60

Provenance: Mary Hamilton Campbell, Lady
Ruthven; by whom bequeathed to the Gallery,
1885 (acc.no.NG 689)

EDINBURGH, NATIONAL GALLERY OF
SCOTLAND

The original canvas has been cut down quite
radically, reducing what was presumably at least a
bust-length portrait to leave the head alone.
Probably at the same time the picture was shaped
into an octagon, and the present four corners are
later additions.[1] Despite these vicissitudes, the
condition of the painting is good, and the quality
of the execution high. To judge from the high
collar and glimpse of a crimson robe, the
anonymous sitter was a Venetian patrician and
official, perhaps a senator. Like the Sutherland
portrait (cat.no.53), the picture has been dated to
about 1549–50,[2] but a date later in the 1550s is
equally possible.

Jacopo Tintoretto VENICE 1519–1594 VENICE

53 ❧ *Portrait of a Man*

Oil on canvas | 74.5 × 61.8cm | *c.*1550–5

Provenance: William Coningham; his sale, Christie's, 9 June 1849 (lot 8), bought by Farrer; in the collection of the 1st Earl of Ellesmere, Bridgewater House, London, by 1851; by descent to the 5th Earl of Ellesmere, later the 6th Duke of Sutherland; by inheritance to the 7th Duke of Sutherland. On loan to the Gallery since 1947

EDINBURGH, NATIONAL GALLERY OF SCOTLAND (DUKE OF SUTHERLAND LOAN)

Although the handling is exceptionally sketchy even for Tintoretto, the unknown sitter is clearly dressed in the kind of fur-lined robes worn by Venetian patricians and office-holders, as seen in numerous other portraits by the artist. One of these, the three-quarter-length *Portrait of Lorenzo Soranzo* of 1553 (Vienna, Kunsthistorisches Museum), may provide both an approximate date for the present portrait and an idea of its original format.[1] The canvas has been cut at both sides and at the bottom, and originally the sitter's hands were probably included; given his physical isolation, however, he is unlikely to have formed part of a larger group portrait, as has been suggested.[2] The now very damaged architectural backdrop presumably served mainly as an imposing foil for the sitter, rather than as an accurate description of his spatial surroundings.

Titian PIEVE DI CADORE c.1485/90–1576 VENICE

54 & 55 ❧ Diana and Actaeon and Diana and Callisto

Diana and Actaeon

Oil on canvas | 184.5 × 202.2cm | 1556–9

Diana and Callisto

Oil on canvas | 187 × 204. 5cm | 1556–9

Inscribed: 'TITIANVS . F.'

Provenance (for both paintings): King Philip II of Spain (died 1598); by descent in the Spanish royal collections to King Philip V, Alcázar, Madrid; by whom presented to the French ambassador, Antoine, Duc de Gramont, 1704; by whom presented to Philippe, 2nd Duc d'Orléans (1674–1723); by descent in the Orléans collection at the Palais Royal, Paris, to Louis-Philippe-Joseph, 5th Duc d'Orléans (Philippe Égalité); by whom sold in 1791 to Viscount Walchiers; François de Laborde de Méréville; exhibited for sale at Bryan's Gallery, London, 1798–9 (nos.240 and 249), but reserved for the 3rd Duke of Bridgewater; by inheritance to the 2nd Marquess of Stafford (later 1st Duke of Sutherland), Stafford House, London; by inheritance to Lord Francis Egerton, later 1st Earl of Ellesmere, Bridgewater House, London; by descent to the 7th Duke of Sutherland. On loan to the Gallery since 1945

EDINBURGH, NATIONAL GALLERY OF SCOTLAND (DUKE OF SUTHERLAND LOAN)

These two mythologies, which rank among the supreme poetic creations of Italian Renaissance painting, were painted by Titian for Philip II of Spain between 1556 and 1559. Their completion was announced in a letter sent to Philip in Ghent in June 1559 ('I have finished the two *poesie* intended for Your Majesty, one of Diana surprised by Actaeon at the fountain, another of Callisto's weakness exposed by two nymphs at Diana's bidding').[1] Titian wrote again in September – by which time Philip had left the Netherlands to return to Spain – to inform him of their imminent dispatch, adding that he had laboured on them for more than three years. Together with a third canvas, *The Entombment* (fig.34), the pair were sent from Venice overland to the port of Genoa. From there they were shipped to Cartagena in south-eastern Spain, resuming their journey by road to Philip in Toledo, where they arrived in the autumn of 1560, before travelling on to Madrid.

The two pictures form part of a series of six large-scale mythologies (or *poesie* as Titian called them) that he executed over a ten-year period, following his meeting with Philip during the Imperial Diet held in Augsburg, southern Germany, in the winter of 1550–1. The others in

the series are the *Danaë* and *Venus and Adonis* (both Madrid, Museo Nacional del Prado), the *Perseus and Andromeda* (London, Wallace Collection) and the *Rape of Europa* (Boston, Isabella Stewart Gardner Museum).[4] These four are much more loosely paired than the two *Diana* pictures; although it has sometimes been supposed that the series was conceived from the outset as an iconographically and intellectually coherent cycle, the documentary and visual evidence indicates rather that it evolved piecemeal, according to changing circumstances. A very general theme underlying the series is that of the loves of the Olympian gods, and of the usually tragic consequences for any mortals who became involved with them. Some of the canvases are also linked by secondary themes: thus the present two *Diana* pictures share with the *Venus and Adonis* the theme of hunting. Unlike Titian's earlier series of mythologies, painted for the Duke of Ferrara between 1518 and 1523 (see cat.nos.17, 18; fig.21), the artist was not provided with a written programme by his patron, but was given the exceptional privilege of selecting his own subjects. Unlike some Italian Renaissance painters, Titian was not particularly learned, and he may have relied on his various literary friends in Venice to suggest to him themes suitable for pictorial treatment. But ultimately he remained free to choose themes that particularly fired his imagination, and also to diverge from his literary sources to give the traditional mythological tales a new personal twist.

As earlier in Ferrara, Titian was concerned about how his mythologies would look as an ensemble, and in a letter about the first pair written to Philip in London in September 1554, he speaks of them making 'the chamber in which they are to hang more attractive'. It is not known whether Philip had in mind any particular destination for the series; perhaps, given the hunting theme underlying three of them, he vaguely intended them to decorate one of his hunting palaces, such as Aranjuez or El Pardo. In any case, Titian can only have been referring to 'the chamber' in the most general terms, since from the 1550s all the existing Spanish royal residences underwent extensive refurbishment, and it is highly improbable that he was instructed to design his paintings for a particular physical space.[5] It is not known where the *Diana* pictures were hung during their first years in Spain, but any arrangement is likely to have been provisional, perhaps for several decades. The first mention of a permanent home does not, in fact, occur until 1623, when they are recorded in the king's private apartments in the Alcázar in Madrid.

The principal literary source for both *Diana* pictures is Ovid's *Metamorphoses*, the most popular of all works of classical literature in the

Italian Renaissance and frequently published in translation. In the story of Diana and Actaeon (*Metamorphoses*, III: 138–253), Ovid tells of how the young huntsman Actaeon one day wandered by mistake into a cave sacred to Diana, goddess of the hunt, where she and her nymphs were bathing at a spring. Furious at being discovered naked, Diana transformed the youth into a stag, whereupon he was chased by his own hounds and torn to pieces. Titian imagines the cave as a sort of Renaissance grotto, in which architecture blends with the forms of nature, and the spring as a fountain carved with classicising ornament.

The rusticated pier is surmounted by a stag's head, the trees are hung with deerskins as trophies of the hunt, and in the far distance on the right Diana is seen again, pursuing her prey. The painter chooses a moment of maximum drama, in which Actaeon – instead of wandering hesitantly, as described by Ovid – bursts into the cave, and confronts Diana at the opposite side of the canvas. The fateful confrontation is given an almost comic echo by Diana's lapdog, which yaps at Actaeon's hounds. Diana's black maidservant hurries to cover her mistress, but while some of her nymphs also react with alarm, others remain unaware of the presence of the intruder. The sense of foreboding communicated by the turbulent sky and the violently tilting axes of the composition is further enhanced by the drama of light and shade that plays over the figures, and by the choppy brushwork characteristic of Titian's late style.

In the story of Diana and Callisto (*Metamorphoses*, II: 401–503), the goddess inflicts an only slightly less cruel punishment on her victim. Callisto was one of her nymphs, who although sworn to chastity, was seduced by Jupiter disguised as Diana herself. When her pregnant condition was discovered, the goddess expelled Callisto from her company. Subsequently – as is illustrated in the drawing by Domenico Campagnola (cat.no.88) – Callisto was transformed into a bear by the vengeful Juno, and was later almost hunted to death by her son. Again Titian focuses on a climactic moment in the story when, suspicious of Callisto's unwillingness to undress for a bathe, Diana orders her to be stripped by her companions. Still wearing her red boots, but with her swollen belly humiliatingly exposed, Callisto is seen on the left, struggling vainly with four of her fellow nymphs. One of the reliefs on the fountain at the centre, representing Diana chasing a stag, provides a thematic link with the Actaeon story. Numerous compositional links confirm that the two *Diana* pictures were meant to be hung as pendants, probably with the *Diana and Actaeon* to the left. Thus the descending diagonal of the stream on the left re-ascends on the right, while further answering diagonals are created by the chains of intensely blue

159

mountains and by the curtains slung at the upper corners of each painting.

It seems that Titian's choice of subject in the *Diana* pictures, as well as in the series as a whole, was in large part prompted by an awareness of the natural erotic tastes of a patron who was still a young man. Both *Diana* pictures are bathing scenes that call for extensive displays of female nudity. Titian's power to evoke through the magic of his brush the soft sensuousness of naked female flesh was one of the most admired aspects of his genius, then as now. His selection of these subjects also allowed great scope for a wide range of other effects of atmosphere, light and texture in the representations of elements and materials such as water, glass, fur and fabric. But beyond all this, the painter was clearly also interested in exploring the deeper meanings of his subjects, and the moral questions they raise regarding guilt and innocence, justice and punishment. Diana is the representative of divine law, and the guardian of the virtue of chastity, but did her victims truly deserve to suffer such cruel fates? By arousing feelings of pity and vicarious fear for Actaeon and Callisto, Titian fully engages the emotions as well as the senses of his viewers.

In 1623, the same year in which all six mythologies were first recorded in the palace of the Alcázar in Madrid, the two *Diana* pictures were packed into crates, ready to be presented as diplomatic gifts from Philip IV to the future Charles I of England, who was wooing the Spanish Infanta.[7] But although Charles did take Veronese's *Venus, Cupid and Mars* (cat.no.69) home with him, the *Dianas* were unpacked again when the marriage negotiations foundered. The Roman patron and connoisseur Cassiano dal Pozzo, who visited Madrid three years later in 1626, seems to have been thinking of the *Diana* pictures in particular when he wrote enthusiastically of Titian: 'It should be noted how frequently he gives beauty and vitality to his figures by placing them near some ancient marble on which he paints figures as if carved in bas-relief in the manner of the ancients. He does this to give beauty to his pictures and to give depth to the stories represented in them by his use of colour and chiaroscuro.'[8] Nearly a century later, in 1704, the *Diana* pictures, together with the *Rape of Europa*, were again identified as a suitable diplomatic gift, and on this occasion they did leave Spain for France. Another century later, in 1798, the three *poesie* arrived in England, where the pair of *Dianas* was bought at the famous Orléans sale by the Duke of Bridgewater. Both paintings – separated, however, by the *Three Ages of Man* (cat.no.15) and a number of other pictures – are clearly visible in a photograph taken in about 1900 on the left wall of the Picture Gallery at Bridgewater House in London (fig.76).

Technical Note

Both paintings were restored by Kennedy North in 1933.[9] Unusually for this date, he left very full dossiers documenting their restoration, including X-radiograph mosaics of the complete compositions – an early use of this technique on such a scale – and extensive detail and macro progress photographs of the work.[10] The reports show that he had removed old paste linings that had probably been carried out in the early nineteenth-century, not long after the pictures arrived in England. He relined the paintings using a wax-resin adhesive and liberally coated the surface with wax instead of the usual finishing varnish. He also made a virtue of removing all varnish and repaintings while not adding any restoration of his own to the various minor damages uncovered. Excessive wax adhesive between the canvases, blisters due to loss of adhesion in the lining, and the coarse weave of the lining canvas contributed to severe deformation of the paintings' surfaces. The surface coating of wax became blanched and very grimy which, taken with their structural shortcomings, left the paintings looking quite neglected. (At around the same time, and using similar methods, Kennedy North was restoring Andrea Mantegna's *Triumphs of Caesar* in the Royal Collection, which attracted considerable adverse criticism.[11])

During the most recent restoration, the pictures were relined to remove the superfluous wax and replace the heavy lining canvas with the aim of recovering something of the original surface texture. The original canvases of the two paintings differ markedly in weight, which has an appreciable effect on their appearance.[12] Both are joined vertically in the centre with sewn seams using the usual loom width of canvas for the time of about a metre, and although the original tacking edges have been removed, evidence of weave distortion from the original stretching seen in X-radiographs shows they have been very little reduced in size. It is not clear what importance should be placed on the use of different weight canvases for such closely related works. Certainly, the heavier weight used for *Diana and Actaeon* allowed or encouraged the painter to adopt a much more vigorous handling of paint. The use of heavier paint and the widespread changes in the composition have resulted in pronounced areas of cracking, notably around Actaeon's upraised hand (fig.134) and in the standing nymph seen from behind at the centre of the painting. Alterations to the architectural elements and to the position of the nymph's hand clutching the pillar are now visible due to the increased transparency, with age, of the overlying paint. The inscription of the artist's name on the pillar is in gold.

In contrast *Diana and Callisto*, being much more thinly painted and with many fewer

Fig.134 | Detail of *Diana and Actaeon* showing drying cracks

Fig.136 | Detail of X-radiograph mosaic of *Diana and Callisto* showing the quiver at the lower right

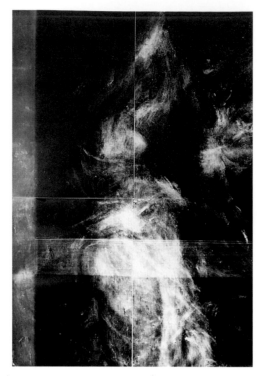

Fig.135 | Detail of X-radiograph mosaic of *Diana and Callisto* showing the nymph at the left

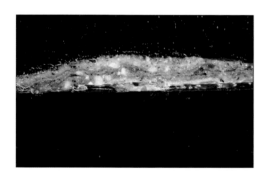

Fig.138 | Cross section of a paint sample taken from *Diana and Actaeon*

Fig.137 | Cross section of a paint sample taken from *Diana and Actaeon*

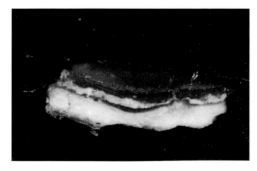

Fig.140 | Cross section of a paint sample taken from *Diana and Callisto*

Fig.139 | Cross section of a paint sample taken from *Diana and Callisto*

alterations in the composition – notable exceptions being the formerly draped figure of the standing nymph at the left (fig.135) and the quiver at lower right, which was originally more or less parallel with the lower edge (fig.136) – has suffered more from loss of paint through abrasion. Titian prepared both paintings with a thin layer of glue-bound gesso which just filled the canvas weave. Due to the thinness of the overlying paint, the ground would have been vulnerable to any aqueous cleaning treatment. This might explain the kind of damage obvious in areas such as Callisto's stomach and, more severely, around Diana's head and across much of her body, which could have occurred relatively early in the painting's history. While damage by abrasion has clearly taken place, the painting must always have been relatively thinly painted and most of the paint surface, notably in the group of nymphs around Callisto and the landscape background generally, is beautifully preserved.

Although Kennedy North stated that he had removed all overpaintings, including drapery from Diana's loins and the inscription of the painter's name, in the *Diana and Callisto* he left the overpainting of Diana's outstretched hand and forearm. This overpainting was also left during the most recent restoration, as there appears to be little of the original paint beneath.

Paint sample cross sections all show the white gesso ground modified by a brown translucent layer, which may be either an *imprimatura* or the artist's initial lay-in. Some of them, such as this typically complex sample taken from the sky near Actaeon's hand (fig.137), reveal multiple layers of paint which reflect the superimposition of successive alterations to the composition rather than the use elaborate layer structures *per se*. A paint sample (fig.138), taken from the lilac-blue drapery of the seated nymph at the left of *Diana and Actaeon* demonstrates how the artist subtly altered colours by varying the proportions of pigments, in this case ultramarine and organic red. Two more samples further illustrate the quality of the pigments Titian used: one (fig.139) shows relatively large particles of malachite, a pigment used in both *Diana* paintings which has also been identified in the *Bacchus and Ariadne* (fig.21);[13] the other (fig.140), taken from the attendant nymph behind the goddess in *Diana and Callisto*, is a fine example of a well-preserved crimson glaze. JD

Andrea Schiavone ZARA(?) (ZADAR) *c*.1510–1563 VENICE

56 ❧ *The Infancy of Jupiter*

Oil on canvas | 181 × 252cm | *c*.1560

Provenance: Henry, 5th Earl of Mulgrave (1755–1831); his posthumous sale, Christie's, 12 May 1832 (lot 47); purchased by Francis, Lord Elcho (later 10th Earl of Wemyss), through the dealer Hickman, *c*.1851–5; by descent to the present owner

THE EARL OF WEMYSS AND MARCH KT

This previously unpublished picture represents a major addition to the oeuvre of Schiavone, and is of special importance as his largest known mythological work. According to ancient legend, Jupiter was the last-born son of the Titan Cronus who, having been warned by an oracle that his son would dethrone him, sought to destroy the infant. To save Jupiter from his father, his mother Rhea entrusted him to the care of the nymphs and the goat Amalthea, who suckled him, while the Curetes, a band of noisy spirits, performed dances so that Cronus would not hear the infant crying. In the frieze-like foreground, the painter shows the infant Jupiter with Amalthea and the nymphs to the left, and the Curetes – playing

Renaissance *viole da gamba* and a recorder – making music on the right. In the left background Rhea is to be seen delivering the child to a nymph under an antique-style portico.

The Infancy of Jupiter is datable to late in the artist's career, and was probably painted shortly before his death in 1563. Compared with his next largest mythology, the *Judgement of Midas* of *c*.1548–50 (Hampton Court, Royal Collection),[1] Schiavone's early interest in the refined elegance of Parmigianino has receded under the impact of the more heroic style of Titian, and in particular the series of mythologies for Philip II of Spain (see cat.nos.54, 55). Schiavone was evidently greatly impressed by the *Diana and Actaeon*, for he painted a number of variants of it. Echoes of Titian's composition are scarcely less evident in *The Infancy of Jupiter* – for example in the atmospheric blending of architecture and foliage in the left background, and in the dramatically descending chain of mountains on the right. Another unmistakable borrowing from the work of Titian in the 1550s is the motif of the nymph on the far right, who holds up a dish in the manner of Titian's *Salome* of about 1555 (Madrid, Museo Nacional del Prado) and its many derivatives.

Consistent with a dating of *The Infancy of Jupiter* to about 1560 is its compositional and stylistic similarity to Schiavone's thematically related *Infant Bacchus and the Nymphs* (formerly Venice, Brass Collection), which has been dated to the same period.[3]

It is odd that there apparently exists no early reference to this ambitious picture. It is first recorded only in 1832, when it was lent to the British Institution by the Countess of Mulgrave;[4] it is clearly visible above the doorway in A.J. Woolmer's painted view of that exhibition (fig.68). Two decades later it is listed by Waagen among the pictures purchased by Lord Elcho between the German scholar's visits to London of 1851 and 1856, and is described by him as 'one of the most important pictures I know by Schiavone'.[5] Waagen went on to observe that 'Like other Venetian painters he was no adept in the difficult task of depicting the human foot, so that in this picture no feet are visible.' During the cleaning of the picture undertaken for the present exhibition, however, it was discovered that none of the plants that previously covered each of the feet was original, and they have now been removed.

Paolo Veronese VERONA 1528–1588 VENICE

57 ❧ The Mystic Marriage of St Catherine

Oil on canvas | 97.7 × 161.2cm | *c*.1555

Provenance: Probably purchased in Venice, 1770–1, by John, 3rd Earl of Bute; by descent to the present owner

PRIVATE COLLECTION AT MOUNT STUART, ISLE OF BUTE

In the best-loved subject associated with Catherine, Princess of Alexandria, the Christ Child tenderly places a ring on the ring finger of her left hand. Accompanying the Holy Family are the Infant Baptist, and a matriarchal figure probably to be identified as the Virgin's mother Anne.

Previously published only once,[1] the Bute picture is clearly an autograph work by Veronese of high quality, probably dating from soon after he settled in Venice in 1553. The sensitively and fluently executed figure of Catherine, with the *changeant* colour effects in her draperies, is particularly close to his ceiling paintings in the sacristy and nave of San Sebastiano (1555–6). This dating invites a reassessment of the picture's relationship with two other versions of the subject associated with Veronese: one on loan to the Yale University Art Gallery (fig.141), and now generally agreed to date from very early in the painter's career of about 1547, before his move from his native Verona to Venice; the other is now in the National Museum of Western Art, Tokyo (fig.142). The composition of the Bute picture bears a general resemblance, in reverse, to that at Yale, but in style it is somewhat more mature, and may be regarded a a slightly later rethinking by the painter of his earlier work. The Tokyo picture, which is less accomplished in its execution than the other two (compare the respective figures of Catherine), has sometimes been attributed for that reason to Veronese's compatriot and former colleague Giovanni Battista Zelotti, and has been interpreted as a laboured variant of the Yale picture, also dating from the late 1540s.[3] But Zelotti was never so compositionally and stylistically dependent on Veronese, and in any case, the Tokyo picture resembles the Bute picture much more closely than the one at Yale. It is more reasonable, therefore, to regard the Tokyo picture as a derivation from the Bute picture, perhaps dating from the late 1550s, and executed in part by an assistant – possibly Veronese's younger brother

Benedetto (born 1538), who is documented as an assistant at San Sebastiano in 1556. Certain aspects of the Bute picture, notably the pose of the Christ Child and the foreshortened lamb, are then repeated in a *Holy Family with the Infant Baptist* (Venice, S. Maria dei Carmini), likewise datable to the later 1550s.[4]

The picture is first certainly documented in a 1799 inventory of the Bute collection,[5] and was probably acquired by the 3rd Earl during his stay in Venice of 1770–1[6]. It was recorded at Luton House by Waagen in 1838,[7] and was exhibited with other works from the Bute collection at the museums of Bethnal Green and Glasgow in 1883.[8]

Fig.141 | Paolo Veronese, *The Mystic Marriage of St Catherine*
New Haven, Yale University Art Gallery (on loan from the Barker Welfare Foundation)

Fig.142 | Paolo Veronese, *The Mystic Marriage of St Catherine*
Tokyo, National Museum of Western Art

Paolo Veronese VERONA 1528–1588 VENICE

58 ❧ *The Adoration of the Shepherds*

Oil on canvas | 95.2 × 115.5cm | *c*.1563–5

Provenance: Cardinal Mazarin, Paris, by 1653; in the possession of his heirs until at least 1714; Louis Fagon, Paris; Pierre Crozat; his sale, Hôtel d'Aligre, 15 March 1779 (lot 18); 4th Earl of Aberdeen, Argyll House, London, by 1816; by descent to the 4th Marquess of Aberdeen and Temair, Haddo House, Aberdeenshire; sale Christie's, London, 1 July 1966 (lot 57); sale, Christie's, London, 29 November 1974 (lot 70)

ON LOAN FROM A PRIVATE COLLECTION, CARE OF THE ASHMOLEAN MUSEUM, OXFORD

As in Jacopo Bassano's slightly earlier *Adoration of the Kings* (cat.no.40), the worshippers at Christ's Nativity are joined by the traditional ox (or rather, cow) and ass, Joseph stands protectively behind the Virgin, and the presence of delapidated antique columns amidst the rustic wooden structure of the stable refers to the imminent collapse of the pagan order with the coming of Christ. In a gesture reminiscent of that of Raphael's *Madonna of Loreto* (Chantilly, Musée Condé), but probably here inspired more directly by a recent *The Adoration of the Shepherds* by Bassano (Rome, Galleria Nazionale d'Arte Antica, Palazzo Corsini; fig.143), the Virgin holds up Christ's sheet to reveal him to the arriving shepherds.

A fine autograph work of Veronese's middle career, the picture represents a variant, intended for private devotion, of two of his much larger-scale versions of the subject: one painted for the chapel of the silk-weavers in Santa Maria dei Crociferi, the other for the ceiling of Santa Maria dell'Umiltà (both are now in the chapel of the Rosary, Santi Giovanni e Paolo, Venice). None of the three is dated, but there is circumstantial evidence for supposing that the Umiltà ceiling – from which the idea of framing the Madonna group with the head of the cow and the kneeling shepherd appears to derive – was executed around 1557–60.[1] Unlike the grander and more formal ceiling painting, the present painting also appears to be responsive to Bassano's version of the subject, which is datable to around 1562. As well as quoting the gesture of the Virgin, Veronese adopts a similar intimacy of man and beast, with the cow nuzzling up to the Christ Child. Like Veronese, Bassano was working for the church of the Umiltà in these very years, and because Bassano was an acknowledged expert in bucolic subjects involving rustic figures and farm animals, Veronese may very well have looked to this very picture, probably painted for a Venetian patron, for inspiration in his own treatment of the theme.[2]

The picture is first recorded in the collection of Cardinal Mazarin (1602–1661) in Paris in 1653. Although the cardinal owned a large number of Venetian paintings, which he imported from Venice throughout the 1640s, little is known of his sources of supply. The picture evidently enjoyed some fame in France, since the sculptor Bernini saw a copy of it in another Parisian palace in 1665, and it was engraved when in the collection of Pierre Crozat in the early eighteenth century.[3] It is first recorded in Britain in 1816,[4] when it was lent to the British Institution in London by the 4th Earl of Aberdeen (1784–1860); he may have acquired it in Paris in 1802 when undertaking his Grand Tour, but more probably in a London saleroom. Lord Aberdeen again lent the picture to the British Institution (of which he was later President) in 1832 and 1836; and it is clearly visible of the left wall in A.J. Woolmer's painted record of the 1832 exhibition (fig.68).

Fig.143 | Jacopo Bassano, *The Adoration of Shepherds*
Rome, Palazzo Corsini, Galleria Nazionale d'Arte Antica

Paolo Veronese VERONA 1528–1588 VENICE

59 ❧ St Anthony Abbot with a Kneeling Donor

Oil on canvas | 198.5 × 117.8cm | c.1565

Provenance: Lendinara (Rovigo), Church of San Francesco, Petrobelli altar, until between 1769 and 1782; William Comyns; his sale, Christie's, London, 6 May 1815 (lot 61), bought by the 2nd Marquess of Stafford (later 1st Duke of Sutherland); Sutherland sale, Christie's, London, 11 July 1913 (lot 94), bought by the National Gallery of Scotland (acc.no.NG 1139)

EDINBURGH, NATIONAL GALLERY OF SCOTLAND

This fragment from a much larger composition shows a kneeling donor, probably Antonio Petrobelli of Lendinara, accompanied by his name-saint, Anthony Abbot. Although Anthony is dressed as an abbot with a crozier rather than in his more usual guise as a humble hermit, he is clearly identifiable by his attributes of a bell (to drive away evil spirits) and a pig (symbolising animal lusts). The device on his *mozzetta* (cape) is probably meant to be read as a capital T, an allusion to the saint's usual T-headed staff. At an

early stage in the evolution of the design, Veronese posed the saint in a more upright position, as is clearly evident from a pentimento behind his head.

On the basis of this and two other surviving fragments of the altarpiece, a *St Jerome with a Donor* at Dulwich (fig.144) and a *Pietà* in the National Gallery of Canada, Ottawa, it has been possible to reconstruct the approximate original appearance of the composition, which would have measured an enormous fifteen feet in height (fig.145).[1] The central, and originally principal figure of the Archangel Michael triumphing over a demon was evidently sacrificed when the painting was removed from its altar in the late eighteenth century and dismembered to create three separate pictures for the art market. The fragmentary parts of St Michael and the demon in the two lower fragments were probably painted out at this time; the archangel's right arm and wing and the demon's left leg were uncovered during the restoration of the Edinburgh canvas in 1958. An idea of the original appearance of the painted architecture, (a semi-circular colonnade of fluted Ionic columns supporting an entablature and set against a background of cloud-streaked sky and silhouetted foliage) is provided by Veronese's late *Annunciation* in Torcello, as well as by an obviously

derivative altarpiece of *St Anne* by his son Gabriele (Liettoli, Parish Church).

The painting was recorded in place above the Petrobelli altar in the church of San Francesco in Lendinara, near Rovigo, by two local historians, Gioacchino Masatto and Francesco Bartoli, shortly before the Franciscan convent was suppressed and the church closed in 1769.[2] According to Masatto, 'on the other altar at the end of the church there is a panel representing at the top the dead Redeemer supported by angels, and below the Archangel Michael in the act of trampling on Lucifer, in the middle of various saints with some portraits. This grandiose work was done by Paolo Veronese in 1565.'[3] An inventory of the church completed in the year of its closure transcribes an inscription at the altar recording that, together with the adjacent sepulchre, it was founded in 1563 by Antonio and Girolamo Petrobelli.[4] Not long afterwards, in 1782, the church and convent were demolished, and thirteen years later another local historian, Pietro Brandolese, commented on the lost altarpiece. He described it as the noble picture once on 'the grandiose and magnificent altar of the noble Petrobelli family . . . Signor Bartoli was convinced that it was by Paolo Veronese and painted in the year 1565; perhaps he deduced this from the date carved on the frieze above the altar table.'[5]

The Petrobelli family, which emigrated from the region of Bergamo to Lendinara around the beginning of the sixteenth century, was one of the wealthiest and most prominent families in the town.[6] As emerges from his will dated 22 December 1569, Antonio Petrobelli was the owner of extensive landed property and livestock; being childless, he named his uncle Girolamo as his universal heir.[7] In the same document Antonio expressed his wish to be buried in front of his altar in the church of San Francesco. The fact that he left an annual sum to the parish of San Michele in Valle Imagna, north west of Bergamo – presumably the village from which his family originated – explains the choice of the dedication of the Petrobelli altar to St Michael. Antonio probably died shortly after making his will; certainly there is no mention of him in his uncle's will, dated 2 March 1587.[8] Girolamo likewise asked to be buried in the family tomb in San Francesco, and made provision for the celebration of a weekly mass at their altar, in perpetuity, for his soul and those of his forebears. By combining the images of the dead Christ, of the Archangel vanquishing the forces of evil and weighing souls in the balance, and of protective name-saints, the altarpiece would have served as an entirely appropriate visual complement to this weekly ceremony.

Brandolese may have been correct in surmising that Masatto and Bartoli inferred their date of 1565 for Veronese's painting from the 1563

Fig.144 | Paolo Veronese, *St Jerome with a Donor* London, Dulwich Picture Gallery

Fig.145 | Graphic reconstruction of the Petrobelli Altarpiece Drawn by Linda Murray

inscription. If so, it is not necessarily reliable, since altarpieces could often be installed years after the erection of their respective altars. The surviving fragments have often, in fact, been dated to the early 1580s, largely because of the iconographic resemblance of the Pietà group in the apex to a similar airborne group in Veronese's *St James* altarpiece of about -1580–2 in San Zulian, Venice.[9] Yet this and other late works by the painter show a deeper, duskier palette and more broken brushwork than the Petrobelli fragments, which exhibit the silvery tonality of his works of the 1560s. It seems likely, in fact, that the painting was indeed commissioned at the time of the foundation of the altar in 1563, and was executed soon afterwards, during the lifetime of Antonio. Stylistically consistent with this dating is the motif of the soaring white fluted columns, which regularly appear in Veronese's work of the 1560s, but which by the 1580s tended to be replaced with columns of rich, polychrome marble.[10] A dating to about 1565 would preclude the participation of either of Veronese's sons, Carletto and Gabriele, neither of whom was born until the late 1560s.[11] The quality of the Edinburgh and Dulwich fragments is in any case high, and contrary to what is often supposed, any workshop assistance is likely to have been limited to the upper part of the composition and the architecture.

In a letter to Pietro Brandolese of 1795, the Venetian collector and dealer Giovanni Maria Sasso deplored the fate of the picture, which because of its large size and static composition had failed to find a buyer on the local art market. So 'it was dismembered and sold in quarters, like butcher's meat', he wrote.[12] All three buyers of the principal fragments were British: Colonel John Campbell (who bought the *Pietà*); the painter Gavin Hamilton, who was also active as a dealer; and an unnamed Englishman. The Dulwich fragment is already recorded in London in the same year, as part of the collection assembled by Noel Desenfans for the King of Poland; it is not clear, however, whether it was this or the Edinburgh fragment that passed through the hands of Gavin Hamilton. In any case, after being acquired from the sale of the dealer Comyns by the 2nd Marquess of Stafford in 1815,[13] the *St Anthony Abbot with a Kneeling Donor* remained at York (later Stafford) House in London for the rest of the nineteenth century,[14] and did not reach Scotland until after it had been sold from the Sutherland collection in 1913.

Giovanni Battista Moroni ALBINO (BERGAMO) 1520/4–1578 ALBINO

60 ❧ Portrait of Don Gabriel de la Cueva, later Duke of Alburquerque

Oil on canvas | 112 × 84cm | 1560

Inscribed on the pedestal: 'AQUI ESTO SIN TEMOR / Y DELA MUERTE / NO HE PAVOR. / M.D.LX / Jo. Bap. Moronus p.' (Here I stand without fear, and of death I have no terror. 1560. Giovanni Battista Moroni painted it)

Provenance: Count Teodoro Lechi, Brescia, by 1812; acquired from his estate by James Irvine for Sir William Forbes of Pitsligo, 1827; by inheritance to Sir John Forbes; Forbes sale, Rainy, London, 2 June 1842 (lot 24), bought by Amery; King William II of the Netherlands, by 1843; his sale, The Hague, 1850, bought by Niewenhuys; the Earls of Warwick, Warwick Castle; Warwick sale, Sotheby's, 13 July 1977 (lot 44), bought by Agnew's; from whom purchased by the Museum, 1979

BERLIN, STAATLICHE MUSEEN, GEMÄLDEGALERIE

Fig.146 | After Giovanni Battista Moroni, *Portrait of Don Gabriel de la Cueva, later Duke of Alburquerque* Solingen, Deutsches Klingenmuseum

Moroni here represents one of the most aristocratic of all his sitters with a masterly balance of richness and restraint. The magnificence of the slashed sleeves, of the elaborately tailored breeches, and of the delicately embroidered collar and cuffs - all in different shades of coral pink - is offset by the sober black of the doublet and cap, and especially by the geometric simplicity of the cool, grey architectural backdrop. In his earlier portraits Moroni frequently posed his sitters against classical architecture in a state of picturesque decay, often invaded by vegetation; here the architectural elements have become almost abstract, and are reduced to a simple, rectilinear grid that echoes and further stabilises the severely vertical pose. The sword and gloves serve as further attributes of nobility, and likewise in keeping with the sitter's elevated rank is his guarded, aloof, even somewhat hostile expression. All of this contrasts with the relaxed elegance with which Titian habitually endowed his princely sitters. Moroni's handling of paint is also characteristically tighter and drier than that of Titian.

Moroni included Spanish mottos in at least two of his other portraits painted around 1560, the more famous of which is the so-called *Knight in Pink* (*Gian Gerolamo Grumelli*) in the Palazzo Moroni, Bergamo.[1] But in these the sitters were Hispanophile members of the provincial Bergamask nobility, whereas the present sitter was a member of a prominent noble family of Castile. Don Gabriel de la Cueva y Girón (1525–71), Count of Ledesma and Huelma, was appointed governor of the kingdom of Navarre in 1560, succeeded his brother as 5th Duke of Alburquerque in 1563, and became governor of Milan in 1564. Although his concern in this last post to maintain the power and prestige of the Spanish crown was to cause tension between himself and the zealous reforming Archbishop of Milan, Carlo Borromeo, Cueva was deeply religious, and was no less committed than Borromeo to the cause of ecclesiastical reform.[2]

Moroni's sitter is identified as Cueva on the basis of a copy now in the Deutsches Klingenmuseum, Solingen (fig.146), which amplifies Moroni's inscription with the words 'El Duque y Conde', and which carries a long Italian inscription on the reverse listing all Cueva's titles. Although the copy slightly subverts the severity of Moroni's composition by introducing a hat badge with a pendant pearl, and by providing the pilaster with relief ornament and a base, it appears to date from not long after the original, and the fact that the Spanish motto was certainly used by the Cueva family confirms the reliability of the information given by the Italian inscription. The sitter's features are also consistent with those of Cueva recorded on a medal by Pietro Paolo Galeotti, struck when, as Duke of

Alburquerque, he was governor of Milan. It is odd, nevertheless, that the painter does not show him wearing his insignia as knight of the Order of Alcántara, with which he was invested in 1543, and it is odd, too, that the date on the copy is 1559 rather than 1560. Nothing is known of the circumstances under which Cueva sat to Moroni. But perhaps he visited Milan, or even Bergamo, where the painter was based, in 1559 immediately before becoming governor of Navarre; in this case, the inscription on the original portrait in Berlin might record the date of completion.[3]

The identity of the sitter had been forgotten by 1812, when Moroni's portrait was described as being of a 'Portuguese Warrior' in the distinguished collection of the Napoleonic general Teodoro Lechi in Brescia.[4] According to the catalogue of the collection of a subsequent owner, King William II of Holland, Lechi had acquired the picture in Genoa,[5] a city with a long history of close contacts with Spain. It was bought from Lechi's estate in 1827, together with Veronese's *The Martyrdom and Last Communion of St Lucy* (cat.no.71) and another portrait by Moroni – the *Lawyer* in the National Gallery, London – by James Irvine on behalf of Sir William Forbes of Pitsligo. In a letter of 10 July to Forbes in Paris, Irvine compared the portrait favourably with the so-called *Titian's Schoolmaster*, then in the collection of the Marquess of Stafford, and the most famous Moroni in Britain: 'This is the more imposing picture and full of character. He leans on a pedestal on which there is an inscription in Portuguese or Spanish, which is then translated in the printed catalogue, under which is the name of the painter and the date. He is dressed in crimson and black.' Five months later, on 19 December, Irvine wrote to Forbes, by then back in Scotland, suggesting that he ship his purchases from the Lechi collection from Leghorn to Leith by way of Rotterdam rather than London, as a way of incurring lower customs duties.[6] However, Forbes died before his pictures arrived, and both his Moronis were sold by his son in 1842.[7] After its brief ownership by the Dutch king, the painting belonged to the Earls of Warwick at Warwick Castle, before being bought by the Berlin gallery in 1979.

AQVI ESTO SIN TEMOR
Y DELA MVERTE.
NO HE PAVOR.

M · D · LX ·

Io: Bap. Moronus. p.

Giovanni Battista Moroni ALBINO (BERGAMO) 1520/4–1578 ALBINO

61 ❧ *Portrait of a Man*

Oil on canvas | 98 × 24cm | 1561

Inscribed on the column: 'M.D.LXI / Io. Bap. Moronus p.'; and on the letter: 'Mag.[nifico] … Dottor(?) Brescia(?)'

Provenance: Alexander, 10th Duke of Hamilton, Hamilton Palace, by 1851; Hamilton Palace sale, Christie's, 1882 (lot 719), bought by Viscount Powerscourt; Earl of Portarlington; Robert Langton Douglas, London; Marcel Nicolle, Paris, before 1920; private collection, Denmark, by 1920; Trotti, Paris; Ehrich Gallery, New York, 1933; Agosti and Mendoza collections sale, Galleria Pesaro, Milan, 1936 (lot 322, bought in); Stramezzi collection, Crema, 1937; private collection, Düsseldorf, 1938; by descent to the present owner

PRIVATE COLLECTION

With its simplicity of pose and setting and its subdued colour range, this portrait of an unknown sitter marks a moment of transition from Moroni's earlier, more flamboyant style to the subtly modulated monochromatism of his late career. The truncated marble column which serves as an arm-rest is a motif adopted from the slightly earlier portrait of *Canon Lodovico Terzi* in the National Gallery, London, and may be seen as a vestige of the type of ruined classical architecture that so often accompanied Moroni's more aristocratic sitters of the 1550s. As in his later portraits of scholars and priests, the setting here is more neutral, with the head emphasised by a glow of light. In common with many of Moroni's portraits, the head here appears rather too large for the body – the result, perhaps, of the two parts having been studied separately.[1] There is no clear indication of the sitter's profession or social rank. It may be noted, however, that although sober in colour, his costume is extremely expensive in its elaborate tailoring and its lavish use of fur trimming.

The earliest reference to the portrait is by Waagen, who noted it on his visit to Hamilton Palace in 1851.[2] After being acquired from the Hamilton Palace sale in 1882 by Lord Powerscourt, it was lent by him to the exhibition of Venetian art at the New Gallery, London, in 1894–5. In 1920 it was lent from a Danish private collection to an exhibition at the Statens Museum for Kunst, Copenhagen.[3] Thereafter it has remained in private hands, and has rarely been seen in public.[4]

Giovanni Battista Moroni   ALBINO (BERGAMO) 1520/4–1578 ALBINO

62 ❧ *Portrait of Giovanni Bressani*

Oil on canvas | 116.2 × 88.8cm | 1562

Inscribed on the inkwell: 'IO. BAP. MORON. / PINXIT QUEM NON VIDIT, (Giovanni Battista Moroni painted him whom he did not see); and on the sheet of paper at lower centre: 'CORPORIS EFFIGIEM ISTA QUIVEM BENE ACTA TABELLA / EXPRIMIT, AST ANIMA TOT MEA SCRIPTA MEI. / M.D.LXII.' (This painted picture well depicts the image of my body, but that of my spirit is given by my many writings. 1562).

Provenance: Count Giambattista Zanchi, Bergamo, by *c.*1760; from whom acquired by Girolamo Manfrin, Venice, 1785; purchased from the Manfrin collection by Alexander Barker, probably in 1856; by whom sold to Baron Meyer de Rothschild, Mentmore, Buckinghamshire, by 1860; by inheritance to his daughter Hannah de Rothschild, and to her heirs, the 5th and 6th Earls of Rosebery, Mentmore; Mentmore sale, Sotheby's, 5 May 1977 (lot 2049), but withdrawn from the sale and purchased by private treaty by the Gallery (acc.no.NG 2347)

EDINBURGH, NATIONAL GALLERY OF SCOTLAND

Fig.147 | Arsensio, *Portrait Medal of Giovanni Bressani* Bergamo, Accademia Carrara

Although the two inscriptions look too crude to be autograph, they probably date from soon after the execution of the picture, and there is no reason to question the validity of the information they provide. Without identifying the sitter directly, they confirm that he was a writer, and imply that he had already died before Moroni painted the portrait in 1562. When it was in the collection of Count Zanchi in the late eighteenth century, the sitter was mistakenly identified as the owner's ancestor, Giovanni Crisostomo Zanchi, who did not die until 1566.[1] Only in 1979 was the sitter's identity correctly estab-

lished, on the basis of a medal struck in 1561 (fig.147), as the Bergamask humanist and poet Giovanni Bressani, who had died the previous year.[2]

Giovanni Bressani (1489/90–1560) was the dominant literary figure in sixteenth-century Bergamo, and his prolific output included thousands of verses in Latin, Italian and local dialect, as well as novellas and other prose works.[3] He was the friend and mentor of other local poets, including the noblewomen Isotta Brembate and Lucia Albani, both of whose portraits had been painted by Moroni.[4] When

173

CORPORIS EFFIGIEM ISTA QVIDEM BENE PICTA TABELLA
EXPRIMIT, AST ANIMI TOT MEA SCRIPTA MEI.
M.D.LXII.

School of the Veneto
63 ❧ *Portrait of a Lady*

he died the members of his literary circle collaborated to produce a collection of funerary verses in his honour; presumably both the portrait medal of 1561, signed by the otherwise little-known medallist Arsensio,[5] and the present portrait painted by Moroni, were similarly commissioned as posthumous tributes by the same group of friends, pupils and admirers.

The compositional formula used for this portrait is based on one that Moroni had devised some two years previously for another man of letters, the so-called *Portrait of a Magistrate* of 1560 (fig.41), and he was frequently to adapt it throughout the 1560s and early 1570s, especially for representations of soberly-clad men of contemplation. Bressani is shown in three-quarter length, seated on a chair placed at right angles to the picture plane, and turning his head to meet the eyes of the spectator. As in the *Portrait of a Magistrate*, the colour range is characteristically cool and restrained, and consists essentially of blacks, whites and subtly modulated greys. Apart from the telling touch of coral-pink in the fringes on the chair-back, these muted tones are enlivened simply by the ivories of the book-bindings and the flesh, and by the olive-green of the table-cloth. But the pose and expression are rather less spontaneous than in the *Portrait of a Magistrate*, and much less so than in later examples of the type, such as the celebrated *Titian's Schoolmaster* of about 1570 (Washington, National Gallery of Art).[6] The figure of Bressani is also smaller in relation to the picture field than in these other portraits, and much greater emphasis is given to the still-life detail, in a way that recalls the Netherlandish tradition of representing scholars in their studies. The objects on the table include a bronze inkwell in the form of a foot, of a type inspired by ancient Roman lamps,[7] and a container for sand with which to dry the ink, in addition to the plenitude of books and papers. While obviously appropriate to Bressani's profession, these objects push the sitter back into space, making him more remote, and further reducing the effect of psychological immediacy that is usually so pronounced in Moroni's portraits. It is as if the painter, while aiming to provide Bressani's friends with a vivid likeness with which to remember him, also wished to create an effect of repose and distance appropriate to a posthumous image.[8]

After Girolamo Manfrin had acquired the picture for his famous collection in Venice in 1785,[9] it was quickly forgotten that the sitter was even a Bergamask, and by the mid-nineteenth century he was romantically identified as Michelangelo.[10]

Oil on canvas | 55 × 45.5cm | *c*.1565–70

Provenance: Probably purchased by Alexander William, Lord Lindsay, later 25th Earl of Crawford and 8th Earl of Balcarres

PRIVATE COLLECTION

The traditional attribution of this sensitive and unpretentious portrait to Jacopo Bassano is not supported by comparison with the few certain portraits by him, but no convincing alternative has been advanced.[1] From the evidence of the costume, its date may be narrowed down to about 1565–70.[2] Possible candidates for its author might be Giovanni Antonio Fasolo (*c*.1530–1572),[3] working in Vicenza, or the Paduan Francesco Apollodoro (*c*.1531–1612).[4]

64 ❧ An Allegory of Prudence

Oil on canvas | 75.5 × 68.4cm | c.1560–70

Inscribed at upper left: 'EX PRAETE / RITO'; at upper centre: 'PRAESENS PRVDEN / TER AGIT'; and at upper right: 'NI FVTVRV[M] / ACTIONE[M] DE / TVRPET' ('From the [experience of the] past, the present acts prudently, lest it spoil future action').[1]

Provenance: Pierre Crozat, Paris, by 1740; Duc de Tallard, Paris; his sale, Remy et Glomy, Paris, 22 March to 7 May 1756 (lot 84); Chevalier Menabuoni, by 1766; Lucien Bonaparte, Rome; his sales, Christie's, London, 6 February 1815 (lot 119, bought in) and Stanley, London, 16 May 1816 (lot 167, bought in), and Paris, 25 December 1822 to 10 January 1823 (lot 28); acquired by the 4th Earl of Aberdeen from Samuel Woodburn, 1826; by descent to the 7th Earl of Aberdeen, London and Haddo House, Aberdeenshire; Baron Alfred Charles de Rothschild, 1917; by whom bequeathed to Almina, Countess of Caernarvon, 1918; Francis Howard, London, by 1924; his sale, Christie's, London, 25 November 1955 (lot 44), bought Leggatt, London; with David Koetser, London; by whom presented to the Gallery, 1966 (acc.no.6376)

LONDON, NATIONAL GALLERY

In this explicitly symbolic configuration, each of the three portraits is aligned with the head of an animal below, and with an inscription above. The Latin of the inscriptions is not grammatically correct, but the general meaning is that the present does well to profit from the past when planning future action.[2] The three heads thus stand for past, present and future, and the central idea – emphasised by the word 'PRVDENTER' at the top – is that action should be guided by prudence.

Similar triple heads appear in a number of manuals of hieroglyphic lore consulted by sixteenth-century Venetians, beginning with the famous *Hypnerotomachia Poliphili* of 1499 (see cat.no.164). In one woodcut of the *Hypnerotomachia*, for example, the heads are anthropomorphic, while on the next page there is a zoomorphic image, combining the heads of the same three animals represented in Titian's painting.[3] In Pierio Valeriano's *Hieroglyphica* of 1556 the same zoomorphic image is defined as an emblem of the virtue of prudence.[4] Giordano Bruno, in his *De gli eroici furori* of 1585, explains the specific meaning of each of these animals, with the wolf consuming the past, the lion ready for present action, and the dog full of hope for the future.[5] X-radiographs (fig.148) show that the animals were added after the figures. It has been suggested that this alteration may have been made after Titian's death, implying that the animals were not necessarily originally intended by him.[6] Equally, however, Titian could have introduced them himself as his composition and its meaning evolved.

The hawk-nosed old man in profile bears a distinct resemblance to Titian himself in old age, as he recorded himself in the self-portrait of about 1565–70 in the Prado Museum (fig.149). On this basis, an ingenious and now widely accepted theory was put forward that the other two heads represent Titian's son and artistic heir, Orazio Vecellio (1515–1576), and his young cousin Marco Vecellio (1545–1611), an assistant in the family workshop.[7] The picture would thus constitute a sort of artistic testament, expressing the hope that the painter's heirs would benefit prudently from his legacy. A problem with this theory is that there is no independent evidence for the appearance of Marco (or of any other member of Titian's family of that generation); furthermore, the X-radiograph shows that the figure on the right was originally bearded. On the other hand, it may plausibly be argued that the central head is compatible with the portrait of Orazio as he appears in a wax roundel in the present exhibition (cat.no.202), and that both images directly reflect the active concern that Titian showed throughout his life for the social and professional advancement of his family.[8]

Although the lettering of the inscription is also definitely crude, the variability of the finish need not imply, as has been suggested, that the picture is largely the work of Titian's assistants.[9] The bold sketchiness of the head of the old man is particularly eloquent of the idea of the past dissolving into night as the wheel of time turns towards the light of the future.[10] An overall sketchiness of handling would also be appropriate if, as has been proposed, this canvas was painted as the cover for another picture, an idea supported by the allegorical content and the almost heraldic composition.[11] Such covers, particularly for portraits, were not uncommon in this period, and in addition to their practical, protective function, they were often used to provide an allegorical gloss on the primary image beneath.

Detached from its original context, the picture became difficult for subsequent owners to decipher. In the catalogue of the Tallard sale of 1756, for example, the central head is improbably identified as a portrait of Alfonso d'Este, Duke of Ferrara, between Pope Julius II on the left and (possibly) the Emperor Charles V on the right.[12] The heads were similarly described when the picture was lent by the 4th Earl of Aberdeen to the British Institution in 1828 ('An allegorical portrait or triple head, representing Charles V, Pope Paul, and Alphonso, Duke of Ferrara').[13] But already in the Lucien Bonaparte sale of 1816, and later, when lent by the 7th Earl of Aberdeen to the old masters exhibition at the Royal Institution in Edinburgh, it was called more simply 'The Triple Mask'.[14]

Fig.148 | X-radiograph mosaic

Fig.149 | Titian, *Self-Portrait*
Madrid, Museo Nacional del Prado

65 ✿ *Salome with the Head of St John the Baptist*

Oil on canvas | 90 × 82.5cm | *c*.1560–70

Provenance: King Charles I; Commonwealth sale, 1649–51, reserved for Oliver Cromwell; recovered after the Restoration for King Charles II; by descent in the Royal Collection until after 1736; private collection, Scotland; Christie's, 9 December 1994 (lot 348), bought by Colnaghi; from whom purchased by the present owner, 2001.[1]

MILAN, KOELLIKER COLLECTION

This picture is of special interest both as an unpublished version of a composition by Titian, and as a picture that once belonged to King Charles I, as is shown by his monogram on the reverse (the initials CR surmounted by a crown). Only recently did it pass from an anonymous private collection in Scotland via the London art market to its present owner; the circumstances of its arrival in Scotland are not known.

The iconography of Salome, the corrupted step-daughter of King Herod (Mark 6: 21–8), closely resembles that of the Old Testament heroine Judith, since both involve a young woman holding a man's decapitated head. In another version of the present composition, currently in Detroit (fig.150), the black servant similarly appears in the lower right corner, as he does in Titian's portrait of *Fabrizio Salvaresio* of 1558 (Vienna, Kunsthistorisches Museum), and also in the much earlier *Laura Dianti* of about 1529 (Kreuzlingen, Kisters collection). The fact, however, that the principal figure is putting the decapitated head into a sack clearly identifies the Detroit figure as Judith. In the present work, by contrast – and also in a variant now on the New York art market [2] – the woman holds her grisly trophy on a dish, identifying her as Salome in the act of taking the head of St John the Baptist to her mother Herodias.

Intriguingly, another version of the head of Salome appears in an X-radiograph of Titian's *Empress Isabella of Portugal* (Madrid, Museo Nacional del Prado), traditionally dated to 1545–8, showing that the portrait of the empress was painted on a canvas previously used for a Salome / Judith composition (fig.151).[3] This would appear to suggest that the compositional idea for the latter likewise dates from around the mid-1540s.[4] However, the painterly breadth of handling in the present picture, in which a general sketchiness is combined with a selective focus on particular details, notably Salome's jewellery, is even more pronounced than in the *Diana and Actaeon* and *Diana and Callisto* paintings of 1556–9 (cat.nos.54, 55), and is characteristic of Titian's work of the last decade or so of his life. In common with most other pictures datable to this late period, including the Detroit *Judith with the Head of Holofernes*, the *Salome* raises difficult questions about the extent to which the work was executed by Titian's assistants, and also about whether he considered it finished in its present state. Judgements on these issues are further complicated in the present case as a result of later interventions. When it appeared on the London art market in 1994 it had been enlarged on all four sides (to measure 123.8 × 99cm) and extensively overpainted. While Titian's own assistants may have been responsible for at least some of this overpaint, in an effort to give the surface a more finished appearance and to make the picture more marketable, the additions (together with further integrating overpaint) must have dated from after 1667, since the dimensions recorded in the royal inventory of that year correspond to those of the picture in its present, restored state.[5] The recent removal of the additions and overpaint has revealed the execution to be of much higher quality than was previously suspected. It has also revealed areas that Titian may not have fully resolved, such as the position of the upper edge of the dish, of which several variant positions are now visible as pentimenti. The figure of the page-boy at the lower right has suffered some abrasion and has also sunk into the dark background, making him rather difficult to discern. Further pentimenti are evident in the X-radiograph (fig.151), which shows that the maidservant's cloak originally covered her neck, and that Salome's right arm was originally draped. These changes to the original design help confirm the close involvement by the master in the execution.

The picture is not listed in the partial inventory of Charles I's collection compiled in 1637–9 by Abraham van der Doort, but it may be identified with an item listed in the Commonwealth sale of the late king's goods of 1649–51, as follows: 'Herod holding sᵗ John head in a platter. by Tytsyan. 150. 00. 00. Reserved: with His Highness'.[6] 'His Highness' must refer to Oliver Cromwell, who must have chosen it as one of a small number of pictures withdrawn from sale to furnish the former royal palaces. Perhaps he interpreted it as a representation of the virtuous tyrannicide Judith; in any case, it is easy to imagine that the theme of decapitation may have held a particular fascination for him. The picture may then be identified with an item recorded in the inventory of 1660–1 of goods recovered for the Crown by Colonel William Hawley as 'A Harodias with A John Baptist head in A platter and her maide by her',[7] and it appears in a succession of royal inventories from the reigns of Charles II (*c*.1666–7), James II (1688), William III (1697), Queen Anne (*c*.1705–10), and George II (*c*.1732–6).[8] There is no mention of it, however, in an inventory of *c*.1785–90, and it is likely therefore to have been sold or otherwise disposed of from the Royal Collection at some point during the preceding fifty years.

Fig.150 | Titian, *Judith with the Head of Holofernes*
Detroit Institute of Arts, Gift of Edsel B. Ford (35.10)

Fig.151 | X-radiograph mosaic

Jacopo Tintoretto VENICE 1519–1594 VENICE

66 ✠ Christ Carried to the Tomb

Oil on canvas | 164 × 127.5cm | c.1565

Provenance: Painted for the Dal Basso chapel, San Francesco della Vigna, Venice; Marquis of Caracena, Milan and Madrid, by 1668; acquired in Spain by Philippe, Duc d'Orléans, 1707/8; by descent in the Orléans collection at the Palais Royal, Paris, to Louis-Philippe-Joseph, Duc d'Orléans (Philippe Égalité); by whom sold in 1791 to Viscount Walchiers; François de Laborde de Méréville; exhibited for sale at Bryan's Gallery, London, 1798–9 (no.208), but reserved for the 3rd Duke of Bridgewater; by inheritance to the 2nd Marquess of Stafford (later 1st Duke of Sutherland), Stafford House, London; by inheritance to Lord Francis Egerton, later 1st Earl of Ellesmere, Bridgewater House, London; by descent to the 5th Earl of Ellesmere (later 6th Duke of Sutherland) by whom placed on loan to the Gallery in 1945; purchased from the Ellesmere Trustees by private treaty with the aid of the National Heritage Memorial Fund, 1984 (acc.no.NG2419)

EDINBURGH, NATIONAL GALLERY OF SCOTLAND

Tintoretto shows the dead Christ being carried by a group of disciples from the scene of the Crucifixion at the top left to the cave of the sepulchre. In the right foreground the Virgin Mary, attended by two of the other Maries, falls into a swoon. As is evident from early reproductive engravings by Jacob Matham, dated 1594 (fig.152) and Lucas Kilian (c.1602–3), the picture format was originally arched. The upper, lunette-shaped portion, which featured a flying angel carrying the crown of thorns, was cut off relatively early in picture's history. The feet of the angel, subsequently overpainted, were revealed when the picture was restored in 1984.

The picture was originally painted as an altarpiece for the third chapel on the left in the Franciscan Observant church of San Francesco della Vigna in Venice. It was recorded there by Vasari in 1568: 'A fainting Virgin with the other Maries and some prophets by his [Tintoretto's] hand may be seen at the altar of the Deposition from the Cross in San Francesco della Vigna'; and by Francesco Sansovino in 1581: 'The third [chapel], in the middle of which are buried members of the Basso family, was painted by Jacopo Tintoretto.'[1] But in 1642 Carlo Ridolfi reported that the picture had been mutilated and stolen from the chapel, leaving behind the upper lunette with the angel;[2] and in 1664 Marco Boschini stated that the dedication of the chapel

Fig.152 | Jacob Matham, *Christ carried to the Tomb* (after Jacopo Tintoretto)
London, British Museum

had been changed in honour of the Spanish Franciscan, Pascal Baylon, and that a new altarpiece representing this saint had been put in place.[3]

San Francesco della Vigna is the most important church built by the leading Venetian architect of the sixteenth century, Jacopo Sansovino. The principal initiative for rebuilding the previous medieval structure was taken by Doge Andrea Gritti (see cat.no.37), who enlisted the support of a group of patricians with whom he had close political and family affiliations. In return for its financial support, in 1537 each family was given patronage rights for one of the side chapels, and assumed responsibility for its decoration and upkeep. Several of the original altarpieces, including those by Federico Zuccaro, Paolo Veronese, Battista Franco and Giuseppe Salviati, commissioned respectively by the Grimani, Giustinian, Barbaro and Dandolo families, remain in place in their original chapels.[4] Two drawings by Franco for his altarpiece in the Barbaro chapel are included in the present exhibition (cat.nos.97, 98).

The third chapel on the left was originally assigned to another patrician family, which, however, did not meet its obligations for the chapel's upkeep, and in 1548 the friars ceded it to the brothers Zuane and Zuan'Alberto dal Basso. Although belonging to the non-noble citizen class, the Dal Basso brothers were exceedingly wealthy, and probably saw the ownership of a chapel in San Francesco, with its ducal associations, as a valuable sign of social prestige. In the 1550s and 1560s they were recurrent office-holders in the richest and most dynamic of the Venetian devotional confraternities, the Scuola Grande di San Rocco.[5] It may have been in that context that they became acquainted with Tintoretto, who famously won the competition to decorate the Scuola's boardroom in 1564.

The subject of Tintoretto's altarpiece was obviously highly appropriate for a chapel where, as Francesco Sansovino specifically mentions, the Del Basso had their family sepulchre directly in front of the altar. But the subject was clearly also chosen to reflect the dedication of the altar to the Deposition, as indicated by Vasari – or more precisely, as specified at the time of its consecration in 1582, to the Pietà.[6] This concept refers as much to the sorrow of the Virgin as to the suffering of Christ, and it is appropriate, therefore, that the figure of the swooning Virgin should loom so prominently in the immediate foreground. The motif of the swoon was one of Tintoretto's favourites, and it appears regularly in his many depictions of Christ's Passion, as a way of arousing in the devotee powerful feelings of empathetic anguish. Partly for that reason, but also for theological reasons, representations of the swooning Virgin were also actively promoted

by the Franciscan order. In contrast to the Dominicans, who maintained that the Virgin did not suffer from ordinary human frailty, and that she was, in any case, fully aware of the imminent Resurrection, the Franciscans interpreted the Virgin's swoon as a spiritual death, parallel to that of Christ himself, so reinforcing the idea that she was actively co-operative in his redemptive self-sacrifice.[7] In his principal work for a Franciscan church, Tintoretto thus gives expression to the characteristically Franciscan doctrine of the Virgin Mary as Co-Redeemer.

Besides mentioning the swooning motif, Vasari records that Tintoretto painted 'some prophets' for the Dal Basso chapel. These have long since disappeared, but by analogy with the neighbouring Dandolo chapel, they probably consisted of a pair of figures – perhaps an Old Testament prophet and a classical sibyl – painted in fresco in niches on either side of the altarpiece. The photomontage (fig.153) shows a view of the Dandolo chapel, with Matham's engraving of Tintoretto's *Christ Carried to the Tomb* superimposed over the existing altarpiece by Salviati, to give an approximate idea of the appearance of the painting in its original frame. It shows how the frame would have provided an important visual complement to Tintoretto's composition by giving stronger articulation to its vertical axis, and to the horizontal axis where Christ's head is aligned with the capitals, and also by serving as a repoussoir, pushing the figures more deeply into pictorial space. The photomontage further provides a reminder of the picture's original

Fig.153 | Photomontage of the Dandolo Chapel, San Francesco della Vigna, with Matham's engraving after Tintoretto's *Christ Carried to the Tomb* superimposed over the altar

placement above a church altar, and of the close visual and ideological connection between the naked and bleeding figure of Christ, and the bread and wine of the mass celebrated at the altar table immediately below.

The commission for Tintoretto's painting is not documented, and traditionally it has been dated on stylistic grounds to about 1565.[9] More recently, it has been suggested that an earlier date is more likely, since there was every reason for the Dal Basso brothers to meet their obligation to decorate their chapel immediately after taking possession of it in 1548.[10] However, several of the patrons of the other chapels – for instance the Bragadin and the Barbaro – delayed at least fifteen years before commissioning an altarpiece and the stylistic argument for the traditional dating remains compelling. In the 1550s, and especially before about 1555, Tintoretto employed a richer palette, more sculptural forms, and a clearer spatial logic. Here the colours have become subordinate to the flickering chiaroscuro, forms are evoked by a web of sketchy highlights, and spatial relationships have become unclear and contradictory. These features are entirely typical of Tintoretto's work of the mid-1560s, as exemplified above all by his great *Crucifixion* and other documented works for the boardroom of the Scuola di San Rocco, and they are also evident in the *Christ Washing the Disciples' Feet* from the church of San Trovaso, which in the nineteenth century was at Hamilton Palace (fig.35).[11] The traditional conclusion that the *Christ Carried to the Tomb* was painted not long before Vasari's visit to Venice in 1566 also fits with the suggestion made above that the Dal Basso brothers chose Tintoretto for the commission in the immediate context of his activity for the Scuola in 1564–5.[12]

By the beginning of the seventeenth century the Dal Basso family had become extinct, and vandalisation and theft of the picture may have been prompted by the neglected state of the chapel. As has recently been discovered, the picture was acquired at some point in the middle years of the seventeenth century by the Spanish nobleman Don Luis de Benavides Carrillo de Toledo, Marquis of Caracena (1606–1668), a long-time resident of the Spanish province of Milan (1648–56 as governor).[13] The fate of the painting after his death is unclear, but it was acquired in Spain in 1707/8 by the Duc d'Orléans for his celebrated collection at the Palais Royal in Paris. It was probably while in either the Caracena or Orléans collections that the picture was enlarged on all four sides with strips of canvas, which were removed during the restoration of 1984.

Follower of Jacopo Tintoretto   VENICE 1519–1594 VENICE

67 ❧ *Portrait of a Gentleman*

Oil on canvas | 127 × 98cm | *c*.1580

Provenance: Giovanni Battista Grimaldi, Genoa, by 1781; by inheritance to Marchesa Teresa Grimaldi Pallavicini; from whom purchased by Andrew Wilson on behalf of the Royal Institution, Edinburgh, 1830 (acc.no.NG 3)

EDINBURGH, NATIONAL GALLERY OF SCOTLAND

When acquired for the Royal Institution in 1830 the picture was attributed to Jacopo Bassano and it was exhibited as such at the Bassano exhibition in Venice in 1957.[1] It was on that occasion, however, that doubts about the traditional attribution surfaced, and since then the portrait has been generally regarded as closer to the orbit of Tintoretto than of Bassano.[2] The difficulty in resolving the question is that while there exist almost no universally accepted portraits by Bassano dating from late in his career, those by Tintoretto are unsufficiently close to the present portrait to inspire confidence in an attribution to him either. Nevertheless, there do exist telling points of contact with the portraiture of Tintoretto, both in terms of pictorial handling and of composition. The head may be compared, for example, with that of the *Vincenzo Morosini* of about 1580 (London, National Gallery); and the dignified format, with looming columns glimpsed above a tall pedestal, resembles that of the *Giovanni Paolo Cornaro* of 1561 in Ghent (Museum voor Schone Kunsten).[3] Even closer in composition are two portraits by Tintoretto's son Domenico: a *Young Man* in the Nationalmuseum, Stockholm, whose pose, black costume, and accessories of curtain, pedestal and column are almost identical to those of the Edinburgh *Portrait of a Gentleman*;[4] and another anonymous portrait of a gentleman (in Scotland in the collection of the Duke of Sutherland until 1976), who once more holds a glove, and likewise stands in front of a table furnished with a folded letter and a crucifix (fig.154).[5] This last portrait is dated 1589, and both from its style and from the costume it looks rather later than the Edinburgh

picture, which perhaps therefore dates from around 1580. The similarities of composition with the two portraits by Domenico, who was born in 1560, make it tempting to regard the picture as an early work by him, but it is perhaps wiser to leave open the question of which of Tintoretto's assistants or close followers was responsible for it.

The portrait was part of one of the earliest batches of old master paintings acquired by the Edinburgh Royal Institution, the organisation that evolved into the National Gallery of Scotland. In 1830, on the instructions of the directors of the institution, the Scottish painter and dealer Andrew Wilson acquired a group of paintings from various aristocratic families in Genoa, and shipped them to Edinburgh.[6] As well as the present portrait and Paris Bordon's *Venetian Women at their Toilet* (cat.no.48), both bought from the Marchesa Pallavicini, the group included Guercino's *Virgin and Child with the Infant Baptist* and three major Van Dycks, all of which remain in the National Gallery of Scotland. Since according to the Marchesa she inherited the portrait from the Grimaldi family, it probably corresponds to a 'Portrait of an old man by Tintoretto' recorded in the Genoese palace of Giovanni Battista Grimaldi in 1781.[7]

Fig.154 | Domenico Tintoretto, *Portrait of a Man with a Folded Letter and a Crucifix*
Private Collection. Formerly in the collections of the Earls of Ellesmere and the 6th Duke of Sutherland.

Jacopo Tintoretto VENICE 1519–1594 VENICE

68 ❧ A Procurator of St Mark's

Oil on canvas | 138.7 × 101.3cm | *c.*1570–90

Provenance: Francis, 10th Earl of Wemyss, Gosford, East Lothian, by 1886; Wildenstein and Co., New York, by 1929; acquired by Samuel H. Kress, 1949; by whom presented to the Gallery, 1952 (acc.no.1952.5.79)

WASHINGTON, NATIONAL GALLERY OF ART, SAMUEL H. KRESS COLLECTION

The unknown sitter wears the robes of a Procurator of St Mark's. Apart from the office of doge, this was the only one in the Venetian constitution to which the patrician holder was elected for life, and it carried with it enormous economic power and political influence. It also carried with it, as an external token of its prestige, the privilege of wearing a gown with 'ducal' sleeves. These were sleeves that did not narrow at the wrist, but were wide open, providing the opportunity for the display of an expensive ermine lining to the crimson toga.[1] Tintoretto maximises the intended effect by showing the inside of the left sleeve fully from the front. Likewise part of the procurator's official costume is the brocaded stole that the sitter wears over his left shoulder.

The frontal, seated pose and the near full-length format are uncharacteristic for the painter, who customarily portrayed his sitters standing in three-quarters view, and in waist or knee length. The unusual effect of majesty, which is further enhanced by the imposing scale and low viewpoint, is arguably greater, in fact, than in Tintoretto's various portraits of doges, and may be compared rather with that found in later ducal portraits such as those by Palma Giovane and Leandro Bassano in the present exhibition (cat.nos.80, 81). The grandeur, however, is here achieved at the cost of psychological penetration, and the *Procurator of St Mark's* lacks the touching combination of dignity and frailty found in the very finest of Tintoretto's late portraits.

The painting is generally accepted as a late work, dating from the last two decades of the painter's life, but it is difficult to date it more precisely.[2] It was lent by the Earl of Wemyss to the Royal Academy exhibition in 1886 (cat.no.144: 'A Venetian Senator' by Tintoretto),[3] but it is not known when he acquired it.

Paolo Veronese VERONA 1528–1588 VENICE

69 ✤ *Venus, Cupid and Mars*

Oil on canvas | 165.2 × 126.5cm | *c.*1580–5

Provenance: Duke of Lerma, La Ribera, near Valladolid; acquired by King Philip III of Spain, 1606; by inheritance to Philip IV, 1621; presented by him to Charles, Prince of Wales (later King Charles I), 1623; Commonwealth sale, 1649–51, bought by Jan Baptist Gaspars; Sampson Gideon, Belvedere House, Kent, by 1761; by descent at Belvedere House to Lord Eardley, Lord Sale and Sele, and Sir Culling Eardley; purchased for the Royal Institution, Edinburgh, 1859 (acc.no.NG 339)

EDINBURGH, NATIONAL GALLERY OF SCOTLAND

Fig.155 | Paolo Veronese, *Studies of Venus and Cupid*
London, British Museum

Fig.156 | X-radiograph mosaic

The fame of the mythologies that Titian painted for Philip II of Spain in the 1550s and 1560s (cat.nos.54, 55) stimulated a wider taste among patrons for mythological and erotic pictures, which Veronese, with his opulent and sensuous style, was perfectly qualified to exploit. In his *Venus and Adonis* (fig.27), Titian had portrayed the final, passionate embrace between the goddess of love and her doomed lover, the beautiful young huntsman Adonis. Veronese depicts an altogether less tragic episode, the story of Venus's adulterous affair with Mars, the god of war. Still wearing his breastplate and helmet, Mars has succeeded in half-undressing the goddess, but to his evident irritation, her attention is distracted by the antics of Cupid and a lapdog. In a humorous parody of the activities of the adult lovers, the dog – usually a symbol of fidelity – appears to have become excited, and is attempting to mount the boy. This playful and witty, but also very human treatment of the subject is characteristic of Veronese's approach to mythological painting in general.

A pen and ink drawing in the British Museum (fig.155) shows the painter experimenting with the poses of Venus, Cupid and the dog.[1] In the sketch on the right Venus holds a mirror (inscribed 'specchio'), suggesting that Veronese's first idea was to paint a *Venus with a Mirror*, as in a picture datable to the mid-1580s in the Joslyn Art Museum, Omaha. In the sketch on the left, where her pose is more fully integrated with that of Cupid, she already appears to be holding up a fan. The painter seems to have changed the subject to *Venus, Cupid and Mars* only after beginning work on the canvas. This is confirmed not just by the awkwardness of the pose and scale of Mars in relation to the other figures, but by the fact – revealed in the X-radiograph – that the

flesh areas of Venus and Cupid were executed over a light underpainting (fig.156).[2] The rest of the canvas, by contrast, including the figure of Mars – and also Venus's right leg, which is not included in the preparatory drawing – was executed over a less carefully prepared dark ground. As a result, the colours in these areas have become darker and duller than in the figures of Venus and Cupid.

The original tonal balance and chromatic intensity of the painting has also been upset by the darkening to near-black of the original greens of the foliage, Cupid's wings and the pattern on Venus's cloak. Nevertheless, the quality of handling in the well-preserved areas of Venus's head and body, Cupid and the dog is high,[3] and is consistent with the supposition that the Edinburgh picture represents the autograph original of a number of replicas and variants executed by Veronese's workshop.[4] On grounds of style, it is usually and plausibly dated to the early 1580s;[5] probably soon after the larger and grander *Venus and Mars* in the Metropolitan Museum, New York, which Veronese painted as one of a group of mythological pictures for the Emperor Rudolf II around 1578–80.

The superior quality of the Edinburgh picture in relation to the other known versions of the composition also supports the recent suggestion that it is identical with one of two works (the other being Giambologna's marble group of *Samson and a Philistine*, now in the Victoria and Albert Museum) that Charles, Prince of Wales, admired when he saw them in the former collection of the Duke of Lerma near Valladolid in 1623.[6] The diplomatic gift by Philip IV to Charles of these and other major works of art may be seen, in fact, as the most positive result of the otherwise ill-fated mission by the prince to win the hand of the Infanta of Spain. Nothing is known of how and when Lerma imported the picture from Venice, but it is not impossible that he was responsible for the original commission. When the future chief minister of Philip III arrived at the Spanish court in 1574, he was deeply impressed by the paintings sent by Titian to Philip II,[7] and he would naturally also have known the work of Veronese, who supplied an *Annunciation* for the high altar of the Escorial in 1583. Alternatively, Lerma's admiration for that work may have prompted him to buy the *Venus, Cupid and Mars* from an original, Venetian owner. After the dispersal of Charles I's collection, all trace of the picture was lost for a century. While it is just possible that it corresponds to one recorded in the collection of Lelio Boscoli in Parma in 1690,[8] it now seems more likely that this is one of the several shop versions, and that the original remained in England, where it reappeared in the collection of Sampson Gideon in 1761.[9]

Paolo Veronese VERONA 1528–1588 VENICE

70 ❧ *The Baptism of Christ*

Oil on canvas | 108.5 × 89cm | *c*.1580–5

Provenance: Probably Muselli collection, Verona, by 1648; probably Philippe, 2nd Duc d'Orléans, Paris, by 1723; probably Sir Richard Sullivan; his sale, Christie's, London, 9 April 1808 (lot 7, bought in); George Hibbert; his sale, Christie's, London, 13 June 1829 (lot 39), bought by Charles Stirling of Cawder (died 1830); by inheritance to his nephew, Sir William Stirling-Maxwell; by descent to Col. W.J. Stirling of Keir; his sale, Sotheby's, London, 3 July 1963 (lot 48); with Julius H. Weitzner and Hallsborough Gallery, London; Lady Virginia Duffield, Geneva, from *c*.1970; from whom purchased by the Getty Museum, 1979

LOS ANGELES, J. PAUL GETTY MUSEUM

For much of the Renaissance period, the gospel story of the Baptism of Christ in the River Jordan by St John the Baptist (Matthew 3: 13–17; Mark 1: 9–11; Luke 3: 21–2; John 1: 29–34) was chosen for pictorial representation chiefly to honour the Baptist. Earlier examples by Veronese and his studio include those in the parish church of Latisana and in the sacristy of the church of the Redentore in Venice, both of which date from the 1560s and were commissioned for altars dedicated to the saint. In the wake of the Counter-Reformation, however, the subject was increasingly adopted to stress the status of Baptism as one the Seven Sacraments of the Catholic church, instituted by Christ himself, and to counter the relative indifference towards towards sacramental theology shown by the Protestant reformers. Such is its significance in Veronese's paintings in the Brera, Milan, painted in about 1582 for the chancel of San Nicolò ai Frari, and for the nave of the Redentore, executed after his death in 1588 by his heirs.[1] Nothing is known of the commission of the present work, which to judge from its relatively modest dimensions was painted for private devotion in the home, possibly for a patron named Giovanni Battista. The solemn event is depicted with an intensity and fervour that closely reflect the religious climate and sacramental veneration of the post-Tridentine period.[2] As in Titian's *Death of St Peter Martyr* altarpiece, the huge, swaying trees part to reveal an angelic glory in the sky, while further drama is created by the sudden contrast between brightly irradiated forms and areas of deep shadow.

The Baptism of Christ is generally agreed to be a late work by Veronese, close in style and date to *The Martyrdom and Last Communion of St Lucy* (cat.no.71), with its similar mood of Counter-Reformation religiosity, and its similarly expressive use of broken brushwork. There is some critical disagreement about the extent of shop participation in the execution. But while certain passages – for instance, the head of the angel behind Christ and the angelic glory above – fall short of Veronese at his best, the overall pictorial quality is high, and the evocation of the landscape is highly poetic.[3] When acquired by the Getty Museum the picture was somewhat larger (114 × 91cm), but strips along all four sides were recognised as additions, and were removed.[4] It may be questioned, however, whether the painter really intended the Baptist's left arm to be cut at the wrist by the right edge, and it is possible that the strips were added to replace damaged areas of original canvas.

The picture was recorded by Waagen in 1857 at Keir House, near Dunblane, in the collection of William Stirling (later Sir William Stirling-Maxwell),[5] who had inherited it from his uncle Charles Stirling of Cawder (1771–1830). Its previous history is confused because several representations of the Baptism by Veronese are recorded in the early sources, and in London salesrooms at the beginning of the nineteenth century. But there are good reasons for identifying the present work with one listed by Ridolfi in 1648 in the collection formed in the early seventeenth century by Cristoforo Muselli in the painter's native city of Verona, since it is consistent with the descriptions provided both by Ridolfi and by a subsequent inventory of the Muselli collection.[6] Probably some time in the early eighteenth century the picture was taken to France, where it was acquired by the Regent, Philippe, Duc d'Orléans.[7] It then re-surfaced in London in 1808, when it was consigned for sale by Sir Richard Sullivan (but failed to sell), and again at the sale of George Hibbert in 1829, when it was acquired by Charles Stirling for his house at Cawder (Cadder), near Glasgow.[8]

Paolo Veronese VERONA 1528–1588 VENICE

71 ✤ The Martyrdom and Last Communion of St Lucy

Oil on canvas | 139.7 × 173.4cm | c.1582–8

Provenance: Belluno, Chiesa di Santa Croce; probably removed from the church and sent to Milan c.1808–11; Count Teodoro Lechi, Brescia, by 1814; acquired from his estate by James Irvine on behalf of Sir William Forbes of Pitsligo, Fettercairn, Kincardineshire, 1827; Forbes sale, Rainy, London, 2 June 1842 (lot 30, bought in); by descent to Diana Bowes-Lyon (Mrs Peter Somervell); Somervell sale, Christie's, London, 10 April 1981 (lot 78), bought Matthiesen Fine Art Ltd, London; from whom purchased by the Gallery, 1984 (Gift of the Morris and Gwendolyn Cafritz Foundation and Ailsa Mellon Bruce Fund, acc.no.1984.28.1)

WASHINGTON, NATIONAL GALLERY OF ART

St Lucy was a virgin martyr of Syracuse, who was put to death at the beginning of the fourth century during the persecutions of the Emperor Diocletian. Thanks to the presence of her relics in the Venetian church dedicated to her (on the site of the present railway station), she enjoyed a widespread cult in Venice and the Veneto. According to the account of her life given in *The Golden Legend*, numerous unsuccessful attempts were made to force her to abjure her Christian faith. Whole teams of oxen were unable to drag her to a brothel. In exasperation, the Roman governor commanded that she be burnt at the stake, but before this could happen one of his henchmen plunged his sword into her throat. She remained alive long enough for a priest to arrive to administer the last rites.

While alluding to the episodes of the burning and the oxen in the sketchily executed background, Veronese conflates in the foreground the two aspects of the story that would have been of particular import in the post-Tridentine church: Lucy's martyrdom, and her reception of the Sacrament of Eucharist. Even as she sacrifices her life for the love of Christ, she endorses the belief that the soul's salvation is achieved only through the Sacraments of the Catholic church; while the executioner bends over her almost tenderly to perform his brutal task, she gazes in tearful rapture at the eucharistic wafer. The violence of martyrdom, as well as its transcendent glory, is also powerfully expressed by the fluency and rapidity of the painter's brushwork, and by the sombre beauty of the palette.[1]

The picture is not dated, but there is general consensus that it was painted in the last decade of Veronese's life, between about 1582 and his death in 1588.[2] Stylistically it is very close to the documented *Miracle of St Pantaleon* of 1587 (Venice, Church of San Pantalon), in which a vested priest similarly ministers to a suffering victim with deep compassion.

Almost certainly commissioned for the chapel of St Lucy in the church of Santa Croce in Belluno, the picture probably hung on a side-wall to complement an existing carved wooden triptych above the altar, with a statue of St Lucy at the centre.[3] The church was administered by a locally powerful devotional confraternity, the Compagnia della Croce, which in the last two decades of the sixteenth century commissioned a cycle of ten Passion scenes from leading Venetian painters, including Palma Giovane, Domenico Tintoretto, Paolo Fiammingo, and Veronese's son, Carletto Caliari. It is likely that the same Compagnia was also at least partly responsible for the commission of Veronese's *The Martyrdom and Last Communion of St Lucy*. The picture was removed from the church during the Napoleonic suppressions of 1808–11, and was probably initially destined for the Brera Gallery in Milan.

However, after the collapse of the Napoleonic regime in Italy in 1813–14, the picture was acquired by Count Teodoro Lechi for his collection in Brescia, and it was from the Lechi collection that James Irvine acquired it (by then entitled *The Martyrdom of St Justina*) for Sir William Forbes in 1827, together with other pictures, including Moroni's *Portrait of Don Gabriel de la Cueva* (cat.no.60).

In his correspondence with Forbes, Irvine felt the need to apologise for the subject of this picture. In a letter of 10 July 1827, he wrote: 'I forgot to say that the P. Veronese is the best of several he [Lechi] has got, but the subject will not perhaps please you. The saint is receiving the sacrament while the executioner is plunging a dagger in her breast, but it is less shocking than such subjects generally are.' Then, after visiting Brescia in October to conclude the purchase, he sought to provide more reassurance: 'The Paul Veronese exceeded my expectation on seeing it down, and I think it may be called his finest work and much superior to all the others in this collection.'[4] Sir William died in the following year without ever seeing the collection that Irvine had so expertly assembled for him, and it was in vain that the latter tried to elicit some enthusiasm for it from Sir William's son and heir.[5] Sir John Forbes later tried to sell the picture in London, but without success. Soon afterwards, even an agent as skilful and experienced as William Buchanan failed to sell it to the King of Holland[6] and the picture was to remain with Forbes's descendants until it was sold in 1981.

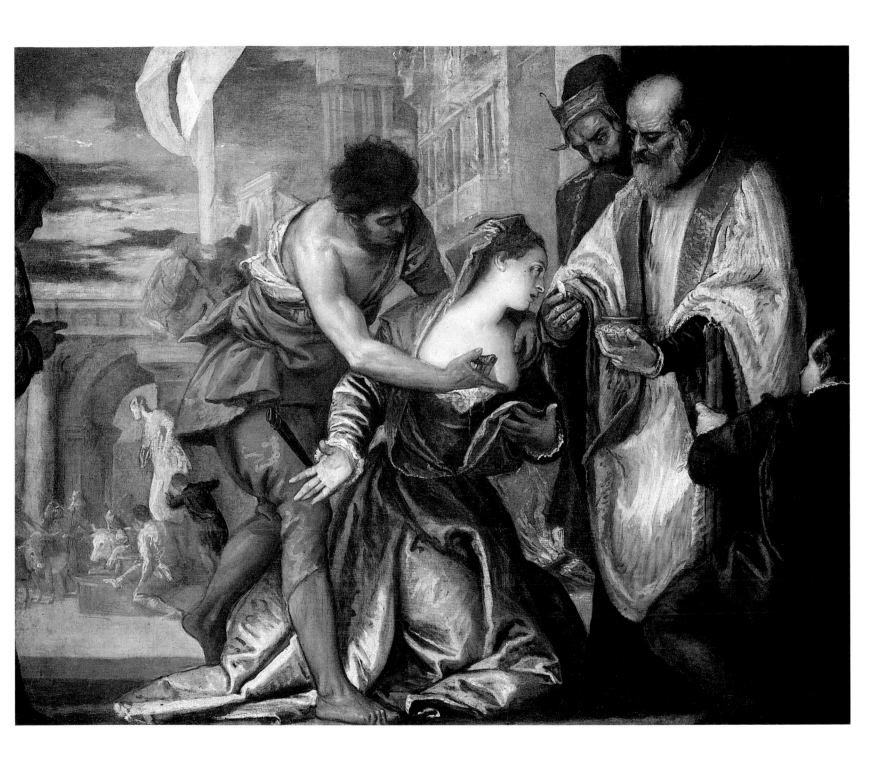

Francesco Bassano BASSANO DEL GRAPPA 1549–1592 VENICE

72 ❧ The Israelites Drinking the Miraculous Water

Oil on canvas | 103 × 138cm | c.1575–7

Provenance: Alexander William, Lord Lindsay, later 25th Earl of Crawford and 8th Earl of Balcarres

PRIVATE COLLECTION

Old Testament scenes such as this, in which numerous small-scale figures and farm animals populate a verdant, undulating landscape, were produced in great quantity by the Bassano family workshop in the last two decades of the sixteenth century. The type developed naturally from Jacopo's representations of New Testament subjects with bucolic accessories, such as the Adoration of the Shepherds and the Adoration of the Kings (see cat.40); and beginning with his *Jacob's Journey* of about 1564 (fig.60), he created a huge demand for his new range of Old Testament subjects, which remained highly popular among collectors in succeeding decades and centuries. Two distinct episodes from the Book of Exodus are shown here. In the foreground the Israelites and their animals, having suffered terribly from thirst during their journey through the desert, are seen refreshing themselves with the water that Moses has miraculously caused to flow from a rock (Exodus 17: 1–7; Numbers 20: 2–13). In the background, Moses – identified by the horns of light emanating from his head – and Aaron lead the Israelites further on their journey towards the Promised Land, symbolised by the radiance above the horizon, while God's blessing is indicated by the shaft of light descending from heaven.

The composition represents a conflation of two related pictures by Jacopo Bassano: *The Journey to the Promised Land* in the

Gemäldegalerie, Dresden (fig.157), datable to about 1573[1] and *The Israelites Drinking the Miraculous Water* in the Prado, Madrid (fig.158), recently dated to about 1566–7. Thus most of the figures in the foreground, including the goat on the right, correspond to their counterparts in the Prado picture, while the ascending diagonal in the right background with Moses and Aaron, and also the dog at the bottom left, correspond to the Dresden picture. In the latter composition, Jacopo may have decided to reverse the background scene, and similarly to reverse the figure of the man with a barrel and a donkey, as a way of better balancing it with that of its pendant picture representing the *Journey of Tobias*, also now in Dresden. In any case, the fact that the Dresden *Journey to the Promised Land* was painted as one of a pair raises the possibility that the present picture was likewise originally paired with a representation of another Old Testament journey.

While some details of the present version do not occur in either the Prado or the Dresden pictures, probably all of them recycle motifs already in circulation in the productive Bassano workshop. The combination of the duck and the hen in the left foreground, for example, recurs in Leandro's *The Presentation of Christ in the Temple* in the present exhibition (cat.no.74). From the early 1570s until his departure for Venice in 1578, Leandro's elder brother Francesco was the assistant principally responsible for producing variants on Jacopo's compositions, and like another version of the same subject, formerly in the Kisters collection, Switzerland,[2] together with a study in the Uffizi for the girl drinking in the central foreground,[3] the present picture is most plausibly attributed to him.[4] A likely date would then be around 1575–7.

Although pictures such as these must have

owed their popularity in late sixteenth-century Venice to their genre-like detail, and to their vision of a bucolic world based in large part on the Venetian *terraferma*, the biblical subject is certainly more than a mere pretext for the picturesque, and some sort of moralising message was in all likelihood intended. It has been suggested, for example, that as in Jacopo's much earlier *The Adoration of the Kings* (cat.no.40), the composition presents two antithetical moral choices for its Christian viewers.[5] According to this reading, while Moses and Aaron show the path of virtue to their obedient followers, the Israelites in the foreground represent those who foolishly and sinfully prefer to gratify their material and sensual appetites. This is probably to go too far: the miraculous, life-saving water was, after all, a gift from God; and like the gift of manna to the travelling Israelites, it was commonly interpreted in Christian exegesis in sacramental terms. Nevertheless, it does seem likely that the picture is meant to suggest the more general idea of human life as a pilgrimage towards salvation.

Like two of the pictures attributed to Leandro in the present exhibition (cat.nos.74, 75), *The Israelites Drinking the Miraculous Water* belonged to Alexander William, Lord Lindsay, later 25th Earl of Crawford (1812–1880), one of the most important of British collectors of the mid-nineteenth century. It remains unclear, however, whether Lord Lindsay bought all or any of the three himself, or whether he inherited them from his father-in-law, Lieutenant-General James Lindsay of Balcarres.[6]

Fig.157 | Jacopo and Francesco Bassano, *The Journey to the Promised Land*
Dresden, Staatliche Kunstsammlungen, Gemäldegalerie Alte Meister

Fig.158 | Jacopo Bassano, *The Israelites and the Miraculous Water*
Madrid, Museo Nacional del Prado

Attributed to Leandro Bassano and workshop BASSANO DEL GRAPPA 1557–1622 VENICE

73 ❦ The Element of Water

Oil on canvas | 106.6 × 143.7 | *c*.1600

Provenance: Leith-Hay family, Leith Hall; bequeathed to the National Trust for Scotland with the contents of the house, 1945

THE NATIONAL TRUST FOR SCOTLAND, LEITH HALL (ABERDEENSHIRE)

In the 1570s Jacopo Bassano and his eldest son Francesco created a number of cycles of pictures with secular subjects, including the *Months of the Year*, the *Four Seasons* and the *Four Elements*.[1] As in Old Testament subjects such as *The Israelites Drinking the Miraculous Water* (cat.no.72), these pictures are conceived in terms of busy, everyday activity, with a distant landscape providing the backdrop for a densely populated foreground. In the case of the *Four Elements* cycle – of which no complete set survives – the key to each subject is provided by a mythological deity riding through the sky in a chariot at the top of the composition.

The present, previously unpublished picture may be interpreted as a later, smaller-scale variant of a composition by Jacopo and Francesco known in two main versions, in the Minneapolis Institute of Arts (fig.159), and in the Ringling Museum, Sarasota. The most direct reference to the element of water is provided by the detailed representation of a fish market in the left and central foreground, where a fishmonger is seen bargaining with two richly-dressed customers while his assistants carry in baskets of seafood. But further references to the unifying theme are provided by the drinking girl and the water-carrying woman in the right foreground, and especially by the river in the background, with its washerwomen on the bank and boats with fishermen. The appropriate presiding deity is Neptune. While the subject would certainly have been meant to carry some wider allegorical message – referring, for instance, to the benefits of water and its produce for human health and happiness – it is more debatable whether it was also meant to point up a moralising contrast between the triviality of much of human activity and the permanence of the natural order.[2]

Compared with the Minneapolis picture,

perhaps datable to the late 1570s,[3] the Leith Hall version is somewhat perfunctory in both composition and handling. Several of the details have been omitted (for instance, the two men behind the fishmonger, and the dog in the right middle-ground) to allow the composition to be compressed and Neptune has lost his trident. The perspective of the foreground still life has been tilted up, and the foreshortening is less expertly drawn. The surfaces of the draperies are blander and lack the animating sparkle of Jacopo's brushwork. The colours are also brighter and more decorative, in a way that recalls the style of Jacopo's younger son Leandro (see cat.no.74). To judge from the principal surviving version of the *Element of Earth* (Baltimore, Walters Art Museum), which is universally attributed to him, Leandro was responsible for painting his own cycle of the *Four Elements*, perhaps dated around 1581. The Leith Hall picture cannot belong to this cycle, since the Baltimore picture is considerably larger, and shows a characteristically hard and precise treatment of detail; it may, however, have once belonged to a smaller-scale version of the series produced in Leandro's workshop some years after the deaths of both Jacopo and Francesco in 1592. As in the earlier, larger versions of the composition, the figure of the girl drinking from a tub repeats that in the various versions of *The Israelites Drinking the Miraculous Water*.

Nothing is known of the circumstances surrounding the acquisition of the picture by the Leith-Hay family. But perhaps the presence of this and two other Italian old masters at Leith Hall may be most plausibly linked with Lt-Colonel Sir Andrew Leith-Hay (1785–1862), who served in the Peninsular War, became MP for Elgin in 1836, and was a gifted amateur painter.

Fig.159 | Jacopo and Francesco Bassano, *The Element of Water*
The Minneapolis Institute of Arts (Bequest of Miss Tessie Jones, by exchange, the Ethel Morrison Van Derlip Fund and the John R. Van Derlip Fund)

Leandro Bassano BASSANO DEL GRAPPA 1557–1622 VENICE

74 ⁊❧ *The Presentation of Christ in the Temple*

Oil on copper | 55 × 44.5cm | *c.*1590

Provenance: Alexander William, Lord Lindsay, later 25th Earl of Crawford and 8th Earl of Balcarres

PRIVATE COLLECTION

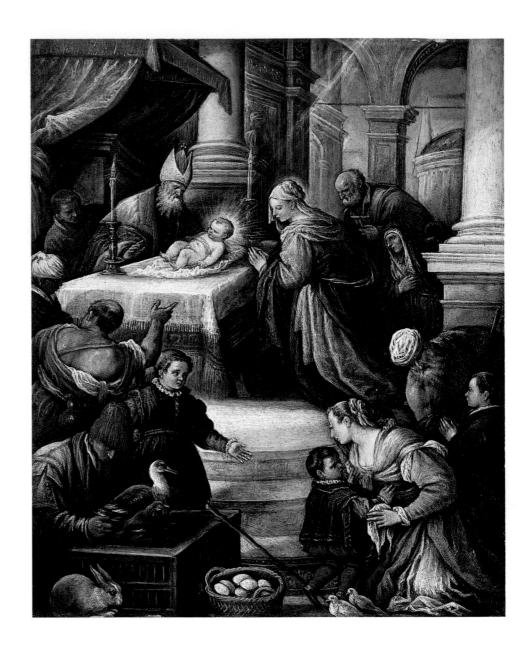

The story of the presentation of Christ in the temple, which is celebrated on the Christian feast of Candlemas, is recounted in Luke 2: 22–39. According to Mosaic law, every first child should be formally presented to God by its parents in the temple, and at the same time the mother should be purified with the ritual sacrifice of a pair of turtle doves. To this offering, represented at the bottom right, the painter has added a selection of other livestock, as well as a basket of eggs.

The composition closely follows those of two large-scale altarpieces signed by Francesco Bassano, one now in the Národní Galerie, Prague, which is datable to about 1590 (fig.160),[1] and the other in the Musée des Beaux-Arts, Rouen.[2] Presumably the present, much-reduced version on copper was painted for private devotion in the home, in a way that is illustrated in Leandro Bassano's *Portrait of a Widow at her Devotions* in the present exhibition (cat.no.75). The changes introduced into this smaller version include: the insertion of a kneeling and praying child at the far right; the clothing of the near-naked child at the centre in a costume that is fashionable and expensive; and the change of sex of the child on the left from a boy to a girl.

Given the free exchange of compositions and motifs within the Bassano family workshop, it is not necessary to assume that Francesco must also have painted this reduced version.[3] Indeed, the decorative palette and the particular quality of the brushwork, modelling by streaks or striations, seem amply to justify the traditional attribution to Leandro.[4] Likewise convincingly attributed to Leandro are a number of stylistically similar paintings on copper that have appeared at auction in recent years.[5]

Fig.160 | Francesco Bassano,
The Presentation of Christ in the Temple
Prague, Národní Galerie

Leandro Bassano BASSANO DEL GRAPPA 1557–1622 VENICE

75 ❧ *Portrait of a Widow at her Devotions*

Oil on canvas | 105 × 88.5cm | *c.*1590–1600

Provenance: Alexander William, Lord Lindsay, later 25th Earl of Crawford and 8th Earl of Balcarres

PRIVATE COLLECTION

This dignified portrait confirms the general verdict that Leandro was often more vital and original as a portraitist than as a painter of religious and genre subjects, where he tends to be mechanical and repetitious.[1] The paraphernalia of devotion that feature here so prominently, including a prie-dieu, a prayer book and a rosary, are found in numerous other Venetian portraits of this period (see also cat.no.67) and are symptomatic of the pervasive influence of the Counter-Reformation. Of particular interest here is the fact that the sitter's pious contemplation is apparently being stimulated by a domestically-scaled painting of a type very similar to Leandro's own *Presentation of Christ in the Temple* (cat.no.74). The choice of the subject of the birth of the Virgin suggests a particular devotion on the part of the sitter to the Virgin Mary and her mother St Anne, who was believed to have conceived her immaculately.

Like the *Presentation of Christ in the Temple* and the *Israelites Drinking the Miraculous Water* (cat.no.72), the portrait belonged in the mid-nineteenth century to Lord Lindsay, but it is not clear whether he acquired it on the market or inherited it from a relative.[2]

Leandro Bassano BASSANO DEL GRAPPA 1557–1622 VENICE

76 ❧ *Fra Gioacchino Torriani*

Oil on canvas | 96.5 × 81.3cm | *c*.1600

Inscribed at the upper left: 'FR[ATER] IOACHINUS / TURRIANUS / VENETUS'; and at the upper right: 'HUIUS CON[VENTUS] FILI[US] / TOTIUS ORD[INIS] PRAE[DICATORUM] / G[E]N[ER]ALIS MAG[ISTE]R'; and on the book: 'IN TE D[OM]INE SPERAVI'. (Brother Gioacchino Torriani of Venice, son of this convent, Master General of the Order of Preachers; In thee, O Lord, do I put my trust); on the back of the original canvas: 'FR[ATER] IOACHINUS TURRIANUS / VENETUS / HUIUS CON[VENTUS] FILI[US] / TOTIUS ORD[INIS] PRAE[DICATORUM] / G[E]N[ER]ALIS MAG[ISTE]R / LEANDRO BASANO PIN[XIT]' (Brother Gioacchino Torriani of Venice, son of this convent, Master General of the Order of Preachers. Leandro Bassano painted it).

THE DOMINICAN FRIARS IN SCOTLAND

The crudely written inscriptions at the upper left and right are clearly later additions, but they are probably correct in indicating that the portrait was meant to represent the Venetian Fra Gioacchino Torriani (1417–1500). After twice serving as prior of the convent of Santi Giovanni e Paolo in Venice (1465–9, 1475–6), Torriani held office as Master of the Dominican order from his election at the Chapter General of 1487 until his death. The Chapter was held at his mother-house of Santi Giovanni e Paolo, and with his reformist sympathies he was thought to be a suitable personality to reconcile the Conventual and Observant factions within the order. But he was no longer young, and was ill-equipped to lead the order during the turbulent decade dominated by the activities of the fanatical prior of San Marco in Florence, Fra Girolamo Savonarola. Eventually Savonarola's persistent denunciations of Pope Alexander VI Borgia forced Torriani to take the pope's side, and in 1498 he agreed to have him tried, tortured and executed. Torriani, who was a great bibliophile and the author of two theological treatises, donated many of his Greek and Latin codices to Santi Giovanni e Paolo in 1494. He died in 1500, and was buried in the choir of Santa Maria sopra Minerva in Rome.[1]

The inscription at the top also makes it clear that the portrait was painted for Torriani's own convent of Santi Giovanni e Paolo, while the quotation from the opening line of Psalm 71 inscribed on the open book (which, by contrast, is clearly original) perhaps expresses a particularly appropriate sentiment in view of Torriani's turbulent career as master. Dating, however, from about a century after his death, the portrait cannot be regarded as a reliable likeness of him, especially since the features do not at all resemble those of Torriani as recorded in his lifetime by an anonymous Florentine medallist, where he is shown as clean-shaven and with a hooked nose.[2] Presumably the painter used a contemporary Dominican as a model for an imaginary portrait of an illustrious former prior and benefactor of the convent.

Although the portrait is unpublished, and the history of its ownership is entirely unknown, the attribution to Leandro Bassano inscribed on the reverse is perfectly plausible. Stylistically it is particularly close to Leandro's portrait of his father Jacopo (Vienna, Kunsthistorisches Museum), but a similar combination of naturalism and Counter-Reformation severity is also to be found in the *Portrait of a Widow at her Devotions* in the present exhibition (cat.75). Furthermore, Leandro is known to have carried out numerous commissions for Santi Giovanni e Paolo and for devotional confraternities attached to the church. He contributed narrative scenes, for example, to the decoration of the sacristy and of the chapel of St Hyacinth, and altarpieces for the confraternities of St Vincent Ferrer and the Trinity.[3] Of even greater relevance is the fact that he painted the portrait of a *Dominican as St Thomas Aquinas* for one of the various confraternities that had their meeting rooms in the cloister of the convent.[4] Since that picture is of approximately the same dimensions (92 × 74cms) as the present one, it is possible that the *Fra Gioacchino Torriani* was likewise painted for a confraternity meeting room, as part of a series, perhaps, of imaginary portraits of learned Dominicans with prominently displayed books.

Pauwels Franck, called Paolo Fiammingo ANTWERP c.1540–1596 VENICE

77 ❧ *The Annunciation to Joachim*

Oil on canvas | 160 × 118.1cm | *c.*1590

Provenance: Claude Phillips; by whom bequeathed to the Glasgow Museum, 1924 (acc.no.1591)

GLASGOW MUSEUMS: KELVINGROVE ART GALLERY AND MUSEUM

The subject is taken from apocryphal accounts of the life of the Virgin Mary, including the very popular thirteenth-century compendium *The Golden Legend*. It concerns Mary's elderly parents, Joachim and Anne; in a scene that obviously parallels the gospel account of the Annunciation, the Angel Gabriel appears to Joachim, and tells him that his wife, hitherto barren, will miraculously bear a child. This event is usually supposed to have taken place when Joachim had retreated to the desert, since the whole point of the story was that the Virgin, like Jesus himself, was conceived immaculately. But although the painter shows Joachim at home with Anne, who is busy sewing, the two are physically separated, and the miraculous nature of the event is amply emphasised by the shaft of light that radiates from the airborne angel, and by his pointing gestures towards Anne and up to heaven.

When the picture was bequeathed to the Glasgow Museum it carried a now descredited attribution to Jacopo Bassano.[1] In more recent years the museum has adopted instead an attribution to the Flemish-born painter Lodowijk Toeput (*c.*1550–1604/5), or Pozzoserato as he was called in Italy. More convincing, however, is the attribution to another Netherlandish painter active in Italy: Pauwels Franck, or Paolo Fiammingo.[2] Paolo worked for some years around 1570 in the studio of Jacopo Tintoretto, chiefly as a specialist in landscape backgrounds. In its composition and general conception the picture is clearly deeply indebted to Tintoretto's

Fig.161 | Jacopo Tintoretto, *The Annunciation* Venice, Scuola di San Rocco

Annunciation of 1583–7 in the lower hall of the Scuola di San Rocco, in which the Angel Gabriel similarly swoops into a humble, partly delapidated domestic interior (fig.161). Entirely characteristic of Paolo is the dislocation between the foreground figures and the landscape background, which is seen from a high viewpoint, and is full of genre-like incident. On the right labourers are busy pruning and harvesting, while at the centre others are trampling grapes to make wine. Equally characteristic of Paolo's style is the luxuriantly ornamental foliage. But he was an eclectic painter, and did not draw only from Tintoretto. The light palette, for example, and the shot colours in the angel's drapery, are more reminiscent of Veronese; while the domestic scene on the left, including the sleeping dog (which ultimately derives from its counterpart in Titian's *Venus of Urbino*, fig.22), clearly owes much to Jacopo Bassano. The crossed-legged figure of the sleeping Joachim is based on one of the soldiers in Dürer's *Resurrection* woodcut of 1510 from his *Large Passion* series.[3]

78 ❧ *Christ Healing the Woman with the Issue of Blood*

Oil on copper | 20.6 × 77.6cm | *c.*1600–10

Provenance: Probably Giovanni Maria Sasso, Venice; from whom acquired by Giacomo della Lena, Venice; from whom purchased by Alexander, Marquess of Douglas (later 10th Duke of Hamilton), 1803/4; Hamilton collection, Hamilton Palace and Brodick Castle; bequeathed with Brodick Castle to the Trust, 1957.

THE NATIONAL TRUST FOR SCOTLAND,
BRODICK CASTLE, ISLE OF ARRAN

Both the traditonal attribution to Veronese and the identification of the subject as Christ and the adulteress are incorrect. In the story of the adulteress (see cat.no.13), the woman is led to Christ by the Pharisees, who demand that he condemn her to death. It appears that the true subject of the picture is story of the woman with the issue of blood (Matthew 9: 20–2; Mark 5: 25–34; Luke 8: 43–8). Jesus was moving among a jostling throng of his disciples towards the house of Jairus, an elder of the synagogue, when he felt a faint touch on the hem of his garment, whereupon the afflicted woman was instantly cured. When he challenged her to come forward, she humbly knelt before him, and he told her 'Daughter, thy faith hath made thee whole.' The exotically-dressed figure near the right of the composition, clearly meant as a Jew, may be identified as Jairus, whose dead or dying daughter Jesus had been called to heal. The porch on the left marks the entrance to Jairus's house, where Jesus will perform his next miracle.

Veronese represented this story in a picture once owned by the 1st Duke of Hamilton (Vienna, Kunsthistorisches Museum),[1] but the present work is related to his style in only a very generic way. It may be attributed rather to the Vicentine painter Alessandro Maganza, by analogy with works such as the *Wedding Feast at Cana* in San Barnaba, Mantua, the *Adoration of the Kings* of about 1597 in San Domenico, Vicenza, and especially the Passion cycle, including an *Ecce Homo* (fig.162) of around 1600–5, in the chapel of the Holy Sacrament in Vicenza Cathedral.[2] Characteristic of Maganza is the eclectic mixture of Veronese (particularly evident in the head of Christ) and Tintoretto (in the elongated proportions, and in the treatment of the drapery folds), as are also the compositional devices of an insistent isocephalism, and of placing figures in half length in the immediate foreground. Compared with these large-scale canvases, the present work has a decorative preciosity associated with the use of a

copper support, popularised in north-east Italy at the end of the sixteenth century by northern European visitors such as Denys Calvaert and Hans Rottenhammer.

The pair of escutcheons at the upper left of the composition are presumably those of the original owner and his wife. However, attempts to identify the arms among those of noble Vicentine families of the period has so far been unsuccessful.[3]

Before passing to the National Trust for Scotland in 1957, Brodick Castle and its contents were the property of the Dukes of Hamilton. Sometimes thought to have formed part of the legacy of William Beckford to his daughter Susan, wife of the 10th Duke, the picture is more likely to be identical with a *Christ and the Adulteress*, or *Christ and the Samaritan Woman*, attributed to Veronese, bought by the future duke in Venice in 1803/4 from the dealer Giacomo della Lena.[4] According to the correspondence between seller and buyer, the picture had previously belonged to the important late eighteenth-century Venetian collector and dealer, Giovanni Maria Sasso (*c.*1742–1802).[5]

Fig.162 | Alessandro Maganza, *Ecce Homo*
Vicenza Cathedral

School of Verona

79 ❧ *Portrait of a Bearded Man*

Oil on slate | 51.5 × 44cm | *c*.1600

Provenance: 'Lewis Ricardo'; from whom purchased, through 'Morley', by Francis, Lord Elcho, later 10th Earl of Wemyss; by descent to the present owner

THE EARL OF WEMYSS AND MARCH KT

This powerful and arresting portrait, which is published here for the first time, was acquired by Lord Elcho from 'Lewis Ricardo thro' Morley' as a self-portrait by Jacopo Tintoretto.[1] Waagen agreed with this description,[2] and the directness and intensity with which the sitter is portrayed are indeed reminiscent of Tintoretto's three self-portraits in the Victoria and Albert Museum, the Philadelphia Museum of Art, and the Louvre.[3] But in 1894 Bernard Berenson attributed it instead to Jacopo Bassano.[4]

Although the quality of the picture is worthy of these great names, the graphic description of the hairs of the beard is not characteristic of either – even when account is taken of the unusually hard support of polished slate. This support was frequently adopted by painters working in Verona in the late sixteenth and early seventeeenth centuries, and it seems very possible that this portrait may have originated in that city. One suggested candidate for its author is Marcantonio Bassetti (1586–1630),[5] a disciple of both Tintoretto and Bassano whose portraits frequently combine, as here, a direct naturalism with a simplification of volume and a strong sense of inner life. An alternative suggestion is that the portrait may be by Bassetti's compatriot Claudio Ridolfi (1560–*c*.1644).[6] But given the dearth of really convincing comparisons by either of these artists, it seems preferable for the time being to leave the question of the authorship of this engaging portrait open.

Attributed to Leandro Bassano BASSANO DEL GRAPPA 1557–1622 VENICE
80 ❧ *Portrait of Doge Marcantonio Memmo*

Oil on canvas | 137 × 107cm | *c.*1612–15

Provenance: Acquired by Andrew Wilson in Genoa for the 5th Earl of Hopetoun; by descent to the present owner.

FROM THE COLLECTION OF HOPETOUN HOUSE, SOUTH QUEENSFERRY

Compared with the portrait of the same sitter by Palma Giovane in the present exhibition (cat.no.81), this work shows the doge in a more elaborate gown, with ermine-lined sleeves, and his family coat of arms displayed on the left. The pictorial handling is also rather different, with rougher brushwork, and a more graphic treatment of the hair and beard, in a way that is characteristic of Leandro Bassano. In his *Life* of Leandro, Ridolfi mentions that he painted the portraits of several doges, including Memmo.[1] A weaker version of the present portrait in the Galleria dell'Accademia, Venice, usefully shows the composition in its original format, without the later fifteen-centimetre additions below and to the right.[2]

According to records at Hopetoun, the picture was bought by Andrew Wilson in Genoa in about 1828, when it was described as 'A Doge of Genoa of the Spinola family by Tintoretto.'[3] This may imply that like Van Dyck's *Portrait of Marchese Spinola* at Hopetoun, Wilson acquired it from the Spinola family in Genoa. In 1830, the picture was lent by the 5th Earl of Hopetoun to the fourth exhibition of old masters at the Royal Institution in Edinburgh. Having visted Hopetoun in 1851, Waagen denied the attribution to Tintoretto, and proposed instead that it was by Palma Vecchio.'[4] A probable explanation for this very odd attribution is that Waagen remembered seeing the very similar portrait by Palma Giovane, then at Bridgewater House, where the names of Palma Senior and Palma Junior had become confused (cat.no.81).

Fig.163 | Jacopo Tintoretto, *Portrait of Doge Nicolò da Ponte*
Formerly New York, Piero Corsini Inc.

Palma Giovane VENICE c.1548–1628 VENICE

81 ❧ Portrait of Doge Marcantonio Memmo

Oil on canvas | 112 × 93cm | c.1612–15

Provenance: Queen Christina of Sweden (1626–1689), Palazzo Riario, Rome, by c.1662; by whom bequeathed to Cardinal Dezio Azzolino (died 1689); by inheritance to his nephew Marchese Pomponio Azzolino; from whom purchased in 1692 by Prince Livio Odescalchi (died 1713); by inheritance to Prince Odescalchi-Erba; from whom purchased in 1720 by Philippe, 2nd Duc d'Orléans (died 1723); by descent in the Orléans collection at the Palais Royal, Paris, to Louis-Philippe-Joseph, 5th Duc d'Orléans (Philippe Égalité); by whom sold in 1791 to Viscount Walchiers; François de Laborde de Méréville; exhibited for sale at Bryan's Gallery, London, 1798–9 (no.24), but reserved for the 3rd Duke of Bridgewater; by inheritance to the 2nd Marquess of Stafford (later 1st Duke of Sutherland, 1758–1833), Cleveland House, London; by inheritance to Lord Francis Egerton (later 1st Earl of Ellesmere), Cleveland (later Bridgewater) House, London; by descent to the present owner.

PRIVATE COLLECTION

Marcantonio Memmo (1536–1615) was elected doge of Venice on 24 July 1612. It was the crowning achievement of a long career in government service, during which he had held office as provincial governor of the *terraferma* cities of Palmanuova, Brescia, Treviso, Verona, Vicenza and Padua. However, by the time of his election, Memmo was elderly and infirm, and had difficulty in performing his ceremonial duties because of the weight of his richly brocaded ducal robes. He reigned for a mere three years, and was buried in Palladio's church of San Giorgio Maggiore.[1]

Despite the brevity of his reign, Memmo found time to commission a tomb monument in San Giorgio and a large votive picture by Palma Giovane for the Doge's Palace, celebrating his many governorships (fig.42).[2] He presumably also commissioned the two compositionally similar portraits in the present exhibition, respectively attributable to Palma and Leandro Bassano (cat.no.80). In terms of its style and pictorial handling – softer, smokier and blander than that of Leandro – the present work is entirely characteristic of Palma, and closely resembles the votive picture.

In composition, both portraits of Memmo are ultimately dependent on Raphael's *Portrait of Pope Julius II* in the National Gallery, London, and Titian's *Portrait of Pope Paul III* (fig.24), in which the sitter is similarly shown majestically en-throned in three-quarter length and three-quarter view. A more immediate prototype for Palma would have been Tintoretto's *Portrait of Doge Nicolò da Ponte* of c.1580 (fig.163), a recent predecessor of Memmo.[3] As in all dogal portraits, the sitter is shown wearing his robes of office, the characteristic horned cap (*corno*), and a cloak of gold brocade covered with a shorter cape of ermine. Palma's version is distinguished from that of Leandro by the somewhat simpler gown beneath the cloak, by the placing of a glove in the sitter's left hand, and by the rampant unicorn finials on the back of the throne.

Although previously unpublished, Palma's portrait is known in a number of other versions, including examples in the Museo Civico, Padua,[4] at Apsley House, London,[5] and in the Städelsches Kunstinstitut, Frankfurt.[6] All three of these, however, are rather weaker in quality than the present work.

When the picture was in the collections of Queen Christina of Sweden and the Dukes of Orléans, it bore an obviously incorrect attribution to Palma Vecchio, which may have stemmed from a confusion with his younger namesake.[7] In his catalogue of the collection of the Marquess of Stafford, where the picture was engraved, William Young Ottley advanced the much more plausible attribution to Tintoretto. This suggestion was ignored, however, by subsequent experts, including Buchanan and Waagen, who adhered to the traditional attribution to Palma Vecchio.[8]

II DRAWINGS

DRAWING IN RENAISSANCE VENICE

Aidan Weston-Lewis

Discussions of drawing in Venice in this period have very often been framed in relation to contemporary practice in central Italy, particularly in Florence. This is mainly because there are some interesting passages in the famous *Lives of the Modern Painters, Sculptors and Artchitects* by the Tuscan artist Giorgio Vasari in which he articulated what he perceived to be the main differences between the theory and practice of drawing (*disegno*) in the two artistic centres. The term *disegno* as Vasari used it in fact carries several different but related meanings, covering 'design', 'composition' and sometimes the whole intellectual process of invention, as well as the practical art of drawing. His account, which appears at the beginning of his biography of Titian in the context of his shift of allegiance from his master Giovanni Bellini to the new manner introduced by Giorgione, provides a convenient springboard from which to address the subject:

Giorgione da Castelfranco, being dissatisfied with the methods then in use, began to give his pictures more softness and greater relief. Despite his development of a fine style, however, Giorgione still used to work by setting himself in front of living and natural objects and reproducing them as best he could with colours applied in patches of harsh or soft tints according to life, without making drawings; for he firmly believed that to paint directly with colours, without recourse to drawing on paper, was the truest and best method of working and the true art of design. He failed to see that whoever wants to balance his compositions and arrange his various inventions well must first set them down on paper in various ways to see how everything goes

together ... Moreover, the use of drawings furnishes the artist's mind with beautiful conceptions and helps him to depict everything in the natural world from memory; he has no need to keep his subject in front of him all the time or to conceal under the charm of his colouring the lack of knowledge of how to draw, as was the case for many years with the Venetian painters Giorgione, Palma, Pordenone and the rest.[1]

In similar vein, later in his *Life of Titian*, in his description of the artist's only trip to Rome in 1545–6, Vasari recounts how he and Michelangelo together went to visit Titian and saw a painting of *Danaë* (fig.25): *... and naturally, as one would do with the artist present, they praised it warmly. After they had left they started to discuss Titian's method and Buonarroti commended it highly, saying that his colouring and his style pleased him very much but that it was a shame that in Venice they did not learn to draw well from the beginning and that those painters did not pursue their studies with more method. For the truth was, he went on, that if Titian had been assisted by art and design as much as he was by nature, and especially in reproducing living subjects, then no one would achieve more or work better, for he had a fine spirit and a lively and entrancing style.*[2]

These passages are fascinating not least because they penetrate to the heart of the theoretical debate about the relative merits of the pre-meditated, rational, intellectualised Tuscan approach to painting enshrined in the notion of *disegno*, and the more intuitive, naturalistic, spontaneous methods associated with Venetian *colore* (or *colorito*). Although Vasari's attitude was bound up with his preoccupation with promoting the status of painting as an intellectual activity and as a liberal art, there is a good deal of truth in his analysis – if not in what he concluded from it – particularly when applied to painters such as Giorgione, Palma Vecchio and even Titian himself (but less so to Pordenone, who he also names), by whom very small numbers of drawings have survived.

It has been estimated that seven times more Florentine drawings survive from the quattrocento and early cinquecento than Venetian ones.[3] This cannot simply be an accident of fate, particularly when one considers that in Venice painters' workshops were often collaborative family enterprises that were passed down, with their studio properties, from one generation to the next. It seems very likely that, just as Vasari maintained, proportionately far fewer drawings were produced in Venice than in Florence. There are nevertheless many exceptions to this rule, for sizeable bodies of drawings survive by such artists as Jacopo Bellini and Carpaccio in the earlier period, and some cinquecento Venetian draughtsmen – Battista Franco, Tintoretto, Veronese, Farinati and Palma Giovane – were as prolific and versatile as most of their central Italian counterparts. It may be no coincidence, however, that the most productive of these, Franco and Palma, had spent much of their formative period outside Venice, in Rome, Florence and Urbino.

If applied more widely to Venetian draughtsmanship in general, there are other respects in which Vasari's argument exaggerates and distorts what must in any case have been a complex and varied picture. His implication that Venetian artists did not make preparatory drawings at all, for instance, is patently untrue; and his statements primarily concern preparatory drawings, whereas in Venice other categories of drawing were equally or more important. He also underpins his argument with a set of values that most Venetians would have found completely alien.

Vasari's premise was that the approach to composition he advocated was the only valid one open to a painter. The Bolognese artist Annibale Carracci (1560–1609), himself an exceptional draughtsman, forcefully challenged this assumption. In the margin of his copy of Vasari's *Lives*, next to the passage quoted above where he insists that the painter must make preparatory compositional drawings before taking up his brush, he made the following annotation: 'As if one can't set down [the design] in various different ways on the panel, and then cancel and rework them as one would on paper; but there isn't enough space here for me to demonstrate what bollocks this dimwit Vasari is talking.'[4] Carracci knew Venice well, was personally acquainted with Veronese, Tintoretto and Jacopo

Bassano and greatly admired their work, and his views are likely to have been very much in line with theirs. That the method he describes corresponds to much contemporary Venetian practice is borne out by the evidence of X-radiographs, which often show numerous and major changes of composition made during the course of painting. And this in turn informs our understanding of the role of preparatory drawing in Venetian practice. An artist such as Veronese may have made numerous exploratory pen sketches on a particular theme but followed none of them when he took up his brushes and began painting (see cat.no.105).

Notwithstanding such important differences of approach, it remains true that every category of drawing made in Florence was also made in Venice and in the artistic centres of the *terraferma*; most are represented in this exhibition, although regrettably there is not a single sheet from the fifteenth-century. Certain types and techniques of drawing are particularly associated with the Venetian school: the use of soft black chalk as a medium, for example, and of blue rag-paper as a support. Red chalk was seldom used in Venice itself, it seems, although more frequently on the mainland by such artists as Pordenone and Romanino (cat.no.86). The distinctive technique of executing figure drawings largely or entirely with the brush, in grey or brown wash heightened with white on blue paper, was popularised by Vittore Carpaccio, and taken up by such artists as Bartolomeo Montagna, Lorenzo Lotto (cat.no.84), and even Albrecht Dürer. Landscape had long been important to Venetian painters, and in the early decades of the sixteenth century Titian and Domenico Campagnola established what was to become a long and highly influential Venetian tradition of elaborate pen and ink landscape drawings (cat.nos.88, 91), produced in tandem with woodcut prints on similar themes. Another popular and enduring category of drawing in Venice was the large-scale portrait, usually drawn in black chalk. The tradition goes back at least to Pisanello and Mantegna, and there are superb examples by Gentile and Giovanni Bellini, Titian, Palma Vecchio (cat.no.82), Lotto (cat.no.83), Jacopo Bassano, and later by Veronese and Palma Giovane (cat.no.117). Bassano also developed a highly original and chromatically rich type of drawing using a combination of coloured chalks on blue paper. A relatively high proportion of finished compositional drawings by Venetian draughtsmen survives whereas, with no local 'Accademia del disegno' as in Florence, the tradition of life-drawing from the nude model was less well-established. There are, of course, important exceptions: Jacopo Tintoretto's surviving drawn oeuvre consists almost entirely of figure studies, with scarcely any compositional drawings.

As we have already noted, a fundamental difference with central Italy is that as a general rule Venetian draughtsmen seem to have been altogether less consistent and methodical in the way that drawings were used in the preparatory process for paintings. We can be much less confident than would be the case with Fra Bartolomeo or Raphael or Andrea del Sarto that the survival of a preparatory drawing for a particular figure in an altarpiece by, say, Titian or Lotto, would necessarily imply that equivalent studies had been made for the other figures in the picture. An explanation that might at least in part account for why this difference arose stems from the absence of a strong tradition in Venice of true fresco painting (*buon fresco*), in which the paint has to be applied rapidly to a fresh layer of damp plaster (the *intonaco*). In central Italy this demanding technique had come over the course of the fifteenth century increasingly to involve the use of a full-scale preparatory drawing or cartoon, from which the outlines of the design could be transferred by a variety of mechanical means to the surface of the plaster. The production of such an elaborate full-size cartoon would in turn have required that the composition as a whole and its component parts and figures would have needed to be studied separately in drawings, hence the proliferation of preparatory studies. A method that had evolved in the context of fresco painting in Tuscany had by the early sixteenth century also come to be used for works on panel, notably by Raphael and artists in his circle, and was thus absorbed into standard workshop procedure.

Cartoons were produced in Venice, but not normally for paintings. They would have been indispensable, for example, for the production of figured stained glass, for the creation of the elaborate mosaics in San Marco, which continued throughout this period, and for articles such as embroidered vestments (see cat.no.118) and elaborate *intarsia* (marquetry) panels, such as those designed by Lotto for Santa Maria Maggiore in Bergamo, the cartoons for which we know he valued highly and preserved.[5]

The drawings catalogued here all belong to the National Gallery of Scotland, a few of them are on permanent deposit from the Royal Scottish Academy. The majority of these originate from three nineteenth-century Edinburgh collections, namely those of Lady Murray of Henderland, a descendant of the painter Allan Ramsay; of the antiquarian and bookseller David Laing, who bequeathed a large body of drawings and prints to the Royal Scottish Academy in 1879; and of William Findlay Watson, whose bequest to the Gallery was received in 1881 (see further the appendix of collectors). Sadly, no great tradition of collecting drawings emerged in Scotland during the seventeenth and eighteenth centuries as it had done in England and France, with the result that there are no great public or private collections of old master drawings here to rival those of the British Museum, the Royal Collection, the Ashmolean Museum in Oxford, or the Duke of Devonshire at Chatsworth. A few Scots did assemble sizeable collections of drawings, for example Robert Udny and especially John Malcolm of Poltalloch (whose outstanding collection was purchased en bloc by the British Museum in 1895),[6] but as was the case with some of the picture collections, they tended to keep their drawings at their London residences, and they therefore do not qualify for inclusion in this exhibition.

Palma Vecchio SERINA (VENICE) c.1480–1528 VENICE

82 ❧ Self-portrait

Black and white chalk on blue paper; the lower left corner made up | 25.7 × 18.4cm

Inscribed on the verso in pen and ink: 'H.º 473 / del Palma Vechio dipinto da / lui In Serinalda / nella palla di S. Giovanni Batt.ª / nel studio Arconati / # / 2'.[1]

Provenance: Sir Peter Lely (Lugt 2093; only the 'P' registered clearly); Keith Andrews, Edinburgh (by 1962), by whom bequeathed to the Gallery in 1989 (acc.no.D 5296)

EDINBURGH, NATIONAL GALLERY OF SCOTLAND

The inscription on the back of the sheet, which states that this head was painted by Palma in the altarpiece of St John the Baptist in his home village of Serinalta, is so specific as to lend it credibility.[2] However, no corresponding figure appears in either of the artist's surviving polyptychs painted for Serina, and no altar there is known to have been dedicated to John the Baptist.[3]

The drawing gives every appearance of being a self-portrait, although scholarly opinion has been divided over this issue.[4] The contrapposto pose can readily be understood in terms of the artist gazing over his right shoulder into a mirror while recording his impressions on a sheet of paper directly in front of him. It is precisely this placement of the shoulders more or less at right angles to the surface plane which distinguishes this drawing from Palma's painted portraits, in which the torsos are invariably less sharply angled into the picture space. The sitter's gaze is also penetrating and acutely analytical in a manner frequently encountered in self-portraits.

The question of the reliability of Vasari's statement that Palma died aged forty-eight now enters the equation. For if it is agreed that this is a self-portrait, and that the features are those of a man of about thirty, a birth date of 1479/80 would imply that it was drawn around 1510. The features, with broad cheekbones, heavy jaw, finely chiselled nose and sensitive mouth, are compatible – once allowance is made for the passage of time – with two probable self-portraits from late in Palma's career, one sketched on the back of a *Portrait of a Woman* formerly in the Contini-Bonacossi Collection, Florence (fig.164), the other in the train of the Magi in an altarpiece of the *Adoration of the Kings with St Helen* commissioned in 1525 (fig.165).[5] The latter is not now generally accepted as a self-portrait,[6] although it was in the past, and the connection with the present drawing is compelling.[7] More equivocal, although not impossible, is the identity of this sitter with the beardless man in a problematic portrait in Munich, which Vasari, in both editions of his Life of Palma Vecchio, described at length as a self-portrait.[8]

The only other drawing by Palma with which the present portrait can meaningfully be compared is a *Portrait of a Young Woman* in the Louvre (fig.166).[9] Although this sheet, like the Edinburgh one, has been dated to the 1520s, it has also been pointed out that very similar female heads appear in a succession of paintings by Palma, beginning with the early *Virgin and Child with Saints Jerome and Helen* at Rovigo.[10] If, as has been generally assumed, the Louvre drawing was studied from life, it would seem logical to place it chronologically at the beginning of this sequence, before any of the painted renditions. It could thus be argued that its stylistic similarites with the study in the Louvre support an early dating for the Edinburgh *Self-portrait*.

Academic arguments aside, the technical freedom of this study, especially the sketchy delineation of the neck and collar, is exceptional among Venetian portrait drawings of the early sixteenth century.

left to right

Fig.164 | Palma Vecchio, *Self-portrait*
Formerly Florence, Contini-Bonacossi Collection

Fig.165 | Palma Vecchio, *The Adoration of the Kings with St Helen* (detail)
Milan, Pinacoteca di Brera

Fig.166 | Palma Vecchio, *Portrait of a Young Woman*
Paris, Musée du Louvre

Lorenzo Lotto VENICE c.1480–1556/7 LORETO

83 ❧ *Portrait of a Bearded Man*

Black and white chalk on slightly faded blue-grey paper | 23.7 × 17.8cm

Inscribed at the lower left, in ink: 'Lorenzo Lotto'

Provenance: A. Paul Oppé, London; with H.M. Calmann, London; from whom purchased, 1966 (acc.no.D 4908)

EDINBURGH, NATIONAL GALLERY OF SCOTLAND

This attractive, somewhat quirky portrait study bears an inscribed attribution to Lotto in an eighteenth- or nineteenth-century hand, the accuracy of which has never been doubted.[1] The straightforward, unidealised presentation of the sitter and the attention to detail in the description of the features, hair and beard are typical of Lotto's portraiture. No corresponding painted portrait is known, and it is quite possible that this was made as an independent work in its own right, perhaps for one of the artist's friends or acquaintances. The sympathetic portrayal of the subject's distinctive, somewhat chunky features negates what might otherwise have been a rather formal, distancing, three-quarter-face presentation of the sitter; Lotto's other portraits are almost invariably full-face, with the sitters directly confronting the viewer.

The drawing has been dated on stylistic grounds to around 1535–40, although in truth the evidence for this is slight, there being no other datable drawings of this type by Lotto. Had it been a widespread fashion, the sitter's extraordinary beard, divided as it is into four elongated cones, might have provided a clue as to its date; but the closest parallels for this quirk of personal grooming are to be found not in portraiture of this period, but among some of Lotto's own male saints, notably St Christopher in the altarpiece of about 1535 in the Palazzo Apostolico, Loreto,[2] and, in variant form, Saints John the Baptist and Jerome in the Sedrina altarpiece of 1542.[3]

The strong physiognomic resemblance between the sitter in this drawing and the jeweller in Lotto's celebrated triple portrait in Vienna (fig.167) has not hitherto been noted.[4] Especially similar are the broad brow, the small, wide-set, almond shaped eyes, and the shape of

the ear. To be sure, the sitter's hair is less tightly curled in the drawing, his beard is fuller and longer and his brow more wrinkled, but such changes could be explained by a lapse of, say, ten years between the painting and the drawing. The sitter in the Vienna portrait, which is usually dated to about 1530, has tentatively but quite plausibly been identified as Bartolomeo Carpan, a goldsmith and jeweller from Treviso who ran a workshop in Venice. We have no proof that Lotto knew Carpan at that date, but there is strong circumstantial evidence to suggest that he probably did; what is certain is that by 1542 Carpan was one of the artist's closest and most trusted friends. For those for whom the appearance of the man in the drawing is not compellingly close to the Vienna jeweller, one might speculate – allowing for a family resemblance – that it could portray instead one of Bartolomeo Carpan's two brothers, Antonio or Vettor, who were also jewellers and were similarly among Lotto's dearest friends.[5]

Fig.167 | Lorenzo Lotto,
Portrait of a Goldsmith in Three Positions
Vienna, Kunsthistorisches Museum

Lorenzo Lotto

213

Attributed to Lorenzo Lotto VENICE c.1480–1556/7 LORETO

84 ✤ The Temptation and Expulsion from Paradise [AFTER MICHELANGELO] [RECTO]; A Profile Portrait of a Man and a Sketch of Romulus and Remus Nursed by the She-Wolf [VERSO]

Brush and grey-brown wash, heightened with white (partially oxidised), over black chalk, on paper washed blue on both sides; verso: black chalk only | 20.4 × 37.9cm

Provenance: David Laing; his bequest to the Royal Scottish Academy, 1879; on loan to the Gallery since 1974 (acc.no.RSA 809)

EDINBURGH, NATIONAL GALLERY OF SCOTLAND

above Fig.168 | Michelangelo, *The Fall of Man and Expulsion from Paradise*
Rome, Vatican Palace, Sistine Chapel

below left to right

Fig.169 | Lorenzo Lotto, *Portrait of a Lady as Lucretia* (detail)
London, National Gallery

Fig.170 | Lorenzo Lotto, *St Martin and the Beggar*
Los Angeles, J. Paul Getty Museum

Fig.171 | | Infrared reflectogram mosaic of recto

This drawing, which is published here for the first time, is for the most part a faithful copy of the corresponding frescoed scene by Michelangelo on the ceiling of the Sistine Chapel in the Vatican Palace (fig.168). Eve is shown receiving fruit from the serpent coiled round the tree of the knowledge of good and evil. Having eaten the fruit despite being warned not to by God, Adam and Eve are driven out of Paradise. This scene was part of the first half of the Sistine Ceiling to be painted, which was completed in August 1510. The only notable difference between the drawing and the fresco is that the copyist has – somewhat bizarrely – turned Michelangelo's female serpent into a male by amputating her breast. The inelegant, bumpy contour of Adam's buttock at the left of the drawing exaggerates the gently swelling profile in the fresco.

The attribution of the copy to Lorenzo Lotto proposed here is based on its style and technique. It was previously filed among the anonymous copies after Michelangelo; a tentative suggestion that it might be by the Emilian artist Girolamo da Carpi is not convincing, but the technique of brush and wash on blue paper certainly points to a North Italian, and specifically to a Venetic, hand. Features such as the almost continuous dark contours drawn with the tip of the brush, and the way the forms are modelled by superimposing brushed hatching strokes – in some areas parallel, elsewhere more broken and choppy – over broader areas of pale wash, recur in other drawings by Lotto. The closest parallels are actually with the 'painted' drawing of Lucretia in the portrait belonging to the National Gallery (fig.169; cat.no.32). Both that figure and the St Martin in the signed drawing now in the Getty Museum (fig.170) share the schematic, mask-like features of the figures in the Edinburgh sheet – one of the few respects in which the copyist imposes his personal stamp on Michelangelo's prototype.

We know from documentary sources that payments were made to Lotto in 1509 for work carried out in the papal apartments known as the Stanze in the Vatican Palace, a project over which Raphael had control. More recently, the execution of one of the frescoes in the Stanza della Segnatura – *Trebonian Presenting the Pandects to the Emperor Justinian* – has been convincingly attributed to Lotto, following a design by Raphael, and dated to 1511.[1] Since the first half of the Sistine Ceiling was unveiled in the summer of that year, this is perhaps the most likely date of Lotto's copy; by October he was recorded in the Marche. However, the even more recent proposal that Lotto returned to Rome and was responsible for painting the ceiling of the Stanza d'Eliodoro, probably in 1514, leaves open the possibility that the Edinburgh copy may have been made a little later.[2]

Examination of the drawing using an infrared camera has revealed a fascinating and quite unexpected black chalk underdrawing (fig.171). This shows the copyist rather tentatively mapping out the broad outlines of the composition before taking up his brush. The many alterations to the contours, some of them quite radical, no doubt reflect the difficulties inherent in copying a large frescoed scene on the ceiling from the floor of the chapel below.

Conservation of the drawing in preparation for this exhibition also revealed its very interesting verso.[3] The fine profile portrait of a man has the appearance of being copied from a Roman imperial bust, and it has been suggested that it may represent the Emperor Domitian, although no specific prototype has so far been identified. On the other hand, the soft, fleshy appearance of the features might suggest instead a more recent, Renaissance prototype; comparison with a profile relief portrait of Francesco Sforza attributed to Giancristoforo Romano (Florence, Museo Nazionale del Bargello), for example, offers compelling parallels.[4] The slighter sketch below represents the mythical founders of Rome, Romulus and Remus, being nursed by the she-wolf. It was almost certainly copied not from a

free-standing sculpture but from an ancient Roman funerary relief, such as that on the *Funerary Altar of C. Julius Phoebus Rufioninus*, now in the in Uffizi in Florence.[5] First recorded in the house of Paolo Planci in Rome in 1521, this features a very similar arrangement to Lotto's drawing, with the standing wolf peering round towards the two suckling infants, who face each other, but are there seated rather than kneeling on one leg. The infrared image of the verso greatly enhances its legibility (fig.172). Only one other copy attributed to Lotto of a work of antique sculpture – after a fragmentary group of *Hercules and Antaeus* then in the Belvedere Courtyard in the Vatican – has been identified.[6] That drawing has extensive white chalk highlights, but the refined handling of the black chalk is comparable to the verso of the present sheet.

This drawing represents a major addition to the slim corpus of about twenty known drawings by him. It is one of the earliest drawings by him identified to date; the only copy by him of a work by a living artist; and the only evidence we have of Lotto paying the slightest attention to the work of Michelangelo.

Fig.172 | Infrared reflectogram mosaic of verso

Girolamo Romanino BRESCIA 1484/7–*c*.1560 BRESCIA

85 ✠ *A Seated Man Wearing a Broad-Brimmed Hat* [RECTO]
An Infant Kneeling before a Woman Seated on a Dais [VERSO]

Pen and brown ink | 20.1 × 19.9cm

Inscribed on the verso in ink: '[illegible word, scored out] / 'Titiano / : 17'

Provenance: Jonathan Richardson Senr (Lugt 2184); Barry Delany (Lugt 350); David Laing; by whom bequeathed to the Royal Scottish Academy, 1879; transferred to the Gallery, 1910 (acc.no.D 704)

EDINBURGH, NATIONAL GALLERY OF SCOTLAND

The genre-like studies on both sides of this sheet, especially the cloaked and cross-legged peasant on the recto, are remarkably informal for a drawing of the first half of the sixteenth century.[1] The rough, incisive pen-work of the sketch on the verso is in many ways more typical of Romanino's draughtsmanship than the more precise and carefully executed recto, but there is little doubt that both sides are by him.[2] The seated man has been associated with the central figure in a small panel by Romanino in a private collection representing Apollo and Marsyas (fig.173).[3] Although the correspondence is by no means exact, so distinctive is the figure in the painting – seated, cloaked, bearded and gazing directly out at the viewer from beneath his broad-brimmed hat – that it is difficult to believe that he was not modelled on the drawing, which was evidently done from life. On account of its strongly Giorgionesque character, the painting has been dated to about 1513–14, when the artist was resident in Padua. But on grounds of style it has been suggested that the drawing must date from later in Romanino's career.[4]

Fig.173 | Girolamo Romanino,
Apollo and Marsyas and Four Pastoral Figures
Private Collection

Attributed to Girolamo Romanino BRESCIA 1484/7–c.1560 BRESCIA

86 ❧ *The Deposition of Christ* [RECTO AND VERSO]

Brush and greenish-ochre and brown washes, heightened with white, over black chalk, on pale brown paper (recto); red chalk and red wash (verso) | 26.6 × 17.9cm

Provenance: David Laing; by whom bequeathed to the Royal Scottish Academy, 1879; on loan to the Gallery since 1974 (acc.no.RSA 897)

EDINBURGH, NATIONAL GALLERY OF SCOTLAND

This drawing, which is published here for the first time, is clearly by the same hand as a double-sided sheet attributed to Romanino recently on the New York art market and now in a private collection (figs.174, 175).[1] The recto of that sheet and both sides of the Edinburgh drawing are variant designs for the same project, most likely for an altarpiece. The verso of the Edinburgh drawing shares with both sides of the New York sheet the distinctive technique combining red chalk and red wash. No painting of this subject by Romanino is known or recorded, but the style of the drawings, with their stocky, plebeian figure types and rugged execution – highly expressive but singularly lacking in grace and refinement – indicate strongly that they are indeed by him. It has to be said, however, that there is nothing else quite like these sheets among the Romanino drawings so far identified.[2] The strong chromatic contrast between the two sides of the Edinburgh drawing is striking, and the use of the greenish-yellow wash on the recto, in particular, is unusual in a sixteenth-century drawing.

We can only speculate about the circumstances that gave rise to these drawings. The presence of two studies of *Christ Carried to the Tomb* – the event that immediately follows the *Deposition* – on the verso of the New York drawing might indicate that the two episodes were to form part of a larger series of scenes from the Passion of Christ. Alternatively, the emphatic focus on the body of Christ in all of these studies might suggest that they were made in connection with a commission, lost or unrealised, for a chapel or confraternity dedicated to the Holy Sacrament or to the Corpus Domini.[3]

Figs.174 and 175 | Attributed to Girolamo Romanino,
The Deposition of Christ (recto)
and *Studies for the Entombment* (verso)
Private Collection

Giovanni Antonio de' Sacchis, called Pordenone PORDENONE *c.*1484–1539 FERRARA

87 ❧ *The Continence of Scipio*

Pen and brown ink and wash, heightened with white, over black chalk, on blue paper; laid down | 19.6 × 25cm

Inscribed on the front and back of the old mount, in ink: 'del Purdenone'

Provenance: An unidentified collector's mark in the form of a daisy-wheel and distinctive gold-embossed mount (not in Lugt); David Laing; his bequest to the Royal Scottish Academy, 1879; on loan to the Gallery since 1976 (acc.no.RSA 923)

EDINBURGH, NATIONAL GALLERY OF SCOTLAND

During the second Punic War against the Carthaginians, the Roman general Scipio Africanus captured the Spanish city of New Carthage and was offered a beautiful maiden as one of the prizes of victory. Having heard that the girl was betrothed, Scipio, in a legendary act of restraint and decency, declined the prize and returned the girl to her fiancé. Pordenone shows an enthroned Scipio commanding his incredulous soldiers to release the girl to the deferential youth in the centre. Behind him are the girl's parents, who had brought gold as a ransom for their daughter (which explains the open treasure-chest in the left foreground); this Scipio gave back to the youth as a wedding present. The story is recounted in Livy's *History of Rome* (26: 50).

This little-known drawing is a fine and characteristic example of a type of highly worked-up compositional drawing by Pordenone that has been termed – for obvious reasons – a *disegno finito* or highly finished drawing.[1] Some of these are so precise that they have the appearance of copies or *ricordi* (accurate copies made after a finished painting), but the present sheet is relatively loose in its handling for a drawing of this kind, and includes a pentimento (visible alteration) to the position of the youth's head in the centre, and an alternative sketch for an arm at the right edge. No painting or fresco of the *Continence of Scipio* by Pordenone is known or recorded, but the theme would have been a very suitable one for a decoration celebrating a betrothal or a wedding. If the drawing was indeed made as a preparatory *modello* for a painting, the intended location must have been high, for the very low viewpoint adopted for the drawing indicates that it was designed to be seen from well below.[2]

The drawing probably dates from about 1530–5, the period when the majority of the artist's drawings of this kind seem to have been made, notably in association with his extensive fresco cycle in the church of the Madonna di Campagna in Piacenza. The Edinburgh drawing has particular affinities with a sheet in the Uffizi representing the *Rejection of Joachim's Offering*, which has been tentatively connected with the Piacenza cycle,[3] and its composition is similar to that of a lost fresco of *Pelias Persuading Jason to go in Search of the Golden Fleece*, executed in 1533–4 on the garden façade of the Palazzo Doria in Genoa, which is known through two preparatory drawings and a drawn copy.[4]

del Pordenone

Domenico Campagnola VENICE c.1500–1564 PADUA

88 ❦ *Landscape with Juno and Callisto*

Pen and brown ink | 35.7 × 48.9cm

Inscribed in ink at the lower left: 'Tiziano'

Provenance: Prince Wladimir Argoutinsky-Dolgoroukoff (Lugt Suppl. 2602d); sale Sotheby's, London, 4 July 1923 (lot 3); sale Sotheby's, London, 15 March 1966 (lot 34); bought Colnaghi, London; from whom purchased, 1966 (acc.no.D 4911)

EDINBURGH, NATIONAL GALLERY OF SCOTLAND

This large and impressive drawing illustrates an episode from the fable of the unfortunate nymph Callisto, as recounted by Ovid in the *Metamorphoses* (11, 410–507). She was one of Diana's chaste and beautiful maidens who was seduced by the ever-lusty Jupiter, who deceived her by assuming the guise of her mistress. When the resulting pregnancy was discovered, Callisto was cruelly banished by Diana; and having subsequently given birth to a son, Arcas, she was punished again by Jupiter's jealous wife Juno, who transformed her into a bear. In Campagnola's drawing we see Juno leaping from her chariot drawn by peacocks to grasp a lock of Callisto's hair, whereupon the maiden's arms immediately began to sprout fur. Once her metamorphosis was complete, Arcas no longer recognised her, and she spent the next fifteen years desperately wandering the wilderness. Eventually they met, he as hunter, she as potential prey, but at this point Jupiter finally intervened to avert further tragedy and immortalised Callisto by transforming her into the constellation of Ursa Major, the Great Bear.

The present drawing has, with good reason, been associated with a sheet by Campagnola in Detroit, very close in style and of almost exactly the same dimensions, illustrating a slightly later moment in the story: a distraught Callisto, now fully transformed into bear, is shown before her startled infant son Arcas, who naturally enough fails to recognise her (fig.176).[1] A third drawing that must have formed part of the same series – presumably the first in the sequence – has recently emerged and is now in a private collection (fig.177).[2] Its subject has been described as *Cephalus and Procris*, but in fact it must represent the seduction of Callisto by Jupiter in the guise of Diana, witnessed by Jupiter's eagle and the nymph's hunting dogs. The setting is the dense virgin woodland where Callisto had laid down to rest, as described by Ovid. Campagnola portrays Jupiter wearing flowing, effeminate garments, but with his own bearded features rather than those of Diana, presumably to facilitate recognition of the story. All three of these drawings carry old inscribed attributions to Titian; those on the

sheets in Detroit and in a private collection are clearly in the same hand. The series must originally have included at least one additional episode, for it is highly unlikely that the crucial scene of the exposure of Callisto's pregnancy – as represented by Titian in one of his great *poesie* for Philip II (cat.no.55) – would have been omitted.

The dating of all but the earliest of Campagnola's landscape drawings and prints is problematic. The Edinburgh drawing was at one time placed at the very end of his career, by analogy with a pair of landscape drawings in the Albertina, Vienna, one of which is dated 1558.[3] However, the similarities are not especially close, and the Callisto drawings seem to fit better stylistically into the artist's middle period, perhaps around 1540.[4] With their dense and varied compositions and masterly evenness of touch, the quality of the draughtsmanship is higher than that of the two sheets in Vienna, and of other landscape drawings generally assigned to Campagnola's last years. The rather large scale of the figures relative to the landscape – particularly in the Edinburgh sheet – also supports an earlier dating. As has been noted in relation to the drawing in Detroit, the style is similar in many respects to a *Landscape with an Old Woman Holding a Spindle* in the Metropolitan Museum of Art, New York, which in turn is particularly close in handling to a group of Campagnola's landscape woodcuts that have been dated to the 1530s and early 1540s.[5]

It is conceivable that the Callisto drawings were themselves intended as designs for a series of ambitious woodcuts, never realised; but it is perhaps more likely that they were made as independent works in their own right, to be displayed framed or kept in a portfolio in some connoisseur's study, to be perused at leisure. One imagines that it was drawings of precisely this kind that were so admired by collectors during Campagnola's lifetime. As early as 1537, for example, the Venetian writer Marcantonio Michiel noted landscapes by Campagnola in both pen on paper and in distemper on canvas in the house of the Paduan collector Marco Mantovano Benavides; similarly, the patrician Gabriele Vendramin owned a large number of Campagnola's landscape drawings, some of them apparently kept in a long, narrow (presumably landscape-format) volume.[6]

Fig.176 | Domenico Campagnola, *Landscape with Callisto Transformed into a Bear after giving Birth to Arcas*
Detroit Institute of Arts

Fig.177 | Domenico Campagnola, *Landscape with the Rape of Callisto*
Private Collection

Domenico Campagnola VENICE *c*.1500–1564 PADUA

89 ✤ *The Holy Family outside the Stable*

Pen and ink | 35.2 × 27.1cm

Inscribed on the verso, in ink: '15' and 'Titian fe. 1.4'; and on the back of the mount, in pencil: 'Dom: Campagnola' (twice)

Provenance: Sir Peter Lely (Lugt 2092); William Gibson; David Laing; his bequest to the Royal Scottish Academy, 1879; on loan to the Gallery since 1966 (acc.no.RSA 134)

EDINBURGH, NATIONAL GALLERY OF SCOTLAND

The Virgin Mary is shown breastfeeding a fairly hefty infant Christ outside the stable, while Joseph, behind, is absorbed in a book and a rather comical-looking ox observes the scene from the left. Although the drawing was formerly attributed to Palma Giovane,[1] the earlier suggestion of Campagnola inscribed on the mount is certainly correct.[2] It displays the overall refinement and consistency of touch typical of his mature drawing style, but is less dry and mechanical in its handling than some of Campagnola's later drawings, such as the Apocalypse series (mainly preserved at the Royal Library, Windsor Castle, and generally dated to about 1550),[3] and the extended series of scenes from the life of Christ, of around the same date.[4] A date for the present drawing in the mid-1540s would seem plausible. The figure types and treatment of the draperies are close to those in a drawing at Chatsworth of an analogous subject, the *Holy Family with St Elizabeth and the Infant St John*.[5]

Attributed to Paris Bordon TREVISO 1500–1571 VENICE
90 ❧ *A Left Foot*

Black and white chalk on blue paper
15.5 × 12.2cm

Provenance: David Laing; by whom bequeathed
to the Royal Scottish Academy, 1879; transferred
to the Gallery, 1910 (acc.no.D 1486)

EDINBURGH, NATIONAL GALLERY OF
SCOTLAND

This simple but rather beautiful study has hitherto
been catalogued among the anonymous late
sixteenth-century Venetian drawings, but seems in
fact to date from earlier in the century and to
originate from the circle of Titian.[1] The tentative
attribution proposed here to Titian's pupil Paris
Bordon is based on stylistic comparison with some
of the numerous sheets by him drawn in this
typically Venetian technique of black and white
chalk on blue paper.[2] The soft, rippling contours
of the toes and the spare use of white heightening
recur in other drawings from Bordon's maturity.
Like the present drawing, several of these are
studies of details of figures and drapery which
were then incorporated into paintings by the artist
(fig.178). This study of a foot in fact corresponds
quite closely, but not exactly, to the left foot of St
Sebastian in Bordon's damaged altarpiece of the
*Virgin and Child Enthroned with Saints Sebastian and
Roch* in the Chiesa Arcipretale in Valdobbiadene,
near Treviso.[3] More generally, the sharp division
in the lighting of the foot between the shadowed
lower leg and ankle and the brightly illuminated
bridge and toes is a peculiarity which recurs
frequently in Bordon's paintings of all periods. On
balance, a date relatively early in his career for this
drawing seems most likely.

A newly revealed sketch of drapery on the verso
of this sheet is consistent with Bordon's drawing
style, but is too fragmentary to confirm the
attribution of the drawing to him.

Fig.178 | Paris Bordon, *Two Studies of an Arm*
London, Victoria and Albert Museum

Venetian School

91 ❧ *Landscape with Wooded Bluffs and a Watermill* [RECTO]
Sketch of a Standing Young Woman and a Reclining Figure [VERSO]

Offset woodcut print and pen and ink (recto); black chalk (verso); a collector's mark cut out from the lower left corner (made up)
24.9 × 26.6cm

Inscribed at the lower right, in ink: 'Rijmsdyk's [cancelled] Museum.'; and on the verso, in pencil: 'Titian'

Provenance: Jan van Rijmsdijk (Lugt 2167); David Laing; by whom bequeathed to the Royal Scottish Academy, 1879; on loan to the Gallery since 1966 (acc.no.RSA 20)

EDINBURGH, NATIONAL GALLERY OF SCOTLAND

This landscape is much more complicated than it might appear at first glance. It could equally well have been included in the print section of this catalogue, since most of the image almost certainly originated as a counter-proof or an offset from a woodcut print. It is one of a group of about a dozen landscape and figure 'drawings', traditionally attributed to Titian or his circle, which were exposed as deliberate but very early forgeries in a controversial article published in 1979.[1] The substance of the arguments presented there is for the most part persuasive, but scholarly opinion since has been sharply divided over the issue of the precise status of these sheets.[2] In one camp are those who continue to believe that they are preparatory drawings for parts of the woodcuts designed by Titian to which they relate so closely; in the other are those who are persuaded that they are derived from the woodcuts – offset impressions made in a print workshop which were then worked up in pen and ink for sale. The most celebrated sheet to be

left to right

Fig.179 | Attributed to Titian, *A Group of Trees*
New York, Metropolitan Museum of Art, Rogers Fund, 1908 (08.227.38)

Fig.180 | After Titian, *St Jerome in the Wilderness*
Private Collection

Fig.181 | After Titian, *St Jerome in the Wilderness*, printed in reverse with the pirated sections outlined in red

questioned was the *Group of Trees* in the Metropolitan Museum of Art in New York, and much of the debate has centred on that drawing (fig.179).

The Edinburgh landscape relates in a complex way to a woodcut of *St Jerome in the Wilderness* after a design by Titian, which is generally dated to around 1530 (fig.180).[3] The wooded bluff that occupies most of the left portion of the 'drawing', and the rather indistinct rocky river bed and stump at the bottom, correspond precisely in terms of scale and detail, but in reverse, to the upper and lower right corners of the woodcut. The simplest way of illustrating this relationship is to reproduce the print in reverse with the relevant sections marked out (fig.181). It appears that the Edinburgh landscape was created as follows: an impression of the woodcut was taken from the block in the normal way; while still wet, this was cut up into sections; two of these sections were then brought together and an offset or counter-proof of them was made onto a new sheet; once dry, the resulting image was then partially strengthened in pen and ink, and the water-mill and other buildings at the upper right were added freehand. When the woodcut was cut into sections, the lower portion was deliberately silhouetted round the back of the sleeping lion, leaving the blank area at the lower right of the Edinburgh sheet.[4]

Like all of the sheets in this problematic group of works, the one in Edinburgh has a rather blurred, faded, washed-out appearance, which could readily be explained by the fact that most of what we see was generated mechanically in the form of a rather weak offset. Some of the fainter hatching lines, especially those on the bank at the centre left, have a broken, dotted appearance, as if the ink from the print did not 'take' to the paper properly; this is particularly clear under high magnification. Printer's ink has been detected in the Metropolitan Museum's *Group of Trees* (fig.179), and it is very likely that it is present here too, although it has not been analysed. Following examination of the drawing under infrared and ultraviolet light, as well as under the microscope, what is certain is that the buildings and other free-hand additions to the Edinburgh landscape were done in a different ink to the offset areas.

It has been argued that the Edinburgh sheet and the others like it originated in a Venetian print workshop around 1515–25, and that they were created as deliberate forgeries of Titian's drawing style for sale on the open market.[5] Although we have little firm evidence (see cat.no.88), there must have been a reasonably healthy demand in Venice for landscape drawings and prints, or so many would not have been produced. Yet it seems unlikely that the production of these hybrid images was market-driven, especially since their creation as outlined above would have entailed the mutilation of perfectly good impressions of the woodcuts. A less venal explanation could be that they were creative experiments, a time- and labour-saving means of generating new and unexpected compositions by effectively cannibalising and collaging together disparate components of an existing image. If successful the results could, of course, be offered for sale.

Although it has been claimed that the black chalk sketch of two (and possibly more) figures on the verso of this sheet must be much later than the recto,[6] there seems no reason why this should necessarily be so. It is reproduced here as an infrared image, which greatly enhances its legibility.

91 verso

Domenico Brusasorci VERONA c.1516–1567 VERONA

92 ❧ *The Circumcision*

Pen and brown ink and wash, heightened with white bodycolour (partially oxidised), on brown prepared paper | 32.7 × 25.2cm

Inscribed on the lowest step below the Virgin, in ink: '1547'; and on the verso in pencil: 'Francesco Salviati' and 'Nº 3'

Provenance: William Findlay Watson; by whom bequeathed to the Gallery, 1881 (acc.no.D 3077)

EDINBURGH, NATIONAL GALLERY OF SCOTLAND

In accordance with Mosaic law, the infant Jesus was taken to the temple to be circumcised and named eight days after he was born (Luke 2: 21). Brusasorci here shows the precocious infant passively submitting to the operation, gently supported by Joseph, while the Virgin Mary perches rather awkwardly on the steps before the altar. Testifying to the significance of the event – the first occasion on which the Redeemer shed blood – are two child angels above, one of whom holds a wreath of victory. The brief gospel account provides no justification for the host of witnesses crammed into the interior, among whom the monumental foreground figures bearing a torch and a censer lend a touch of authenticity and atmosphere to the scene.

The fact that this highly finished, painterly drawing bears the date 1547 makes it a particularly useful point of reference for the oeuvre of an artist for whom we have few securely datable works. Indeed, on the only occasion that it has been published with its correct attribution, it was presented as the key benchmark for Brusasorci's early chronology,[1] although archival discoveries since then have added a few more firm dates.[2] The elaborate technique and high degree of finish might lead one to conclude that this drawing was conceived as a finished work in its own right; if preparatory for a painting, one has the impression from the densely packed composition that this would have been a small-scale work. No painting of this subject by Brusasorci is known or recorded in the early sources.

The drawing illustrates well Brusasorci's rather eclectic style, grafting as it does elements derived from Mantuan and Emilian mannerism – notably the figure types of the high priest and the Virgin – and from contemporary Venetian art, onto a core rooted in the art of his native Verona.[3] It compares particularly well with his painting of the *Attempted Healing of a Possessed Boy* in San Giorgio in Braida (fig.182), for which a date of about 1545–7 is widely accepted.[4] The highly wrought execution of this drawing, in which all of the contours and outlines are very precisely defined in dark ink, is typical of Brusasorci's more elaborate, *modello*-type drawings, among them the other sheet by him in Edinburgh (see cat.no.93), the compositional study at Chatsworth for his altarpiece in Sant'Eufemia, Verona (see fig.183), and a drawing of *Christ appearing to St Thomas* in the Victoria and Albert Museum, which has not to my knowledge hitherto been associated with Brusasorci but is certainly by him.[5]

During conservation in preparation for the exhibition, infrared examination of the drawing revealed that the torch-bearer at the lower left was originally shown bearded and in near profile, in which guise he would have resembled quite closely the apostle with a large book in the left foreground of the *Attempted Healing of a Possessed Boy* (fig.182).

Fig.182 | Domenico Brusasorci, *The Attempted Healing of a Possessed Boy*
Verona, Church of San Giorgio in Braida

Domenico Brusasorci VERONA c.1516–1567 VERONA

93 ❧ The Coronation of the Virgin, with the Apostles at her Tomb Below

Pen and brown ink and wash, heightened with white, over black chalk, on paper washed pale brown; squared in black chalk | 54 × 30cm

Inscribed faintly at the lower right in white chalk: '88'

Provenance: Sale Sotheby's, London, 3 July 1996 (lot 53), bought Colnaghi; from whom purchased by the Gallery with the aid of the National Art Colletions Fund, 1999 (acc.no.D 5484)

EDINBURGH, NATIONAL GALLERY OF SCOTLAND

This recently discovered drawing is a major and entirely characteristic addition to the small group of sheets that can be reliably attributed to Brusasorci. It shows the Virgin Mary being crowned as Queen of Heaven by the Holy Trinity, with the apostles gathered around her empty tomb below gazing up in wonder at the joyous event. As was recognised when the drawing appeared on the London art market,[1] it is especially close in scale, technique and handling to a preparatory study at Chatsworth for the artist's altarpiece of *The Virgin and Child with Saints Sebastian, Monica, Augustine and Roch and two Donors of the Da Cerea Family* (Verona, Sant'Eufemia), which is the benchmark for Brusasorci as a draughtsman (fig.183).[2] The altarpiece is usually dated to the first half of the 1550s.[3] Some of the figure types and the handling of the draperies in the Edinburgh sheet also find particularly close parallels in a large drawing in the Louvre of the *Parable of the Wedding Feast*,

which also dates from this same period.[4]

The present drawing is of special interest in that it is preparatory for a fresco on the lateral wall of a side-chapel in Leon Battista Alberti's great basilica of Sant'Andrea in Mantua (fig.184). Until the discovery of its connection with the drawing, the fresco had not previously been associated with Brusasorci's name.[5] It was traditionally thought to be by the Mantuan mannerist painter Ippolito Andreasi (1548–1608), although that attribution had been questioned in the most recent literature; and it was considered to date from much later in the century, around 1589–91, when the chapel was under the patronage of Federico Cattaneo, a former minister to Duke Guglielmo Gonzaga who was then dean (*primicerio*) of Sant'Andrea.[6] Close comparison with other frescoes by Brusasorci – notably those decorating the Cappella della Muletta (or della Maestà) in Santa Maria in Organo, Verona, and the *Conversion of St Paul* and *Martyrdom of St Ursula and her Companions* in Santissima Trinità in the same city, all of which have recently been dated to around 1552–3 – leaves little room for doubt that the Mantuan fresco is also by him, and probably of about the same date (compare figs.185, 186).[7] The same is true of the pendant fresco representing the *Birth of the Virgin* on the opposite wall of the chapel.[8] This is therefore a rare instance when a major project can be added to an artist's oeuvre on the basis of the identification of a preparatory drawing. Furthermore, the two scenes in Sant'Andrea are much better preserved than most of Brusasorci's other frescoes.

The scale and clarity of the drawing suggest that it may have served as a *modello* to be shown to the patron for approval before being squared up for enlargement. The proportions of the fresco are even taller and narrower than those of the drawing, and to help bridge the gap between the heavenly and terrestrial realms Brusasorci introduced a landscape with a large tree, a pair of musician angels, and a child angel lowering the Virgin's girdle to St Thomas. The frescoed heaven is also more densely populated with cherubim than the drawn one, and monochrome winged angels or victories bearing palm fronds

above Fig.183 | Domenico Brusasorci, *The Virgin and Child with Saints*
Chatsworth, The Duke of Devonshire and the Trustees of the Chatsworth Settlement

above right Fig.184 | Domenico Brusasorci, *The Coronation of the Virgin, with the Apostles at her Tomb Below*
Mantua, Basilica of Sant'Andrea

right Fig.185 | Domenico Brusasorci, detail of Fig.184

far right Fig.186 | Domenico Brusasorci, *The Resurrection of Lazarus* (detail)
Verona, Church of Santa Maria in Organo, Cappella della Muletta

After Jacopo Sansovino FLORENCE 1486–1570 VENICE
94 ❧ *St John the Evangelist*

were introduced into the spandrels above the arch. These additions, with the possible exception of the last, are likely to have been included in the full-scale cartoon for the fresco, the use of which can be inferred from the presence of indirect incision around the main contours, which was produced when the outlines of the cartoon were re-drawn with a sharp stylus so as to transfer the design to the damp plaster.

It may be noted that the fresco appears in several respects distinctly weaker than the preparatory drawing, which opens up the possibility that it may have been executed by an assistant or collaborator to Brusasorci's design. On the other hand, the artist's frescoes frequently display weaknesses and gaucheries that are largely absent from his drawings and his works in oil. The physiognomies and gestures of the apostles betray Brusasorci's close study of Titian's *Assumption of the Virgin* (c.1530–5) in the Duomo in Verona,[9] while some of the more mannered elements, such as the contorted, muscular arm of an apostle resting on the tomb at the lower centre, reflect the influence of Giulio Romano and his Mantuan followers.

Brusasorci's links with Mantua, which is in any case only a short distance from his native Verona, are well established. He was one of four Veronese painters commissioned in 1552 by Cardinal Ercole Gonzaga to paint small altar-pieces for newly-built altars in the city's Duomo; the *St Margaret in Prison* he supplied is still in situ.[10] The pictures were actually painted in Verona, but their delivery to Mantua may have provided the occasion for the commission of the Sant'Andrea frescoes from Brusasorci. It is to be hoped that archival research may in the future shed some light on the circumstances of this commission. Brusasorci's third and last important Mantuan commission came in 1564, when he was chosen to paint the principal altarpiece of *The Martyrdom of St Barbara* for the new church of Santa Barbara, situated within the Ducal Palace complex.[11]

Red chalk and red wash on discoloured cream paper; squared in black chalk | 26.2 × 12.3cm

Provenance: Possibly Allan Ramsay; Lady Murray of Henderland; by whom presented to the Gallery, 1860 (acc.no.D 1896)

EDINBURGH, NATIONAL GALLERY OF SCOTLAND

Fig.187 | Jacopo Sansovino, *St John the Evangelist* Venice, Basilica of San Marco, detail of Sacristy Door

Previously described as St James the Great, the true identity of this figure was established when it was noticed that it corresponded closely to the bronze high-relief figure of St John the Evangelist in the upper left border of Sansovino's sacristy door in the Basilica of San Marco, Venice, one of the sculptor's most spectacular works in bronze (fig.187).[1] St John, who is accompanied below by his identifying eagle, is paired with St Matthew on the opposite side of a large relief of the *Resurrection of Christ*; on the lower half of the door, the other two Evangelists flank a relief of the *Entombment*. The sacristy door was commissioned in 1546 by the Procurators of San Marco, who employed Sansovino as *proto* (chief architect), but its execution was extremely protracted and it was only installed in 1572, two years after its maker's death.

This drawing departs in a number of minor but significant respects from Sansovino's relief figure: there are some differences in the arrangement of his drapery, the niche and the book supporting his left foot are absent in the drawing, and the rendition of the features, clothing and overall pose is more relaxed and naturalistic. It is no doubt these discrepancies, together with the fact that the drawing is squared up for enlargement, that have led to its being claimed, albeit tentatively, as the sculptor's preparatory study for the bronze.[2] However, although it is undoubtedly a drawing of considerable quality, it simply does not have the appearance of a sculptor's working drawing, and the handling is quite different from the few other figure studies attributed to Sansovino.[3] On balance it seems most likely that it is an adaptation, by an accomplished artist, of Sansovino's figure of St John the Evangelist, which may have been squared up for use in another context.

The drawn figure gives the impression of being fully in the round rather than in high relief, and it may be that it was derived from a lost terracotta or wax model by the sculptor, rather than directly from the bronze figure on the sacristy door. The technique of red chalk with red wash is unusual for a drawing made in Venice; the copyist may conceivably have been a Lombard draughtsman.

233

Andrea Schiavone ZARA(?)(ZADAR) *c*.1510–1563 VENICE

95 ❧ *An Archer Seen from Behind*

Black and white chalk on grey-blue paper
18.3 × 11.9cm

Inscribed on the verso in ink: 'Ex Collectione
Regis Caroli 1:^(mi)' and, in pencil: 'a/i / Barker
[illegible word] 1880 / 2 = c / [?] / July 10 /
1840'

Provenance: Nicholas Lanier (Lugt 2885);
Jonathan Richardson Senr (Lugt 2183, with his
mount and shelf-marks on back); John Barnard
(Lugt 1419–20, with his shelf-marks on the
back); Sir Joshua Reynolds (Lugt 2364);
Bindon Blood (Lugt 3011, with his inscription
on the verso); David Laing; by whom bequeathed to the Royal Scottish Academy, 1879;
transferred to the Gallery, 1910 (acc.no.D 1764)

EDINBURGH, NATIONAL GALLERY OF
SCOTLAND

Although rather badly rubbed, this is a characteristically impressionistic and diaphanous
figure study by Schiavone, the equivalent in
chalk to his scintillating brushwork in oil.[1] The
figure may well represent Apollo as the god of
archery, one of his many incarnations. The
drawing relates closely to the figure in a small
canvas by Schiavone in the National Gallery,
London, and may well have been made in that
connection (fig.188). The differences are that his
weight is on the opposite leg in the drawing, his
bow is aimed higher and he appears already to
have released his arrrow.[2] The pose is also very
similar, but in reverse, to the figure of
Ganymede in Schiavone's etching of *Ganymede
and Hebe*.[3]

   As with so much of Schiavone's work, the
influence of Parmigianino, particularly of his
etchings, permeates this drawing; indeed, it was
previously attributed to the great Parmese
master.[4]

Fig.188 | Andrea Schiavone, *Landscape with a Mythological
Figure, possibly Apollo*
London, National Gallery

Giuseppe Salviati CASTELNUOVO DI GARFAGNANA *c.*1520–*c.*1570 VENICE

96 ❧ *Cloelia Fleeing from the Etruscan King Porsena*

Pen and brown ink and wash, heightened with white, over black chalk; laid down
14.1 × 18.1cm

Inscribed faintly on the old mount, in pencil: 'Salviati 1510–1573'

Provenance: Sir Peter Lely (Lugt 2092); William Findlay Watson; by whom bequeathed, 1881 (acc.no.D 3139)

EDINBURGH, NATIONAL GALLERY OF SCOTLAND

In the early history of Rome a peace treaty was drawn up between the Romans and the Etruscans, under the terms of which the Romans handed over as hostages to the Etruscan King Lars Porsena ten daughters and ten sons of patrician Roman families, of whom Cloelia was one. She mounted a daring escape from the enemy camp, crossing the River Tiber on horseback and persuading her companions to swim after her. But for fear of rekindling hostilities, the girls were sent back, whereupon Porsena, in admiration of her courage, granted Cloelia and her companions freedom. In his drawing, Salviati shows the girls stealing out of the Etruscan encampment while the guards sleep. Occupying the lower left corner of the drawing are an old river god with an overturned urn issuing water, signifying the Tiber, and the she-wolf suckling the infants Romulus and Remus, symbol of Rome.

The drawing has been associated with a lost fresco of this subject by Salviati on the façade of the Casa Loredan in Campo Santo Stefano, Venice, which has been dated to the mid-1550s.[1] Ridolfi described the scene as 'Cloelia with her companions, when they are crossing the Tiber, while King Porsena's sentinels sleep.'[2] It was one of a series of scenes from the early history of Rome on the façade, which was described in effusive terms in the early sources. Even in Ridolfi's day some of the scenes were in a ruinous condition, and no trace of them remains. A second drawing of this subject by Salviati, formerly in the grand-ducal collections in Weimar, has also been linked with the Casa Loredan fresco.[3] It is conceived rather differently to the Edinburgh drawing, with the sleeping soldiers and two girls in the foreground, but with a mounted Cloelia already crossing the Tiber in the middle distance. This latter detail would seem to conform better to Ridolfi's description.

The Edinburgh drawing is smaller in scale and rather different in handling to the Weimar drawing and to other sheets by the artist assigned to the 1550s, and the possibility that it was made in connection with some earlier project, perhaps in the mid-1540s, cannot be excluded.[4] The maiden seen from behind at the rear of the group, looking over her shoulder in lost profile, is a recurrent type in Salviati's work.

An alternative attribution of the drawing to Lambert Sustris (*c.*1515 – after 1591), a Netherlandish artist active in Venice and the Veneto, has recently been proposed, but the figure style seems altogether more elegant and the handling more refined than in other drawings attributed to Sustris.[5]

Battista Franco VENICE (?) c.1510–1561 VENICE

97 & 98 ❧ *God the Father* and *The Baptism of Christ with Saints Bernardino of Siena and Francis*

God the Father

Black, red and white chalk on blue paper; various spots and stains | 29.2 × 24.3cm

Inscribed in ink on the mount by Jonathan Richardson: 'Battista Franco' and on the back of the mount with his shelf mark and inscription: 'In the latter part of his life (Vasari says) Battista finding his expenses at Rome too great for his Inc[ome].../ that 'tis chargeable living there & he had not much employment, nor a ready Sale for those Pictures he made un.../ return'd to Venice his Native place, where he made in the Ch: of S. Francesco della Vigna a Picture in Oyl, of our L[ord bap] / tized by S. John, above is God the Father of wch probably this is the Drawing. / Jonathan Richardson.'

Provenance: Jonathan Richardson Senr (Lugt 2184, with his mount); Sir Joshua Reynolds (Lugt 2364); Sir Thomas Lawrence (Lugt 2445); David Laing; by whom bequeathed to the Royal Scottish Academy, 1879; transferred to the Gallery, 1910 (acc.no.D 1590)

EDINBURGH, NATIONAL GALLERY OF SCOTLAND

The Baptism of Christ with Saints Bernardino of Siena and Francis

Pen and brown ink and wash on discoloured white paper; backed and inlaid into the mount 18.7 × 21.5cm

Inscribed on the mount in ink: 'Bat.^a Franco Venez.^o'

Provenance: William Young Ottley (Lugt 2662, with his mount); Sir Thomas Lawrence (Lugt 2445); David Laing; by whom bequeathed to the Royal Scottish Academy, 1879; transferred to the Gallery, 1910 (acc.no.D 1591)

EDINBURGH, NATIONAL GALLERY OF SCOTLAND

Despite their very different appearance, these two drawings are both preparatory studies for the same altarpiece of the *Baptism of Christ*, which is still in its original location in the Venetian church of San Francesco della Vigna (fig.189).[1] The picture was ordered from Franco around 1552–4 by the distinguished Venetian patrician and Patriarch-elect of Aquileia Daniele Barbaro for his family chapel in the church. According to his biographer Vasari, it was this major public commission that established Franco's reputation in his native city, to which he had recently returned after some two decades away working in Rome, Florence and the Marche.

The monumental conception of the figure of God the Father reflects the enduring impact of Franco's study of Michelangelo's Sistine Ceiling, notably of his imposing figures of God the Father in the various Creation scenes.[2] But as has often been remarked, the chromatic richness of the sheet, combining as it does three coloured chalks on blue paper, lends it a particularly Venetian air, although it in fact pre-dates most of the drawings in this technique by the Venetian artists with which it is most closely associated, such as the Bassano and Caliari. The Edinburgh *God the Father* is in fact unique among Franco's drawings in its combination of media, although one other drawing by him, in the Louvre, does feature on the same sheet a figure study in black and white chalk with a separate sketch of the legs in red chalk.[3] With the exception of the folds of God's mantle, which are simpler in the painting, the study corresponds closely to the figure as executed, although much of the vigour and vitality of the drawing has been lost in translation.

The second drawing, which is preparatory for the principal register of the altarpiece, is altogether more typical of Franco's draughtsmanship.[4] Executed with a fine pen and delicate washes, its high degree of finish suggests that it may have been intended as a final *modello* for the main figure group in the altarpiece, although in the event all six figures represented underwent significant changes. In the altarpiece, the two angels in the middle-distance are shown standing rather than kneeling, and the poses and draperies of each of the four main protagonists were modified, as were the attributes of the Franciscan saints. In the light of such major alterations, it is highly likely that Franco made another, intervening compositional drawing, now lost, which approximated more closely the painting as executed. Given the importance of the commission and the thoroughness of Franco's preparatory method, the four principal figures – each of which has such a self-contained, statuesque quality in the final painting – are likely also to have been studied individually in separate drawings. Apart from the two sheets in Edinburgh, however, the only other surviving preparatory drawing for the *Baptism of Christ* altarpiece is a study in Yale University Art Gallery for two of the diminutive figures in the scene of purgatory at the bottom of the painting.[5]

The anachronistic inclusion of two later saints in the biblical scene of the Baptism is unusual, and the juxtaposition of that scene with the representation of purgatory shown in the lowest register of the altarpiece is unique in Italian art. This complex iconography was almost certainly devised not by the artist but by the patron Daniele Barbaro himself, and it reflects aspects of his personal religious beliefs and concerns and those of the observant Franciscans to whom the church belonged.[6]

Fig.189 | Battista Franco, *The Baptism of Christ*, Venice, Church of San Francesco della Vigna, Barbaro Chapel

Battista Franco VENICE (?) c.1510–1561 VENICE

99 ❧ A Boy with Upraised Hands: Study for the Young Spectator in the 'Martyrdom of St Lawrence'

Black chalk on discoloured white paper; cut irregularly and laid down | 17.4 × 20.5cm

Inscribed on the mount, in ink, in Jonathan Richardson's hand: 'Battista Franco', and, in another hand, 'Despair'; on the back of the mount, in ink, Richardson's shelf mark

Provenance: Sir Peter Lely (Lugt 2092); Jonathan Richardson, Senr (Lugt 2183, with his mount); Sir Joshua Reynolds (Lugt 2364); William Findlay Watson; by whom bequeathed to the Gallery, 1881 (acc.no.D 2893)

EDINBURGH, NATIONAL GALLERY OF SCOTLAND

This study of a boy, not hitherto connected securely to a known work,[1] corresponds closely with the distressed youth to the left of centre in an engraving of the *Martyrdom of St Lawrence* (fig.190). This undescribed print, of which the only known impression is in the Bibliothèque Nationale in Paris, is of considerable importance as it documents a lost composition by Franco.[2] Although the Paris engraving bears the name of Battista's son, the engraver and publisher Giacomo Franco,[3] the existence of three preparatory drawings for it by the elder Franco confirms his responsibility for its design. A splendid, unpublished, double-sided drawing in Berlin includes, on the recto, an elaborate study in red chalk for the pose of the recumbent St Lawrence (fig.191) and, on the verso, exploratory poses for his tormentors (fig.192).[4] Stylistically, the Berlin drawing fits perfectly well in Franco's oeuvre.[5] A further red chalk study by Franco for the arm of the kneeling executioner who adds wood to the fire is in the Victoria and Albert Museum, London.[6] Named in Franco's will and testament of 20 March 1555 as the principal heir to his father's estate,[7] Giacomo was still a boy when Battista died six years later. He may have inherited from his father either a full compositional drawing of the *Martyrdom of St Lawrence*, now untraced, which served as the basis for the engraving; or, since the style of the engraving is very close indeed to Battista's

autograph prints, a finished or nearly finished engraved plate, to which he added his own name. But it is perhaps even more likely that Giacomo's print is a reduced copy after a lost engraving by his father.[8]

Perhaps inspired by Titian's treatments of this theme (see cat.no.146; figs.239–40), Franco probably designed the engraving during his final years in Venice (*c*.1552–61). It is comparable to other prints that on stylistic grounds may be assigned to this late period.[9] Two of the executioners in the print, one holding the rope on the left, the other lighting the fire on the right, reappear in paintings by Franco executed in Venice.[10] A dating to his last Venetian period is further supported by the expert use of black and red chalk for the preparatory studies. Following his return to his native city, Franco began to favour the chalk medium for figure studies preparing prints and paintings as he responded to his new surroundings (see also cat.no.97).[11] While the forms remain essentially Michelangelesque, the artist's later studies often display an interest in rich, textured surfaces, effects usually associated with Venetian draughtsmen such as Titian and Paris Bordon. In the present drawing, Franco uses black chalk to achieve the soft modelling of the boy's face and to articulate the delicate interplay of shadow and light on the folds of his tunic. AVL

left Fig.190 | Battista Franco, *The Martyrdom of St Lawrence* Paris, Bibliothèque Nationale

below left Fig.191 | Battista Franco, *Reclining Figure: Study for St Lawrence* Berlin, Staatliche Museen zu Berlin, Kupferstichkabinett

below right Fig.192 | Battista Franco, *Figure Studies for the Martyrdom of St Lawrence* Berlin, Staatliche Museen zu Berlin, Kupferstichkabinett

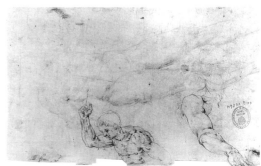

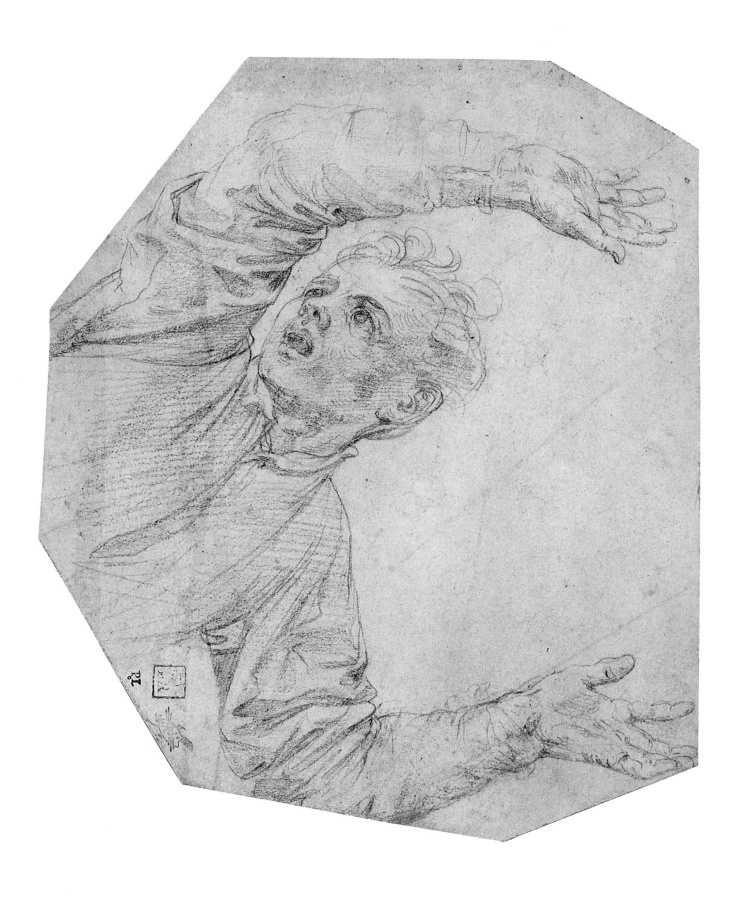

239

Battista Franco VENICE (?) c.1510–1561 VENICE

100 ❧ The Resurrection

Pen and brown ink, the contours lightly incised with a stylus; laid down | 21.4 × 14.6cm

Provenance: Jan Pietersz. Zoomer (Lugt 1511); Thomas Hudson (Lugt 2432); Richard Cosway (Lugt 629);[1] Sir Thomas Lawrence (Lugt 2445); David Laing; his bequest to the Royal Scottish Academy, 1879; transferred to the Gallery 1910 (acc.no.D 634)

EDINBURGH, NATIONAL GALLERY OF SCOTLAND

A fine example of Franco's scrolling, calligraphic penwork, this spirited drawing was reproduced faithfully, in reverse, in the artist's own etching of this subject (fig.193).[2] The two are identical in scale, and so closely does the drawing correspond to the print that it seems very likely that it was used directly in its production, especially given the presence of incised indentations. Not much is known about the methods used in the sixteenth century to transfer designs to printing plates, but in this case two possibilities present themselves. The principal contours of the drawing could have been incised through the paper directly into the etching ground with a stylus, the resulting image clarified and reinforced with an etching needle, and the plate then bitten in the acid bath. This method would have been especially effective in transmitting to the print the freshness and vitality of touch so evident in the drawing. Alternatively, the verso of the sheet could have been darkened and the contours on the recto then lightly incised to register the design like a carbon-copy on the surface of the etching ground. These lines would then have been re-drawn with the etching needle to expose the copper and the plate bitten in the normal way. It may be noted that there appears to be considerable discolouration on the verso of the sheet, especially at the margins (although since the drawing is stuck down on its mount, it is impossible to assess this evidence fully). In either of the foregoing scenarios, the modification between drawing and print to the profile of the risen Christ, the strengthening of the radiating strokes surrounding his aura and other areas of shading, and the removal of the shield on which the foreground soldier rests, could easily have been introduced freehand directly into the etching ground.

As was his wont, for this composition Franco adapted figures from other masters whose work he admired. The soldier seen from behind in the foreground of the drawing was evidently derived from one of the fallen soldiers in the *Battle of Constantine and Maxentius* in the Sala di Costantino in the Vatican, executed by Raphael's workshop around 1520.[3] The rather meaningless gesture of the helmeted soldier at the right of the drawing suggests that he too may have been borrowed from another source, and his upper half indeed corresponds quite closely, although in reverse, to another figure in the same Sala di Costantino fresco. Most significantly, because it helps us to date the print, Franco's risen Christ seems clearly to betray a knowledge of Francesco Salviati's *Resurrection* fresco in the Cappella della Pietà in Santa Maria dell'Anima in Rome (note, especially, the unusual profile view of Christ's face in the final print).[4] Franco's etching, and the preparatory drawing for it, must therefore post-date the unveiling of Salviati's decorations in

1550. Although it is tempting to argue that the composition might date from prior to Franco's departure from Rome, while the various sources upon which it drew were still close at hand, it was in all likelihood executed during his final Venetian period. The few prints for which the artist used etching alone are unanimously dated to these last years.[5] It may be noted that the Edinburgh design has remarkably little in common with either of Franco's own frescoed Resurrections, in Santa Maria sopra Minerva, Rome (which Vasari implies was painted in 1550),[6] and the lunette in the Cappella Grimani in San Francesco della Vigna, Venice, dating from some ten years later (for which there is a preparatory drawing at Chatsworth and a related print).[7]

Fig.193 | Battista Franco, *The Resurrection* London, British Museum

101 ❧ *Portrait of a Bearded Man* [RECTO]; *Study of a Right Hand and Forearm* [VERSO]

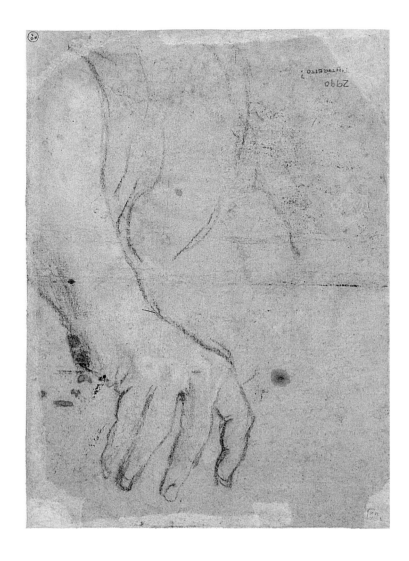

Black chalk on faded blue paper; part of left edge and lower left corner made up; various stains
30.4 × 22.5cm

Inscribed on the verso in a modern hand: '2990 TINTORETTO?'

Provenance: William Findlay Watson; by whom bequeathed to the Gallery, 1881 (acc.no.D 2990)

EDINBURGH, NATIONAL GALLERY OF
SCOTLAND

The sitter on the recto is shown in an informal pose, almost frontally, in slightly more than half-length, seated in a chair and with his hands folded on his lap. The head and facial features are treated in a very summary fashion, a feature that suggests that this sketch may have been made from a surrogate sitter to establish the pose of a portrait for which the head had already been – or was yet to be – painted from life.[1] No corresponding painted portrait by Jacopo Bassano, or from his workshop, is known, and in none of those that have been identified does the sitter clasp his hands on his lap in so informal and relaxed a manner. Nor is the handling of the chalk typical of Jacopo Bassano, but then there are no other drawings by him of quite this type with which to compare it.[2] However, the way the hands are drawn, both those on the recto and the larger study on the verso, seems very convincing as the work of Jacopo (the verso might be compared with the forearm of the figure in the right foreground of the *Adoration of the Kings*, cat.no.40). The free and rapid execution – which recalls some of Tintoretto's drawings – would suggest a relatively

late date in Bassano's career, perhaps in the 1560s or 1570s.

The striking informality with which the sitter is presented, with the focus on his clasped hands, is strangely reminiscent of some late nineteenth-century portraits by artists such as Cézanne and Van Gogh.

Attributed to Jacopo Tintoretto VENICE 1519–1594 VENICE

102 ❧ *A Man with his Arms Outstretched*

Black chalk on faded blue paper; squared in black chalk; various spots and stains; a small loss at the centre of the top edge made up; laid down
34.4 × 23.5cm

Inscribed at the lower right in ink: 'Giacomo Tintoretto'

Provenance: Benjamin West (Lugt 419); David Laing; his bequest to the Royal Scottish Academy, 1879; transferred to the Gallery, 1910 (acc.no.D 758)

EDINBURGH, NATIONAL GALLERY OF SCOTLAND

The traditional attribution of this drawing to Jacopo Tintoretto is retained here, albeit tentatively, although the authorship has been questioned in the past,[1] and the sheet has recently been reattributed by one authority to his son Domenico, whose drawing style, especially in his early years, was very close to that of his father (see following entry).[2] To be sure, it is not the most typical drawing by Jacopo, but its quality is high and it displays a number of the idiosyncracies one associates with the elder Tintoretto. The greatly elongated limbs and the unusual viewpoint, which makes it seem as if the artist drew the figure from above, give the drawing an unsettling, unstable quality which one finds in numerous figure studies by Jacopo. It has been suggested that the figure may have been drawn not from life but from one of the wax or clay models that the artist is reported to have suspended from his studio ceiling to help him with difficult foreshortenings,[3] although the fact that the figure is clothed might argue against this. The disproportionately small head, the distinc-

Fig.194 | Jacopo Tintoretto, *Study of a Man Balancing on a Ladder*
Rotterdam, Museum Boijmans van Beuningen

Fig.195 | Jacopo Tintoretto, *Study of a Seated Man*
London, British Museum

tive shorthand used for the enormous hand and feet, and the alteration to the position of the left leg are also characteristic of the Jacopo's drawings. The closest stylistic parallels are with sheets dating from the 1560s, notably with some of the studies for the great *Crucifixion* in the Scuola di San Rocco in Venice (fig.194).[4] Another particularly convincing comparison is offered by a drawing of a *Seated Man* in the British Museum (fig.195), which has recently been connected convincingly with a Tintoretto painting of the *Martyrdom of St Lawrence* datable to the early 1570s, although here again the master's responsibility for the drawing has been contested.[5]

That the Edinburgh drawing is squared up suggests strongly that it was used for a figure in a painting, but no corresponding figure has been identified among the surviving works of either Jacopo or Domenico.[6] Although the viewpoint is higher in the drawing, the pose of the figure is similar to that of Moses in the painting from Frankfurt, which was probably painted by Jacopo with workshop assistance (fig.65).

There is an undisputed drawing by Jacopo Tintoretto in the British Museum with an inscribed attribution in the same hand as the one on the present drawing.[7]

Black chalk on faded blue-grey paper; a small patch inserted at the lower left edge
24.5 × 16.8cm

Inscribed at the lower left in ink: 'Dom.ᶜᵒ Tintoretto'

Provenance: David Laing; his bequest to the Royal Scottish Academy, 1879; transferred to the Gallery, 1910 (acc.no.D 1655)

EDINBURGH, NATIONAL GALLERY OF SCOTLAND

This slight but highly accomplished drawing is strongly reminiscent of the style of Domenico's father Jacopo, and the possibility that it may in fact be by the older artist should not be com-pletely excluded.[1] The bulbous, curving contours used to describe the well-developed muscles are a hallmark of Jacopo's figure drawings, although in the latter they are usually both stronger and more broken than here. The dynamic pose of the model, with the head seen from the top and the upper torso and left arm strongly foreshortened, is rendered with great mastery and economy of means. Figures in poses like this recur frequently in the work of both Jacopo and Domenico, but no perfect match has been found. Since Domenico, along with his sister Marietta and brother Marco, trained in his father's studio and assisted him on many projects, it is hardly surprising that his style, especially in his earlier years, should resemble Jacopo's so closely.

Attributed to Domenico Tintoretto VENICE 1560–1635 VENICE

104 ❧ *The Head of Giuliano de' Medici* [AFTER MICHELANGELO] [RECTO AND VERSO]

Black chalk or charcoal, heightened with white chalk, on brown paper; various spots, stains and repairs, especially on the verso | 35.3 × 25cm

Provenance: Possibly Allan Ramsay; Lady Murray of Henderland; by whom presented, 1860 (acc.no.D 1855)

EDINBURGH, NATIONAL GALLERY OF SCOTLAND

According to the early sources, Jacopo Tintoretto built up an outstanding collection of casts and models after the Antique and Michelangelo, in some cases spending huge sums in order to obtain them.[1] These were used very much as teaching tools and studio properties and a large number of drawings after them survives, by Jacopo himself and by members of his workshop.

Michelangelo's statue of Giuliano de' Medici in the New Sacristy of San Lorenzo, Florence, seems to have been represented in the Tintoretto workshop in two forms: a small-scale model of the whole figure which, since it shows variations relative to the final marble, may have recorded a lost autograph model by Michelangelo;[2] and a cast after the head alone (fig.196). It is the latter that is copied in the studies on both sides of this sheet, and in a large number of other drawings from the Tintoretto shop.[3] These show the head from a variety of different angles, and there are often many surviving drawings recording it from more or less the same viewpoint, with only very minor variations, like the studies on either side of this sheet. To absorb Michelangelo's style through the study of these casts seems to have become something of an obsession for Jacopo, and it was one that he imparted to his pupils. The appearance of the head seems to change remarkably when studied from different angles and under different lighting conditions, which may account in part for its enduring appeal. In the present drawings, for example, and even more so in a double-sided sheet at Christ Church for which a similarly low viewpoint was chosen,[4] Giuliano's features have curiously taken on something of the emotionally charged expressions of Michelangelo's *Slaves* in the Louvre. The bold chiaroscuro contrasts generated by the juxtaposition of rich black and white chalks in drawings like this give the impression that they may have been drawn by candle-light.

The tentative attribution of the present drawing to Domenico is based on the fact that several strongly contrasted studies after sculpture like this appear on the backs of oil *modelli* in the British Museum that are definitely by him, including one after the same cast of Giuliano de' Medici.[5]

Fig.196
Michelangelo, *Head of Giuliano de' Medici*
Florence, Church of San Lorenzo, New Sacristy

Paolo Veronese VERONA 1528–1588 VENICE

105 ❧ *Studies for a Baptism of Christ* [RECTO AND VERSO]

Pen and brown ink and wash | 21.9 × 9.4cm

Inscribed on the mount in ink: 'Paulo Veronese'; and on the verso in ink: 'B A B nº 123' and 'P. Ver:ˢᵉ 3.1'; and in pencil: '1 – 6'

Provenance: William Gibson (with his price code on the verso); Sir Joshua Reynolds (Lugt 2364); his posthumous sale, H. Phillips, London, 5 to 26 March 1798 (lot 1461, one of four drawings); private collection, Perth; sale Sotheby's, London, 26 June 1969 (lot 8), bought by Hans Calmann; from whom purchased by the Gallery, 1970 (acc.no.D 4945)

EDINBURGH, NATIONAL GALLERY OF SCOTLAND

Veronese was one of the greatest Venetian draughtsmen of the sixteenth century, and this sheet, although sadly rather faded, is entirely typical of his drawings in pen and ink: very freely drawn and with delicate dabs of wash selectively applied for emphasis and clarification. We witness the artist thinking on paper, so to speak, dashing down on both sides of the paper a succession of alternative ideas for a composition of the *Baptism of Christ*, experimenting with new solutions and returning to and refining ones already formulated, with an impressive fertility of invention.[1] In all of these sketches Veronese focused on the relationship between the two key protagonists, to the exclusion of the angels and other figures that populate his paintings of this subject. In some sketches Christ half-kneels while the Baptist stands, in others the reverse is true; in some Christ's pose inclines towards the Baptist, in others it arcs away from him; and so forth.

More than a dozen paintings of the *Baptism* were produced by Veronese and his studio, making it one of his most popular subjects (see cat.no.70).[2] None of the sketches on the present sheet corresponds exactly to any of the painted versions although, given the finite number of basic variations on the theme available, they inevitably share numerous features in common. There is a general consensus that the Edinburgh drawing is a very late work, probably of about the same moment as another sheet of studies of the same subject in the Fogg Art Museum (fig.197), which has on the verso the draft of a letter dated 4 February 1588, a little more than two months before the artist's death.[3] Partly on that basis, as

well as on compositional grounds, both drawings have been linked with an altarpiece in the Church of the Redentore which was probably commissioned from Veronese in late 1587 or early 1588, and which was executed and signed by his heirs after his death (fig.198).[4] An alternative view is that the Edinburgh and Fogg drawings should be considered as preparatory for the much smaller autograph painting of this subject in the Palazzo Pitti, Florence (fig.199),[5] although that picture is usually dated slightly earlier.[6]

left to right

Fig.197 | Paolo Veronese, *Studies for a Baptism of Christ*
Cambridge, Mass., Harvard University Art Museums, Fogg Art Museum

Fig.198 | Workshop of Paolo Veronese, *The Baptism of Christ*
Venice, Church of the Redentore

Fig.199 | Paolo Veronese, *The Baptism of Christ*
Florence, Palazzo Pitti, Galleria Palatina

Attributed to Bartolomeo Passerotti BOLOGNA 1529–1592 BOLOGNA

106 ❧ *A Spaniel* [AFTER PAOLO VERONESE]

Brown and white oil paint on brown prepared paper; laid down | 25.4 × 32.1cm

Inscribed at the lower right in ink: 'passarota in Verona feci[t]' ·

Provenance: David Laing; by whom bequeathed to the Royal Scottish Academy, 1879; transferred to the Gallery, 1910 (acc.no.1674)

EDINBURGH, NATIONAL GALLERY OF SCOTLAND

This fine oil study of a Cavalier King Charles spaniel relates very closely to the small dog in the centre foreground of Paolo Veronese's large canvas of *Susanna and the Elders* in the Kunsthistorisches Museum, Vienna (fig.200).[1] It has been argued that the Edinburgh drawing is Veronese's autograph preparatory study for the dog in the painting.[2] Although the handling is not incompatible with Veronese's – as a direct comparison with the similar spaniel in his *Venus, Cupid and Mars* (cat.no.69) makes clear – there are no other oil studies like this among his surviving drawings.[3] But it is the very specific inscription on the drawing that casts most doubt on the attribution to Veronese himself: why would anyone have invented this information?

For his part, Passarotti seems to have been particularly fond of dogs, if the large number that appear as accessories in his portraits – and in a few subject pictures – is anything to go by,[4] so it is entirely plausible that he should have elected to copy this particular detail from a Veronese composition. And another oil sketch on paper by him, showing the *Head of St John the Baptist*, has recently come to light.[5] This was a type of drawing that became particularly popular in Bologna towards the end of the sixteenth century in the circle of the Carracci.

If accurate, the inscription is of particular interest on another count, in that it establishes that Veronese's *Susanna and the Elders*, and by implication the nine other paintings in the same series, were in Verona in the late sixteenth century and had presumably been painted for a client in the artist's native city.[6] If so, they were soon removed from their original setting, for it has recently been established that the series was purchased by the Flemish diplomat Charles de Croy, possibly when he was in Venice in 1592.[7] The cycle originally consisted of five scenes each from the Old and the New Testaments and is usually dated to very late in Veronese's career, around 1585, by which time the artist had been based in Venice for some thirty years. This dating would imply that the copy must have been done late in Passerotti's life too, although he is not known to have been in Verona. The possibility that the inscription refers not to Bartolomeo Passerotti but to one of his four artist sons cannot be ruled out, except perhaps on qualitative grounds.

Paolo Farinati VERONA 1524–1606 VERONA

107 ❧ *Five Putti Playing Among the Branches of a Tree*

Brush and brown wash over black chalk on paper washed brownish-yellow; laid down 22.8 × 34.6cm

Inscribed on the backing sheet, in ink: '9 Drawings by Corregio, Par… / o. 10. 6'

Provenance: Sir Peter Lely (Lugt 2092); David Laing; by whom bequeathed to the Royal Scottish Academy, 1879; transferred to the Gallery, 1910 (acc.no.D 706)

EDINBURGH, NATIONAL GALLERY OF SCOTLAND

Fig.200 | Paolo Veronese, *Susanna and the Elders*
Vienna, Kunsthistorisches Museum

This charming drawing, executed almost entirely with the brush, is a characteristic late sheet by Farinati, perhaps dating from the 1590s.[1] No related painting or fresco by the artist is known, but the light-hearted subject matter, with putti gambolling in the branches and collecting fruit (the two fruits in the upper left corner appear to be pomegranates), suggest that if may have been a design for part of the decoration of a country villa.

Paolo Farinati VERONA 1524–1606 VERONA

108 ❧ Elijah and the Chariot of Fire

Pen and brown ink and wash, heightened with
white (partly oxidised), over black chalk, on
discoloured cream paper; laid down
41.6 × 26.3cm

Provenance: Sir Peter Lely (Lugt 2092); David
Laing; by whom bequeathed to the Royal
Scottish Academy, 1879; on loan to the Gallery
since 1966 (acc.no.RSA 154)

EDINBURGH, NATIONAL GALLERY OF
SCOTLAND

This drawing was formerly thought to represent
the mythological scene of Phaethon driving the
chariot of the sun.[1] In fact its true subject is the
Old Testament prophet Elijah being borne off to
heaven on a miraculous chariot of fire (II Kings
2: 9–15), which Farinati has rendered somewhat
prosaically as a Roman-style two wheeled chariot
drawn by two tandem pairs of horses. There is no
mention of the charioteer in the biblical account.
The drawing is preparatory for Farinati's fresco
of this subject on the right lateral wall of the
Marogna family chapel in the Veronese church of
San Paolo in Campo Marzio (fig.201), to which it
corresponds closely in all but a few minor details
(for example, the positioning of the charioteer's
right heel in relation to Elijah's leg, the distance
between their heads, and the introduction in the
fresco of a semi-circular projection at the rear of
the chariot). The execution of the drawing is
relatively loose for a study of this kind by
Farinati, and there are a number of visible
alterations, notably to the profile of the charioteer. The encroaching entablature shown towards
the top of each side of the drawing reflects the
real architecture of the chapel. The precociously
baroque character of the design, with the agitated
horses sweeping deep into the pictorial space, has
a particularly dramatic impact in the narrow
confines of the chapel, notwithstanding the
damage the fresco has suffered.

The chapel was built for the brothers Antonio
Maria and Giambattista Marogna, who ordered
an altarpiece from Paolo Veronese representing
*The Virgin and Child Enthroned with Saints Anthony
of Padua and John the Baptist and the two Donors*,[2]
and fresco decoration from Farinati, much of
which has disappeared due to damp. Opposite
the Elijah scene is a now fragmentary representa-

tion of *Jonah Cast into the Sea*, while above on the
ceiling there is a *Resurrected Christ* and *Angels with
the Symbols of the Passion*. It is generally assumed
that the entire decoration was completed by
1565, the date inscribed over the entrance arch to
the chapel.[3]

A related drawing in the Louvre tallies even
more closely with the fresco than the Edinburgh
drawing does (fig.202).[4] It may have been the
final *modello* for the fresco, but could equally well
be a *ricordo* of it – that is, an autograph drawn
copy of the final fresco made for future reference.
Many of Farinati's more highly finished drawings
have the appearance of *ricordi*, and there is
mention in his account book of an album of
drawings on blue paper which may have been
records of this kind.[5]

Fig.201 | Paolo Farinati, *Elijah and the Chariot of Fire*
Verona, Church of San Paolo, Marogna Chapel

Fig.202 | Paolo Farinati, *Elijah and the Chariot of Fire*
Paris, Musée du Louvre

Paolo Farinati VERONA 1524–1606 VERONA

109 ❧ The Jewish Forces Vanquishing the Supporters of Haman

Pen and brown ink and wash, heightened with white (partly oxidised to pink), over black chalk, on blue paper | 23.7 × 43.5cm

Inscribed on the verso in ink: 'na Tintoret'; and, in black chalk: 'nr to Farinato'

Provenance: E. Peart (Lugt 892); David Laing; by whom bequeathed to the Royal Scottish Academy, 1879; on loan to the Gallery since 1966 (acc.no.RSA 153)

EDINBURGH, NATIONAL GALLERY OF SCOTLAND

The subject was previously erroneously identified as the *Sabine Women Flinging themselves between the Romans and the Sabines*.[1] The drawing is in fact directly preparatory for part of the frescoed frieze representing scenes from the Old Testament story of Esther and Ahasuerus in the main reception room in the former Casa Sebastiani (also variously referred to as Bastiani or Sansebastiani), now the Biblioteca Civica, in Verona (fig.203).[2] The details of this commission are helpfully set out in Farinati's own journal.[3] An entry dated 12 May 1586 records the artist's undertaking to paint a frieze with eight scenes from the story of Esther for the patron 'Zanieronimo Bastiani' (Count Giovanni Girolamo Bastiani). He began work on the frieze the following spring, on 14 April, and it was completed on 20 June. He received a total of 90 ducats, paid in four instalments, the final one on the last day of August 1587. Bastiani was clearly confident in Farinati's abilities, since before the artist had even commenced work on the Esther frieze he ordered a second frieze and other decorations from him for other rooms in the palace.[4]

The biblical account tells how the wicked chief minister Haman had persuaded his master Ahasuerus, powerful king of Persia, to allow him to exterminate all the Jews in his kingdom. Ahasuerus's queen Esther, who unknown to him was herself Jewish, heard of the plot, exposed Haman's treachery and saved her people. Haman was hanged, and the Jewish forces exacted a terrible revenge on his supporters who rose up against them. This is the episode represented in the present drawing. A preparatory study for the portion of the scene to the immediate left of the Edinburgh drawing is in the National Gallery of Canada (fig.204).[5] The dismembered, sword-wielding arm at the left edge of the Edinburgh study in fact belongs to the soldier at the right of the Ottawa drawing. The correspondence between the two preparatory drawings and the fresco as executed is very close, with the exception of the soldier at the extreme right of the

Edinburgh sheet. His pose implies that he was conceived as the closing figure at the end of the frieze, but in the fresco itself he was transformed into a female warrior posed very differently. Two further fleeing horsemen are interposed between her and the telamon figure who terminates that wall at the corner. The fact that there are ruled framing lines at the top and bottom of the Edinburgh drawing, but not at the sides, indicates that the original sheet may have been much larger, and that it was cut into sections. Further studies for episodes represented on other walls of the room are in the British Museum, the Pierpont Morgan Library, and the Louvre.[6] All of these are about the same size and are drawn on blue paper in the same combination of media as the present sheet.

Although he was hugely prolific in other areas, Farinati made the painting of friezes in palaces in and around his native Verona a particular specialism. He had already treated the story of Esther in an earlier frieze, which no longer survives, in the Palladian Palazzo Della Torre.[7] The preparatory drawings for this earlier project are distinguished by being drawn on pale brown rather than blue paper. Although many of the episodes selected for the Sebastiani frieze inevitably repeated those in the Della Torre one, the battle scene was a new introduction.

Fig.203 | Paolo Farinati, *The Jewish Forces Vanquishing the Supporters of Haman* (detail)
Verona, Biblioteca Civica

Fig.204 | Paolo Farinati, *The Jewish Forces Vanquishing the Supporters of Haman*
Ottawa, National Gallery of Canada

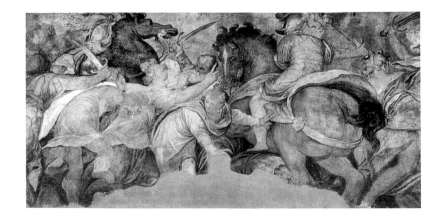

Paolo Farinati VERONA 1524–1606 VERONA

110 ❦ *The Virgin and Child* [RECTO]; *The Resurrected Christ between Two Male Saints* [VERSO]

Black and white chalk (partly oxidised to pink), with brown wash, on blue paper; verso: pen and ink only | 23.7 × 43.5cm

Inscribed on the verso in ink: 'P. Farinato / 6'.

Provenance: Sir Peter Lely (Lugt 2092); Jonathan Richardson Snr (Lugt 2184); William Gibson (not in Lugt); David Laing; by whom bequeathed to the Royal Scottish Academy, 1879; transferred to the Gallery 1910 (acc.no.D 749)

EDINBURGH, NATIONAL GALLERY OF
SCOTLAND

Contrary to what has been asserted, the study of the *Virgin and Child* on the recto is neither severely rubbed nor strengthened by a later hand;[1] its slightly unusual appearance results from the fact the artist himself clarified and reinforced the contours of a brush and wash drawing using black chalk or charcoal, evidently while it was still damp.

The verso of this drawing represents another, less familiar aspect of Farinati's draughtsmanship, although among the hundreds of surviving sheets by him there are a number of others executed in the same sketchy pen and ink manner.[2] The central figure has been interpreted as St John in the act of baptising, but it appears rather to represent the resurrected Christ holding his customary long banner with his left hand and raising his right in benediction. He is flanked on his proper right by a deacon saint, tonsured and

wearing a dalmatic, and on his left by a bishop saint, with his mitre and an open book. What must have been a very similar composition by Farinati, featuring *The Saviour between Saints Peter and John the Baptist*, is recorded on the high altar of the parish church in San Giovanni Lupatoto near Verona.[3] Below the drawing of Christ there is a seemingly unrelated fragmentary sketch of a putto with his right arm raised. The verso of this sheet was evidently drawn first, and the paper later trimmed to frame the more finished drawing on the recto. The inscription on the verso is in the hand of the English painter and collector William Gibson (1645–1703), and represents a price code inscribed on his drawings for the benefit of his widow (see also cat.no.111).[4] Neither of the drawings on this sheet has been connected to a painting by Farinati.

Paolo Farinati VERONA 1524–1606 VERONA

111 ❦ *The Virgin and Child under a Tree* [RECTO]; *Two Studies of a Figure Holding an Open Book* [VERSO]

Pen and brown ink and brown and grey wash, heightened with white, over black chalk, on blue paper; verso: brush and brown wash over black chalk | 27.7 × 21.1cm

Inscribed on the verso in ink: 'P. Farinato / 5.2'; and on two slips cut from the old mount: 'Paulo Farinati', in Richardson's hand, and with his shelf marks

Provenance: Sir Peter Lely (Lugt 2092); William Gibson (not in Lugt); Jonathan Richardson Snr (Lugt 2183); David Laing; by whom bequeathed to the Royal Scottish Academy, 1879; transferred to the Gallery 1910 (acc.no.D 1577)

EDINBURGH, NATIONAL GALLERY OF SCOTLAND

The attractive, highly finished drawing of the seated Virgin suckling the infant Christ on the recto, complete with its framing architecture at the left and landscape setting, is a characteristic late work by the artist. The blank features of the Virgin and the handling of the media are similar to a drawing at Chatsworth of *The Virgin and Child with Saints Benedict, Justina of Padua and Julian of Rimini*, which is preparatory for a small painting on copper datable to 1591.[1] To judge from the various free-hand and ruled lines towards the margins, Farinati clearly gave some thought as to how best to frame the figure group. This might imply that the drawing was made in preparation for a painting or a print, although no corresponding work appears to survive. Several prints on similar themes designed by Farinati do, however, exist (see cat.nos.149, 150).

The delicate studies on the verso, drawn entirely with the brush, seemingly represent two alternative ideas for the same figure. The inscription is in the hand of William Gibson (see cat.no.110).

Palma Giovane VENICE c.1548–1628 VENICE

112 🎋 *The Annunciation* [RECTO]; *The Presentation of Christ in the Temple* [VERSO]

Pen and brown ink and wash over black chalk on pale buff paper (verso: pen and brown ink only) 17.4 × 24.6cm

Inscribed at the lower left, in ink: 'Keerom'; numbered in pencil at the lower left: '21'

Provenance: Jan Pietersz Zomer (Lugt 1511); William Findlay Watson; by whom bequeathed to the Gallery, 1881 (acc.no.D 2917)

EDINBURGH, NATIONAL GALLERY OF SCOTLAND

The composition of the *Annunciation* on the recto of this sheet corresponds quite closely, but in reverse, to Palma Giovane's large painting of this subject now in Munich, and was almost certainly made in connection with it (fig.205).[1] The Munich *Annunciation* is the only surviving canvas from a series of four scenes from the Life of the Virgin painted by Palma in 1581–2 for the church of the Jesuit fathers (the 'Preti di Gesù') in Venice, later known as the Chiesa dell'Umiltà and long ago destroyed. Two canvases from the series were installed in each of the chapels flanking the high altar of the church: the *Annunciation* and the *Presentation of the Virgin in the Temple* in the one to the left, and the *Visitation* and the *Presentation of Christ in the Temple* in that to the right.[2] The cycle is mentioned in print as early as 1584 by the Florentine Raffaello Borghini, but had already been removed from the church and dispersed by the time Carlo Ridolfi was writing in the 1640s.[3]

The connection between the *Annunciation* drawing and the Jesuit commission is underscored by the sketch of the *Presentation of Christ in the Temple* on the verso, which was evidently preparatory for the canvas of this subject from the same cycle, now lost. A more fully worked-up study for this scene was formerly in the C.R. Rudolf collection (fig.206; present whereabouts unknown). The subject of these drawings and the lost painting has sometimes been described erroneously as the *Circumcision*,[4] but no blade is visible in either drawing, and the action centres on the High Priest receiving the baby Jesus from Mary. The *Presentation of Christ* is in fact more appropriate than the *Circumcision* to a Marian cycle of paintings, for it is linked with the purification of the Virgin and the feast of Candlemas.

The recto and verso of this sheet present very different graphic styles. The recto is unusually highly finished and precise in its execution for Palma. With its delicate washes and rather decorative treatment of the draperies, it betrays lingering Zuccaresque influences from the years the artist spent in Rome. The sketchy, rather messy pen-work on the verso, on the other hand, is reminiscent of Veronese's late drawing style.[5]

On both sides of the drawing Palma included free-hand framing lines to indicate the long horizontal format required.

Palma's point of departure for his drawing of the *Annunciation* was clearly Jacopo Caraglio's beautiful engraving after a lost altarpiece by Titian (cat.no.130). His decision to reverse the composition between the drawing and the painting now in Munich presumably had to do with its relation to its intended setting. The painted Virgin appears to gesture with her right hand towards something beyond the picture field to the left – possibly the altar of the chapel. That the artist switched the direction of lighting as well as the design between drawing and painting may have been intended to tally with the real source of illumination in the chapel.

The instruction *Keerom* ('turn over') inscribed on the recto of the drawing was probably added by the Dutch collector Jan Pietersz Zomer, whose collector's mark appears at the lower right.[6]

Fig.205 | Palma Giovane, *The Annunciation* Munich, Alte Pinakothek

Fig.206 | Palma Giovane, *The Presentation of Christ in the Temple* Formerly C. R. Rudolf Collection

Palma Giovane VENICE c.1548–1628 VENICE

113 ❧ *Solomon and the Queen of Sheba*

Pen and brown ink and wash over black chalk; squared in black chalk, and the top row of squares numbered from 1 to 10 in black chalk; laid down; two losses at lower edge of sheet 13.8 × 19.1cm

Inscribed on the mount, in ink: 'Jacopo Palma'; numbered on the back of the mount, in ink: '1033'

Provenance: Jonathan Richardson Snr. (with his mount, Lugt 2995); David Laing; his bequest to the Royal Scottish Academy, 1879; transferred to the Gallery, 1910 (acc.no.D 723)

EDINBURGH, NATIONAL GALLERY OF SCOTLAND

Intrigued by tales of Solomon's wisdom and the magnificence of his court, the Queen of Sheba journeyed to Jerusalem and sought an audience with him (I Kings 10: 1–13). Palma shows her standing before Solomon's throne, gesturing towards her camel-train laden with gifts of gold, spices and precious stones. Although the drawing is squared, presumably to facilitate enlargement of the design, no painted version of this subject by Palma is known or recorded. There is, however, another drawing of the same subject by him, similar in design to the Edinburgh sheet, in the Moravská Galerie in Brno, Czech Republic.[1]

The drawing has been dated to the 1590s,[2] but it may in fact be rather earlier, since the wiry, meandering lines used to evoke the hair of the women at the right and the camel-train behind recall the graphic style of Taddeo Zuccaro, whose drawings Palma would have known during his formative years in Rome.

The sheet is stuck down onto its mount, but a drawing on the verso including at least two figures can be detected through the paper at the upper right.

Palma Giovane VENICE c.1548–1628 VENICE

114 ❧ *A Man Seen from Behind*

Black chalk, heightened with white, on blue
paper; laid down | 29.2 × 16.1cm

Inscribed on the backing paper in pencil:
'Londonio of Milan / B. Milan 1723 / animal
painter'

Provenance: David Laing; his bequest to the
Royal Scottish Academy, 1879; on loan to the
Gallery since 1966 (acc.no.RSA 309)

EDINBURGH, NATIONAL GALLERY OF
SCOTLAND

Ignoring the inscription on the back, this
drawing was previously catalogued as anonymous seventeenth-century Bolognese school.[1]
The drawing is in fact a preparatory study for a
figure in the left foreground of Palma's large
votive painting showing *Doge Alvise Mocenigo
Giving Thanks to the Virgin for the Victory of Lepanto*
in the Venetian church of San Fantin (fig.207).[2]
The picture was probably painted in 1596 or
shortly afterwards, for this date is inscribed on a
drawing of a girl (in fact the artist's own young
daughter Virginia) in Munich, which was used
for the pose of the girl in the foreground of the
painting. The San Fantin painting was in any
case certainly finished by 1604, when it is
recorded in Giovanni Stringa's edition of
Francesco Sansovino's *Venezia Citta Nobilissima*,
published in that year.

A second drawing by Palma from the same
album in Munich is a sketchier study for the same
figure as the Edinburgh drawing and the group of
figures around him (fig.208). It shows a number
of variations relative to the final painting and
must have preceded the present sheet in the
preparatory process.

Fig.207 | Palma Giovane, *Doge Alvise Mocenigo Giving
Thanks to the Virgin for the Victory of Lepanto*
Venice, Church of San Fantin

Fig.208 | Palma Giovane, *A Figure Seen from Behind with
other Figures Around*
Munich, Staatliche Graphische Sammlung

Palma Giovane VENICE c.1548–1628 VENICE

115 ❧ St Martin and the Beggar, with the Virgin and Child Flanked by a Bishop Saint and a Pilgrim Saint Above

Cream oil paint over black chalk or charcoal on coarse textured buff paper; squared in black chalk | 39.1 × 25.9cm

Inscribed on the back of the old mount in ink: 'N. 44 / Tintoretto bought at Hudson's Sale AD: 1779'

Provenance: Thomas Hudson (Lugt 2432); his sale, Langford's, London, 15 March 1779 (and following eleven evenings); David Laing; his bequest to the Royal Scottish Academy, 1879; transferred to the Gallery, 1910 (acc.no.D 697)

EDINBURGH, NATIONAL GALLERY OF SCOTLAND

St Martin was an early Christian saint from Hungary who served in the Roman army and later, around 370 AD, became bishop of Tours in France. One winter while serving in the army in Gaul, he came upon an old beggar freezing from the cold and divided his military cloak in two and shared it with the unfortunate man. That night Christ appeared to Martin in a dream wearing the portion of the cloak he had given away. The scene shown here, in which a mounted St Martin divides his cloak with his sword, is the most frequently represented episode from his legend.

It has been suggested that this drawing may have been made in connection with a lost altarpiece of this subject – which also, unusually, included a bishop saint – formerly in the church of San Martino on the Venetian island of Murano, but the early sources disagree about the attribution of that painting.[1] Marco Boschini states that it was by Jacopo Tintoretto, but 'restored', and in large part repainted, by Palma Giovane, in which case a full compositional study by Palma would hardly have been necessary.[2] Carlo Ridolfi, on the other hand, attributed the altarpiece to Pietro Malombra.[3]

Much more direct is the relationship between the Edinburgh drawing and the high altarpiece in the parish church of Zanano di Sarezzo near Brescia, which has been attributed, together with the drawing, to Palma's little-known Brescian pupil Camillo Rama (fig.209).[4] The drawing, however, is of very high quality and is entirely characteristic of Palma's *modelli* of this kind. A likely scenario is that Palma executed the drawing specially to assist his pupil, or – less likely given the rather specific iconography of the altarpiece – that Rama availed himself of a drawing by Palma already in existence.

About fifteen drawings by Palma executed in this distinctive technique are known, several of which are preparatory for datable commissions.[5] These earliest of these is a study in the Albertina for a *Christ on the Cross with the Virgin and Saints* in the church of Zoccolanti in Potenza Picena, which is dated 1599; the latest is a sheet in the Louvre which is preparatory for an altarpiece in the Venetian church of San Geremia datable to the second decade of the seventeenth century.[6] The Edinburgh sheet falls squarely within this range, for the Zanano di Sarezzo altarpiece is dated 1609, so the drawing must have been made in that year or earlier.

The old attribution of this sheet to Tintoretto probably referred to Domenico Tintoretto, who produced many *modelli* of this kind in preparation for his paintings, rather than to his more celebrated father Jacopo. Pen and ink drawings by Palma Giovane of *St Martin and the Beggar*, differently composed, are in the British Museum and in an album of drawings by the artist in the Museo Correr in Venice.[7]

Fig.209 | Attributed to Camillo Rama, *St Martin and the Beggar*
Zanano di Sarezzo, Parish Church

Palma Giovane VENICE c.1548–1628 VENICE

116 ❧ *Two Allegorical Figures of Painting and Sculpture and a Sketch of St Jerome* [RECTO]
The Annunciation and Figure Studies [VERSO]

Pen and ink | 36.1 × 24.3cm

Inscribed by the artist on the recto, in ink: 'a venti quatro hore vine un vento cusi ardente che / pareva fiame di focho che molti pensavano che si abrugiase / case dove chi a lasciate un caldo intolerabille'('at twenty four hours [i.e. midnight] there came such a scorching wind, like flames of fire, that many [people] thought that houses were burning from which an intolerable heat remained'; and below: 'scultura'('sculpture'); 'pittura' ('painting'); 'bortolomio Scandilino in lion di f…'; and, on the verso, in ink, in a different hand: 'G.P. no: 151'

Provenance: So-called Sagredo-Borghese collection (with the characteristic inscription on the verso); Doge Nicolò Sagredo (by c.1651); his brother, Stefano Sagredo; his nephew, Zaccaria Sagredo; his wife, Cecilia Sagredo; probably Sagredo sale, Prestage, London, 9 January (postponed from 5 January) 1764;[1] David Laing; his bequest to the Royal Scottish Academy, 1879; transferred to the Gallery, 1910 (acc.no.D 1173)

EDINBURGH, NATIONAL GALLERY OF SCOTLAND

These vigorous pen sketches are characteristic examples of Palma Giovane's draughtsmanship from around 1610. The emphatic use of parallel hatching has been linked to his activity as a printmaker at that period of his career. In 1611 a group of twenty-seven etchings by him was published in Venice by Giacomo Franco in the form of a drawing manual entitled *De excellentia et nobilitate delineationis libri duo* ('Two books on the excellence and nobility of drawing'; see cat.no.154).[2] One of these etchings shows personifications of Painting and Sculpture (fig.210)[3] and, notwithstanding significant differences, it seems likely that the principal sketch on the recto of the present sheet represents an early idea for that print. The female personification of Sculpture in the drawing was transformed in the print into a young man holding a statuette of Jupiter, and each figure is now accompanied by various identifying attributes. A lost *Allegory of Painting* by Palma, executed in distemper (*guazzo*) on paper, is recorded as part of the ceiling decoration in the Scuola dei Pittori (confraternity of painters) in Venice,[4] but the presence of the personification of sculpture alongside that of painting in the Edinburgh drawing and in the related etching effectively rules out any connection with that project.

Two published drawings by Palma that are

particularly close in handling to the recto of this
drawing are a sheet of figure studies, mainly for a
group of the Three Graces, in the Fondazione
d'Arco in Mantua, which is dated 1611, and
another in the British Museum, which has been
linked to a painting datable to that same year.[5]
The latter, like the Edinburgh drawing, also
features a subsidiary sketch of St Jerome beating
his chest in penitent self-punishment.

The sketch of the *Annunciation* on the verso of
this sheet is one of countless painted and drawn
treatments of this subject by Palma (see also
cat.no.112). The horizontal format indicated by
the framing lines in the drawing, and the
prominent inclusion of the dove of the Holy
Ghost at the upper centre, towards which Gabriel
gestures energetically, link the sketch most
closely with a painting in the church of Santi
Simeone, Giuda e Bartolomeo (called San
Gaetano) in Padua (fig.211), although there are
also some significant differences.[6] An unpublished drawing in the British Museum, also from
the Sagredo collection, features two further
studies for the same painting.[7]

Fig.210 | Palma Giovane,
An Allegory of Painting and Sculpture
London, British Museum

Fig.211 | Palma Giovane,
The Annunciation
Padua, Church of San Gaetano

Palma Giovane VENICE c.1548–1628 VENICE

117 ✠ *Self-portrait* [RECTO]; *Study of a Man's Legs* [VERSO]

Black and red chalk, with accidental touches of ochre chalk, on blue paper (verso: black chalk only) | 23.9 × 20.1cm

Inscribed at the lower left in ink: 'Palme effigies ab ipsomet delineata anno Dñi 1614. Die 15 Decemb.' ('The portrait of Palma drawn by himself in the year of our Lord 1614, on 15th December'); numbered on the verso in black chalk: '16'

Provenance: William Findlay Watson; by whom bequeathed, 1881 (acc.no.D 2237)

EDINBURGH, NATIONAL GALLERY OF SCOTLAND

Although the inscription on the recto is not in Palma's own hand, there is no reason to doubt its accuracy. Comparison with numerous other painted and drawn self-portraits by the artist, such as the one in the Pinacoteca Querini-Stampalia in Venice (fig.212) of about 1606,[1] leaves no doubt that the features are indeed his own. Palma would have been in his mid-sixties in 1614, although he scarcely looks older in the drawing than he does in the Querini-Stampalia painting. An unusual *Self-portrait in a Monk's Habit* in the Bardisian collection, painted on slate, may date from around the same time as the Edinburgh drawing, or even somewhat later, although it has hitherto been associated chronologically with the Querini portrait of about 1606.[2] The technique of this drawing, using coloured chalks on blue paper, shows the influence of the Bassano family and was used only occasionally by Palma.

The fragmentary sketch of legs on the verso of this sheet cannot be linked to a particular painting by the artist, although similar 'zig-zag' arrangements of male legs occur repeatedly in Palma's work, particularly in his representations of the dead Christ and of St Sebastian.

Fig.212 | Palma Giovane, *Self-portrait* Venice, Pinacoteca Querini-Stampalia

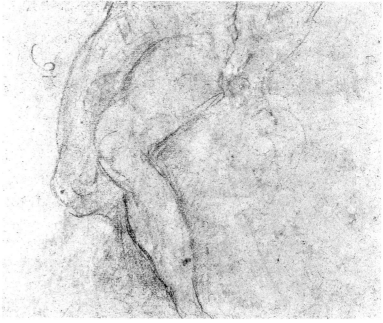

Palma Giovane VENICE *c.*1548–1628 VENICE

118 ❧ *Christ Standing in a Chalice Supported by Angels*

Pen and brown ink over charcoal or black chalk dots ('spolveri') pounced from another sheet; laid down, with all four corners made up
26.9 × 19.3cm

Inscribed on the chalice, in ink: 'Palma'; at the lower right, in pencil: 'Palma'; on the verso, in ink: 'Palma Veccia' (twice) and 'No.46'

Provenance: William Findlay Watson; by whom bequeathed, 1881 (acc.no.D 3099)

EDINBURGH, NATIONAL GALLERY OF SCOTLAND

In this powerfully symbolic, eucharistic image, the limp body of Christ is held up by angels in a chalice, into which blood gushes from a wound in his side. The purpose was to express forcefully in visual terms the Catholic doctrine of transubstantiation, that is the belief that the bread and wine consecrated by the priest actually become the body and blood of Christ, to be consumed by the faithful during Mass. This was one of the key issues that divided the Catholic and Protestant churches, the latter believing the bread and wine of the Eucharist to be purely symbolic of the body and blood of Christ.

Palma's drawing, which probably dates from relatively late in his career, may have been made as a design for the decoration of a tabernacle door (a tabernacle being the place where the consecrated Host was reserved for use in the Mass), or more likely for the embroidered decoration of a liturgical vestment. An earlier example of this imagery being used for an embroidered panel on a chasuble – the overgarment worn by a priest during Mass – is preserved in the Duomo of Motta on the Venetian mainland.[1] The commission for Palma's design may have come from one of the many lay confraternities (*scuole*) in Venice dedicated to the Sacrament, which devoted themselves to the maintenance of tabernacle altars in the city's churches, and to supplying the vessels and vestments used in the Mass.[2]

Of interest from a technical point of view is the presence in this drawing of numerous dotted contours, indicating that the underlying design was transferred from another drawing by 'pricking' or perforating its main outlines and then 'pouncing' or dabbing chalk or charcoal dust through the holes. The artist then worked up and revised this design using pen and ink. A closely related drawing by Palma in the Museo Correr in Venice (fig.213) has faint framing lines, which indicate that the object for which the design was intended was to be oval in shape.[3]

Fig.213 | Palma Giovane, *Christ Standing in a Chalice Supported by Angels*
Venice, Museo Correr

Palma Giovane VENICE c.1548–1628 VENICE

119 ✤ *St Francis Receiving the Stigmata*

Pen and brown ink and wash, heightened with white (partially oxidised), over traces of black chalk, on brown paper | 38 × 23.9cm

Inscribed on the verso in ink: 'Carrache 4' and 'Vieux Palma'

Provenance: David Laing; his bequest to the Royal Scottish Academy, 1879; on loan to the Gallery since 1966 (acc.no.RSA 223)

EDINBURGH, NATIONAL GALLERY OF SCOTLAND

While praying at La Verna in 1224, St Francis experienced a vision of a seraph in the form of a cross, from which he miraculously received wounds in his hands, feet and the side of his chest corresponding to those inflicted on Christ at the Crucifixion. These wounds, known as the stigmata, remained visible until his death two years later.

This dramatic compositional drawing is preparatory for Palma's altarpiece in the Chiesa dell'Angelo Raffaele in Venice (fig.214).[1] Signed and dated 162[5] (the last digit is indistinct), this is the latest of four surviving altarpieces of this subject by the artist, and others are recorded in the early sources. Although there is no indication of a curved top in the drawing, its design lends itself readily to the arched format of the altarpiece. The dramatic and moving conception of the saint in the drawing, with his face cast into shadow and his mystical experience internalised, was modified in the final painting, where his pose is more open and accessible to the worshipper.

Fig.214 | Palma Giovane, *St Francis Receiving the Stigmata* Venice, Chiesa dell'Angelo Raffaele

Leandro Bassano BASSANO DEL GRAPPA 1557–1622 VENICE

120 ❧ *The Adoration of the Shepherds* (after Jacopo Bassano)

Black and red chalk on blue-grey paper
23.7 × 29.6cm (excluding later additions of
2.6cm at the left edge and 0.7cm at the right
edge)

Provenance: Jonathan Richardson Senr (Lugt
2184); Edward Bouverie (Lugt 325); William
Findlay Watson; by whom bequeathed to the
Gallery, 1881 (acc.no.D 2232)

EDINBURGH, NATIONAL GALLERY OF
SCOTLAND

This is a loose copy after the lower portion of
Jacopo Bassano's altarpiece painted in 1568 for
the church of San Giuseppe (St Joseph) in his
native town of Bassano del Grappa, and now in
the Museo Civico there (fig.215).[1] This soon
became one of Jacopo's most celebrated works,
and it was widely praised and imitated. The
drawing was once considered to be by Jacopo
himself, but there is now a general consensus
that it is by his second son Leandro.[2] Drawings
such as this would have been one of the means by
which compositions were recycled in the Bassano
workshop, in which numerous versions and
variants of successful designs were often produced. No painted version of this composition in
the horizontal format of the drawing is known,
but there is a signed variant by Girolamo
Bassano, Leandro's younger brother, in the
Kunsthistorisches Museum in Vienna which is
more or less square in shape.[3] In his copy
Leandro rather fudged the area at the left above

Fig.215 | Jacopo Bassano, *The Adoration of the Shepherds*
Bassano del Grappa, Museo Civico

St Joseph, which in the altarpiece is occupied by Saints Victor and Corona – who with Joseph were the co-patrons of the church – and by a portrait of the donor. These venue-specific figures in the original would have been less appropriate in any spin-off versions of the composition (in the above-mentioned variant by Girolamo, the artist omitted the donor and secularised the two saints).

The handling of this drawing is very similar to a group of other compositional drawings by Leandro, including three examples in the British Museum (the *Adoration of the Shepherds*,[4] the *Parable of Dives and Lazarus*,[5] and a study for an altarpiece formerly in the church of Santa Lucia, Venice);[6] one in the Fitzwilliam Museum (fig.216);[7] and one in the Uffizi in Florence.[8] The strips of paper added to each side of the Edinburgh sheet have been thought to be original by some writers, but they must be later additions dating from no earlier than the eighteenth century. It may be noted that Edward Bouverie placed his collector's mark in the lower left corner of the original sheet rather than on the addition.

Fig.216 | Leandro Bassano, *Christ in the House of Simon* Cambridge, Fitzwilliam Museum

Brush and brown wash over black chalk on blue paper; the sheet made up of two pieces of paper joined horizontally about 8.8cm from the bottom edge | 39.4 × 21.5cm

Inscribed in brown ink at the lower right: 'Benedetto Calliari'; on the verso, in brown ink: 'B. C. Nᵒ.3'; and in pencil, on a slip cut from the old mount: 'Benedetto Cagliari / Brother of Paul Veronese'

Provenance: Count J. von Ross (Lugt 2693); William Findlay Watson; by whom bequeathed to the Gallery, 1881 (acc.no.D 2225)

EDINBURGH, NATIONAL GALLERY OF SCOTLAND

Occupying the entire sheet is the massive figure of St Jerome supporting his head with his right hand, gesturing forcefully with his left, and gazing intently towards what was presumably intended to be a crucifix beyond the left edge of the drawing. The traditional attribution of this sheet to Paolo Veronese's younger brother Benedetto Caliari – as attested by no fewer than three old inscriptions – seems to be correct, although no other drawing by him quite like this is known.[1] Nor can it be connected with any painted St Jerome by Benedetto. The figure type and gestures nevertheless find close parallels among his paintings, for example his *St Peter Appearing to St Agatha in Prison* painted in the late 1560s for the church of Santa Maria degli Angeli on Murano (now in the church of San Pietro there).[2] The pose of the saint in the drawing is based closely on the *Penitent St Jerome* in Paolo Veronese's altarpiece in the Venetian church of Sant'Andrea della Zirada, with the exception of the proper right hand, which in the painting is shown clutching the stone with which the saint beat his breast in contrition.[3]

On the verso is a slight sketch in black chalk of a male nude, shoulders to buttocks, and a separate sketch of a lower left leg.

Pietro Malombra VENICE 1556–1618 VENICE

122 ❧ St Stanislaus Raising a Dead Man, with St Hyacinth Kneeling before the Trinity Above

Pen and brown ink and wash, heightened with white, over traces of black chalk, on blue paper 38.5 × 20.6cm

Provenance: Sir Peter Lely (Lugt 2092); David Laing; by whom bequeathed to the Royal Scottish Academy, 1879; on loan to the Gallery since 1966 (acc.no.RSA 221)

EDINBURGH, NATIONAL GALLERY OF SCOTLAND

Malombra's contribution to Venetian painting around 1600 is obscured by the fact that most of the paintings ascribed to him in the early sources are lost or unrecognised. Those that have come down to us show him to have been a painter of modest talents, but the few drawings by him that have been identified are rather more distinctive.

The drawing shown here was long thought to be by a Veronese artist; an inscription on the old mount (now removed from the drawing) attributes it to Paolo Farinati, and later an attribution to Marco del Moro was suggested.[1] It is in fact of some importance as the touchstone for Malombra as a draughtsman, being the only sheet that can be firmly connected to a surviving painting by him.[2] It is preparatory for the altarpiece painted for the altar of the Polish Nation in the left aisle of the Basilica of St Anthony (the Santo) in Padua (fig.217).[3] This was the most prestigious of three commissions executed by Malombra for churches in Padua; it is signed and is described in Carlo Ridolfi's *Life* of the artist.[4] An inscribed tablet set into the wall next to the altar bears the date 1607, which must reflect the year the altar was consecrated. It seems likely that the altarpiece was painted by that date or shortly afterwards, although it has also been argued on stylistic grounds that it dates from several years later, around 1612.[5] In 1809 the original altar was replaced with a grander one transferred from another Paduan church, into which Malombra's picture was inserted.[6] Comparison between the preparatory drawing and the altarpiece indicates that the latter may have been cut slightly at each side at that time to fit the new altar,[7] which would explain the rather abrupt truncation of some of the marginal figures in the painting, as well as its unusually tall, narrow proportions. Having been replaced with a new altarpiece in 1979, Malombra's picture now hangs on one of the piers in the right aisle of the basilica.

In the foreground of the drawing Stanislaus Szczepanowski, Bishop of Cracow and patron saint of Poland, accompanied by acolytes, is shown miraculously raising a youth, Piotrawin, from the dead. Behind, in the middle distance, the resurrected Piotrawin testifies before the enthroned king of Poland on behalf of the bishop, who had been falsely accused of usurping some land from him. In an unconnected scene above, Hyacinth (Iaccho Odrowąż), a popular Polish Dominican missionary who had recently (1594) been canonised by Pope Clement VIII, is shown kneeling before the Holy Trinity, receiving a holy vestment bearing an inscription from the Virgin Mary.[8] The most notable difference between the preparatory drawing and Malombra's altarpiece is the insertion in the lower right corner of the rather striking portrait of its patron, Girolamo Czyżowski.[9] This had the

effect of pushing the main action further back into the picture space. And whereas in the drawing Piotrawin is daringly posed in the foreground with his back to the viewer, in the painting he has been swivelled round and transformed into a more familiar, Lazarus-like character – although his massive and sharply foreshortened left leg projecting out towards the viewer at the centre is hardly conventional. The precise, highly finished nature of the Edinburgh drawing suggests that it may have been made to be shown to Czyżowski for approval of the design; and it was presumably at this stage that he instructed that his own image should be introduced.

One of the few other drawings that can be convincingly attributed to Malombra, a *Coronation of the Virgin* in the Akademie der Bildenden Künste in Vienna, shows a similar compositional arrangement to the Edinburgh sheet, with a cloudy barrier dividing the scene into two distinct zones.[10] The technique and figure types in the Edinburgh drawing are very similar to those in a drawing of the *Miracle of the True Cross* recently on the New York art market and now in the Horvitz collection; this has hitherto been attributed to the Veronese artist Battista Zelotti, but can now confidently be added to the slim corpus of drawings by Malombra.[11]

Fig.217 | Pietro Malombra,
St Stanislas Raising a Dead Man, with St Hyacinth Kneeling before the Trinity Above
Padua, Basilica del Santo

Antonio Vicentino, called Tognone ACTIVE IN VICENZA c.1560–75
123 ❧ *The Judgement of Midas*

Pen and brown ink and wash, heightened with white, on blue paper; laid down; a collector's mark cut out from the lower right margin (now made up) | 20.4 × 20.6cm; a segment 2.3cm deep added at the top and another 0.3cm wide at the left side

Inscribed on the mount in ink: 'Tognon di Vicenza'; and on the back in black chalk: 'Tait [illegible word] 897 / May 18 / 1840'

Provenance: Bindon Blood (Lugt 3011, with his inscription on the verso); David Laing; by whom bequeathed to the Royal Scottish Academy, 1879; on loan to the Gallery since 1966 (acc.no.RSA 156)

EDINBURGH, NATIONAL GALLERY OF SCOTLAND

The drawing illustrates a seldom represented moment in Ovid's tale of the musical contest between Apollo and Pan, who are shown at the lower right and left respectively. The contest was judged by the mountain god Tmolus, seated at the centre, who pronounced Apollo the winner; but King Midas who was also present rashly disagreed – the episode shown here – and Apollo punished him by giving him ass's ears. There is a very similar circular drawing at Windsor Castle on a closely related theme – Apollo flaying Marsyas following his victory in another musical contest (fig.218),[1] and the two designs must have been made in connection with the same project.[2] Like the present drawing, that sheet bears an old attribution to the otherwise virtually unknown 'Tonion di vincenza', who is to be identified with Antonio da Vicenza, called Tognone, a pupil of Battista Zelotti (*c*.1526–1578) to whom Carlo Ridolfi dedicated a short biography.[3] During a brief artistic career which he abandoned to become a soldier, Tognone seems to have specialised in mural decorations, none of which appear to have survived.

Although notably feeble in execution, the style of the two drawings is closely dependent on that of Zelotti, and their compositions are similarly indebted to ceiling paintings by Zelotti such as his three roundels for the ceiling of the Biblioteca Marciana in Venice and the frescoed *Council of the Gods* in the Palazzo Chiericati in Vicenza.[4] The tentative attribution to Tognone of a drawing of the *Flight into Egypt* in the Uffizi seems very plausible on stylistic grounds by comparison with the Edinburgh and Windsor roundels.[5] Two further drawings at Windsor, possibly copies after a painted work by Zelotti, seem also to be by the same hand.[6]

Fig.218 | Antonio Vicentino, *An Allegorical Scene* Windsor Castle, Royal Library

Attributed to Alessandro Maganza VICENZA 1556–1632 VICENZA
124 ✣ The Holy Family with Angels

Pen and brown ink and wash over graphite on
discoloured cream paper; laid down
25.3 × 19.7cm

Provenance: Unidentified collector's mark at the
lower right, largely obliterated; William Findlay
Watson; by whom bequeathed to the Gallery,
1881 (acc.no.D 3110)

EDINBURGH, NATIONAL GALLERY OF
SCOTLAND

Previously catalogued as early seventeenth-
century Veronese school,[1] the re-attribution of
this sheet to Alessandro Maganza,[2] who headed a
productive family workshop in Vicenza, seems
very plausible if not completely watertight. The
drawing styles of the various members of the
Maganza workshop, which at times are almost
indistinguishable, have only recently begun to be
clarified.[3]

The hint of landscape indicates that the
subject of this drawing is the rather rare one of
the Holy Family attended by angels during the
Rest on the Flight into Egypt, an episode
recorded in the *Golden Legend* and other late
medieval sources. One angel fastens a makeshift
canopy, while the other presents the infant Jesus
with fruit and a flower. Maganza painted a
picture of this subject for the church of San
Gaetano in Brescia, probably around 1600–5.[4] It
is possible that the drawing may be an early
design for that painting, although it differs
significantly from the composition as delivered.

Stylistically the Edinburgh sheet compares
well with a drawing of a similar subject by
Maganza at Christ Church, notably in the
somewhat stilted poses of the angels (fig.219).[5]
On the other hand, it also has much in common
with a compositional drawing of the *Madonna of
the Rosary with Saints* in the Pierpont Morgan
Library, which has recently been tentatively
attributed to Alessandro's son, Giambattista
Maganza il Giovane.[6]

Fig.219 | Alessandro Maganza, *The Virgin and Child
with Angels*
Oxford, Christ Church Picture Gallery

Federico Zuccaro SANT'ANGELO IN VADO (MARCHE) 1540/42–1609 ANCONA

125 ✠ *Two Infant Angels on Clouds Bearing a Cross* [AFTER TITIAN]

Black and red chalk | 18.4 × 13.8cm

Provenance: Nicholas Lanier (Lugt 2885); Jonathan Richardson Senr (Lugt 2183); Henry Stephen Olivier (Lugt Suppl. 1373); Giles Robertson; by whom presented to the Gallery, 1976 (acc.no.D 5024)

EDINBURGH, NATIONAL GALLERY OF SCOTLAND

This is a copy, with some minor variations, of the upper portion of Titian's celebrated altarpiece known as the *Madonna di Ca' Pesaro* or *Pesaro Madonna* in the church of the Frari in Venice (figs.20, 220).[1] Executed between 1519 and 1526, this was the second major commission Titian painted for that important church, having recently completed the great *Assumption of the Virgin* for the high altar (see fig.19). In his copy Zuccaro omitted the left wing of the rearmost angel, and the left arm of his companion, and there are a number of other small differences of pose and detail, none of which amounts to a wilful intent on the copyist's part to modify Titian's original. It could simply be that it was difficult to see some of the details of the upper part of the altarpiece from the floor of the nave far below, and Zuccaro's view would have been steeply foreshortened. We can only speculate as to why this particular part of the picture caught his eye.

Zuccaro was one of the most prolific and successful artists of his generation. Originally from Sant'Angelo in Vado near Urbino in the Marche, he was based mainly in Rome, but travelled and worked extensively within Italy and beyond, even paying a visit to the court of Elizabeth I in London. He made a large number of drawn copies of works by other masters he saw on his travels, almost invariably in the combination of red and black chalk used for the present sketch, and he may have carried with him sketchbooks reserved for this purpose.[2] Many of these copies show slight variations relative to their models. A huge number of Zuccaro's copies was owned by the seventeenth-century banker and connoisseur of drawings Everhard Jabach, in Paris, who may have acquired them en bloc.[3]

Zuccaro visited Venice on three occasions – in 1563–5 (when he carried out the decoration of the Grimani chapel in San Francesco della Vigna), in 1582 (during a period of exile from the papal court) and again in 1603 – and made numerous copies after paintings by Titian, Tintoretto and Veronese.[4] He continued to make copies late into his career and his drawing style changed very little, so it is difficult to date this drawing with any certainty. However, there seems to be some consensus that most of his copies after Venetian paintings are likely to have been made during his protracted first stay there, when their impact would have been greatest.

Fig.220 | Titian, *The Madonna di Ca' Pesaro* (detail)
Venice, Church of Santa Maria Gloriosa dei Frari

Bernardo Strozzi GENOA 1581–1644 VENICE

126 ✿ *St John the Baptist* [AFTER TITIAN]

Black chalk with touches of white on grey-brown paper | 44.4 × 21.4cm (max.); cut irregularly

Provenance: David Laing; by whom bequeathed to the Royal Scottish Academy, 1879; on loan to the Gallery since 1974 (ACC.NO. RSA935)

EDINBURGH, NATIONAL GALLERY OF SCOTLAND

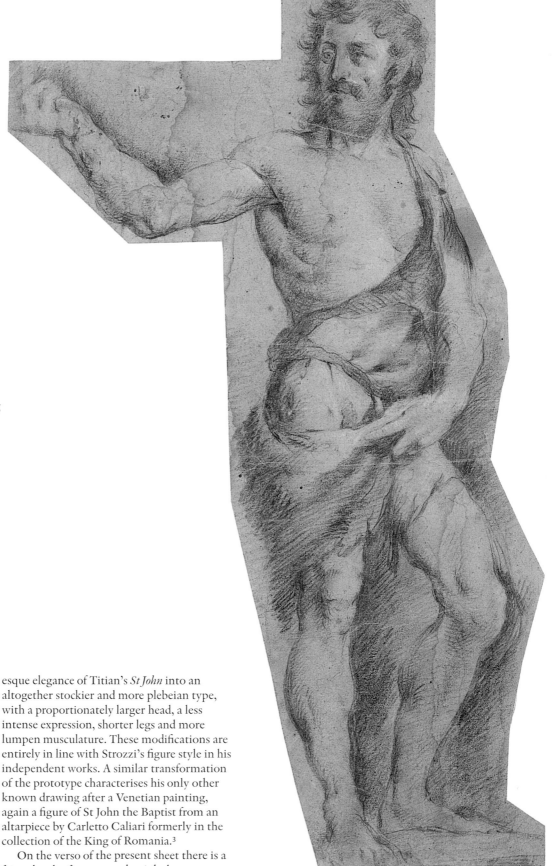

Strozzi was arguably the most accomplished Genoese artist of his generation. Having trained as an artist, around 1598 he became a Capuchin monk, but after about ten years he was given permission to leave his monastery in order to provide for his widowed mother and unmarried sister. He worked with great success and productivity in his native city for over two decades, but a protracted dispute with his Capuchin brethren led to his fleeing to Venice in 1633, where he remained for the rest of his life. He was sometimes known there as 'il Prete Genovese', the Genoese priest.

This drawing must date from this last decade of Strozzi's career.[1] It is a fairly faithful copy of Titian's *St John the Baptist* (fig.221), which was painted a century earlier for the chapel belonging to Vincenzo di Giacomo Polani situated to the right of the high altar in the Venetian church of Santa Maria Maggiore.[2] The commission is not documented, and the picture is variously dated between the early 1530s and about 1550. In his copy Strozzi transformed the idealised, statu-

Fig.221 Titian, *St John the Baptist*
Venice, Galleria dell' Accademia

esque elegance of Titian's *St John* into an altogether stockier and more plebeian type, with a proportionately larger head, a less intense expression, shorter legs and more lumpen musculature. These modifications are entirely in line with Strozzi's figure style in his independent works. A similar transformation of the prototype characterises his only other known drawing after a Venetian painting, again a figure of St John the Baptist from an altarpiece by Carletto Caliari formerly in the collection of the King of Romania.[3]

On the verso of the present sheet there is a faint sketch of a torso and a right leg.

III PRINTS

PRINTMAKING IN THE AGE OF TITIAN

Michael Bury

By the very end of the fifteenth and the early years of the sixteenth century, Venice had established itself as one of the most important centres for printmaking in Europe. Fundamental for this development was the city's position as an international commercial centre, open to several of the great trade routes through Europe and the Mediterranean. These provided paths for the distribution of printed materials, but they also led to a constant stream of potential clients, of the greatest diversity, passing through the city.[1] More directly significant for print production was the fact that by the end of the fifteenth century the city had become the most important centre in Europe of the book-printing industry and of the book trade. It has been estimated that in the second quarter of the sixteenth century Venice dominated Italian book production, surpassing on its own, and by a substantial margin, the whole of the rest of the peninsula.[2]

The illustrated book required the work of woodcutters, for it was not until the second half of the sixteenth century that engraved illustrations began to replace woodcuts. It was in the 1490s that there began to emerge printmakers of extraordinary refinement who produced work of the finest quality. This is seen in books such as Ketham's *Fascicolo di Medecina,* printed by Johannes and Gregorius de Gregoriis in 1494, and the *Hypnerotomachia Poliphili* of 1499, printed by Aldo Manuzio (see cat.no.164).[3] In the closing years of the fifteenth century, alongside the production of book illustrations, there began to appear independent woodcuts of an ambitious

kind, often conceived on a monumental scale. On the one hand, their publication was in the control of men like the Nuremberg merchant Anton Kolb, or printers like Bernardino Benalio and Gregorio de' Gregoriis who produced books as well as prints; on the other hand of those such as Benedetto Bordon, Giovanni da Brescia and Domenico delle Greche, who described themselves as painters.[4] This fundamental polarity continued throughout the century.

It has often been proposed that woodcuts and engravings should be considered separately; there is much to recommend that approach because they involved different techniques, and different structures of manufacture and sale prevailed. But there is, nevertheless, clear evidence of convergence as well as divergence. Designers of woodcuts did not usually cut the blocks themselves, so painters such as Jacopo de' Barbari and Domenico Campagnola, who practiced engraving (see cat.nos.127, 128, 129), could also turn their hands to designing woodcuts. The nature of the subjects treated in woodcut and in engraving also showed a certain convergence. The learned subject matter of pagan mythology and history, for example, can be found represented in both media: cases would be Jacopo de' Barbari's woodcuts of *Satyrs* (fig.222), or the *Triumph of Caesar* by Jacob of Strassburg. One factor that may have encouraged this crossover was the example of Albrecht Dürer, the most admired printmaker of the period, whose works showed that both media could produce remarkable but distinctive effects, demonstrating that there was every reason to cultivate both. In Venice, the woodcut was to become a medium that elicited grand performances even from artists of the calibre of Titian.

There is some doubt about how Titian's woodcuts came into existence. However, it seems likely that for the most part they were commissioned by professional printers and print dealers, and that Titian produced drawings for a fee. This would have been the method adopted in the cases of the *Triumph of Christ* and the *Crossing of the Red Sea*, designed in the second decade of the century when Titian was still at the start of his career. As far as we know, Titian's name did not appear on early editions of these prints, a point that has recently received partial confirmation from the evidence of Ferdinand Columbus's inventory. Columbus, who died in 1539, owned early editions of some of these woodcuts, which no longer survive, and Titian's name never appears.[5]

The first indication that Titian initiated the making of a print does not involve a woodcut, but an engraving. This is the fine *Annunciation* (cat.no.130) of about 1537, engraved by the Veronese printmaker Jacopo Caraglio. The composition records an altarpiece the painter had made for the nuns of Santa Maria degli Angeli on Murano. In the event, the nuns were unable to afford it and Titian decided to present it instead either to the Emperor Charles V or to the Empress Isabella. An inscription on the engraving makes explicit both Titian's responsibility for the design and also the destined recipient, the emperor. Much later in his career, Titian's gift to Pius V of a devotional image of *The Martyrdom of*

St Peter Martyr was also commemorated by an engraving (cat.no.134). In these cases the painter's responsibility is clear and the manifest intention was to proclaim his own achievement and the high status of those he served. Because in both cases the original paintings have disappeared, we cannot know directly how faithful the prints were to the originals. However, with the *Annunciation* it can be deduced that certain alterations must have been made. In particular, there is a visual statement of the Imperial gift: the presence in the heavens of angels carrying the two columns with the motto 'PLUS ULTRA', the personal *impresa* (device) of Charles V. These can never have formed part of the altarpiece. It may further be guessed that the painting had a round top, made rectangular in the print. Such adjustments to the *Annunciation* fit well with what happened in the later engravings that Titian had made.

The most important collaboration between Titian and an engraver was his arrangement with the Netherlander, Cornelis Cort. We do not know the circumstances of Cort's arrival in Venice, but it is clear that when he arrived he worked very closely indeed with Titian in the period 1565–6 (cat.nos.142, 143, 144, 145). The painter chose very carefully six compositions for Cort to work with: a mixture of secular and sacred, including compositions in which landscape had a very important role and others where figures were dominant. Cort's success in Titian's eyes is indicated by the fact that in 1571 he returned, and produced two further engravings: *The Martyrdom of St Lawrence* (cat.no.146) and

left to right

Fig.222 | After Jacopo de' Barbari, *The Combat between Men and Satyrs*
Vienna, Graphische Sammlung Albertina

Fig.223 | Giulio Sanuto, *Venus and Adonis*
London, Victoria and Albert Museum

Fig.224 | Giovanni Britto, *Portrait of Titian* (after Titian)
Amsterdam, Rijksmuseum

Tarquin and Lucretia. Whereas in early states of the first group of six works Cort's name did not appear anywhere on the engravings, he was credited with the work on the later two. Initially Titian can only have regarded Cort as his executive arm, but once his fame had increased, it became useful to advertise the fact that it was he who had been responsible for the engravings. Titian prepared special drawings for Cort. This can be deduced from the fact that when taking existing compositions as the model, the painter seems never to have just had them copied. *The Martyrdom of St Lawrence* is a good example, where the engraved composition was developed from a conflation of his two painted versions, one in Venice and the other at El Escorial. The motivation behind such procedures was the need to ensure that the designs worked effectively in the black and white medium of the print.

There were other engravers who used Titian's designs. Martino Rota, it has been argued, stepped in and became Titian's collaborator following Cort's departure from Venice in 1566.[6] However, in cases like Rota's *The Martyrdom of St Peter Martyr* (cat.no.147), the evidence is against this theory, for what was produced is a straightforward reproductive engraving after the altarpiece in Santi Giovanni e Paolo. The case of Giulio Sanuto is more complex. He was an illegitimate son of one of the leading members of the great Sanuto clan and, although he appears to have operated in some respects as a professional engraver, he tried as much as possible to work outside the normal commercial publishing structures.[7] His *Venus and Adonis* of 1559 shows important differences from Titian's paintings of this subject, not least in the adoption of a vertical format.[8] Whether it was done with the painter's approval and with the aid of a drawing that he provided is unclear. It was certainly not well received in some quarters. The Netherlandish humanist, Lampsonius, in his letter to Titian of 1567, mentioned two engravings of *Venus* that in his view did not do honour to Titian's reputation.[9] Sanuto's was one of them (fig.223); the other was the anonymous one exhibited here (cat.no.140).

While many of the woodcuts that Titian designed were commissions from commercial printers or print dealers and his involvement would have been relatively limited, there is one that suggests a much closer relationship, more comparable to what can be observed with the engravings. This is the *Six Saints* (cat.no.132), which relates closely to the lower half of his painted altarpiece for the Venetian church of San Nicolò ai Frari (fig.230). According to Vasari, Titian drew the composition on the block, which others cut and printed. Comparison between the altarpiece and the woodcut shows a significant alteration to the figure of St Sebastian. The naturalism of the painted saint was the object of comment, not necessarily favourable, among contemporaries.[10] In the print the figure is completely different, being given a much more orthodox contrapposto pose. The fact that St Sebastian was the object of special attention is also confirmed by the evidence of a plug: a piece of the original block, corresponding to the saint's head, was cut out and a new piece of wood inserted. These could be signs that Titian was motivated by the same concerns in this woodcut as he was in the engravings. The saint's naturalism worked well in oil paint, but in the linear drawing of the woodcut it might have been judged weak, so it was redesigned. This in turn would suggest that Titian regarded the print as a means of displaying his powers of invention. The fact that only a part of the altarpiece is represented, with an emphasis on the figures to the exclusion of any background, makes it difficult to think that it was intended to attract buyers as either a devotional or a subject print. However, it must be admitted that the idea that it was conceived as an exemplum of the painter's achievement as a designer is made less plausible by the absence Titian's name.

We have the names of two woodcutters working in Venice in the middle of the century who in one way or another can be connected with Titian: Giovanni Britto and Nicolò Boldrini. There was also a master who signed himself with the monogram 'B' with a horizontal line (possibly an 'I') through the middle of the 'B'. There has been a tendency to suppose that there were no others, and even to conflate the monogrammist with one or other of the named cutters.[11] The situation is one of complete scholarly confusion, with each writer on the subject contradicting his predecessors without any substantial evidence to go on. Britto is a particularly good example. Although he commonly described himself as *intagliatore* (cutter), all his documented activity was in publishing. In 1543 he was involved in the publication of an unillustrated book printed in Venice by Marcolini, and his name on a portrait of Titian of about 1550 (fig.224), and on another of Charles V, is there as printer or publisher, not as cutter.[12] One very important issue that is usually not discussed is whether in fact it is possible to discriminate between individual cutters by means of visual analysis. As with all woodcuts, the possibility that the artist responsible for the original invention either drew on the block or provided a drawing that could be directly transferred, means that a single woodcutter might produce very different results depending on his model. It is highly questionable whether one should expect to find different personal styles.[13] The invisibility of the cutter, whose task was to cut the drawing into the block as precisely

and accurately as possible, may have been the principal criterion for judging his excellence. It may be relevant that the practice of inscribing a woodcut with the name of someone who explicitly identified himself as the cutter begins rather late and is largely confined to those responsible for chiaroscuro woodcuts; for example Nicolò Boldrini's *Venus* after Titian of 1566.[14]

The chiaroscuro woodcut is a special case. It had been developed in Germany in the early years of the sixteenth century as a means of providing tonal and colouristic effects in a printed image.[15] It involved the creation and deployment of two or more blocks: one, known as the key block, printing black and the others providing tone. The distribution of the design through the different blocks in such a way that they would cumulatively produce a successful image, was one aspect of the special complexity of this medium. Another was the problem of printing, requiring the exact registration of the different blocks on the paper. The technique was known in Venice in the second decade of the century, when Ugo da Carpi applied for a privilege to cover what he claimed, falsely, to have been his own invention. Ugo made a particularly beautiful *St Jerome* after Titian, but soon moved to Rome where he became famous producing works after compositions by Raphael and Parmigianino. Nicolò Vicentino's *An Allegory of Time* after Pordenone (cat.no.131) is a fine example of this technique, probably produced in Venice in the 1530s.

Although woodcuts continued to be produced in Venice in the second half of the sixteenth century with a great degree of creativity and skill – as seen in the work of Giovanni Britto, Nicolò Boldrini, Andrea Schiavone and Giuseppe Scolari – and although they remained relatively significant if judged by the standards of what happened elsewhere in the peninsula, nevertheless copperplate prints came to predominate. It was in the 1550s that this change became overwhelmingly evident. A symbolic moment in the emerging supremacy of engraving was Giacomo Gastaldi's map of *Piedmont*, which Matteo Pagano issued on wood in 1555 and which in the following year was engraved on copper by Fabio Licinio (1521–1565).[16] There were precedents for this: Gastaldi's world map was engraved in 1546, already anticipating the resurgence of a medium that had been used for maps in the fifteenth century.[17]

The demand for engraved maps may be part of the explanation for the phenomenon of the shift from woodcut to engraving as the preferred medium. The importance of the printed map within the economy of Venetian print production was considerable: Venetian maps had come to dominate the European markets and the output was enormous.[18] But the advantages of the copperplate had become evident in other areas too. The greater sharpness and precision of engraving, with its ability to manage fine detail, seem to have made it the preferred medium for many categories of subject matter. In figural prints there were already anticipations in the later 1530s and early 1540s of what was to come, as is shown by Caraglio's engraving of the *Annunciation* after Titian (cat.no.130), and also Licinio's engraved *Annunciation* after Pordenone of 1544.[19] The potential of engraving was especially clearly demonstrated to the book culture of mid-sixteenth century Venice by Enea Vico (1523–1567), through his engraved series of the coins of the Roman emperors for Antonio Zantani's *Le imagini con tutti i riversi trovati et le vite de gli imperatori* of 1548, with its engraved titlepage.[20] Cort's engravings after Titian were also a symptom of this change.

From the middle of the century there were other important Venetian developments in copperplate printmaking. One especially remarkable artist, who worked in a combination of etching and engraving, was Battista Franco (cat.nos.135, 136, 137, 138). Originally from Venice, he had gone to Rome in his youth where he absorbed the example of central Italian artists, especially Michelangelo. It was not until the early 1550s that he returned to Venice, and his work remained heavily indebted to central Italian design ideas. He would work up the bulk of the composition using etching and then refine areas such as the internal modelling of the figures with engraving. This technique was picked up by other Venetians, as may be seen in the case of the *Venus and Adonis* (cat.no.140), where the procedure is comparable.

Etching was, of course, a technique that could be learned relatively easily by painters and draughtsmen. Unlike engraving, which required a lengthy period of training before the burin could adequately be mastered, the etching needle could easily be made to obey the artist's will. Another Venetian painter who took it up was Andrea Meldolla, called Schiavone, using it in combination with drypoint to produce work characterized by a free and informal manner.[21] There were also a few Veronese painters who turned their hands to etching, including Battista and Marco Angolo del Moro, and Paolo and Orazio Farinati (cat.nos.148, 149, 150). It is not at all clear what the context of their printmaking operations was. There is much evidence that Battista del Moro, the most prolific of them, spent considerable amounts of time in Venice at various moments of his career. Venice had the infrastructure – the suppliers of materials, the printers and the agents for distribution – that a commercial printmaker would require. It may be supposed that this would have been a precondition for the professional engagement that characterised his activity in this field.[22]

The creativity of Venetian printmaking at the middle of the century can be seen not only in originality of design, but also in content. Certain categories of subject matter were first developed in Venice and especially cultivated there: Christian allegories illustrating the consequences of different sorts of behaviour, an example being the so-called *Sieve of Death*;[23] moralistic subjects such as the *Tree of Madness* (*L'Arboro della pazzia*); and humorous subjects with a satirical edge, such as the *World Turned Upside Down* (*Il mondo alla riversa*) or the *Land of Cockaigne*.[24] Although often described as popular prints, it has become clear that this gives a very misleading idea of the kind of interest they had. The people who bought such works were of the most varied status, including those who would also be buying prints with devout or erudite content.[25] These 'unofficial' themes go along with a concern with the modern world, which differentiates Venice from the other great centre of print production in the peninsula, Rome.[26] A large element of Roman output was concerned with the remains of classical antiquity and there were numbers of prints that recorded, reproduced or developed compositions of great masters such as Michelangelo and Raphael, even long after their deaths. In Venice there was much more of a sense of engagement with the present and prints of reportage seem to have flourished there. Also, important new types emerged as, for example, generic representations of religious and state ceremonies, describing the essential elements of their ideal forms rather than recording particular instances.[27]

After the terrible plague of 1575–7, there seems to have been a certain decline in the range and vitality of Venetian printmaking. There were negative signs even before the plague had shown its full virulence, as for example Natale Bonifacio's departure from Venice to Rome in about 1575.[28] In certain important areas of production, in particular maps, the plague coincides with a catastrophic decline.[29] The lists of Georg Willer describing the maps available at the Frankfurt book fair of 1573 still point to the dominant position of Venice in this area;[30] after the plague, output dropped to almost nothing. Another indicator is the sudden fall, after 1575, in the number of applications to the Venetian Senate for privileges to protect the publication of prints.[31]

It is difficult to judge relative decline and it is easy to exaggerate the situation. The evidence of the activities of *librai* (booksellers) like Luca Bertelli and his brother Donato is that they ran apparently flourishing businesses after the time of the plague. They were prepared to take risks and embark on creative new ventures. For example Luca and Orazio Bertelli played a major role in the publication of some engravings by Agostino Carracci when he was in Venice in 1582.[32] Agostino set a very high standard with his prints after works by the two greatest Venetian painters of the period, Veronese and Tintoretto (cat.nos.151, 152). Agostino knew these painters and presumably discussed his projects with them. They would have been interested in co-operating because of the way that Titian had demonstrated, through his collaboration with Cort, how effective the print could be in advertising an artist's achievement to a wide public.

In the 1590s a small number of creative figures emerged. They included the fine etcher Odoardo Fialetti (1573–1637/8), who came to Venice from Bologna.[33] But the most prominent was probably Giacomo Franco, the illegitimate son of Battista, and himself an engraver, who rapidly established a dominant position in the local print markets.[34] He published pattern books for sewing and lace making, writing books, devotional images, maps and views of many parts of the world, but particularly specialised in views of Venice and representations of the costumes, customs and ceremonies of the city (see cat.no.169). He further acquired a huge stock of older plates, including his father's, which he reprinted with his own address added.[35] The quality of his production was always professional. One venture of the greatest interest was his invitation to his friend Jacopo Palma to contribute to a drawing book, the *De excellentia et nobilitate delineationis libri duo* (cat.no.154). By this means he elicited some idiosyncratic but energetic etched work from the painter.[36] The other very significant figures who emerged on the Venetian scene in the 1590s were the Sadelers. Jan, Raphael and Aegidius moved to Venice from Verona around 1596–7 and introduced many northern genres into the city, such as an engraved series of flowers in vases.[37] They also gave a great boost to the reputation of the Bassano family (see cat.nos.155, 156).[38]

Jacopo de' Barbari ACTIVE VENICE 1497–BEFORE 1516 MALINES *or* BRUSSELS
127 ✿ *Apollo and Diana*

Latin Terms commonly found on Prints

Invenit (*i.* or *in.* or *inv.*) from *invenire*, to invent: used to indicate the person responsible for the design or invention of the underlying visual idea of the print, or a key element of it.

Pinxit (*pinx.*) from *pingere*, to paint: used to indicate the painter who made the picture reproduced in the print

Delineavit (*del.*) from *delineare*, to draw: used to indicate the person who made the drawing used for the print

Fecit or *faciebat* (*f., fe* or *fac.*) from *facere*, to make: used to indicate either the person who designed the original composition or the person who made the matrix

Incidit or *incidebat* (*inc.*) from *incidere*, to cut into or to engrave; *Sculpsit* (also *scalpsit*) or *sculpebat* (*sc.* or *sculp.*) from *sculpere* (or *scalpere*), to carve or cut: used to indicate the person responsible for making the matrix

Excudit or *excudebat* (*exc.* or *excud.*) from *excudere*, to print: bused to indicate the person responsible for printing from the matrix

Formis (*for.*) from *forma*, pattern, stamp or printer's forme: used to indicate the person who had control of the printing matrix

Engraving | 14.9 × 9.4cm (trimmed)
At the upper left there is a caduceus, the artist's personal device.

EDINBURGH, NATIONAL GALLERY OF SCOTLAND

The two pagan gods Apollo and Diana are shown as the sun and the moon. Apollo stands on the crystalline sphere of the fixed stars holding his drawn bow as an attribute, without paying attention to where it is pointing. Diana, her back turned and holding a stag, drops away below Apollo, her thighs visible through the transparent sphere. Beyond the fixed stars there are further spheres.

De' Barbari probably designed as well as executed this engraving. It is undated, and there has been considerable disagreement about the date.[1] Some scholars have considered it to have been done in Venice, while others have placed it a few years later, after De' Barbari had left Venice. In April 1500 he was appointed portrait painter and miniaturist by the Emperor Maximilian, with instructions to reside in Nuremberg.[2] It has often been noticed that there is a close relationship with Dürer's engraved *Apollo and Diana* (fig.225), which can be dated to around 1503–4,[3] and it is usually supposed that De' Barbari influenced Dürer rather than the other way around.

The learned subject matter and refined technique suggest that this print was made to be bought by highly educated collectors.

Fig.225 | Albrecht Dürer, *Apollo and Diana*
London, British Museum

Domenico Campagnola VENICE *c*.1500–1564 PADUA

128 ❧ *A Battle of Nude Men*

Engraving | 22.4 × 23.1cm (trimmed) | 1517

Inscribed at the lower left: 'DOMINICVS / CA[M]PAGNOLA / .1517.'

Provenance: James McCallum (Lugt 1409 bis); by whom presented to the Hunterian (acc.no.GLAHA 49)

GLASGOW UNIVERSITY, HUNTERIAN ART GALLERY

Fig.226 | Marcantonio Raimondi, *A Lion Hunt*
London, British Museum

This extraordinary composition of naked battling figures enclosed by trees seems to be an attempt to create an enlivened modern version of an antique battle scene like those found on ancient Roman sarcophagi.[1] The dog in the foreground is based on the dog in Marcantonio Raimondi's engraving of the *Lion Hunt* (fig.226), itself derived from a sarcophagus relief, and the screen of trees also recalls that composition.[2] Leonardo da Vinci's drawings for the *Battle of Anghiari* were also fundamental for Campagnola's conception. Some of the drawings that seem to have been especially influential are now in Venice and this may indicate that they were already there and accessible to Campagnola by 1517.[3]

Domenico Campagnola produced about thirteen engravings with very diverse subject matter in the years 1517 and 1518. He was responsible for their design as well as execution. In many of them he tried to maximise the emotional expressiveness of his figures and, as in this case, was prepared to distort his forms in a radical way to achieve it.

Domenico Campagnola VENICE *c.*1500–1564 PADUA

129 ❧ *The Execution of St Catherine*

Engraving | Diameter 18.9cm (trimmed) | 1517

Inscribed at the upper left: 'DOMINICVS / CAMPA / GNO / LA'; and at the bottom: 'MDXVII.'

Provenance: William Bell Scott (Lugt 2607); Dr James McCallum (Lugt 1409 bis); by whom presented to the Hunterian (acc.no.GLAHA 3624)

GLASGOW UNIVERSITY, HUNTERIAN ART GALLERY

The pagan emperor Maximinus condemned the Christian princess Catherine to die on a wheel, but the execution failed when angels destroyed the lethal device; she had to be beheaded instead.

Campagnola's engraving technique has been described as breaking with the past by adapting the mode of the quick pen sketch, with 'rapidly flowing lines which follow the forms they delineate and group them into contrasting areas of light and shade'.[1] A drawing in the Ecole des Beaux-Arts in Paris has several studies for the figure of St Catherine kneeling below the throne of the emperor (fig.227). The care Campagnola took with the design shows that the apparent sketchiness and spontaneity of his engraving was in fact a carefully calculated effect. In this print the search for expressive effect through figural distortions and disconcerting changes in proportions is especially marked.

The copperplate used to print *The Execution of St Catherine* may have been engraved on the reverse with another composition, the *Pentecost*.[2]

Fig.227 | Domenico Campagnola, *Figure Studies for the Martyrdom of St Catherine*
Paris, Ecole nationale supérieure des Beaux-Arts

Jacopo Caraglio VERONA *c.*1505–1565 CRACOW(?)

130 ❧ *The Annunciation* [AFTER TITIAN]

Engraving | 45.5 × 34.6cm (trimmed)

Inscribed at the lower right: 'TITIANI FIGVRARVM / AD CAESAREM EXEMPLA' (Copies of the figures of Titian [sent] to the Emperor); and at the lower left: 'IACOBVS / CARALIVS / .FE.'

Provenance: Professor W.R. Scott; by whom bequeathed to the Hunterian, 1940 (acc.no.GLAHA 10293)

GLASGOW UNIVERSITY, HUNTERIAN ART GALLERY

This engraving relates to an altarpiece painted by Titian for the nuns of Santa Maria degli Angeli on Murano around 1536.[1] Because the nuns were not prepared to pay the price of 500 ducats demanded, in 1537 Titian presented the picture instead either to the Emperor Charles V or to the Empress Isabella. Pietro Aretino identified the intended recipient as the empress in a letter to Titian dated 9 November 1537; but Giorgio Vasari, in 1568, wrote that it was sent to the emperor, and the inscription on the print itself refers to the emperor. Titian received a pension worth 100 scudi a year by way of reward.[2]

It is likely that Titian himself commissioned the engraver Caraglio to make this print. By that means he was able publicly to announce his gift and its illustrious recipient. He was later to do the same with *The Martyrdom of St Peter Martyr* that he presented to Pius V (see cat.no.134). Titian often reworked his compositions to make them suitable for representation in the black and white graphic medium. It is difficult for us to judge this point in the present case because of the loss of the original painting. One indicator of differences between the painting and the print is provided by Cassiano dal Pozzo's description of the picture, which he saw in Spain in 1626. He recorded that the prayer desk at which the Virgin kneels was '*formato da un Aquilone*', which seems to imply that is was eagle-shaped. The original altarpiece also probably had an arched top. This can be deduced from the presence in the upper corners of the print of angels holding the emblems of Charles V – the two pillars and the '*Plus ultra*' motto – which are very unlikely to have been included in the altarpiece.

Attributed to Giuseppe Nicolò Vicentino BORN VICENZA, ACTIVE *c*.1510–*c*.1550

131 ✧ *An Allegory of Time* [AFTER PORDENONE]

Chiaroscuro woodcut from four blocks
32 × 43.1cm

Provenance: Dr James McCallum (Lugt 1049
bis); by whom presented to the Hunterian
(acc.no.GLAHA 265)

GLASGOW UNIVERSITY, HUNTERIAN ART
GALLERY

The reclining winged figure is holding a verge
escapement and has a snake around his ankles,
which is biting its own tail. The escapement was
a mechanism used to regulate the motion of the
geared wheels and pinions of mechanical clocks,
before the introduction of the pendulum. A boy
with wind-blown hair seems to be taking the
mechanism from the older man. It has been
suggested that the boy is Eros, intent on inter-
rupting the continuity of time; against this is the
fact that he is not winged.[1] The snake is a symbol
of eternity and the reclining figure is sometimes
identified as Saturn: in the Renaissance, the
figures of Time (Cronus) and Saturn were often
conflated.[2]

The design follows very precisely a drawing by
Pordenone (fig.228), formerly at Chatsworth,
which may well have been made specifically for
this purpose and is almost exactly the same size
as the print.[3] The invention was first conceived
for the fresco decoration of one of the bays in the
attic storey of the facade of the Palazzo Martino
d'Anna on the Grand Canal in Venice, painted by
Pordenone in the 1530s (fig.229).[4]

The older attribution of the woodcut to Ugo
da Carpi has convincingly been shown to be
wrong, and the name of Nicolò Vicentino
proposed instead.[5] A later state of the woodcut
carried the address of Andrea Andreani, who is
known to have acquired Nicolò's blocks much
later in the sixteenth century.[6] Strong support for
this attribution comes from the observation that
an offset from one of Nicolò's signed prints
appears on the verso of an impression of the
Allegory of Time in the British Museum.[7]

Fig.228 | Pordenone, *Study for the Allegory of Time*
Formerly Chatsworth, The Duke of Devonshire and the
Trustees of the Chatsworth Settlement

Fig.229 | Pordenone, *Design for the Façade of the
Palazzo d'Anna, Venice*
London, Victoria and Albert Museum

Attributed to Nicolò Boldrini BORN VICENZA, ACTIVE IN VENICE c.1530–1570

132 ❦ *Six Saints* [AFTER TITIAN]

Woodcut | 37.1 × 52.9cm

EDINBURGH, NATIONAL GALLERY OF
SCOTLAND

This woodcut is closely related, in reverse, to the group of saints in an altarpiece Titian painted for the church of San Nicolò della Lattuga (San Nicolò dei Frari) in Venice (fig.230).[1] In the painting Saints Sebastian, Francis, Anthony of Padua, Peter, Nicholas and Catherine stand below a heavenly apparition of the Virgin and Child. In the past there has been considerable disagreement about the date of the painting, although there now seems to be a growing consensus that it was completed around 1520–5.[2] It was a celebrated work, mentioned during Titian's lifetime by Lodovico Dolce with high praise.[3]

Vasari asserted explicitly that the composition of the woodcut 'was by Titian himself, drawn on the wood and then cut and printed by others'.[4] It is not a record, let alone a reproduction, of the painting. In particular, the figure of St Sebastian was re-designed; this figure presumably continued to trouble the artist because a plug of wood was inserted, replacing the head originally cut.[5] Dolce commented on the naturalism of the Sebastian in the altarpiece, a point that Vasari reiterated while evidently finding it problematic. He wrote that the figure was taken directly from nature 'without any artifice', but for all that, he wrote, 'it is held to be beautiful'. However, what in paint could be greeted as a miracle of naturalism, might seem weak in the black and white lines of a print and Titian presumably reworked the image in order to make it more successful in graphic terms.

Dates have confidently been advanced for this woodcut – usually in the 1530s – but there is little firm evidence about when it was produced; we know only that Vasari's mention of it in the 1568 edition of his *Lives* means that it must have been in existence by then. Nor is there any substantial evidence to support the attribution of the woodcutting to Boldrini, which has been customary since the middle of the nineteenth century.[6]

In this print it seems likely that it was the artistry in the design and grouping of figures that was the intended object of attention. The subject matter cannot have been of central importance for, by isolating the saints from the heavenly apparition above them and placing them against a plain background, their movements and expressions become motiveless.

Fig.230 | Titian, *The Virgin and Child in Glory
with Six Saints*
Rome, Pinacoteca Vaticana

Venetian School MID-SIXTEENTH CENTURY

133 ❧ *The Stigmatization of St Francis* [AFTER TITIAN]

Woodcut | 29.6 × 42.3cm

Provenance: Dr James McCallum (Lugt 1409 bis); by whom presented to the Hunterian (acc.no.GLAHA 3308)

GLASGOW UNIVERSITY, HUNTERIAN ART GALLERY

This woodcut shows St Francis with his friend and disciple Leo at La Verna, receiving the vision that was to imprint his hands, his feet and his side with the wounds of Christ. At the centre of the explosion of divine light, in the upper right corner, is a simple cross rather than the seraph with six shining wings that was described in the written accounts. The image is surprising and dynamic, with the saint, his back turned to us, caught in his moment of rapture. A screen of trees contains and focuses this visionary drama.

There are no letters on the print itself to indicate authorship. However, in 1568 Vasari mentioned a woodcut which he stated was by Titian, and Ridolfi also described it as by him in his life of the artist published in 1648.[1] The originality of the diagonal composition links it with other designs by the painter from the 1520s, like the *Martyrdom of St Peter Martyr*.[2] There is, however, a remarkable similarity between the figure of St Francis and the apostle in the foreground of Titian's altarpiece of *Pentecost* in

Santa Maria della Salute, and this has led one scholar to suggest that the design for the woodcut should be dated around 1550.[3]

This woodcut, which unlike the *Six Saints* is fully realised in pictorial terms, could have been bought as a devotional image. There have been various ideas about who was responsible for the cutting of the woodblock. The names of Giovanni Boldrini and Giovanni Britto have been proposed,[4] but there does not seem to be any compelling reason for believing either name to be correct.

Venetian School SECOND HALF OF THE SIXTEENTH CENTURY

134 ❧ *The Martyrdom of St Peter Martyr* [AFTER TITIAN]

Engraving | 43.7 × 34.2cm (trimmed)

Inscribed in the lower margin:
'TITIANVS.VECELLIVS. EQVES. CAES. PIO.V.
PONT. MAX. FACIEBAT / Lucae Bertelli Formis'
(Tiziano Vecellio, Imperial Knight, made this
for Pope Pius V)

EDINBURGH, NATIONAL GALLERY OF
SCOTLAND

This is the only visual record of a lost painting by
Titian which we know from letters of 1 March
and 17 May 1567 was sent by him to Cardinal
Alessandro Farnese in Rome, with the intention
that he should present it to Pope Pius V on
Titian's behalf.[1]

St Peter Martyr was a Dominican monk
whose relentless pursuit of heretics led to his
appointment as Inquisitor-General by Pope
Honorius III (reigned 1216–27). He died in 1252
at the hands of assassins hired by men whom he
had denounced. They attacked him at the
entrance to a wood while he was journeying with
a companion from Como to Milan. Some
accounts of the event state that, failing to kill him
immediately, Peter had time to trace the word
'Credo' ('I believe', the first word of the Creed)
on the ground with his finger before his assailants
completed their task. That is the episode shown
in the present print. The subject was an especially
appropriate one for Pius V (reigned 1566–72)
who, before his election as pope, had been a
Dominican monk and who had himself held the
position of 'Inquisitor-General of Christendom'.

The print may have been published first by
Titian himself. The example shown here carries
the address of the Venetian print dealer Luca
Bertelli, but there are earlier impressions without
it and it is possible that Titian, having first made
use of the plate for his own purposes, subsequently sold it to Bertelli.[2] If that was the case, it
may be that the print did not follow precisely the
composition of the painting. Titian was very
sensitive to the importance of adapting compositions made for paintings so that they would work
effectively in graphic terms (see cat.no.146). The
composition is related to another lost painting by
Titian, namely the altarpiece representing the
same subject that Titian had completed for Santi
Giovanni e Paolo in Venice in 1530 (see
cat.nos.147, 159). However, the visual drama of
that earlier picture was modified. It may be
supposed that the painting was a relatively small-
scale work, intended for the pope's private

apartments rather than for a church.

The attribution of this engraving to Cornelis
Cort which is sometimes proposed is not
sustainable,[3] although the style does show the
strong influence of Cort. If Titian originally
commissioned it himself, he may have asked the
engraver to imitate Cort's manner. Mariette
believed that the engraver was Gaspare Osello
(fl.1557/8–1577).[4]

Battista Franco VENICE (?) c.1510–1561 VENICE

135 ❧ The Flagellation of Christ

Etching and engraving | 42.2 × 54.5cm
(trimmed)

Inscribed at the lower left: '[Battista] Franco
facciebat' (the first word cut off in this impression); and at the lower right: 'Batista franco
fecit / Giacomo franco forma'

Provenance: Professor W.R. Scott; by whom
bequeathed to the Hunterian, 1940
(acc.no.GLAHA 23949)

GLASGOW UNIVERSITY, HUNTERIAN ART
GALLERY

Christ tied to the column is assaulted by five
men, each of whom is given a highly distinctive
pose. They all stand on a narrow stage in front of
an almost abstract background. Franco was
himself responsible for the design of this print, as
is evident from the fine drawings by him – one
for Christ and the other for the figure on the
extreme left – which exist in the Metropolitan
Museum of Art and at Windsor Castle respectively (figs.231, 232).[1] His method of composition involved assembling independently derived
parts to make up his figures. For example, the
raised arm and head of the man second from the
left is derived from the fleeing companion of the
saint in Titian's altarpiece of the *Martyrdom of St
Peter Martyr* (see cat.nos.147, 159), while the legs
of the foreground figure, on the right, are those
of the saint's assassin in the same altarpiece. Each
of the figures was conceived and formed as a
separate unit, and then pieced together with the
others to make up the whole composition. In
Franco's mind there must have been vivid
memories of Sebastiano del Piombo's famous
Flagellation in the Roman church of San Pietro in
Montorio (fig.233).

The print must date from Franco's residence
in Venice between 1552 and his death in 1561.
This is an example of the second state of the
print, with the address of Battista's heir Giacomo
Franco added.[2]

left to right

Fig.231 | Battista Franco, *Study for Christ in the Flagellation*
New York, Metropolitan Museum of Art, Rogers Fund
(1962.119.10)

Fig.232 | Battista Franco, *Drawing for a Torturer in the
Flagellation*
Windsor Castle, Royal Library

Fig.233 | Sebastiano del Piombo, *The Flagellation*
Rome, Church of San Pietro in Montorio

Batista franco fecit
Giacomo franco for

Battista Franco VENICE (?) c.1510–1561 VENICE

136 ❧ *The Entombment*

Etching and engraving | 30.4 × 22.6cm
(trimmed)

EDINBURGH, NATIONAL GALLERY OF
SCOTLAND

In this print,[1] Franco's customary rhetoric of
anatomically complex figures is given up in
favour of a direct pathos. The diagonal structure
of the composition and the prominence of the
figure seen from the back holding the cloth at
Christ's feet suggest that Franco was influenced
by Titian's composition of the *Entombment*
delivered by Titian to Philip II in 1559 (replacing
one lost in transit two years earlier, see fig.34).[2] If
so, it would indicate that the print dates from late
in Franco's career. There is a realism in the
treatment of the figures that suggests a desire to
emulate northern models, especially Dürer (for
example, the engraved *Entombment* from his
Passion series).

Battista Franco VENICE (?) c.1510–1561 VENICE

137 ❧ *The Virgin and Child with the Infant St John*

Etching and engraving | 24.9 × 36.8cm

Inscribed at the lower edge: 'Batista franco fecit'

Provenance: Sir John St Aubyn (Lugt 1534)

EDINBURGH, NATIONAL GALLERY OF
SCOTLAND

This print must have been designed and executed
during Franco's period in Venice between 1552 and
1561, as the very Venetian-looking buildings in the
background testify.[1] The figures show a combination of the Michelangelesque, as in the figure of the
prophetic Virgin, and the Venetian, as in the Christ
Child throwing up his arms to embrace his mother,
an ecstatic pose reminiscent of some of the angels
in Titian's *Assumption* in the Frari (fig.19).

   This is the second state of this print, a state
before the addition of the letters having been
recorded.[2] The present impression is a late one,
taken after the plate had been heavily worn and
re-cut.

Etching and engraving | 120 × 351 mm | 1563

Inscribed at the lower left: '.B. F .V. IN. .NN. exc.1563.'

Provenance: Professor W.R. Scott; by whom bequeathed to the Hunterian, 1940 (acc.no.GLAHA 6293)

GLASGOW UNIVERSITY, HUNTERIAN ART GALLERY

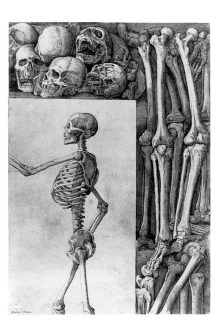

Fig.234 | Battista Franco, *A Skeleton, and additional Studies of Skulls and Bones*
Vienna, Graphische Sammlung Albertina

This frieze of densely packed skulls, it has been argued, was contrived to show the anatomical structure of the head from various aspects, with and without the jaw. The arrangement is, therefore, didactic, not simply grimly ornamental.[1]

The skulls in the right half of this print are the same as those at the top of Franco's remarkable study of a skeleton with borders of bones (fig.234).[2] Franco's skeleton is obviously only a fragment of a larger composition and a convincing reconstruction of the whole project has been made.[3] In the present anonymous print, the continuation of the frieze of skulls and the fact that it is in the same direction as Franco's print means it is unlikely to have been copied from the latter, but probably from a preparatory drawing for it. The presence of a part of a heel and ankle at the right edge, exactly as in Franco's print, makes clear that the putative drawing included the vertical border with bones. An anonymous Flemish metalpoint drawing of three skulls in the British Museum shows the skull to the right of centre (the one facing left) and the two skulls to the left (the ones facing right) the same way round as in the print, and so were probably copied from it.[4]

The letters 'NN exc.' in the inscription identify the engraver and print dealer Nicolò Nelli as the person responsible for printing the plate. Nelli was active in Venice from about 1552 until about 1579.[5] Whether he himself actually etched and engraved this print, or employed someone else to do so, is not clear.

Giulio Sanuto VENICE ACTIVE *c*.1540–AFTER 1588 VENICE

139 ❧ *Apollo and Marsyas* [AFTER AGNOLO BRONZINO]

Engraving on three plates | 54 × 132cm | 1562

Inscribed at the lower edge of the left-hand plate: 'APOLLINIS ET MARSIAE / FABVLA EX CLARISS / PICTORIS ANTONII / DE CORREGGIO PICTVRA' ('The story of Apollo and Marsyas from the painting by the most famous painter Antonio da Correggio'); and on the right-hand plate, a long dedicatory inscription beginning: 'ALL' ILLVSTRISSIMO ET / ECCELLENTISS. SIGNOR DONNO / ALFONSO II, DA ESTE, DVCA QVINTO DI FERRARA ...' and ending 'In Vinegia Il di XVIII di Luglio M D L XII. / DI V.E. / Divotiss. et humiliss. / servitore / Giulio Sanuto' ('To the most illustrious and most excellent Lord Alfonso d'Este, 5th Duke of Ferrara ... in Venice on 18 July 1562, your Excellency's most devoted and humble servant, Giulio Sanuto')

Provenance: With Lutz Riester, London and Freiburg; from whom purchased, 1986

EDINBURGH, NATIONAL GALLERY OF SCOTLAND

Fig.235 | Agnolo Bronzino, *Apollo and Marsyas*
St Petersburg, State Hermitage Museum

This ambitious print illustrates several episodes from the story of Apollo and Marsyas.[1] On the right is shown the musical competition between Apollo and the arrogant Marsyas, who had rashly dared to challenge the sun god; the goddess Pallas Athena (Minerva) and King Midas sit in judgement. In the centre Marsyas is flayed alive by Apollo as punishment for his hubris. King Midas did not escape punishment either, for he had mistakenly judged Marsyas the winner, and his ears grew long like those of an ass. He hoped to keep his shame hidden by covering his head, but at the left is illustrated how his ears were inadvertently revealed by his barber who, having discovered the truth and being desperate to speak about it, whispered the secret into a hole in the ground. Reeds grew up over the spot and released the shameful news to the wind.

The inscription identifies the source of the composition as a painting by Correggio, but this was a mistake. The source was, in fact, a panel on a harpsichord painted by the Florentine artist Bronzino around 1530 (the panel, long removed from the instrument, is now in the Hermitage Museum, St Petersburg, fig.235). It is likely that around 1538 the harpsichord had been given to Giulio Sanuto's father, Francesco, by the Duke of Urbino, and when transported from Urbino to Venice, knowledge of its true authorship had been lost. Sanuto elaborated the original composition through the addition of landscape elements and, most strikingly, by the introduction of a group of Apollo and the Muses derived from Marcantonio Raimondi's engraving of Raphael's *Parnassus* (see fig.100).[2]

Sanuto's engraving is very ambitious in scale, being slightly larger in size than the painting from which it derives. The print was dedicated to Alfonso d'Este, Duke of Ferrara, who was a great music lover, and impressions of it were presented to him in 1562. Alfonso, as the flattering inscription on the print makes clear, was exactly the opposite of Midas, a prince who was eminently capable of judging every sort of excellence. He could be expected to reward Sanuto appropriately for his virtuoso performance. Sanuto himself must have been entirely responsible for the print: not only did he adapt Bronzino's design and execute it, but also saw to its printing and distribution.

Venetian School THIRD QUARTER OF THE SIXTEENTH CENTURY

140 ❧ *Venus and Adonis* [AFTER TITIAN]

Etching and engraving | 41.2 × 32.5cm

Inscribed in the lower margin: 'Aurea formosum Cypris dilexit Adonin / Deliciae iuvenis, devia, tela, canes. // Sic miser imprudens caelestem linquit Amantem, / Casurus properans dente ferocis Apri.' ('Golden Venus loved the beautiful Adonis, a youth who delighted in unfrequented places, weapons and dogs. So he, unfortunate and imprudent, left his heavenly lover, hastening away to be killed by the tusk of the wild boar.')

Provenance: Sir Joshua Reynolds (Lugt 2364)

EDINBURGH, NATIONAL GALLERY OF SCOTLAND

In Ovid's account (*Metamorphoses*: book x) Venus, who loved the mortal Adonis, warned him of the dangers of hunting but, while she was away, he went out and was killed by a wild boar. Titian varied the invention, showing Adonis breaking away from Venus' embrace, thus conflating elements of the story in order to make it more effective as a visual drama. Love (Cupid) sleeps under a tree. This was one of Titian's most famous compositions, originally conceived for Philip II around 1553–4. Many painted versions and copies are known (fig.236). The inclusion in the print of a tiny scene of the death of Adonis in the background and the presence above, in the heavens, of Venus in her chariot drawn by birds, show the tragic outcome of Adonis's imprudence (*Metamorphoses*, book x, 708–24, where the birds are described as swans; elsewhere Ovid specifies that they were doves, as they are represented here).

It is interesting that the printmaker used etching for the landscape, whereas the figures are mainly engraved.[1] The softer effects of etching contrast with the sharper and more precise qualities of engraving. The treatment of the shadows in the figures is badly misjudged. The lines are so close together that they register as a smudge. This must be one of the prints that was strongly criticised by the Netherlandish humanist, Lampsonius, in a letter he wrote to Titian in 1567.[2] There is an engraved copy, in reverse, by the so-called Master of the Name of Jesus, a printmaker who was active in Venice around the years 1556 to 1572.

A number of factors make it clear that the print was not conceived as a straightforward reproduction of Titian's painted composition: the changes to the content of the print relative to the painted versions; the change in the format from horizontal to vertical; and the absence of any notice of Titian's responsibility for the design. It would have been sold as an independent subject print.

Fig.236 | Titian, *Venus and Adonis*
Madrid, Museo Nacional del Prado

Venetian School SECOND HALF OF THE SIXTEENTH CENTURY

141 ❧ St Anthony of Padua

Engraving (main image) and etching (border)
36.8 × 25.4cm (trimmed)

Inscribed in the margin: 'Divus Antonius
Vlisbonae hyspaniarum Civitas / ortus, qui cum
ad usum rationis pervenit Augus / tinianae
religionis habitum sumpsit. // Cupiens
martirium ad seraphicam religionem / se
transtulit Patavium veniens signis, et / miraculis
illustravit. / Venetijs per Lucam Bertellum.' ('St
Anthony, born at Lisbon, city of Spain, who
when he reached the age of reason adopted the
habit of the Augustinian order. Seeking martyrdom, he transferred to the Franciscans and
coming to Padua made it famous through signs
and miracles')

EDINBURGH, NATIONAL GALLERY OF
SCOTLAND

This representation of the Franciscan St Anthony
of Padua in a landscape belongs to a type of non-
narrative image of single saints in landscape
settings which appeared in the second half of the
sixteenth century. Another example of this type
is Cornelis Cort's fine engraving of St Dominic
after Bartolomeus Spranger, of 1573.[1]

The image of St Anthony and the landscape
are engraved, while the decorative border is
etched, probably by a different hand. The
presence of the border suggests that the print was
intended to be pinned up for use as a devotional
image, rather than mounted in an album. It was
published in Venice by Luca Bertelli, an important print dealer in Padua and Venice, who was
active from about 1564 to 1589. The long
inscription indicates that Paduan local pride may
have been significant factor in the marketing of
this print.

Cornelis Cort EDAM c.1533–1578 ROME

142 ❧ *Landscape with Angelica and Ruggiero* [AFTER TITIAN]

Engraving | 30.2 × 44.1cm (trimmed)

Inscribed at the lower left: 'Cun privilegio 1565'; and at the lower right: 'Titianus'

Provenance: Pierre Mariette (Lugt 1788; with his inscription 'P. Mariette 1678' on the verso); Louis Chauveau (according to an inscription on the verso); Sir Thomas Lawrence (Lugt 2446); Professor W.R. Scott; by whom bequeathed to the Hunterian, 1940 (acc.no.GLAHA 52272)

GLASGOW UNIVERSITY, HUNTERIAN ART GALLERY

The scene represented is loosely based on Lodovico Ariosto's great epic romance poem *Orlando Furioso* of 1532. Angelica lies at the mercy of a dragon, while from the cloud above springs forth her rescuer, the knight Ruggiero mounted on a mythical beast called a hippogryph. Unlike Ariosto's Angelica, the woman in the print is not chained to a rock at the sea's edge, nor does she appear at all worried by the stare of the monster. In some of his painted *poesie* on Ovidian themes, Titian did not feel constrained to follow precisely his literary sources but made his own inventions out of them,[1] and he seems to have done the same here. The print is closely related to a surviving drawing by Titian, now in Bayonne (fig.237).[2]

This engraving was one of the first of six that Cort produced for Titian in the years 1565–6.[3] The engraver, who came from the Low Countries, had been invited to work with Titian and their collaboration was evidently a close one. Titian seems to have chosen carefully the subject matter and types of composition for this group of prints, in order to achieve variety and to display the range and quality of his powers of invention. The other prints in the group represent *Mary Magdalene*, *St Jerome Reading in the Desert* (cat.no.143), *The Adoration of the Trinity*, *Diana and Callisto* (derived from a version of cat.no.55) and *Tityus* (cat.no.144). In each case the print exists in an early state with the name of Titian but without the name of Cort; the engraver's name was added only in later states of each of them. This suggests that initially Cort was seen merely as an executive instrument of Titian's publishing intentions; only once Cort's reputation was well established was his role explicitly acknowledged.

Fig.237 | Titian, *Landscape with Angelica and Ruggiero*
Bayonne, Musée Bonnat

Cornelis Cort EDAM c.1533–1578 ROME

143 ❧ *St Jerome Reading in the Desert* [AFTER TITIAN]

Engraving | 29.2 × 25.5cm (trimmed)

Inscribed at the lower right: 'Cun privilegio' and 'Titianus I[n]ventor / 1565'

(acc.no.GLAHA 7669)

GLASGOW UNIVERSITY, HUNTERIAN ART GALLERY

St Jerome, with his books, sits in thought beside a great rock to which cling storm-blasted trees and a cross roughly fashioned from sticks. A wide mountainous landscape provides a wild setting for the saint's outdoor study.[1]

In a letter written to Titian in 1567, the Netherlandish humanist Lampsonius praised all six of the engravings that Cort had made after Titian's designs, but singled out this one for special praise. More than any other engraver who tackled his compositions, Lampsonius wrote, Cort gave grace to the wildness of Titian's landscapes, and he went on: *Unique in the world is that desolate and lonely little landscape with St Jerome. It gives me the greatest pleasure to imagine what it would be like painted by the felicitous hand of your Lordship, with the figure of St Jerome life size, as I persuade myself your Lordship may have done. And in fact your Lordship has, to a high degree, taken over from all our Flemings the reputation for landscape, a type of painting … in which we thought to hold the field.*[2]

A printed double line, like a frame, defines the edge of the image, but these lines are crossed at the top by the trees. This gives an effect of informality, like a drawing. In this impression something seems to have gone wrong (see the upper right) in the process of printing, leaving a rather ugly discoloured mark on the paper in that area.

Cornelis Cort EDAM *c*.1533–1578 ROME

144 ❧ *Tityus* [AFTER TITIAN]

Engraving | 38.2 × 31.4cm (trimmed)

Inscribed on the rock near the lower edge: 'Titianus 1566'; and at the lower edge: 'Cun Privilegio'

Provenance: Sir Joshua Reynolds (Lugt 2364)

EDINBURGH, NATIONAL GALLERY OF SCOTLAND

Fig.238 | Titian, *Tityus*
Madrid, Museo Nacional del Prado

In the *Odyssey* (XI: 576–81), Homer referred to Tityus who, having violated Leto, was punished by having his liver (the supposed seat of desire) preyed upon by two vultures. Ovid (*Metamorphoses*, IV: 451–61) grouped Tityus with the other giants Tantalus, Sisyphus and Ixion, all four of whom were condemned to eternal torment for their crimes.

This is another of the six engravings that Cort executed for Titian in the years 1565 and 1566 (see also cat.nos.142, 143, 145).[1] There is a painting of the same subject in the Prado, executed by Titian in the late 1540s for the Regent of the Netherlands, Mary of Hungary (fig.238).[2] The engraving reverses the composition of the painting. There are other important differences too, of which the most significant are the substitution of rocks for the two tree trunks to which Tityus's feet are chained, and the alteration to the position of his lower arm and hand. In the painting he grips the rock in tense struggle whereas in the engraving it falls loose. The addition of an area of cloudy sky above the figure and the slight increase in the lateral space decisively relaxes the compressed tension of the painting. The differences between print and picture could be explained either by Cort's having used a preliminary drawing by Titian for the painting, or by supposing that Titian made a drawing specially for the engraver. The cumulative evidence for the whole group of Cort's engravings makes the second explanation the more likely.

After Cornelis Cort EDAM *c.*1533–1578 ROME
145 ❧ *St Mary Magdalene* [AFTER TITIAN]

Engraving | 25.2 × 19.2cm (trimmed)

Inscribed at the lower edge: 'Sadeler exc'; and in lower margin: 'ILLACRYMANS SANCTI DVM PEDES MOESTA MAGISTRI / TERGIT PECCATRIX REDVCEM COMPLECTITVR CHRISTVS.' (When the weeping, sorrowful sinner washed the feet of her holy master, Christ embraced the one who returned to the fold)

EDINBURGH, NATIONAL GALLERY OF SCOTLAND

This is a reduced-size copy, in reverse, of Cort's engraving of the saint, one of the six prints he made in Titian's workshop in the years 1565 and 1566.[1] It was published by one of the Sadelers, probably after their arrival in Venice in 1596–7. As it carries no indication of Titian's name or its origins in an engraving by Cort, it was presumably intended as an independent subject print, not as a reproduction. This kind of piracy, re-using the compositions of others without any acknowledgement, was commonplace at this period. In 1567 Titian had obtained from the Venetian Senate a fifteen-year privilege to protect his prints.[2] But this would have expired in 1582 at the latest, if not in 1576 when he died.

ILLACRYMANS SANCTI DVM PEDES MOESTA MAGISTRI·
TERGIT PECCATRIX REDVCEM COMPLECTITVR CHRISTVS·

Cornelis Cort EDAM *c.*1533–1578 ROME

146 ❧ *The Martyrdom of St Lawrence* [AFTER TITIAN]

Engraving | 48.5 × 34cm (trimmed)

Inscribed on the gridiron: 'TITIANVS INVENT. AEQVES CAES'; and on the pedestal of the statue: 'Invictis. PHILIPPO / Hispaniarum Regi / D (Titian, Imperial knight, invented this // For the most invincible Philip, King of Spain); and at the bottom: 'Cun prevel. 1571 Cornelio cort fe.'

EDINBURGH, NATIONAL GALLERY OF SCOTLAND

The deacon Lawrence was martyred by being roasted alive on a gridiron. The composition of this engraving relates to two painted versions of the subject by Titian. The earlier is in the church of the Gesuiti in Venice (begun in 1548 and still unfinished in 1557, fig.239).[1] The other is at the Escorial and was sent from Venice to Spain at the end of 1567 (fig.240).[2] The print is, however, an original composition, containing elements from each of the painted versions: the angels with the palm of martyrdom derive from the Escorial version, while the figures below are close to those of the Gesuiti altarpiece. The explanation must be that Titian made a design especially for Cort to work from which incorporated elements from each painting.[3]

The elimination in the print of any architectural space, and the filling of the background with the billowing smoke of the fire rising into the heavens, was a masterful idea. For the smoke, fitfully illuminated by the fire and by torches, is both visually effective and at the same time symbolically significant. It is out of the smoke of martyrdom rising to heaven that the angels appear, bearing the reward for Lawrence's sacrifice. Through his virtuoso command of lines that curve and swell, Cort was able to sustain visual drama over the whole surface. The result is a tour de force in which the central idea is never lost.

It is an indication of Titian's appreciation of what Cort had achieved in the 1560s that the engraver returned to Venice around 1570 and

undertook a further collaboration with the aged painter. This print is one of two products of this second partnership, the other being the engraving of *Tarquin and Lucretia. The Martyrdom of St Lawrence* was dedicated to Philip II, King of Spain. One of the impressions sent to the king, printed on silk, can still be seen in his private apartment at the Escorial.

Fig.239 | Titian, *The Martyrdom of St Lawrence*
Venice, Church of the Gesuiti

Fig.240 | Titian, *The Martyrdom of St Lawrence*
El Escorial, Real Monasterio de San Lorenzo, Old Church

305

Martino Rota SEBENICO c.1520–1583 PRAGUE

147 ❧ *The Martyrdom of St Peter Martyr* [AFTER TITIAN]

Engraving | 39.6 × 27.1cm (trimmed)

Inscribed on the tablet on the tree: 'TICIANVS / INVENTOR / MARTINVS / ROTA SIBESIS / . F.'; and at the lower left: 'STEFANO / SCOLARI / FORMIS'

EDINBURGH, NATIONAL GALLERY OF SCOTLAND

This is a reproduction of the very famous altarpiece that Titian painted for the church of Santi Giovanni e Paolo in Venice; delivered in 1530, it was destroyed by fire in 1867.[1] This engraving is an important piece of evidence in the reconstruction of its appearance. It was Titian's first important treatment of the subject of the martyrdom of the Dominican saint Peter Martyr. The assassination of the monk took place at the entrance to a wood while he was journeying with a companion from Como to Milan. While his companion flees, Peter gestures up towards a vision of angels who hold a palm of martyrdom and thus announce heaven's reward for his sacrifice.

Because the altarpiece has been destroyed, it is difficult to be certain about how closely the engraving followed it.[2] However, there are a number of visual sources, including several early painted copies – among them the seventeenth-century one by Johann Carl Loth that was installed in place of Titian's original following its destruction[3] – and the etching by Lefevre (cat.no.159), which suggest that Rota's print was very close indeed to the painting. When he collaborated with Cornelis Cort (see cat.nos.142, 143, 144, 145, 146), Titian prepared designs that usually deviated from his original painted compositions in order to ensure that they would be effective as prints. In this regard, the presence in Rota's engraving of the arched top of the altarpiece is particularly revealing when one considers that Titian's *Martyrdom of St Lawrence* was carefully adapted for the rectangle of Cort's engraved plate (cat.no.146). The indicators are that, unlike Cort, Rota operated independently of Titian, making his own drawing from the painting and then engraving it.

This is a late, second state of the print. Stefano Scolari, whose address appears on this impression, was active as an etcher and print publisher in Venice in the years 1644 to 1687.

TICIANVS
INVENTOR
MARTINVS
ROTA.SIBE
F:

TICIANVS
INVENTOR
MARTINVS
ROTA.SIBE
F:

Battista del Moro VERONA c.1514–1573 VENICE

148 ❧ *An Allegory of Fame*

Etching | 33.2 × 22.3cm

Inscribed at the lower right: 'Batt.a cognominato / del Moro'; and in the lower margin: 'Io son colei che ognuno al mondo brama, / Perche per me dopo la morte vive / E se vitio o virtude opera trama / Tal che a le spoglie o al degno imp[er]io arrive // Per quello infamia son per questa Fama. / E a colui per me solo si ascrive / Del Biasmo il suono ond'a costei si dona / De la gloria le palme e la corona.' (I am she whom everyone in the world longs for, because through me they live after death. And if vice or virtue operates so as to obtain [respectively] plunder or honourable empire, I am infamy for the former and for the latter fame. [Vice] has only blame from me while [virtue] has glory, palms and crown.)

Provenance: Professor W.R. Scott; by whom bequeathed to the Hunterian in 1940 (acc.no.GLAHA 6006)

GLASGOW UNIVERSITY, HUNTERIAN ART GALLERY

A winged, female personification of Fame with trumpet and wreath stands on a sphere while below, looking up towards her, are two standing figures. On the left is a female personification of Virtue, with instruments of cultural, scientific and military use at her feet; on the right a male satyr as a personification of Vice. In the verses below, Fame announces that she will make infamous the deeds of Vice, while those of Virtue she will make famous. Military achievement and rule seem to be the central points of focus, to judge by the content of the verses and by the prominent trophies of arms and armour suspended from lions' heads at each side.

This is one of Battista del Moro's most beautiful etchings.[1] The relationship with his drawing for a ceiling decoration in the Palazzo Murari at Verona has been noted.[2] This connection makes clear that the design of the etching was Battista's own and allows it to be dated to around 1560. How Battista organised his printmaking and publishing business is not at all clear. However, he spent a great deal of time in Venice, where he eventually died in 1573; it may be that it was there, rather than in Verona, that his plates were printed and distributed. It was in Venice that there existed the developed infrastructure to support such operations.[3]

Paolo Farinati VERONA 1524–1606 VERONA

149 ✤ *Charity*

Etching | 22.4 × 23.5cm (trimmed)

Inscribed at the lower left: '.P.F'.

EDINBURGH, NATIONAL GALLERY OF
SCOTLAND

The identification of the subject as a personification of Charity is traditional.[1] The fact that one
of the children sits separately from the woman
and is leaning on a rabbit might suggest instead
that it is an allegory of Fecundity. The spiral shell
above the artist's initials appears on most of
Farinati's prints and seems to have been a
personal device or rebus.

   The figure style and the way that the composition works combines a knowledge of
Michelangelo – the female figure is reminiscent
of figures such as the woman with the child in the
Zorobabel, Abiud and Eliachim lunette of the
ancestors of Christ on the Sistine ceiling – with
Raphaelesque elements. The presence at that
time in the Canossa collection in Verona of
Raphael's Madonna, known as *La Perla* (now in
the Prado, Madrid, fig.241) evidently had a major
influence on Farinati.

   Paolo Farinati produced a small group of
etchings after his own inventions. Twelve have
been identified, of which four bear the dates
1566, 1567, 1568 and 1578.[2] They were presumably all first published by Farinati himself.
Subsequently a few of them came into the hands
of commercial dealers: the second state of the *St
John the Evangelist* carries the address of Justus
Sadeler; and similarly, later examples of the *Venus
and Cupid* have the address of Pietro Stefanoni.
The subjects of seven of Farinati's prints are
mythological. One striking characteristic of them
is that rather little attention is paid to the setting,
with the result that they have the appearance of
printed drawings.

Fig.241 | Raphael, *The Virgin and Child with St Elizabeth
and the Infant St John the Baptist ('La Perla')*
Madrid, Museo Nacional del Prado

Orazio Farinati VERONA 1559–1616 VERONA

150 ❧ *The Virgin and Child with St John the Baptist*

Etching | 24.7 × 22cm (trimmed)

Inscribed at the lower centre: 'Gasparo dalolio exc'; and at the lower right: 'P.Fari I' (this impression is trimmed at the bottom, leaving only the tops of the remaining letters of the inscription – 'HO.F.F.' – visible).

EDINBURGH, NATIONAL GALLERY OF SCOTLAND

The composition was designed by Orazio's father, Paolo Farinati, and is an elegant variation on Raphaelesque models, in particular the *Madonna under the Oak Tree* in the Prado, Madrid, and Giulio Romano's *Madonna della Gatta* in the Museo Nazionale di Capodimonte, Naples (fig.242).

Orazio was responsible for an even smaller number of etchings than his father.[1] All five are after his father's inventions, two of them being rather ambitious large compositions: the *Crossing of the Red Sea* and the *Deposition*.[2] The date of the present work is not known, but the fact that the first states of two of his five known etchings are both dated 1583 may provide an indication.

This is an example of the fourth state of this print, with the four corners of the plate cut. Already at an early stage the bottom left corner of the plate had broken off and the other corners may have been cut in order to achieve a symmetrical appearance. It has been suggested that the plates used by Orazio may have been of a soft metal such as pewter, which may account for an early fracture of this kind.[3]

Fig.242 | Giulio Romano, *Madonna della Gatta*
Naples, Museo Nazionale di Capodimonte

Agostino Carracci BOLOGNA 1557–1602 PARMA

151 ✤ *The Mystic Marriage of St Catherine* [AFTER PAOLO VERONESE]

Engraving | 51.3 × 34.9cm (trimmed) | 1582

Inscribed at the lower left: 'Paulli Caliarij Veronensis opus / in ecclesia D. Caterinae Venetijs'; and at the lower right: 'Agu Car fe 1582'

Provenance: Pierre Mariette Senior (Lugt 1788; with his inscriptions 'P. Mariette 1666' on the recto and 'P. Mariette 1663' on the verso)

EDINBURGH, NATIONAL GALLERY OF SCOTLAND

Veronese's celebrated composition was painted around 1575 for the high altar of the church of Santa Caterina in Venice (fig.243).[1] It shows the visionary scene of St Catherine of Alexandria's marriage to Christ: the infant places a ring on her finger while angels celebrate (see also cat.no.57 and figs.141, 142).

The print follows the painting very closely, although the proportions have been altered so as to reduce the height relative to the width.[2] There are similar changes to the proportions in other engravings of Agostino's done in 1582 after paintings by Veronese. He may have felt that a less vertically elongated format suited better the character of a print. Agostino's visit to Venice in 1582 marked a turning point in his career as an engraver, for it was there that he really mastered

Fig.243 | Paolo Veronese,
The Mystic Marriage of St Catherine
Venice, Galleria dell'Accademia

the skill of finding equivalents in black and white lines for subtle pictorial effects of texture and colour. During the course of this trip he seems to have engraved no fewer than six of Veronese's compositions, and it is very likely that he established contact with the painter. In at least one case there is quite strong evidence to suppose that he was commissioned by Veronese to produce an engraving, and that might have been the situation with the present print too.[3] Titian's success in having fine prints made after his inventions may have encouraged Veronese to think along the same lines when he came across an engraver of Agostino Carracci's brilliance.

Agostino Carracci BOLOGNA 1557–1602 PARMA

152 ❧ *The Temptation of St Anthony* [AFTER JACOPO TINTORETTO]

Engraving | 50.4 × 32.8cm (trimmed)

Inscribed at the lower left: 'Iacobi Tintoreti pictoris / Veneti prestantissimi / inventum.' (An invention of Jacopo Tintoretto, most excellent Venetian painter.); at the lower centre: 'Antonius, cum Daemones vario sub aspectu ipsum infestantes / perpetua patientia superasset, viso Domino confortantur.' (Anthony, when through constant endurance he was overcoming the demons that attacked him in various guises, is given strength by seeing the Lord.); and at the lower right: 'Lucae Berteli For. / Anno M.D.L.XXXII'

EDINBURGH, NATIONAL GALLERY OF SCOTLAND

St Anthony Abbot, whose identifying attributes are a crutch, bell and pig, was an Egyptian hermit saint of great asceticism who was subjected to terrible temptations by devils. They offered him the possibility of indulging every sensual appetite and when he resisted they became ever more aggressive. Here his powers of resistance are strengthened by the appearance of Christ. The print reproduces the design of an altarpiece painted by Tintoretto for the church of San Trovaso, Venice (fig.244).

Although it carries no indication of author-ship, the engraving has generally been accepted as the work of Agostino.[1] Presumably Luca Bertelli commissioned him to cut the plate. The adjustment of the proportions of the original painting to a squarer format fits perfectly with Agostino's treatment of Veronese's compositions at this same period. Also characteristic of Agostino's adaptation of his sources is the opening up of the space in the foreground and at the side, thus releasing some of the compression of the original composition. What is relatively unusual in terms of Agostino's practice is that the print reverses Tintoretto's design. There are, in his oeuvre, other examples of reversal, but on the whole he meticulously observed the direction of the original compositions from which he was working.[2]

Fig.244 | JacopoTintoretto, *The Temptation of St Anthony*
Venice, Church of San Trovaso

Agostino Carracci BOLOGNA 1557–1602 PARMA

153 ❧ *Portrait of Titian*

Engraving | 32.4 × 23.1cm (trimmed)

Inscribed in the upper margin: 'TITIANI
VECELLI PICTORIS CELEBERRIMI AC /
FAMOSISSMI VERA EFFIGIES' (The true
portrait of Titian Vecellio, the most celebrated
and famous painter); and in the lower margin:
'ILL.mo ET R.mo D. DNO. HENRICO CAETANO
S.R.E. CARD. AMPL.mo BON.ae LEGATO /
EXIGVVM HOC MVNVS IMAGINIS TITIANI
PICT. CVIVS NOMEN ORBIS CONTINERE NON
VALET SVBMISSE DICAT SACRATQVE /
HVMILL.S DEDIT.S Q. SERVVS AVGVST.
CARRATIVS. 1587' (To the most illustrious and
Reverend Lord Enrico Caetano S.R.E. Cardinal,
most distinguished Legate to Bologna; this
small tribute of the image of Titian, the painter
whose name the world is not great enough to
contain, your humble and devoted servant
Agostino Carracci submissively dedicates and
consecrates).

PRIVATE COLLECTION

Fig.245 | Titian, *Self-portrait*
Berlin, Staatliche Museen zu Berlin, Gemäldegalerie

This image of Titian is very closely related, in
reverse, to the self-portrait now in Berlin that
was in Venice until the early nineteenth century
(fig.245).[1] However, missing in the print is one of
the key features of the painting: the gold chain
that the Emperor Charles V bestowed on Titian
in 1533 when he was knighted. As the print is a
celebration of the painter, it seems unlikely that
the engraver would have omitted the chain had it
been present in his prototype. This suggests that
Agostino may have worked from a different
version of the self-portrait.

This is an impression of the third state of the

engraving. When it was first made in 1587 it may
have formed part of Agostino's project to establish
a print business in Bologna.[2] Both this print and
his *Ecce Homo* after Correggio of the same year are
dedicated to Enrico Caetano.[3] Caetano, who had
been appointed titular Cardinal of Santa
Pudenziana in 1585, was the papal legate to
Bologna in 1587 and was known as a collector.[4]
His interest in prints may have been considerable,
for he was one of those mentioned in 1593 as
being potentially interested in purchasing the
extremely important collection that had been put
together by Cardinal Scipione Gonzaga.[5]

Palma Giovane VENICE c.1548–1628 VENICE

154 ✠ *Samson and Delilah*

Etching | 14.7 × 20.9cm (trimmed)

Inscribed at the lower left: 'Jacobus Franco formis con Privilegio'; and at the lower right: 'Palma'

EDINBURGH, NATIONAL GALLERY OF SCOTLAND

Delilah reduced Samson to powerlessness by surreptitiously cutting his hair while he slept on her lap. The composition is close to a painting by Palma of the same subject in a private collection in Florence.[1] A variety of alternative designs for a composition of this subject are to be found on a sheet in the album of drawings by Palma in the British Museum, but none relate directly to this print.[2]

It is usually claimed that this etching was made for Giacomo Franco's *De Excellentia et Nobilitate Delineationis Libri Duo*, published in 1612, one of a number of books that appeared in Venice around that time to help amateurs acquire a grounding in drawing.[3] In January 1612 the Venetian Senate granted Franco a thirty-year privilege to cover three books entitled *Della nobilta del dissegno*.[4] The precise contents of this work remain uncertain. It seems likely that the *Samson and Delilah* had been intended to form part of the 1612 volume, for that would explain the presence of Franco's privilege; but in the event it may never have been included. It has been noted that in the 1612 volume Palma's participation was nowhere mentioned, whereas in the *Regole per imparar a disegnar*, which was a new edition published in 1636, long after Giacomo Franco's death, his role was emphatically asserted.[5]

The use of prints to provide models for people learning to draw was well established by this time.[6] Armenini, commenting on the practice in 1586, warned that a lot of time could be wasted copying refined engravings like those of Dürer, which anyway might do more harm than good by instilling an overly laborious approach.[7] Palma's loose style evidently avoided such dangers.

This impression is printed on unusually heavy paper.

Palma Giovane *Samson and Delilah* (detail of signature)

Jan Sadeler ANTWERP 1550–1600 VENICE

155 ❧ *The Adoration of the Shepherds* [AFTER JACOPO BASSANO]

Engraving | 20.8 × 27cm

Inscribed in the upper margin: 'COGNOVIT BOS POSSESSOREM SVVM, ET ASINVS PRESEPE DOMINI SVI. ISRAEL AVTEM ME NON COGNOVIT. Isai.1' (see below); and in the lower margin: 'MAG.CO ATQ. EGR.gio Viro IACOB.O KENING ALIAS PINICIANO GERMANICO / Ioa. Sadeler.s Belga tabell.m hanc ab exemplari Iac.i Bass.is pict. ill. desu[m]ptam / grati ac benevoli animi ergo D.D. M.D.XCIX. / Cu[m] privil. Sum[m]i Pontif. et Caes. M.tis' (To the magnificent and distinguished Jacob Kening known as 'Piniciano Germanico', this plate, undertaken after an original by the illustrious painter Jacopo Bassano, Jan Sadeler from Flanders presents and dedicates in a grateful and friendly spirit')

Provenance: Pierre Mariette (Lugt 1788, with his inscription 'Mariette' on the verso)

EDINBURGH, NATIONAL GALLERY OF SCOTLAND

The passage in the upper margin is adapted from Isaiah 1: 3: 'The ox knoweth his owner and the ass his master's crib: but Israel does not know me.' This passage came to be applied to the Christ Child born in a stable, who was thus the fulfilment of Old Testament prophecies. The original painting by Bassano from which this print derives has not been traced, although variants are known. Animals are given particular prominence, including the hen in a basket that the two shepherds in the foreground have brought as a gift.

The print bears a dedication to Jacob Kening, a German jeweller and art dealer.[1] Jan Sadeler had come to Venice in 1596–7 with his brother Raphael, and died there in 1600. In 1581 they had been granted a privilege by the Holy Roman Emperor to protect their work against copyists in the lands of the empire, and this was renewed in 1593. In 1598 they were granted a papal privilege as well. Both these privileges are recorded in the inscription.

315

Raphael Sadeler ANTWERP 1561–1632 MUNICH

156 ❧ *The Adoration of the Kings* [AFTER JACOPO BASSANO]

Engraving | 26.6 × 20.7cm (trimmed)

Inscribed at the lower edge: 'Iacob.de P.Bassan. pinx'; at the lower right: 'Cum priviliegio sum / Pontificis et S.C.M. / Rapha. Sadeler scalpsit'; and in the lower margin: 'EX AVGVSTO MVSAEO ADM. R.di PRIS MAGRI FRIS PAVLI CAGGIOLI VENETI ORD.is / PRAEDICATORVM IN CON.tu SS. IOANNIS ET PAVLI. M.D.IIC.' (From the distinguished museum of the reverend prior, master brother Paolo Caggiolo of Venice, of the order of Preachers in the convent of SS. Giovanni e Paolo, 1598)

EDINBURGH, NATIONAL GALLERY OF SCOTLAND

Raphael Sadeler came to Venice in 1596–7 with his brother Jan and set up a business making and publishing prints. He left to settle in Munich in 1604. This print reproduces a painting by Jacopo Bassano now in the Galleria Borghese in Rome, which came from the convent of the Dominicans of Santi Giovanni e Paolo in Venice (fig.246). According to the inscription, the painting was in the collection of Paolo Caggiolo, who was prior of the convent.

The imperial and papal privileges are recorded in the lower right corner.[1] It is interesting that while they were resident in Venice, the Sadeler brothers do not seem to have sought to obtain a privilege from the Venetian Senate to protect their work in the city. The possible reasons for this may have been that they regarded it as valueless because of inadequate enforcement, or alternatively that they thought that their principal markets would lie outside Venetian territories.[2]

Fig.246 | Jacopo Bassano, *The Adoration of the Kings*
Rome, Galleria Borghese

Cornelis Visscher HAARLEM 1628/9–1658 AMSTERDAM

157 ❧ *Abraham's Journey* [AFTER JACOPO BASSANO]

Etching and engraving | 32.2 × 38.8cm

EDINBURGH, NATIONAL GALLERY OF
SCOTLAND

The Old Testament story of Abraham's journey
from Haran to Canaan (Genesis 12) provided
Bassano with an opportunity to indulge his
passion for genre-like subjects in which prominence was given to animals, still-life and landscape elements (see also cat.nos.72, 73).

This print was published in Amsterdam in a
volume entitled *Variarum imaginum a celeberrimis
artificibus pictarum caelaturae* (Engravings of
various painted images by celebrated artists).[1] It
reproduces a painting (now lost), probably by
Jacopo Bassano, which in the middle of the
seventeenth century was in the collection of
Gerrit Reynst in Amsterdam. Several similar
compositions from the Bassano workshop are

known, but the one from the Reynst collection
cannot now be traced.

Although Visscher was never in Italy, he made
a number of prints after Venetian masters,
including Palma Vecchio, Titian, Veronese and
Tintoretto.

Valentin Lefèvre BRUSSELS *c.*1637–1677 VENICE

158 ✤ *The Three Ages of Man* [AFTER TITIAN]

Etching | 24.3 × 35.1cm

Inscribed in the lower margin: 'V. lefebre del et sculp. TITIANVS VECELLIVS CAD. INVENT. & PINXIT. J.Van Campen. Formis. Venetijs.'

EDINBURGH, NATIONAL GALLERY OF SCOTLAND

This etching records a composition of Titian's that is similar, but not identical, to *The Three Ages of Man* (cat.no.15).[1] The most significant differences are the presence of more buildings in the background; the sprouting branches of the pollarded tree at the right; the fact that two rather than just one of the babies are winged; the fact that the girl holds only one flute; and the absence of the old man with skulls in the middle-ground. These changes result in a shift in the subject of the print, which is now more insistently about love than the three ages of man. X-ray examination of the Sutherland picture has revealed that some of the differences evident in the etching were present in the initial laying-in of the painting, but were subsequently modified by Titian (see fig.88). This suggests that Lefèvre's model could have been another version of Titian's painting, now lost, which reflected an earlier stage of its evolution.

The present etching was included in the collection of prints by Lefèvre reproducing works by Titian, Veronese and Tintoretto published by Jacob van Campen in 1682.[2] The title page carries the inscription: *Opera Selectiora, quae Titianus Vecellius Cadubriensis, et Paulus Calliari Veronensis inventarunt et pinxerunt.* In a little booklet that was published by Antonio Bosio in Venice in 1683 to accompany the plates, this etching is described as 'Pastor e pastorella con Groppo de puttini, in paese, di Titiano in Casa de particolari' (Shepherd and shepherdess with a group of children in a landscape by Titian, in a private collection).[3] The colophon of the booklet reveals that the plates could either be purchased as a set in the street called the Merzaria or as separate sheets at what may have been Bosio's own shop at Santa Maria Formosa.[4]

V. lefebre del. et sculp.   TITIANVS VECELLIVS. CAD. INVENT. & PINXIT.   J. Van Campen. Formis. Venetijs.

Valentin Lefèvre BRUSSELS c.1637–1677 VENICE

159 ❧ *The Martyrdom of St Peter Martyr* [AFTER TITIAN]

Etching | 54.3 × 33.5cm (trimmed)

Inscribed in the lower margin: 'V. lefebre del. Et sculp. N.o 9 TITIANVS VECELLIVS CAD. INVENT. & PINXIT J. Van Campen. Formis. Venetijs. / Invidus hic fremat nec imitabile dicat.' (Let the envious one [?painter] here growl and not say that this [painting] can be imitated.)

EDINBURGH, NATIONAL GALLERY OF SCOTLAND

This etching reproduces, in reverse, the altarpiece Titian painted in the later 1520s for the church of Santi Giovanni e Paolo in Venice. The painting was immensely celebrated but was destroyed in a fire in 1867. This etching was included in the collection of prints by Lefèvre reproducing works by Titian, Veronese and Tintoretto that was first published by Jacob van Campen in 1682 under the title *Opera Selectiora, quae Titianus Vecellius Cadubriensis, et Paulus Calliari Veronensis inventarunt et pinxerunt*.[1] These etchings could be bought either as a series, with a title page, or as individual sheets (see cat.no.158).

319

DELLE
METAMORFOSI
D'OVIDIO
LIBRO PRIMO.

ARGOMENTO.

Distingue Dio il gran Chaos, e'l mondo forma:
Cangia l'Età, i Giganti, e Licaone:
Manda il Diluuio: e'l Sasso si trasforma
In noua gente: vcciso è'l fier Pitone:
Dafne, & Io, con Mercurio han varia forma:
Diuien Siringa fistola, e'l Pauone
Con gl'occhi d'Argo la sua coda s'orna:
Io nel primier sembiante suo ritorna.

1

E FORME
in Noui
corpi tras-
formate
Grã desio di
cãtar m'in
fiamma il
petto,
Da i tẽpi pri
mi a la fe-
lice etate,

Che fu capo à l'Imperio Augusto eletto.
Dei, c'hauete non pur quelle cangiate,
Ma tolto à voi più volte il proprio aspetto,
Porgete à tanta impresa tale aita,
C'habbiano i versi miei perpetua vita.

2

E tu, se ben tutto hai l'animo intento,
Inuittissimo HENRICO, al fero Marte
Mentre io sotto il tuo nome ardisco, e tento
Di figurar sì bei concetti in carte,
Fammi del fauor tuo talhor contento,
Che le tue gratie a noi largo comparte:
Che, s'esser grato a te vedrò il mio carme,
Farò cantar le Muse al suon de l'arme.

Inuo-
tione

3

Pria che'l Ciel fosse, il mar, la terra, e'l foco;
Era il foco, la terra, il ciel, e'l mare:
Ma'l mar rendea il ciel, la terra, e'l foco,
Deforme il foco, il ciel, la terra, e'l mare.
Che iui era e terra, e cielo, e mare, e foco,
Doue era e cielo, e terra, e foco, e mare;
La terra, il foco, e'l mare era nel cielo;
Nel mar, nel foco, e ne la terra il cielo.

Caos.

IV BOOKS & MANUSCRIPTS

opposite | Enlarged detail from cat.no.165

Werner Rolewinck
160 ❧ *Fasciculus Temporum*

Vellum binding on boards | 31 × 43cm (folio)
1479

Incipit: *Fasciculus Tempor[um] omnes antiquor[um] cronicas complectens: incipit feliciter*. (A 'nosegay' of the times, comprising all the chronicles of the ancients: it begins happily ...)

Colophon: 'Chronica qu[ae] d[icitu]r fascicul[us] tempor[um]: edita in alma universitate colonie agrippine a quoda[m] devoto cartusiensi: [et] imp[re]ssa Venetiis singulari industria atq[ue] impensa Georij Walch almani. a[n]no d[omi]n[i] 1479.' (The chronicle which is called 'a nosegay of the times': produced in the nurturing University of Cologne by a certain Carthusian monk: and printed at Venice by the singular diligence and expense of Georg Walch of Germany. In the Year of Our Lord 1479.)

Provenance: Marco Contardini (according to an inscription on leaf 64 in a contemporary hand); Liaio Soranzo, 1752 (according to an inscription on the front free endpaper); Consul Joseph Smith, after 1755 (with his armorial bookplate on the front pastedown); his posthumous sale, 25 January 1773 and following days (lot 822 or 823), bought by the Advocates' Library, Edinburgh, 1773;[1] transferred to the National Library on its foundation in 1925 (shelfmark: Inc.137)

EDINBURGH, NATIONAL LIBRARY
OF SCOTLAND

Within twenty years of Johann Gutenberg printing his first Bible at Mainz in 1455, Venice had become the most important centre of the European book trade, a position it would hold for fifty years. Not only did the city offer a rich cultural environment, but, perhaps more importantly, it provided access to a good paper supply from nearby Padua and the trade networks that enabled Venetian books to be exported all over the known world.

The woodcut shown here is the first recorded printed image of Venice. It occurs in the first Venetian edition of the *Fasciculus Temporum*, a chronicle of world history written by the German scholar and Carthusian monk Werner Rolewinck (*c*.1425–1502), and accompanies an account of the founding of the city. It is clearly recognisable today as a representation of the Piazzetta San Marco, with the Doge's Palace, the domes of the Basilica of St Mark's, the statues and the bridge to the Riva degli Schiavoni. A closer examination, however, reveals that the view is reversed: looking from the opposing bank, the order should be the statues, the palace and then the bridge. Presumably this error happened because of 'teething troubles' with the process of printing an illustration. It has been suggested that the original sketch was made directly onto the block of wood from which it was printed, and thus what looked correct on the block was reversed on paper.[2]

Rolewinck's chronicle was first published in Cologne, where he lived. The first edition (1473) was without illustrations; the second (1474) contained among other illustrations one of contemporary Cologne, including the cathedral which was then under construction.[3] That edition, which was one of Walch's source texts, probably inspired him to include a picture of Venice in his own production.

Little is known about Georg Walch, other than that he was a German who published four books in Venice from 1479 to 1482 – one of many foreigners involved in the Venetian book trade. Some were Germans who brought the new technology to the city; others included Nicholas Jenson from France and Aldo Manuzio (see cat.no.162), who was Italian but not a citizen of the Republic. Walch's edition may also have involved the printer Erhard Ratdolt (see cat.no.161), who produced his own edition the following year.[4] He replaced Walch's illustration with another view of the same scene, this time with the monuments in the right order. HV

Standard Bibliographical References

BMC V
London: British Museum, *Catalogue of books printed in the XVth century now in the British Museum, vol.5: Venice*, London, 1963–7.

BM STC Italian
London: British Library, *Short-title catalogue of books printed in Italy and of Italian books printed in other countries from 1465 to 1600 now in the British Library*, 2nd edn., London, 1986.

Brunet
J.-C. Brunet, *Manuel du libraire et de l'amateur de livres*, 5th edn., 6 vols., Paris, 1860.

GW
K.W. Hiersemann, *Gesamtkatalog der Wiegendrucke*, Leipzig, 1925–40.

Hain
L. Hain, *Repertorium Bibliographicum*, Stuttgart, 1826–8.

¶ Arcturus rex britanie noīatissim⁹ in victorijs: quadrigentosssexagita viros gladio suo interfecit. Ecclesie dei subuenit: ⁊ fidez valde ampliauit: oēsq̧ terras francie: datie: norwegie ⁊c̄. sibi seruire coegit. Perditur tandē: nec vsq̧ hodie scitur vbi manserit.

¶ Dubricius p̄mas anglie: vir sanctus: miraculis clarus: post heremita: coronauit arcturum.

¶ Iste zeno fuit arrian⁹: ⁊ totaliter crudelis ꝯ catholicos. Fed⁹ init cū gothis: ⁊ filiuz Leonis īterficere volens: alter similis ei offertur. Ipse theodericū puer: postea regem gothoꝝ a patre suo in obsidē accepit.

Zeno annis 12.

Imperatores

¶ Helizei pphete ossa transferūtur de samaria in alexādriam.
¶ Marci euāgeliste corp⁹ transfert̄ ad venetias de alexādria.
¶ Letanie minores instituūtur a mamerto epo vienen̄.
¶ Remigi⁹ remenſ eps: q post clodoneū regez frācie ꝯuertit.
¶ Perpetuus episcopus turonenſ.
¶ Prosper eps vir clarus scia sanctitate vite: de aqtanie terra.
¶ Theodorus eps syrie scripsit cronicaz: ⁊ plura alia.
¶ Cyprian⁹ amsilienſ epus: vir supra moduz misericors: totuz quod habuit fratrib⁹ in necessitate dedit.
¶ Hereſ acephaloꝝ fuit: que impugnauit ꝯciliuz calcedonēse.
¶ Meretrix q̄dam peperit infantes 7 vno ptu: ⁊ in piscinaz piecit: ⁊ vnus factus est rex lōgobardoꝝ.

¶ Etthicius senator i burgūdia tpe famis 4 milia paupū sustētauit: ⁊ celestis pmissiōis vocē audiuit.

¶ Fulgentius eps ruspen̄. claret: luculentissim⁹ doctor: scia ⁊ fide plenus. afer.

¶ Anglia i flore tpe arcturi: cui ter dena regna seruierūt: sȝ tpe puo. Et nō signuz īfallibile: qn̄ videlȝ militaris celsitudo bellū delectabilr appetit: ⁊ occasionez q̄rit: tūc seqͥ finis cōiter miserabilis: iux̄ illō pphe. Dissipa gētes q̄ bella volūt. O si hoc tpe britones q nūc dnr anglici prudētia ꝟa gubernassent: toti⁹ europe dn̄i fuissent. Sȝ duz uolunt fortiter cōtra fortes agere: pariter cuz fortibus ī quos impegerunt: ceciderūt. Est siquidez miserabilis victoria: quādo victor paucos aut nullos milites retinet. Unde audacia plurimū nocet: quādo puidentia non gubernatur. sic arcturo cōtigit.

Anno mūdi 5663

Pape

sardus

Hilari⁹ p̄ an. 6. mē. 3 di. 6.

tyburtin⁹

Siplicius an. 15. mē. 2. di. 7.

Anno xp̄i 464

¶ Iste hilarius dedicauit ecclesiam beati stephani iuxta basilicam beati laurencij. Hic cōstituit: vt nullus pontifex sibi successorem cōstituat: vt habetur. viij q. i. plericq̧. Sepelitur in monasterio sancti laurencij: quod ipse cōstruxit.

¶ Iste simplicius diuisit vrbem in qnq̧ regiones: ⁊ plures ecclesias dedicauit. Hic cōstituit vt clericus inuestituraz nō recipiat a laico: quod fuit post per alios magis roboratum: vt patet. xvi. q. vi. per totum. Sepelitur in vaticano.

¶ Uenetiaꝝ ciuitas.

¶ Uenetiaꝝ ciuitas inclyta conditur: aut potius ampliat̄ circa hec tempa: āno 450. non a pastoribus sicut Roma: sed a potentioribus ⁊ ditioribus puinciarū aduenis: illic ppter persecutionē Attile confugientibus. Miruz est: ⁊ summo extollēdum laudis p̄conio: potuisse a tot tāq̧ diuersis vrbiuz ⁊ oppidoꝝ populis conditam ciuicatem per annos mille cum tali incremēto: ac glorie splendore: vnanimiq̧ sagacitate conseruare.

Euclid
161 ❧ *Elementa Geometriae*

Leather binding with blind-stamped decoration
32 × 42cm (folio) | 1482

Incipit: *Praeclarissimus liber elementorum Euclidis perspicacissimi: in artem Geometrie incipit qua[m] foelicissime* (The most famous book of the Elements of the most acute Euclid: in the art of geometry it begins thus most happily ...)

Colophon: 'Opus elementoru[m] euclidis megarensis in geometria[m] arte[m] In id quoq[ue] Campani p[er]spicacissimi Co[m]mentationes finiu[n]t. Erhardus ratdolt Augustensis impressor solertissimus. venetijs impressit. Anno salutis. M.cccc.lxxxij. Octavis. Calen. Jun.' (Here ends the work of the Elements of Euclid of Megara in the art of geometry, also the commentaries on it of the most acute Campanus. Erhard Ratdolt of Augsburg the extremely skillful printer. Printed at Venice. In the year of our salvation 1482 on 25th May.)

The original binding has been repaired, and over the original blind-stamped centrepiece, first an armorial seal and the name 'Thomas' have been stamped in gold, and subsequently 'Advocatorum Bibliotheca' in a gold wreath.

Provenance: Unidentified armorial crest illuminated in blue, red and gold on sig. a2; an early provenance inscription has been erased; the Advocates' Library, Edinburgh (acquired between 1808 and 1874); transferred to the National Library on its foundation in 1925 (shelfmark: Inc.143)

EDINBURGH, NATIONAL LIBRARY
OF SCOTLAND

The *editio princeps* of Euclid's treatise on geometry is one of the finest printing achievements of the fifteenth century. As the printer Erhard Ratdolt (1447–1528) himself states in his dedication, this work had previously not appeared in print because no-one had been able to produce the necessary diagrams.[1] Ratdolt never explained the means by which he overcame the technical obstacles, although his solutions included the use of at least 420 woodcuts or metal plates and successfully printing in the margins of the text.[2]

Ratdolt was perhaps uniquely equipped amongst the early printers to overcome these hurdles. Born in Augsburg, he may have gained expertise in working with woodblocks through the family woodcarving business. He also seems to have printed with the astronomer Johann Muller Regiomontanus (1436–1476) in Nürnberg. The first book he printed in Venice was a copy of Regiomontanus's *Calendarium*, a production involving the printing of astronomical wheels and diagrams. Ratdolt probably initially came to Italy as part of Regiomantus's entourage, and he remained there after his mentor's death. He returned to Augsburg in 1486 at the request of its bishop to print for the diocese, and died there in 1525.

By 1482 Ratdolt was printing on his own in Venice. The designer of the decorative border and decorated initial is unknown, as is the illuminator of the National Library of Scotland's copy. Ratdolt's earlier collaboration with the illustrator Bernard Maler, like his training with Regiomontanus, shows a man concerned with book design, and in particular the use of decorative elements such as title pages, illustrations, borders, and decorated initials – all features that, along with the geometric diagrams here and the ability to print in several colours, he either invented or took to a new level of production.[3]

Ratdolt was well aware of the importance of his printing achievements, as his dedication shows. This dedication was addressed to Giovanni Mocenigo, doge of Venice from 1478 to 1485, and Ratdolt presented him with an illuminated vellum copy in which the dedication was printed in gold.[4] The present copy is one of a number that seem to have been produced for a second tier of patrons, with the decorative border printed then illuminated by hand.

Probably to increase the usefulness of his edition, Ratdolt here printed the Latin translation produced by an English philosopher, Adelard of Bath (*c*.1100–1150), rather than the Greek original, with notes by the commentator Johannes Campanus Novariensis. His text may not have been at the forefront of contemporary scholarship, but Ratdolt's edition is a monument to the liminal moment between the manuscript tradition and the art of the printed book. HV

¶Preclarissimus liber elementorum Euclidis perspi/
cacissimi: in artem Geometrie incipit quãfoelicissime:

Unctus est cuius ps nõ est. ¶Linea est
lõgitudo sine latitudine cui⁹ quidẽ ex/
tremitates st̃ duo pũcta. ¶Linea recta
ẽ ab vno pũcto ad aliũ breuissima exte/
sio i extremitates suas vtrũq₃ eoꝝ reci
piens.¶Supficies ẽ q̃ lõgitudinẽ ꞇ lati
tudinẽ tm̃ h₃:cui⁹ termi quidẽ sũt linee.
¶Supficies plana ẽ ab vna linea ad a/
liũ extẽsio. i extremitates suas recipiẽs
¶Angulus planus ẽ duarũ linearũ al/
ternus ꝓtactus:quaꝝ expãsio ẽ sup sup
ficiẽ applicatioq₃ nõ directa. ¶Quãdo aũt angulum ꝓtinẽt due
linee recte rectiline⁹ angulus noiaꝛ. ¶ Cm̃ recta linea sup rectã
steterit duoq₃ anguli ytrobiq₃ fuerit eq̃les:eoꝝ vterq₃ rect⁹erit
¶Lineaq₃ linee supstãs ei cui supstat ꝑpendicularis vocaꝛ.¶An
gulus ỹo qui recto maioꝛ ẽ obtusus diciꝉ.¶Angul⁹ ỹo minoꝛ re
cto acut⁹appellaꝉ.¶Termin⁹ẽ qd vniuscuiusq₃ tnis ẽ.¶Figura
ẽ q̃ tmino vl̃ termis ꝓtinef.¶Circul⁹ẽ figura plana vna q̃dem li
nea ꝓtẽta: q̃ circũferentia noiaꝛ:in cui⁹medio pũct⁹ẽ. a quo⁹oẽs
linee recte ad circũferẽtiã exeũtes sibiinicez sut equales. Et hic
quidẽ pũct⁹cẽtrũ circuli dr̃.¶Diameter circuli ẽ linea recta que
sup ei⁹centꝛ trãsiens extremitatesq₃ suas circũferẽtie applicans
circulũ i duo media diuidit.¶Semicirculus ẽ figura plana dia/
metro circuli ꞇ medietate circũferentie ꝓtenta.¶Portio circu/
li ẽ figura plana recta linea ꞇ parte circũferẽtie ꝓtẽta: semicircu/
lo quidẽ aut maioꝛ aut minoꝛ. ¶Rectilinee figure sũt q̃ rectis li/
neis cõtinent quarũ quedã trilatere. q̃ trib⁹rectis lineis: quedã
quadrilatere q̃ q̃tuoꝛ rectis lineis. q̃dã mltilatere que pluribus
q₃ quatuoꝛ rectis lineis continenꝉ. ¶ Figurarũ trilaterarũ:alia
est triangulus hñs tria latera equalia. Alia triangulus duo hñs
eq̃lia latera. Alia triangulus triũ inequalium laterũ. Haꝛ iterũ
alia est oꝛthogoniũ:vnũ .s. rectum angulum habens.Alia ẽ am/
bligonium aliquem obtusum angulum habens. Alia est oꝛigoni/
um:in qua tres anguli sunt acuti.¶Figurarũ autẽ quadrilateraꝛ
Alia est q̃dratum quod est equilaterũ atq₃ rectangulũ. Alia est
tetragon⁹long⁹:q̃ est figura rectangula : sed equilatera non est.
Alia est helmuaym: que est equilatera : sed rectangula non est.

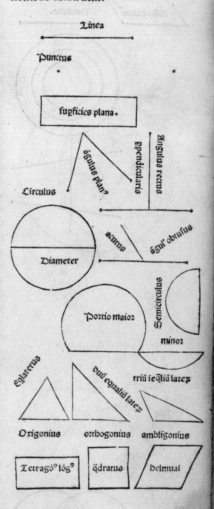

De pꝛincipijs ꝑ se notis: ꞇ pmõ de diffini/
tionibus earandem.

Linea

Punctus

supficies plana.

Angulus planus

ꝑpendicularis

Angulus rectus

Circulus

Diameter

acutus

ãgꝉi obtusus

Semicirculus

Portio maioꝛ

minoꝛ

Eqlaterus

duũ equaliũ lateꝛ

triũ se q̃liũ lateꝛ

Oꝛigonius

oꝛthogonius

ambligonius

Tetragõ⁹ lõg⁹

q̃dratus

helmuai

Pietro Bembo

162 ❧ Gli Asolani

Quarter-bound in blue morocco with marbled boards | 22 × 25cm (octavo) | 1505

Title: Gli Asolani di messer Pietro Bembo

Colophon: 'Impressi in Venetia nelle Case d'Aldo Romano nel anno. MDV. del mese di Marzo.' (Printed in Venice in the house of Aldus the Roman in the year 1505 in the month of March.)

Provenance: H.C. Hollway-Calthrop (with his armorial book-plate); Professor William L. Renwick (1889–1970), Regius Professor of Rhetoric and English Literature at Edinburgh University (with his book label); by whom presented to the National Library, 1964 (shelfmark: Ren.25)

EDINBURGH, NATIONAL LIBRARY OF SCOTLAND

While some early printers attempted to rival the splendours of illuminated manuscript, others moved towards an austere minimalism, combining beautiful typography with a masterly use of the space around a text. One of the key figures in this development was Aldo Manuzio (1449–1515), or Aldus as he is generally known in English. Originally a teacher, he was driven to become a printer by the desire to share the newly rediscovered literature of classical Greece with as wide an audience as possible; it was the presence in Venice of Greek exiles from Constantinople that led him to establish his press there in 1494.

Aldus was an eminent classical scholar in his own right, but among his many distinguished collaborators was Pietro Bembo (1470–1547), the epitome of the cultured Renaissance Venetian. The scion of a distinguished patrician family, Bembo preferred a life of courtiership and study to politics. His association with Aldus began when Bembo supplied him with a manuscript of the Greek grammar of Constantine Lascaris, which was Aldus's first publication. In 1501 Bembo edited the poems of Petrarch and Dante as the first vernacular works in the seminal series of Aldine octavo pocket-sized classics. *Gli Asolani*, the first of Bembo's own vernacular works to appear in print, was written in the Tuscan dialect he would later advocate in his *Prose della volgar lingue* (1525).

One contemporary who preferred Aldus's scholarly publications dismissed *Gli Asolani* as 'a few odds and ends in the vernacular, about love'.[1] But in its vision of a court where witty and poetic ladies and gentlemen would debate the finer points of neo-Platonic and Petrarchan love, it offered a synthesis of humanist ideas whose influence would extend across Europe, most notably through Baldassare Castiglione's *Il Cortegiano*, where Bembo himself figures as a character. Bembo began work on *Gli Asolani* in the late 1490s while he was studying philosophy at the court of Ferrara and at the same time was embroiled in a Petrarchan affair with a married woman. Set at the court of Caterina Cornaro, the exiled Queen of Cyprus (and a relation of Bembo's), the work is a dialogue which ends with an encomium on the renunciation of earthly for heavenly desire.

The National Library of Scotland's copy is one of those which contains the dedication to Lucrezia Borgia (1480–1519), with whom Bembo had embarked on a relationship in 1501 at Ferrara. Her name may be synonymous today with sexual intrigue thanks to the propaganda of the Borgias' political opponents, but Bembo here praises her as 'longing ... to clothe her soul with comely virtues'.[2] *Gli Asolani* was not published until their affair had cooled; one reason that not all copies contain the dedication may be that there was a delay in Bembo obtaining permission to publish it.[3]

The book is printed in the italic font cut for Aldus by Francesco Griffo, who also cut the roman font named for Bembo which was first used in Aldus's edition of his *De Aetna* (1496) and still is in use today, its austerity eminently befitting a work which advocates the renunciation of material beauty for 'another world which is neither material nor evident to sense, but completely separate from this and pure'.[4] HV

A MADONNA LVCRETIA ESTEN=
SE BORGIA DVCHESSA ILLV=
STRISSIMA DI FERRARA.

PIETRO BEMBO.

E io non ho a V . S . piu tosto quegli ragiona=
menti mandati , che essendo l'anno passato in
Ferrara le promisi giunto che io fussi qui di
mandare; iscusimi appo lei la morte de lmio caro fratel
lo Carlo; che io oltre ogni mia credéza ritrouai di que
sta uita passato : laqual morte si mi stordi; che a guisa
di coloro , che dal fuoco delle saette tocchi rimangono
lungo tempo sanza sentimento , non ho peranchora ad
altro potuto riuolger lanimo , che alla sua insanabile et
penetreuolissima ferita. Percio che io non solamente ho
un fratello perduto; ilche suole tuttauia esser graue et
doloroso per se; ma ho perduto un fratello , che io solo
hauea , et che pur hora nel primo fiore della sua gio-
uanezza entraua; et il quale per molto amore di me ogni
mio uolere facendo suo nessuna cura maggiore hauea ,
che di tutte le cure alleggiarmi ,si che io a gli studi del
le lettere , che esso sapea essermi sopra tutte le cose cari ,
potessi dare ogni mio tempo et pensiero ; et oltre a cio
di chiaro et di gentile ingegno , et per molte sue par =
ti meriteuole di peruenire a glianni della inchineuole
uecchiezza; o certo almeno a cui si conuenia , percio che
egli era alla uita uenuto doppo me , che anchora doppo me se ne dipartisse : lequai tutte cose quanto habbiano sanza fine fatta profonda la mia piaga ; V . S . da
quelle due , che la inguriosa fortuna in ispatio di poco
tempo a lei ha date , potra istimare . Hora; poscia che
altro fare non se ne puo , et che in me per la tramissio
ne di questo tempo uolgare et commune medicina piu to
sto che per altro rimedio, il dolore et le lachrime han=
no in parte dato luoco alla ragione et al diritto cono =
scimento,

Francesco de' Lodovici
163 ❧ *Triomphi di Carlo*

Bound in green morocco with gilt edges and gilt borders | 22 × 31cm (quarto) | 1536

Title: *Triomphi di Carlo di messer Francesco D'i Lodovici … M D XXXVI.* (The Triumphs of Carlo by Mr Francesco D'i Lodovici … 1536)

Colophon: 'Il fine della seconda parte, & di tutto esso libro, intitolato I TRIOMPHI DI CARLO, di messer Fra[n]cesco d'i Lodovici Vinitiano, Stampato in Vinegia per Mapheo Pasini & Francesco Bindoni co[m]pagni al segno dell'angiolo Raphaello apresso san Moise l'anno della nostra salute M D XXXV. del mese di Settembre.' (The end of the second part, and of the whole book, entitled The Triumphs of Carlo, by Mr Fransceco d'i Lodovici of Venice, printed in Venice by the partners Maffeo Pasini & Francesco Bindoni at the sign of the angel Raphael; printed at San Moise in the year of our salvation 1535 in the month of September.)

Edition: First published in 1535, this is the second edition of 1536

Provenance: Thomas Gaisford (with his armorial bookplate);[1] John A. Fairley, 1909 (with his bookplate, dated); the Trustees of William Robert Reid; by whom presented to the Library in 1926 [2] (shelfmark: L.C. 1811)

EDINBURGH, NATIONAL LIBRARY OF SCOTLAND

The image of the author presenting his work to a patron at the head of the text was a long-standing tradition of manuscript illumination which was brought across to printed books. In this woodcut the author Francesco de' Lodovici presents a richly bound copy of his epic romance on Charlemagne, Orlando and Rinaldo to the Doge Andrea Gritti (see cat.nos.37, 196, 197); since Gritti is recognisable, it must be assumed that this is also a portrait of Lodovici.

It is unknown whether this woodcut symbolises an actual presentation. In manuscript, the illustration would accompany the copy actually presented to the dedicatee, but this image is intended to impress the general readership addressed in the preceding foreword, and survived into the work's second edition. It is possible that a copy was presented to Gritti exactly as shown here, but equally likely that the author never even met his patron. The work is, however, dedicated 'all'illustrissimo signor Andrea Gritti' at the head of the first page, and book one is addressed directly to him: 'di voi sol famossissimo GRITTI / Donar quest' opra' (To you alone, most famous Gritti / I give this work; lines 14–15).

However, there is a third figure in the image: the sun, whose rays directly touch the poet. This may represent the inspiration of Apollo, or more generally divine inspiration as symbolised by the sun, but given its portrait quality it may also be a representation of the woman Lodovici elsewhere called his Muse.[3]

By the 1530s, this was just one of the ways in which an author could be presented in the printed text. Rejected here were images which might have given the poet greater authority – showing him in the act of writing or reading in his study, for example, or looking out at the readers he addresses, or as a classicised authorial figure crowned with a laurel wreath and set in a medallion. The visual image of the doge as patron receiving the text would lend authority to a 'new book of romance, newly composed' as Lodovici describes his tale on the title page. But Lodovici's humble presentation of his work to the doge is balanced by the rays of the sun which directly touch him; the author in print is not here simply a humble suppliant but also an inspired creator. HV

Francesco Colonna

164 ❧ *Hypnerotomachia Poliphili*

Red morocco half-binding, with marbled boards
31 × 41cm (folio) | 1545

Title: *La Hypnerotomachia di Poliphilo, cioè pugna d'amore in sogno. Dov'egli mostra, che tutte le cose humane non sono altro che sogno: & dove narra molt'altre cose degne di cognitione. Ristampato di novo, et ricorretto con somma diligentia, à maggior commodo de i lettori.* (The Hypnerotomachia of Poliphilo, that is, the strife of love in a dream. In which it is shown that all human things are nothing other than a dream: and where many other things are told worthy of memory. Newly reprinted, and corrected with all diligence, for the greater convenience of the readers.)

Colophon: 'In Vinegia, nell' anno M. D. XLV. In casa de' figliuoli di Aldo.' (In Venice, in the year 1545. In the house of the sons of Aldus.)

Provenance: Advocates' Library, Edinburgh, acquired between 1776 and 1807; transferred to the National Library on its foundation in 1925 (shelfmark Ac.3.8)

EDINBURGH, NATIONAL LIBRARY
OF SCOTLAND

Acclaimed as the most beautiful printed work of the Renaissance, the *Hypnerotomachia* – 'the strife of love in a dream', in the words of its earliest English translator – possesses an allure that is only increased by the mystery surrounding its production.[1] Published anonymously, its author is generally assumed to be Francesco Colonna (1433–1527), a Dominican monk who seems to have led a controversial and not necessarily moral life, and whose name can be found in the acrostic formed from the first letter of each chapter.

The book is a confused if not wilfully obscure combination of romance and dream-vision which is as much about a humanist's delight in encountering the fragmented ruins of the classical past as it is a psychological – and highly erotic – exploration of desire. The text has been seen as the perfect subject for Jungian analysis (one such critique carried a foreword from Jung himself) and as nothing more than the 'prurient imagination of a diseased monk'.[2] Written in a unique combination of Latin, Italian, and the odd word of Arabic, Hebrew and Chaldic (not to mention the hieroglyphics which appear in the illustrations), its language reflects the macaronic word-games popular at the University of Padua in the late fifteenth century.

But the influence of the *Hypnerotomachia* lay not in its text – it is perhaps the least-read book to have such an effect – but in its design. Probably undertaken by the great printer Aldo Manuzio (see cat.no.162) purely as a commission, it was his only illustrated book and his first vernacular publication. The type was cut by his equally eminent designer Francesco Griffo; the illustrator is unknown but the painter Benedetto Bordone has been suggested. The influence of many artists has been seen in the 170 woodcuts, that of Andrea Mantegna in particular. Both the typography and the illustrations have been universally praised for their simplicity and harmony, but it is the perfect combination of the two which gives the book its unique visual appeal.

'Let he who can imagine these things judge what voluptuous pleasure they gave me', says Poliphilo in his account of the triumph of Priapus, the largest and most detailed of a series of triumphs described in the text,[3] and illustrated here in a way which leaves little to the imagination (and in practice was often censored in individual copies). This book could never have been intended for a wide audience, but in placing word and image side by side so that each is an integral part of the reader's experience, it creates a pattern of perfection that artists have sought to imitate for hundreds of years.

This copy is an example of the second Aldine edition of the *Hypnerotomachia*, published in 1545 by Aldus's son Paolo Manuzio (1512–1574). His reprint reproduces the original layout and illustrations in full, using nearly all of the original blocks. It was perhaps part of his programme of restoring the reputation of the house of Aldus when he took control of the business in the 1540s, breaking with his father's partners, who had carried it on since Aldus's death. His edition stimulated fresh interest in this work, particularly in France, where a translation appeared in 1546, with three subsequent editions by 1600. HV

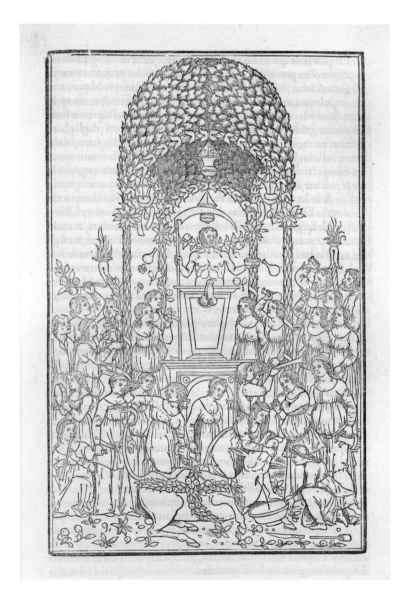

LA HYPNEROTOMACHIA DI POLIPHILO,
CIOE' PVGNA D'AMORE IN SOGNO.
DOV'EGLI MOSTRA, CHE TVTTE LE COSE
HVMANE NON SONO ALTRO CHE

Sogno: & doue narra molt'altre cose degne

di cognitione.

AL DVS

RISTAMPATO DI NOVO, ET RICORRETTO

con somma diligentia, à maggior commodo

de i lettori.

IN VENETIA, M. D. XXXXV.

Ovid

165 ❧ *Le metamorfosi*, translated by Giovanni Andrea dell'Anguillara

Calf binding with gilt tooling on spine
24 × 34cm. (quarto) | 1584

Title: *Le metamorfosi di Ovidio ridotte da Gio Andrea dell'Anguillara in ottava rima: con le annotationi di M. Gioseppe Horologgi, & gli argomenti, & postille di M. Francesco Turchi. In questa nuova impressione di vagle figure adornate.* (The metamorphoses of Ovid abridged by Gio. Andrea dell'Anguillara in *ottava rima*: with the annotations of Mr Giuseppe Horologgi, and with the arguments, and glosses of Mr Francesco Turchi. Decorated in this new edition with skilful illustrations.)

Imprint: 'M.D.L.XXXIV. In Vin. Presso Bern. Giunti.' (1584. In Venice. At the press of Bernardo Giunti.)

Provenance: Acquired by the Advocates' Library in 1790; transferred to the National Library on its foundation in 1925 (shelfmark: K.55.d)

EDINBURGH, NATIONAL LIBRARY
OF SCOTLAND

Ovid's *Metamorphoses* was perhaps the most influential classical text of the Renaissance in both art and literature. The verse translation produced by Giovanni Andrea dell'Anguillara (*c*.1517–1572) was first published in 1561 and became the most popular Italian version in the latter part of the sixteenth century. The annotations by Giuseppe Orologi and Francesco Turchi first appeared in subsequent editions of the 1560s.

The engravings in the 1584 edition were produced by Giacomo Franco, whose other notable books included *Habiti d'huomeni et donne venetiane* (1610). Franco produced thirty-one prints in all for this edition: an illustrated title page, fifteen full-page prints, and fifteen decorative borders enclosing the *argomenti* to each book. His full-page prints were also issued independently as a set. Anguillara's text was as much influenced by the great Italian epic poet Lodovico Ariosto as it was by Ovid; Franco's design for the title page was similarly influenced by an edition of Ariosto's *Orlando Furioso* published in the same year with engravings by Girolamo Porro.[1] Anguillara's portrait, crowned with laurel, is enclosed in a medallion at the top of the page, and where Porro has Venus and Mars forming the pillars which hold up the arch framing the title, Franco has Minerva and Mercury, with Mercury in particular in a much more dynamic pose. The arms on the title page are those of the printer Bernardo Giunti.

Franco's plates illustrate the entire range of metamorphoses in each book of the poem. The plate for Book I begins at the top with God separating the Earth from the Heavens, and sweeps round anti-clockwise through the fall of the giants and the flood, to mythological figures such as Apollo and Daphne, and Argus and Io, who are moving away from the foreground where the animals of the golden age are shown.

One of many vernacular versions of Ovid published during the sixteenth century, this edition, the first of two published in 1584, exemplifies the interplay between art and the printed word. Such editions were often the source of Ovidian stories for artists, while their illustrations reflect back not only the text but also the iconography of Ovidian paintings.[2] HV

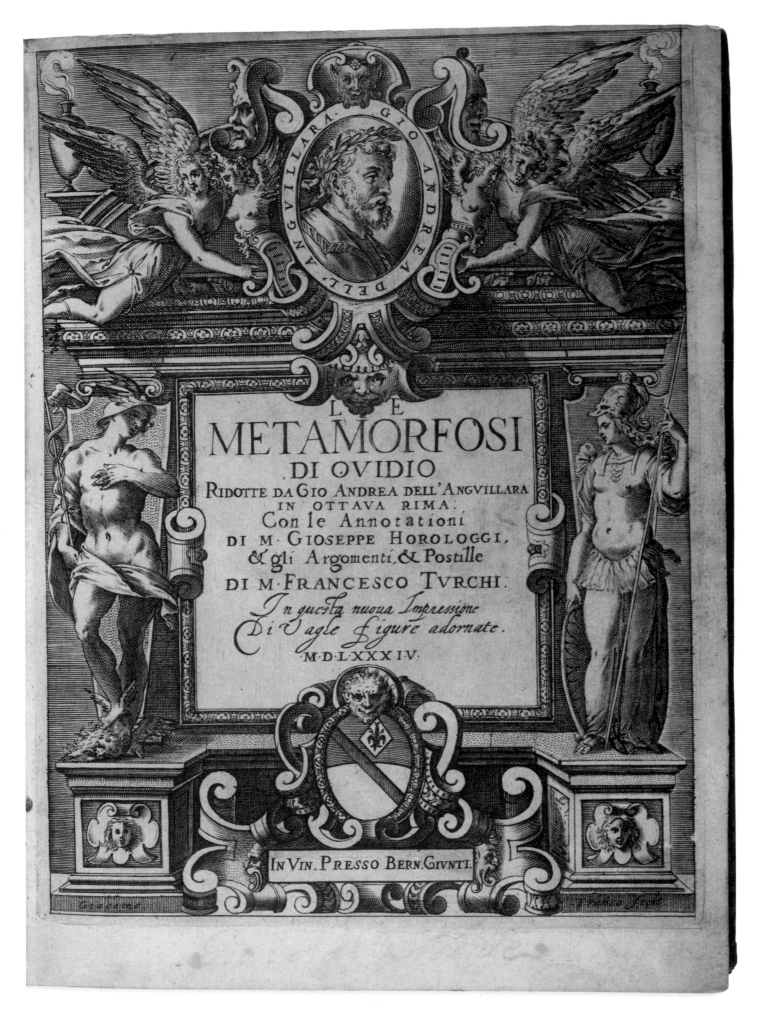

LE
METAMORFOSI
DI OVIDIO
Ridotte da Gio Andrea dell'Angvillara
in ottava rima:
Con le Annotationi
DI M. GIOSEPPE HOROLOGGI,
& gli Argomenti, & Postille
DI M. FRANCESCO TVRCHI.
In questa nuoua Impressione
Di Vaghe figure adornate.
M·D·L·XXXIV·

IN VIN. PRESSO BERN. GIVNTI.

Cesare Vecellio ACTIVE 1570–DIED 1601
166 ❧ *Habiti antichi e moderni de tutto il mondo*

Contemporary vellum binding on boards
17.5 × 30cm (octavo) | 1598

Title: *Habiti antichi et moderni de tutto il mondo. Di Cesare Vecellio. Di nuovo accresciuti di molte figure. Vestitus antiquorum, recentiorumque totius orbis. Per Sulstatium Gratilianun Senapolensis latinae declarati*

Imprint: In Venetia, Apresso i Sessa. M.D. XCVIII.'

Provenance: Acquired by the Royal Scottish Museum, Edinburgh, 1888; presented to the National Library, 1950 ([Ac]. 3/3)

EDINBURGH, NATIONAL LIBRARY
OF SCOTLAND

With its profusion of woodcuts and its bilingual text in Italian and Latin, this work purports to offer a highly-illustrated survey of the costume of all lands and all periods. In fact the emphasis is on Italy, and the differences of dress among the principalities and city states are demonstrated.

As befits a book of this nature printed in Venice, the costumes of the Republic through time form the subject of a large number of the illustrations, all set within mannerist frames. Vecellio's compendium was only one of a number of such productions which capture the glamour and exoticism of Venice in its time of greatness. Ancient, medieval and early renaissance costumes are all dealt with, but a major portion of the book illustrates the costume of the age of Titian and Veronese.

The whole gamut of society is here, ordered and characterised by distinctive dresses, from the Doge and Dogaressa, through the Procurators of St Mark's, members of the Council of Ten, senators, magistrates, admirals and generals of the Republic, nobles and gentlefolk, priests and nuns, craftsmen, the poor, and even galley-slaves. The infamous prostitutes appear in their professional costumes, though their black veils over one eye should not be confused with widow's weeds.

The elegant noblewoman, shown here in festive costume with a flag-shaped fan and with her hair dressed in the horn-like curls fashionable at the time, sums up the richness of life in late sixteenth-century Venice. The pose of the figure, not to mention the attire, is very similar to that of pharaoh's daughter in Giambattista Tiepolo's much later painting of *The Finding of Moses* (Edinburgh, National Gallery of Scotland), in which the costumes hark back to the age of Veronese. IGB

Andrea di Pietro della Gondola, called Palladio PADUA 1508–1580 VICENZA *or* MASER

167 ❧ *I Quattro libri dell' architettura di Andrea Palladio*

Leather binding with gold-tooled borders
32 × 46cm (folio) | 1616

Title: *I Quattro libri dell' architettura di Andrea Palladio. Ne' quali, dopo un breve trattato de' cinque ordini, & di quelli avertimenti, che sono più necessarii nel fabricare; si tratta delle case private, delle vie, dei ponti, delle piazze, de i xisti, & de' tempi*

Imprint: In Venetia, Appresso Bartolomeo Carampello, 1616

Fourth edition, 1616

Provenance: Dalrymple family, Newhailes, Midlothian; Newhailes Library and muniments accepted by HM Treasurer from the Trustees of Sir Mark Dalrymple Bt, in lieu of estate duty, and allocated to the National Library, 1978 (shelf mark: Nha.M84)

EDINBURGH, NATIONAL LIBRARY OF SCOTLAND

Palladio was arguably the most famous, and certainly the most imitated, architect in history. His buildings were long admired and much visited, but his *Quattro Libri* was even more widely influential, shaping the tastes and architectural aspirations of generations. In his villa designs especially he provided not only models for imitation, but offered a window onto an idealised world and a way of life.

His great book was first published in Venice in 1570. This fourth edition appeared only two years after Inigo Jones had travelled to Vicenza to discover Palladio at the fountainhead, a journey that would ultimately lead to England and Scotland becoming, as it were, Palladio's spiritual second home. The woodblocks used in this edition were those of the first, but by 1616 they had deteriorated, having become worn and worm-eaten, and the quality of the printing had declined.

'In the history of architecture, Palladio's treatise occupies a key position. It combines the humanistic literary tradition of the editions and commentaries of Vitruvius with the illustrated pattern-books written by architects for practical use … Palladio's own buildings take their place beside the buildings of antiquity; in fact they bear the stamp of antiquity as illustrations of ancient private houses built according to Vitruvius's text.'[1] The *Quattro Libri* shows Palladio as both theorist and practitioner of architecture. It has been observed that Palladio's book rendered the image fully as important as the word as a means of conveying information and style in the arts.[2] Illustration and descriptive text are placed on the same or on the facing page for ease of use; plan and elevation of a building are set one above the other so the concept of the structure is readily conveyed.

Book II is devoted to private houses, both urban palaces and rural villas, Palladio's own domestic designs succeeding his reconstructions of ancient edifices and the form of these being shown adapted to the requirements of Palladio's day. The opening illustrated shows villas of two distinct types. On the left is the Villa Foscari at Malcontenta on the Brenta canal, not far inland from Venice. Built for Alvise and Nicolò Foscari in the 1550s, this is one of the architect's characteristic designs for a large and imposing villa of two principal storeys, where a pedimented temple portico is set high on a podium. Opposite, on the right, is the nearly contemporary Villa Barbaro at Maser, Treviso, deep in the Venetian *terraferma* and some distance north of La Serenissima herself. Built for another pair of brothers, Daniele and Marcantonio Barbaro, Palladio's most distinguished patrons, this was a very different kind of villa. Its physical form consisted of one major storey with a temple front and arcaded wings for farming functions:

whereas the Villa Foscari was a non-agricultural *villa suburbana*, the Barbaro house was properly a *casa di villa* at the centre of a working estate. Both were country retreats, though of differing remoteness, and both were lavish in architectural and decorative terms, but their basic purpose was different. Both display the temple front that was Palladio's hallmark, and his lasting legacy in domestic architectural design. Though a working farmhouse, modest in its setting and with a secret garden and grotto against the hillside behind, the Maser villa is particularly richly decorated with frescoes by Paolo Veronese which offer 'a paradoxical mix of realistic illusion and classical evocation'.[3] Architecture and painting complement each other perfectly, and together form one of the greatest achievements of the late Venetian Renaissance. Palladio is said to have died at Maser, effectively a member of the Barbaro household, having been mentioned in Daniele's will as 'Palladio our architect'.[4]

This copy of the *Quattro Libri* comes from the Dalrymple family library at Newhailes, Midlothian, a house originally built by and for the architect James Smith (*c*.1645–1731), a figure of some importance in the dissemination of Palladianism in Britain. IGB

NON Molto lungi dalle Gambarare sopra la Brenta è la seguente fabrica delli Magnifici Signori Nicolò, e Luigi de' Foscari. Questa fabrica è alzata da terra vndeci piedi, e sotto vi sono cucine, tinelli, e simili luoghi, & è fatta in volto cosi di sopra, come di sotto. Le stanze maggiori hanno i volti alti secondo il primo modo delle altezze de' volti. Le quadre hanno i volti a copula: sopra i camerini vi sono mezati: il volto della Sala è à Crociera di mezo cerchio: la sua imposta tanto alta da piano, quanto è larga la sala: la quale è stata ornata di eccellentissime pitture di Messer Battista Venetiano.

Messer Battista Franco grandissimo disegnatore a nostri tempi hauea ancor esso dato principio a dipingere vna delle stanze grandi; ma soprauenuto dalla morte ha lasciata l'opera imperfetta. La loggia è di ordine Ionico La Cornice gira intorno tutta la casa, e fa frontespicio sopra la loggia, e nella parte opposta. Sotto la gronda vi è vn'altra cornice, che camina sopra i frontespicij. Le camere di sopra sono come mezati per la loro bassezza, perche sono alte solo otto piedi.

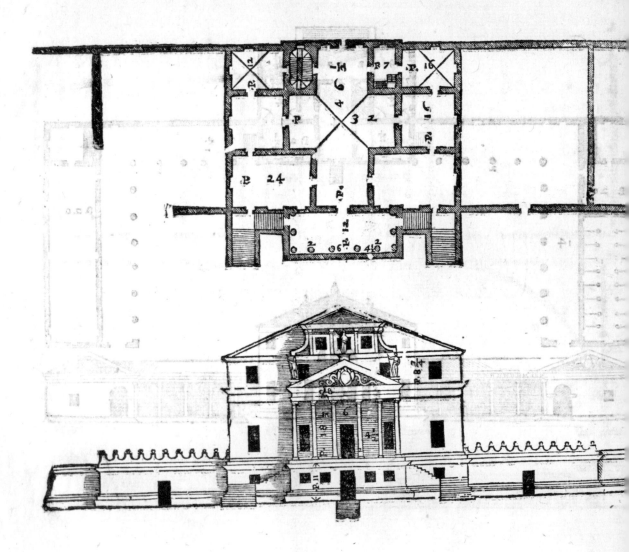

LA SOT-

LA Sottoposta fabrica è à Masera, Villa vicina ad Asolo, Castello del Triuigiano, di Monsi-gnor Reuerendissimo Eletto di Aquileia, & del Magnifico Signor Marc'Antonio fratelli de' Bar-bari. Quella parte della fabrica, che esce alquanto in fuori, ha due ordini di stanze, il piano di quel-le di sopra è a pari del piano del cortile di dietro, oue è tagliata nel monte rincontro alla casa vna fontana con infiniti ornamenti di stucco, e di pittura. Fa questa fonte vn laghetto, che serue per pe-schiera; da questo luogo partitasi l'acqua scorre nella cucina, & dapoi irrigati i giardini, che sono dalla destra, e sinistra parte della strada, la quale pian piano ascendendo códuce alla fabrica, fa due peschiere co i loro beueratori sopra la strada cómune, donde partitasi, adacqua il Bruolo, il quale è grandissimo e pieno di frutti eccellentissimi, e di diuerse seluaticine. La facciata della casa del pa-drone ha quattro colóne di ordine Ionico: il capitello di quelle de gli angoli fa fronte da due parti, i quali capitelli come si facciano, porrò nel libro dei Tempij. Dall'vna, e l'altra parte vi sono loggie, le quali nell'estremità hanno due colombare, e sotto quelle vi sono luoghi da fare i vini, e le stalle, e gli altri luoghi per l'vso di Villa.

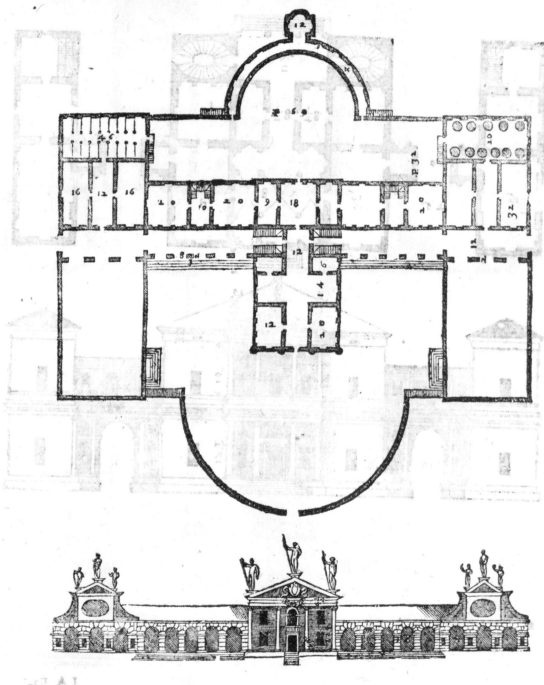

Giulio Savorgnan 1516–1595

168 ❧ *Regole della Fortificatione dell' Illmo. Sigre. Julio Savorgnano*

manuscript: ii + 29 folios | 25 × 36cm
Late sixteenth-century

Provenance: The Kerrs of Newbattle Abbey,
Midlothian; by descent to the 11th Marquess
of Lothian, by whom bequeathed to the
National Library, 1950 (MS 5735)

EDINBURGH, NATIONAL LIBRARY
OF SCOTLAND

The precise nature and status of this manuscript is unclear. Its contemporary title attributes it to Giulio Savorgnan, the most distinguished member of a large family of Venetian soldiers and military engineers, who is not recorded as having published a treatise on fortification. Savorgnan worked on the defences of Venetian outposts in the Adriatic and Mediterranean, serving at Zara, Zante, Candia and in Cyprus. Relief plans of some of these fortifications can be seen on Giuseppe Sardi's baroque façade of Santa Maria del Giglio (Zobenigo) in Venice, a church which Ruskin branded a 'manifestation of insolent atheism'.

Fortifications such as these are evidence of Venice's attempt to assert control of its far-flung territories. Military needs conditioned planning and indeed shaped urban development. Artillery fortifications, with their triangular bastions serving as gun-platforms, ravelins, protective outworks and complex, sometimes geometrically perfect, radial plans reached an apogee in the mainland fortress of Palmanova, situated on the Friuli plain in the path of potential Austrian and Ottoman invasions. Palmanova was Savorgnan's greatest achievement; its nine-sided polygonal plan has been likened to a gigantic snowflake.[1] Many fortress engineers worked together in interconnecting groups and circles,[2] and Savorgnan is known to have worked with Bonaiuto Lorini and Vincenzo Scamozzi at Palmanova from 1593. Both of the latter published works on fortification, and the present manuscript includes a drawing after one of Lorini's plans. The so-called '*Regole*' of Savorgnan may therefore be regarded as something of an amalgam of late-sixteenth century Venetian practice in the art and science of military architecture. This was a period when 'civil

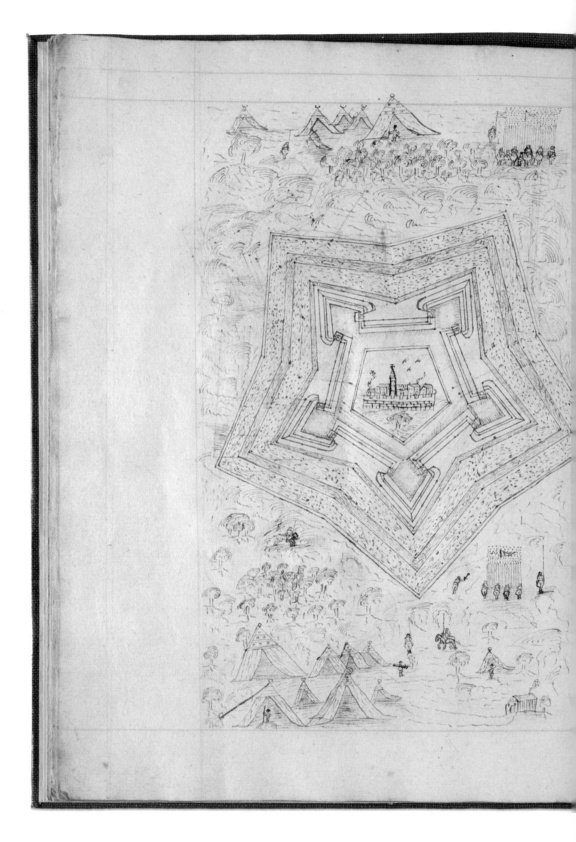

architecture was outstripped not only in print but in prestige' by the literature of fortification, a publishing genre which flourished in the sixteenth century, when many eminent architects were also highly regarded and much patronised as engineers.[3]

The manuscript includes many drawings of what would have been called the 'traces' (ground plans) of bastioned fortifications, together with illustrations of siege-works, fire plans, calculations of trajectories, and details of ordnance and ballistics, a topic of particular interest for Savorgnan. These drawings have a distinctly amateur feeling, and it is difficult to believe that they are anything other than remote descendants of the productions of the Venetian military engineer's own drawing-board. This reminds us that fortification was seen as an element of the gentleman's education, along with architecture and mathematics. Treatises on the subject were read avidly by professionals and amateurs alike, and no doubt (as in this instance) copied, adapted and debased in the process. Venetian achievement in the field was internationally renowned, and early Scottish travellers will have interested themselves in this aspect of the art and civilisation of the Republic.

The radial plan on the right-hand page (folio 20) of the manuscript illustrated here may represent either an actual or an ideal fortification: it has the nine bastions of Palmanova, and a schematic representation of its street-plan, but has a *mastio* or keep at the centre rather than Palmanova's *piazza d'armi*, and the drawing is in fact closer in its detail to the ideal radial town plan proposed by Bonaiuto Lorini and published in his *Delle fortificationi libri cinque* (Venice, 1596). Vitruvius had seen the perfect town as circular, with a central forum and radiating, concentric streets. Renaissance practice sometimes followed ancient theory: 'The radial plan, with its regular geometry, a fantasy of humanistic cosmology, was transformed into a military machine.'[4]

This manuscript seems to have been in the collection of the Kerr (or Ker) family of Newbattle Abbey, Midlothian, by the mid-seventeenth century. It was probably acquired either by Robert Kerr, 2nd Earl of Lothian, while a student at Padua in 1599–1600; or else by Sir William Kerr, 3rd Earl of Lothian, who was in Italy in 1625. IGB

Manuscript vi + 197 folios in a contemporary red morocco Venetian binding | 16 × 27cm | 1596–9

Provenance: William Hog, 1660; Marquesses of Lothian (with their eighteenth-century book-plate, probably that of William, 3rd Marquess, *c.*1690–1767); Lothian sale, New York, 1932 (lot 28); Sotheby's, London, 24 June 1975 (lot 201), where bought by the Library with the aid of the National Art Collections Fund (MS 16000)

EDINBURGH, NATIONAL LIBRARY
OF SCOTLAND

An Album Amicorum is literally a 'book of friends', but is more properly to be understood as a record of friendships and shared experiences during a period of life. The custom of keeping such books originated among German students, who would ask their friends and any notables whom they met to inscribe their names and chosen mottos, or to supply details of their coats of arms which local heraldic painters would prepare for insertion in the books. A variety of other illustrative matter was also sometimes added, and these loose sheets were bound up as a volume such as Balfour's. Only four Scottish *alba amicorum* are known, and of these the present example is by far the most interesting.

Balfour, later first Lord Balfour of Burleigh (died 1619), was a distinguished diplomat in the service of King James VI and I. His album reflects his social, cultural and intellectual contacts. Royal autographs, mottos and arms of contemporary celebrities are represented in quantity. But the real importance and charm of the volume lies in its assemblage of watercolour and gouache paintings of scenes and characters in Italy, accumulated during Balfour's Continental travels – really a proto-Grand Tour – between 1596 and 1599. The series of Venetian and Paduan subjects is especially interesting and exotic. These striking images – the equivalents of picture-postcards today – encapsulate so much of what Venice meant to Scottish travellers of the period, and indeed afterwards in the classic age of the Grand Tour: a place of dangerously tempting luxury and idle dalliance, of un-Presbyterian pleasure and worldly wickedness.

Most of these figure- and costume-studies, or topographical *veduti*, seem to have been executed in a Venetian atelier specifically for the tourist market.

There seems to be some relationship between the brightly coloured costume illustrations in such albums, and the woodcuts in contemporary costume books by Cesare Vecellio (cat.no.166) and Giacomo Franco, although this connection has been doubted.[1] In the Balfour album, classes or types of Venetian character are represented: the Doge himself; gorgeously attired ladies with elaborate coiffures and peacock-feather fans; and shameless courtesans out to corrupt innocent young men from Scotland. There are scenes of flirtation, of courtesy and of the mad goings-on of Carnival and masquerade. A dramatic depiction of one of the celebrated (and frequently lethal) street-fights between student factions in Padua adds a disagreeable note as antidote to other scenes of naughty happenings in gondolas. The salacious element in the paintings is notable: in the picture of a young man bending to pick up a lady's glove one has the opportunity to lift a paper flap which serves as her veil to glimpse (as the youth is clearly attempting to do) not only her face but her décolletage beneath; one may raise the 'curtain' flap on the gondola *felze* to view the amorous activity within the cabin; or one can lift the 'skirt' flap to reveal the remarkable underwear and enormous chopines (*zoccole*) beneath the street costume of a courtesan. The vanity of the Venetian woman is well symbolised by the painting of the lady seated on her roof-terrace illustrated here: mirror in hand, she bleaches her chemically-treated dark hair blonde in the sunlight, with the tresses spread through the aperture in the crown of her wide-brimmed *solana* straw hat which otherwise protects her complexion. This image is very similar to the illustration of the same subject in Vecellio's book.[2] IGB

Georgio Sideri CALAPODA (?) (CRETE) DOCUMENTED 1537–1581 CRETE

170 ❧ *Portolan Chart of the Mediterranean and Atlantic Coasts of Europe*

Manuscript and watercolour on vellum
58 × 99cm | MS 20995

EDINBURGH, NATIONAL LIBRARY
OF SCOTLAND

Sailing directions, sometimes called *portolani* or port books, were used by mariners long before the first sea charts appeared in the late thirteenth century. These port books listed place names and harbours around coasts, recording hazards and navigation aids. Portolan charts augment this information in a graphic form. It is perhaps no coincidence that they first emerge in the century after the magnetic compass reached Europe. By 1560, when this chart was hand drawn, chart-making workshops had developed in a few important seaports around the Mediterranean.[1] Different elements in the chart might be prepared by various people with specialist skills, such as cartographic drafting, calligraphy, and ornamentation.

The chart has an irregular shape because, as was common practice, it was drawn on an animal skin to resist salt water. The compass roses with radiating rhumb lines were used to construct the chart and to assist the navigator in setting a course. Red text signifies harbours and points of interest for the seaman, and prominence is given to Jerusalem and sites of religious significance. Information is restricted to the coasts, while the empty interiors offer scope for fanciful illustration (note the Red Sea).

An ornamental portolan chart such as this was probably not intended to be used at sea, but would have been commissioned for display by a wealthy trader or important official. This is a late example; modelled on charts of the previous century, it was deliberately designed to look antique. Inscribed in the 'neck' are the date and the name of the chart-maker Georgio Sideri (Zorzi Sideros), also known as Calapoda, perhaps from the town near Chania in Crete which may have been his birthplace. The master of a merchant ship, between 1538 and 1554 Sideri sailed to Venice, where he also had family connections. His surviving charts date from 1537 to 1565; this chart was produced during the time when he was resident in Venice, before returning to live in Crete after 1564.

In his depiction of Italy, Sideri gave particular prominence to Venice and Genoa, the two great rival maritime powers on opposite sides of the peninsula, showing a blue crescent for the Venetian lagoon, while Genoa's magnificent harbour is shown with many wharves. Other towns do not merit such individual detail. The Venetian connection is further confirmed by the inclusion of the coat of arms of the Bragadin family in the 'neck', which suggests that the chart is likely to have been made for a member of this influential patrician family; one possible candidate is the celebrated naval commander Marcantonio Bragadin (1523–71).

As the centre for maritime trade in the mid-sixteenth century, Mediterranean shores are shown in some detail, with only a rudimentary outline of the British Isles on the edge of Europe. Until the devastating plague of the mid-1570s, Venice was the European centre for the production of printed maps.[2] But the focus for map-making expertise was about to change, as Europe turned towards world-wide exploration and trade, and new map-making centres developed in the Low Countries, which were better positioned for world travel. DW

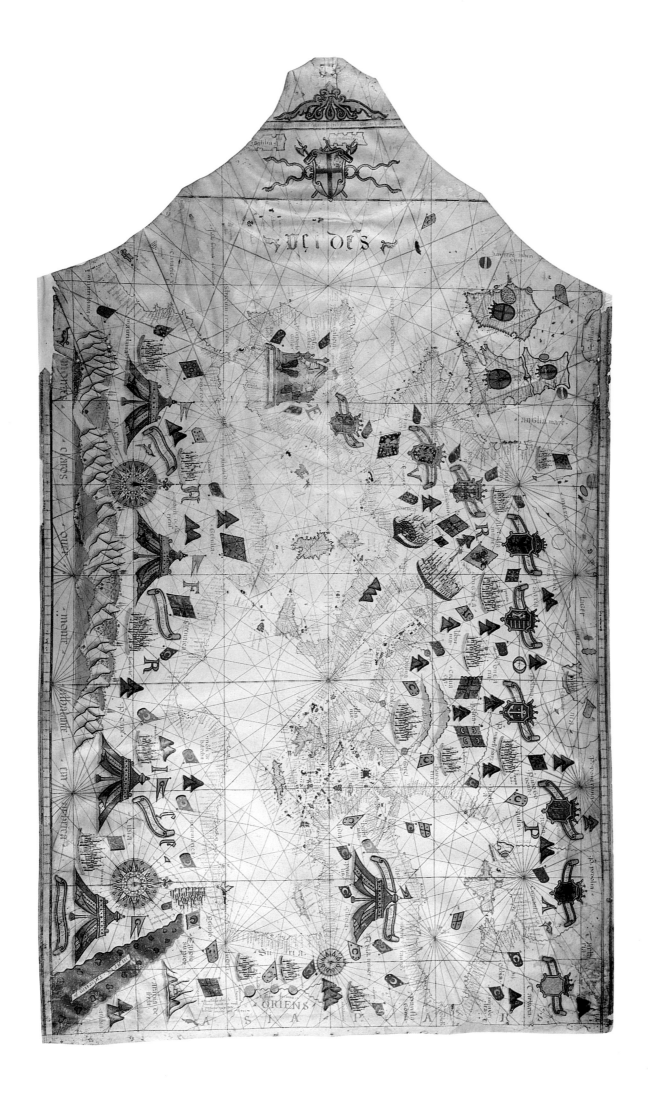

V SCULPTURE & DECORATIVE ARTS

Venetian *or* Lombard SECOND HALF OF THE FIFTEENTH CENTURY

171 ❧ *A Well-head carved with Cornucopia, Cherubs' Heads and Shields of Arms*

Istrian stone (limestone) | 89 × 125 × 125cm

Provenance: Bought in Venice or north eastern Italy by the Rt Hon. George Augustus Cavendish Bentinck (1821–1897) and probably installed in the castle on Brownsea Island off Poole, Dorset; presented by him to the Victoria and Albert Museum in 1893; transferred to the National Museums, 1992 (acc.no.A.1922.56)

EDINBURGH, NATIONAL MUSEUMS
OF SCOTLAND

The well-head is in the form of a massive capital developing from a circular base into a square head. The structure is supported on pairs of curved cornucopia back to back that form shoulders resting on broad acanthus leaves beneath. In the apron-shaped space between the horns of the cornucopia alternate frontal cherub masks and shields of *testa di cavallo* (horse's head) form. The heraldry, previously unidentified, appears to be that of the Foscarini family of Venice and Strà, namely Or (gold) with lozengy a bend dexter Azure (a bend formed of diamond patterns in blue on a gold ground).[1]

Well-heads like this were placed in the centre of Venetian courtyards and *campi* and had wrought iron superstructures attached from which buckets were drawn up and down. This example is closely reminiscent of another with cherub heads and acanthus now in the Campo San Zaccaria, Venice, which was confiscated from an antique dealer and placed there by the Venetian authori-

ties in 1932 (fig.247).[2] Three other handsome examples are in the collection of the Earl of Wemyss at Gosford House, and a fourth is at the War Memorial, Aberlady, East Lothian.

Fig.247 | Venetian School, *A Well-head carved with Cherub's Heads, Volutes, Vases and Acanthus Foliage Decoration* Venice, Campo San Zaccaria

School of the Veneto *or* Venice *c.*1480–1510
172–175 ✤ *Two Corinthian and Two Composite Capitals*

Istrian stone (limestone) | 26 × 34.5 × 28.5cm
(A.1893.236); 30.5 × 37 × 19cm (A.1893.237);
39.5 × 51.5 × 53cm (A.1893.241); 41 × 43 × 46cm
(A.1893.244)

Provenance: The Rt Hon. George Augustus Cavendish
Bentinck (1821–1891), Brownsea Island, Dorset; by
whom bequeathed to the Victoria and Albert Museum,
1892; transferred to the Royal Museum, 1893
(acc.nos.A.1893.236, 237, 241, 244)

EDINBURGH, NATIONAL MUSEUMS OF SCOTLAND

These capitals, two from columns and two
from pilasters, are almost certainly from the
interiors of suppressed and subsequently
demolished churches. Some indeed may have
formed part of the integral architecture of
altars designed by artists of the generation of
Giovanni Bellini, Basaiti and Cima da
Conegliano, for very similar fictive capitals
are repeated in their works.[1]

Pietro da Fano FANO ACTIVE 1462–1464 VENICE (?)

176 ❧ *Doge Pasquale Malipiero*

Obverse: Doge Pasquale Malipiero (born 1385, Doge of Venice 1457–62), shown in profile to left, wearing cap and robes, with a small crown below. Inscribed around the edge: 'PASQVALLS. MARIPETRVS. VENETVM. D. DVX'

Reverse: His wife Giovanna Dandolo, shown in profile to left, in a flat cap and veil. Inscribed around the edge: 'INCLITE. IOHANNE. ALME VRBIS. VENEZIAR[VM]. DVCISSE'

Bronze (cast) | 9.2cm diameter

Provenance: W. Ready, London; from whom purchased by the Royal Museum, 1883 (acc.no.A.1883.5.9)

Literature: Armand, 1883–7, I, cat.no.35, 4; III, 5 B; Hill, 1930, cat.no.409; Hill and Pollard, 1967, cat.no.135

EDINBURGH, NATIONAL MUSEUMS
OF SCOTLAND

The medallist produced another medal of Malipiero's wife combined with a reverse bearing the artist's signature. Another portrait medal of the doge is known by Marco Guidizani, who was active in Venice around 1454–62, an example of which is in the Bargello, Florence.[1] A portrait of Malipiero by Gentile Bellini is recorded which corresponds closely to the Guidizani medal.[2]

Malipiero, a soldier and diplomat, was the first doge habitually to wear silk robes. His influential and powerful dogaressa introduced the lace industry into the lagoon, while the first book printed in Venice was dedicated to her. Bartolomeo Colleoni (of Verrocchio equestrian statue fame) was appointed General of the

Serenissima's land forces by him in 1458. When Pope Pius II held a diet at Mantua in 1459 so that he could mount a crusade against the Turks, Malipiero refused to join the proposed Holy League; without Venetian galleys to carry the troops the crusade proved impossible. Under this doge Antonio Gambello built the ceremonial land gate (1460) to the Arsenale (fig.248), which is generally claimed to be the first example of Renaissance classical architecture in Venice. Malipiero, 'dux pacificus' (the peace loving doge), died on 7 May 1460 and was buried in Santi Giovanni e Paolo.[3] His tomb next to the sacristy door (fig.249) is the first work executed in Venice by the great sculptor Pietro Lombardo (c.1435–1515).

Fig.248 | Antonio Gambello, *Gateway to the Arsenale*, Venice

Fig.249 | Pietro Lombardo, *Tomb of Doge Pasquale Malipiero*
Venice, Church of Santi Giovanni e Paolo

Attributed to Nicolò di Giovanni Cocari called Nicolò Fiorentino ACTIVE IN PADUA 1443–AFTER 1477 DALMATIA (?)
177 ✢ *Relief of the Virgin and Child*

Terracotta | 74 × 36cm

In a late-fifteenth century polychrome wooden tabernacle frame, 152 × 76cm

Provenance: Adolf von Beckerath, Berlin (1834–1915); his posthumous sale, Lepke, Berlin, 23 May 1916 (lot 79); Camillo Castiglione, Vienna; possibly his sale, F. Müller, Amsterdam, 17–20 November 1925; Onnes de Nijerode, Château de Nijerode; his sale, Ant. W.M. Mensing in association with F. Müller, Amsterdam, 4–7 July 1933 (lot 203); M. Jaarsma, Amsterdam; his sale, Maak van Way, Amsterdam, 15–18 April 1947 (lot 252); with Richard Philp, London; from whom purchased with the aid of the Patrons of the National Galleries of Scotland, 1997 (acc.no.NG 2665)

EDINBURGH, NATIONAL GALLERY
OF SCOTLAND

The terracotta is modelled in high relief, with the Virgin conventionally clothed, three-quarter length, facing to the left, holding the naked Christ Child before her on a narrow ledge. He looks down, his right hand is raised in benediction and his left clasps his mother's right hand.

The surface of the relief is abraded and weathered and shows slight traces of the original gesso and paint. A thermo-luminescence test using a sample taken from the middle of the back shows that the relief was fired between 350 and 600 years ago.[1] Framed in a polychrome wooden tabernacle, probably about 1470–1500 (Umbrian or Florentine), the decoration of which was described in the 1916 Von Beckerath sale catalogue as in 'the manner of the Carrand Master'.

This relief, originally gessoed and painted, was probably not a house altar, but intended to be placed high above a doorway, or perhaps high on the corner of a street, which explains the exaggerated length of the Virgin's neck and head and the marked forward inclination of the Christ Child's head. It would, therefore, have been similarly sited to, say, the Donatello School *Virgin and Child with Angels* in the Via delle Fogge, Verona,[2] or the *Madonna and Angels* given to Michelozzo in the Chiostro delle Medicherie, Arcispedale di Santa Maria Nuova, Florence.[3]

When the relief was offered in the Von Beckerath sale in 1916 it was described as by a 'Follower of Donatello'. Von Beckerath's collection consisted of magnificent quattrocento Italian sculpture, majolica, textiles, and old master paintings. The relief then passed into Camillo Castiglione's collection in Vienna. Castiglione owned a major collection of bronzes that was the subject of a catalogue compiled by

178 ✤ *A Writing Casket, with Putti Holding Ribbons Flanking a Medusa's Head on the Lid*

Leo Planiscig,[4] and it was probably he who first proposed the attribution of this terracotta to Giovanni da Pisa.

Giovanni di Francesco da Pisa ('Zuan da Pisa') was one of Donatello's main apprentices working on the Altare del Santo, Padua (1444–7) along with Nicolò Pizzolo, Urbano da Cortona, Antonio Chellini, and Francesco del Valente. On 8 July 1447 he received payment for the terracotta altarpiece in the Ovetari chapel of the Eremitani Church, Padua.[5] There is, however, confusion over whether this work is by Giovanni da Pisa or by Pizzolo.[6] Also attributed to him is the limestone octagonal Madonna relief formerly in the sacristy of the same church.[7] Giovanni may have been the same sculptor referred to by Filarete in his *Tratto d'Architettura*, written between 1461 and 1464, whom he described as having died recently at Venice.[8] Other works have been added to his oeuvre which are not entirely convincing, such as the *Madonna in a Niche*, also from the Von Beckerath collection, now in Berlin.[9]

The present *Virgin and Child* relief is undeniably close to Donatello, but a firm attribution to Giovanni da Pisa can hardly be sustained with so little documented material. However, while in Padua, Donatello exercised a great influence on other sculptors working in Venice, the Veneto, and Dalmatia. The idiosyncratic morphology of the Virgin's head and the classicising quality of the Eremitani's two sculptures appear markedly different to the Edinburgh relief. In the latter, the flat swirling wet-fold draperies, and the compact bullet-headed Christ Child, have a much greater stylistic resemblance to the statues of the Evangelists and the reliefs of angels by Nicolò Fiorentino in the Blessed Orsini's chapel in Trau (Trogir) Cathedral, Spalatro (Croatia), of *c*.1468–72.[10] Nicolò Fiorentino was also a collaborator of Donatello's in Padua (1443–4, 1448–9), but later worked extensively in Dalmatia, a Venetian possession, where he is last recorded in 1477.

Bronze of rich brown metal with black lacquer patina

7 × 20.4 × 11cm

Provenance: Robert Napier, by 1865;[1] his posthumous sale, Christie's, London, 17 April 1877 (lot 910), bought T.M. Whitehead on behalf of the Royal Museum (acc.no.A.1877.20.37)

EDINBURGH, NATIONAL MUSEUMS OF SCOTLAND

The lid, within a border of palmettes, consists of the frontal head of Medusa in low relief at the centre, enclosed within a fruiting laurel wreath flanked by two standing putti holding ribbons. The front and back are formed by reliefs of a Bacchus mask within a wreath of cornucopia supported by flanking centaurs galloping with nymphs on their backs; beneath their hooves respectively are Pan pipes and a lyre. At each end is a Medusa head above a leafy garland suspended from bulls' skulls (bucrania). The casket is constructed of individually cast panels soldered together.

This writing casket, with variations, exists in more than forty-five examples. They have been attributed to many different workshops, and the influence of both Mantegna and Donatello has been noted by several authors. A fine example of this casket in the National Gallery of Art, Washington, has been attributed to the Paduan sculptor Severo Calzetta da Ravenna, who is

mentioned in the *De Sculptura* of Pomponius Gauricus (1504) and is known from two signed works, a *Statue of St John the Baptist* in Padua (documented to 1500) and a bronze *Dragon Inkstand* (formerly with Blumka, New York).[2] Together with a writing casket at Munich and a bowl in Vienna, it has been argued that all these artefacts were designed in a single studio. However, in the context of a discussion of a related bronze casket in the Thyssen-Bornemisza collection, some doubt has been cast on the attribution of these works to Severo.[3] The argument in favour of Severo's authorship depends on a presumed similarity between the reliefs on the caskets and the satyr-masks on the Vienna bowl and the head of the dragon on the Blumka bronze, but this connection is far from watertight.[4] The bronze relief of centaurs carrying nymphs was copied in marble on the frieze surrounding the seated statue of Pliny the Elder on the façade of Como Cathedral, which was carved by the sculptors Tommaso and Jacopo Rodari da Maroggia (from the Ticino) in 1480. Other well known bronze plaquettes also appear copied in marble on the northern portal of the cathedral and date from the 1490s.

The manifest stylistic connections between the reliefs on the casket and Andrea Mantegna's work suggests a sculptor close to him, like the Mantuan medallist and jeweller Cristoforo di Geremia (died 1476), or his nephew, the medallist known by his pseudonym as 'Lysippus Junior', who was active through the pontificate of Sixtus IV della Rovere (1471–84).[5] The argument that the model for these caskets may have originated in Rome or Mantua before 1480 does not exclude the likelihood that many of them were made in Paduan workshops.[6]

Attributed to Bartolomeo Bellano PADUA 1437/8–1496/7 PADUA
179 ✠ *Relief of St Jerome in the Wilderness*

Terracotta, partly painted | 47.8 × 36.7cm

Provenance: With Heim Gallery, London; from whom purchased by the Museums, 1980 (acc.no.A.1980.146)

EDINBURGH, NATIONAL MUSEUMS
OF SCOTLAND

St Jerome sits on a bench outside a cave, wearing a short hair tunic, his arms and legs bare. He reads the Vulgate, which rest on his lap. Beside him, to the left, is his cardinal's hat and before him to the right his lion, seated. To the right, in the background, is a wooded hilly landscape and sky, painted naturalistically, with the horizon crowned with a fortified wall.

St Jerome (or Eusebius or Hieronymus) was born in Dalmatia around 347 AD and died in Bethlehem in 419/20. He is generally considered one of the most learned of the Latin Fathers of the Church, translating the Bible into Latin (the Vulgate), devising education theory and formulating much of the Christian canon. He received the cardinal's hat from Pope Damasus, whose secretary he was in Rome, and was active in setting up the monastic movement. In 375–8 Jerome went into the desert at Chalcis searching for inner peace. In 386 he moved to Bethlehem where he continued his studies and set up a monastery. This relief would appear to show his hermit cell outside the walls of Bethlehem.

This conventional image grows out of paintings by Bellini and his followers, such as Cima (see cat.nos.2, 10). It was also a popular subject for reliefs issuing from Donatello's workshop in Padua.[1] This Donatellesque relief, with its vigorous naturalism, is especially reminiscent of Bellano's style, which has its point of departure in such reliefs as the *Ford Nativity* in Detroit, a Ghibertian relief that may be by the young Donatello.[2] The Edinburgh relief is, however, later and by a quite distinctive hand.

Workshop of Severo da Ravenna FERRARA OR RAVENNA 1465/75 – BEFORE 1538 RAVENNA

180 ❧ *Statuette of David with the Head of Goliath* (after Bartolomeo Bellano)

Bronze of rich brown metal with dark blackish patina | 25.3 × 10cm (diameter of base)

Inscribed on the under-part of the socle with dots created by a pointed punch or drill: 'MARCO. ANTONIO. RAVENNA A.F.G [or C]. F.'

Provenance: Robert Napier, by 1865;[1] his posthumous sale, Christie's, London, 17 April 1877 (lot 911), bought T.M. Whitehead on behalf of the Royal Museum (acc.no.A.1877.20.44)

EDINBURGH, NATIONAL MUSEUMS OF SCOTLAND

David wears a short belted tunic, with long sleeves and knee-length boots. His hair hangs to his shoulders in ringlets. Over his right shoulder is slung a satchel, on a long strap, which rests against his left hip. In his right hand he holds a sword hilt (the blade broken) and in his left is a sling and stone. He stands with his right leg behind Goliath's massive bearded head and his left foot rests on the giant's neck.

The story of David, the Israelite shepherd boy who slew the Philistine giant, Goliath, with his sling-shot is a classic parable of superior odds being overcome by faith, daring and skill, a subject especially appealing in war-torn Renaissance Italy (I Samuel 17). The image is a known model by Bellano of around 1470–80, fine examples of which are in the Philadelphia Museum of Art (Fulc collection, 29cm high, on circular base) and the Metropolitan Museum of Art, New York (C. Ruxton Love Jr collection, 28.5cm high, gilded and mounted on a moulded circular base).[2] They are closely related both in modelling and finish to Bellano's documented relief in the choir of the Santo at Padua and ultimately derive from Donatello's bronze David in the Bargello, Florence, dating from around 1440. Bellano would have known this from the time he spent in Florence assisting Donatello with the pulpits of San Lorenzo. A number of bronzes of secondary quality deriving from the Philadelphia – Metropolitan Bellano model are recorded, and have been variously ascribed to the Bellano workshop or more specifically Severo da Ravenna. Examples are in the Victoria and Albert Museum, London, the Metropolitan Museum of Art, New York (Untermeyer collection), the National Gallery of Art, Washington (Widener collection), the Museo Correr, Venice, and the Staatliche-Museum, Berlin (Isaac Falcke collection).[3] Many of these variants and copies appear to have issued from Severo's Paduan workshop, and the beautiful cast in the National Museums of Scotland fits into this category.[4] However, it bears the unique 'signature' of Marco Antonio da Ravenna who, it has been suggested, was the son of Severo. A 'Marcantonio' is recorded as having worked on the sculptural decoration of the cloister of Santa Maria in Porto, Ravenna, in 1506.[5] But it is also possible that the curiously formed inscription is not so much a signature as an indication of ownership.

181 ✤ *Triangular Box with a Seated Figure of St John the Evangelist on the Cover*

Bronze, the base of rich brown colour, the cover with dark blackish patina | 27 × 16 × 15cm

Provenance: Robert Napier; his posthumous sale, Christie's, London, 18 April 1877 (lot 1060), bought by T.M. Whitehead on behalf of the Royal Museum (acc.no.A.1877.20.46 & A)

EDINBURGH, NATIONAL MUSEUMS OF SCOTLAND

The tall triangular base is supported on lion's paw feet issuing from acanthus fronds above. A shallow apron beneath terminates in an anthemion-shaped pendant.[1] This type of plinth appears in a drawing by Giulio Romano (fig.250). It ultimately depends on classical bronze prototypes. The historiated sides include a frieze of nude boys flanking a bifurcate mermaid.

The base section is very closely related to other bronzes demonstrably from Severo da Ravenna's workshop, like the *Spinario* in the Metropolitan Museum of Art, New York,[2] which has an identical nude boy frieze and acanthus leaf fronds, and a three-wick oil lamp in the Frick Collection, New York, which is similarly constructed to the Scottish base with lion's paw feet and pendant anthemion. Another closely related inkstand was in the Heinz Schneider collection, Cleveland.[3]

The cover with the figure of the Evangelist is much later and comparable to a figure of St Mark supported on a more elaborate base at Kingston Lacy, Dorset (National Trust), and another inkstand with St John the Evangelist, offered at Sotheby's, New York, 31 May 1990 (lot 92). Such figures are often loosely associated with the name of Nicolò Roccatagliata.

Fig.250 | Giulio Romano, *Design for an Incense Burner*
Chatsworth, The Duke of Devonshire and the Trustees of the Chatsworth Settlement

Workshop of Severo da Ravenna FERRARA *or* RAVENNA 1465/75–BEFORE 1538 RAVENNA

182 ❧ *A Kneeling Satyr Holding a Shell*

Bronze of coppery brown metal with a blackish varnish, a little rubbed | 25.1 × 16.6 × 16.6cm

Provenance: Probably Clarence H. MacKay, Roslyn; Anne Maxwell MacDonald; by whom presented to Glasgow Museums, 1967 (acc.no.PHS.23)

GLASGOW MUSEUMS: POLLOCK HOUSE

The satyr, kneeling on his left knee, is bearded, has pointed ears and two short horns, furry legs and cloven hoofs. He holds up a shell in his right hand, while with his left arm he gestures downward, with his fingers open and facing towards the ground. The figure stands on a shallow triangular plinth with a roughened surface to indicate soil, which is supported at the corners by lion's paw feet.

This familiar design of a bronze inkwell, with the shell providing the reservoir, was clearly very popular in Padua from around 1500 until the second half of the sixteenth century and even later. The subject varies greatly in modelling, base forms and attributes but, historically, has usually been associated with the name of Riccio. Five examples were included in the first serious catalogue of Riccio's work: two in the Barsanti collection, Rome; another in the Kaiser Friedrich Museum, Berlin; the same model on a very tall base is in the Kunsthistorisches Museum, Vienna; and a fifth, which appears to be identical with the present bronze, which was then in the collection of Clarence H. MacKay at Roslyn.[1] There is also an etching of what appears to have been a good cast of this model in the collection of Jacob de Wilde in 1703.[2]

However, the emergence from a private collection of an example of the satyr inkwell bearing the signature 'SE' (for Severo) prompted a reconsideration of the old attribution to Riccio. In fact, stylistically the satyr, and indeed many others of this type, are closely comparable in detail to the two documented bronzes by Severo da Ravenna.[3] A group of eight of these kneeling satyr inkwells were exhibited together in Frankfurt in 1985–6, which provided a very clear indication of the variation in the quality of such models.[4] The Glasgow cast seems closely similar to one in the Palazzo Venezia, Rome.[5]

What appears to have been intended as a companion piece shows a seated satyress, sheltering a young male satyr, holding up an inkwell in her right hand.[6]

Galeazzo Mondella, called Moderno VERONA 1467–1528 VERONA

183 ❧ *Plaquette of the Crucifixion*

Gilt bronze | 11.2 × 7.7cm

Provenance: With A. Darer, London; from whom purchased by the Patrons of the National Galleries of Scotland, 1999 (acc.no.NG 2712)

Literature: Molinier, 1886, I, cat.no.171; Bange, 1922, cat.no.454; Pope-Hennessy, 1965, cat.no.147; Cleveland, 1975, cat.no.42; Toderi and Vannel Toderi, 1996, cat.no.143

EDINBURGH, NATIONAL GALLERY
OF SCOTLAND

Christ's cross is situated centrally, flanked by the crosses of the thieves. Beneath the crosses is a dense crowd of figures including, to the left, the fainting Virgin Mary, the standing figure of St John and, in the centre, Mary Magdalene embracing the cross. To the right stands a group of soldiers, including one naked and one holding a shield emblazoned with the Gorgon's head.

It has been suggested that the image may derive from Ercole de'Roberti's lost Crucifixion fresco of 1482–6 from the Garganelli chapel in San Petronio, Bologna, which in turn may derive from Antonio Vivarini's *Crucifixion* of around 1440, now at Ravenna.[1]

Galeazzo Mondella, called Moderno VERONA 1467–1528 VERONA

184 ❧ *Plaquette of St Sebastian*

Bronze with very dark brown patina; a small circular casting fault in the field | 7.7 × 5.6cm

Provenance: With Jan Lis, London; from whom purchased by the Patrons of the National Galleries of Scotland, 1990 (acc.no.NG 2529)

Literature: Molinier, 1886, I, cat.no.182; Bange, 1922, cat.no.433; Pope-Hennessy, 1965, cat.no.154; Cleveland, 1975, cat.no.45; Toderi and Vannel Toderi, 1996, cat.no.145

EDINBURGH, NATIONAL GALLERY
OF SCOTLAND

St Sebastian, pierced with arrows, stands bound to a Corinthian column within classical buildings. To the right is a fragment of a ruined building with a relief of a Roman soldier, possibly Mars, and beneath is an eagle perched on a globe. Attached to the building to the left are reliefs of horsemen top and bottom and, in the centre, an armed female figure, possibly Minerva.

It has been suggested that the St Sebastian is derived from Giovanni da Treviso's figure of the saint in his *Madonna del Fiore* painted for Treviso Cathedral in 1487. That figure in turn was probably inspired by Mantegna's celebrated St Sebastian now in the Franchetti collection at the Ca' d'Oro, Venice.[1] For this reason the plaquette has been dated to shortly after 1487, although a later date of around 1500 has also been proposed.[2]

Andrea del Briosco, called Riccio TRENT 1470–1532 PADUA

185 ✸ *Plaquette with Two Winged Putti Stealing a Book from a Sleeping Youth*

Bronze of pale brown metal, a little abraded
6.3cm diameter

Provenance: Malvezzi Collection, Bologna;
with Alain Moatti, Paris; from whom purchased by the Patrons of the National Galleries
of Scotland, 1989 (acc.no.NG 2500)

Literature: Molinier, 1886, I, cat.no.238; Bange,
1922, cat.no.390; Pope-Hennessy, 1965,
cat.no.219; Edinburgh, 1989, cat.no.33

EDINBURGH, NATIONAL GALLERY
OF SCOTLAND

An allegorical scene with a sleeping youth seated
on his cloak with his head supported on his left
hand. His left elbow rests on an ornamental
spouted vase from the neck of which issue three
laurel branches. In the youth's right hand is an
open book which two putti are trying to steal. In
the central background is a date palm. In the
exergue is the Greek inscription: ΣΕΜΝΗ
ΚΛΟΠΙΑ ('noble theft').

The same composition recurs on the reverse of
a medal of Girolamo Donati (died 1511) by
whom Riccio, sometime after 1492, was commissioned to make the bronze doors for the reliquary
of the Holy Cross in the church of the Servi,
Venice, along with four reliefs of scenes from the
Legend of the True Cross.[1] The crossed palm
branches and laurel in the exergue are paralleled
by the crossed laurel branches at the base of the
tabernacle door, while the vase filled with laurel
branches recurs in Francesco Colonna's
Hypnerotomachia Poliphili (see cat.no.164).[2] The
exact explanation of the allegory is obscure, but
was probably personal to Donati, the concept
being reminiscent of an 'ex-libris'.

Andrea del Briosco, called Riccio TRENT 1470–1532 PADUA

186 ✸ *Plaquette of Nessus Carrying off Dejaneira*

Bronze of pale brown metal with a rich dark
brown patina, pierced at the top for suspen-
sion 5.4 × 6.1cm

Provenance: With Alessandro Castellani,
Rome; bought at his sale, March-April 1884,
for the Royal Museum (acc.no.A.1884.44.46)

Literature: Molinier, 1886, I, cat.no.229;
Bange, 1922, p.53, cat.no.387, pl.37; Planiscig,
1927, pl.536

EDINBURGH, NATIONAL MUSEUMS
OF SCOTLAND

The centaur Nessus carries the Calydonian
princess Dejaneira, who was betrothed to Hercules,
across the raging waters of the river Evenus. Fierce
Nessus later attempted to take advantage of
Dejaneira, who cried out to her husband-to-be for
protection. Hercules killed Nessus with an arrow,
the tip poisoned by the blood of the Lernaean
serpent (Ovid, *Metamorphoses*: book IX).

Within a double-moulded rim Nessus gallops to
the right holding the struggling naked figure of
Dejaneira to the left. Versions of this lively bronze,
which dates from the artist's maturity, are in many
other collections. There are, for example, good
casts in the Victoria and Albert Museum (Salting
Bequest, acc.no.m.673–1910); the British Museum
(acc.no.1915–12–16–95) and the Metropolitan
Museum of Art, New York (Eric Lederer collection, acc.no.1986.319.312).

Andrea del Briosco, called Riccio TRENT 1470–1532 PADUA

187 ❧ *Plaquette with the Sacrifice of a Swine*

Bronze of rich dark brown metal with warm golden varnish | 7.7 × 9.1cm

Provenance: Mrs T.S. Smith, Edinburgh; by whom presented to the Royal Museum, 1928 (acc.no.A.1928.214)

EDINBURGH, NATIONAL MUSEUMS OF SCOTLAND

The composition, surrounded by a moulded rim, represents the sacrifice of a swine within the interior of a temple. Two kneeling youths perform the slaughter. A bearded priest stands to the right of centre holding a libation cup while, to the left, stand two courtly women. To the extreme left are two trumpeters and, to the right, a youthful and an old patrician. Three signed examples in Berlin, London (British Museum) and Vienna (ex-Figdor collection) confirm Riccio's authorship of this plaquette.[1]

The subject is not identified, but it may be the same as the engraving by Girolamo Mocetto (*c*.1454/58–*c*.1531) of *The Killing of the Sow*.[2] The two kneeling youths recur in one of Riccio's reliefs from the Della Torre monument of about 1516–21, formerly in Verona and now in the Louvre,[3] while the whole composition, with many differences, recurs in a sacrifice scene on Riccio's *Paschal Candlestick* of 1507–16 in the Santo in Padua.

Attributed to Andrea del Briosco, called Riccio TRENT 1470–1532 PADUA

188 ❧ *Plaquette of the Triumph of a Hero*

Bronze of brown metal, gilded and abraded on highlights | 7.6 × 10.3cm

Provenance: Miss Brown of Lanfine; by whom bequeathed to the Museum, 1897 (acc.no.97.190G5)

Literature: Molinier, 1886, I, cat.no.233; Bange, 1922, p.50, cat.no.368; Planiscig, 1927, p.361, cat.no.492; C. Seymour de Ricci, *The Gustave Dreyfus Collection: Reliefs and Plaquettes*, Oxford, 1931, p.110, cat.no.140; Pope-Hennessy, 1965, p.69, cat.no.232; Toderi and Vannel Toderi, 1996, p.113, cat.no.206

GLASGOW MUSEUMS: KELVINGROVE ART GALLERY AND MUSEUM

In the centre a nude male stands on a dais and to the left is a winged Victory, who rests her left hand on his shoulder. Between them is a vase with two branches of laurel and a snake and to the left are two girls in chitons, one holding a standard, the other a laurel branch. To the right of the image, sharing the dais, is a kneeling male nude, holding a bull which is to be sacrificed. A priest, about to sacrifice the bull, stands to the right and a further three priests or acolytes to the right of centre. Behind are (right) a ruined arch and (centre) a palm and laurel tree. The image is recessed within a narrow rim, and pierced at top centre, bottom right and left corners for fixing.

The subject matter is unexplained. The

plaquette has been accepted by most authors as by Riccio, although some believe it to be the work of an assistant ('neither the pronouncedly linear treatment of the nude figures nor the uncertain definition of the space confirms exactly to Riccio's authenticated works').[1]

In the context of the publication of an example of the plaquette in the Louvre, it has been proposed that the traditional title of the plaquette is inaccurate, and that it represents not an antique triumph but a glorification. It has been argued that it is a relatively late work, recalling the reliefs on Riccio's Della Torre monument, probably following an idea by Riccio in his maturity but executed by a collaborator.[2]

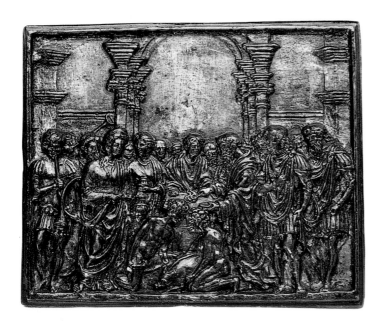

Workshop of Desiderio da Firenze DOCUMENTED IN PADUA 1532–1545
189 ❧ Triangular Perfume Burner with Winged Demi-figure Handles

Bronze of warm brown metal
14.5 × 18.5 × 16cm

Provenance: Stefano Bardini, Florence; his sale, Christie's, London, 5–7 June 1899, where bought by the Royal Museum (acc.no.A.1899.133 & A)

EDINBURGH, NATIONAL MUSEUMS OF SCOTLAND

The triangular box has winged demi-figure handles terminating in foliage scrolls which form the feet. The sides are decorated in low relief with vine tendrils and palmettes with, at the centre, a lion's head with open jaws and wild mane, below a shallow voluted apron. The separate triangular cover is ornamented with a frieze of leafy palmettes, the pyramidal top with three leafy masks, their mouths open and with further holes pierced between the masks, providing in total six holes. The cover is surmounted by a seated naked child.

This container of triangular form, with variations of handles, feet, and figure(s) on the cover, exist in at least twelve examples, including another in the National Museums of Scotland (see Cat.no 190), lacking its cover and with bold, volute handles substituting the winged demi-figures. Another example, with putti sitting on the three corners of the lid and a triton blowing a horn at the central apex, was in the Heinz Schneider collection, Cleveland.[1]

The attribution of these utensils to Desiderio da Firenze is based on stylistic comparison with the sculptor's documented voting urn in the Bottacia collection of the Museo Civico, Padua.[2] The urn was commissioned by the Consiglio of the Comune of Padua between 7 March 1532 and 8 February 1533.[3] A closely related *Paschal Candlestick* is in the Cleveland Museum of Art (Bequest of John L. Severance, acc.no.42.802).

A group of related oil lamps, candlesticks, incense burners and bells are much cruder than the voting urn. They share, however, so many features in common that they probably issued from the same Paduan workshop, operating in the second quarter of the sixteenth century.

Workshop of Desiderio da Firenze DOCUMENTED IN PADUA 1532–1545
190 ❧ Triangular Sand-box with Volute Handles

Bronze of brown metal | 6.3 × 14 × 11cm

Provenance: C. Richetti, Venice; from whom purchased for the Royal Museum, 1868 (acc.no.A.1868.54.3)

EDINBURGH, NATIONAL MUSEUMS OF SCOTLAND

The triangular box with bold volute handles rests on three ball feet. The cast ornament on the sides is identical to the *Triangular Perfume Burner* also in the National Museum of Scotland (cat.no.189). This example lacks its original cover, so might originally have served either as a sand-box or a perfume burner.

A late sixteenth-century Venetian *Portrait of a Scholar with an Inkstand* in the National Gallery of Scotland shows a very similar inkstand in use.[1]

Giammaria Mosca, called Padovano   PADUA 1495/9–1574 CRACOW

191 ❧ Relief of Mucius Scaevola

White marble; a small loss at the lower left of the base made up in resin and a diagonal split at the upper right filled | 34.5 × 21cm

Provenance: The Dukes of Leeds, Hornby Castle by 1927; by descent to the 10th Duke of Leeds Will Trust; sale, Christie's, London, 7 July 1987 (lot 135), bought Daniel Katz Ltd., London; from whom purchased with the aid of the National Art Collections Fund (William Leng Bequest), 1988 (acc.no.NG 2460)

EDINBURGH, NATIONAL GALLERY
OF SCOTLAND

The subject is taken from Livy's *Annals* 2: 12–13. In 507 BC Rome was besieged by the Etruscans under Lars Porsena, King of Clusium. Caius Mucius, a young Roman noble, penetrated the Etruscan camp, but instead of assassinating Porsena, killed the king's aide by mistake. Captured by the guards, he thrust his own right hand into the flames of a nearby altar to show how cheaply he valued his own life. Duly impressed, Porsena let him go free. 'Scaevola' means left-handed.

The young Roman Mucius Scaevola is shown unarmed and bare legged wearing a cuirass and thonged Roman kilt. He stands taking his weight on his left leg and places his right hand in a flaming brazier supported on a tripod. The hero, his head covered in dense curly hair, suffers the pain wide-eyed and open-mouthed, looking upwards. He stands on a narrow ledge, pressed up against a low parapet, with the walls of a square tower to the left. Within this deceptively simple composition there is a great subtlety and sophistication, from the swelling movement of the tightly confined body to the carefully managed limbs betraying a masterly comprehension of anatomy.

This tablet was conceived as one of a series of Roman gods, goddesses, heroes and heroines all of a similar size and format that could presumably have been bought individually, in pairs, or even in larger sets.[1] Each seems to represent one of the human virtues as praised in classical literature. Here we have the heroes of antiquity replacing the prophets and saints of the Old and New Testaments. Thus Mucius Scaevola represents Fortitude; Venus Anadyomene, Truth; Lucretia, Chastity; Portia, Conjugal Loyalty; Eurydice, Fidelity; and so on. It was previously suggested that a prime series formed part of the 'Camerino d'Alabastro' or 'Studio di Marmo' of Alfonso I d'Este, Duke of Ferrara, but this has now been discounted.[2] This tablet is known in three examples; the other two are in the Staatliche Kunstsammlungen, Dresden, and the Bargello Museum in Florence. They have all been damaged but the finest example, in sculptural quality and condition, is that in Edinburgh, which was confirmed when all three reliefs were recently displayed together in Ferrara.[3] The Dresden replica of the relief has an inscription cut on the left side of the altar, CON / STA / N[TIAE] and on the right side, R[OMANA], an epithet previously applied to Mucius Scaevola by an anonymous author in *De Viris Illustribus*, XII–'Vir Romanae constantiae'. The series has generally been assigned dates within the 1520s, but more precise dating within the decade, without new documentation, is unrealistic.

The style of the Edinburgh tablet is quite consistent with Mosca's documented relief of *The Miracle of the Unbroken Glass* (1520–7) in the shrine of the saint in the church of San Antonio, Padua (the Santo). The figure of the standing warrior in *The Miracle of the Unbroken Glass* is closely comparable.[4] The style owes much to the Lombardo family, especially to Tullio, but the conception and execution is less monumental and more self-consciously elegant. Mosca indulges in elaborate contrapposto – the pose in which one part of the body is twisted in the opposite direction from the other – and sometimes even avoids making his draperies reveal the underlying form of the body. There is also a connection with the early style of the engravings of Domenico Campagnola – for example, his *Shepherd and the Old Warrior*. Campagnola, who would certainly have known Mosca, settled in Padua around 1520 and remained there for the rest of his life.

Padua was a notable centre of learning concentrated around the ancient university founded by the Emperor Frederick II in 1238. The city by legend was founded by the Trojan hero Antenor and it was later the birthplace of the historian Livy (who related the story of Mucius Scaevola) and the first-century Roman poet Valerius Flaccus. In the early sixteenth century an intellectual circle flourished in Padua conscious of their antique ancestry and dedicated to reconstructing classical culture, among them Pietro Bembo, Nicolò Leonico Tomeo, Pomponius Gauricus and Giambattista Leone. According to the Venetian patrician and humanist Marcantonio Michiel (1484–1552), the philosopher Giambattista Leone commissioned the marble relief of *The Judgement of Solomon* by Giovanni Maria Mosca as a present to 'an English bishop'. Neatly fitting this description is the damaged relief in the Louvre, Paris which stylistically is similar to the Edinburgh relief, especially in the figure of the executioner.[5] The base is inscribed 'Posthumus', one of Leone's names, while the English bishop can be identified as the future Archbishop of Canterbury, Cardinal Reginald Pole (1500–1558), who from 1520 to 1526 was studying at Padua with Leone. The latter also commissioned the great bronze paschal candlestick by Riccio for the basilica of San Antonio.

Such reliefs as *Mucius Scaevola* were produced for the pleasure of learned men at Padua and Venice, in much the same way as bronze plaquettes and statuettes. These marble reliefs were relatively small, easily portable, and clearly not intended to be attached to walls as at least two of them, the *Philoctetes* in the Hermitage, St Petersburg, and the *Eurydice* in the Museo di Capodimonte, Naples, bear beautifully cut long inscriptions on the reverse.[6] Some of these reliefs were probably commissioned as tokens to friends and relations who the donors believed manifested, or should manifest, some of the same virtues as the gods and heroes of antiquity.

361

Giammaria Mosca, called Padovano PADUA 1495/9–1574 CRACOW

192 ❧ *Relief of a Satyress Triumphant*

Bronze of chestnut brown metal with dense black patina | 19.5 × 11.7 × 3.5cm

Fragmentary inscription on the back: '[…]N / STIDOMI[…] / RAO[…]'

Provenance: Possibly acquired by Sir John Clerk, 2nd Bart of Penicuick (1676–1755; in Italy 1697–9), or by his son Sir James Clerk, 3rd Bart (1709–1782, in Italy 1733–6); by descent to Sir Robert Clerk, 11th Bart

EDINBURGH, NATIONAL MUSEUMS OF SCOTLAND (ON LOAN FROM SIR ROBERT CLERK, 11TH BART OF PENICUIK)

The satyress is copied closely from a group of figures on a marble bacchic sarcophagus in the Gabinetto Segreto of the Museo Nazionale Archeologico, Naples, which was well known in the Renaissance when it was in the garden of San Marco, Rome. The relief was reproduced in an engraving by Marcantonio Raimondi (*c*.1480–1534). In the original image the satyress explicitly clasps the erect phallus of a priapic term, with which she attempts to pleasure herself. In the bronze relief the satyress holds a flute instead of a phallus, and the term is omitted. Behind the bronze satyress stands a dying tree to which are attached, and stacked, musical instruments, while she places her right hoof on an elaborately decorated helmet. The iconography may represent the abandonment of virtue for carnal pleasure, with the acts of virtue symbolised by the helmet and musical instruments lying forsaken on the ground. Abandonment is suggested by the dying tree and carnal pleasure by the action of the satyress. Indeed, the relief seems to be an early variation on the *Amor vincit Omnia* (Love conquers all) theme.[1]

Another version of this relief, in the Cleveland Museum of Art, was formerly in the collection of the Counts Donà dalle Rose in Venice.[2] Both reliefs were usually attributed to Riccio and dated to the 1520s until it was convincingly argued that the Cleveland relief, along with a relief of *Artemis as Protector of Wild Animals* (Vienna, Kunsthistorisches Museum) and a relief of *Dido's Suicide* (Rome, Palazzo Venezia) were all characteristic examples of Mosca's style. It has been further suggested that they may have been cast by the founder Guido Aspetti, called 'Lizzaro', who according to Marcantonio Michiel owned some clay models of Mosca's and may have made these casts.[3]

Simone Bianco LORO CIUFENNA BEFORE 1512–AFTER 1553 VENICE

193 ✤ *Bust of Cleopatra*

White marble, the back hollowed out except for a central support | 41cm high

Provenance: Daniel Katz Ltd, London; from whom purchased, 2002 (acc.no.NG 2762)

EDINBURGH, NATIONAL GALLERY
OF SCOTLAND

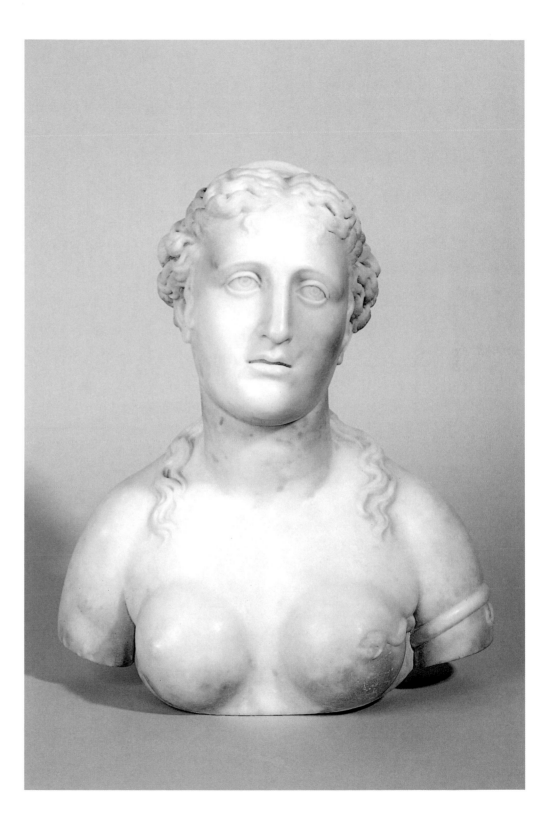

Cleopatra VII, daughter of Ptolemy XII Auletes, was born in 69 BC. She was co-ruler of Egypt with her brothers and successive husbands Ptolemy XIII and Ptolemy XIV, and was the mother of Ptolemy XV Caesar. Cleopatra met Mark Anthony in Tarsus (41 BC) and bore him twins, Alexander Helios and Cleopatra Selene. Anthony helped to re-establish her rule within all former Ptolomeic territories and thus evoked Octavian's anger. After Cleopatra's fleet was defeated in the subsequent war, at Actium, Anthony committed suicide. The queen copied him on 10 August 30 BC; legend has it by the bite of a cobra or asp.[1]

This bust is strongly influenced by the ideal portrait sculptures of Tullio and Antonio Lombardo, which were themselves contemporary interpretations of classical images.[2] Other sculptors working in his immediate circle, and providing rather similar 'all antica' busts, were Giammaria Mosca and Antonio Minelli.

Simone Bianco was Florentine by birth but is first recorded working in Treviso. Seven of his busts are signed in Greek 'Simon Lenkos Venetos Epoiei' (Simone Bianco of Venice Sculptor).[3] Stylistic and technical comparisons between this bust and, for example, the signed female bust in the Statens Museum fur Kunst, Copenhagen, demonstrate that both were carved by the same hand. They share the same distinctive facial type, but also the precision of carving the elaborately tressed hair.

Several of the letters of the writer Pietro Aretino indicate that some of Simone's busts were sent to the King of France in the mid-1530s.[4] It has been established convincingly that Simone's busts related closely to the Cleopatra type were carved towards the end of the 1520s and we can assume that they may have been made for one of his established Venetian collectors, like Andrea Odoni.[5]

Giovanni Falier (or Faletro) ACTIVE IN VENICE, EARLY SIXTEENTH CENTURY
194 & 195 ❧ *Andrea Gritti, Procurator of St Mark's*

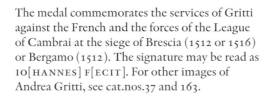

Obverse: Andrea Gritti, Procurator of St Mark's (born 1455, Doge of Venice 1523–38), shown in profile to left in armour and cloak. Inscribed around the edge: 'ANDREAE GRITO PROCVR[ATORI] D[IVI] MARCI'; and below: 'IO F'

Reverse: The Siege of a City, with Gritti commanding, mounted on a horse, before a city with the wall breached; before him a nude man seen from behind. Inscribed above: 'OPT[IME] DE PATRIA MERITO'; and below: 'GRAT[IA] CIV[IVM]'

Bronze (cast) | 6.5cm diameter

Provenance: [cat.no.194] W. Ready, London; from whom purchased by the Royal Museum, 1883 (acc.no.A.1883.5.10); [cat.no.195] Rosenheim Collection; Spink and Son Ltd, London; from whom purchased by the Royal Museum, 1923 (acc.no.A.1923.448)

Literature: Armand, 1883–7, I, cat.no.122; Hill, 1930, cat.no.464; Hill and Pollard, 1967, cat.no.156

EDINBURGH, NATIONAL MUSEUMS OF SCOTLAND

The medal commemorates the services of Gritti against the French and the forces of the League of Cambrai at the siege of Brescia (1512 or 1516) or Bergamo (1512). The signature may be read as IO[HANNES] F[ECIT]. For other images of Andrea Gritti, see cat.nos.37 and 163.

Giovanni Falieri (or Faletro) ACTIVE IN VENICE, EARLY SIXTEENTH CENTURY
196 ❧ *Andrea Gritti, Procurator of St Mark's, at a Siege*

Bronze intaglio medal die | 6.7cm diameter

Provenance: With Delehar Ltd, London; from whom purchased with funds given by Mr Dennis Ward in memory of his wife, 1990 (acc.no.NG 2659)

EDINBURGH, NATIONAL GALLERY OF SCOTLAND

The scene may have been intended to represent the siege of Brescia (1512 or 1516) or siege of Bergamo (1512), at both of which Gritti performed the prime heroic role. The intaglio die was cast for impressing leather book covers or perhaps the pommels of swords and daggers in so-called 'cuir bouilli'.[1]

Andrea Spinelli PARMA 1508–1572 VENICE
197 ❧ *Portrait of Doge Andrea Gritti*

Obverse: Portrait of Doge Andrea Gritti (born 1455, Doge of Venice 1523–38), shown bust length in left profile, wearing a ducal cap and robe. Inscribed around the edge: 'ANDREAS GRITI DVX VENETIA R[VM] MDXXIII'

Reverse: *The Church of San Francesco della Vigna, Venice*. Inscribed around the edge: 'DIVI FRANCISCI MD XXXIIII'; and below: 'AN[DREAS] SP[INELLI] F[ECIT]'

Gilt bronze medal, struck | 3.6cm diameter

Provenance: Sale, Sotheby's, London, 24 May 1988 (lot 53), bought by the Gallery (acc.no. NG 2482)

Literature: Armand, 1883–7, I, cat.no.155; Hill and Pollard, 1967, cat.no.413

EDINBURGH, NATIONAL GALLERY OF SCOTLAND

This is the foundation medal, dated 1534, for Sansovino's new church of San Francesco della Vigna. The temple-front façade was added in the 1560s by Andrea Palladio, which was his first major ecclesiastical commission. Gritti lived in a palace in the *campo* immediately in front of San Francesco. The church contained Jacopo Tintoretto's fine *Christ Carried to the Tomb* (cat.no.66), while two drawings by Battista Franco in the exhibition (cat.nos.97–8) are preparatory studies for his Baptism altarpiece, which is still in the church.

Gritti reigned for fifteen years. He had read philosophy at Padua University and spoke five languages fluently, including English. Indeed, he went on a Venetian diplomatic mission to England. Gritti fought gallantly against the League of Cambrai and in 1519 was appointed generale da mar (admiral) against the Turks. It was he who caused the construction in stone of the Fondamente delle Zattere in Venice. Gritti appointed Sansovino *proto* (chief architect) of San Marco, and also appointed Pietro Bembo state historian and Pietro Aretino state poet. He honoured and protected the courtesans of Venice and did much to re-establish and uphold the splendours of the *Serenissima*. He was buried in the basilica of Santi Giovanni e Paolo, but later in 1580 his heirs erected a mausoleum for him in San Francesco.[1]

Attributed to Andrea Spinelli PARMA 1508–1572 VENICE
198 ❧ *A Horse Attacked by a Lion*

Obverse: A Horse Attacked by a Lion

Reverse: Eternity. Inscribed around the edge: 'SEMPITERNITAS'

Bronze medal (struck), abraded 3.2cm diameter

Provenance: Sale, Glendinning's, London, 10 June 1987 (lot 318), bought by the Patrons of the National Galleries of Scotland (acc.no.NG 2468)

Literature: Edinburgh, 1989, cat.no.15

EDINBURGH, NATIONAL GALLERY OF SCOTLAND

Eternity is personified by a female figure holding a globe on which is the phoenix on its pyre. Another medal with an identical reverse is in Washington, but with an image of Fame on the obverse dated 1541;[1] another similar example is in Vienna. The lion being attacked by a horse is a motif derived from classical sculpture, notably a fragmentary group in the Capitoline Museums in Rome.

Attributed to Valerio Belli VICENZA c.1468–1546 VICENZA

199 ❧ *The Adoration of the Shepherds*

Tablet of rock crystal engraved in intaglio, with a lunette-shaped top | 10.6 × 7.7 × 0.4cm

Provenance: With Alessandro Castellani, Rome; his sale, Rome, March-April 1884 (lot 764), bought for the Royal Museum (acc.no.A.1884.44.7)

EDINBURGH, NATIONAL MUSEUMS OF SCOTLAND

Inside a ruined building consisting of part barn, part temple, a manger stands to the right of centre. The Holy Family is distributed along the bottom of the tablet as a frieze. St Joseph, to the right, leans forward, steadying himself on the manger, while adoring the Christ Child. Christ is cradled in his mother's arms, who kneels to the left. The shepherds enter the building from the left, unusually approaching the drama from behind the Virgin Mary, and one of the shepherds kneels, left of centre, and illuminates the nativity with his torch. Angels flutter above while one clings to a column and gazes down at the crib.[1]

Valerio Belli was probably the most famous of all the Italian Renaissance engravers of gems and was a friend of both Michelangelo and Raphael. Although born in Vicenza, he was probably trained in Venice and was to work for both Pope Clement VII and Pope Paul III. The rock crystal

carvings set into the reliquary of the Holy Cross (c.1508) in the Treasury of San Marco, Venice, are probably by Belli.

This piece, which is apparently unpublished,[2] was attributed to Valerio Belli in the 1884 Castellani sale and appears to be an early work, related in subject to a relief in the Museo Civico, Udine, which bears what appears to be Belli's signature. An unsigned replica is in the Walters Art Gallery, Baltimore. The authenticity of both has recently been doubted, with the suggestion that they may even date from the early nineteenth century. In the present example the quality of the intaglio cutting of the rock crystal is of a very high order, while the design is sophisticated and highly original. Whether the design was Belli's own or provided by another artist, perhaps Girolamo da Carpi or Enea Vico, is not known.

Attributed to Giovanni Bernardi da Castel Bolognese   CASTEL BOLOGNESE 1494–1553 FAENZA

200 ✢ *The Emperor Charles V*

The Emperor Charles V (1500–1558), shown in profile to right wearing fur-lined robes and cap. Inscribed around the edge: 'CAROLUS. V. IMP. BONON. CORONATUS. M.D.XXX'

Bronze (cast) | 8.2cm diameter

Provenance: With A. Darer, London; from whom purchased, 1994 (acc.no.NG 2629)

Literature: Armand 1883–7, I, cat.no.137; Kris, 1929, I, p.62; II, p.55 fig.229; Hill and Pollard, 1967, cat.no.484c

EDINBURGH, NATIONAL GALLERY
OF SCOTLAND

This medal was issued on the occasion of the coronation of the Emperor Charles V in Bologna in 1530. It is a uniface example of a medal that in its double-sided form has a reverse showing a river god representing the Tiber and an inscription.

Giorgio Vasari states that Bernardi made a medal struck from engraved dies to celebrate Charles V's coronation in Bologna. Stylistically, however, this medal, which is cast, shows little relationship to Bernardi's exquisite work and it has been argued that it must be by another hand.[1] On the other hand, the medal may be uncharacteristic of Bernardi's work because it

had to be made in a hurry and, moreover, was required to be especially large and showy.

Charles V was born in Bruges 1500, King of Spain 1516, Holy Roman Emperor 1519–56 and died in 1558. The Emperor and his son, the future King Philip II of Spain, were Titian's most important patrons.

Leone Leoni   AREZZO c.1509–1590 MILAN

201 ✢ *The Emperor Charles V and Philip, Infante of Spain*

Obverse: The Emperor Charles V (1500–1558) and 2Philip, Infante of Spain (1527–1598), both shown bearded and in armour, jugate, to the right. Inscribed around the edge: 'IMP. CAR. V · ET · PHI · PRINC · ISP'

Reverse: The Twin Columns of Hercules, set in a stormy sea, supporting the imperial crown, with a fluttering banderole inscribed 'PLUS OULTRE', surrounded by the linked collar of the order of the Golden Fleece.

Silver (struck) | 4.1cm diameter

Provenance: Sale, Sotheby's, London, 5 October 1989 (lot 213); sale, Bonham's, London, 17 May 1994, where bought by Richard Falkiner Ltd on behalf of the Gallery (acc.no.NG 2600)

Literature: Armand, 1883–7, II, cat.no.183; F. Kenner, 'Leone Leonis Medaillen für den Kaiserlichen Hof', *Jahrbuch der Kunsthistorischen Sammlungen in Wien*, XIII, 1892, pp.55–93; E. Plon, *Les maîtres italiens au service de la maison d'Autriche …*, Paris, 1887, pl.XXXI, figs.8–9; K. Domanig, *Porträtmedaillen des Erzhauses Österreich von Kaiser Friedrich III bis Kaiser Franz II*, Vienna, 1896, cat.no.48; M. Cano, 'Catálogo de medallas' in Madrid, Museo del Prado, *Los Leoni (1509–1608): Escultores del Rinascimento italiano al servicio de la corte de España*, exh. cat. by J. Urrea *et al.*, Madrid, 1994, p.184, cat.no.38; Duisburg, 1994, p.347, cat.no.209

EDINBURGH, NATIONAL GALLERY
OF SCOTLAND

The medal was struck before Philip became King of Spain in 1555. It is included here because Charles V and Philip II were the major patrons of Titian in his later career, with Philip commissioning the *Diana and Actaeon* and *Diana and Callisto* (cat.nos.54, 55).

Italian *c.1560–70*

202 ❦ *Portrait Medallion of Titian and his Son Orazio*

Coloured wax, enriched with gold, seed pearls, and diamond or topaz (pendant) and chalcedony(?) (finger-ring), mounted on glass; in a glazed frame of turned, ebonised and gilded wood | 13 × 12.9 × 2.3cm

Inscribed around the top, in yellow wax: 'TITIANI PICT. ET FILII EFIGIES.'; and on the scroll beneath Titian's hand, in red wax: 'HORA . ES . FILI'

Provenance: William, 12th Duke of Hamilton, by 1876;[1] sale, Christie's, Hamilton Palace sale, 19 July 1882 (lot 2018), bought by Williams; with P. & D. Colnaghi & Co. Ltd, London, 1981;[2] with J. Kugel Antiquaires, Paris, from whom purchased by the Museums (acc.no.K.2004.38)

EDINBURGH, NATIONAL MUSEUMS OF SCOTLAND

Fig.251 | Attributed to Agostino Ardenti, *Portrait Medal of Titian and his Son Orazio* Brunswick, Maine, Bowdoin College Museum of Art (Gift of Amanda Marchesa Molinari)

This high-quality wax portrait of Titian holding a miniature of his cherished second son, the painter Orazio Vecellio (*c.*1515–1576), is clearly indebted to Titian's portraits of himself (figs.149, 245). As in the self-portraits, Titian is shown wearing his characteristic dark skull-cap, a coat with huge brown fur lapels, and the heavy gold chain presented to him by the Emperor Charles V in 1533. It seems likely that the composition is related in some way to a self-portrait that the artist sent to Philip II of Spain in 1552–3, which was destroyed in 1604. That lost work depicted the great Venetian painter holding a miniature of Philip, clad in armour, and served to convey and demonstrate Titian's devotion and commitment to the future emperor.[3] Such an image would have provided an excellent point of departure for this remarkable expression of fatherly love and pride in a (not particularly gifted) son, and also helps explain the magnificence of the miniature-frame.

At present, it is far from clear who modelled the wax and where it stands in relation to an almost identical, if rather crude, cast medal of Titian and Orazio, in copper alloy and lead, which measures 10.3cm in diameter and bears two different inscriptions: 'TITIANI PICTORIS EXIMII. EFFIGIESI. A.' at the top, and 'HORATIVS . FIL' on the scroll (fig.251).[4] The authorship of this medal is problematic, but it has been attributed to the little-known medallist Agostino Ardenti, a native of Faenza active around 1563.[5] It has been argued that Agostino signed his medals 'AA', while his brother, the painter and sculptor Alessandro Ardenti, used the letters 'AAR' and an 'AR' monogram. Photographs of examples of the Titian medal show only one unambiguous 'A', although there may be the beginnings of a second 'A' on at least one cast. Nevertheless, the link with 'AA' and Agostino Ardenti seems to be confirmed by comparison with a medal of the woodcarver Andrea Foscho of Faenza, which is unequivocally signed 'A.A.' on the left-hand side.[6] The fact that Foscho was active in Venice between about 1566 and 1582, and worked successfully with Palladio on the Ducal Palace, strengthens the case that Agostino Ardenti could have executed the medal of Titian.

The wax of Titian has been attributed to two 'big name' Milanese medallists and gem engravers, in apparent ignorance of the existence of the medal attributed to Ardenti. It was first associated with Giovanni Antonio de' Rossi (1517–after 1571).[7] However, there are insufficient stylistic similarities with De' Rossi's medals, with waxes by him of *Pope Pius V* and with his cameo of *Cosimo de' Medici and his Family* (Florence, Palazzo Pitti) to support this view. Moreover, De' Rossi was working in Rome from 1560. More recently, an alternative attribution to the even

more celebrated Antonio Abondio (1538–1591) has been put forward.[8] But again there are few stylistic parallels and a possible problem, for Abondio was employed in Innsbruck and Ambras and then in Vienna after 1565–6, and is not known to have visited Venice during this period.

Research is continuing to establish whether Agostino Ardenti could have been responsible for the wax, either as a development of the model for the medal or as a parallel exercise. The alternative is that the wax is after the medal, and was produced to meet the growing taste and demand for such 'Kunstkammer' pieces – especially at the Austrian Habsburgh court – in the late sixteenth century.[9] A much more interesting issue, though, is exactly how the medals and wax (which do not seem to be *ad vivum* portraits) are connected with Titian's promotion of Orazio as an artist and organiser and his determined efforts to ensure the continuing status and prosperity of the Vecellio family.

Nothing is currently known about the early history of the wax. It does not seem to have been owned by the maniacal collector William Beckford (1760–1844) and to have been inherited by his daughter, Susan, the wife of the 10th Duke of Hamilton. Such indicators as there are suggest that *Titian and his Son Orazio* was acquired by Alexander, 10th Duke of Hamilton (1767–1852). The 10th Duke lived in the north-east of Italy in the 1790s and early 1800s, and visited Italy frequently in the 1810s and 1820s. He bought items, including Roman cameos, from Giovanni Maria Sasso, Count Leopoldo Cicognara and other Venetian and Italian dealers, and was criticised by his brother as early as 1816 for his apparently large collection of 'precious Stones, miniatures & manuscripts'.[10] In 1876 the wax was in the library of Hamilton Palace, which had been created by the 10th Duke for his outstanding collection of illuminated manuscripts. It was in one of the two *pietre dure* cabinets that the duke had purchased from the George Watson Taylor sale in 1832 and soon installed in his new library.[11] The 1876 inventory indicates that these cabinets were used to store a stocking and letters from the Princess Pauline Borghese and some of the 10th Duke's other prized possessions.[12] GE

Alessandro Vittoria TRENT 1525–1608 VENICE

204 & 205 ❧ *Tommaso Rangone of Ravenna*

Obverse: Tommaso Rangone of Ravenna (1493–1577), shown bearded, in profile to right, in a gown. Inscribed around the edge: 'THOMAS PHILOLOGVS RAVENNAS'

Reverse: The Origin of the Milky Way: Jupiter, as an eagle, brings the infant Hercules to Juno, who lies recumbent and sleeping within the Milky Way; below, lilies grow out of the ground and three birds are in flight. Inscribed around the edge: 'A IOVE ET SORORE GENITA'

Bronze (cast) | 3.8cm diameter | (cat.no.204)

Provenance: Lord Carmichael of Skirling; by whom presented to the Royal Museum, 1906 (acc.no.A.1906.446)

EDINBURGH, NATIONAL MUSEUMS OF SCOTLAND

Bronze (cast), worn | 4.2cm diameter (cat.no.205)

Provenance: Sale, Glendining's, London, 10 June 1987 (lot 301), bought by the Patrons of the National Galleries of Scotland (acc.no.NG 2467)

Literature: Armand, 1883–7, II, cat.no.196, 20; Hill and Pollard, 1967, cat.no.417b; Edinburgh, 1989, cat.no.16

EDINBURGH, NATIONAL GALLERY OF SCOTLAND

Tommaso Rangone (1493–1577), known as Philologus, was born with the surname Gianozzi, but took his new surname after serving under Conte Guido Rangoni. Tommaso studied at Padua and in 1518 became a professor of philosophy and later of astronomy. He moved to Venice as a medical doctor. He restored the church of San Giuliano, employing Sansovino and Alessandro Vittoria. Sansovino was responsible for sculpting the statue of Rangone above the main doorway (fig.252).

The reverse illustrates the story of the creation of the Milky Way. Jupiter wanted to give his son Hercules the immortality due to a son of a god and so carried the child to the sleeping Juno to be fed. The milk that fell in the heavens created the Milky Way and, falling to earth, created lilies. The choice of the image was a reference to Rangone's own adoption and it can be seen as a forerunner of Jacopo Tintoretto's painting of the same subject now in the National Gallery, London. Tintoretto was a close friend of Rangone.[1]

The problem of attribution for this medal is complex. It has been variously attributed in the past to both Sansovino and Vittoria. However, in 1974 a list of portrait medals of Rangone was found amongst the Rangone papers and the name Matteo Pagano is specified as one of the medallists responsible; he may be identical with the obscure Venetian woodcarver Paganus a Fide.[2] The explanation seems to be that the two examples of the medal exhibited here are by Vittoria, but that other versions of it exist, with a different portrait and different lettering, one dated 1562, and it is these that are probably the work of Matteo Pagano.[3]

Fig.252 | Jacopo Sansovino,
Bronze Statue of Tommaso Rangone
Venice, Church of San Giuliano, Façade

Workshop of Alessandro Vittoria TRENT 1525–1608 VENICE
206 ❧ *Statuette of Jupiter Holding a Thunderbolt*

Bronze of coppery alloy with chocolate brown and black patina, the highlights rubbed
33.7 × 13.3 × 12cm (diameter of base)

Provenance: Daniel Katz Ltd, London (as Tiziano Aspetti); from whom purchased, 2002

EDINBURGH, NATIONAL GALLERY OF SCOTLAND

The bearded god stands, naked, gesturing with his left arm across his breast and in his right hand he clasps a thunderbolt. He stands on a circular socle with his right leg raised placed on the back of an eagle. The circular flat base is drilled for attachment to a support, probably as an andiron.

The bronze has only a loose, generic relationship to Aspetti, to whom it was previously attributed, but is much closer to Vittoria, with its swaggering contrapposto and robust musculature. In fact, it is a slightly less good replica of a bronze by Vittoria in the Kunsthistoriches Museum, Vienna.[1] The pose appears to have been influenced by Giambologna's *Neptune Fountain* in Bologna (1563–6). Formerly dated to the mid-1560s,[2] there is now a consensus of opinion that the Vienna bronze dates from about 1580, nearer the *St John the Baptist* in the Duomo, Treviso. The figure also is reminiscent of Vittoria's figure of a *River God* in a spandrel of the Libreria Marciana, finished in the early 1580s.

This model and a figure of *Juno with her Peacock* appear as the terminals of a pair of andirons in the Victoria and Albert Museum, London,[3] and another pair in the Queen's House, Greenwich.

Attributed to Alessandro Vittoria TRENT 1525–1608 VENICE
207 ❧ *Head of an Elderly Warrior*

Terracotta | 29 × 20 × 22cm

Provenance: With Heim Gallery, London;[1] from whom purchased by the Museums, 1972 (acc.no.A.1972.137)

EDINBURGH, NATIONAL MUSEUMS OF SCOTLAND

This terracotta shows the head of a powerful old man, balding and with high, emphatic cheekbones, sunken eye-sockets, furrowed brow, and full beard. The head was modelled to slot into the top of a separately modelled torso and includes an armoured collar with slashed linen shirt worn beneath.

This fine bust is little known, and if not by Vittoria himself, is certainly by a sculptor in Vittoria's immediate circle. The sitter has not been identified but must have been modelled at much the same time as the *Bust of Sebastiano Venier* now in the Palazzo Ducale, Venice, which Vittoria left to the Republic in his will of 1608.[2] The Venier bust appears to date from the end of the 1580s or early 1590s. As far as Vittoria's vigour as modeller is concerned, the Edinburgh bust appears to be of fine quality and arguably as good or better than his heads of *Tommaso Rangone* and *Pietro Zen*.[3] Such busts were commissioned to rival in sculpture the painted portraits of Titian, Tintoretto and Veronese.

Circle of Alessandro Vittoria TRENT 1525–1608 VENICE

208 ❧ *Doorknocker with Neptune Standing between two Sea Horses*

Bronze of pale grey brown metal, unpatinated
42 × 31cm

Provenance: Robert Napier, by 1861;[1] his
posthumous sale Christie's, London, 18 April
1877 (lot 1075), bought T.M. Whitehead on
behalf of the Royal Museum
(acc.no.A.1877.20.42)

EDINBURGH, NATIONAL MUSEUMS
OF SCOTLAND

Neptune, rising from a shell, is shown bearded
and naked holding a trident in his right hand and
his left hand resting on the leafy tail of a sea
horse. The sea god is flanked by a pair of sea
horses, their tails entwined behind Neptune's
back. The figure represents the god as wrathful,
hurling invective against the winds, in his
'Quos Ego' guise as described by Virgil (*Aeneid* 1:
125–40). The same subject was engraved by
Marcantonio Raimondi after Raphael. That
image was in turn the source of a plaquette by
Giovanni Bernardi da Castel Bolognese (1496–
1553).[2] A related stone relief appears on the
façade of the Scuola di San Rocco, Venice.[3] The
ultimate source was an antique prototype like the
front of a *Sarcophagus with Neptune, Nereids and
Tritons* in the Giardino della Pigna in the
Vatican.[4]

   This is a rich and vigorous model, although
the cast is flawed, with considerable patching to
the torso visible from the back. The model is by
an artist deeply influenced by Jacopo Sansovino,
and has traditionally been attributed to
Alessandro Vittoria, Sansovino's assistant for
twelve years,[5] but the modelling seems inferior to
his autograph work. Two much later casts of the
same model also belong to the National Museums of Scotland.[6] The model was evidently very
popular and continued to be manufactured well
into the nineteenth century, often with a family
shield of arms (or *stemma*) above supported by
the tails of the sea horses. Examples are in the
Museo Correr, Venice, Alnwick Castle, Northumberland, the Ashmolean Museum, Oxford,
Budapest, Vienna, and in many other collections.[7] They relate closely to a terracotta *Neptune
and a Dolphin* attributed to Vittoria in the British
Museum, London.[8]

   A companion bronze knocker showing a
marine *Venus Flanked by Putti Riding on Dolphins* is
known (two versions are in the Kress collection);
this model is not by Vittoria but by a follower,
possibly Tiziano Aspetti (1565–1607).[9]

Venetian SECOND HALF OF THE SIXTEENTH CENTURY

209 ❧ *Doorknocker with a Pair of Entwined Dolphins Suspended from a Mask of Neptune*

Bronze of warm brown metal with a rich dark
patina | 43.7 × 29.6cm

Provenance: P. Norton, London; Robert Napier,
by 1861;[1] his posthumous sale Christie's,
London, 18 April 1877 (lot no.1076); bought
T.M. Whitehead on behalf of the Royal Museum (acc.no.A.1877.20.47)

EDINBURGH, NATIONAL MUSEUMS
OF SCOTLAND

Two dolphins are shown with their coiled tails
flanking a mask of Neptune (not Jupiter, as
described in 1861 exhibition). The dolphins are
suspended forming a lyre shape, their heads
terminating at a horned and bearded satyr mask.
The style of this bronze grew out of the circle of
Jacopo Sansovino. A rather similar model in the
Bayerisches Nationalmuseum in Munich shows a
bifurcate Triton, and provides parallels with a
fine black chalk study from the circle of
Sansovino of a *Doorknocker with Demi-figures of
Neptune and Amphitrite* (Munich, Staatliche
Graphische Sammlung).[2]

The 1877 Napier sale catalogue records that
the doorknocker was 'For thirty years on the
door of Mr P. Norton's house, Soho Square'.

North Italian, possibly Veneto LATE SIXTEENTH CENTURY

210 ❧ *Statuette of Satyress Carrying a Child*

Bronze of warm brown metal, much worn, with blackish patina remaining within the relief; on a turned porphyry socle | 22.8 × 9.5cm

Provenance: With A. Myers & Son, London; from whom purchased by the Royal Museum, 1883 (acc.no.A.1883.47.1)

EDINBURGH, NATIONAL MUSEUMS OF SCOTLAND

The crouched old satyress with wizened face and sagging breasts is naked, but for a cloth cap and fig leaf. She carries a plump satyr child on her left hip. Another cast of the bronze belonged to the French antiquarian Paul Petau in 1610,[1] which may be identical with the example now in the Louvre.[2] It was then reproduced accurately by Charles Patin in his Paris publication of 1697 (fig.253). A further cast is in the Ashmolean Museum, Oxford, where the figure surmounts an inkstand.[3] The type of satyress image grows out of the Riccio tradition in Padua but this vigorously modelled figure, with its nicely observed and finely expressed details, looks later. The suggestion that it might be Venetian and date from about 1575 is not persuasive.[4]

Fig.253 | Plate from Charles Patin, *Imperatorum Romanorum …*, Paris, 1697

Attributed to Tiziano Aspetti PADUA 1557/9–1606 PISA

211 ❧ *Statuette of St Mark Writing his Gospel*

Bronze of dark brown metal with black patina on a later turned granite base with ormolu plinth | 17.8cm high (excluding base)

Provenance: 17th Earl of Perth, Stobhall, Perthshire

PRIVATE COLLECTION

The bearded St Mark, patron saint of Venice, is seated wearing a tunic tied at the waist and a cloak over his shoulders, which billows out behind and then falls in generous crumpled folds around his lap and knees. The saint sits on his winged lion and writes the gospel, which he holds in his left hand, and holds a stylus in his right. The figure is supported on a shallow hexagonal plinth.

This neat little bronze is demonstrably Venetian of the 1590s and is stylistically reminiscent of Girolamo Campagna (1549–*c*.1625). It may be compared, for example, with his bronzes of the four Evangelists for the high altar of San Giorgio Maggiore (1589–92) and the pair of *Angels Holding Candlesticks* in the church of the Carmine (*c*.1590–2).[1]

But the form of this tall, slender saint with pinched features, tidy beard and long limbs, is even more closely reminiscent of the relief figures by Tiziano Aspetti on the two signed panels of *the Martyrdom of St Daniel* in the shrine of St Daniel in the Duomo at Padua.[2] It is also similar to a seated figure of *Minerva with a Putto* attributed to Aspetti in Stockholm, which shares many of the same stylistic features and is also on a distinctive hexagonal base (fig.254).[3] Aspetti was probably Campagna's pupil, which may explain why this bronze closely resembles his style.

Fig.254 | Attributed to Tiziano Aspetti, *Minerva with a Putto* Stockholm, Nationalmuseum

Venetian LATE SIXTEENTH CENTURY

212 ❧ *Plaquette of the Coronation of the Virgin*

Bronze of brown colour with darker brown lacquer patina, rubbed | 13.3 × 8.8cm

Provenance: T. Chapman, auctioneer, Edinburgh; from whom purchased for the Royal Museum, 1873 (acc.no.A.1873.21.27)

EDINBURGH, NATIONAL MUSEUMS OF SCOTLAND

Christ is seated in clouds at the upper right in the act of crowning the Virgin Mary, who kneels in supplication, at the left, with her hands crossed on her breast. Both Christ and the Virgin are supported in the heavens by flying cherubs, while others fly around holding circlets of roses and festoons of rosary beads.[1] The plaquette is sometimes found within a cast integral frame consisting of strapwork in the so-called Sansovino taste (examples in the Staatliche Museen, Berlin, the Museo Bardini, Florence and the Museo d'Arti Applicate, Milan).

The plaquette has been attributed to a follower of Sansovino,[2] and the style does indeed suggest a Venetian origin. It has been thought to date from between 1573 – when Pope Gregory XIII, after the great naval victory of Lepanto over the Turks on 7 October 1571, proclaimed this day as the festival of the Madonna of the Rosary – and 1582, when the Cappella del Rosario in the church of Santi Giovanni e Paolo in Venice was founded. The image has been said to derive from the destroyed altarpiece by Cima da Conegliano in that chapel, but the direct source is clearly much later and resembles an artist of Tintoretto's generation.[3]

The traditional ascription of this plaquette to Jacopo Sansovino or a follower has been questioned, and it has been associated instead with a silver pax of the *Assumption of the Virgin* in the Treasury of the Frari, Venice, which bears on the reverse a long inscription and the date 1595. Although the plaquette is somewhat cruder, it has been argued that it is by the same designer as the *Coronation of the Virgin* relief. The putti and 'vermiculated' clouds point to an artist, perhaps a Venetian goldsmith, in the circle of Roccatagliata and a connection with Nicolò and Sebastiano Roccatagliata's signed altar frontal of 1633 in San Moisè has been proposed.[4]

Workshop of Nicolò Roccatagliata GENOESE, ACTIVE IN VENICE 1593–AFTER 1636
or Giuseppe de Levis ACTIVE IN VERONA 1552–1611/14
213 ❧ *An Inkstand Supported on Three Winged Harpies*

Bronze of rich brown metal, the black varnish patina much rubbed | 8 × 13.5 × 13.5cm

Provenance: Sir Joseph Noel Paton (1821–1900); acquired by the Royal Museum, 1905 (acc.no.A.1905.893)

EDINBURGH, NATIONAL MUSEUMS OF SCOTLAND

Three harpies, belted below their bare breasts, with lion's-paw feet and leafy tails, have their hair gathered and falling in loose tresses to their shoulders. They wear voluted Phrygian-type caps and their wing tips are knotted together with bunches of drapery to support a shallow bowl ornamented with bobbin-and-bead moulding.

Closely related harpies support a cognate inkstand formerly in the collection of Sir John Martin-Hervey and a pair of three light candle-

Venetian LATE SIXTEENTH *or* EARLY SEVENTEENTH CENTURY

214 ❧ *An Altar Candlestick*

Bronze of coppery alloy, the pricket replaced
57.5cm high

Issuing from three shaped, scrolling brackets
enclosing reliefs of three standing hermit saints
in ovals (one missing), the candelabrum shaft
consists of two tiers of vases supported on the
first tier by three winged caryatids, and on the
second by three seated putti; the upper pear-
shaped balustre supports a shallow ribbed drip
pan.

 This type of candlestick, with variations,
frequently occurs and is generally associated with
the workshop of Nicolò Roccatagliata, but also
issued from other Venetian foundries. The
attribution is ultimately based on rather similar
putti appearing on the bronze candelabra and
sconces on the high altar of San Giorgio
Maggiore, Venice (1593–6).[1] A fine pair is in the
National Gallery of Art, Washington,[2] and
another pair, gilded and with the arms of the
Moro family of Venice, was on the London art
market in 1994.[3] A third pair in the collection of
the Earl of Rosebery at Dalmeny is now wired for
electricity.

sticks now in the Art Institute Chicago (also
from the Martin-Hervey collection). This group
has been published as the work of Giuseppe de
Levis, although it has been noted as anomalous
that while the inkstand is signed by him, the
candlesticks bear no signature.[1] The candlesticks
are very similar to a salt with gadrooned bowl
surmounted by three putti supporting a marine
Venus on their shoulders (Dresden, Grünes
Gewölbe Museum), which is usually given to
Roccatagliata, with persuasive stylistic analogies
to other signed bronzes.[2] A third bronze probably from the same foundry – a gadrooned
inkstand supported on the backs of three putti,
their wing tips tied together – is in the Frick Art
Museum, Pittsburg.[3] The Frick bronze is
cautiously attributed to either Roccatagliata or
De Levis, and this seems the wisest solution in
our present state of knowledge of this area. It is
quite possible that Roccatagliata was responsible
for the model and De Levis for casting it.

Venetian, possibly Nicolò Roccatagliata GENOESE, ACTIVE IN VENICE 1593–AFTER 1636
or Andrea di Alessandri ACTIVE IN VENICE, *c*.1550–AFTER 1575
215 ❧ *An Andiron with a Figure of Jupiter*

Bronze of deep golden brown patina
119 × 54cm; the figure of Jupiter, with integral
base: 54cm high, the base 12.5cm diameter
c.1570–1630

Provenance: Soranzo family, Venice; probably
bought by John Stuart, 3rd Earl of Bute, during
his stay in Venice 1769–71;[1] thence by descent at
Luton Park (later Luton Hoo), Bedfordshire,
until the fire of 1843, when transferred to Mount
Stuart, Isle of Bute; sale, Christie's, London, 3
July 1996 (lot 27), bought by a French private
collector; its export was deferred and it was
purchased by the Gallery with the aid of the
National Heritage Memorial Fund and the
National Art Collections Fund, 1997
(acc.no.NG 2660)[2]

EDINBURGH, NATIONAL GALLERY
OF SCOTLAND

Jupiter, bearded and naked but for drapery
around his loins, facing half right, with a thunderbolt in his right hand and his eagle behind
him at the left. The god stands on a turned
circular plinth that rests on an urn ornamented
with monster masks and is supported on three
addorsed winged harpies with (later) candle
nozzles issuing from behind their heads. The urn
is supported on a richly ornamented base
consisting of the Soranzo arms, in a cartouche,
flanked by an elderly satyr and satyress, kneeling
and scowling, with curious short wings in
substitution for their arms; above them is a
further voluted cartouche on which are seated a
pair of putti, with a stylised herm between them.

Such handsome andirons must originally have
graced the fireplaces of numerous palazzi in
Venice and the Veneto. During the winter
months, especially, the architecture of the
chimneypiece itself and its characteristic frescoed
or stuccoed trapezoid *suprastufo* would have
become the central focus of the room, and these
tall bronze pyramidal compositions, supporting
and shielding the cast iron armatures on which
the logs would have been placed, must also have
provided a significant focus. The bronzes are
made up of sections bolted or fused together and
usually culminate with deities as finials. The
concept probably goes back to an idea of Jacopo
Sansovino, although no documented Sansovino
andirons are known. Many have been attributed
to his assistants and followers, such as Vittoria,
Campagna, Aspetti, Andrea Bresciano and, a
little later, Segala and Roccatagliata. Some must
have issued from the foundries in and around the
Arsenale, Venice, but others were certainly cast in
Padua, Brescia, and Verona.[3]

In spite of the spate of recent archival research
on these foundries, it is true to say that, apart
from the recognisable cognate group of signed
works form the foundry of De Levis in Verona,
we are not yet in a position to make many firm
attributions to particular designers, modellers, or
workshops. Most appear not to have been
designed for specific sites, but were bought 'off
the peg' from foundries, where the Renaissance
buyer could choose his combination of disparate,
independent sections, and could also specify the
inclusion of his own coat of arms. Familiar
arrangements exist today, for example when
buying chocolate Easter eggs, where the purchaser selects the favoured chocolates from a
variety of choices and then has the egg personal-
ised with an inscription, perhaps trailed in
coloured icing.

Closely related to the Bute andiron is a pair in
the Metropolitan Museum, New York, with
statuettes (that may, however, have been added
later) of Mars and Venus.[4] The vase element of
the Bute andirons, with harpies, and the
cartouche, with seated putti, are repeated, but
seated lions supporting shields have been
substituted for the satyr and satyress. A squat
vase with monster masks on the shoulders, linked
by festoons of fruit, has been added immediately
beneath the statuettes. Although not of such fine
quality as the Bute andiron, the Metropolitan
variant probably originated from the same
foundry. The pose of the Bute Jupiter is repeated
in a figure of Adonis (or Meleager) surmounting
an andiron with the arms of Barbaro in the
Victoria and Albert Museum.[5] Here the foundry
has replaced Jupiter's bearded head with the
clean shaven Adonis and substituted a hunting
dog for Jupiter's eagle. Noticeably, Jupiter's
drapery is hitched up by a strap hanging from his
right shoulder to below his left hip and this
accounts for a generous tuck in his loin cloth. The
same tuck reappears in Adonis's drapery, but has
become meaningless because Adonis has no such
strap.[6] This is a clear indication of the precedence
of the more dynamic Bute andiron over the
Victoria and Albert Museum's Adonis example.

When the Bute andiron was offered for sale by
Christie's it was attributed to Nicolò
Roccatagliata: 'The putti, with their distinctively
proportioned bodies, hooded eyes, and curling
hair piled up over the forehead, are particularly
reminiscent of other putti known to be from the
hand of Roccatagliata.' This attribution was
based on the documented pair of candelabra in
San Giorgio Maggiore, Venice (fig.255), and on a
pair of andirons attributed to him in the Bargello,
Florence. A recent detailed study of the Edinburgh andiron and its pair (for which see below)
has led to the alternative suggestion that it might
be by Andrea di Alessandro, called Bresciano,[7]
but on balance the Roccatagliata attribution
seems a little more persuasive.

The Bute andiron has a companion, in the
collection of the heirs of Sir Brinsley Ford, which
is now lacking its statuette finial.[8] After the 3rd
Earl of Bute bought the pair, Robert Adam
converted them into handsome candelabra,
replete with tall altar-shaped pedestals resting on
winged lion's-paw feet, ram's heads on the
shoulders, from which suspended festoons of
husks. This companion andiron was engraved in
1774 with Robert Adam's additions in R. and J.
Adam's *The Works of Architecture of Robert and
James Adam*, London, 1778, I, section 3, pl.VIII.
We learn that it was originally surmounted by a
figure of Hercules and that the pair stood in
niches in the withdrawing room of the earl's
house at Luton Park, Bedfordshire. A companion
pair, of a different pattern but certainly by
Andrea di Alessandri, *c*.1565–70, had also been
acquired by the 3rd Earl and, to judge from the
same engraving, underwent a similar transformation in Adam's hands.[9]

We may know how the Earl of Bute displayed
these andirons at Luton Hoo, but we know little
of their earliest destination with the Soranzo
family. The Soranzo were one of the twenty-four
so-called 'case vecchie', who were said to have
founded Venice before the ninth century. Two
portraits of members of the Soranzo family
belong to the Earl of Harewood, including a
handsome full-length male portrait by Paolo
Veronese dating from the mid-1570s. It is
tempting to believe that Veronese's sitter may
have originally owned these andirons.[10]

Fig.255 | Nicolò Roccatagliata, detail showing the bronze
candelabrum
Venice, Church of San Giorgio Maggiore

Italian, probably Venetian *c.1560–70*

216 ❧ *Cassone Carved in Relief with Mermen, Nereids and Putti*

Walnut wood | 79.5 × 175 × 62cm

Provenance: With Alessandro Castellani, Rome; his sale March-April 1884, where purchased for the Royal Museum (acc.no.A.1884.44.8)

EDINBURGH, NATIONAL MUSEUMS OF SCOTLAND

The chest, of swelling convex form, is deeply carved with a marine *thaos* frieze of nereids, tritons and putti flanking an elaborate blank cabochon cartouche; this rests on a narrower concave frieze of scallop shells and gathered drapery and is surmounted by a concave rinceau frieze with a scallop shell at the centre enclosing the key escutcheon. The composition is held together by statuesque mermaids. The hinged lid is decorated with stiff leaf mouldings.

Such a marriage chest or *cassone* was filled with linen and presented, as part of a dowry, to the betrothed maiden. This *cassone* may originally have had a shield of arms that has now been erased. Heraldry was often much in evidence on these prestigious pieces of useful furniture. Several *cassoni* of this very robust form are known. One, with the bas-relief against a gold ground, is in the civic collections of Milan, where it is described as Venetian, mid-sixteenth century.[1] Another is in the Schlossmuseum, Berlin,[2] and three more are in the Hermitage, St Petersburg (from the Botkin Collection).[3] Another example in the Lehman Collection at the Metropolitan Museum, New York, is described as Roman.[4]

Venetian or Veneto *c.1560–80*

217 & 218 ❧ *A Pair of Chairs of so-called 'Sgabello da pozzo' Type*

Walnut, carved, parcel gilt and silvered
113 × 38.6 × 43.5cm

Provenance: With Daniel Katz Ltd, London;
from whom purchased, 1989

EDINBURGH, NATIONAL GALLERY
OF SCOTLAND

This form of chair, or more correctly stool with a back, consists of four boards joined by mortise-and-tenon joints, namely: a pierced back splat of inverted lyre form, elaborately carved and ornamented with scrolls, cinquefoils and acanthus foliage enclosing a blank silvered shield; a solid seat with a shallow dish shaped depression on top, presumably to take a cushion; a richly carved fronting board below the seat in the form of a grotesque mask flanked by addorsed winged harpies, their tails terminating in satyr-masks; and a back board, which repeats the silhouette of the fronting board, but is plain and undecorated.

The 'sgabello' probably takes its name from the diminutive and dialect form of 'scagno' or 'scanno' (stool), 'scanello' (little stool).[1] A sixteenth-century Venetian inventory appears to describe twelve such stools as 'scagni de nogara intagliade et doradi col pozo' or stools of walnut carved and gilded with backs.[2] The 'pozo' appears to have been a corruption of 'd'appoggio', meaning something to rest or lean against. Such stools, with or without backs, were made in long sets and were lined up against the walls of the 'portego' of Venetian palaces in the second half of the sixteenth century.

There appears to be little literature on the design and development of these pieces of seat

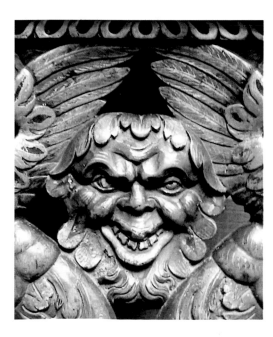

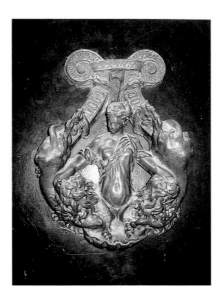

Fig.256 | Bernardino India, *Decorative Design with Venus Holding an Apple* Formerly London, Art Market

Fig.257 | Attributed to Danese Cattaneo, *Doorknocker with Fortitude Holding Two Lions* Venice, Private Collection

Fig.258 | Battista del Moro, detail from *Pandora* Florence, Galleria degli Uffizi

furniture. They are self-consciously designed exemplars of Mannerism that appear to have been invented by an artist, or artists, in the immediate circle of Andrea Palladio. Palladio himself in his *Quattro Libri dell'Architettura* (1570; see cat.no.167) notably does not provide designs for furniture; much of the furniture in his villas and palaces was probably designed by an associate, such as the Veronese painter and prolific designer Bernardino India (1528–1590). A characteristic sheet by India (fig.256) is stylistically very similar to this furniture.[3] He sometimes provided the figurative elements in Palladio's architectural drawings and carried out

the fresco decoration of Palladio's Palazzo Thiene and Villa Poiana. It is known that India was a friend of the sculptor and poet Danese Cattaneo (1509–1572), who had been a pupil of Jacopo Sansovino.[4] India certainly designed handsome stucco chimneypieces,[5] and may even have designed some distinctive bronze door-knockers, perhaps modelled by Cattaneo (fig.257).[6] Other artists from Verona may have been involved in designing furniture of this kind. For example, the decoration on the box at the lower left of Battista del Moro's etching of *Pandora* of 1557 is very similar in style to these chairs (fig.258).[7]

Venetian *c.1570–1600*

219 & 220 ❧ *A Pair of Walnut and Parcel Gilt Cassoni*

55.9 × 156.2 × 55.7cm

Provenance: Carse Antiques, Perthshire; from whom purchased by the Patrons of the National Galleries of Scotland, 1986

EDINBURGH, NATIONAL GALLERY OF SCOTLAND

The *cassoni* (chests) have a blank central, horizontal panel framed with moulding of fruit and foliage and flanked to right and left by panels with leafy monster masks. Below is a shallow slightly projecting gadrooned base, supported at the front by two narrow bracket feet in the form of paired dolphins, their tails entwined.

Cassoni such as these, originally made to contain clothes or linen, are among the commonest type of furniture to survive from the Renaissance. One of these chests is inscribed 'China Room' inside the lid. Both have been badly eaten by worm and the interior soft-wood carcasses have been rebuilt and the tops of the lids replaced. A similar *cassone*, more elaborate in design, with putti and foliage carved in the central reserve, is in the Museo Correr, Venice, another is in the Museo Civico di Storia e Arte, Trieste and a third in the Palazzo Comunale, Gubbio.[1]

Veneto-Saracenic *c.1460–1500*

221 ✤ *A Candlestick Decorated with an Inscribed Shield*

Brass | 18 × 9.2cm

Provenance: With Galleria Sangiorgi, Rome; from whom purchased by the Royal Museum, 1926 (acc.no.A.1926.226)

EDINBURGH, NATIONAL MUSEUMS OF SCOTLAND

The tall turned candlestick shaft issues from a high incurved conical foot and broad flat drip tray, engraved with foliage and a European tilting shield (with knotched lance rest) charged with a chevron and the gothic letters LSD.

A candlestick of similar form appears on a shelf in the left background of Vittore Carpaccio's *Vision of St Augustine*, painted in about 1502 in the Scuola degli Schiavoni, Venice. A corresponding armorial Mamluk (Damascus) candlestick of about 1400 is in the British Museum, and others are in the Correr Museum, Venice, with the arms of Zen (or Contarini) and with the arms of Malipiero.[1]

The distinctive style of metalwork known as Veneto-Saracenic is often believed to have been made in Venice by Moorish craftsmen, but it seems more likely to have been made in Mamluk workshops in Syria and Egypt specifically to be traded with Venice.[2] Metalwork decorated in the moresque style, with most elaborate interlaces, often follows European shapes and examples frequently bear the heraldry of celebrated Venetian families like the Priuli, Pisani, Corner and Badoer. Similar ornament on metalwork, copied at second hand through prints by the likes of Zoppino,[3] exerted a great influence on European painting and decorative art, and in particular on potters like Jacomo da Pesaro.

Veneto-Saracenic MID- TO LATE SIXTEENTH CENTURY

222 ✤ *A Candlestick Decorated with Foliate Medallions and Interlaces*

Brass, with inlaid threads of silver | 18 × 17.8cm

Provenance: Robert Napier; his posthumous sale, Christie's, London, 18 April 1877 (lot 1077); bought T.M. Whitehead on behalf of the Royal Museum (acc.no.A.1877.20.48)

EDINBURGH, NATIONAL MUSEUMS OF SCOTLAND

A cast brass candlestick, turned, engraved and inlaid with silver; it has a broad convex moulded base with concave waist and generous drip pan supporting a vase-shaped nozzle.

This profile of candlestick finds parallels in bronzes made by Giuseppe de Levis of Verona and by Roccatagliata in Venice in the last quarter of the sixteenth century. It may have been made by an Islamic craftsman in Venice, but is more likely to have issued from a workshop in Syria or Egypt, made specifically for export to Venice.

Veneto-Saracenic LATE SIXTEENTH CENTURY

223 ❧ *A Round Brass Box and Cover Engraved with Interlaces*

5 × 12cm

Provenance: With Mackay and Chisholm, Edinburgh; from whom purchased by the Royal Museum, 1880 (acc.no.A.1880.13.3 & A)

EDINBURGH, NATIONAL MUSEUMS OF SCOTLAND

The box is of cast brass, turned and engraved with foliate medallions, quatrefoils and interlaces inlaid with silver and black pitch. The differences in the decorative designs and in the quality of execution reveal that the lid and container come from two different boxes and are a later 'marriage'. Both parts were probably made in Egypt for the Venetian trade. This sort of metalwork was thought previously to have been made in Venice by Islamic craftsmen, the so-called Azzimini.[1]

Venetian LATE FIFTEENTH CENURY

224 ❧ *A Copper Dish with Enamelled and Gilt Decoration*

46.9cm diameter

Provenance: Baron Gustave de Rothschild; purchased by Sir William Burrell, 1937; by whom presented to the City of Glasgow, 1944 (acc.no.26.21)

GLASGOW MUSEUMS: THE BURRELL COLLECTION

This copper dish has repoussé decoration picked out in coloured enamels (rich blue, green, turquoise, white and red) and fine gilded detailing. The reverse is enamelled in blue, aubergine and white, sprinkled with gilt stars and a band of grouped stylised leaves. In the centre of the dish is a rivet-attached enamelled disk displaying a stylised sprig of laurel and the motto 'VT LAVRVS VIRTVS'.

The dish may have been designed originally with a central well emplacement to take a matching ewer, in which case the enamel disk depicting a laurel tree with a motto may have been added later when the dish was adapted for decorative purposes.

Very little research has been undertaken on Venetian enamels of this type, which seem to have been made from the last quarter of the fifteenth century until the second decade of the sixteenth.[1] The shapes often follow those of contemporary northern repoussé brass work, while the decoration is similar to contemporary Venetian glass. A fine Venetian enamel dish of about 1500 was in the collection of the late Lord Perth. One of the largest groups of Venetian enamels is in the Cini Collection at the Palazzo Loredan a San Vio, Venice.

Venetian (Murano) *c.*1500

225 ❧ *A Clear Glass Tazza Decorated with Florets*

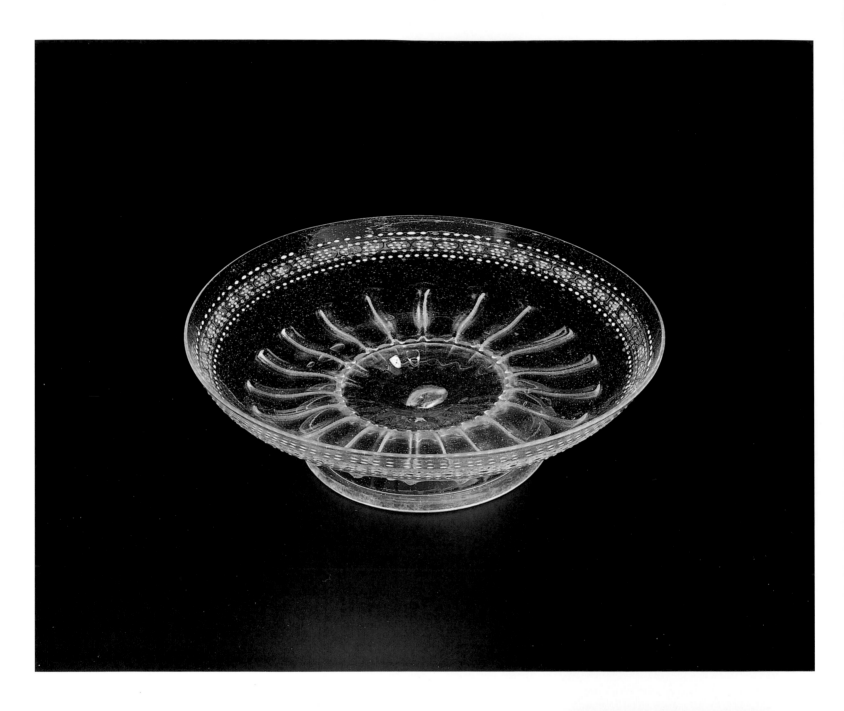

6.6 × 23.7cm

Provenance: With Salviati & Co., Venice; from whom purchased by the Royal Museum, 1873 (acc.no.A.1873.23.49)

EDINBURGH, NATIONAL MUSEUMS OF SCOTLAND

This dish or *tazza* has a spreading foot with a folded rim. Vertical ribbing is decorated with a band of florets below the rim and enamelled in dots of blue, red and pink and partly gilded. Another very similar *tazza* is in the British Museum.[1]

Fig. 259 | Andrea del Sarto, detail showing glass bowl from his *Portrait of Domenico di Jacopo Becuccio, called 'Becuccio Bicchieraio'* Edinburgh, National Gallery of Scotland

Venetian (Murano) *c*.1500

226 ✿ *A Clear Glass Dish with Twelve Ribs Extending out from the Centre in the Form of the Sun's Rays, with a Folded Rim*

6.4 × 39cm

Provenance: With Salviati & Co., Venice, from whom purchased by the Royal Museum, 1873 (acc.no.A.1873.23.61)

EDINBURGH, NATIONAL MUSEUMS OF SCOTLAND

Probably Venetian (Murano) *c*.1500–1520

227 ✿ *A Clear Glass Bowl on a High Foot decorated with Dark Blue Trails*

15.2 × 26.6cm

Provenance: With Salviati & Co., Venice; from whom purchased by the Royal Museum, 1873 (acc.no.A.1873.23.67)

EDINBURGH, NATIONAL MUSEUMS OF SCOTLAND

The bowl is on a high spreading ribbed foot, the folded rim of which is decorated with a dark blue trail; there is another trail about three centimetres below the rim and a third forming the folded foot.

Very similar bowls are in the British Museum[1] and in the Museo Vetrario, Murano.[2] The bowl is similar to a vessel in the foreground of Andrea del Sarto's *Portrait of Domenico di Jacopo Becuccio, called 'Becuccio Bicchieraio'*, a Florentine maker of glass vessels, in the National Gallery of Scotland (fig.259).[3] As Florence was certainly a centre of glass manufacture, with the Medici glass house then situated to the north of the Palazzo Medici gardens at San Marco, it is possible that the dish in the Sarto portrait is indeed not Venetian but Florentine.[4]

Venetian (Murano) *c.*1500–20

228 ❧ *A Clear Glass Bowl on a Tall Foot*

17 × 28.1cm

Provenance: Charles Davis, London; by whom
presented to the Royal Museum, 1905
(acc.no.A.1905.392)

EDINBURGH, NATIONAL MUSEUMS
OF SCOTLAND

A shallow bowl with gently flaring sides and
folded rim resting on a tall waisted folded foot;
decorated below the rim with a fish-scale motif,
gilded and enamelled with dots of blue, red and
green.

Illustrated opposite

Venetian (Murano) *c.*1513–34

229 ❧ *A Clear Glass Dish Enamelled with Medici Papal Arms*

7 × 24.5cm

Provenance: Sale Sotheby's, London, 28 June
1971 (lot 164), bought by the Royal Museum
(acc.no.A.1971.307)

EDINBURGH, NATIONAL MUSEUMS
OF SCOTLAND

A shallow dish on a low foot with spiral ribs
radiating from the centre towards the border, the
rim is decorated with a broad frieze of fish scale,
which is gilded and enamelled with dots of blue,
red and white. In the centre are the arms of a
Medici pope: either Leo X (Giovanni de' Medici,
1513–21) or Clement VII (Giulio de' Medici,
1523–34).

Several dishes of this pattern with Medici
arms are recorded: examples are in the
Kunstmuseum, Dusseldorf, the Metropolitan
Museum, New York (two, one of them in the
Lehman Collection), the British Museum, and
the Corning Museum of Glass.[1] There is a
variation in the painting of the heraldry, with
some appearing with the crossed keys partly
hidden by the shield. Another dish of this shape
and similar decoration, but with the lion of St
Mark in the centre, is in the British Museum.[2]

Venetian (Murano) THIRD QUARTER OF THE SIXTEENTH CENTURY

230 ❦ *A Glass Plate with Diamond Point Engraved and Gilt Decoration*

26.5cm diameter

Provenance: Earl of Clanwilliam; H. Hübner; from whom purchased with the aid of the Local Museums Purchase Fund and the National Art Collections Fund (acc.no.E.1980.64)

GLASGOW MUSEUMS: ART GALLERY AND MUSEUM, KELVINGROVE

The plate is of clear glass with a shallow centre with a slight kick and a broad folded rim. Three concentric bands of granular gilding bordered with trailed *lattimo* threads separate three bands of diamond-point engraving. Of these, the inner band features satyrs and cornucopias, the middle one, eagles on swags suspended from lion masks, and the outer one, arch and feather decoration.

Only five other examples of this type of plate are known to exist: two in the British Museum,[1] and one each in Cologne,[2] Liège and Toledo, Ohio. Related plates are recorded with the arms of Pope Pius IV (Pope 1559–66).[3]

Venetian (Murano) MIDDLE *or* SECOND HALF OF THE SIXTEENTH CENTURY

231 ❦ *A Clear Glass Goblet on a Foot*

10.8 × 15.5cm

Provenance: With Salviati & Co., Venice; from whom purchased by the Royal Museum, 1873 (acc.no.A.1873.23.3)

EDINBURGH, NATIONAL MUSEUMS OF SCOTLAND

The goblet has a semi-circular bowl with a narrow stem, a knop and a folded foot. There are traces of a gilded border to the rim and striped gilding on the knop. This is the sort of glass goblet held by figures in Veronese's various versions of *Christ in the House of Levi*.

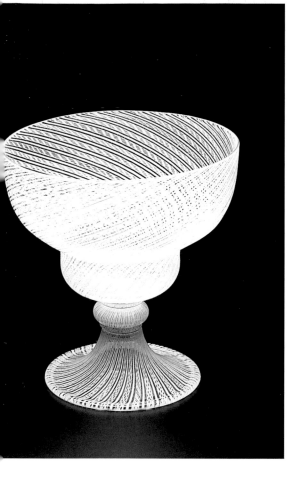

Venetian (Murano)

LATE SIXTEENTH CENTURY

232 ❧ *A Goblet with 'vetro a retorti' Decoration*

13.7 × 12.5cm

Provenance: Robert Napier; his posthumous sale, Christie's, 4 June 1877 (lot 2388); bought T. M. Whitehead on behalf of the Royal Museum (acc.no.A.1877.20.78)

EDINBURGH, NATIONAL MUSEUMS
OF SCOTLAND

Venetian (Murano) *c.1600–30*

233 ❧ *A Wine Glass with Baluster Stem*

15 × 9.9cm

Provenance: With Salviati & Co., Venice; from whom purchased by the Royal Museum, 1873 (acc.no.A.1873.23.6)

EDINBURGH, NATIONAL MUSEUMS
OF SCOTLAND

Venetian (Murano) *c.1600–30*

234 ❧ *A Funnel-shaped Drinking Glass*

15 × 7.9cm

Provenance: With Salviati & Co., Venice; from whom purchased by the Royal Museum, 1873 (acc.no.A.1873.23.20)

EDINBURGH, NATIONAL MUSEUMS
OF SCOTLAND

The bowl is of hemispherical form leading into a compressed bulb and supported by a knop between clear mereses and a folded spreading foot.

'Vetro a retorti' is a luxury filigree glass technique developed in Venice in the second quarter of the sixteenth century. It consists of spiralling, opaque white canes embedded in the colourless glass matrix.

A similar goblet, but with a shaped bowl, is in the British Museum.[1]

This is a 'cristallo' conical bowl wineglass with baluster stem and folded foot.

This is a 'cristallo' funnel-shaped drinking glass with a baluster stem.

Probably Veneto *c.1500–50*

235 ❧ *An Inkpot in the Form of a Tortoise or Terrapin*

Slipware with 'sgraffito' decoration
8 × 10 × 11.2cm

Provenance: With Guggenheim, Venice;[1] from
whom purchased, 1873 (acc.no.A.1873.47.5)

EDINBURGH, NATIONAL MUSEUMS
OF SCOTLAND

The inkpot is in the shape of a tortoise or
terrapin, with a flat, oval-shaped base, an oval
dome for the shell and a short, flared, narrow
neck at the top, which is the aperture for quills.
It has four applied short feet and the tail and
head are incised with details. Two volutes extend
between the head and tail to form a handle. It is
modelled in rich dark brown earthenware
covered with a white slip incised and cut, and the
decoration picked out in green, blue and yellow
clear lead glaze. It is decorated with scrolling
leaves and tendrils and there are two bands of
incised dashes with dots in the centre on the
handle and neck edge. Two of the feet are broken,
and the neck and edge of the body are chipped.[2]

A similar inkpot in the British Museum is
dated 1525 and relates to pieces found in the
Venetian Lagoon.[3]

Ceramics of curious or sophisticated form
such as this were often copied, via bronzes, from
artefacts originally conceived to be executed in
precious metal. Small bronze tortoises and
terrapins, many probably cast from life, and
apparently made in Padua in the early sixteenth
century, are in the Palazzo Venezia, Rome, the
Hermitage, St Petersburg, the Boijmans-van
Beuningen Museum, Rotterdam and in a private
collection in Germany, while another, ascribed to
Severo da Ravenna, is in Padua.[4]

The design resembles a drawing by Giulio
Romano (1499–1546) for a salt cellar, which was
probably intended to be cast in silver for the
Gonzaga Court at Mantua (fig.260).[5]

Fig.260 | Giulio Romano, *Design for a Salt Cellar
in the Shape of a Tortoise or Terrapin*
Chatsworth, The Duke of Devonshire and the Trustees of the
Chatsworth Settlement

Probably Veneto *c.1530–40*

236 ❧ *A Flask in the Form of a Scallop Shell*

Slipware with 'sgraffito' decoration
21 × 17.9cm

Provenance: Stefano Bardini, Florence; his sale
Christie's, London, 5–7 June 1899 (lot 119 or
123), bought by the Royal Museum
(acc.no.A.1899.130)

EDINBURGH, NATIONAL MUSEUMS
OF SCOTLAND

The flask is moulded in the form of a shell, on an
oval base with a short cylindrical narrow neck
and four applied loop handles. The red-brown
earthenware is covered with white slip, incised
and cut away, with the details picked out in
green, blue and yellow, clear lead glaze. It is
decorated with scrolling foliage, modelled lion-
mask heads on each handle, and triangular motifs
with dashes on the neck and lower foot.[1]

This shape is unusual for a ceramic flask, and
is probably based on embossed leather ('cuir-
bouilli') pilgrim flasks, the scallop shell form
being the badge of St James of Compostela,
patron of pilgrims.

Similar pottery examples are in the Victoria
and Albert Museum.[2] The same vertical lines of
scrolling foliage can be seen on a flask in the
Museo Civico di Palazzo Schifanoia, Ferrara,
where it is described as East Emilian, second half
of the sixteenth century.[3]

Probably Veneto 1564–1600

237 ❧ *A Basin with Abimelech Restoring Sarah to Abraham*

Slipware with 'sgraffito' decoration | 9.4 × 45cm

The basin is set on a short recessed foot. It is of dark brown earthenware covered (except on the base) with a white incised slip, picked out in green, blue, orange and purple clear lead glaze. The subject of the decoration is Abimelech restoring Sarah to Abraham. In the centre Abraham stands accepting a bag of gold held out by Abimelech, and with the other hand he indicates Sarah, who stands in profile with a greyhound seated at her feet, and two oxen, sheep and servants behind. The encounter takes place on a pavement in an architectural setting with small figures leaning over a balcony above.

The base of the building, on the left, is inscribed, 'ABRAAMO GENESI', the base of a column to the right 'REBECHA–CAPI. 20' and there is an inscription beside the central steps 'RE ABIMELH'. The basin is also inscribed on the underside: 'DE GENESI C.XX INGERAR. FINGE. ABRAAME LA PAURA / CHE SARA ESUA. NON MOGLIE MA / SORELLA. ABIMELECH INTROALLE REGIE MURA SER / P[R]ESA GODER LA DONA BELLA MA[...]LM / HUOI[?] GUISTO CURA MINA CANDO[...]TE AL / RE FAVELLA COSI SALV. A MENDUEL LASCIA FORI ET / DATI L LOR[?]O BSTIAMIA [R]GNE NTO E ORO'

Restored and repainted in three sections on the guilloche rim and on a patch in the centre.

Provenance: With Guggenheim, Venice; from whom purchased, 1873 (acc.no.A.1873.47.4)

EDINBURGH, NATIONAL MUSEUMS OF SCOTLAND

Abraham tried to pass on his wife Sarah to Abimelech, King of Gerar, by pretending she was his sister. When God told Abimelech before the marriage he returned Sarah and her dowry to Abraham. 'And Abimelech took sheep, and oxen and men servants and women servants and gave them unto Abraham, and restored him Sarah his wife' (Genesis 20).

The figures are copied from a woodcut by Pierre Eskrich that appeared in the Italian, and French, editions of *Figure de la biblia illustrate de Stanze Tuscane per Gabriele Simeoni* and *Figures de la Bible, Les verses par Gueroult*, published by Guillaume de Roville in 1564. The inscription on the underside of the basin is lifted from the printed text of the Italian edition (fig.261).

The setting shows a knowledge of Sebastiano Serlio, for example the *Tragic scene* woodcut from his *Libro primo d'architettura* (Venice, 1551, fol.29v). Detailed narrative scenes of this kind are uncommon on earthenwares decorated *a sgraffito*. The potter was obviously hoping to compete successfully with contemporary rival potters who were producing *istoriato* (figure-painted) maiolica. There is an *istoriato* painted dish in the Victoria and Albert Museum of the same obscure subject, which is possibly Venetian in origin, and dated 1576.[2]

Fig.261 | Pierre Eskrich, *Abimelech Restoring Sarah to Abraham*, woodcut from Guillaume de Roville, *Figure de la biblia illustrate de Stanze Tuscane per Gabriele Simeoni*, 1564

397

Workshop of Domenico da Venezia VENICE 1520/25–1569/74 VENICE

238 & 239 ✦ Two Vases of 'Vaso a bombola' Form with Decoration 'a frutti'

Maiolica decorated in colours | 36 × 29cm

Provenance: Probably Alexander William, Lord Lindsay, later 25th Earl of Crawford and 8th Earl of Balcarres (1812–1880)

PRIVATE COLLECTION

The vases are of generous form with swelling body and narrow base and neck, painted in vivid blue, green, yellow and orange-brown with branches of fruit and foliage against a white ground. Above the base and below the neck there is a broad orange-brown band bordered with blue stripes. The base is flat with no foot rim and the clay pale buff in colour.

Such vases, richly decorated with fruit, date from the early 1560s and are thought originally to have contained conserved fruits or marmalade. They were used as containers for export especially to the Low Countries, which explains why Delft potters copied both their form and decoration.[1]

Domenico da Venezia signed a dish now in the Schlossmuseum in Berlin, a drug pot in Frankfurt-am-Main, and three dishes in the Herzog Anton Ulrich-Museum, Brunswick. One of the latter is signed and inscribed 'al ponte selo p[er] andar a san polo', while another is signed 'Domenego Becer feci'. In a document of 1547 Domenico is described as 'depentor over bochaler' (painter or rather potter), which has led to the suggestion that he was not only a potter but perhaps also a painter on canvas.[2]

A set of vases 'a bombola' by Domenico, but decorated with trophies and dated 1562, are in the Museo Regionale, Messina.[3]

Workshop of Domenico da Venezia VENICE 1520/25–1569/74 VENICE
240 ❧ *A Jar with Putti in Cartouches*

Maiolica decorated in colours | 29 × 28.1cm
*c.*1560–70

Provenance: Robert Napier; his posthumous sale
Christie's, London, 4 June 1877 (lot 2482), bought
by the Royal Museum (acc.no.A.1877.20.118)

EDINBURGH, NATIONAL MUSEUMS
OF SCOTLAND

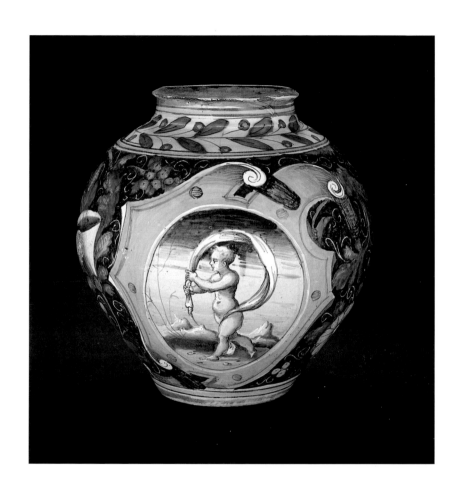

The jar has a bulbous body tapering to a slightly
flaring mouth, and is painted in dark blue, light
green, yellow, orange, purple, black and white. It is
decorated on one side with a cartouche showing
cupid lying in the centre holding a ball aloft; on the
other side there is another cartouche with a cupid
holding a billowing sail aloft, with a tree and
mountains on the horizon. Both are allegories of
fortune. Between the cartouches the dark blue
ground is incised with scrolling lines revealing the
white ground beneath.[1]

The cupid and strapwork decoration on this jar
are similar to those found on the series of jars made
for the apothecary of the Grande Ospedale in
Messina.[2] One of these, now in the Museo
Nazionale in Messina, is similar in shape and style
to the present example, and is signed 'Domenego da
Uénezia, 1562', one of the few signed pieces from
this prolific workshop.[3]

Workshop of Domenico da Venezia VENICE 1520/25–1569/74 VENICE
241 ❧ *A Plate with Nymphs, a Satyr and Cupid in a Landscape*

Maiolica decorated in colours | 3.6 × 24.8cm
*c.*1565–70

Provenance: H.S. James; sale, Dowells, Edinburgh,
1878 (date unrecorded), bought by the Royal
Museum (acc.no.A.1878.13.20)

EDINBURGH, NATIONAL MUSEUMS
OF SCOTLAND

The shallow plate has a flattened convex centre and
broad sloping border and is painted in dark blue,
green, orange, purple, black and white. It is
decorated with a satyr chasing a nymph and Cupid
is depicted with his bow, talking to a seated woman,
set against a wild mountainous landscape with a
distant city to the right. The rim is edged with
orange.[1]

This work relates to a whole series of Venetian
plates decorated thematically on the subject of love,
showing Cupid, satyrs, nymphs and various female
figures.[2]

Workshop of Domenico da Venezia, or possibly Urbino

242 ❧ *A Dish with a Soldier and Two Women Praying to an Idol*

Maiolica decorated in colours | 6.3 × 24.3cm
*c.*1560–70

Provenance: Robert Napier; his posthumous sale
Christie's, London, 4 June 1877 (lot 2462),
bought by the Royal Museum
(acc.no.A.1877.20.98)

EDINBURGH, NATIONAL MUSEUMS
OF SCOTLAND

The shallow dish has an upturned rim on a low
foot and is painted in dark blue, yellow, orange,
green, black and white. It is decorated with an
image of a kneeling woman praying to a small
male statue; a soldier and a woman stand together
behind her; a mountainous landscape with a
castle in the left background and a lake to the
right. A thin yellow band on the border extends
over rim to the underside. The dish is inscribed in
the centre of the underside in dark blue: '*lidolo*'
('the idol'). Broken and made up in one small area
in the rim.[1]

This dish relates thematically to a series on the
subject of love, some of them inscribed, and
described as the 'Triumph of Venus'. The setting,
although generalised, is reminiscent of the area
around Bracciano, north of Rome. The figures
are clearly copied from an unidentified print,
which was also the source for another Venetian
dish in the Fitzwilliam Museum, Cambridge,
inscribed on the reverse '*rapimento di giganti*'
(Raped by Giants).[2] Other similar dishes are in
the Herzog Anton Ulrich-Museum, Brunswick.[3]

Probably Workshop of Domenico da Venezia   VENICE 1520/25–1569/74 VENICE
243 ❧ *A Bowl with the Triumph of Galatea*

Maiolica decorated in colours | 25 × 42.1cm
1567

Provenance: Auguste Ricard de Montferrand, St
Petersburg; sold London, Christie's 14–16
November 1859 (lot 364), bought J.C. Robinson
for the Royal Museum (acc.no.A.510.12)

EDINBURGH, NATIONAL MUSEUMS
OF SCOTLAND

The bowl has a large curved body, flaring slightly
to the rim with a recessed spreading foot. It is
painted in dark blue, light green, orange, yellow,
purple and brown and decorated with a scene of
the triumph of Galatea. She stands in the centre
with a female attendant on the left, both of them
on dolphins. Below a putto rides a dolphin
holding his reins; behind a sea monster swims
with a nereid, naked but for billowing drapery; to
the right a youthful triton blows into a conch
shell, with a second young triton to the left
brandishing a trident. Above are two winged
putti, one shooting arrows at Galatea, while
overhead, a putto flourishes a laurel wreath. The
bowl is dated on the underside in purple: '1567'.
The bowl is chipped, patched and repainted in

several places, notably on the foot, outer walls
and inner bowl and extensively repainted in the
centre of the bowl. There is a single unrepaired
crack extending from the rim to the centre.[1]

Galatea, a sea nymph, was loved by the youth
Acis. He, however, was killed by the cyclops,
Polyphemus, who was obsessed by his unrequited
love for Galatea (Ovid, *Metamorphoses*: book
XIII, 750–897).

A similar bowl, with the same type of
decoration on the outside, was sold at the
Somerhill sale, Sotheby's, London, June 1981 (lot
423), attributed to the Venetian School.
However, the scene of Diana and Actaeon in the
centre was painted by a different painter, as were
the scrolling branches of fruit.

School of Pesaro, painted by the 'Zenobia painter' *c.1550–60*

244 ❧ *A Dish with Joseph sold by his Brothers into Slavery* (after a design by Battista Franco)

Maiolica decorated in colours | 5.1 × 32.5cm

Provenance: Auguste Ricard de Montferrand, St Petersburg; his sale, Christie's, London, 14–16 November 1859 (lot 310), bought by J.C. Robinson for the Royal Museum (acc.no.A.510.13)

EDINBURGH, NATIONAL MUSEUMS OF SCOTLAND

The dish has a wide depression and narrow sloping border. It is painted in pale blue, green, yellow, orange, dark orange, dark brown, black and white and decorated with a scene of Joseph being handed over by his brothers to five Ishmaelites, whose leader wears a distinctive tall hat. At the far left, in the middle ground, are two camels. To the right of the central, circular brick well, stand six of Joseph's brothers beneath a tree. The thin yellow band edging the rim extends to the underside, and there is a another yellow band on the underside below the border.[1]

Joseph's jealous brothers planned to murder him when he was sent to Dothan by their father, Israel, to mind sheep. One brother, Reuben, suggested that they hid Joseph in a pit, so that he, Reuben, could secretly save him. Whilst in the pit another brother, Judah, suggested they sell him as a slave for twenty pieces of silver to some passing Ishmaelites. Upon arrival in Egypt the Ishmaelites sold Joseph to Potiphar, an officer of Pharaoh and captain of the guard (Genesis 37: 17–28).

The 'Zenobia painter' is named after the scenes from the story of Zenobia, Queen of Palmyra, represented on two plates.[2] One of these bears a descriptive title on the underside;[3] the other, in the Victoria and Albert Museum, is decorated with the same subject and is inscribed and dated '*fato in Pesaro 1552*' (made in Pesaro). Two of the other plates in the group have figures whose facial characteristics and mannerisms are very similar to those on the present dish.[4]

The distinctive plump figures with short tunics, barefoot and with baggy trousers gathered at the knee, spread across the circular dish in a broad frieze, betray the style of their designer, Battista Franco. Venetian by birth, Franco spent much of his career in Rome and Florence as a painter and above all as a designer. He was employed by Guidobaldo II, Duke of Urbino, to design maiolica services for his factory at Castel Durante (modern Urbania). The designs were also used by other maiolica painters in the Marches at Urbino and Pesaro. Other drawings for a series of Joseph subjects by Franco have been identified.[5]

403

Italian, probably Venetian

SIXTEENTH CENTURY

245 ❧ *A Length of Velvet with Artichoke Patterns*

Pile-on-pile velvet, in a deep apricot coloured velvet and gilt metal thread (the metal thread wound round a silk core), with a Florentine artichoke pattern within ogives | 74.5 × 55.5cm

Provenance: With Mayorcas Ltd, London; from whom purchased by the Royal Museum, 1977 (acc.no.A.1977.155)

EDINBURGH, NATIONAL MUSEUMS
OF SCOTLAND

This sumptuous textile is of a historic type that probably originated in the early fifteenth century. Indeed, the pattern is similar to that worn by the Virgin Mary in the Bartolomeo Vivarini triptych in this exhibition (cat.no.1). So little contextual evidence survives about such textiles that this length should best be described as 'possibly' Venetian, but it might equally well be Spanish.[1]

Italian, possibly Venetian

LATE SIXTEENTH *or* EARLY SEVENTEENTH CENTURY

246 ❧ *A Length of Silk Woven with Pomegranate Devices*

Brocatelle silk, woven in orange silk, on a light grey ground, with a bold repeating design consisting of pomegranate devices contained in ogival panels, faded | 54.6 × 74.3cm

Provenance: R. Arditti; from whom purchased by the Royal Museum, 1930 (acc.no.A.1930.246)

EDINBURGH, NATIONAL MUSEUMS
OF SCOTLAND

Textiles of this type were made throughout Italy and although they are often described as Florentine they could equally well have been made in Venice, and would certainly have been worn in Venice. Textile manufacture and trade in silk velvet and samite (cloth of gold) was started in the early fourteenth century by Guelf exiles from the Republic of Lucca. The Lucchese obtained protection from the Servite Order and set up their own Scuola di Santa Croce (named after the miraculous Volto Santo crucifix at Lucca) in Rio terà della Maddalena at San Marcuola, while a 'confraternita dei tesitori di sete' (confraternity of silk weavers) had its seat in the Campo dell' Abbazia.[1]

Italian, possibly Venetian LATE SIXTEENTH or EARLY SEVENTEENTH CENTURY
247 ❧ *A Sample of Figured Silk Velvet with Running Scroll*

26 × 75cm

Provenance: With Hakky Bey, Paris; from whom purchased by the Royal Museum, 1891 (acc.no.A.1891.314)

EDINBURGH, NATIONAL MUSEUMS
OF SCOTLAND

As is the case with the other textiles in this exhibition, it is difficult to be categoric about the exact origin and date of this sample.[1] At the time of its purchase it was thought to be Florentine, *c*.1500.

Italian, possibly Venetian FIRST HALF OF THE SEVENTEENTH CENTURY
248 ❧ *A Red Velvet Border with Foliage Pattern*

Part of a red velvet ciselé band, or border, showing a repeated design of foliage and pomegranates on a wavy stem | 26.7 × 125cm

Provenance: Miss D. Hamilton, Edinburgh; by whom presented to the Royal Museum, 1963 (acc.no.A.1963.322)

EDINBURGH, NATIONAL MUSEUMS
OF SCOTLAND

A ciselé velvet is one with the main element in cut pile and with outlines and details in uncut pile. Previously thought to be sixteenth century, a slightly later date for this textile has recently been proposed.[1]

Venetian *c.1600–20*

249 ✾ *A Section of Cut Velvet*

Crimson velvet pile on a warp of couched yellow silk | 79 × 80cm

Provenance: Probably originally in the church of San Trovaso, Venice; purchased *c.*1970 in Venice

PRIVATE COLLECTION

A broad frieze of vertical oval foliate medallions is enclosed by interlaced 'C' scrolls beneath a narrow band of scales; below that is a shaped apron forming lappets consisting of 'D' shaped networks of lozenges enclosed by semi-circular wreaths of leaves. The yellow ground has been meticulously darned over many centuries. It was conserved by Sheila Landi of the Victoria and Albert Museum in about 1971.

Probably from the church known in Venice as San Trovaso (properly Santi Gervasio e Protasio), where other identical fragments still

form part of the sumptuous festive decorations of the nave, cladding the walls, wainscotting and pilasters. The velvet was probably supplied after 1583 when they began rebuilding the church, which had been burnt down. Around 1600–4, when the church was nearing completion, the altarpieces were supplied by Domenico Tintoretto, Pietro Malombra and Palma Giovane.[1] A velvet drapery somewhat resembling this appears in Veronese's *Venus, Cupid and Mars* (see cat.no.69).

APPENDIX I: ARTISTS' BIOGRAPHIES
INCLUDING PRINT DEALERS AND PRINT PUBLISHERS

SMALL CAPITALS are used to indicate cross-references within these biographies.

TIZIANO ASPETTI
1557/9–1606

Aspetti was from a dynasty of sculptors and bronze founders in Padua and presumably learnt his craft in the family workshop. He probably moved to Venice in 1577 where he was closely associated with Girolamo CAMPAGNA, with whom he may have completed his training. He soon gained the support of the powerful Patriarch of Aquileia, Giovanni Grimani, who employed him to restore antique marbles and who was probably instrumental in helping Aspetti secure a number of prominent public commissions in Venice in the later 1580s, among them for marble statues and reliefs for the Palazzo Ducale, the Mint and the Rialto Bridge. In the early 1590s Grimani commissioned a series of bronze figures from him for his chapel in San Francesco della Vigna and for the exterior façade of the church (the latter dating from later in the decade, after Grimani's death). Aspetti spent much of the 1590s executing works for his native Padua, including bronze reliefs for the Duomo and the prestigious commission for the bronze figures on the altar of the shrine of St Anthony in the Basilica del Santo. Most of his later career was spent in Tuscany, principally in Pisa, where he died. As with so many Paduan *bronzisti* of the Cinquecento, many small-scale bronzes are attributed to Aspetti and his workshop and he is also known to have made statuettes in silver.

Literature: C. Kryza-Gersch in Padua, 2001, pp.343–65; C. Kryza-Gersch in Boström, 2004, pp.95–7

See cat.no.211

JACOPO DE' BARBARI
active 1497–died before 1516

Barbari was a painter, engraver and designer of woodcuts. He was probably born in Venice, where he worked until about 1500. On 8 April 1500 he was appointed portraitist and miniature painter to the Emperor Maximilian I and was instructed to reside in Nuremburg. He subsequently worked in Saxony and the Netherlands. He died at Malines or Brussels before 1516. None of his prints is dated, apart from the 1500 woodcut map of Venice published by the Nuremburg merchant, Anton Kolb, which Barbari is believed to have designed (fig.3). He signed his engravings with a caduceus.

Literature: Hind, 1938–48, V, pp.141–58; Levenson, Oberhuber and Sheehan, 1973, pp.341ff.; Zucker, 1999, pp.1–47

Cat.no.127

FRANCESCO BASSANO (FRANCESCO DAL PONTE THE YOUNGER)
1549–1592

Son of JACOPO BASSANO, Francesco was the principal assistant in the family workshop from the early 1560s, and seems to have played a particularly important role in the execution and replication of his father's increasingly popular biblical genre pictures. In 1578 he moved to Venice, where he was immediately commissioned to paint four battle scenes for the new ceiling of the post-fire Sala del Maggior Consiglio in the Palazzo Ducale. In the 1580s he contributed to the history cycle in the same room, as well as to other major decorative projects in Venice, Brescia and Bergamo, while also continuing to practise the family specialism of genre pictures for private collectors. In 1591 he attempted suicide, and later died from his injuries.

Literature: Arslan, 1960; L. Alberton Vinco da Sesso in Turner, 2000, pp.140–1

See cat.no.72

JACOPO BASSANO (JACOPO DAL PONTE)
c.1510–1592

Named after his native town on the Venetian *terraferma*, Jacopo Bassano was the son of a minor local painter, Francesco dal Ponte the Elder, from whom he received his initial training. After a brief period as an assistant to BONIFACIO VERONESE (c.1533–5), Jacopo returned to Bassano and became a leading partner in the busy family workshop. There he remained for the rest of his long career, assisted from the 1570s by his three painter-sons, FRANCESCO the Younger, LEANDRO and Girolamo. Despite his choice of a small and provincial place of residence, Jacopo's style never ceased to evolve over a period of nearly six decades; despite his specialisation in subjects that called for rustic figures and settings, his art was conceptually and technically highly sophisticated. Although he received few commissions for public buildings in Venice, he enjoyed considerable success with Venetian collectors, especially from the mid-1560s onwards.

Literature: Arslan, 1960; Fort Worth, 1993; Aikema, 1996; L. Alberton Vinco da Sesso in Turner, 2000, pp.135–9

Cat.no.40; see also cat.no.101

LEANDRO BASSANO (LEANDRO DAL PONTE)
1557–1622

Son of JACOPO and younger brother of FRANCESCO BASSANO, Leandro was active in the family workshop from an early age, and became Jacopo's principal assistant after the departure of Francesco for Venice in 1578. Even after his own

move to the metropolis in 1588 – where he enjoyed considerable success as a painter of large-scale historical and religious paintings and of portraits – Leandro continued to produce replicas and variants of Jacopo's popular biblical genre compositions, and series such as the *Seasons* and the *Elements*. Although certain aspects of Leandro's style are distinctive and easily recognisable, the high degree of collaboration within the Bassano workshop often makes it difficult to distinguish his hand from that of Francesco and the other members of the family.

Literature: Arslan, 1960; L. Alberton Vinco da Sesso in Turner, 2000, pp.141–2

Cat.nos.74–6, 120; see also cat.nos.73, 80

BATTISTA DEL MORO (GIOVANNI BATTISTA ANGOLO DEL MORO)
c.1514–1573

Del Moro was a painter and etcher, born in Verona, the son-in-law and pupil of Francesco Torbido, il Moro, whose nickname he adopted. He was active in Verona and Venice, where he died. Some seventy-five individual etchings have been ascribed to him, to which must be added the series of *Twelve Caesars* (Bartsch, XVI, p.79, nos.1–12) and the *Compartments* (Bartsch, XVI, pp.83–91, nos 13–33), wrongly attributed by Bartsch to Andrea Schiavone.

Literature: Bartsch, XVI, pp.173ff.; Meyer, 1872–85, III, pp.36–9; Bury, 2003

Cat.no.148

FRANCESCO BECCARUZZI
1490/3–before 1563

Resident principally in the Venetian mainland city of Treviso, Beccaruzzi's career as a painter of altarpieces and frescoes for local churches is relatively well documented. Because much of this work is lost, his chronology remains obscure and attributions to him remain problematic. To judge, however, from an important surviving altarpiece such as the *Stigmatization of St Francis* of 1545 (Conegliano, Duomo), his chief sources of inspiration were locally available works by TITIAN, PORDENONE and PARIS BORDON.

Literature: G. Fossaluzza, 'Profilo di Francesco Beccaruzzi', *Arte Veneta*, XXXV, 1981, pp.71–83

Cat.no.39

BARTOLOMEO BELLANO
1437/8–1496/7

Bellano was one of the most important Paduan bronze sculptors in the second half of the fifteenth century. He was the son of a goldsmith, but the main influence on his style was that of Donatello, who was resident in Padua from 1443 to 1454. The young Bellano accompanied his

master on his return to Florence and assisted him on such late works in bronze as the statue of *Judith* and the San Lorenzo pulpits. After executing a bronze statue of Pope Paul II in Perugia in 1467, Bellano returned to Padua and was commissioned to execute reliefs for the reliquary cupboard in the sacristy of the Santo, his most important work in marble. Bellano's two outstanding commissions in bronze are the series of ten reliefs of scenes from the Old Testament executed between 1484 and 1490 for the exterior of the choir screen in the Basilica del Santo, and the *Monument to Pietro Roccabonella* of 1491–5 in San Francesco, Padua (dismembered, but most elements extant). It was probably Bellano who was responsible for introducing the art of the small bronze into Padua from central Italy.

Literature: V. Krahn in Turner, 2000, pp.153–5; V. Krahn in Padua, 2001, pp.63–91

Cat.no.179; see also cat.no.180

VALERIO BELLI
c.1468–1546

Belli was a gem-engraver, goldsmith and medallist from Vicenza, who was active principally in Rome at the papal court, briefly in Venice after the Sack, and, for the latter part of his career, in his native city. His real specialisms were cutting rock-crystal and gems, and carving dies for coins and medals. Amongst his most celebrated works is a silver-gilt casket with twenty-four engraved crystal scenes from the Passion of Christ, which was sent by Pope Clement VII to France to celebrate the marriage in 1532 of the future Henri II to Catherine de' Medici.

Literature: Burns, Collareta and Gasparotto, 2000

See cat.no.199

GIOVANNI BELLINI
c.1438–1516

Son of the painter Jacopo Bellini and younger brother of Gentile, from 1453 Giovanni was also the brother-in-law of Andrea Mantegna. Although his birth-date has traditionally been set around 1433, this may be about five years too early, since there exists good evidence that his earliest works date from around 1460, and that he continued working with his father until the mid-1460s. By the beginning of the 1470s he was generally recognised as Venice's leading painter of altarpieces and of smaller devotional works such as half-length Madonnas. Official recognition of his pre-eminent position in all branches of Venetian painting came in 1479, when he was appointed to work alongside his brother Gentile on the history cycle in the Sala del Maggior Consiglio in the Palazzo Ducale. Partly in response to the burden of work imposed by this appointment, Giovanni came to employ numerous assistants, and by about 1500 he stood at the head of what was probably the largest painter's workshop in fifteenth-century Italy. Despite the artistic revolution created by Giorgione during the first decade of the sixteenth century, Bellini continued to dominate artistic life in Venice up to the time of his death.

Literature: Robertson, 1968; Goffen, 1989; Tempestini, 1992; P. Humfrey in Turner, 2000, pp.166–78; Humfrey, 2004

Cat.nos.2–4; see also cat.nos.5, 17

LUCA BERTELLI
active 1564–1589

Bertelli was a book and print dealer and publisher active in Padua in the mid-1560s, and in Venice, where he had a shop at San Bartolomio. In 1578 he was described as 'Luca Bertelli fu de Ms Piero libraro a S. Bartholamio'. Bertelli published single-sheet prints from 1565, including prints by Agostino Carracci, Giacomo Franco and Martino Rota, and prints after designs by Michelangelo, Veronese, Titian, Domenico Campagnola, Raphael, Farinati, and Clovio; also maps, ornament prints and polemical prints.

Literature: Meyer, 1872–85, III, pp.702–3; F. Borroni in *Dizionario Biografico degli Italiani*, IX, 1967, pp.492–3; Borroni Salvadori, 1980, p.lxix, note 1

SIMONE BIANCO
active 1512–1553

Vasari states that Simone was Florentine, but all documents relating to him are from Venice and the Veneto, and seven of his busts are signed in Greek with variations on 'Simone Leukos [meaning 'bianco' or white] Venetos'. He is first documented in Treviso in 1512. Marcantonio Michiel records two works by Simone in the celebrated collection of Andrea Odoni in Venice. He knew Pietro Aretino and is mentioned several times in his correspondence. Aretino singled out for comment a bust of the wife of Nicolò Molino, possibly identifiable with a bust now in Berlin, which he had viewed with TITIAN and SANSOVINO. All of Simone's known works are idealised, *all'antica* portrait busts, mainly in marble, of the kind popularised by Antonio and Tullio Lombardo around the turn of the sixteenth century.

Literature: R.A. Branstator in Turner, 2000, p.204

Cat.no.193

NICOLÒ BOLDRINI
active 1547–1566

A woodblock cutter from Vicenza who was active in Venice, a marriage contract of June 1547 is the earliest reference to Boldrini. His only dated work is the 1566 *Venus and Cupid* after Titian. There are signed prints by Boldrini after

PORDENONE and DOMENICO CAMPAGNOLA. Both he and GIOVANI BRITTO are sometimes identified with the artist who used a monogram consisting of a B with a horizontal I through the centre.

Literature: Bartsch XII.126–9; Passavant, 1860–64, VI, pp.217–18; Washington, 1976, pp.236ff

Cat.no.132

BONIFACIO VERONESE (BONIFACIO DE' PITATI)
1487–1553

Known as Bonifacio (or Bonifazio) Veronese after his birthplace, he was resident in Venice as early as 1505; nothing further, however, is known of him until the mid-1520s, by which time he was practising a style closely related to that of his master PALMA VECCHIO. In 1529 he embarked on the principal commission of his career: an extensive series of canvases painted to decorate the many government offices housed in the Palazzo dei Camerlenghi at Rialto. Bonifacio evidently made use of a large team of assistants for this enterprise, with the result that his works are often variable in quality. However, on the positive side, his workshop appears to have provided the training ground for major painters of the younger generation, including JACOPO BASSANO, SCHIAVONE and JACOPO TINTORETTO.

Literature: Simonetti, 1986; T. Nichols in Turner, 2000, pp.1260–1; Cottrell, 2000; P. Cottrell, 'Corporate colors: Bonifacio and Tintoretto at the Palazzo dei Camerlenghi in Venice', *Art Bulletin*, LXXXII, 2000, pp.658–78

Cat.nos.31, 45, 49; see also cat.no.44

PARIS BORDON
1500–1571

Born in Treviso on the Venetian mainland, Paris came to Venice as a child and received his artistic education under TITIAN. By the 1520s he was producing his own versions of the whole range of domestic pictures popularised by Titian and PALMA VECCHIO (Holy Families in a landscape, half-length beauties, reclining nudes, and so forth), as well as church altarpieces. The climax of this earlier, Titianesque period was reached with the large-scale narrative canvas of the *Fisherman Delivering the Ring* (fig.4), painted for the Scuola di San Marco in Venice, and datable on external evidence to 1534–5. According to Vasari, Bordon visited the court of Francis I at Fontainebleau in 1538, where he received commissions from leading members of the French court; some recent scholars, however, have doubted this date, and have postponed the French visit to 1559–61. The matter obviously has important implications for a proper understanding of Bordon's still problematic chronology.

In the last decade of his life he seems to have withdrawn to his native Treviso, where he was active as a painter of altarpieces of increasingly feeble quality.

Literature: Canova, 1964; Fossaluzza and Manzato, 1987; C. Mandel in Turner, 2000, pp.230–3

Cat.nos.29, 30, 46–8, 50; see also cat.no.90

GIOVANNI BRITTO
active c.1543–1550

Britto was a German woodcutter and publisher active in Venice. His name appears in the colophon of the 1543 translation of Joannes Servilius's *La congiuratione de Gheldresi contra la città d'Anversa* by F. Strozzi, printed by Francesco Marcolini: 'In Vinegia per Giovanni Britto Intagliatore'. Two prints are signed in a similar manner: the woodcut *Portrait of Titian* (fig.224), and a view of Boulogne during the siege of 1549, both datable to around 1550. Both he and NICOLÒ BOLDRINI are sometimes identified with the woodcutter who signed himself with a monogram consisting of a B with a horizontal I through the centre, who was active in Germany from 1531 and in Venice from 1536.

Literature: F. Borroni in *Dizionario Biografico degli Italiani*, XIV, 1972, pp.351–2; Washington, 1976, pp.191–2

DOMENICO BRUSASORCI (DOMENICO RICCIO OR RIZZI)
c.1516–1567

One of the leading artists of mid-sixteenth-century Verona, Brusasorci was a painter of large-scale frescoes and altarpieces for the city and its surrounding region. He preceded his younger contemporary PAOLO VERONESE in introducing borrowings from Parmigianino and Giulio Romano into the local tradition, and remained more consistently attached to the fashionable style of Mannerism throughout his career.

Literature: Stefani Mantovanelli, 1979; D. Gisolfi in Turner, 2000, p.286

Cat.nos.92, 93

BENEDETTO CALIARI
1538–1598

The younger brother of PAOLO VERONESE, whom Benedetto had followed to Venice by 1556. Although responsible for some independent works, he was active principally as an assistant to his brother, collaborating on large-scale commissions and executing variants of his designs.

Literature: D. Gisolfi in Turner, 2000, p.306

Cat.no.121

GIROLAMO CAMPAGNA
1549–1621/5

Originally from Verona, where he was probably apprenticed to Danese Cattaneo, Campagna was one the most successful and prolific sculptors in both marble and bronze in late sixteenth- and early seventeenth-century Venice. His first major commission, completed in 1577, was to execute the last of the major reliefs for the shrine of St Anthony in the Santo in Padua, and he then won the competition for a new altar in the same chapel. The 1580s and 1590s brought a series of major commissions in Venice, including marble statues for the Palazzo Ducale, the balustrade of the Libreria Marciana and the Mint; two groups of the *Virgin and Child* for San Salvatore and San Giorgio Maggiore; and important large-scale bronze figures for the high altars of the latter church and of the Redentore. Campagna's success continued well into the following century; his last major work was the high altar of the Scuola Grande di San Rocco. He died, presumably in Venice, some time between 1621 and June 1625.

Literature: P. Rossi in Padua, 2001, pp.331–41; V. Avery in Boström, 2004, pp.238–40

DOMENICO CAMPAGNOLA
c.1500–1564

Campagnola was a painter, draughtsman, engraver and designer of woodcuts who was born in Venice of German parentage. He was the pupil of Giulio Campagnola (c.1482 – after 1515), whose name he adopted and from whom he inherited a life-long interest in printmaking. He spent most of the latter part of his career in Padua, where he is documented by 1531. All thirteen of his engravings bear the dates 1517 and 1518. He also designed a number of woodcuts, some of which are similarly dated 1517. Campagnola was a prolific draughtsman, making an important contribution to the development of landscape drawings in the manner of TITIAN; he was certainly more talented as a graphic artist than as a painter.

Literature: Bartsch, XIII, pp.377–87; Hind, 1938–48, V, pp.207–15; Washington, 1976, pp.120–75; Turner, 2000, pp.307–9

Cat.nos.88, 89, 128, 129

DOMENICO CAPRIOLO
c.1494–1528

Born in Venice and probably trained there in the Bellinesque tradition, Capriolo moved in about 1517 to the mainland city of Treviso, where he spent the remainder of his short career. His various signed and dated paintings, which include portraits, altarpieces and smaller devotional works, form the basis for the reconstruction of a larger oeuvre. Initially influenced chiefly by PALMA VECCHIO and SAVOLDO, Capriolo's style was later deeply affected by the presence in Treviso of PORDENONE.

Literature: Fossaluzza, 1983; M. Lucco in Turner, 2000, pp.316–17

Cat.no.21

JACOPO (GIAN GIACOMO) CARAGLIO
*c.*1505–1565

Caraglio was an engraver, goldsmith, gem-cutter and architect from Verona, who was also active in Rome in about 1524–7 and in Venice from about 1533; by 1539 he had left Italy for Poland and settled in Cracow. There he seems to have abandoned engraving and worked as a goldsmith, gem-cutter and architect. He was knighted in 1552.

Literature: Bartsch XV, pp.59ff; M. Cirillo Archer, *The Illustrated Bartsch*, 28, *Italian Masters of the Sixteenth Century: Commentary*, New York, 1995, pp.73–216

Cat.no.130

GIOVANNI CARIANI (GIOVANNI DE' BUSI)
*c.*1485–after 1547

Born near Bergamo and presumably trained there, Cariani moved to Venice before 1509. However, he subsequently returned to Bergamo for further periods of residence (1517–23; 1528–30), apparently in response to local commissions for altarpieces and portraits. Although there survives a reasonably large number of documented works, his chronology remains difficult to plot, largely because of a stylistic eclecticism that responded variously to Sebastiano del Piombo, TITIAN, PALMA VECCHIO, LOTTO and others. Capable of producing works of very high quality, Cariani was an erratic artist, and especially after about 1530 he descended into a mannered provincialism.

Literature: R. Pallucchini and G. Rossi, *Giovanni Cariani*, Milan, 1983; M. Lucco in Turner, 2000, pp.320–21; Bergamo, 2001

Cat.no.22

AGOSTINO CARRACCI
1557–1602

A painter, engraver and print publisher from Bologna, Carracci was also active in Venice, Rome and elsewhere. His first certain dated works in engraving are of 1576. He worked for Domenico Tibaldi in Bologna around 1579–81, but was established as an independent printmaker by 1582. In 1581 he may have been in Rome. He was in Venice in 1582 and again in 1588–9 and was back in Rome towards the end of the 1590s. Agostino produced single-sheet engravings after Peruzzi, Sammacchini, Correggio, Barocci, Vanni

and others, and developed particularly fruitful relationships in Venice with VERONESE and TINTORETTO (see cat.nos.151, 152). The latter was godfather to his son Antonio, born in 1589. He published many of his own plates; others were published by Tibaldi, Luca and Orazio Bertelli, Rascicotti and Florimi.

Literature: Bartsch, XVIII, pp.29ff; Washington, 1979; Bohn, 1995

Cat.nos.151, 153

VINCENZO CATENA
*c.*1470/80–1531

To judge from a number of signed works, Catena was a pupil and close follower of GIOVANNI BELLINI, whose designs for figures of Madonnas and Saints he regularly adopted. After about 1515 he became more responsive to the work of younger painters such as PALMA VECCHIO, especially in the landscape backgrounds to his devotional pictures – without, however, abandoning the Bellinesque basis of his style. Catena seems to have enjoyed considerable contemporary esteem as a portrait painter, and his sitters included leading humanists as well as Doge Andrea Gritti (London, National Gallery).

Literature: Robertson, 1954; P. Rylands in Turner, 2000, pp.347–9

Cat.nos.7, 8

GIOVANNI BATTISTA CIMA DA CONEGLIANO
1459/60–1517/18

A native of the *terraferma* town of Conegliano in the province of Treviso, Cima seems to have established himself in Venice by the mid-1480s, where he may have trained under Alvise Vivarini, and where he was to remain throughout his professional life. His major works consist almost exclusively of altarpieces, mostly representing the Virgin and Child enthroned with Saints, but also showing narrative scenes such as the *Incredulity of Thomas* of 1504 (London, National Gallery). The other main activity of his workshop was the production of small-scale panels for private devotion, such as half-length Madonnas, or representations of St Jerome in the desert (cat.no.10). Like his older contemporary GIOVANNI BELLINI, Cima had a particular talent for landscape painting, and his religious subjects typically show backgrounds of light-filled pastures, receding to distant blue mountains, and filled with naturalistic detail.

Literature: Humfrey, 1983; P. Humfrey in Turner, 2000, pp.373–8

Cat.no.10; see also cat.no.9

CORNELIS CORT
*c.*1533–1578

Cort was an engraver from Edam in the Netherlands. He was active in Antwerp around 1560–65; in Venice 1565–6; in Rome 1566–9; in Florence in 1569; in 1571 he was again in Venice and in 1572 back in Rome, where he died before 17 March 1578. His engravings after designs by TITIAN established his reputation in Italy (see cat.nos 142–5). There is some evidence that he may have tried to publish his own work in Rome in the 1570s. There were an unusually large number of copies made after his engravings by contemporary or slightly later printmakers (see cat.no.146), indicating the perception of the importance of his work (Sellink, 2000, I, p.xxvii).

Literature: Bierens de Haan, 1948; Sellink, 2000

Cat.nos.143, 144, 146; see also cat.no.145

DESIDERIO DA FIRENZE
active 1532–after 1545

He was a sculptor and founder of Florentine origin active in Padua. Only one work can be securely ascribed to him on the basis of documents, namely the *Voting Urn of the Greater Council of the Comune of Padua* (Padua, Museo Civico), for which Desiderio received a downpayment in 1532. In 1545 he was jointly commissioned with Tiziano Minio to execute the prestigious bronze cover for the baptismal font in San Marco, Venice, although their respective roles in this work remain to be clarified. A number of other elaborate bronze artefacts, such as the *Perfume Burner with a Satyr* recently acquired by the Ashmolean Museum, Oxford, as well as a group of small bronze statuettes with mythological and erotic subjects, can convincingly be ascribed to Desiderio.

Literature: Turner, 2000, pp.442–3; F. Pellegrini in Padua, 2001, pp.173–87

See cat.nos.189, 190

DOMENICO (DOMENEGO) DA VENEZIA
*c.*1520/25–1569/75

A maker of maiolica in Venice, he is described in the sources as both 'bocaler' and 'depentor', indicating that he was both a potter and a painter. He ran the most prolific maiolica workshop in Venice in the second half of the sixteenth century, specialising in broadly painted *istoriato* dishes and large storage jars with fruit and flower decoration. He is often known by the dialect form of his name, Domenego, with which he signed some of his wares. Some have his address on the back: 'on the stonemason's bridge on the way to S. Polo'.

Literature: Concina, 1975

See cat.nos.238–43

ORAZIO FARINATI
1559–1616

He was a painter and etcher from Verona, the son and collaborator of PAOLO FARINATI. He produced five etchings after his father's designs, two of which are dated 1583. By 1593 three of his plates were in the hands of the print dealer GASPARE DALL'OGLIO.

Literature: Bartsch, XVI, pp.168–72; Albricci, 1980; Boston, 1989, pp.63–5

Cat.no.150

PAOLO FARINATI
1524–1606

A leading painter of later sixteenth-century Verona, Farinati remained more faithful than his slightly younger contemporary VERONESE to the fashionable Mannerism of their youth. He was a highly prolific and accomplished draughtsman; eleven etchings are also attributed to him. Farinati's later career is particularly well documented thanks to the survival of his detailed account-book covering the years 1573 onwards.

Literature: Bartsch, XVI, pp.164–8; Puppi, 1968; Albricci, 1980; Boston, 1989, pp.61–3; D. Gisolfi in Turner, 2000, pp.499–500

Cat.nos.107–11, 149

BATTISTA FRANCO (GIOVANNI BATTISTA FRANCO, CALLED IL SEMOLEI)
*c.*1510–1561

A native Venetian, Battista moved at an early age to Rome, where he fell under the spell of Michelangelo. Most of his career was spent in Rome, Florence and the Marches, but around 1552 he returned to Venice, where he was commissioned to paint the *Baptism* for the chapel of Daniele and Marcantonio Barbaro in San Francesco della Vigna (see cat.nos.97, 98). In 1556–7 he contributed three roundels to the ceiling of the Library Reading Room, and in the later 1550s he also worked in the Palazzo Grimani at Santa Maria Formosa and in the Grimani chapel at San Francesco della Vigna. His work in that chapel was completed after his death by FEDERICO ZUCCARO. Franco was a prolific printmaker, usually reproducing his own designs in a combination of etching and engraving. An important group of his prints, which he seems to have published himself, dates from his late, Venetian period. Many of his plates were inherited by his natural son GIACOMO FRANCO.

Literature: Bartsch XVI, pp.109–72; M. Sica in Turner, 2000, pp.590–1; Maastricht, 2003, pp.136–43, 158–71

Cat.nos.97–100, 135–7; see also cat.no.138

GIACOMO FRANCO
1550–1620

The natural son and heir of BATTISTA FRANCO, he was a designer, engraver, printer, dealer and publisher of books and prints in Venice. He was described as 'Intagliator di rame' in the necrology of San Moisè; in his will he described himself as 'dessegnador'. He may have taken over his father's shop at Santa Fosca, but by 1595 he was established 'all'Insegna del Sole' in the Frezzeria. In 1579 a 'Jacopo Franco' was inscribed in the Arte dei Stampatori e Librari of Venice, and Giacomo was matriculated in the guild of Venetian painters from 1606–19. Giacomo's first dated print is from 1572 and he executed plates for NELLI, the BERTELLI and other publishers. He specialised in prints showing Venice, its life and customs. He inherited at least some of his father's plates and later acquired a number of plates that had originally carried the address of Orazio and Luca Bertelli (for example, Agostino Carracci engravings after Veronese and Tintoretto; see cat.nos.151, 152).

Literature: Cicogna, 1824–53, IV, 1834, pp.334–5, V, pp.431–44; Washington, 1979, p.497; C. Stefani in *Dizionario Biografico degli Italiani*, 50, 1998, pp.181–4

See cat.no.165

GIORGIONE
(GIORGIO DA CASTELFRANCO)
1477/8–1510

Ever since the first edition of Vasari's *Lives of the Artists* (1550), Giorgione has been universally acknowledged as the founder of the 'modern style' (that is, the High Renaissance) in Venetian painting. Giorgione's fame is based, however, on exceptionally little reliable contemporary information about his life and work, and from the sixteenth to the nineteenth centuries his name became associated with a very heterogeneous body of pictures. These included works in the present exhibition now attributed to painters as diverse as TITIAN (cat.no.13), GIOVANNI DA ASOLA (cat.no.16), ROMANINO (cat.no.24), SAVOLDO (cat.no.41), LOTTO (cat.no.32) and MORETTO (cat.no.43), as well as (but controversially) to Giorgione himself (cat.no.12). Today critics are agreed on his authorship of only a handful of pictures, including the *Laura* (fig.14), which is inscribed with the date 1506 on the back, and the *Tempest* and *Three Philosophers* (fig.13), both of which were recorded in Venetian collections as by Giorgione before 1543. However, it is obvious even from these that he was highly inventive in style, composition, technique and iconography, and it is equally clear that the characteristically mysterious and poetic mood of Giorgione's pictures exercised an extraordinary fascination for his contemporaries.

Literature: Paris, 1993; Anderson, 1997; P. Humfrey and M. Kemp in Turner, 2000, pp.664–75

See cat.no.12

GIOVANNI DA ASOLA
active 1512–1531

The work of Giovanni and of his son Bernardino is poorly documented, and the reconstruction of their careers remains controversial. But it is known that Giovanni reached Venice from his native Asola (between Cremona and Mantua) in about 1512, and there are good reasons to attribute to him a dated *Resurrection* of 1516 in San Francesco della Vigna (fig.90), together with a group of other works similarly influenced by GIORGIONE, TITIAN, ROMANINO and the Ferrarese painter Dosso Dossi.

Literature: Lucco, 1996–9, I, p.87, III, p.1295

Cat.no.16

GIROLAMO DA SANTACROCE
c.1480/5–c.1556

Documented as a pupil of Gentile Bellini, Girolamo evidently also had close contacts with the workshop of GIOVANNI BELLINI, whose designs he frequently replicated in his own altarpieces and domestic Madonnas. Despite his superficial accommodation of the styles of leading members of the younger generation such as TITIAN and PALMA VECCHIO, Girolamo perpetuated fifteenth-century stylistic habits into the middle of the sixteenth century.

Literature: A. Tempestini in Turner, 2000, pp.1473–4

Cat.no.20

JACOMETTO VENEZIANO
active 1472–1497

Virtually nothing is known of the life and works of Jacometto beyond what is said of him by the Venetian patrician and connoisseur Marcantonio Michiel, who recorded a number of small works by him in Venetian collections between 1520 and 1543. Only one of these works is now certainly identifiable: a *Portrait of Alvise Contarini*, and its pendant, *A Nun of San Secondo*, now in the Lehman Collection at the Metropolitan Museum of Art, New York (fig.79). Stylistically these show a close knowledge both of Flemish painting and of the art of Antonello da Messina, and they provide a basis for attributing a number of other works, mainly portraits, to Jacometto.

Literature: P. Humfrey in Turner, 2000, pp.821–2

Cat.no.6

VALENTIN LEFÈVRE
c.1637–1677

Lefèvre was a painter and etcher from Brussels who was active mainly in Venice. The official notification of his death, on 2 September 1677, states that he was about forty years old. An inventory of his possessions was drawn up on 5 September and, in his testament of 27 August 1677, fifty-two etched plates were left to Isabella, daughter of Giovanni 'Vuanbele fiamengo sartor', with the rider that she could dispose of them as she wished. Plates that were etched by Lefèvre were published posthumously in the *Opera Selectiora, quae Titianus vecellius Cadubriensis, et Paulus Calliari Veronensis inventarunt et pinxerunt*, published by Jacob van Campen in Venice in 1682. To accompany the plates, a small booklet was published entitled *Notitia dove si ritrovano li originali di Titiano et Veronese intagliati da Valentino le Febre di Bruscellles et publicati da Giacomo van Campen in Venetia 1683*, printed by Antonio Bosio.

Literature: Ruggeri, 2001

Cat.nos.158, 159

BERNARDINO LICINIO
c.1490–c.1549

Licinio belonged to the generation of Venetian painters whose careers began around the time of the death of GIORGIONE, and for whom both he and the young TITIAN were fundamental sources of inspiration. Licinio painted a large number of religious works, but his somewhat prosaic and literal style was arguably better suited to his portraiture.

Literature: Vertova, 1980; Turner, 2000, pp.874–5

Cat.no.23

LORENZO LOTTO
c.1480–1556/7

Lotto's career was one of constant movement. Born and presumably trained in Venice, perhaps under Alvise Vivarini, his earliest independent activity took place in Treviso (c.1503–6). In 1506 he moved to the Marches, and then in 1512 to Bergamo, where again he remained for several years. In 1525 he returned to Venice, but his residence there was interrupted by further extended visits to the Marches (1538–40) and to Treviso (1542–5). In 1549 he finally abandoned Venice for the Marches, where he died seven years later at Loreto. Lotto was active above all as a painter of religious subjects, but was also a painter of some of the most psychologically penetrating portraits of the sixteenth century.

Literature: Humfrey, 1997; Washington, 1997; D. Oldfield and L. Matthew in Turner, 2000, pp.919–25

Cat.nos.11, 32, 33, 83; see also cat.no.84

ALESSANDRO MAGANZA
1556–1632

Alessandro was the principal member of a family of artists, and one of the leading painters in Vicenza at the end of the sixteenth and beginning of the seventeenth centuries. His work is characterised by an eclectic synthesis of the styles of VERONESE, TINTORETTO and PALMA GIOVANE.

Literature: Vicenza, 1980, pp.106–20; M. Binotto in Lucco, 1996–9, II, pp.785–6

Cat.no.78; see also cat.no.124

PIETRO MALOMBRA
1556–1618

A native Venetian, Malombra was reportedly a pupil of GIUSEPPE SALVIATI, with whom he continued to share an interest in Roman painting, and in particular of Michelangelo, as well as in the local work of TINTORETTO. Closely involved in the large-scale redecoration of the Palazzo Ducale after the fires of 1574 and 1577, Malombra was also active as a painter of altarpieces, mythologies and celebratory mythological allegories.

Cat.no.122

MODERNO (GALEAZZO
MONDELLA)
1467–1528

Moderno was a medallist, gem engraver, and arguably the most accomplished maker of bronze plaquettes of the Italian Renaissance. He came from Verona and appears to have worked mainly there and for the Gonzaga court at Mantua to the west. His early style reflects the prevailing style in Verona and above all the art of Andrea Mantegna. Moderno and Antico (Pier Jacopo Alari-Bonacolsi) appear to have adopted their pseudonyms simultaneously in Mantua around 1487, the former indicative of his independence from classical models. Later in his career Moderno's most important patron was Cardinal Domenico Grimani, who helped foster a clientele for his work in Venice. A coherent group of twelve of his plaquettes is signed.

Literature: D. Lewis in Luchs, 1989, pp.105–41; D. Lewis in Turner, 2000, pp.1099–1100

Cat.nos.183, 184

MORETTO DA BRESCIA
(ALESSANDRO BONVICINO)
c.1498–1554

Moretto spent virtually the whole of his uneventful career in his native Brescia, practising above all as a painter of religious subjects for the churches of the city and its province. Occasionally he also received commissions from the neighbouring cities of Milan, Bergamo and Verona. His only non-religious pictures are portraits, largely of prominent members of Brescian society.

Moretto's work shows a clear preference for timeless, meditative themes over dramatic narratives and, as is increasingly recognised, it closely reflects the spirit of the Catholic Reform movement, in which Brescia played a prominent early role.

Literature: Brescia, 1988; A. Bayer in Turner, 2000, pp.1109–13

Cat.no.43

GIOVANNI BATTISTA MORONI
1520/4–1578

A native of Albino in the province of Bergamo, Moroni received his artistic education, presumably in the later 1530s or early 1540s, under MORETTO in Brescia. After an early career in Trento and perhaps other north Italian cities, he returned to his native region, settling first in Bergamo and then, after 1561, in his home town of Albino. Here, despite his provincial isolation, he enjoyed a highly successful career as a painter both of altarpieces for local churches, and of portraits of the local nobility and prosperous middle classes.

Literature: Gregori, 1979; F. Frangi in Turner, 2000, pp.1116–18; Fort Worth, 2000

Cat.nos.60, 61, 62

GIAMMARIA MOSCA
(IL PADOVANO)
c.1495/9–1574

Mosca was principally a sculptor in marble, but is known, earlier in his career, to have supplied models in terracotta, wax and plaster to be cast in bronze. He was a native of Padua, where he trained first in the workshop of the sculptors Giovanni and Antonio Minello (1507–12), and then with the goldsmith Bartolomeo Mantello. His earliest extant work, a bronze high relief of the *Beheading of St John the Baptist* (Padua, Duomo), dates from 1516 and was cast by the bronze founder Guido Aspetti, called Lizzaro, with whom Mosca collaborated periodically until Aspetti's death in 1528. During the 1520s Mosca spent periods living in Venice, and executed a number of commissions there. His most important commission during his Paduan years was for one of the series of large marble reliefs in the shrine of St Anthony in the Santo, the protracted and interrupted execution of which lasted from 1520 to 1529, and even then was completed by assistants. Another important relief of *The Judgement of Solomon* (Paris, Musée du Louvre) was carved in the mid-1520s for the Paduan philosopher Giambattista Leone, who presented it to the Englishman Reginald Pole. Around 1530 Mosca moved to Poland to work at the court of King Sigismund I, and was to remain there until his death over forty years later.

Literature: Markham Schulz, 1998; M. De Vincenti in Padua, 2001, pp.223–37

Cat.nos.191, 192

NICOLÒ NELLI
active 1552–died 1579/86

Nelli was an engraver, etcher, print dealer and publisher in Venice; in his will of 1570 he described himself as 'intagliator di stampe di rame'. He had a shop at the Rialto in 1570 and in 1574–6 his address was 'Al segno de l'arca di Noe'. On 19 February 1567 he was granted a privilege for a tree of the Ottoman Sultans (ASV, Senato Terra, filza 46, f.136v), and on 12 October 1569 he was granted a twenty-year privilege by the Venetian Senate for 'li dissegni suoi novi', which included geographical, 'popular' and devotional prints, portraits and histories (ASV, Senato Terra, filza 54). Nelli was the half-brother of GASPARE OSELLI. His first dated prints are from 1563 and he made prints for Ferrando Bertelli and provided illustrations for several books, including the *Naspo Bizaro* of Alessandro Caravia (1565). He issued series of prints on particular themes such as portraits, proverbs, and birds, and also published prints by Gaspare Oselli, Giovanni Battista Fontana, GIACOMO FRANCO and others.

Literature: F. Piloni, 'Nuovi contributi per Nicolò Nelli e Gaspare Osello', *Grafica d'arte*, 29, 1997, pp.8–9; F. Piloni, 'Nicolò Nelli: contributi per un catalogo', *Grafica d'arte*, 31, 1997, pp.7–14; Van der Sman, 1999, pp.2–9

GASPARE DALL'OGLIO
active 1593–1603

Gaspare was a printer and print dealer from Bologna, active in Brescia and Venice. His sons Ortensio and Ottavio married the daughters of JAN SADELER; there may have been a family connection with Camillo Procaccini, who married a Francesca dall'Oglio. Gaspare was responsible for publishing Francesco de' Marchi's book *Della architettura militare libri Quattro*, published in Brescia in 1599. He was recorded in Venice in November 1599. His address appears on plates by Annibale Carracci, ORAZIO FARINATI and Camillo Procaccini, but not usually on the first states. Orazio Farinati's *Crossing of the Red Sea* bears his address with the date 1583, later altered to 1593. It is possible that the earlier date should be taken seriously and Dall'Oglio's documented activity amended accordingly.

Literature: Albricci, 1980, pp.23–6; G. Dillon, S. Marinelli and G. Marini, *Museo del Castelvecchio, Verona. La collezione di stampe antiche*, Milan, 1985, p.33

GASPARE OSELLO
(GASPAR AB AVIBUS)
active 1557/8–1577

Osello was an engraver active in Venice and the half-brother of NICOLÒ NELLI. His first dated works are of 1557–8 (*Austriacae Gentis Imagines*). Quite a number of his prints are copies of earlier engravings by Giorgio Ghisi, Marcantonio and others.

Literature: S. Seccareccia, 'Gaspare Osello, contributi per un catalogo', *Grafica d'arte*, 27, 1996, pp.8–13; Van der Sman, 1999, pp.2–9; G. Streliotto, *Gaspar ab Avibus, incisore cittadellese del XVI secolo*, Cittadella, 2000

PALMA GIOVANE
(JACOPO PALMA IL GIOVANE)
c.1548–1628

The great-nephew of PALMA VECCHIO, Palma Giovane was the leading painter in Venice after the deaths of VERONESE and TINTORETTO. His formative years were spent at the court of Urbino and in Rome; when he returned to Venice in the early 1570s he was already a mature artist, practising a style at first reflecting the Roman late Mannerism of the Zuccaro, but then increasingly consisting of an eclectic synthesis of the major Venetian masters of the later sixteenth century. An immensely productive painter, Palma served the needs of counter-reformation religion in Venice by filling the city's churches and the meeting rooms of devotional confraternities with vast numbers of altarpieces and narrative cycles. He also played a major role in the large-scale redecoration of the Palazzo Ducale after the fires of 1574 and 1577.

Literature: Mason Rinaldi, 1984; P. Rylands in Turner, 2000, pp.1177–8

Cat.nos.81, 112–19, 154

PALMA VECCHIO
(JACOPO PALMA IL VECCHIO)
c.1480/90–1528

A native of Serina, near Bergamo, Palma appears to have settled in Venice by about 1510. As is evident from a number of references in the *Notebooks* of Marcantonio Michiel, and also from an inventory of the painter's studio compiled after his death, Palma specialised in pictures destined for a domestic context: Holy Families with Saints in a landscape, half-length female beauties, and reclining nudes. He also painted a number of altarpieces for churches in Venice, the Veneto and his native region. Once mature, Palma's style did not change greatly, and most of his works remain difficult to date with any precision.

Literature: Rylands, 1992; P. Rylands in Turner, 2000, pp.1174–7; Bergamo, 2001

Cat.no.82

PAOLO FIAMMINGO
(PAUWELS FRANCK)
c.1540–1596

A native of Antwerp, Paolo had reached Italy by 1573, and he probably settled in Venice in about 1580. There he seems to have worked first as a specialist in landscape backgrounds in the workshop of TINTORETTO, before gaining independent recognition as a painter of altarpieces, historical pictures and especially of mythological allegories.

Literature: Meijer, 1975; Mason Rinaldi, 1978

Cat.no.77

POLIDORO DA LANCIANO
1515–1565

A native of Lanciano in the Abruzzi, Polidoro had reached Venice by 1536, where he became a close follower of TITIAN. In the past a large number of Titianesque pictures have been attributed to him, but since only one securely documented work is known, the *Descent of the Holy Spirit* of 1545 (fig.106), many of these attributions have to be treated with caution.

Literature: T. Nichols in Turner, 2000, p.1268; Mancini, 2001

PORDENONE (GIOVANNI ANTONIO DE' SACCHIS)
c.1483/4–1539

Born and trained in the Friulian town from which he takes his name, Pordenone was above all a painter of large-scale murals for churches, and of altarpieces. After an early career spent in his native region on the Venetian *terraferma*, he began to receive a number of important commissions for churches in Lombardy and Emilia: at the cathedral in Cremona (1520–22); at Cortemaggiore near Piacenza (c.1529–30); and at the Madonna di Campagna, Piacenza (1530–35). From 1527 until his death in 1539 he resided mainly in Venice, where his most important works included fresco decorations, now largely lost, in the choir and semi-dome of San Rocco, in the cloister of Santo Stefano, and on the façade of the Palazzo d'Anna (see fig.229).

Literature: Cohen, 1996; P. Casadio in Turner, 2000, pp.1283–6

Cat.no.87

RICCIO (ANDREA BRIOSCO)
1470–1532

The son of a Milanese goldsmith, Riccio was probably born in Trent but was active mainly in Padua, where he was probably an assistant to BARTOLOMEO BELLANO. He worked mainly in bronze and in terracotta, and was an outstanding exponent of the art of the small bronze, specialising in poetic mythological and pagan figures and objects such as oil lamps. He completed Bellano's *Monument to Pietro Roccabonella* in 1498, and in 1506–7 he executed two bronze reliefs to complete the series of Old Testament scenes made by Bellano for the choir screen of the Basilica del Santo. Riccio's most important commissions were the monumental bronze *Paschal Candelabrum* made for the Santo (1507–16) and the *Monument to Girolamo and Marcantonio della Torre* for San Fermo, Verona (the bronze reliefs from which are now in the Louvre). Later in his career he executed some major works in polychrome terracotta, notably a *Virgin and Child* group for the altar of the Scuola del Santo, and a group of the *Lamentation over the Body of Christ* for the Paduan church of San Canziano, of which only fragments survive. Many of Riccio's patrons were among the leading scholars and humanists at the University of Padua.

Literature: C. Avery in Turner, 2000, pp.1338–42; C. Avery *et al.* in Padua, 2001, pp.93–129

Cat.nos.185–7; see also cat.no.188

NICOLÒ ROCCATAGLIATA
*c.*1560–*c.*1636

Nicolò was a Genoese sculptor, principally in bronze, who is documented in Venice in the 1590s and again in 1630s, but who was probably also active in his native city. His eighteenth-century biographer Soprani stated that he trained as a marble sculptor in Venice and was employed by JACOPO TINTORETTO as a maker of models. Only a few works can be attributed to Roccatagliata with any certainty. He executed a group of bronzes for San Giorgio Maggiore, Venice, in 1593–6, including statuettes of *St George* and *St Stephen* and two large candelabra. In 1633 he signed a bronze altar frontal in the church of San Moisè, executed jointly with his son Sebastiano. A signed standing *Virgin and Child* by Nicolò is in the Musée National de la Renaissance, Écouen. A large number of bronze statuettes, andirons, candlesticks, doorknockers and the like, of very variable quality, are attributed to his workshop.

Literature: C. Kryza-Gersch in Boström, 2004, pp.1436–8

See cat.nos.213, 215

GIROLAMO ROMANINO
1484/7–*c.*1560

Although based for most of his career in and around his native city of Brescia, Romanino was a frequent traveller to other artistic centres in northern Italy, from which he absorbed a wide range of heterogeneous influences. He had already visited Venice by about 1510, and a stay in nearby Padua in 1513–14 consolidated his interest not just in TITIAN, but also in the expressionistic art of Dürer. Highly gifted as a fresco painter as well as of altarpieces,

Romanino worked in Cremona in 1519–20 and in Trento in 1531–3, where he again came into fruitful contact with German art. Uneven as well as eccentric, Romanino was often also highly original as a painter.

Literature: Nova, 1994; A. Nova in Turner, 2000, pp.1361–3

Cat.nos.24, 85; see also cat.no.86

MARTINO ROTA
*c.*1520–1583

He was an etcher, engraver and print publisher from Sebenico, active in Venice, Graz, Vienna and Prague. Rota's earliest dated print is from 1558 although he probably worked in Venice until late 1572: plates of about 1571/2, with subjects related to the victory over the Turks at Lepanto seem to have been produced in Venice. Rota was producing portraits in Vienna by 1573 and in 1576 he was described as painter to Maximilian II. He went to Prague around 1580. His work in Venice was published by, among others, L. Guarinoni, Luca and Ferrando BERTELLI, Camocio, Giovanni Mastini, Benedetto Stefani, Claudio Duchetti (Duchet), NELLI, and Bolognino Zaltieri.

Literature: Bartsch, XVI, pp.245–85; M. Pelc, *Martin Rota Kolunica*, Zagreb, 1977

Cat.no.147

JAN SADELER
1550–1600

An engraver and print publisher from Antwerp, he was active there and in Cologne, Mainz, Frankfurt, Munich, Verona and Venice. He left Munich in 1595 and went to Verona, moving on to Venice with his brother RAPHAEL SADELER in 1596–7. He was granted an imperial privilege in 1581, which was renewed in 1593; a papal privilege followed around 1598.

Literature: Hollstein XXI, pp.83–190, XXII, pp.97–165; Sénéchal, 1987; Bassano, 1992, p.26

Cat.no.155

RAPHAEL SADELER
1560/61–1632

He was a painter, engraver and print publisher from Antwerp who, like his brother JAN SADELER, was active in Cologne, Antwerp and Munich. The two brothers moved from Munich to Verona in 1595 and then to Venice around 1596–7. In 1604 Raphael returned to Munich. A papal privilege protecting his prints was granted in about 1598.

Literature: Hollstein XXI, pp.213–65; XXII, pp.183–210; Sénéchal, 1987

Cat.no.156

GIUSEPPE SALVIATI (GIUSEPPE PORTA)
*c.*1520/5–after 1575

Born in the province of Lucca in Tuscany, Giuseppe Porta studied under Francesco Salviati in Rome and adopted his name, accompanying his master to Venice in 1539. After Francesco's departure in 1541, Giuseppe remained in the city, becoming one of the leading local exponents of Mannerism. He was active above all as a painter of large-scale public works, including a number of altarpieces for Venetian churches, and mythological allegories for the Palazzo Ducale and Marciana Library.

Literature: McTavish, 1981; R. Branstator in Turner, 2000, pp.1437–8

Cat.no.96

JACOPO SANSOVINO (JACOPO TATTI)
1486–1570

He was born in Florence and apprenticed to the sculptor Andrea Sansovino, whose name he adopted. After about five years in Rome studying antique sculpture (1506–11), Sansovino returned to Florence where he received some important sculptural commissions and also took up architecture. He returned periodically to Rome but after the Sack in 1527 he fled to Venice, and settled there permanently. Over the next four decades Sansovino played a central role in shaping sculpture and architecture in the city. He won powerful friends and patrons, among them TITIAN and Pietro Aretino, and was appointed to the post of *proto*, or chief architect, to the Procurators of San Marco. In that capacity he designed and supervised the construction of such celebrated landmarks as the Marciana Library, the Mint (Zecca), and the Loggetta at the base of the bell-tower; the bronze sacristy doors in San Marco and the marble statues of *Mars* and *Neptune* on the Scala dei Giganti in the Palazzo Ducale. He also designed important churches (San Francesco della Vigna, San Giuliano) and palaces (Palazzo Dolfin and Palazzo Corner, both on the Grand Canal) and also the buildings of the Fabbriche Nuove at Rialto. Many of the best sculptors in the second half of the Cinquecento trained in Sansovino's busy shop, notably ALESSANDRO VITTORIA.

Literature: Howard, 1975; Boucher, 1991; B. Boucher in Turner, 2000, pp.1465–70

See cat.no.94

GIULIO SANUTO
active 1540–after 1588

Sanuto was an engraver active in Venice and, at some time in the later 1540s or early 1550s, in Rome. His first dated print is from 1540. From 1557 he was engraving maps in Venice which were published by Giordano Ziletti and others.

Literature: Bartsch, XV, pp.499–501; Passavant, 1860–64, VI, pp.104–7; Edinburgh, 1990

Cat.no.139

GIOVANNI GIROLAMO SAVOLDO
*c.*1480/5–after 1548

Savoldo was presumably trained in his native Brescia, but by about 1520 he had settled in Venice. Although he received a number of commissions for altarpieces, most of his pictures consist of variations on Giorgionesque themes, and show single or small groups of figures in close-up, often in unusual and poetic lighting conditions (such as twilight, firelight or moonlight). The deeply meditated and conceptually inventive character of his art seems, in fact, to have been much appreciated by connoisseurs, both in Venice and Brescia. In modern Italian art historiography a lively debate has centred on the question of whether Savoldo should be regarded primarily as a Lombard painter, whose earthy naturalism foreshadows that of Caravaggio, or as a Venetian.

Literature: Gilbert, 1986; Brescia, 1990; Frangi, 1992; C. Gilbert in Turner, 2000, pp.1489–92

Cat.no.41

SCHIAVONE (ANDREA MELDOLLA)
*c.*1515–1563

A native of the Venetian colonial city of Zara (Zadar) in Dalmatia (hence his nickname, meaning Slavonian), Schiavone seems to have arrived in Venice in the mid- to late 1530s. Throughout his career he practised as an etcher as well as a painter and his earliest etchings, datable to around 1538, already show the strong influence of Parmigianino. A relatively large number of Schiavone's paintings are small-scale mythologies, presumably originally incorporated into domestic furniture; but he also painted altarpieces, organ shutters, and other large-scale religious pictures. Together with other leading Venetian painters of the mannerist tendency, Schiavone participated in the decoration of the ceiling of the Reading Room of the Marciana Library in 1556–7.

Literature: Richardson, 1980; F. Richardson in Turner, 2000, pp.1502–4

Cat.nos.56, 95

STEFANO SCOLARI
active 1644–1687

An etcher and print publisher active in Venice, with an address at San Giuliano, he acquired and reissued large numbers of older plates. For example, he owned many previously in the possession of GIACOMO FRANCO, the BERTELLI and Francesco Valegio; and several of the plates made by CORNELIS CORT after TITIAN. On a map of the Trevigiano, he is described as Stefano Mozzi Scolari. He was the publisher of *Viaggio da Venezia a Costantinopoli per mare e per terra e insieme quello di Terra Santa*.

Literature: R. Almagià, *Carte geografiche a stampa di particolare pregio e rarità dei secoli XVI e XVII esistenti nella Biblioteca Apostolica Vaticana*, (Monumenta Cartographica Vaticana II), Vatican City, 1948, p.118

SEVERO (CALZETTA) DA RAVENNA
*c.*1465/75–before 1538

The son of a Ferrarese sculptor practising in Ravenna, Severo is documented there in 1496 and was well established by 1500, when he received the important commission for a life-size statue of *St John the Baptist* for the Basilica del Santo in Padua – his only known work in marble. The style of his early works is strongly indebted to that of the Lombardo family, which has led to the suggestion that he may have spent some time in Pietro Lombardo's workshop in Venice. Severo is known above all as a modeller, caster and finisher of small-scale bronze statuettes and vessels, including saints, pagan deities and fantastic subjects such as sea-monsters. He was based in Padua from 1502–9 but returned to Ravenna following the upheavals of the War of the League of Cambrai. There he set up what appears to have been a hugely prolific workshop-foundry, in which versions and multiples of his own and other's models were produced in quantity. Little is known of his later career in Ravenna, but the recent re-reading of a document in the Mantuan archives has led to the important discovery that he supplied a figure of *Hercules* to Isabella d'Este, Marchioness of Mantua, in 1528, so his clientele was not entirely local.

Literature: Turner, 2000, pp.1524; J. Warren in Padua, 2001, pp.131–67

See cat.nos.181, 182

DOMENICO TINTORETTO (DOMENICO ROBUSTI)
1560–1635

Domenico was the son and principal assistant of JACOPO TINTORETTO on many of his large-scale projects of the 1580s and 1590s. But he was already in demand as a painter in his own right before his father's death in 1594, and his particular talent for portraiture was recognised with commissions both from leading Venetians and from foreign courts.

Literature: Turner, 2000, pp.1608–9

Cat.no.103; see also cat.no.104

JACOPO TINTORETTO (JACOPO ROBUSTI)
1519–1594

Born in Venice, Tintoretto spent his whole life in the city and worked almost exclusively for Venetian patrons. His nickname, signifying that he was the son of a textile dyer, served to advertise his self-identification with the social world of tradesmen and artisans. Although he was eventually to work in the Palazzo Ducale, his most characteristic patrons were the Venetian devotional confraternities, or Scuole. Perhaps because of the hostility of TITIAN, he was slow to gain official recognition. The *Miracle of the Slave*, however (Venice, Galleria dell' Accademia), painted in 1548 for the very public setting of the Scuola di San Marco, marked an important breakthrough; and from the early 1550s onwards his biography corresponds to a sequence of major decorative commissions for Venetian public buildings. His long association with the Scuola di San Rocco began in 1564 with the decoration of its *albergo* (board room), and this was followed by that of the large Chapter Hall (1575–81), and later by that of the Lower Hall (1582–7). Meanwhile he continued to work for smaller devotional confraternities, most notably for the parish-based Scuole del Sacramento. Tintoretto was evidently a man of deep and passionate religious sensibility, who felt a natural sympathy with the spiritual and philanthropic ideals of these institutions of lay devotion. Although generally less successful than his rival VERONESE in gaining commissions from the Venetian government and the ruling patriciate, Tintoretto did enjoy favour as a painter of dignified and restrained official portraits.

Literature: De Vecchi, 1970; Rossi, 1974; Pallucchini and Rossi, 1982; Nichols, 1999; T. Nichols in Turner, 2000, pp.1595–1608

Cat.nos.52, 53, 66, 68, 102; see also cat.no.51

TITIAN (TIZIANO VECELLIO)
*c.*1485/90–1576

Sixteenth-century documents and sources provide conflicting evidence regarding Titian's birth date, but there is now a growing consensus that he was born between 1485 and 1490, and that his earliest independent works date from shortly before 1510. The identification of these works is still a matter of controversy, however, as is the precise nature of the young Titian's relationship with the somewhat older GIORGIONE. Still much discussed, for example, are the attributions of paintings such as the *Christ and the Adulteress* (cat.no.13) and the *Concert Champêtre* (fig.15). But the problems of dating and attribution become less acute by the middle of the second decade, and with the *Assumption of the Virgin* (fig.19), completed in 1518, Titian reached full

maturity. Already the dominant personality in Venetian painting, he was equally versatile and inventive in every type of pictorial commission, and he quickly became one of the most sought-after painters in all Italy. The cycle of mythologies for the Duke of Ferrara (1518–23; fig.21) was followed by a series of commissions in the 1520s and 1530s from the Duke of Mantua; the early 1530s also saw the beginnings of his long relationship with the Emperor Charles V, who knighted him in 1533. During this period he made frequent trips to Ferrara, Mantua, and other north Italian cities, although he did not visit Rome and Florence until as late as 1545–6. In 1548 and again in 1551–2, he crossed the Alps to attend the imperial court at Augsburg, and on the latter occasion he consolidated his acquaintance with the emperor's son Philip, who was King of Spain from 1555. From this time onwards Philip was Titian's major patron; without ever visiting Spain in person, the painter sent regular consignments of pictures from his studio in Venice to the Spanish court.

Titian's later career is exceptionally well documented, and there exists an extensive correspondence between the painter and King Philip and his agents. There remain, however, three inter-related areas of critical controversy, all of which concern his workshop practices. Like GIOVANNI BELLINI before him, Titian could only meet the huge demand for his pictures by employing a large number of assistants; the efficiency with which the shop operated means that assessing the extent of the collaboration in a particular picture is often one of fine critical judgement. The two other areas of controversy derive from his habit of executing pictures over a period of years, sometimes even decades, stopping work and then resuming again after long interruptions. As a result, certain pictures are difficult or impossible to date accurately. Similarly, it is often difficult to decide whether or not a particular picture should be regarded as finished. These are all matters that affect the interpretation of several of the paintings by or associated with Titian in the present exhibition.

Literature: Pallucchini, 1969; Wethey, 1969–75; Hope, 1980; Washington, 1990; Manca, 1993; Goffen, 1997; C. Gould in Turner, 2000, pp.1609–22; Joannides, 2001; London, 2003; Madrid, 2003

Cat.nos.13–15, 19, 25, 34–6, 54, 55, 64; see also cat.nos.18, 28, 37, 38, 65

FRANCESCO VECELLIO
*c.*1485/95–1559/60

The brother of TITIAN, Francesco was also his occasional assistant, but there is doubt as to which of the two was the elder. Apparently little in demand in Venice itself, Francesco was active above all as a painter of altarpieces for the Venetian mainland, especially in the regions of Belluno and his native Cadore.

His style remained closely based on Titian's work of the second decade.

Literature: S. Claut in Turner, 2000, p.1695

See cat.nos.26, 27

PAOLO VERONESE (PAOLO CALIARI)
1528–1588

Trained in his native city of Verona, Veronese's earliest independent works, datable to about 1546, were painted for local patrons and buildings, but already by 1550–1 he was working for the Venetian patrician families the Soranzo and the Giustinian. As a result of these connections he was invited in 1553 to participate in the ceiling decoration of a series of council chambers in the Palazzo Ducale and about two years later he finally abandoned Verona to settle in Venice, where he enjoyed an almost uninterrrupted series of public successes. In 1555 began his decade-long association with the church of San Sebastiano, and in 1562–3 he executed another major commission for a monastic patron, the huge and festive *Wedding Feast at Cana* for the refectory of San Giorgio Maggiore (Paris, Musée du Louvre). An almost equally grand banquet scene, however, the so-called *Feast in the House of Levi* (Venice, Galleria dell' Accademia). incurred the disapproval of the Inquisition, and thereafter Veronese's paintings became noticeably more serious in mood and sombre in colour. At the same time, his continuing taste for sensuous texture and his natural wit ideally qualified him as a painter of erotic mythologies.

Literature: Washington, 1988, Fehl, 1992; Pignatti and Pedrocco, 1995; D. Gisolfi in Turner, 2000, pp.1727–39; Cocke, 2001

Cat.nos.57–9, 69–71, 105; see also cat.no.106

(GIUSEPPE) NICOLÒ VICENTINO
*c.*1510–*c.*1550

A woodblock cutter and probably a printer who was known as a maker of chiaroscuro woodcuts. There are five that carry his signature, after designs by Parmigianino and Maturino; others have been attributed to him, including works after Pordenone (see cat.no.131) and Raphael. It seems likely that Andrea Andreani (1558/9–1629) later acquired all his blocks, and reissued many of them.

Literature: Passavant, 1860–4, VI, pp.212–13; C. Karpinski, *The Illustrated Bartsch*, 48, *Italian Chiaroscuro Woodcuts*, New York, 1983, pp.26–7, 85, 144, 150, 154, 182 and 189

Cat.no.131

CORNELIS VISSCHER
c.1629–c.1658

Visscher was an engraver and etcher from Haarlem who made prints after paintings by BASSANO, Ostade and Brouwer, as well after his own inventions. He contributed to the book *Variarum imaginum a celeberrimis artificibus pictarum caelaturae elegantissimis tabulis repraesentatae*, published at Amsterdam 1660–71; it had been commissioned by Gerrit Reynst.

Literature: J. Wussin, *Cornel Visscher*, Leipzig, 1865; Hollstein, XL, pp.9–216

Cat.no.157

ALESSANDRO VITTORIA
1525–1608

Vittoria was the most accomplished and versatile sculptor active in Venice in the second half of the sixteenth century. He probably received his initial training in his native Trent under the Paduan sculptors Vincenzo and Gian Girolamo Grandi. He went to Venice in 1543 and entered the workshop of the foremost sculptor and architect in the city, JACOPO SANSOVINO. Vittoria was an independent sculptor by 1550, the year of his earliest known sculpture, a *St John the Baptist* for a holy-water stoop (Venice, San Zaccaria). He was in Trent in 1551 and then in Vicenza (1551–3), where he executed stucco decorations in Palladio's Palazzo Thiene. A bitter falling-out with Sansovino was healed through the mediation of Pietro Aretino, and Vittoria returned to Venice and collaborated with him on major projects during the 1550s. After Sansovino's death in 1570, he became the most sought-after sculptor and designer in the city. His major works include the stucco decorations of the Scala d'Oro in the Palazzo Ducale and in the Marciana Library; statues for altars in many Venetian churches, including San Francesco della Vigna, the Frari, Santa Maria del Giglio, San Giuliano and San Salvatore; and, as an architect, the façade of the Scuola di San Fantin and the Palazzo Balbi. Justly ranked amongst his greatest creations are the many strikingly life-like portrait busts he executed in terracotta, marble and bronze. He also modelled some superb bronze statuettes and reliefs.

Literature: Martin, 1998; Trent, 1999; T. Martin in Turner, 2000, pp.1777–81; V. Avery in Boström, 2004, pp.1736–40

Cat.nos.204, 205; see also cat.nos.203, 206–8

BARTOLOMEO VIVARINI
c.1430–after 1491

The younger brother of Antonio Vivarini, and uncle of Alvise, Bartolomeo's most characteristic works are altarpieces, many of which are signed and bear dates ranging from 1450 to 1491. The signature on virtually all the works of the 1450s is paired with that of Antonio, whose pupil he evidently was, and whose specialisation and clientele he largely inherited. Historically the most significant period of Bartolomeo's career was between about 1460 and 1475. His works of this phase reveal a concern to adapt the still prevalently Gothic style of his brother to the modern style made current in Padua by Andrea Mantegna and the other followers of Francesco Squarcione. But although advanced in the early 1460s, this style had become old-fashioned by the mid-1470s; Bartolomeo was never to accommodate himself to the innovations in form, colour and light introduced into Venetian painting by GIOVANNI BELLINI.

Literature: Pallucchini, 1962; J. Steer in Turner, 2000, pp.1784–6

Cat.no.1

FEDERICO ZUCCARO
1540/1–1609

The leading painter in late sixteenth-century Rome, Federico was a native of Sant'Angelo in Vado near Urbino, and he collaborated extensively with his elder brother Taddeo until the latter's early death in 1566. Federico travelled widely in and beyond Italy, and in 1574 he visited France, Antwerp and England, where he is supposed to have painted a portrait of Queen Elizabeth. He made three visits to Venice: first in 1562–5, on the invitation of Giovanni Grimani, Patriarch of Aquilea, when he completed the decoration of the Grimani chapel in San Francesco della Vigna; then in 1582–3, when he painted a scene for the Sala del Maggior Consiglio in the Palazzo Ducale; and finally in 1603. Federico practised his late Mannerist style with self-conscious deliberation, and his establishment of an academy in 1593 in his own palace in Rome was followed in 1607 by his publication of a treatise propounding his ideals of beauty and design, *L'Idea de' Scultori, Pittori e Architetti*.

Literature: Acidini Luchinat, 1998–9; L. de Girolami Cheney in Turner, 2000, pp.1802–5

Cat.no.125

APPENDIX II: PRINCIPAL SCOTTISH COLLECTORS & ADVISERS

Peter Humfrey

SMALL CAPITALS are used to indicate cross-references within this index.

4TH EARL OF ABERDEEN

The collection of the Earls of Aberdeen at Haddo House, Aberdeenshire, is itemised in two inventories of 1899 and 1901. Consisting chiefly of Italian pictures, the collection was formed by George Hamilton Gordon, 4th Earl (1784–1860), at the beginning of the nineteenth century, and included two important Venetian works: Titian's *Allegory of Prudence* (cat.no.64), and Veronese's *Adoration of the Shepherds* (cat.no.58). Lord Aberdeen had a distinguished political career. Having served as Foreign Secretary under the Duke of Wellington in 1818 he rose to become Queen Victoria's Prime Minister from 1852 to 1855. He was also closely interested in the arts. After taking in Greece on his Grand Tour of 1802–4, he wrote regular articles on Greek architecture for the *Edinburgh Review*, for which he was satirised by his kinsman Lord Byron as 'the travell'd thane, Athenian Aberdeen'. He became a trustee of the British Museum in 1812 and a founding trustee of the National Gallery of Scotland in 1824. He was one of the vice-presidents of the Royal Institution in Edinburgh in 1826 and he later served as President of the British Institution. Another major Italian picture in his collection was Sebastiano del Piombo's handsome *Portrait of Antonio Francesco degli Albizzi* (Houston, Museum of Fine Arts), but he sold this in about 1829 while the collection was still in London; unlike the pictures by Titian and Veronese, the portrait never reached Scotland. Part of the collection remains at Haddo House, now the property of the National Trust for Scotland, but most of the best pictures were dispersed during the course of the twentieth century.

Literature: Paul, 1904–14, I, pp.94–5; Smith, 2003

2ND MARQUESS OF BREADALBANE

John Campbell, 4th Earl and 1st Marquess of Breadalbane (1762–1834) was in Rome and Naples in 1782–3, and was a patron of the Scottish painter Jacob More (Ingamells, 1997, pp.120–1). When he visited Edinburgh in 1804, WILLIAM BUCHANAN thought that he would be a likely buyer of old masters (Brigstocke, 1982, p.296). His son and namesake the 2nd Marquess (1796–1862) served as MP for Perthshire before he succeeded his father in 1834, and was later president of the Society of Antiquaries of Scotland. He employed Gillespie Graham to complete the remodelling of his family seat of Taymouth Castle, begun by his father at the beginning of the century, and entertained Queen Victoria there in 1842 (Millar, 1890, pp.144–56). His picture collection included several works acquired on a tour of Italy in 1830, among them Rubens's *Feast of Herod* (Edinburgh, National Gallery of Scotland), and a group of six Neapolitan pictures that he presented in 1833 to the Literary and Antiquarian Society of Perth (now Perth Museum and Art Gallery; information provided by Robin Rodger). His Venetian pictures, perhaps acquired on the same tour, included a *Holy Family with St John* attributed to Titian (Breadalbane sale, Christie's, 5 June 1886), Sebastiano del Piombo's *Portrait of a Man* (on the New York art market in 1981: see M. Hirst, *Sebastiano del Piombo*, Oxford, 1981, p.149), and Veronese's idealised representations of the fathers of geography, Ptolemy and Averroes (Los Angeles County Museum of Art; figs.29, 30). These pictures were inherited by Breadalbane's niece and her husband, the Hon. Robert Baillie-Hamilton, and the last three were lent by them to the Royal Academy exhibition in 1881 (Graves, 1913, p.938). Breadalbane also made purchases in London; in 1855, for example, he acquired the version of Titian's *Man with a Blue Sleeve* previously in the collection of JAMES DENNISTOUN.

Literature: Paul, 1904–14; Edinburgh, 1992, pp.158–9

5TH DUKE OF BUCCLEUCH & 7TH DUKE OF QUEENSBERRY

From the eighteenth century the Dukes of Buccleuch kept important art collections at their Scottish houses of Dalkeith Palace, Bowhill and Drumlanrig Castle, and in England at Boughton House, Northamptonshire, and Montagu House in London. But although their collections (in part inherited from the Dukes of Montagu and of Queensberry) included Italian as well as Dutch and British pictures of great distinction, there appear to have been no Venetian Renaissance pictures of significance. Jacometto's *Portrait of Alvise Contarini* (cat.no.6) formed part of an otherwise predominantly British collection of 750 portrait miniatures formed by Walter Francis, 5th Duke of Buccleuch (1806–1884).

Literature: Paul, 1904–14, II, p.245; Edinburgh, 1992, p.159; Lloyd, 2003

WILLIAM BUCHANAN

Buchanan (1777–1864) was one of the most important British art dealers in the period following the French Revolution, and was responsible for importing masterpieces of the calibre of Titian's *Bacchus and Ariadne* (fig.21), Raphael's *Alba Madonna* (Washington, National Gallery of Art), and Velázquez's *Rokeby Venus* (London, National Gallery) from southern Europe into Britain. The son of a wealthy Glasgow merchant and hatmaker, Buchanan at first intended to enter the legal profession. But having met JAMES IRVINE in Edinburgh in 1799 he became interested in the opportunities created for the art market by the dramatic political and social upheavals taking place on the Continent. Between 1802 and 1806, first in Edinburgh and then in London, Buchanan acted in partnership with Irvine in Rome, importing the *Bacchus and Ariadne* and selling it to the 8th BARON KINNAIRD in 1806–7. Later he turned his attention to Spain, using G.A. Wallis as his agent on the spot. After the fall of Napoleon he succeeded in importing entire major collections to London, including those of Lucien Bonaparte and Talleyrand. In his *Memoirs of Painting* (1824), Buchanan provided a detailed account of the influx of old master paintings into England over the preceding twenty-five years, beginning with the Orléans sale in 1798, and of his role in what he regarded as a glorious and patriotic enterprise. In 1827 he was in contact with the Royal Institution in Edinburgh, offering it five pictures, three of which were Venetian, and around 1830 he acted as an adviser to Sir John FORBES OF PITSLIGO. By that time he was becoming an increasingly marginal figure in the London art world, and in later life he returned to Scotland.

Literature: Buchanan, 1824; C. Clark, 'In search of Buchanan', *Scottish Art Review*, XI, 4, 1968, pp.27–9; Herrmann, 1972, pp.127–39; Haskell, 1976, pp.45–51; Brigstocke, 1981; Brigstocke, 1982; Turner, 1996, V, pp.71–2

SIR WILLIAM BURRELL

Sir William Burrell (1861–1958) was the greatest Scottish collector of the late nineteenth and early twentieth centuries. Although his taste was unprecedentedly catholic, it was consciously opposed to the tastes that had prevailed in the eighteenth and early nineteenth centuries. He may also have avoided Venetian Renaissance pictures because he considered them to be overpriced. In any case, his only known purchase in this area was a *Virgin and Child* by Giovanni Bellini, formerly in Palazzo Barberini, Rome (cat.no.4).

Literature: Marks, 1983; Edinburgh, 1992, pp. 159–60; Hamilton, 2003

3RD EARL OF BUTE

John Stuart, 3rd Earl of Bute (1713–1792; fig.59), besides being Prime Minister to George III and one of the leading statesmen of his day, was an important patron of the arts and one of the great collectors of the later eighteenth century. He did not undertake the Grand Tour to Italy in his youth, and his first passion was for Dutch painting. From the later 1760s, however, perhaps inspired by the need to furnish his new seat at Luton Park in Bedfordshire, built for him by Robert Adam in 1766–74, he began acquiring larger-scale Italian pictures. In Venice in 1768 he commissioned Sir James Wright, the British Resident, to buy for him Tiepolo's *Finding of Moses* (Edinburgh, National Gallery of Scotland), then attributed to Veronese (Brigstocke, 1993, p.161). Soon afterwards, in 1770–1, Bute was back in Venice for six months, and it was presumably during this stay that he bought the impressive set of Venetian pictures by Titian, Paris Bordon, Tintoretto, Veronese and others that today hang mainly in the Drawing Room at Mount Stuart (cat.nos.38, 42, 44, 50, 57; fig.61). The Bute collection at Luton is recorded in a manuscript inventory of 1799 (copy in the library of the National Gallery, London); and although a major sale (which included the Tiepolo) took place in 1822, there remained plenty for Waagen to admire in the late 1830s (1838, III, pp.373–4). After a fire at Luton Park in 1843, the family sold the house, and around this time both the Royal Scottish Academy and the Royal Institution unsuccessfully attempted to negotiate the rehousing of the collection in Edinburgh. The collection was exhibited at the Bethnal Green Museum, London, at the Corporation Galleries in Glasgow, and at Manchester between 1882 and 1885, and from about 1891 to 1916 it was kept at St John's Lodge in Regent's Park, London. The pictures were subsequently dispersed among the various family homes until about 1947, when they were reunited at Mount Stuart.

Literature: Richter, 1883; Paul, 1904–14, II, pp.301–2; Edinburgh, 1992, p.160; F. Russell in the Turner, 1996, XXIX, p.796; Russell, 2003. Further information kindly provided by Andrew McLean

CAMPBELL OF SUCCOTH

In 1854 Waagen (III, pp.291–4) recorded his visit to the collection of Sir Archibald Campbell, 3rd Baronet, at Garscube near Glasgow. According to Waagen the collection was formed chiefly by the owner's grandfather, Sir Ilay Campbell, 1st Baronet and Lord President of the Court of Session (1734–1823). But probably an even greater interest in collecting was shown by Sir Archibald, 2nd Baronet (1769–1846), who had Garscube rebuilt in 1826–7 by William Burn. It was Sir Archibald, for example, who bought a *Virgin and Child with Saints* attributed to Moretto in Italy in 1827 on the advice of ANDREW WILSON, and who was present at the sale of LORD CLERK OF ELDIN's pictures in Edinburgh in 1833. Waagen had particular praise for the Italian pictures, of which four were Venetian. One of these was a *St Jerome in a Landscape* attributed to Titian, but perhaps a copy (Wethey, 1969, p.134); this had been acquired by ANDREW WILSON from the Doria collection in Genoa in 1804, but was sold on by him in 1807 (Brigstocke, 1982, p.505), perhaps to Sir Ilay. Waagen also recorded a picture attributed to Palma Vecchio, but which in fact was Bonifacio's *Rest on the Flight into Egypt* now in Adelaide (fig.126); the 'Moretto', probably in fact by Gian Pietro Silvio (see Humfrey, 2003b, pp.18–19); and a *Lamentation* signed by Palma Giovane (Mason Rinaldi, 1984, p.86). The last two were lent by Sir George Campbell, 6th Baronet, and by Sir Ilay Campbell, 7th Baronet, to the Glasgow

Art Gallery from 1962 to 1978, but were sold soon afterwards.

Literature: Edinburgh, 1992, p.161; Humfrey, 2003b, pp.19–20

SIR JAMES CARNEGIE: SEE 9TH EARL OF SOUTHESK

25TH EARL OF CRAWFORD & 8TH EARL OF BALCARRES

Alexander William Lindsay, 25th Earl of Crawford and 8th Earl of Balcarres (1812–1880), known for most of his life as Lord Lindsay, was the author of a pioneering and influential study of early Italian painting, the *Sketches of the History of Christian Art* (1847), as well as a passionate bibliophile and collector of pictures. He made frequent trips to Italy, staying at the villa acquired by his father at Fiesole, and the collection he formed between the 1840s and the 1870s consisted above all of pictures of the Tuscan and Umbrian Quattrocento. But Lindsay's scholarly seriousness as an art historian sometimes led him to buy pictures outside his preferred area, and he may also have inherited Venetian cinquecento pictures, for instance by the Bassano family (cat.nos.72, 74, 75), from his father-in-law, Lieutenant-General James Lindsay of Balcarres. Lord Lindsay kept his collection at the family homes of Haigh Hall, Lancashire, and Dunecht, Aberdeenshire, neither of which was visited by Waagen.

Literature: Paul, 1904–14, III, pp.47–8; H. Brigstocke, 'Lord Lindsay and the Sketches of the History of Christian Art', *Bulletin of the John Rylands University Library Manchester*, LXIV, 1, 1981; Edinburgh, 1992, p.162; Edinburgh, 2000

JAMES DENNISTOUN

James Dennistoun of Colgrain and Camieskam, Dumbartonshire (1805–1855), was important as an antiquarian and as an early admirer of fourteenth- and fifteenth-century Italian painting, especially Umbrian, before he became a collector. He made several extended visits to Italy and the Continent (1825, 1836–9, 1842–6, 1851), and in 1851 he published a major work of scholarship, the *Memoirs of the Dukes of Urbino*. Like his correspondent LORD LINDSAY, he did not particularly favour Venetian cinquecento painting, but he did own a version or copy of Titian's *Portrait of a Man with a Blue Sleeve* (London, National Gallery), an engraving of which was used to illustrate the *Memoirs* (III, p.265), and a *Virgin and Child on a Grassy Bank* attributed to the School of Titian. He also owned two important Venetian fifteenth-century works, Giorgio Schiavone's polyptych now in the National Gallery, London (fig.67), and Cima's *Virgin and Child* in Detroit (fig.8), both of which he acquired in Edinburgh in 1841–2, and both of which were recorded by Waagen when he visited Dennistoun's house at 113 George

Streeet, Edinburgh, in 1851 (III, pp.281–2). The Schiavone and the *Virgin and Child on a Grassy Bank* had previously belonged to JAMES JOHNSTON OF STRAITON. After Dennistoun's death his pictures, the majority of which were early Florentine and Sienese, were sold at Christie's in London (14 June 1855).

Literature: H. Brigstocke, 'James Dennistoun as a collector and traveller', and 'James Dennistoun's second European tour 1836–1839', *Connoisseur*, 184, 1973, pp.90–7, 240–9; H. Brigstocke, 'James Dennistoun and the *Memoirs of the Dukes of Urbino*', in C. Richardson and G. Smith (eds.), *Britannia, Italia, Germania: Taste and Travel in the 19th Century*, Edinburgh, 2001, pp.98–124

5TH EARL OF DUNMORE

On his second visit to Scotland in 1856 Waagen (1857, pp.453–7) visited Dunmore Park, near Falkirk, and recorded a number of Italian pictures. These had probably been collected by the 7th Earl's grandfather, George Murray, 5th Earl (1762–1836), for whom William Wilkins had rebuilt the house (now ruinous) in 1820–5 in the Tudor-Gothic style (J. Gifford and F. Arnell Wilson, *The Buildings of Scotland: Stirling and Central Scotland*, New Haven and London, 2002, p.452). The 5th Earl was brother-in-law of the 10th DUKE OF HAMILTON, and the 7th was brother-in-law of the 9th EARL OF SOUTHESK. Waagen lists six Venetian pictures, including a *Joseph and Potiphar's Wife* by Giuseppe Salviati, a *Finding of Moses* by Tintoretto, and a *Portrait of Admiral Vincenzo Cappello* (fig.116), also attributed to Tintoretto, but in fact a version of the portrait by Titian (cat.no.35). Of these only a late masterpiece by Veronese, the *Martyrdom of St Catherine* subsequently in the collection of the Earls of Haddington at Mellerstain, has entered the modern literature (see Piero Corsini Inc, New York, *Important Old Master Paintings*, dealer catalogue, New York, 1990, pp.54–7; Pignatti and Pedrocco, 1995, p.492).

Literature: Paul, 1904–14, III, pp.392–5

LORD ELCHO: SEE EARL OF WEMYSS

LORD ELDIN

John Clerk (1757–1832), raised to the bench as Lord Eldin, was a member of the cadet branch of the Clerk family of Penicuik, and a founding director of the Royal Institution in Edinburgh. The sale of his pictures at his house in Picardy Place in March 1833, at which many collectors and notables were present (including Sir ARCHIBALD CAMPBELL), is famous above all for the disastrous collapse of the drawing-room floor, resulting in death and human injury as well as the probable destruction of works of art. The outstanding picture in Eldin's collection, which included forty Italian as

well as Flemish, Dutch and French old masters, was Jacopo Bassano's *Adoration of the Kings* (cat.no.40), then attributed to Titian, which had been exported from Genoa in 1805 by ANDREW WILSON. Eldin also owned a *Venus Disarming Cupid* attributed to Veronese (now at Gosford House), bought three years later by the 8th EARL OF WEMYSS.

Literature: Brown, 1987; Edinburgh, 1992, p.161; Brown, 2003a and 2003b

7TH EARL OF ELGIN & 11TH EARL OF KINCARDINE

Thomas Bruce, 7th Earl of Elgin and 11th Earl of Kincardine (1766–1841) is famous above all for having instigated the removal of the Parthenon sculptures from the Acropolis in Athens from 1801 to 1811, initially during his period of service as British ambassador to the Ottoman Empire. But he was also a founding director of the Royal Institution in Edinburgh, and acquired a collection of old masters for his family home of Broomhall in Fife, a selection of which were seen by Waagen (1857, pp.443–5), when they were on loan to the Corporation Art Gallery in Glasgow in 1856. These included Sebastiano del Piombo's *Portrait of a Woman* (Earl of Harewood collection), and the *Portrait of a Blacksmith*, traditionally attributed to Moroni, reattributed by Waagen to Moretto, and now more commonly given to Paolo Farinati (fig.74). Elgin also bought pictures on the London art market in the late 1820s on behalf of his kinsman by marriage CHARLES STIRLING OF CAWDER.

Literature: Paul, 1904–14, III, pp.492–3

THOMAS ERSKINE OF LINLATHEN

In 1854 Waagen (III, p.315) recorded that at Linlathen, 'seat of Mr Erskine, in the neighbourhood of Dundee', there were 'good Italian pictures, purchased in Rome by the advice of M. Colombo'. This collector was Thomas Erskine of Linlathen (1788–1870), a distinguished spiritual writer and close friend of Thomas Carlyle (Irving, 1881, p.133). Erskine undertook three extended trips to the Continent (in 1822–5, 1826–7, 1844–6), visiting Rome on all three occasions. In 1827 he also visited Venice, where he 'bought two or three pictures, but no great things'. In his voluminous correspondence he makes occasional reference to his love of art, and in particular to the spiritual inspiration of great religious art; he does not, however, mention his dealings with Colombo in Rome (see W. Hanna (ed.), *Letters of Thomas Erskine of Linlathen*, 2 vols., Edinburgh, 1877, especially I, pp.66, 92, 96, 99–100). In 1828 JAMES IRVINE offered him a *Portrait of Pietro Aretino in Profile* attributed to Titian, originally acquired for Sir William FORBES OF PITSLIGO, but eventually sold it instead to Erskine's brother-in-law, CHARLES

STIRLING OF CAWDER (Jaffé, 1971, p.702). Two of the pictures that had belonged to Erskine, Bonifacio's *Holy Family with the Young St John the Baptist and St Catherine of Alexandria* (cat.no.31) and a portrait attributed to Bronzino, were lent to the Royal Academy exhibition of 1896 by his nephew J.E. Erskine (Graves, 1913, I, pp.77, 109)

JAMES EWING

James Ewing (1775–1853) made his fortune as a West India merchant in Glasgow, and in later life was closely involved in civic affairs, serving for many years as director of Glasgow's Chamber of Commerce. In 1832 he was elected both provost of the city and as one of Glasgow's first two MPs. In 1838 he bought the Dumbartonshire estate of Strathleven, with its house of 1710 by James Smith. In 1844–5 he undertook a tour of Italy, and recorded his itinerary and impressions in a series of letters to his friend Mr Mathieson, later privately printed. In May–June 1845 he spent four weeks in Venice, and it was on this occasion that he bought Titian's *Portrait of Jacopo Dolfin* (cat.no.34). A marble bust of Ewing by William Brodie is in the Merchants House, Glasgow.

Information kindly provided by Ewing's descendant, Alexander Hamilton.

SIR WILLIAM FORBES OF PITSLIGO

The eminent banker Sir William Forbes, 6th Baronet (1739–1806), undertook a Grand Tour of Italy in 1792–3 (Ingamells, 1997, pp.369–70), but it was his son Sir William, 7th Baronet (1773–1828), who had his Kincardineshire home of Fettercairn rebuilt by William Burn, and then set about furnishing it with a collection of Italian pictures of exceptional quality. Forbes was the banker and a governor of the Royal Institution in Edinburgh, and the brother-in-law of its secretary, James Skene of Rubislaw. His collection was formed in Italy by JAMES IRVINE, whom Forbes had met in Rome, and whose family from Drum Castle in Aberdeenshire were neighbours. Among the Venetian pictures acquired within little more than a year in 1827–8 were *A Man with Dividers* attributed to Gentile Bellini (London, National Gallery); Paris Bordon's early *Rest on the Flight into Egypt* (whereabouts unknown; see Pfäffikon, 1978, p.98); Catena's *Rest on the Flight into Egypt* (fig.10), then attributed to Giovanni Bellini; Lotto's *Portrait of a Lady as Lucretia* (cat.no.32), then attributed to Giorgione; Lotto's *Portrait of an Architect* (cat.no.33); Moroni's *Portrait of a Lawyer* (London, National Gallery) and *Portrait of Don Gabriel de la Cueva* (cat.no.60); Titian's *Doge Andrea Gritti* (cat.no.37) and *Two Boys of the Pesaro Family* (cat.no.36); and Veronese's *Martyrdom and Last Communion of St Lucy* (cat.no.71). Forbes, however, died in October 1828 without ever seeing the collection that Irvine had put together for him, and his interest in pictures was not shared by his son Sir John, who almost immediately began selling the collection off piecemeal. Early buyers included Sir Archibald CAMPBELL OF SUCCOTH and Sir James Carnegie (EARL OF SOUTHESK). Some of the other pictures were put up for auction at Rainy's, London, 2 June 1842, but several (including the Veronese) did not sell, and were inherited by the descendants of Sir John's daughter, Lady Clinton.

Literature: Jaffé, 1971; Brigstocke, 1982, pp.25–30, 480–507

JOHN GRAHAM-GILBERT

After ARCHIBALD MCLELLAN, the painter John Graham-Gilbert (1794–1866) was the most important donor of Italian paintings to the Glasgow Museum. The son of a West Indies merchant, Graham (as he was born) was trained at the Royal Academy Schools in London, spent two years in Italy as a young man. He was elected to the Royal Scottish Academy in 1830, and returned to his native Glasgow to follow a successful career as a portrait painter in 1834. His already prosperous financial circumstances were further improved by his marriage to Miss Gilbert of Yorkhill, 'a lady of fortune', enabling him to make frequent return visits to Italy, and especially to indulge his passion for collecting. As a painter Graham-Gilbert was much influenced by his close study of Italian old masters, and the bequest by his widow in 1877 to the Glasgow Museum included many of his copies after Venetian painters such as Titian, Palma Vecchio and Veronese. In addition to the pictures by Giovanni Bellini (cat.no.3) and Paris Bordon (cat.no.29) included in the present exhibition, Graham-Gilbert owned works by Palma Vecchio (fig.75), Giovanni da Asola (cat.no.16), and the school of Tintoretto.

Literature: J. Laird, *Descriptive Catalogue of the Collection of Old Paintings formed by the late John Graham Gilbert Esq, RSA, of Yorkhill* (MS of 1877, Glasgow Art Galleries); Pinnington, 1898, pp.16–18; Irwin and Irwin, 1975, p.221; Hamilton, 2003

14TH BARON GRAY

Francis, 14th Baron Gray (1762–1842) inherited the Kinfauns estate, to the east of Perth, from his mother, and had Kinfauns Castle rebuilt in a medievalising, castellated style by Robert Smirke in 1820–2 (Paul, 1904–14, IV, p.294). A major architectural feature was the Gothic Long Gallery, and as if to fill it Gray accumulated an impressive collection of Italian, Netherlandish and British paintings. A catalogue of the collection, written by the eminent portraitist Francis Grant (*Catalogue of Pictures Ancient and Modern of Kinfauns Castle, chiefly collected by Francis, Lord Gray*) was published in 1828. The Venetian pictures included a portrait of 'Count Castilignone' (presumably meant to be Baldassare Castiglione, 1478–1529), attributed to Giorgione; Paris Bordon's *Holy Family with St Jerome* (fig.129); and a *Marriage of St Catherine* by Lorenzo Lotto. The last was almost certainly a version of Lotto's popular and much replicated *Holy Family with St Catherine* of 1533 in the Accademia Carrara, Bergamo. According to the Revd Thomas Dibdin, who provided a general account of the collection and its owner, Lord Gray bought both in Italy and in Britain, including at the sale of LORD ELDIN in Edinburgh in 1833 (Dibdin, 1838, II, pp.934–43).

9TH AND 10TH DUKES OF HAMILTON & BRANDON

The collection formed by Alexander Hamilton, 10th Duke (1767–1852; fig.56), at his ancestral seat of Hamilton Palace in Lanarkshire, was the largest and most important in Scotland for most of the nineteenth century. Several of his eighteenth-century ancestors had undertaken the Grand Tour and had shown more than a passing interest in art (Ingamells, 1997, pp.445–60), but after the confiscation and sale of the great collection formed by the 1st Duke between 1638 and 1643, the family had made relatively few acquisitions of Italian Renaissance pictures. A new interest was shown, however, by Alexander's father Archibald, 9th Duke (died 1819), who had been in Italy between 1758 and 1761, and bought works in Italy and London in the 1790s. An undated inventory of his collection includes Tintoretto's *Moses Striking the Rock* (fig.65) and a *Portrait of a Venetian Admiral* attributed to Tintoretto.

From the beginning Alexander, who spent several years in Italy, including Venice, around this time, collected on a much more lavish scale. His motives were by no means purely aesthetic, and as was the case with his later rebuilding on a grandiose, almost regal scale of Hamilton Palace in 1822–31, a prevailing concern was one of prestige. He acquired a large and very distinguished collection of French furniture and decorative arts, much of it with royal and imperial connections (Edinburgh, 1985, pp.71–93). His largely traditional tastes in painting included an admiration for the great names of the Venetian Cinquecento, as well as for the Bolognese Seicento. His already splendid collection was further enriched in 1844 when his wife inherited the pictures belonging to her father William Beckford (1760–1844), one of the leading collectors of the early nineteenth century, whose very broad tastes included a precocious interest in the so-called Primitives.

Hamilton Palace was visited in 1851 by Waagen (1854, III, pp.294–309), who declared that it was the chief reason for his visit to Scotland. But as usual he listed and described only selected highlights, and the most complete published inventory of the collection was compiled by the auctioneers Christie's in 1882, in the catalogue of perhaps the most spectacular art sale of the nineteenth century. A short list of the Venetian fifteenth- and sixteenth-century pictures in the Hamilton sale includes – in addition to Tintoretto's *Moses Striking the Rock* mentioned above – Cima's *St Jerome in the Desert* (cat.no.10); Catena's *Portrait of a Young Man* (cat.no.7); a *Virgin and Child* by a follower of Bellini (cat.no.5); Girolamo dai Libri's *Virgin and Child with Saints* (fig.66); a *Mythological Scene* attributable to Bonifacio (fig.17); Bonifacio's *Resurrection* and Oliverio's *Portrait of a Man* (both Dublin, National Gallery of Ireland); Titian's *Portrait of Admiral Vincenzo Cappello* (cat.no.35); Moroni's *Portrait of a Man* of 1561 (cat.no.61); Tintoretto's *Christ Washing the Disciples' Feet* (fig.35) and *Resurrection* (Oxford, Ashmolean Museum); and Veronese's *Portrait of Admiral Girlamo Contarini* (fig.40). Other pictures attributed to Titian, Schiavone, Tintoretto and Veronese are at present untraced.

A major buyer at the Hamilton sale was the National Gallery, London, but many other pictures were soon to be exported to Germany and the United States; astonishingly, not a singe item was bought by the National Gallery of Scotland. Apart from Titian's *Portrait of Admiral Vincenzo Cappello*, which belonged to the Earls of Rosebery at Dalmeny from 1893 to 1939, the only Hamilton pictures to remain in Scotland were those that had previously been placed in another of the family's residences, Brodick Castle on Arran, probably by William, the 11th Duke. These included the picture here attributed to Maganza (cat.no.78). Another series of sales took place in 1919, and Hamilton Palace was demolished in the 1920s.

Literature: A.A. Tait, 'The Duke of Hamilton's palace', *Burlington Magazine*, CXXV, 1983, pp.394–402; Edinburgh, 1992, p.165; Evans, 2003. Further information kindly provided by Godfrey Evans

4TH AND 5TH EARLS OF HOPETOUN

The 2nd and 3rd Earls of Hopetoun were both eighteenth-century Grand Tourists, as was the maternal uncle of the 2nd Earl, the 2nd Marquess of Annandale (1688–1730), who returned to Scotland in 1721 with booty comprising three hundred paintings, as well as engravings, books and classical marbles (Ingamells, 1997, p.560). All of this he later left to his nephew for his mansion of Hopetoun House, on the Firth of Forth, enlarged on a grand scale by William Adam from the 1720s. But neither Annandale nor the eighteenth-century earls showed any particular interest in Venetian painting, and it was not until 1819 that the 4th Earl (1765–1823), who as General Sir John Hope had distinguished himself in the Peninsular War, bought the huge *Hunting Scene* (cat.no.39), then attributed to Titian, on the advice of ANDREW WILSON. After the 4th Earl's sudden death in 1823, Wilson continued to work for John Hope, the 5th Earl (1803–1843), and the *Portrait of Doge Marcantonio Memmo* (cat.no.80) was one of a number of pictures Wilson bought for Hopetoun during an extended stay in Genoa from 1826 to 1831. The other pictures recorded by Waagen on his visit in 1851 (III, pp.309–12) were mainly Dutch.

Literature: Paul, 1904–14, IV, pp.501–4; Skinner, 1968; Edinburgh, 1992, pp.165–6

JAMES IRVINE

Like ANDREW WILSON, James Irvine (1759–1831) was a painter who became more important as a dealer. The younger son of the 17th Laird of Drum, Aberdeenshire, Irvine attended the Royal Academy Schools in London in 1777, and by 1780 had settled in Rome. He had begun to deal in pictures by the mid-1780s, and had formed his own modest collection by 1790. A particularly intense phase of his dealing career began in 1802, when after meeting WILLIAM BUCHANAN on a return visit to Scotland, he went into business partnership with him, and regularly exported pictures back to London from Rome. After Buchanan turned his attention to Spain around 1806, Irvine continued to work for British customers from his Italian base. In 1818 he made a trip to the New World, visiting Havana, New York and Boston. In his later career he used his nephew Charles as his London agent. The most productive episode of this period, particularly as regards the collecting of Venetian pictures, came at the very end, when he assembled a collection of extraordinarily high quality in a very short space of time for Sir William FORBES OF PITSLIGO. After Forbes's death in 1828, Irvine first offered one of these pictures, a *Portrait of Pietro Aretino in Profile* attributed to Titian, to THOMAS ERSKINE OF LINLATHEN and then to Erskine's brother-in-law, CHARLES STIRLING OF CAWDER. Irvine's renewed links with Scotland were further strengthened when in the same year he sent his own painting of *Satan Rising from Chaos* to the Royal Scottish Academy, and was elected a member (Gordon, 1976, pp.33–4).

Literature: Jaffé, 1971; Bristocke, 1981; Brigstocke, 1982; Ingamells, 1997, pp.543–4

JAMES JOHNSTON OF STRAITON

According to the *Catalogue of the Johnston Collection of Pictures* (Edinburgh, 1835), James Johnston began collecting pictures on a winter tour of the Continent in 1829–30, and subsequently bought more during his 'residence of several seasons in London'. The collection housed at

Straiton House in Wemyss Place, Edinburgh, formed part of the grandly titled Caledonian Museum of Practical Science, and was hailed at its opening in 1833 as the 'Louvre Ecossais' (Forbes, 1996, p.48). The catalogue listed no fewer than 650 paintings, including works attributed to Giorgione, Titian, Tintoretto and Veronese. Although it admitted that some of these may not have been authentic, there certainly were some important originals, including the mid-fifteenth-century polyptych by Giorgio Schiavone (fig.67), which was bought at the Johnston sale at C.B. Tait, Edinburgh, 14 January 1842, by JAMES DENNISTOUN. Dennistoun also bought a *Holy Family* attributed to Titian, which according to the Johnston catalogue (p.43, cat.no.641) came from the Balbi Palace in Genoa. According to the catalogue of the Dennistoun sale of 1855 (Christie's, 14 June, lot 45) this showed the 'Virgin and Child on a grassy bank', with a composition close to that of pictures at Hampton Court and Palazzo Pitti. Just such a composition appears in the *Virgin and Child with St Catherine(?) and the Child Baptist* now in the Kimbell Art Museum, Fort Worth, which may therefore be identical with the Johnston-Dennistoun picture.

7TH AND 8TH BARONS KINNAIRD

On his second visit to Scotland in 1856, Waagen (1857, pp.445–8) visited Rossie Priory, near Dundee, seat of George, 9th Baron Kinnaird. The family collection was formed by the owner's grandfather George, 7th Baron (1754–1805), who restored his family's fortune by marrying Elizabeth Ransom, heiress of Ransom's (later Barclay's) Bank in London. He had bought a number of Dutch and Flemish paintings from the Orléans collection (Edinburgh, 1992, p.167), as well as a number of Italian pictures from London salerooms around the beginning of the nineteenth century. Charles, 8th Baron (1780–1826), whose tastes were more Italianate, bought on an even more lavish scale, and in 1806/7 acquired Titian's great *Bacchus and Ariadne* (fig.21), as well as a picture called *Sophonisba*, both newly imported from Italy by JAMES IRVINE and WILLIAM BUCHANAN (Brigstocke, 1982, pp.504–5). Mounting debts forced Kinnaird to sell the *Bacchus and Ariadne* and a number of other pictures in 1813 (at Phillips, London, 3–4 March). But the 8th Baron – a close friend of Lord Byron – continued to travel to Italy and to buy paintings and classical antiquities, which were housed in the newly rebuilt and refurbished Rossie Priory (by William Atkinson, 1807–15). Among the Venetian pictures noted by Waagen was Licinio's *Allegory of Love* (cat.no.23), Tintoretto's *Conversion of Saul* (Washington, National Gallery of Art), Veronese's *St Clare Receiving the Palm* (whereabouts unknown), and Titian's *Sophonisba*. This last work – a 'beauty' similar to his *Woman in a Fur Wrap* in the Kunst-

historisches Museum, Vienna – has now disappeared, but it was copied in an enamel made for Kinnaird in 1813 by Henry Bone (sold at Bonham's, London, *Fine Portrait Miniatures*, 22 May 2003, lot 126). Also in the collection, but not recorded by Waagen, were a Bellinesque double portrait (Berenson, 1957, fig.254), and Titian's *Portrait of Giulio Romano* (fig.114). The Kinnaird collection was dispersed during the course of the twentieth century, notably at a sale at Christie's, London, 21 June 1946.

Literature: Millar, 1890, pp.11–40; Paul, 1904–14, V, pp.213–14

DAVID LAING

The son of an Edinburgh bookseller, David Laing (1793–1878) was largely self-educated but rose to become librarian to the Writers to the Signet and a member of the Society of Antiquaries. He played a prominent role in the literary life of Edinburgh and shared with his friend Sir Walter Scott a passion for Scottish literary and historical texts, some of which he edited for publication. On his death he bequeathed his very substantial collection of Scottish and old master drawings to the Royal Scottish Academy, specifying that they should be 'classed and bound in volumes, excluding such as may be reckoned not worth preservation'. Unfortunately, the mass of Laing's correspondence and personal papers now belonging to Edinburgh University Library sheds no light on where, when or from whom he acquired his drawings, but it is very likely that this was for him a sideline to activities as a collector of books and manuscripts. Ownership of the majority of the drawings was transferred to the National Gallery of Scotland in 1910; further significant batches of drawings from the Laing bequest were discovered later in the Royal Scottish Academy, and these were placed on permanent loan to the National Gallery in 1966 and 1974 respectively.

Literature: Edinburgh, 1976

LORD LINDSAY: SEE EARL OF CRAWFORD

3RD EARL OF LOTHIAN AND 8TH MARQUESS OF LOTHIAN

Two members of the Lothian family have played a particularly important role in the history of collecting in Scotland, William Kerr, 3rd Earl (c.1605–1675) and his namesake the 8th Marquess (1832–1870). The 3rd Earl was prominent in mid-seventeenth-century Scottish politics as a leading Covenanter, but from the 1640s he also found time to create an important library and a very large collection of pictures at his home of Newbattle Abbey, near Dalkeith. Mainly Dutch, Flemish and British, the pictures also included two portraits attributed to Tintoretto, possibly the earliest examples of Venetian cinquecento painting to be imported into Scotland.

The 8th Marquess of Lothian also had high political ambitions after a brilliant undergraduate career at Oxford, but persistent ill health forced him to abandon these at an early date for the more sedentary life of a scholar and collector. He made several picture-buying trips to Italy, concentrating in particular on Florence and Rome. Following the lead of writers and collectors such as LORD LINDSAY and JAMES DENNISTOUN, he was attracted above all to the fifteenth-century Florentines and Umbrians, but this did not preclude a more traditional admiration for Venetian painters of the generation of Titian. His Venetian purchases included Bonifacio's huge *Return of the Prodigal Son* (cat.no.49), and a *Virgin and Child* now attributed to a follower of Titian (cat.no.28), which was bequeathed with seventeen other pictures to the National Gallery of Scotland by the 11th Marquess in 1941. A major masterpiece acquired by Lothian shortly before his premature death in 1870, but sold by the 9th Marquess to the Berlin Museum in 1892, was Albrecht Dürer's *The Madonna of the Siskin*, painted in Venice in 1506 (fig.9).

Literature: Thompson, 1972, pp.111–12; Edinburgh, 1992, p.167; Wenley, 1993; Wenley, 2003

ARCHIBALD MCLELLAN

In his will of 1853 Archibald McLellan (1796–1854), who during the course of the previous thirty years had assembled the greatest non-aristocratic collection of pictures in Scotland, left it to the city of Glasgow with the intention that it should form the basis of a civic art gallery. McLellan was a wealthy coach-builder and harness-maker, who played an active role in civic life, serving as convener of the Trades Guild and a baillie on the Town Council, and was closely involved in the restoration of Glasgow Cathedral. He was also a friend of leading artists of his time such as Wilkie, Chantrey and JOHN GRAHAM-GILBERT. He was perhaps inspired in his endeavour of forming a collection for Glasgow that included works from all the principal European schools by the example of Robert Foulis in the eighteenth century. As early as 1838, the Revd Thomas Dibdin, who visited McLellan for dinner on his tour of Scotland, declared that 'his house teems with art' (Dibdin, 1838, II, p.773). A representative sample of McLellan's collection, which included works from all the principal European schools, was recorded by Waagen, who visited the owner at Mugdock Castle in 1851, and made a number of re-attributions (1854, III, pp.286–91). These were duly incorporated into the initial catalogue, drawn up after McLellan's death in 1854, when an impressive total of 510 pictures was displayed in three purpose-built galleries in Sauchiehall Street. Waagen visited these on his second trip to Scotland in 1856, and made several

further reattributions, including of the now famous *Christ and the Adulteress* (cat.no.13) from Bonifacio to Giorgione (1857, pp.457–62). McLellan owned a number of other Venetian pictures, including works by Catena (cat.no.8), Paris Bordon (cat.no.30), one now attributed to Francesco Vecellio (cat.no.27) and Tintoretto (cat.no.51), as well as the huge Bellinesque *Virgin and Child Enthroned with Saints and Musician Angels* (fig.72) formerly in the Palazzo Balbi, Venice, and later in the Solly collection, which Waagen oddly considered to be an early work by Giorgione.

Literature: The McLellan Gallery. Catalogue of Pictures bequeathed to the People of Glasgow by the late Archibald McLellan, Glasgow, 1855; Pinnington, 1898, pp.9–14; E. Gallie, 'Archibald McLellan', *Scottish Art Review*, v, 1, 1954, pp.7–12; M. Park, 'The McLellan bequest', *Scottish Art Review*, XVII, 1991, pp.22–5; Edinburgh, 1992, pp.168–9; Hamilton, 2003

LADY MURRAY OF HENDERLAND

Lady Murray was the wife of the nephew of the celebrated Scottish portrait painter Allan Ramsay. After her husband's death, in 1860 she presented a very substantial group of over 300 of Ramsay's drawings to the National Gallery of Scotland, which had just opened the previous year. With these was a small but significant number of continental drawings, mainly Italian. Most of these are assumed to have been collected by Ramsay himself, who made four trips to Italy.

ROBERT NAPIER

The eminent marine engineer and shipbuilder Robert Napier (1791–1876) began his career as an apprentice to his father, a blacksmith from Dumbarton. By 1823 Napier had constructed his first marine engine, and by the 1840s he was providing the steam engines for much of the Royal Navy and for the entire Cunard fleet. In his later years he lived at West Shandon on Gareloch, in a villa he had built for himself and his sumptuous art collection. This consisted of oriental porcelain, silver, bronzes, furniture and clocks, as well as of contemporary and old master paintings. Inventories of the collection are provided in a privately printed catalogue of 1865 by Sir J.C. Robinson, and by the catalogue of the Napier sale at Christie's in 1877 (11–17 April). His Venetian pictures included Bonifacio's *The Holy Family with St Elizabeth, the Infant St John the Baptist and two Shepherds* (fig.18) now in the Los Angeles County Museum of Art, as well as others attributed to Titian, Paris Bordon, Jacopo Bassano, Tintoretto and Veronese. Some fine renaissance bronzes and pieces of maiolica were bought at his posthumous sale by the Royal Museum of Scotland in Edinburgh (see cat.nos.178, 180, 184, 208, 209, 240, 242).

Literature: Irving, 1881, p.385; *Dictionary of National Biography*, XL, London, 1894, pp.74–5; Edinburgh, 1992, p.169

5TH EARL OF ROSEBERY

Archibald Primrose, 5th Earl of Rosebery (1847–1929), was a distinguished historian as well as an active Liberal politician, who succeeded Gladstone as Prime Minister in 1894. He inherited two considerable art collections, housed at his own family seat of Dalmeny, close to the Firth of Forth, and at Mentmore, the Buckinghamshire mansion built by his father-in-law, the fabulously wealthy Baron Mayer de Rothschild. Moroni's *Portrait of Giovanni Bressani* (cat.no.62) was part of the Mentmore collection. Rosebery did not add greatly to the old masters in either collection, but in 1893 he did buy for Dalmeny Titian's *Portrait of Admiral Vincenzo Cappello* (cat.no.35), previously at Hamilton Palace. He had bought Jacques-Louis David's *Portrait of Napoleon in his Study* (Washington, National Gallery of Art) at the Hamilton Palace sale of 1882, and for him part of the attraction of Titian's picture may have been its long association with the Hamilton collection, and perhaps also its military subject.

Literature: Paul, 1904–14, VII, pp.227–8

MARY, LADY RUTHVEN

Mary Hamilton Campbell, Lady Ruthven (1789–1885) was a talented amateur watercolourist who left three old master paintings, two fine watercolours by G. B. Lusieri, a terracotta after Michelangelo, and two antique marble steles to the National Gallery of Scotland on her death. The daughter of Walter Campbell of Shawfield, she married James, 7th Baron Ruthven (1777–1853) in 1813, and in the 1820s the couple lived in Athens. As a person who 'takes a true interest in matters of art', she provided Waagen with a letter of introduction to visit Rossie Priory, even in the absence of its owner, LORD KINNAIRD (Waagen, 1857, p.445). The three old masters she left to the gallery include the *Portrait of an Archer* attributed to Giorgione (cat.no.12) and Tintoretto's *Portrait of a Bearded Man* (cat.no.52). To judge from the provenance of the former, she and her husband may have bought the pictures in London in 1827, presumably for their seventeenth-century home of Winton House, Pencaitland.

Literature: Paul, 1904–14, VII, pp.390–1

9TH EARL OF SOUTHESK

An impressive collection of largely Italian pictures at Kinnaird Castle, near Brechin, was formed between about 1820 and 1870 by Sir James Carnegie, 5th Baronet and 16th Laird (1799–1849), and his son, also Sir James, 6th Baronet and, from 1855, 9th Earl of Southesk (1827–1905). From the manuscript catalogue of the collection compiled by the latter shortly before his

death, it is evident that the 5th Baronet, who bought important pictures by Lodovico Carracci, Domenichino and Albani in Bologna in 1826, had a traditional taste for the Bolognese Seicento. Significantly in the present context, he also bought Moretto's *King David with a Donor* (cat.no.43) with an attribution to Domenichino.

Lord Southesk had an early career in the army before serving as Lord Lieutenant of Kincardineshire from 1849 to 1856, and he later went on to write a number of antiquarian and art-historical works, including *Britain's Art Paradise*, in which he compared contemporary British painters such as Millais, Leighton and Poynter highly unfavourably with old masters such as Jan van Eyck, Crivelli and Giovanni Bellini (Southesk, 1871). By 1854 he was the owner of Lotto's *Portrait of a Lady as Lucretia* (cat.no.32), then attributed to Giorgione, which he (or his father) probably bought directly from his neighbour Sir John FORBES OF PITSLIGO, but which he sold on to R.S. Holford in London in 1855. Perhaps this was because he increasingly shared the new taste for the Primitives, as is reflected in his purchase of a number of fifteenth-century pictures in Florence in 1865, and two years earlier at the sale of the pioneering collection assembled by the Revd Walter Davenport Bromley. The latter group included works by or attributed to Jacobello del Fiore, Squarcione, and Giovanni Bellini (cat.no.2). The Jacobello was lost together with other important works of art in a serious fire at Kinnaird Castle in 1921, and others have been sold subsequently.

Literature: Millar, 1890, pp.245–71; Southesk, 1904; Paul, 1904–14, IX, pp.88–92

CHARLES STIRLING OF CAWDER AND SIR WILLIAM STIRLING-MAXWELL

On his first visit to Scotland Waagen did not visit the collection of William Stirling of Keir, near Dunblane, and he recorded (1854, III, p. 314) just one Italian picture he knew to be in the collection, Signorelli's *Lamentation* (Glasgow, Pollok House). But on his second tour in 1856 Waagen did visit Keir, and recorded two Venetian pictures (1857, p.451), as well as many of the Spanish pictures that Stirling – better known by his later title of Sir William Stirling-Maxwell (1818–1878) – later transferred to Pollok when he inherited the Maxwell baronetcy from his maternal uncle. The two Venetian pictures were a half-length *Concert* attributed by Waagen to Previtali, but still awaiting a satisfactory attribution (see F. Rossi in Bergamo, 2001, pp.214–15), and Veronese's *Baptism of Christ* (cat.no.70). Both of these were inherited by the owner from his uncle Charles Stirling of Cawder (1771–1830), who had bought them at London sales in 1829, apparently through the agency of his

kinsman the 7th EARL OF ELGIN. Three more Venetian pictures acquired by Charles Stirling in the 1820s – Tintoretto's *Portrait of Marco Zane* (Rossi, 1974, p.144), Schiavone's *Ecce Homo* (Richardson, 1980, p.194), and Paris Bordon's *Rest on the Flight into Egypt* (cat.no.46) – were still in the 1850s in the possession of the buyer's widow at Cawder House, near Bishopbriggs, and were not known to Waagen. All five of these Venetian pictures were put up for sale by Col. W.J. Stirling of Keir, grandson of Sir William Stirling-Maxwell, at Sotheby's on 3 July 1963. A *Portrait of Pietro Aretino in Profile* attributed to Titian, sold to Charles Stirling by JAMES IRVINE in 1828 after being refused by Stirling's brother-in-law THOMAS ERSKINE OF LINLATHEN, has not been traced.

Literature: W. Fraser, *The Stirlings of Keir*, Edinburgh, 1858; *Burke's Landed Gentry*, 1914 ed., p.1791

JAMES STIRLING OF GLENTYAN

In 1854 Waagen (III, p.314) referred to a collection of pictures formed by Captain James Stirling of Glentyan, Deputy Lieutenant and MP for Renfrewshire (1789–1872). These included works attributed to Giovanni Bellini, Bonifacio, Tintoretto, Veronese, Zelotti and Moroni. Since, however, Waagen did not actually visit the collection or provide titles, the pictures cannot now be identified. He records that they had been collected on the advice of JAMES IRVINE and a 'Mr Colombo' (who also advised his cousin and close friend THOMAS ERSKINE OF LINLATHEN) in Rome, as well as of the painter William Dyce.

1ST DUKE OF SUTHERLAND

The history of the Sutherland collection is closely bound up with that of the Ellesmere collection, and their corresponding picture galleries – known respectively as the Stafford Gallery and the Bridgewater Gallery – were two of the most important in nineteenth-century London. Both had their origins in the sale in London in 1798 of one of the most celebrated collections of eighteenth-century Europe, that of the Dukes of Orléans, the cadet branch of the French royal family. At the Orléans sale the cream of the Italian pictures, many of which were by the great cinquecento Venetians, were reserved for a syndicate of three English noblemen: Francis Egerton, 3rd Duke of Bridgewater (1736–1803); his maternal nephew, George Leveson-Gower, Earl Gower (1758–1833); and Gower's brother-in-law, the 5th Earl of Carlisle. On the death of his childless uncle, Gower – who subsequently succeeded to the titles of 2nd Marquess of Stafford (through his father) and 1st Duke of Sutherland (through his wife) – inherited some seven eighths of the Italian pictures from the former Orléans collection, and added to it by making

extensive further acquisitions of his own. Displayed at Cleveland House, St James's, in the three decades between 1803 and 1833, a monument to the extraordinary range and quality of the Stafford collection is provided by the sumptuous four-volume illustrated catalogue by William Young Ottley (1818).

After the 1st Duke's death in 1833, the collection was re-divided into its 'Gower' and 'Bridgewater' constituents, with the former passing to the elder son, the 2nd Duke, and the latter (and more important) part to the younger son, Lord Francis Leveson-Gower, who assumed the surname of Egerton in honour of his great-uncle. The collection of the 2nd Duke of Sutherland and his descendants was moved to nearby Stafford House (previously known as York or Gower House), where it was kept until the house was sold in 1912 (and subsequently renamed Lancaster House), and the collection dispersed. It was at the Sutherland sale in the following year that the National Gallery of Scotland purchased Veronese's *St Anthony Abbot with a Kneeling Donor* (cat.no.59).

Meanwhile, Lord Francis Egerton, who was created 1st Earl of Ellesmere in 1846, rebuilt much of Cleveland House, renaming it Bridgewater House, and similarly renaming the Stafford Gallery the Bridgewater Gallery (fig.76). It was his descendant John, 5th Earl (1915–2000), who moved the Ellesmere collection to Scotland after Bridgewater House was seriously damaged by bombardment in the Second World War, and who placed the former Orléans Titians (cat.nos.19, 25, 54, 55), Lotto (cat.no.11) and Tintoretto (cat.no.66) – as well as important Raphaels and Poussins – on long-term loan to the National Gallery of Scotland. At first known as the Ellesmere Loan, this became known as the Sutherland Loan after the 5th Earl inherited the title of 6th Duke of Sutherland from his distant Leveson-Gower cousin in 1963.

Literature: Herrmann, 1972, pp.139–42; Edinburgh, 1992, p.171

JOHN WALDIE

The privately printed *Catalogue of Pictures, Statues etc … at Hendersyde Park* (2nd edition, 1859) also gives an account of the formation of the collection by Waldie in London and Italy during the 1820s and 1830s, and of the building of his house near Kelso from 1803. The Venetian pictures included works attributed to Palma Vecchio, Bonifacio, Schiavone, Moroni, Tintoretto (a large *Esther and Ahasuerus*) and Veronese (a sketch for the *Apotheosis of Venice*, bought from Sir Thomas Lawrence in 1830). A portrait now attributed to Tintoretto in the Museum of Fine Arts, Boston, is probably identifiable with a picture described in the catalogue (p.45) as 'School of Titian. Head of a Man with Lace Frill. Collection

419

of Mr Silvester, 1825.' The collection was subsequently inherited by Waldie's nephew, Sir George Waldie-Griffith, and was dispersed after the death of his son Sir Richard Waldie-Griffith in 1927.

WILLIAM FINDLAY WATSON

Watson (1810–1881) was the son of baker from Leith who was apprenticed aged fifteen to an Edinburgh bookseller, leaving after seven years to set up his own business. Like DAVID LAING, his main interests were in Scottish history, literature and topography. He built up a very large and varied collection of prints, autograph letters and drawings, which he bequeathed to the Board of Trustees for Manufactures in Scotland, which then administered the National Gallery. The majority of the 1400 plus drawings that were allocated to the Gallery are Scottish, but among them are some outstanding sheets by old masters, including a number of Venetian drawings (see cat.nos.96, 99, 118). As is the case with Laing, virtually nothing is known about where Watson acquired his drawings.

Literature: Edinburgh, 1981

EARLS OF WEMYSS & MARCH

Several eighteenth- and nineteeth-century Earls of Wemyss collected paintings, but two of them were of particular importance: Francis, 7th Earl (1723–1808); and his great-grandson Francis, 10th Earl, known for much of his life as Lord Elcho (1818–1914). The 7th Earl's collection was distinguished above all for its Dutch pictures (Edinburgh, 1992, p.171), but towards the end of his long life – stimulated, perhaps, by the completion of his huge new Italianate house of Gosford, designed for him by Robert Adam and built between 1792 and 1803 – he seems to have acquired a new interest in Italian painting. Certainly, WILLIAM BUCHANAN in 1803–4 considered that the Earl had 'a particular rage for naked beauties', and thought that he would be a likely purchaser of Titian's *Venus and Adonis* or *Bacchus and Ariadne* (Brigstocke, 1982, pp.113, 184, 243). Nothing came of these overtures, but the 8th Earl's purchase in 1836 of a *Venus Disarming Cupid* attributed to Veronese from the collection of LORD ELDIN reflects similar taste.

The 8th Earl's grandson, Lord Elcho, had highly developed aesthetic tastes from an early age, and unlike most aristocratic collectors he never made use of agents. While still an undergraduate at Oxford in the late 1830s he offered advice to his father and grandfather on purchases of Italian art (including Savoldo's *Shepherd with a Flute* cat.no.41), and he made his own first acquisitions – including Romanino's *Adoration of the Shepherds*, then attributed to Giorgione (cat.no.24) – on his first trip to Italy in 1842. His buying was in full spate in the 1850s, when Waagen twice visited his house in London, and made a special note of the pictures acquired between 1851 and 1856 (Waagen, 1854, II, pp.82–3; 1857, pp.62–4). As a member of the generation of LORD LINDSAY and John Ruskin (a contemporary at Christ Church), Elcho inevitably shared the growing appreciation of the Primitives, and he was the owner of Masolino's *Annunciation* (Washington, National Gallery of Art) and Botticelli's *Virgin Adoring the Sleeping Christ Child* (Edinburgh, National Gallery of Scotland), as well as of the domestic polyptych by Bartolomeo Vivarini (cat.no.1). But as the range of pictures from Gosford in the present exhibition shows (in addition to those already mentioned, see cat.nos.20, 47, 56, 68 and 79), his tastes remained catholic, and he evidently enjoyed sensuously profane pictures from the Venetian Cinquecento as much as Quattrocento Madonnas. In 1870 Elcho lent eighty-two paintings for exhibition at the South Kensington Museum, and after his succession as 10th Earl in 1883, he rebuilt two of the previously demolished wings of Adam's house, one of which was specifically designed as a picture gallery.

Literature: Paul, 1904–14, VII, pp.512–18; Edinburgh, National Gallery of Scotland, *Pictures from Gosford House lent by the Earl of Wemyss and March*, exh. cat. by C. Thompson, Edinburgh, 1957; Wemyss, 2003

ANDREW WILSON

Wilson (1780–1848) was an Edinburgh-born painter who also acted as a dealer and adviser to collectors. Trained under Alexander Nasmyth and at the Royal Academy Schools in London, he specialised as a landscape painter. His career as a speculator in old master paintings began in Italy in 1803–6, when he succeeded in buying a number of pictures from aristocratic Genoese collections, including Jacopo Bassano's *Adoration of the Kings* (cat.no.40). On his return to Britain he sold the paintings he had acquired (Buchanan, 1824, II, pp.195–202) and resumed his career as a painter and art teacher. He returned to Edinburgh in 1818 to become master at the Trustees' Academy, also becoming closely involved with the organisation of the Royal Institution's exhibitions, and advising the 4th EARL OF HOPETOUN on the refurbishment of Hopetoun House. Wilson spent the years 1826–32 back in Italy, where he continued to work for the Royal Institution and for the 5th EARL OF HOPETOUN, and also for other Scottish collectors such as Sir Archibald CAMPBELL OF SUCCOTH. Among the Venetian pictures he sent back to Scotland during this phase were Leandro Bassano's *Portrait of Doge Marcantonio Memmo* (cat.no.80), Paris Bordon's *Venetian Women at their Toilet* (cat.no.48), and the Tintorettesque *Portrait of a Gentleman* (cat.no.67). Wilson's son, Charles Heath Wilson, important as an art educator, also became an adviser to collectors, including ARCHIBALD MCLELLAN, and accompanied Waagen on several of his excursions in 1851.

Literature: J. Caw, *Scottish Painting Past and Present*, London, 1908, pp.152–3; Skinner, 1968; Thompson, 1972, p.18; Irwin and Irwin, 1975, pp.241–2; Brigstocke, 1982

BIBLIOGRAPHY

ACIDINI LUCHINAT, 1998–9
C. Acidini Luchinat, *Taddeo e Federico Zuccari: fratelli pittori del Cinquecento*, 2 vols., Rome, 1998–9

AIKEMA, 1996
B. Aikema, *Jacopo Bassano and his Public. Moralising Pictures in an Age of Reform, ca. 1535–1600*, Princeton, 1996

ALBRICCI, 1980
G. Albricci, 'Le incisioni di Paolo e Orazio Farinati', *Saggi e Memorie di Storia dell'Arte*, 12, 1980, pp.9–30

AMSTERDAM, 1992
Amsterdam, Rijksmuseum, *Chiaroscuro Woodcuts. Hendrik Goltzius and his Time (1558–1617)*, exh. cat. ed. by N. Bialler, Amsterdam, 1992

ANDERSON, 1997
J. Anderson, *Giorgione: the Painter of Poetic Brevity*, Paris, 1997

ANDREWS, 1968
K. Andrews, *National Gallery of Scotland: Catalogue of Italian Drawings*, 2 vols., Cambridge, 1968 (reprinted 1971)

ARMAND, 1883–7
A. Armand, *Les médailleurs italiens des quinzième et seizième siècles*, 3 vols., Paris, 1883–7

ARMENINI, 1586
G.B. Armenini, *De' veri precetti della pittura*, Ravenna, 1586

ARSLAN, 1960
E. Arslan, *I Bassano*, 2 vols., Milan, 1960

ATHENS, 1995
Athens, National Gallery, *El Greco in Italy and Italian Art*, exh. cat. ed. by N. Hadjinicolaou, Athens, 1995

AULD, 2004
S. Auld, National Gallery, *Renaissance Venice, Islam and Mahmub the Kurd metalworking enigma*, London, 2004

AVERY AND RADCLIFFE, 1983
C. Avery and A. Radcliffe, 'Severo Calzetta da Ravenna: New Discoveries' in *Studien zum Europäischen Kunsthandwerk: Festschrift Yvonne Hackenbroch*, Munich, 1983

BAGATIN, PIZZAMANO AND RIGOBELLO, 1992
P.L. Bagatin, P. Pizzamano and B. Rigobello, *Lendinara: Notizie e immagini per una storia dei beni artistici e librari*, Treviso, 1992

BAGROW, 1948
L. Bagrow, 'A Page from the Distribution of Maps', *Imago Mundi*, V, 1948, pp.53–62

BALLARIN, 1971
A. Ballarin, 'Considerazioni su una mostra di disegni veronesi del '500', *Arte Veneta*, XXV, 1971, pp. 92–118

BANGE, 1922
E.F. Bange, *Die Italienischen Bronzen der Renaissance und des Barock: vol.2, Reliefs und Plaketten (Katalog des Kaiser Friedrich-Museums in Berlin)*, Berlin and Leipzig, 1922

BARBERI, 1969
F. Barberi, *Il Frontispizio nel libro italiano del quattrocento e del cinquecento*, 2 vols., Milan, 1969

BARTSCH, 1803–21
A. von Bartsch, *Le Peintre graveur*, 21 vols., Vienna, 1803–21

BASEGGIO, 1844
G.B. Baseggio, *Intorno tre celebri intagliatori in legno vicentini*, Bassano, 1844

BASSANO, 1992
Bassano del Grappa, Museo Civico, *Jacopo Bassano e l'incisione*, exh. cat. ed. by E. Pan, Bassano, 1992

BEMBO, 1954
P. Bembo, *Gli Asolani*, translated by R.B. Gottfried, Bloomington, 1954

BERENSON, 1901
B. Berenson, 'Venetian painting at the New Gallery 1895' in *The Study and Criticism of Italian Art*, London, 1901, pp.90–146

BERENSON, 1907
B. Berenson, *Venetian Painters of the Renaissance*, 3rd edn., London, 1907

BERENSON, 1916
B. Berenson, *Venetian Painting in America*, London, 1916

BERENSON, 1957
B. Berenson, *Italian Pictures of the Renaissance: Venetian School*. 2 vols., London, 1957

BERGAMO, 1979
Bergamo, Accademia Carrara, *Giovanni Battista Moroni (1520–1578)*, exh. cat. ed. by M. Gregori, Bergamo, 1979

BERGAMO, 2001
Bergamo, Accademia Carrara, *Bergamo: L'altra Venezia. Il Rinascimento negli anni di Lorenzo Lotto 1510–1530*, exh. cat. ed. by F. Rossi, Milan, 2001

BERLIN, 1971
Berlin, Kupferstichkabinett, *Tizian und sein Kreis*, exh. cat. ed. by P. Dreyer, Berlin, 1971

BIERENS DE HAAN, 1948
J.C.J. Bierens de Haan, *L'oeuvre gravé de Cornelis Cort*, The Hague, 1948

BOHN, 1995
B. Bohn, *The Illustrated Bartsch*, 39, *Italian Masters of the Sixteenth Century: Agostino Carracci, Commentary*, part 1, New York, 1995

BORRONI SALVADORI, 1980
F. Borroni Salvadori, *Carte, piante e stampe storiche delle raccolte lafreriane della Biblioteca Nazionale di Firenze* (Ministero per i Beni Culturali e Ambientali. Indici e cataloghi NS, XI), Rome, 1980

BOSCHINI, 1660
M. Boschini, *La Carta del Navegar Pittoresco* (1660), (ed.) A. Pallucchini, Rome, 1966

BOSCHINI, 1664
M. Boschini, *Le Minere della Pittura*, Venice, 1664

BOSTON, 1989
Boston, Museum of Fine Arts, *Italian Etchers of the Renaissance and the Baroque*, exh. cat. by S.W. Reed, R. Wallace *et al.*, Boston, 1989

BOSTRÖM, 2004
A. Boström (ed.), *The Encyclopedia of Sculpture*, 3 vols., New York, 2004

BOUCHER, 1991
B. Boucher, *The Sculpture of Jacopo Sansovino*, 2 vols., New Haven and London, 1991

BRANDOLESE, 1795
P. Brandolese, *Del genio de' lendinaresi per la pittura*, 1795, V. Sgarbi (ed.), Lendinara, 1990

BRESCIA, 1988
Brescia, Monastero di Santa Giulia, *Alessandro Bonvicino il Moretto*, exh. cat. by B. Passamani, Bologna, 1988

BRESCIA, 1990
Brescia, Monastero di Santa Giulia, *Giovanni Gerolamo Savoldo*, exh. cat. ed. by B. Passamani, Milan, 1990

BRIGSTOCKE, 1981
H. Brigstocke, 'William Buchanan: his friends and rivals. The importation of Old Master Paintings into Great Britain during the first half of the nineteenth century', *Apollo*, CXIV, 1981, pp.76–84

BRIGSTOCKE, 1982
H. Brigstocke, *William Buchanan and the 19th-Century Art Trade: 100 Letters to his Agents in London and Italy*, London, 1982

BRIGSTOCKE, 1993
H. Brigstocke, *Italian and Spanish Paintings in the National Gallery of Scotland*, 2nd edn., Edinburgh, 1993

BROWN, 1987
I.G. Brown, *The Clerks of Penicuik: Portraits of Taste and Talent*, Edinburgh, 1987

BROWN, 2003A
I.G. Brown, '"I understood pictures better than became my purse …": the Clerks of Penicuik and Eldin as collectors and connoisseurs', *Journal of the Scottish Society for Art History*, VIII, 2003, pp.27–36

BROWN, 2003B
I.G. Brown, 'Venerating the Venetians? Some Scottish views of the painters of the Golden Age', *Journal of the Scottish Society for Art History*, VIII, 2003, pp.93–6

BRUSCO, 1781
G. Brusco, *Description des Beautés de Gênes*, 2nd edn., Genoa, 1781

BUCHANAN, 1824
W. Buchanan, *Memoirs of Painting, with a chronological History of the Importation of Pictures by the Great Masters into England since the French Revolution*, 2 vols., London, 1824

BURNS, COLLARETA AND GASPAROTTO, 2000
H. Burns, M. Collareta and D. Gasparotto (eds.), *Valerio Belli Vicentino 1468 c.–1546*, Vicenza, 2000

BURY, 1985
M. Bury, 'The Taste for Prints in Italy to c.1600', *Print Quarterly*, II, 1985, pp.12–26

BURY, 2003
M. Bury, 'New Light on Battista del Moro as a Printmaker', *Print Quarterly*, XX, 2003, pp.123–30

BYAM SHAW, 1976
J. Byam Shaw, *Drawings by Old Masters at Christ Church, Oxford*, 2 vols., Oxford, 1976

CALLEGARI, 2000
R. Callegari, 'Il mercato d'arte a Venezia alla fine del Settecento e Giovanni Maria Sasso', in Pavanello, 2000, pp.95–119

CAMPORI, 1870
G. Campori, *Raccolta di cataloghi ed inventari inediti*, Modena, 1870

CANOVA, 1964
G. Canova, *Paris Bordon*, Venice, 1964

CARRARA AND GREGORY, 2000
E. Carrara and S. Gregory, 'Borghini's Print Purchases from Giunti', *Print Quarterly*, XVII, 2000, pp.3–17

CESCHI LAVAGETTO, 1981
P. Ceschi Lavagetto (ed.), *Giornata di Studio sul Pordenone*, Piacenza, 1981

CHARLOTTESVILLE, 1991
Charlottesville (Va), Bayly Art Museum, *Masterpieces of Renaissance and Baroque Printmaking*, exh. cat. ed. by S. Sell, Charlottesville, 1991

CHIARI, 1982
M.A. Chiari, *Incisioni da Tiziano; catalogo del fondo grafico a stampa del Museo Correr*, Venice, 1982

CICOGNA, 1824–53
E.A. Cicogna, *Delle iscrizioni veneziane*, 6 vols., Venice, 1824–53

CLARKE, 2000
M. Clarke *et al.*, *A Companion Guide to the National Gallery of Scotland*, Edinburgh, 2000

CLEVELAND, 1975
Cleveland, Museum of Art, *Renaissance Bronzes from Ohio Collections*, exh. cat. by W.D. Wixom, Cleveland, 1975

CLIFFORD, 2003
T. Clifford, 'Italian art in Scotland in the 18th and early 19th centuries', *Journal of the Scottish Society for Art History*, VIII, 2003, pp.7–16

COCKE, 1984
R. Cocke, *Veronese's Drawings: a Catalogue Raisonné*, London, 1984

COCKE, 2001
R. Cocke, *Paolo Veronese*, Aldershot, 2001

COHEN 1980
C.E. Cohen, *The Drawings of Giovanni Antonio da Pordenone*, Florence, 1980

COHEN, 1996
C.E. Cohen, *The Art of Giovanni Antonio Pordenone: Between Dialect and Language*, 2 vols., Cambridge, 1996

CONCINA, 1975
E.Concina, 'Un contributo alla definizione della cronologia ed all' ambiente di Maestro Domenico da Venezia', *Faenza*, 61, 1975, pp.136–9

CONSTABLE, 1930
W.G. Constable, 'Dipinti di raccolte inglesi alla mostra d'arte italiana a Londra', *Dedalo*, X, 1929–30, pp.723–67

CONTON, 1940
L. Conton, *Le antiche ceramiche veneziane scoperte nella laguna*, Venice, 1940

COTTRELL, 2000
P. Cottrell, *Bonifacio's Enterprise. Bonifacio de' Pitati and Venetian Painting*, Ph.D. thesis, University of St Andrews, 2000

CROWE AND CAVALCASELLE, 1871
J.A. Crowe and G.B. Cavalcaselle, *A History of Painting in North Italy*, 2 vols., London, 1871

CROWE AND CAVALCASELLE, 1877
J.A. Crowe and G.B. Cavalcaselle, *Titian: his Life and Times*, 2 vols., London, 1877

CURNOW, 1992
C. Curnow, *Italian Maiolica in the National Museums of Scotland*, Edinburgh, 1992

D'ONOFRIO, 1964
C. D'Onofrio, 'Inventario dei dipinti del Cardinal Pietro Aldobrandini compilato da G.B Agucchi nel 1603', *Palatino*, pp.15–20, 158–62, 202–11

DA MOSTO, 1966
Andrea Da Mosto, *I Dogi di Venezia*, Venice, 1966

DAVIES, 1961
M. Davies, *The National Gallery Catlaogues: The Earlier Italian Schools*, London, 1961

DETROIT, 1985
Detroit, Institute of Arts, and Fort Worth, Kimbell Art Museum, *Italian Renaissance Sculpure in the Time of Donatello*, exh. cat. ed. by A.P. Darr, Detroit, 1985-6

DE VECCHI, 1970
P. De Vecchi, *L'Opera Completa del Tintoretto*, Milan, 1970

DIBDIN, 1838
T. Dibdin, *A Biobliographical, Antiquarian and Picturesque Tour of the Northern Counties of England and in Scotland*, 2 vols., London, 1838

DOLCE, 1557
L. Dolce, *Dialogo della pittura, intitolato l'Aretino*, Venice, 1557

DREYER, 1979
P. Dreyer, 'Tizianfälschungen des sechzehnten Jahrhunderts: Korrekturen zur Definition der Delineatio bei Tizian und Anmerkungen zur Datierung seiner Holzschnitte', *Pantheon*, XXXVII, 1979, pp.365–75

DREYER, 1980
P. Dreyer, 'Sulle silografie di Tiziano', *Tiziano e Venezia: Convegno internazionale di studi (Venice, 1976)*, Vicenza, 1980, pp.503–11

DUBOIS DE SAINT GELAIS, 1727
L.F. Dubois de Saint Gelais, *Description des Tableaux du Palais Royal*, Paris, 1727

DUISBURG, 1994
Duisburg, Wilhelm Lehmbruck Museum, *Beschwörung des Kosmos: Europäische Bronzen der Renaissance*, exh. cat. by C. Brockhaus *et al.*, 1994–5

DUNKERTON, FOISTER AND PENNY, 1999
J. Dunkerton, S. Foister and N. Penny, *Dürer to Veronese. Sixteenth-Century Painting in the National Gallery*, London, 1999

EDINBURGH, 1883
Edinburgh, Royal Institution, *Works of Old Masters and Scottish National Portraits*, exh. cat., Edinburgh, 1883

EDINBURGH, 1976
Edinburgh, National Gallery of Scotland, *Old Master Drawings from the David Laing Bequest*, exh. cat. by K. Andrews, Edinburgh, 1976

EDINBURGH, 1981
Edinburgh, National Gallery of Scotland, *Drawings from the Bequest of W.F. Watson 1881–1981*, exh. cat. by K. Andrews, Edinburgh, 1981

EDINBURGH, 1985
Edinburgh, Royal Scottish Museum, *French Connections: Scotland and the Arts of France*, exh. cat. ed. by G. Evans, Edinburgh, 1985

EDINBURGH, 1989
Edinburgh, National Gallery of Scotland, *The Patrons of the National Galleries of Scotland: Catalogue One*, exh. cat. by T. Clifford, Edinburgh, 1989

EDINBURGH, 1990
Edinburgh, National Gallery of Scotland, *Giulio Sanuto, a Venetian Engraver of the Sixteenth Century*, exh. cat. by M. Bury, Edinburgh, 1990

EDINBURGH, 1992
Edinburgh, National Gallery of Scotland, *Dutch Art and Scotland: A Reflection of Taste*, exh. cat. by J. Lloyd Williams *et al.*, Edinburgh, 1992

EDINBURGH, 1999
Edinburgh, National Gallery of Scotland, New York, Frick Collection, and Houston, Museum of Fine Arts, *The Draughtsman's Art: Master Drawings from the National Gallery of Scotland*, exh. cat., Edinburgh, 1999

EDINBURGH, 2000
Edinburgh, National Gallery of Scotland, *'A Poet in Paradise': Lord Lindsay and Christian Art*, exh. cat. ed. by A. Weston-Lewis, Edinburgh, 2000

EVANS, 2003
G. Evans, 'The Hamilton Collection and the 10th Duke of Hamilton', *Journal of the Scottish Society for Art History*, VIII, 2003, pp.53–72

FABBRO, 1977
C. Fabbro (ed.), *Tiziano: Le lettere*, Cadore, 1977

FAIRFULL-SMITH, 2001
G. Fairfull-Smith, *The Foulis Press and the Foulis Academy: Glasgow's eighteenth-century School of Art and Design*, Glasgow, 2001

FEHL, 1992
P. Fehl, *Decorum and Wit: the Poetry of Venetian Painting*, Vienna, 1992

FERRARA, 2004
Ferrara, Castello Estense, *Il Camerino di alabastro: Antonio Lombardo e la scultura all'antica*, exh. cat. by M. Ceriana *et al.*, Milan, 2004

FLORENCE, 1976
Florence, Galleria degli Uffizi, *Tiziano e il disegno del suo tempo*, exh. cat. by W.R. Rearick, Florence, 1976

FLORENCE, 1995
Florence, Istituto Universitario Olandese and Amsterdam, Rijksmuseum, *Italian Drawings from the Rijksmuseum, Amsterdam*, exh. cat. ed. by B.W. Meijer, Florence, 1995–6

FLORENCE, 2000
Florence, Galleria degli Uffizi, *Cinque secoli del disegno veronese*, exh. cat. by S. Marinelli, Florence, 2000

FORBES, 1996
D. Forbes, *Artists, Patrons and the Power of Association. The Emergence of a bourgeois artistic Field in Edinburgh, c.1775–c.1840*, Ph.D. thesis, University of St Andrews, 1996

FORLANI TEMPESTI, 2002
A. Forlani Tempesti (ed.), *Calepino di Disegni: Note e saggi su disegni e stampe e sulla loro storia. 1. Disegni dal Veneto fra cinque e seicento*, Rimini, 2002

FORT WORTH, 1993
Fort Worth, Kimbell Art Museum, *Jacopo Bassano c.1510–1592*, exh. cat. ed. by B.L. Brown and P. Marini, Bologna, 1993

FORT WORTH, 2000
Fort Worth, Kimbell Art Museum, *Giovanni Battista Moroni: Renaissance Portraitist*, exh. cat. by P. Humfrey *et al.*, Fort Worth, 2000

FOSSALUZZA, 1983
G. Fossaluzza, 'Profilo di Domenico Capriolo', *Arte Veneta*, XXXVII, 1983, pp.49–66

FOSSALUZZA AND MANZATO, 1987
G. Fossaluzza and E. Manzato (eds.), *Paris Bordon e il suo tempo: Atti del convegno internazionale di studi (Treviso, 28–30 October 1985)*, Treviso, 1987

FOULIS, 1776
R. Foulis, *A Catalogue of Pictures composed and painted chiefly by the Masters of the Roman … etc Schools*, 3 vols., Glasgow, 1776

FRANGI, 1992
F. Frangi, *Savoldo*, Florence, 1992

FRANKFURT, 1985
Frankfurt am Main, Liebieghaus, Museum alter Plastik, *Natur und Antike in der Renaissance*, exh. cat., Frankfurt, 1985–6

FREDERICKSEN, 1988–93
B. Fredericksen (ed.), *The Index of Paintings sold in the British Isles during the Nineteenth Century*, I: 1801–5, Oxford, 1988; II: 1806–10, Oxford, 1990; III, 1811–15, Santa Barbara, 1993

FREEDMAN, 2003
L. Freedman, *The Revival of the Olympian Gods in Renaissance Art*, Cambridge and New York, 2003, pp.111–14

GALLO, 1950
R. Gallo, 'Gioan Francesco Camocio and his Large Map of Europe', *Imago Mundi*, 7, 1950, pp.93–102

GARAS, 1964
K. Garas, 'Giorgione et giorgionisme au XVIIe siècle I', *Bulletin du Musée Hongrois des Beaux-Arts*, XXV, 1964, pp.51–80

GARAS, 1965
K. Garas, 'Giorgione et giorgionisme au XVIIe siècle II', *Bulletin du Musée Hongrois des Beaux-Arts*, XXVII, 1965, pp.33–58

GARAS, 1967
K. Garas, 'Die Entstehung der Galerie des Erzherzogs Leopold Wilhelm', *Jahrbuch der Kunsthistorischen Sammlungen in Wien*, XXVII, 1967, pp.39–80

GEMIN, 1990
M. Gemin (ed.), *Nuovi studi su Paolo Veronese (Atti del convegno internazionale di studi su Paolo Veronese, Università di Venezia, 1988)*, Venice, 1990

GENTILI, 1988
A. Gentili, *Da Tiziano a Tiziano. Mito e allegoria nella cultura veneziana del Cinquecento*, 2nd edn., Rome, 1988

GILBERT, 1986
C. Gilbert, *The Works of Girolamo Savoldo. The 1955 dissertation with a Review of Research, 1955–1985*, New York, 1986

GLASGOW GALLERY, 1864
Glasgow Gallery of Art: Catalogue of Paintings, Glasgow, 1864

GLASGOW, 1990
Glasgow, Hunterian Art Gallery, *The Art of the Print, Part 1: from Mantegna to Goya*, Glasgow, 1990

GLASGOW, 1994
Glasgow, Hunterian Art Gallery, *The Italian Renaissance Print*, exh. cat. ed. by M. Hopkinson, Glasgow, 1994

GOFFEN, 1989
R. Goffen, *Giovanni Bellini*, New Haven and London, 1989

GOFFEN, 1997
R. Goffen, *Titian's Women*, New Haven and London, 1997

GOLDNER, 1981
G. Goldner, 'A *Baptism of Christ* by Veronese in the Getty Museum', *Journal of the J. Paul Getty Museum*, 9, 1981, pp.111–26

GORDON, 1976
E. Gordon, *The Royal Scottish Academy of Painting, Sculpture and Architecture 1826–1976*, Edinburgh, 1976

GOULD, 1975
C. Gould, *National Gallery Catalogues: The Sixteenth Century Italian Schools*, London, 1975

GRABSKI, 1987
J. Grabski, 'Rime d'amore di Paris Bordon: strutture visuali e poesia rinascimentale', in Fossaluzza and Manzato, 1987, pp. 203–11

GRANT, 1828
F. Grant, *Catalogue of Pictures ancient and modern of Kingfauns Castle, chiefly collected by Francis Lord Gray*, Perth, 1828

GRAVES, 1913–15
A. Graves, *A Century of Loan Exhibitions*, 5 vols., London, 1913–15

GREGORI, 1979
M. Gregori, *Giovan Battista Moroni*, Bergamo, 1979

GREGORI, 1986
M. Gregori (ed.), *La Pittura del Cinquecento a Brescia*, Milan, 1986

HALE, 1977
J. Hale, *Renaissance Fortification: Art or Engineering?*, London, 1977

HAMILTON, 2003
V. Hamilton, 'Italian Old Masters in Glasgow: resources for research', *Journal of the Scottish Society for Art History*, VIII, 2003, pp. 87–92

HASKELL, 1976
F. Haskell, *Rediscoveries in Art. Some Aspects of Taste, Fashion and Collecting in England and France*, New York, 1976

HEINEMANN, 1962
F. Heinemann, *Giovanni Bellini e i Belliniani*, 2 vols., Venice, 1962

HELKE, 1999
G. Helke, 'Giorgione als Maler des Paragone', *Jahrbuch des Kunsthistorischen Museums in Wien*, I, 1999, pp. 11–79

HENDERSYDE PARK, 1859
Catalogue of Pictures, Statues etc … at Hendersyde Park, 2nd edn., privately printed, 1859

HERRMANN, 1972
F. Herrmann, *The English as Collectors. A documentary Chrestomathy*, London, 1972

HILL, 1930
G.F. Hill, *A Corpus of the Italian Medals of the Renaissance before Cellini*, 2 vols., London, 1930

HILL AND POLLARD, 1967
Renaissance Medals from the Samuel H. Kress Collection at the National Gallery of Art. Based on the Catalogue of Renaissance Medals in the Gustave Dreyfus Collection by G.F. Hill, revised and enlarged by G. Pollard, London, 1967

HIND, 1935
A.M. Hind, *An Introduction to the History of the Woodcut*, 2 vols., London, 1935

HIND, 1938–48
A.M. Hind, *Early Italian Engraving: A Critical Catalogue*, 7 vols., London, 1938–48

HOLBERTON, 1990
P. Holberton, *Palladio's Villas. Life in the Renaissance Countryside*, London, 1990

HOOD AND HOPE, 1977
W. Hood and C. Hope, 'Titian's Vatican Altarpiece and the Pictures Underneath', *Art Bulletin*, LIX, 1977, pp. 534–52

HOPE, 1980
C. Hope, *Titian*, London, 1980

HOPE, 1982
C. Hope, 'Titian's portrait of Giacomo Dolfin', *Apollo*, CXV, 1982, pp. 158–61

HOPE, 1990
C. Hope, 'Titian, Philip II and Mary Tudor' in *England and the Continental Renaissance: Essays in honour of J.B. Trapp*, ed. by E. Chaney and P. Mack, Woodbridge and Rochester, 1990, pp. 53–65

HOWARD, 1975
D. Howard, *Jacopo Sansovino. Architecture and Patronage in Renaissance Venice*, New Haven and London, 1975

HUMFREY, 1983
P. Humfrey, *Cima da Conegliano*, Cambridge, 1983

HUMFREY, 1990
P. Humfrey, *La pittura veneta del rinascimento a Brera*, Florence, 1990

HUMFREY, 1993
P. Humfrey, *The Altarpiece in Renaissance Venice*, New Haven and London, 1993

HUMFREY, 1997
P. Humfrey, *Lorenzo Lotto*, New Haven and London, 1997

HUMFREY, 2003
P. Humfrey, 'The patron and early provenance of Titian's *Three Ages of Man*', *Burlington Magazine*, CXLV, 2003, pp. 787–91

HUMFREY, 2003 (2)
P. Humfrey, 'G.F. Waagen in Scotland', *Journal of the Scottish Society for Art History*, VIII, 2003, pp. 17–22

HUMFREY, 2004
P. Humfrey (ed.), *The Cambridge Companion to Giovanni Bellini*, Cambridge and New York, 2004

HURT, 1971
J.M. Hurt III, 'An Eighteenth Century Bronze Saturn as a Figure of Time', *Bulletin of the North Carolina Museum of Art*, 10, 3, 1971, pp. 17–28

INGAMELLS, 1997
J. Ingamells, *A Dictionary of British and Irish Travellers in Italy 1701–1800*, New Haven and London, 1997

IRWIN AND IRWIN, 1975
D. and F. Irwin, *Scottish Painters at Home and Abroad 1700–1900*, London, 1975

JAFFÉ, 1971
M. Jaffé, 'Pesaro family portraits: Pordenone, Lotto and Titian', *Burlington Magazine*, CXIII, pp. 696–702

JAFFÉ, 1994
M. Jaffé, *The Devonshire Collection of Italian Drawings: Venetian and North Italian Schools*, London, 1994

JESTAZ, 2000
B. Jestaz, 'Un fonds d'atelier de Battista del Moro', *Mitteilungen des kunsthistorischen Institutes in Florenz*, XLIV, 2000, pp. 292–305

JOANNIDES, 2001
P. Joannides, *Titian to 1518*, New Haven and London, 2001

JOHNSON, 1982
J. Johnson, 'Ugo da Carpi's Chiaroscuro Woodcuts', *Il Conoscitore di Stampe*, 57–58, 1982, pp. 2–87

KENNEDY NORTH, 1932
S. Kennedy North, 'Titian's *Venus* at Bridgewater House', *Burlington Magazine*, LX, 1932, pp. 58–63

KLIBANSKY, PANOFSKY AND SAXL, 1964
R. Klibansky, E. Panofsky and F. Saxl, *Saturn and Melancholy*, London, 1964

KORNELL, 1989
M. Kornell, 'Anatomical Drawings by Battista Franco', *Bulletin of the Cleveland Museum of Art*, 76, 1989, pp. 302–25

KOWALCZYK, 1967
J. Kowalczyk, 'La Cappella della 'Nazione Polacca' a Padova nel Seicento' in *Il Santo. Rivista antoniana di storia, dottrina, arte*, VII, 1, 1967, pp. 67–86

KRIS, 1929
E. Kris, *Meister und Meisterwerke der Steinschneiderkunst*, 2 vols., Vienna, 1929

KRYZA-GERSCH, 1998
C. Kryza-Gersch, 'New Light on Nicolò Roccatagliata and his son Sebastiano Nicolini', *Nuovi Studi*, 5, 1998, pp. 111–26

LAIRD, 1877
J. Laird, *Descriptive Catalogue of the Collection of Old Master Paintings formed by the late John Graham Gilbert Esq, RSA, of Yorkhill*, MS of 1877, Glasgow Museums and Art Galleries

LANDAU AND PARSHALL, 1994
D. Landau and P. Parshall, *The Renaissance Print*, New Haven and London, 1994

LANE, 1973
F.C. Lane, *Venice, a Maritime Republic*, Baltimore, 1973

LAUDER, 1997
A.V. Lauder, 'Un nuovo disegno di Battista Franco per il '"Battesimo di Cristo" della cappella Barbaro', *Arte Veneta*, 50, 1997, pp. 98–107

LAUDER, 2003
A.V. Lauder, 'Absorption and interpretation: Michelangelo through the eyes of a Venetian follower, Battista Franco' in F. Ames-Lewis and P. Joannides (eds.), *Reactions to the Master: Michelangelo's Effect on Art and Artist in the Sixteenth Century*, London, 2003, pp. 93–113

LE BLANC, 1854–89
C. Le Blanc, *Manuel de l'amateur d'estampes*, 4 vols., Paris, 1854–c.1889

LESSMANN, 1979
J. Lessmann, *Italienische Majolika: Katalog der Sammlung Herzog Anton Ulrich-Museum, Braunschweig*, Brunswick, 1979

LEVENSON, OBERHUBER AND SHEEHAN, 1973
J.A. Levenson, K. Oberhuber and J.L. Sheehan, *Early Italian Engravings from the National Gallery of Art*, Washington DC, 1973

LLOYD, 2003
S. Lloyd, 'Italian paintings in the Scottish collections of the Dukes of Buccleuch and Queensberry', *Journal of the Scottish Society for Art History*, VIII, 2003, pp. 37–46

LONDON, 1966
London, Colnaghi's, *Old Master Drawings: a Loan Exhibition from the National Gallery of Scotland in aid of the National Art-Collections Fund*, exh. cat. by K. Andrews, London, 1966

LONDON, 1981
London, P. & D. Colnaghi, *Objects for a 'Wunderkammer'*, dealer catalogue ed. by A. González-Palacios, 1981

LONDON, 1983
London, Royal Academy, *The Genius of Venice*, exh. cat. ed. by J. Martineau and C. Hope, London, 1983

LONDON, 1987
London, British Museum, *Ceramic Art of the Italian Renaissance*, exh. cat. by T. Wilson, London, 1987

LONDON, 1996
London, British Museum, *Old Master Drawings from the Malcolm Collection*, exh. cat. by M. Royalton-Kisch, H. Chapman and S. Coppel, London, 1996

LONDON, 2000
London, National Gallery, *Seeing Salvation: The Image of Christ*, exh. cat. by G. Finaldi *et al.*, London, 2000

LONDON, 2001
London, British Museum, *The Print in Italy 1550–1620*, exh. cat. by M. Bury, London, 2001

LONDON, 2002
London, British Museum, *Albrecht Dürer and his Legacy*, exh. cat. by G. Bartrum *et al.*, London, 2002

LONDON, 2003
London, National Gallery, *Titian*, exh. cat. by D. Jaffé *et al.*, London, 2003

LUCCO, 1989–90
M. Lucco (ed.), *La Pittura nel Veneto: il Quattrocento*, 2 vols., Milan, 1989–90

LUCCO, 1996–9
M. Lucco (ed.), *La Pittura nel Veneto: il Cinquecento*, 3 vols., Milan, 1996–9

LUCHS, 1989
A. Luchs (ed.), 'Italian Plaquettes', *Studies in the History of Art Volume 22*, Washington DC, 1989

LUISETTO, 1986
G. Luisetto (ed.), *Archivio Sartori. Documenti di storia e arte francescana*, II / 1: *La Provincia del Santo e dei Frati Minori Conventuali*, Padua, 1986

MACANDREW, 1985
H. Macandrew *et al.*, 'Tintoretto's *Deposition of Christ* in the National Gallery of Scotland', *Burlington Magazine*, CXXVII, 1985, pp.501–17

MCGRATH, 1997
E. McGrath, *Rubens: Subjects from History*, 2 vols., London, 1997

MCLELLAN GALLERY, 1855
The McLellan Gallery. Catalogue of Pictures bequeathed to the People of Glasgow by the late Archibald McLellan, Glasgow, 1855

MCTAVISH, 1981
D. McTavish, *Giuseppe Porta, called Giuseppe Salviati*, (Ph.D. thesis, Courtauld Institute of Art, University of London), New York and London, 1981

MAASTRICHT, 2003
Maastricht, Bonnefanten Museum, and Bruges, Arenthuis, *Le Siècle de Titien, Gravures vénitiennes de la Renaissance*, exh. cat. by G.J. van der Sman, Zwolle, 2003

MACK, 2002
R. E. Mack, *Bazaar to Piazza: Islamic Trade and Italian Art 1300–1600*, California, 2002

MADRID, 2003
Madrid, Museo Nacional del Prado, *Tiziano*, exh. cat. ed. by M. Falomir, Madrid, 2003

MANCA, 1993
J. Manca (ed.), 'Titian 500' *Studies in the History of Art*, 45, Washington DC, 1993

MANCINI, 2001
V. Mancini, *Polidoro da Lanciano*, Lanciano, 2001

MARIETTE, 1969
P.-J. Mariette, *Notes manuscrites de P.J. Mariette, les grands peintres, I, Ecoles d'Italie*, Paris, 1969

MARINELLI, 1998
S. Marinelli (ed.), *Manierismo a Mantova: La pittura da Giulio Romano all'età di Rubens*, Cinisello Balsamo (Milan), 1998

MARKHAM SCHULZ, 1998
A. Markham Schulz, *Giammaria Mosca called Padovano, a Renaissance Sculptor in Italy and Poland*, 2 vols., University Park, 1998

MARKS, 1983
R. Marks, *Burrell: A Portrait of a Collector*, Glasgow, 1983

MARTIN, 1998
T. Martin, *Alessandro Vittoria and the Portrait Bust in Renaissance Venice*, Oxford, 1998

MARTINONI, 1983
R. Martinoni, *Gian Vincenzo Imperiale: Politico, letterato e collezionista genovese del Seicento*, Padua, 1983

MASON RINALDI, 1978
S. Mason Rinaldi, 'Paolo Fiammingo', *Saggi e Memorie di Storia dell'Arte*, XI, 1978, pp.47–80

MASON RINALDI, 1984
S. Mason Rinaldi, *Jacopo Palma il Giovane*, Milan, 1984

MASON, 1999
S. Mason, 'Per la grafica dei Maganza', *Arte Documento*, 13, 1999, pp.211–15

MASSING, 1977
J.-M. Massing, 'Jacobus Argentoratensis: Etude préliminaire', *Arte Veneta*, XXXI, 1977, pp.42–52

MAURONER, 1943
F. Mauroner, *Le incisioni di Tiziano*, Venice, 1943

MEIJER, 1974
B.W. Meijer, 'Early Drawings by Titian: Some Attributions', *Arte Veneta*, XXVIII, 1975, pp.75–92

MEIJER, 1975
B.W. Meijer, 'Paolo Fiammingo reconsidered', *Mededelingen van het Nederlands Instituut te Rome*, NS II, 1975, pp.117–30

MEILMAN, 2000
P. Meilman, *Titian and the Altarpiece in Renaissance Venice*, Cambridge, 2000

MEMPHIS, 2001
Memphis, Brooks Museum of Art, Athens, Georgia Museum of Art and New Orleans, Museum of Art, *Scottish Treasures: Masterpieces from the National Gallery of Scotland*, exh. cat., Edinburgh, 2001

MEYER, 1872–85
J. Meyer *et al.*, *Allgemeines Künstler-Lexicon*, 3 vols., Leipzig, 1872–85

MIDDLEDORF AND GOETZ, 1944
U. Middeldorf and O. Goetz, *Medals and Plaquettes from the Sigmund Morgenroth Collection*, Chicago, 1944

MILLAR, 1890
A.H. Millar, *The Historic Castles and Mansions of Scotland: Perthshire and Forfarshire*, Paisley, 1890

MOLINIER, 1886
E. Molinier, *Les bronzes de la Renaissance. Les plaquettes. Catalogue raisonné*, 2 vols., Paris, 1886

MONGAN AND SACHS, 1946
A. Mongan and P.J. Sachs, *Drawings in the Fogg Museum of Art*, 2nd edn., 2 vols., Cambridge MA, 1946

MORTIMER, 1974
R. Mortimer, *Italian 16th Century Books (Harvard College Library, Department of Printing and Graphic Arts: Catalogue of Books and Manuscripts Pt II)*, 2 vols., Cambridge Mass., 1974

MORTIMER, 1996
R. Mortimer, 'The Author's Image: Italian Sixteenth-Century Printed Portraits', *Harvard Library Bulletin*, NS, VII.2, 1996, pp.7–87

MOSCHINI MARCONI, 1962
S. Moschini Marconi, *Gallerie dell'Accademia di Venezia: Opere d'Arte del secolo XVI*, Rome, 1962

MOTTURE, 2003
P. Motture (ed.), 'Large Renaissance Bronzes' *Studies in the History of Art Volume 64*, New Haven and London, 2003

NAGLER, 1858–79
G.K. Nagler, *Die Monogrammisten*, 5 vols., Munich, 1858–79

NICHOLS, 1999
T. Nichols, *Tintoretto: Tradition and Identity*, London, 1999

NODARI, 1994
F. Nodari, 'Disegni di Francesco Bassano tra il 1571 e 1590', *Paragone*, 535–7, 1994, pp.48–80

NORRIS AND WEBER, 1976
A.S. Norris and I. Weber, *Medals and Plaquettes from the Molinari Collection at Bowdoin College*, Brunswick, 1976

NOVA, 1994
A. Nova, 'Girolamo Romanino', Turin, 1994

NOVA, 1995
A. Nova, 'The Drawings of Girolamo Romanino, *Burlington Magazine*, CXXXVII, 1995, pp.159–68 (I) and pp.300–6 (II)

OBERHUBER, 1980
K. Oberhuber, 'Titian Woodcuts and Drawings: Some Problems', in *Tiziano e Venezia: Convegno Internazionale di Studi, Venice, 1976*, Vicenza, 1980, pp.523–8

OTTLEY AND TOMKINS, 1818
W.Y. Ottley, *Engravings of the Most Noble Marquis of Stafford's Collection of Pictures in London*, 5 vols., London, 1818

PADUA, 2001
Padua, Musei Civici, *Donatello e il suo tempo: Il bronzetto a Padova nel Quattrocento e nel Cinquecento*, exh. cat. ed. by D. Banzato *et al.*, Geneva and Milan, 2001

PALLUCCHINI, 1962
R. Pallucchini, *I Vivarini*, Venice, 1962

PALLUCCHINI, 1969
R. Pallucchini, *Tiziano*, 2 vols., Florence, 1969

PALLUCCHINI AND ROSSI, 1982
R. Pallucchini and P. Rossi, *Tintoretto: le opere sacre e profane*, 2 vols., Venice, 1982

PALMA 1984
Palma, 'Disegni di Pietro Malombra', *Arte Veneta*, XXXVIII, 1984, pp.72–8

PANOFSKY, 1957
E. Panofsky, *Meaning in the Visual Arts*, New York, 1957

PARIS, 1993
Paris, Grand Palais, *Le siècle de Titien. L'âge d'or de la peinture à Venise* exh. cat. by M. Laclotte *et al.*, Paris, 1993

PARIS, 1993 (2)
Paris, Musée du Louvre, *Le dessin à Vérone au XVIe et XVIIe siècles*, exh. cat. by H. Sueur *et al.*, 1993

PARKER, 1927
K.T. Parker, 'Jacopo Robusti called Tintoretto', *Old Master Drawings*, II, 1927–8, pp.6–7

PASERO, 1935
C. Pasero, 'Giacomo Franco, editore, incisore e calcografo', *La Bibliofilia*, 37, 1935, pp.332–56

PASSAVANT, 1836
J.D. Passavant, *Tour of a German Artist in England, with Notices of Private Galleries*, 2 vols., London, 1836

PASSAVANT, 1860–4
J.D. Passavant, *Le Peintre-graveur*, 6 vols., Leipzig, 1860–4

PAUL, 1904–14
J.B. Paul, *The Scots Peerage*, 9 vols., Edinburgh, 1904–14

PAVANELLO, 2000
G. Pavanello (ed.), *Antonio Canova e il suo Ambiente Artistico fra Venezia, Roma e Parigi*, Venice, 2000

PAVONE, 1985
M.P. Pavone, 'Maestro Domenico da Venezia e la spezieria del Grande Ospedale di Messina', *Faenza*, 1985, pp.49–67

PAZZI, 1993
P. Pazzi, *Introduzione al collezionismo di argenteria civile e metalli veneti antichi*, Treviso, 1993

PEDROCCO, 2001
F. Pedrocco, with the assistance of M.A. Chiari Moretto Wiel, *Titian: The Complete Paintings*, London, 2001

PENNANT, 1774
T. Pennant, *A Tour in Scotland*, 3rd edn., London, 1774

PENNY, 1992
N. Penny, *Catalogue of European Sculpture in the Ashmolean Museum, 1540 to the Present Day*, 3 vols., Oxford, 1992

PFÄFFIKON, 1978
Pfäffikon, Seedamm-Kulturzentrum and Geneva, Musée d'Art et d'Histoire, *Art venitien en Suisse et au Liechtenstein*, exh. cat. by M. Natale, Milan, 1978

PIGNATTI, 1973
T. Pignatti, 'The Relationship between German and Venetian Painting' in J.R. Hale (ed.), *Renaissance Venice*, London, 1973, pp.244–73

PIGNATTI AND PEDROCCO, 1995
T. Pignatti and F. Pedrocco, *Veronese*, 2 vols., Milan, 1995

PINCUS, 2001
D. Pincus (ed.), 'Small Bronzes in the Renaissance', *Studies in the History of Art Volume 62*, New Haven and London, 2001

PINNINGTON, 1898
E. Pinnington, *The Art Collection of the Corporation of Glasgow*, Glasgow, 1898

PLANISCIG, 1921
L. Planiscig, *Venezianische Bildhauer der Renaissance*, Vienna, 1921

PLANISCIG, 1927
L. Planiscig, *Andrea Riccio*, Vienna, 1927

POLLARD, 1984
G. Pollard (ed.), Medaglie italiane del Rinascimento nel Museo Nazionale del Bargello, 3 vols., Florence, 1984

POPE-HENNESSY, 1965
J. Pope-Hennessy, *Renaissance Bronzes in the Samuel H. Kress Collection: Reliefs, Plaquettes, Statuettes, Utensils and Mortars*, London, 1965

POPHAM, 1946
A.E. Popham, *The Drawings of Leonardo da Vinci*, London, 1946

POPHAM AND WILDE, 1949
A.E. Popham and J. Wilde, *The Italian Drawings of the XV and XVI Centuries in the Collection of His Majesty the King at Windsor Castle*, London, 1949

PRIEVER, 2000
A. Priever, *Paolo Caliari, called Veronese*, Cologne, 2000

PUPPI, 1968
L. Puppi (ed.), *Paolo Farinati: Giornale (1573–1606)*, Florence, 1968

PYKE, 1981
E.J. Pyke, *A Biographical Dictionary of Wax Modellers (Supplement)*, London, 1981

RACKHAM, 1977
B. Rackham, *Victoria and Albert Museum: Catalogue of Italian Maiolica*, J.V.G. Mallet (ed.), 2 vols., London, 1977

RADCLIFFE, 1992
A. Radcliffe, M. Baker and M. Maek-Gérard, *The Thyssen-Bornemisza Collection: Renaissance and Later Sculpture, with Works of Art in Bronze*, London, 1992

REARICK, 1958
W.R. Rearick, 'Battista Franco and the Grimani Chapel', *Saggi e memorie di storia dell'arte*, 2, 1958–9, pp.107–39

REDFORD, 1888
G. Redford, *Art Sales*, 2 vols., London, 1888

RENDINA, 1984
C. Rendina, *I Dogi*, Rome, 1984 (reprinted 2002)

RICHARDSON, 1980
F. Richardson, *Andrea Schiavone*, Oxford, 1980

RICHTER, 1883
J.P. Richter, *Catalogue of the Collection of Paintings lent for Exhibition by the Marquess of Bute, K.T.*, London, 1883

RIDOLFI, 1648
C. Ridolfi, *Le maraviglie dell'arte*, Venice, 1648

RIDOLFI, 1914–24
C. Ridolfi, *Le maraviglie dell'arte* (1648), (ed.) D. von Hadeln, 2 vols., Berlin 1914–24

ROBERTSON, 1954
G. Robertson, *Vincenzo Catena*, Edinburgh, 1954

ROBERTSON, 1968
G. Robertson, *Giovanni Bellini*, Oxford, 1968

ROBERTSON, 1971
G. Robertson, 'The X-ray Examination of Titian's 'Three Ages of Man' in the Bridgewater House Collection', *Burlington Magazine*, CXIII, 1971, pp.721–6

ROBINSON, 1865
J.C. Robinson *et al.*, *Catalogue of the Works of Art forming the collection of Robert Napier, of West Shandon, Dumbartonshire*, London, 1865

ROME, 1976
Rome, Gabinetto Nazionale delle Stampe, *Imagini da Tiziano, stampe dal sec. XVI al sec. XIX dalle collezioni del Gabinetto Nazionale delle Stampe*, exh. cat. ed. by M. Catelli Isola, Rome, 1976

ROME, 1978
Rome, Gabinetto Nazionale delle Stampe, *Immagini dal Veronese: Incisioni dal secolo XVI al XIX*, exh. cat. ed. by P. Ticozzi, Rome, 1978

ROSENTHAL, 1981
G. Rosenthal (ed.), *Italian Paintings XIV to XVIII Centuries from the Collection of the Baltimore Museum of Art*, Baltimore, 1981

ROSKILL, 1968
M.W. Roskill, *Dolce's 'Aretino' and Venetian Art Theory of the Cinquecento*, New York, 1968

ROSSI, 1974
P. Rossi, *Jacopo Tintoretto: i Ritratti*, Venice, 1974

ROSSI, 1975
P. Rossi, *I disegni di Jacopo Tintoretto*, Florence, 1975

ROSSI, 1984
P. Rossi, 'Per la grafica di Domenico Tintoretto II', *Arte Veneta*, XXXVIII, 1984, pp.57–71

ROSSI, 1991
F. Rossi, *Il Moroni*, Soncino, 1991

ROWLANDS, 1966
J. Rowlands, 'Two Unknown Works by Palma Vecchio', *Pantheon*, XXIV, 1966, pp.372–7

RUGGERI, 2001
U. Ruggeri, *Valentin Lefèvre (1637–1677)*, Reggio Emilia, 2001

RUHEMANN, 1954
H. Ruhemann, 'The Adulteress before Christ by Giorgione', *Scottish Art Review*, V, 1, 1954, pp.13–18, 31

RUSSELL, 2003
F. Russell, 'John, 3rd Earl of Bute, and Venice', *Journal of the Scottish Society for Art History*, VIII, 2003, pp.23–6

RYLANDS, 1992
P. Rylands, *Palma Vecchio*, Cambridge, 1992

SACCOMANI, 1980
E. Saccomani, 'Domenico Campagnola: gli anni della maturità', *Arte Veneta*, XXXIV, 1980, pp.63–71

SANDRART, 1675
J. von Sandrart, *Academie der Bau-, Bild- und Mahlerey-Künste* (1675), A.R. Peltzer (ed.), Munich, 1925

SANSOVINO, 1581
F. Sansovino, *Venetia città nobilissima*, 1581, G. Martinioni (ed.), Venice, 1663

SAVINI BRANCA, 1965
S. Savini Branca, *Il collezionismo veneziano nel '600*, Florence, 1965

SCHULZ, 1968
J. Schulz, *Venetian Painted Ceilings of the Renaissance*, Berkeley and Los Angeles, 1968

SCHULZ, 1978
J. Schulz, 'Jacopo de'Barbari's View of Venice. Map Making, City Views and Moralized Cartography before 1500', *Art Bulletin*, LX, 1978, pp.425–74

SELLINK, 2000
M. Sellink, *The New Hollstein. Dutch and Flemish Etchings, Engravings and Woodcuts 1450–1700: Cornelis Cort*, 3 vols., Rotterdam, 2000

SÉNÉCHAL, 1987
P. Sénéchal, *Les graveurs des écoles du nord à Venise 1585–1620: Les Sadeler, entremise et enterprise*, unpublished dissertation, Université de Paris – Sorbonne, 1987

SHAPLEY, 1979
F.R. Shapley, *National Gallery of Art, Washington: Catalogue of Italian Paintings*, 2 vols., Washington, 1979

SHIRLEY, 1983
R.W. Shirley, *The Mapping of the World: Early Printed World Maps 1472–1700*, London, 1983

SIMONETTI, 1986
S. Simonetti, 'Profilo di Bonifacio de' Pitati', *Saggi e memorie di storia dell'arte*, XV, 1986, pp.85–134

SKINNER, 1968
B. Skinner, 'Andrew Wilson and the Hopetoun Collection', *Country Life*, 15 August 1968, pp.370–2

SMITH, 2003
C. Smith, 'The 4th Earl of Aberdeen as a collector of Italian Old Masters', *Journal of the Scottish Society for Art History*, VIII, 2003, pp.47–52

SOUTHESK, 1871
James, 9th Earl of Southesk, *Britian's Art Paradise. Notes on some Pictures in the Royal Academy*, London, 1871

SOUTHESK, 1904
James, 9th Earl of Southesk, *Catalogue of Pictures at Kinnaird Castle*, MS, 1904 (typescript at the National Gallery of Scotland)

STEFANI MANTOVANELLI, 1979
M. Stefani Mantovanelli, *Momenti essenziali dell'attività di Domenico Brusasorci e semantica di un'opera*, Verona, 1979

STEFANI MANTOVANELLI, 2000
M. Stefani Mantovanelli, 'Una chiacchierata su Domenico Brusasorci frescante', *Arte Documento*, 14, 2000, pp.104–9

TAFURI, 1984
M. Tafuri (ed.), *'Renovatio Urbis': Venezia nell'età di Andrea Gritti (1523–1538)*, Rome, 1984

TAIT, 1979
H. Tait, *The Golden Age of Venetian Glass*, London, 1979

TASSI, 1793
F.M. Tassi, *Vite de' Pittori, Scultori e Architetti Bergamaschi*, 2 vols., Bergamo, 1793

TEMPESTINI, 1992
A. Tempestini, *Giovanni Bellini*, Florence, 1992

THOMPSON, 1972
C. Thompson (ed.), *Pictures for Scotland. The National Gallery of Scotland and its Collection*, Edinburgh, 1972

THORNTON, 1991
P. Thornton, *The Italian Renaissance Interior 1400–1600*, London, 1991

TIETZE AND TIETZE-CONRAT, 1944
H. Tietze and E. Tietze-Conrat, *The Drawings of the Venetian Painters in the 15th and 16th Centuries*, New York, 1944

TODERI AND VANNEL TODERI, 1996
G. Toderi and F. Vannel Toderi, *Museo Nazionale del Bargello: Plachette Secoli XV–XVIII*, Florence, 1996

TOKYO, 1993
Tokyo, Isetan Museum of Art, Miyazaki, Museum and Cultural Institutions of Miyazaki Prefecture, and Yokohama, Sogo Museum of Art, *Masterpieces from the National Gallery of Scotland*, exh. cat. by T. Clifford *et al.*, Edinburgh, 1993

TOKYO, 1996
Tokyo, National Museum of Western Art, and Nagoya, Aichi Prefectural Museum of Art, *Italian 16th and 17th Century Drawings from the British Museum*, exh. cat. ed. by M. Koshikawa and H. Kurita, 1996

TOOLEY, 1939
R.V. Tooley, 'Maps in Italian Atlases of the Sixteenth Century', *Imago Mundi*, 3, 1939, pp.12–47

TRENERRY, 2000
E. Trenerry (ed.), *Portrait of Sansovino?*, Melbourne, 2000

TRENT, 1999
Trent, Castello di Buonconsiglio, 'La Bellissima Maniera': *Alessandro Vittoria e la scultura veneta del Cinquecento*, exh. cat. ed. by A. Bacchi, L. Camerlengo and M. Leithe-Jasper, Trent, 1999

TREVISO, 1984
Treviso, Palazzo dei Trecento, *Paris Bordon*, exh. cat. ed. by E. Manzato, Milan, 1984

TURNER, 1996
J. Turner (ed.), *The Dictionary of Art*, 34 vols., New York, 1996

TURNER, 2000
J. Turner (ed.), *Encyclopedia of Italian Renaissance and Mannerist Art*, 2 vols., London and New York, 2000

VALCANOVER, 1999
F. Valcanover, *Tiziano. I suoi pennelli sempre partorirono espressioni di vita*, Florence, 1999

VAN BINNEBEKE, 1994
E. van Binnebeke, *Bronssculptur: Beeldhowkunst 1500–1800 in de collectie van het Museum Boymans-van Beuningen*, Rotterdam, 1994

VAN DER SMAN, 1994
G.J. van der Sman, 'Il percorso stilistico di Battista Franco incisore: elementi per una ricostruzione', *Arte Documento*, 8, 1994, pp.101–13

VAN DER SMAN, 1999
G.J. van der Sman, 'Alcune precisazioni su Nicolò Nelli e Gaspare Osello', *Grafica d'Arte*, X, 37, 1999, pp.2–9

VAN DER SMAN, 2003
G.J. van der Sman, Review of 'The Print in Italy 1550–1620', *Simiolus*, 2003, pp.120–4

VAN MARLE, 1923–38
R. van Marle, *The Development of the Italian Schools of Painting*, 19 vols., The Hague, 1923–38

VASARI, 1906
G. Vasari, *Le vite de' più eccellenti pittori, scultori ed architettori*, 9 vols., G. Milanesi (ed.), 2nd edn., with additions and corrections, Florence, 1906

VASARI, 1965
G. Vasari, *The Lives of the Artists: a Selection*, translated by G. Bull, Harmondsworth, 1965

VASARI, 1966–87
G. Vasari, *Le Vite de' più eccellenti Pittori, Scultori e Architettori* (1550 and 1568 editions), R. Bettarini and P. Barocchi (eds.), 6 vols., Florence, 1966–87

VENICE, 1971
Venice, Fondazione Giorgio Cini, and Verona, Museo di Castelvecchio, 'Disegni veronesi del Cinquecento', exh. cat. ed. by T. Mullaly, Vicenza, 1971

VENICE, 1976
Venice, Fondazione Giorgio Cini, *Disegni di Tiziano e della sua cerchia*, exh. cat. ed. by K. Oberhuber, Vicenza, 1976

VENICE, 1981
Venice, Palazzo Ducale, *Da Tiziano al El Greco: Per la storia del Manierismo a Venezia*, exh. cat. ed. by R. Pallucchini, Milan, 1981

VENICE, 1982
Venice, Palazzo Ducale, *Mille anni di arte del vetro a Venezia*, exh. cat. ed. by R. Barovier Mentasti, Venice, 1982

VENICE, 1990
Venice, Museo Correr, *Palma il Giovane 1548–1628. Disegni e dipinti*, exh. cat. by S. Mason Rinaldi, Milan, 1990

VENICE, 1999
Venice, Palazzo Grassi, *Renaissance Venice and the North, Crosscurrents in the Time of Dürer, Bellini and Titian*, exh. cat. ed. by B. Aikema and B.L. Brown., London, 1999

VENTURI, 1901–40
A. Venturi, *Storia dell'arte italiana*, 11 vols., Milan, 1901–40

VERONA, 1980
Verona, Palazzo della Gran Guardia, *Palladio e Verona*, exh. cat. ed. by P. Marini, Verona, 1980

VERONA, 1988
Verona, Museo di Castelvecchio, *Veronese e Verona*, exh. cat. ed. by S. Marinelli, Verona, 1988

VERONA, 1994
Verona, Museo del Castelvecchio, *Disegni veronesi al Louvre 1500 – 1630*, exh. cat. ed. by S. Marinelli, H. Sueur and P. Marini, Milan, 1994

VERTOVA, 1980
L. Vertova, 'Bernardino Licinio', in *I pittori bergamaschi dal XIII al XIX secolo: Il Cinquecento I*, Bergamo, 1980, pp.373–465

VICENZA, 1980
Vicenza, Tempio di Santa Corona, *Palladio e la maniera: I pittori vicentini del Cinquecento e i collaboratori di Andrea Palladio*, exh. cat. by V. Sgarbi, Milan, 1980

WAAGEN, 1838
G.F. Waagen, *Works of Art and Artists in England*, 3 vols., London, 1838

WAAGEN, 1854
G.F. Waagen, *Treasures of Art in Great Britain*, 3 vols., London, 1854

WAAGEN, 1857
G.F. Waagen, *Galleries and Cabinets of Art in Great Britain*, London, 1857

WARD-JACKSON, 1979
P. Ward-Jackson, *Victoria and Albert Museum Catalogues: Italian Drawings, I, 14th–16th Century*, London, 1979

WASHINGTON, 1976
Washington, National Gallery of Art, *Titian and the Venetian Woodcut*, exh. cat. ed. by D. Rosand and M. Muraro, Washington, 1976

WASHINGTON, 1979
Washington, National Gallery of Art, *Prints and Related Drawings by the Carracci Family, A Catalogue Raisonné*, exh.cat. by D. DeGrazia Bohlin, Washington DC, 1979

WASHINGTON, 1988
Washington, National Gallery of Art, *The Art of Paolo Veronese*, exh. cat. by W.R. Rearick, Cambridge, 1988

WASHINGTON, 1990
Washington, National Gallery of Art, *Titian: Prince of Painters*, exh. cat. by F. Valcanover *et al.*, Munich, 1990

WASHINGTON, 1990 (2)
Washington, National Gallery of Art, and Fort Worth, Kimbell Art Museum, *Old Master Drawings from the National Gallery of Scotland*, exh. cat. by H. Macandrew, Edinburgh, 1990

WASHINGTON, 1997
Washington, National Gallery of Art, *Lorenzo Lotto: Rediscovered Master of the Renaissance*, exh. cat. by D.A. Brown, P. Humfrey and M. Lucco, New Haven and London, 1997

WEBER, 1993
A. Weber, *Venezianische Dogenporträts des 16. Jahrhunderts*, Sigmaringen, 1993

WEDGWOOD KENNEDY, 1964
R. Wedgwood Kennedy, 'Apelles Redivivus', in L. Freeman Sandler (ed.), *Essays in Memory of Karl Lehmann*, , New York, 1964, pp.160–70

WEIRAUCH, 1967
H.R. Weihrauch, *Europäische Bronzestatuetten: 15–18 Jahrhundert*, Brunswick, 1967

WEMYSS, 2003
S. Wemyss, 'Francis, Lord Elcho (10th Earl of Wemyss) as a collector of Italian Old Masters', *Journal of the Scottish Society for Art History*, VIII, 2003, pp.73–6

WENLEY, 1993
R. Wenley, 'William, 3rd Earl of Lothian: covenanter and collector', *Journal of the History of Collections*, V, 1993, pp.23–41

WENLEY, 2003
R. Wenley, 'The 8th Marquess of Lothian as a collector of Italian Old Masters', *Journal of the Scottish Society for Art History*, VIII, 2003, pp.77–86

WESTPHAL, 1931
D. Westphal, *Bonifazio Veronese*, Munich, 1931

WETHEY, 1969
H.E. Wethey, *The Paintings of Titian I: The Religious Paintings*, London, 1969

WETHEY, 1971
H.E. Wethey, *The Paintings of Titian II: The Portraits*, London, 1971

WETHEY, 1975
H.E. Wethey, *The Paintings of Titian III: The Mythological and Historical Paintings*, London, 1975

WETHEY, 1987
H.E. Wethey, *Titian and his Drawings, with reference to Giorgione and some Close Contemporaries*, Princeton, 1987

WILLIAMSON, 1903
G.C. Williamson (ed.), *The Anonimo*, London, 1903

WILSON, 1976
A. Wilson, *The Making of the Nuremberg Chronicle*, Amsterdam, 1976

WOLTERS, 1983
W. Wolters, *Der Bilderschmuck des Dogenpalastes*, Wiesbaden, 1983

WOODS-MARSDEN, 1998
J. Woods-Marsden, *Renaissance self-portraiture: the visual construction of identity and the social status of the artist*, New Haven and London, 1998

WOODWARD, 1997
D. Woodward, 'Italian Composite Atlases of the Sixteenth Century' in J.A. Wolter and R.E. Grim (eds.), *Images of the World: the Atlas through History*, Washington 1997, pp.51–70

ZAMPETTI, 1969
P. Zampetti (ed.), *Lorenzo Lotto: Libro di spese diverse*, Florence, 1969

ZERI, 1973
F. Zeri, with the assistance of E.E. Gardner, *A Catalogue of the Collection of the Metropolitan Museum of Art. Italian Paintings: Venetian School*, New York, 1973

ZERNER, 1979
H. Zerner (ed.), *The Illustrated Bartsch 32: Italian Masters of the Sixteenth Century; School of Fontainebleau*, New York, 1979

ZORZI, 1996
M. Zorzi, 'Dal manoscritto al libro' in A. Tenenti and U. Tucci (eds.), *Storia di Venezia, IV: il Rinascimento politica e cultura*, Rome, 1996, pp.817–958

ZUCKER, 1999
M.J. Zucker, *The Illustrated Bartsch, 24: Early Italian Masters, Commentary*, part 4, New York, 1999

NOTES AND REFERENCES

ESSAYS

Venetian Painting in the Age of Titian
PAGES 11–31

1 Recent surveys of Venetian Renaissance painting include N. Huse and W. Wolters, *The Art of Renaissance Venice*, Chicago, 1990; and P. Humfrey, *Painting in Renaissance Venice*, New Haven and London, 1995. A more detailed treatment of some of the themes touched on here is provided by D. Rosand, *Painting in Cinquecento Venice*, revised ed., Cambridge, 1997. For references to monographs on individual painters, see the appendix of artists' biographies.

2 Convenient surveys of Venetian history include D. Chambers, *The Imperial Age of Venice, 1380–1580*, London, 1970; and J.J. Norwich, *A History of Venice*, London, 1982.

3 Helke, 1999.

4 P. Holberton, 'The *Pastorale* or *Fête Champêtre* in the early sixteenth century' in Manca, 1993, pp.245–62.

5 For this picture and its problematic attribution, see Rylands, 1992, pp.274–5.

6 The subject, attribution and provenance of this picture are discussed by Gould, 1975, pp.304–5. See also Evans, 2003, p.58. The National Gallery retains an attribution to a 'Follower of Titian', but it may be accepted as an early work by Bonifacio.

7 The appearance of this portrait is known from the copy by Rubens recently exhibited at the National Gallery of Scotland: see Edinburgh, National Gallery of Scotland, and Nottingham, Djanogly Art Gallery, *Rubens: Drawing on Italy*, exh. cat. by J. Wood, Edinburgh, 2002, p.68.

8 Vasari, 1568, VI, p.164; Vasari, 1965, p.455.

9 M. Roskill, *Dolce's 'Aretino' and Venetian Art Theory of the Cinquecento*, New York, 1968, p.185.

10 English translation by J. Fletcher in D. Chambers and B. Pullan (eds.), *Venice: a Documentary History*, Oxford, 1992, p.421.

11 P. Hills, 'Decorum and desire in some works by Tintoretto', in F. Ames-Lewis and A. Bednarek (eds.), *Decorum in Renaissance Narrative Art*, London, 1992, pp.121–3.

The Age of Titian: The Paintings in Context
PAGES 33–41

1 See especially D. Rosand, *Painting in Cinquecento Venice: Titian, Veronese, Tintoretto*, London, 1982, pp.51–8; Humfrey, 1993, pp.301–4.

2 G. Marchini, *Italian Stained Glass Windows*, London, 1957, pp.61–3. See especially the Lorenzo Veneziano *Saints* made for the Frari, but now in the Accademia, the *Pietà* by Giovanni Bellini in the cupola of Santa Maria dei Miracoli, and the large window in the right transept of Santi Giovanni e Paolo, which seems a combination of three talents – Bartolommeo Vivarini, Cima da Conegliano and Girolamo Mocetto, *c.*1476–1515. E. Castelnuovo, *La Grande Vetrata 2; SS. Giovanni e Paolo*, Venice, 1982.

3 Often created by F. and V. Zuccato, most notably on the façade, and on some of the interior vaults, of the basilica of San Marco: see B. Bertoli, *I mosaici di San Marco: Iconografia dell'Antico e Nuovo Testamento*, Milan, 1986.

4 Schulz, 1968, pp.28–91, figs.84–101.

5 J. Schulz, 'Cristoforo Sorte and the Ducal Palace of Venice', *Mitteilungen des Kunsthistorischen Institutes in Florenz*, X, 1961–3, pp.193–208. Sorte's style betrays none of Giulio's influence, but shows the influence of Perino's style for ornamental dishes of precious metal.

6 G. Giani, *Camini di Venezia*, Milan, 2000.

7 C. Piccolpasso, *The Three Books of the Potter's Art*, R. Lightbown and A. Caiger Smith (eds.), London, 1980 (the original manuscript of about 1557 is in the Victoria and Albert Museum); G. Morazzoni, *La maiolica antica veneta*, Milan, 1955; A. Alvera Bortolotto, *Storia della ceramica a Venezia dagli albori alla fine della Repubblica*, Florence, 1981.

8 T. Clifford and J.V.G. Mallet, 'Battista Franco as a Designer for Maiolica,' *Burlington Magazine*, CXVIII, 1976, pp.387–410.

9 I. Favaretto and M. DaVilla Urbani, *Arazzi e tappeti dei Dogi nella basilica di San Marco*, Venice, 1999.

10 Boucher, 1991.

11 S. Tumidei, 'Scultura e pittura a confronto, a Venezia, nell'età di Vittoria' in Trent, 1999, pp.107–25. Titian's *St John the Baptist* in the Accademia, Venice (fig.221) is particularly Sansovinesque, while Sansovino's pulpit relief of *St Mark Cursing a Woman from Murano* (Venice, San Marco) seems to betray the influence of Titian's Frari *Assumption* (fig.19).

12 D. Thornton, 'The Status and Display of Small Bronzes in the Italian Renaissance Interior', *The Sculpture Journal*, V, 2001, pp.33–41; L. Syson and D. Thornton, *Objects of Virtue: Art in Renaissance Italy*, London, 2001.

13 R. Wittkower, *Palladio and English Palladianism*, London, 1983.

14 D. Howard, *Venice and the East: the Impact of the Islamic World on Venetian Architecture 1100–1500*, New Haven and London, 2000; Mack, 2000.

15 The subject of Venetian enamels has not been properly studied. A large collection belongs to the Cini family in Venice. The forms and decorations resemble contemporary Venetian glass. See V. Krempel, 'Smalti' in *I Quaderni dell'Antiquariato*, Milan, 1981.

16 P. Fortini Brown, *Venice and Antiquity*, London, 1999, p.279.

Collecting Venetian Painting in Scotland
PAGES 43–55

Supplementing the notes to this essay are the information and references provided in the appendix of principal collectors and dealers on pp.407.

1 For the formation and dispersal of Hamilton's collection see Garas, 1967; P. Shakeshaft, '"Too much bewiched with thoes intysing things": the letters of James, third Marquess of Hamilton and Basil, Viscount Feilding, concerning collecting in Venice 1635–1639', *Burlington Magazine*, CXXVII, 1986, pp.114–32; J. Brown, *Kings and Connoisseurs: Collecting Art in Seventeenth-Century Europe*, New Haven and London, 1995, pp.49–57, 161.

2 P. McEvansoneya, 'An unpublished inventory of the Hamilton collection in the 1620s and the Duke of Buckingham's pictures', *Burlington Magazine*, CXXXIV, 1992, pp.524–5.

3 J. Lloyd Williams in Edinburgh, 1992, especially pp.15–17.

4 For the following, see Wenley, 1993.

5 Also passing through the hands of López (*c.*1582–1649) around this time was Titian's *Man with a Blue Sleeve* and *The Virgin and Child with St John the Baptist and an Unidentified Male Saint* (cat.no.25).

6 Oil on canvas, 98 × 74cm. This is probably the picture described in the Newbattle inventory of *c.*1726 (no.62) as 'A Doge of Venice' by Tintoretto: see Wenley, 1993, p.27. Pennant, 1774, p.63, also called it 'The Doge of Venice', but recorded an attribution to Titian. In fact it is a variant in reverse of Veronese's posthumous *Portrait of Agostino Barbarigo* (Cleveland, Ohio, Museum of Art).

7 Brown, 1987, p.7; Edinburgh, 1992, p.161.

8 Brown, 2003a, p.29.

9 Brown, 1987.

10 Basil Skinner, *Scots in Italy in the Eighteenth Century*, Edinburgh, 1996, pp.6–7.

11 B. Lenman, *Integration and Enlightenment: Scotland 1746–1832*, Edinburgh, 1981, pp.34–6.

12 Listed in Clifford, 2003, pp.12–13.

13 J. Macky, *A Journey through Scotland*, London, 1723, pp.278–82; Pennant, 1774, p.235. Macky is referring, of course, to the great Veronese, formerly in the refectory of San Giorgio Maggiore, Venice, and now in the Louvre.

14 According to a document in the Bute archive, the painter John Medina (grandson of the more famous Sir John) submitted an account to Lord Dumfries in June 1759 for cleaning and varnishing various paintings, including 'a large history piece by Bassan'. This reference was kindly provided by Andrew McLean.

15 For the Foulis Academy, see Irwin and Irwin, 1975, pp.85–90; Fairfull-Smith, 2001.

16 Foulis, 1776, II, pp.24–6 ('The picture belonged to a painter, who bestowed it as part of his daughter's portion'). One of Foulis's other 'Titians' – a *Supper at Emmaus*, probably copied from the original now in the Louvre – is just discernible in the engraved view of the exhibition of the Foulis collection in the quadrangle of Glasgow College. The engraving by William Jameson, an academy pupil, after Veronese's *Adoration of the Shepherds* (reproduced by Fairfull-Smith, 2001, p.44), was almost certainly made after Marco Piccioni's engraving after Veronese's original rather than from the original itself, now in a private collection in New York. For this picture and Piccioni's engraving, see F. Zeri, 'Une Adorazione di Pastori di Paolo Veronese', *Antologia di Belle Arti*, II, 1978, pp.107–9.

17 For the Orléans sale, see Buchanan, 1824, I; Herrmann, 1972, pp.133–45; Haskell, 1976, pp.39–44; J. Pomeroy, 'The Orléans collection. Its impact on the British art world', *Apollo*, CXLV, 1997, pp.26–31.

18 E.M. Lee, '*Titianus Redivivus*': Titian in British Art Theory, Criticism and Practice, 1768–1830, PhD dissertation, Yale University, 1997, pp.265ff.

19 Haskell, 1976, pp.42–6; Brigstocke, 1982, p.3.

20 For further information on these three dealers, see the appendix of principal collectors and dealers.

21 Brigstocke, 1982, p.249.

22 Ibid., p.78.

23 Ibid., p.255.

24 Ibid., pp.393, 430.

25 Ibid., p.296.

26 Jaffé, 1971, p.702.

27 Letter of 30 April 1827 from Rome: Skene of Rubislaw MSS, recently acquired by the National Library of Scotland; transcription kindly provided by Helen Smailes. In the same letter Wilson also mentions that he has been buying pictures for Sir Archibald Campbell of Garscube.

28 Forbes, 1996, p.43.

29 Forbes, 1996, pp.41–2.

30 See W. Frost, *A Catalogue of the Paintings in the Collection of Hugh Andrew Johnstone Munro of Novar, 6 Hamilton Place, London*, 1865; the Titian and the Tintoretto are listed on p.16, no.48 and p.15, no.46 respectively. Titian's *Rest on the Flight into Egypt* once belonged to the collection of the Archduke Leopold Wilhelm, and is clearly visible in Teniers's painting in the Prado (fig.57). For the Munro collection, see also Edinburgh, 1992, p.169.

31 See S. Coppel in London, British Museum, *Old Master Drawings from the Malcolm Collection*, exh. cat. ed. by M. Royalton-Kisch, London, 1996, pp.7–20.

32 Evans, 2003, pp.56–7.

33 G. Evans in Edinburgh, 1985, p.73.

34 In 1828 James Irvine missed the opportunity to buy late works by Titian for Sir William Forbes, such as the *Venus with a Mirror* (Washington, National Gallery of Art) and the *St Sebastian* (St Petersburg, Hermitage) because he considered them to be 'the inferior pictures of Titian's old age': see Jaffé, 1971; Brigstocke, 1982, p.28.

35 *Hendersyde Park*, 1859, p.x.

36 For Hamilton and Woodburn, see R.W. Liscombe in the *Dictionary of Art*, 1996, XIV, p.107. In 1804 Buchanan noted that Cosway was 'very intimate with the Marquis of Douglas' (the future 10th Duke); Brigstocke, 1982, p.293.

37 Thompson, 1972, pp.22–6; Gordon, 1976, pp.12–13, 69–70; I. Gow, 'The Northern Athenian Temple of the Arts' in I. Gow and T. Clifford, *The National Gallery of Scotland: an Architectural and Decorative History*, Edinburgh, 1988, pp.11–44.

38 National Archives of Scotland, Royal Institution MSS, NG3/4/9, letter of 22 March 1827. See also Thompson, 1972, p.27.

39 Brigstocke, 1982, p.70.

40 For the provenance of the Borghese *Venus*, see B. Meijer in Venice, 1999, pp.532–3.

41 Brigstocke, 1993, pp.29–30.

42 Thompson, 1972, pp.27–34.

43 See Brigstocke, 1993, pp.67–9, 168–70 respectively.

44 Brigstocke, 1993, pp.186–7. This picture (acc.no.NG103) and Bassano's *Adoration of the Kings* were transferred to the National Gallery of Scotland in 1910.

45 Gordon, 1976, pp.125–8.

46 Quoted in Pinnington, 1898, pp.13–14, and in the introduction to the various editions of the Glasgow Gallery catalogue.

47 The picture was seen by Waagen in 1835 in the collection of Edward Solly in London and was hailed by him as an important early work by Giorgione (Waagen, 1838, II, pp.192–3). Solly had reputedly bought it from the Balbi family in Venice, who had in turn inherited from the Soranzo family. It appears in the Solly sale, Christie's, 8 May 1847 (lot 42), but failed to sell, and it was acquired by McLellan in January 1854, shortly before his death, from Mr Peel of Golden Square, London.

48 Waagen, 1854, III, pp.266–315; Waagen, 1857, pp.429–64. See also G. Waterfield, 'Waagen in England', *Jahrbuch der Berliner Museen*, XXXVII, 1995, pp.47–59; Humfrey, 2003b, with further references.

49 Waagen, 1857, pp.443–4. Following the opinion of Bernard Berenson, the portrait now bears a tentative attribution to Paolo Farinati (see Berenson, 1968, I, p.124, incorrectly as formerly in the Earl of Elgin's collection).

50 Waagen, 1857, p.455.

51 Edinburgh, 1883.

PAINTINGS

1

1 Pallucchini, 1962, p.119; and, for the fullest discussion, Pope-Hennessy, 1987, pp.230–6.

2 Ibid.

2

1 A. Gentili, 'Bellini and landscape', in Humfrey, 2003c, p.168.

2 B. Degenhart and A. Schmitt, *Corpus der italienischen Zeichnungen 1300–1450*, VI.2, Berlin, 1990, pp.458–60.

3 K. Christiansen, 'Bellini and Mantegna', in Humfrey, 2003c, p.57.

4 Crowe and Cavalcaselle, 1871, I, pp.139–40; R. Pallucchini, *Giovanni Bellini: Catalogo della Mostra*, Venice, 1949, p.48; Robertson, 1968, pp.15–16; Goffen, 1989, pp.4–8; M. Lucco, 'Venezia', in Lucco, 1989–90, II, pp.412–13; Tempestini, 1992, p.18.

5 Crowe and Cavalcaselle, 1871, I, p.140; Robertson, 1968, p.15.

6 Lucco, 1989–90, II, p.413.

7 Goffen, 1989, p.4.

8 Lucco (as in note 4), pp.411–12; P. Humfrey, 'Introduction', in Humfrey, 2003c, pp.5–6; Christiansen (as in note 3), pp.52–3.

9 Southesk, 1904, pp.10, 14, 19.

10 Southesk, 1871, p.25.

3

1 It receives no mention, for example, in the monographs on Bellini by Robertson, 1968 and Goffen, 1989. Heinemann, 1962, p.318, no.348, proposed an entirely unjustified attribution to Bellini's follower Francesco Bissolo.

2 See the survey of opinions by Tempestini, 1992, p.130.

3 Tempestini, 1992, p.130.

4

1 Crowe and Cavalcaselle, 1871, I, p.189; G. Lafenestre and E. Richtenberger, *Rome: les musées, les collections particulières, les palais*, Paris, 1905, p.152, no.90.

2 See the survey of opinions in Tempestini, 1992, p.186.

3 Berenson, 1916, p.118.

4 Listed by Heinemann, 1962, p.9, no.36 and figs.388 and 403.

5 Marks, 1983, p.21.

6 'As you know there are always 'wise ones' going about who doubt the authenticity of every other picture and evidently the Bellini did not escape them but these articles are useful as showing how these gentlemen went wrong' (letter to T.J. Honeyman, quoted by Marks, 1983, p.155).

7 'Un Quadro con cornice d'albuccio alla fiorentina tutta dorata mezza figura in tavola la Madonna con N.S. in seno ignudo quale tiene un filo in mano et a piedi a d.o filo vi e legato una Sorte d'erba alto d.o quadro tre palmi e un terzo e largo palmi due e tre quarti di Pierino del Vago' (A picture on panel, with a gilt poplar frame in the Florentine style, showing the Madonna in half length with the Child held close to her. He is nude and holds a thread in his hand, and some sort of plant is tied to the end of the thread. Three palms and a third high by two and three quarter palms wide. By Perino del Vaga). See M.A. Lavin, *Seventeenth Century Barberini Documents and Inventories of Art*, New York, 1975, p.249, no.840. My thanks to Vivien Hamilton for pointing out this reference to me, and especially for her observation that before the picture was cleaned in 1934–5, it was inscribed with the Barberini inventory number 'F.135'. The crude inscription PIRINO DEL VAGO is faintly legible on the back of the panel. See Hamilton, 2003, pp.89–92.

8 See W.L. Barcham and C.R. Puglisi, 'Paolo Veronese e la Roma dei Barberini', *Saggi e Memorie di Storia dell'Arte*, XXV, 2001, pp.57–87.

5

1 The picture is attributed to the workshop of Giovanni Bellini and dated to about 1510 by Zeri, 1973, pp.7–8. Although Berenson (1957, p.32) attributed it to Bellini himself, it has been omitted from all recent monographs on the painter.

2 Waagen, 1838, III, p.118 ('Cordelle Agi', the name with which Previtali sometimes signed his works). Much less plausible was the Berenson's initial re-attribution to Marco Basaiti (Berenson, 1907, p.82).

3 Information kindly provided by Godfrey Evans (see also cat.no.10).

6

1 For these works, see J. Pope-Hennessy, *Italian Paintings (The Robert Lehman Collection)*, I, Princeton, 1987, p.242.

2 Williamson, 1903, p.127.

3 See A. Chong, *European and American Paintings in the Cleveland Museum of Art. A Summary Catalogue*, Cleveland, 1995, p.115.

4 Some evidence for this interpretation is provided by the close repetition of the hart in an engraving by Giulio Campagnola: see Maastricht, 2003, pp.61–2.

5 Williamson, 1903, p.115.

6 A. McKay, *Catalogue of the Miniatures in Montagu House belonging to the Duke of Buccleuch*, London, 1896, p.16; Edinburgh, Scottish National Portrait Gallery, *Portrait Miniatures from the Collection of the Duke of Buccleuch*, exh. cat. by S. Lloyd, Edinburgh, 1996, p.24; Lloyd, 2003, pp.43–4.

7

1 Gould, 1975, pp.52–3.

2 Berenson, 1916, p.248 (c.1500–5); Robertson, 1954, p.46 (c.1508–10).

3 Robertson, 1954, p.46, noted that 'A heade of Vincentius Catena' was included among the pictures put into crates for transport to Scotland in 1642–3 (inventory published by Garas, 1967, p.70). But as kindly pointed out to me by Jeremy Wood, the 1st Duke's Catena almost certainly corresponds to the signed portrait now in the Kunsthistorisches Museum, Vienna.

4 In the files of the National Gallery, London.

8

1 E.M. Dal Pozzolo, 'Il lauro di Laura e delle 'maritate venetiane'', *Mitteilungen des Kunsthistorischen Institutes von Florenz*, XXXVII, 1993, p.287, note 67; A. Tempestini, 'La 'Sacra Conversazione' nella pittura veneta dal 1500 al 1516', in Lucco, 1996–9, III, p.940.

2 Information kindly provided by Jochen Sander of the Städelsches Kunstinstitut.

3 See Heinemann, 1962, pp.30–1, no.118; A. Tempestini, 'Giovanni Bellini and his collaborators', in Humfrey, 2003c, pp.264–7.

4 Robertson, 1954, pp.54–5, suggests a date of around 1507, but this may be slightly too late.

5 McLellan Gallery, 1855, no.118.

6 Waagen, 1857, p.460; Glasgow Gallery, 1864, no.409.

7 Berenson, 1901, p.130.

9

1 Humfrey, 1983, p.100; B. Blass-Simmen, 'Cima da Conegliano: alcuni riflessioni sui disegni', *Venezia Cinquecento* IV, 8, 1994, p.159.

2 A. Tempestini (review of Humfrey, 1983), *Antichità Viva*, XXXV, 1, 1986, p.50. This attribution is much more convincing than one to a Veronese master proposed by E.M. Dal Pozzolo, 'E tutto Cima?', *Venezia Cinquecento* IV, 7, 1994, p.69.

3 Humfrey, 1983, pp.62–6; J. Dunkerton and A. Roy, 'The technique and restoration of Cima's *The Incredulity of S. Thomas*', *National Gallery Technical Bulletin*, X, 1986, pp.7–8; J. Dunkerton, 'Bellini's technique', in Humfrey, 2003c, pp.195–225.

10

1 R. Echols, 'Cima and the theme of Saint Jerome in the Wilderness', *Venezia Cinquecento*, IV, 8, 1994, pp.47–69.

2 L. Menegazzi, *Cima da Conegliano*, Treviso, 1981, p.123; Humfrey, 1983, p.111.

3 Davies, 1961, p.145; Zeri, 1973, pp.7–8. For Strange as a collector, see Callegari, 2000, pp.99–101.

4 Oxford, Bodleian Library, MS Beckford, c. 58, p.22.

5 Waagen, 1838, III, p.118: 'A small St Jerome, admirably finished and of great warmth and depth of colouring, is of the same school [as Bellini], and calls to mind MARCO BASAILI [sic]'.

6 The pair is recorded at Hamilton House in the posthumous inventory of the 11th Duke of 1864: Hamilton Archive, Lennoxlove, M. 4/78, p.137. My thanks to Godfrey Evans for this and for the archival reference in note 4.

11

1 Contrary to what is sometimes reported, the wound on Francis's right hand remains faintly visible, and there must originally have been a similar wound on the damaged left hand. This is confirmed by the existence of an early copy of the painting, in a private collection, where both stigmata are clearly visible (photograph and further information in the Gallery files).

2 See S. Béguin, 'A propos des peintures de Lorenzo Lotto au Louvre', in P. Zampetti and V. Sgarbi (eds.), *Lorenzo Lotto: Atti del convegno internazionale di studi*, Treviso, 1981, p.100; and especially A. Gentili, *I giardini di contemplazione. Lorenzo Lotto, 1503–1512*, Rome, 1985, p.112 (who quotes Christ's words immediately prior to the Crucifixion in Luke 23: 28–31); E.M. Dal Pozzolo, 'Alcune precisazioni intorno al 'Lignum Crucis' di Luca Antonio Busati e all'iconografia della Passione in ambito francescano', *Il Santo*, XXX, 1990–1, pp.112–13.

3 A. Tempestini, 'La *Sacra Conversazione* nella pittura veneta dal 1500 al 1516', in Lucco, 1996–9, III, p.961.

4 Humfrey, 1997, pp.21–2; D.A. Brown in Washington, 1997, pp.91–2.

5 Leonardo's *Madonna Litta* is often identified with a painting recorded by Marcantonio Michiel in the collection of Michele Contarini in Venice in 1543. See D.A. Brown in Venice, Palazzo Grassi, *Leonardo and Venice*, exh. cat., Milan, 1992, p.362; D.A. Brown in Washington, 1997, pp.91–2, with reference to the similar figure of the Virgin in Lotto's *Virgin and Child with Saints* in the Muzeum Narodowe, Cracow.

6 It remains unclear whether Dürer painted the picture while still in Venice, or towards the end of 1506 in Rome. On this subject see, most recently, I. Lübbeke in Venice, 1999, pp.296–9.

7 For this work and the identification of Buscatti as its author, see A. Tempestini, 'I fratelli Busati e il Maestro Veneto dell'Incredulità di San Tommaso', *Studi di Storia dell'Arte*, IV, 1993, pp.27–68. Reflections of Lotto's female saint appear in pictures in Rome, Pinacoteca Vaticana, in Cambridge (Mass.), Fogg Art Museum (formerly New York, Woodner Collection), and in two unknown collections: see Tempestini's figs.16, 18, 53, 56.

8 Dubois de Saint Gelais, 1727, pp.294–5. This catalogue provides a record of the Orléans collection as it existed at the time of the regent's death in 1723. The picture was almost certainly acquired at some time previously by the regent, although for some reason the picture was omitted from a MS inventory of 1724 (for which see C. Stryienski, *Galerie du Régent Philippe Duc d'Orléans*, Paris, 1913, p.151, no.43).

12

1 Anderson, 1997, p.309.

2 Paolo Pino, *Dialogo di Pittura*, Venice, 1548, pp.27v–28r.

3 Helke, 1999, pp.66–7.

4 A. Ballarin, 'Una nuova prospettiva su Giorgione: la ritrattistica degli anni 1500–1503', in *Giorgione: Convegno internazionale di studi per il 50 centenario della nascita*, Castelfranco Veneto, 1979, pp.234, 247, note 41 (where the picture is dated *c.*1501); A. Ballarin in Paris, 1993, p.288; M. Lucco, *Giorgione*, Milan, 1995, p.146 (an early work); Joannides, 2001, p.204. By contrast, T. Pignatti and F. Pedrocco, *Giorgione*, New York, 1999, p.202, remain more cautious, and attribute the picture to an anonymous painter in the circle of Giorgione.

5 See the survey of opinions in Brigstocke, 1993, pp.194–5.

6 'Un giouinetto parimente con molle chioma, & armatura, nella quale gli reflette la mano di esquisita bellezza'; Ridolfi, 1648, I, p.106. This plausible identification was first suggested by Garas, 1964, p.57.

7 'Een Mans konterfeytsel half lijf in't harnas met de hand gahantschoent op't harnas': see Garas, 1964, p.57.

8 Anderson, 1997, p.309.

13 & 14

1 The restoration is described by Ruhemann, 1954, pp.13–18, 31. See also H. Ruhemann, 'The cleaning and restoration of the Glasgow Giorgione', *Burlington Magazine*, XCVII, 1955, pp.278–82.

2 First proposed by E. Tietze-Conrat, 'The so-called *Adulteress* by Giorgione', *Gazette des Beaux-Arts*, XXVII, 1945, pp.189–90, followed by a number of writers in the 1950s and 1960s, and recently revived by A. Ballarin in Paris, 1993, pp.327–39. Further compelling arguments against the identification are provided by Joannides, 2001, p.89.

3 This position is maintained by Wethey, 1969, pp.169–70, who lists earlier opinions.

4 First proposed by L. Hourticq in 1919, the attribution to the young Titian was influentially endorsed by R. Longhi, and has been upheld by a majority of critics in the last thirty years, including Pallucchini, 1969, p.236; F. Richardson in London, 1983, pp.169–70; A. Ballarin, in Paris, 1993, pp.327–39; M. Lucco in Lucco, 1996–9, I, p.58; Anderson, 1997, p.327; Valcanover, 1999, pp.16, 254; Joannides, 2001, pp.89–94.

5 Hope, 1980, p.40; P. Holberton, 'The *pastorale* or *fête champêtre* in the early sixteenth century', in Manca, 1993, pp.257–8.

6 Joannides, 2001, p.93, plausibly suggests that the figure is based on a version of the so-called *Cincinattus* (Paris, Louvre), known to Titian in the form of a drawing or cast.

7 Ruhemann, 1954, pp.13–18.

8 As first suggested by Crowe and Cavalcaselle, 1871, II, p.159, quoting the posthumous inventory of Queen Christina's collection published by Campori, 1870, p.348 ('Un altro quadro con l'istoria di Cristo con l'adultera con varie figure di farisei e soldati, mano di Giorgione, in tela a giacere p.mi sette e mezzo, alto quattro e mezzo, con cornice intagliata alla genovese'). This identification has been widely accepted, but was convincingly rejected by A. Ballarin in Paris, 1993, pp.327–39.

9 See Dubois de Saint Gelais, 1727, p.252; *Galerie du Palais Royal gravée d'après les Tableaux des différentes Ecoles*, 3 vols., Paris, 1808, II, as 'J.A. Regillo' (Pordenone); Garas, 1965, pp.36–7;

C. Furlan, 'Tra Giorgione e il Pordenone: a proposito di alcuni dipinti già nella collezione del duca d'Orléans', in Ceschi Lavagetto, 1981, pp.12–23. Virtually all of Queen Christina's pictures (including two of the Titians from the Sutherland collection in the present exhibition, cat.nos.15, 19) passed in to the Orléans collection in 1720, and the dimensions of the 'Pordenone' *Adulteress* closely correspond to those of Christina's 'Giorgione' (c.100 × 170cm). This picture disappeared around the time of the French Revolution and did not come to England (Buchanan, 1824, I, p.128). From the engraving it appears to have been a Venetian picture of the mid-sixteenth century.

10 See Garas, 1965, pp.36–7; R. Martinoni, *Gian Vincenzo Imperiale. Politico, letterato e collezionista genovese del Seicento*, Padua, 1983, pp.326–8.

11 Waagen, 1857, pp.459–60. See also McLellan Gallery, 1855, no.95 (as Bonifacio); Glasgow Gallery, 1864, no.434 (as 'Giorgio Barbarelli').

15

1 *Tornato poi Tiziano a Vinezia, fece per lo suocero di Giovanni da Castel Bolognese, in una tela a olio, un pastore ignudo et una forese che gli porge certi flauti perché suoni, con un bellissimo paese; il qual quadro è oggi in Faenza in casa il su detto Giovanni':* Vasari (1568), ed. 1966–87, VI, p.159. The translation here is from G. Vasari, *Lives of the Artists: a Selection*, translated by G. Bull, Harmondsworth, 1965, p.448.

2 P.L. Rubin: *Giorgio Vasari: Art and History*, New Haven and London, 1995, p.170.

3 Humfrey, 2003a, p.791.

4 *The Autobiography of Benvenuto Cellini*, translated by G. Bull, Harmondsworth, 1956, p.169.

5 Sandrart, 1925, p.272.

6 Joannides, 2001, pp.199–201.

7 P. Holberton, 'The pipes in Titian's *Three Ages of Man*', *Apollo* CLVII, 2003, pp.26–30. Other recent interpretations include Gentili, 1988, pp.86–9; and Goffen, 1997, pp.26–33.

8 Humfrey, 2003a, p.791.

9 For the theme of music in the picture see, in addition to the studies cited in note 7 above, E. Winternitz, *Musical Instruments and their Symbolism in Western Art*, London, 1967, pp.48–50; G. Studdert-Kennedy, 'Titian: metaphors of love and renewal', *Word and Image*, III, 1987, pp.29–32; A. Rowland-Jones, 'The iconography of the two (or three) recorders', *Recorder Magazine*, March 1997, pp.12–17; A. Rowland-Jones, 'The recorder in the art of Titian', *American Recorder* XLIII, 2, March 2000, pp.7–13; T. Seebass, 'Giorgiones und Tizians *fantasie* mit

Musik', *Imago Musicae*, XVI/XVII, 1999–2000, pp.25–60.

10 Joannides, 2001, pp.193–4.

11 As suggested by R. Longhi, *Viatico per cinque secoli di pittura veneziana*, 1946; reprinted in *Opere complete di Roberto Longhi*, X, Florence, 1978, p.58. Romanino's altarpiece was commissioned in January 1513, and must have been complete by July 1514, when the painter left Padua: see Nova, 1994, pp.217–21. Joannides, 2001, p.194, rejects Longhi's suggestion, and argues that both sets of babies derive from a common source in Mantegna's engraving of a *Bacchanal with a Wine Vat*. But while Titian's figure group clearly depends on that of Mantegna in terms of its composition, that of Romanino does not, but represents rather a response to Titian's interpretation of Mantegna. Particularly close to Titian is Romanino's description of the creases in the infants' flesh, using red outlines and a minimum of modelling.

12 G. Robertson, 'The x-ray examination of Titian's *Three Ages of Man*', *Burlington Magazine*, XCIII, 1971, pp.21–6.

13 Humfrey, 2003a, p.789.

14 Sandrart, 1675, p.272. As kindly pointed out to me by Christian Klemm, the 'Walberg' who sold the picture to Christina was no a descendant of Cardinal Truchsess, as is often supposed, but an 'art-lover' – presumably a dealer – mentioned elsewhere by Sandrart (1675, p.99).

15 Brigstocke, 1993, pp.174–7.

16 Foulis, 1776, II, pp.241–3.

16

1 G. Gronau, 'Notes complémentaires sur Domenico Campagnola', *Gazette des Beaux-Arts*, XII, 1894, 2, pp.433–4 (as Domenico Campagnola); Berenson, 1901, p.137 (as Romanino). Gronau's attribution was adopted in the Glasgow Gallery catalogues between 1895 and 1935, but it was subsequently dropped in favour of the more generic 'Venetian School'.

2 M. Lucco in *Proposte di restauro: Dipinti del primo Cinquecento nel Veneto*, Castelfranco Veneto, 1978, p.101; M. Lucco, 'Venezia', in Lucco, 1996–9, I, p.87; III, p.1295.

17

1 For Bellini's picture, see D. Bull and J. Plesters, *The Feast of the Gods: Conservation, Examination and Interpretation* (*Studies in the History of Art*, 40), Washington, 1990; D.A. Brown in Washington, 1990, pp.198–200; D. Jaffé and S. Carey in London, 2002, pp.108–9, cat.no.15. An indication of the fidelity of the Edinburgh copy is provided not just by the repetition of Bellini's signature – and even of the original's inventory number in the

Aldobrandini collection – but also by its value as a guide to the conservators in the restoration of the original in the later 1980s (Bull and Plesters, p.36).

2 C. D'Onofrio, 'Inventario dei dipinti del Cardinal Pietro Aldobrandini compilato da G.B. Agucchi nel 1603', *Palatino*, 1964, p.205.

3 See the summary of opinions in Brigstocke, 1993, pp.33–5.

4 F. Haskell, 'William Coningham and his collection of Old Masters', *Burlington Magazine*, CXXXIII, 1991, pp.679–80.

5 Edinburgh, 1981, pp.20–1.

18

1 Gould, 1975, pp.271, 273.

2 Evans, 2003, p.57.

3 Waagen, 1854, III, p.200.

4 See Edinburgh, 2000, p.106.

5 P. Humfrey in *Dosso Dossi: Court Painter of Renaissance Ferrara*, New York, 1998, pp.111, 175–6.

6 Letter of 3 December 2003 from Alessandro Ballarin to Aidan Weston-Lewis, citing the article by C. Stefani, 'Considerazioni intorno al viaggio del Cavaliere d'Arpino a Venezia', *Paragone*, LI, 599, 2000, pp.67–77. Professor Ballarin will include the painting, as by the Cavaliere d'Arpino, in the forthcoming fifth volume of his 'Il Camerino delle pitture di Alfonso I'.

7 D. Montelatici, *Villa Borghese fuori di porta pinciana*, Rome, 1700, p.276. Montelatici records three further copies attributed to the Cavaliere after Bacchanals by Titian – apparently the entire compositions – in the villa; none of these has been identified, and it seems highly unlikely that they were all by him.

8 Edinburgh, 2000, p.106.

19

1 Freedman, 2003, pp.111–14.

2 In 1521 the Ferrarese ambassador to Venice reported to his master that Titian looked well but exhausted, adding: 'I suspect that the girls whom he often paints in different poses arouse his desires, which he then satisfies more than his limited strength permits'. See Hope, 1980, p.58.

3 Pliny the Elder, *Natural History*, XXXV: 79–97. The connection between Pliny's description and Titian's picture was first pointed out by Wedgwood Kennedy, 1964, p.162. See further Goffen, 1997, pp.126–32; Freedman, 2003, pp.195–6.

4 See N. Penny in London, 2003, p.104; P. Humfrey, 'Titian's *Bacchanals* for Duke Alfonso's *camerino*: a re-examination of the chronology' in G. Venturi (ed.), *L'Età di Alfonso I e la Pittura del Dosso*, Ferrara, 2004, pp.179–85.

5 D. Rosand, *Myths of Venice: The Figuration of a State*, Chapel Hill and London, 2001, pp.117–18.

6 Ibid. It may also be noted in this connection, as Aidan Weston-Lewis reminded me, that the Venetian patrician Jacopo Pesaro, for whom Titian was painting the Ca' Pesaro altarpiece (Venice, Frari) in these very years (1519–25), was Bishop of Paphos, the very site of the ancient cult of Venus. In this way Pesaro becomes a plausible patron of the *Venus Anadyomene*.

7 Despite Wethey's rejection of the idea (1975, pp.187–8), it is still sometimes suggested that the *Venus* is identical with a picture that Titian was painting for Duke Alfonso on 19 February 1518, and which he describes as a *bagno*. Although the date and the patron might fit, it seems highly improbable that Titian would refer to the figure of the emerging Venus as a *bagno* (a 'baignade', or bathing scene). For an alternative, but no more convincing, identification of the *bagno*, with a correction of the dating of Titian's letter from 1517 to 1518, see W. Hood and C. Hope, 'Titian's Vatican altarpiece and the pictures underneath', *Art Bulletin*, LIX, 1977, pp.546–9.

8 Wedgwood Kennedy, 1964.

9 For Alfonso as the likely patron of this work, see P. Evelyn (Motture) in P. Williamson (ed.), *European Sculpture at the Victoria and Albert Museum*, London, 1996, p.92; A. Sarchi, 'Per Antonio Lombardo: fortuna e collezionismo', *Arte Lombarda*, 132, 2001–2, p.55.

10 For Titian and the *paragone*: L. Freedman, 'The Schiavona': Titian's response to the *paragone* between painting and sculpture', *Arte Veneta*, XLI, 1987, pp.31–40; Goffen, 1997.

11 The use of a classical model was, however, assumed by Brigstocke, 1993, p.177.

12 Brigstocke, 1993, pp.177–8.

13 Goffen, 1997, p.128.

14 Kennedy North, 1932, pp.58–63.

15 J. Dunkerton, 'Titian's Painting Technique' in London, 2003, p.48.

20

1 R. Stradiotti, 'Per un catalogo delle pitture di Girolamo da Santacroce', *Atti dell'Istituto Veneto di Scienze, Lettere ed Arti*, CXXXIV, 1975–6, p.580, plausibly suggests a date of *c*.1520.

2 For example, Berenson, 1957, p.154. When exhibited at the Royal Academy in 1886, however, it was simply called 'Italian'.

21

1 M. Lucco, 'Pordenone a Venezia, *Paragone*, 309, 1975, p.20; M. Lucco, 'La giovinezza del Pordenone (nuove

riflessioni su vecchi studi)', in Ceschi Lavagetto, 1981, p.39. The writer compares the picture with Pordenone's altarpiece of about 1512 in the parish church of Vallenoncello (near Pordenone). M.G. Ciardi Duprè, 'Alessandro Oliverio', in *I pittori Bergamaschi: Il Cinquecento I*, Bergamo, 1980, p.474, no.7, rejects an attribution supposedly made by Berenson, 1957, p.122, to Oliverio; Berenson, however, was actually referring to a quite different picture in Glasgow, the *Virgin and Child enthroned with Saints* (fig.72).

2 G. Fossaluzza, 'Profilo di Domenico Capriolo', *Arte Veneta*, XXXVII, 1983, pp.52–4.

22

1 See A. Weston-Lewis, in Tokyo, 1993, p.145 and in Clarke, 2000, p.31; F. Rossi in Bergamo, 2001, p.152.

2 Rearick (in Florence, Galleria degli Uffizi, *Tiziano e il disegno del suo tempo*, exh. cat. by W.R. Rearick, Florence, 1976, pp.80–1) interprets this picture rather as an image of St George, in which the portrait-like features of the model have been retained. For a similar problem of interpretation in works by Savoldo, see cat.no.41.

3 A. Ballarin in London, Colnaghi, *Gothic to Renaissance: European Painting 1300–1600*, dealer catalogue, (ed.) D. Garstang, London, 1988, pp.30–2; A. Ballarin in Paris, 1993, pp.385–6; M. Lucco, 'Venezia 1500–1540', in Lucco, 1996–9, I, p.115, note 205; E.M. Dal Pozzolo, 'Tra Cariani e Rocco Marconi', *Venezia Cinquecento*, VII, 13, 1997, p.6; F. Rossi, in Bergamo, 2001, p.152.

4 The dating of this work is controversial, but Joannides (2001, pp.249–52) convincingly dates it to about 1516, and identifies the heroine as Judith rather than Salome.

5 A dating to this slightly later phase was argued by A. Weston-Lewis in Tokyo, 1993, p.145.

23

1 Berenson, 1907, p.111, calls the picture 'Portrait of a Lady'.

2 Apart from the fact that the musical score shows notes but no words, the leaps would be much more difficult for the voice than for an instrument. I am grateful to David Bryant for discussing the representation of the music with me.

3 F. Moro in Milan, Palazzo Reale, *L'Anima e il volto. Ritratto e fisionomia da Leonardo a Bacon*, exh. cat. ed. by F. Caroli, Milan, 1998, p.80. See also E. Ginaneschi in Milan, Palazzo Reale, *Il Cinquecento Lombardo. Da Leonardo a Caravaggio*, exh. cat. ed. by F. Caroli, Milan, 2000, p.293.

4 Waagen, 1857, p.446.

5 Vertova, 1980, p.432; G. Fossaluzza, 'Qualche recupero al catalogo ritrattistico del Bordon', in Fossaluzza and Manzato, 1987, p.187.

24

1 Waagen, 1854, II, pp.82–3.

2 Crowe and Cavalcaselle, 1871, II, pp.162–3. G.B. Cavalcaselle's drawing after the picture, now with his papers in the Marciana Library, Venice, is reproduced in Gregori, 1986, p.271.

3 For the dating of c.1524–5 and previous bibliographic references, see Nova, 1994, pp.251–2.

4 Edinburgh, National Gallery of Scotland, Pictures from Gosford House lent by the Earl of Wemyss and March, exh. cat. by C. Thompson, Edinburgh, 1957, p.7; Wemyss, 2003, p.74.

25

1 See the summary of opinions in Brigstocke, 1993, p.171.

2 Recent writers who doubt the identification of the figure as Joseph include A. Weston-Lewis in Clarke, 2000, p.33. Recent writers who accept the identification include Brigstocke, 1993, p.171; Joannides, 2001, p.146; C. Wilson, St Joseph in Italian Renaissance Society and Art, Philadelphia, 2001, pp.195–6, note 11; idem, 'Invention, devotion, and the requirements of patrons: Titian and the new cult of St Joseph', in P. Meilman (ed.), The Cambridge Companion to Titian, Cambridge and New York, 2004, pp.86–8.

3 See, for example, Hope, 1980, p.40, note 19 (c.1507–8); Valcanover, 1999, p.253 (c.1512–13); Joannides, 2001, p.146 (c.1521).

4 For the provenance, see Brigstocke, 1993, pp.171–2. The writer implies that the picture entered the Orléans collection some time between 1724 and 1727, the published date of the catalogue by Dubois de Saint Galais, in which it is first mentioned. But the catalogue was compiled in 1723 immediately after the death of the 2nd Duc d'Orléans, and it was certainly he who acquired it from its previous owner.

5 As kindly pointed out by David Ekserdjian (letter in the Gallery files). See New York, The Drawing Center, Creative Copies: Interpreting Drawings from Michelangelo to Picasso, exh. cat. by E. Haverkamp-Begemann, New York, 1988, pp.98–9.

6 'Nostre Dame qui regarde saint Jean-Baptiste assis tenant son agneau; elle donne son fils à un homme à genoux qui a un manteau rouge avec son habit brun, après Titien', in Mémoires de la Société de l'Histoire de Paris, Paris, 1894, p.255, no.118. This reference kindly communicated by Nicholas Penny (letter in the Gallery files).

26

1 See Wethey, 1987, pp.167–8 and pl.17 (the drawing was then still in the Baer Collection, Stone Mountain, Georgia)

2 McLellan Gallery, 1855, cat.no.107; Glasgow Gallery, 1864, cat.no.159. Waagen omitted it from his description of the McLellan collection.

3 W. Suida, 'Miscellanea Tizianesca IV', Arte Veneta, XIII–XIV, 1959–60, pp.62–5; Pallucchini, 1969, p.245; Fehl, 1992, p.327; Valcanover, 1999, pp.106, 254. These scholars tend to see the picture as an early work by Titian, datable to c.1513–14.

4 Berenson, 1901, p.91; Berenson, 1907, p.122.

5 Wethey, 1969, p.175.

6 As proposed by A. Venturi, Storia dell'Arte Italiana, IX/7, Milan, 1934, p.74; G. Fiocco, Lettere ed arti, II, 1, 1946, p.33. C. Ricketts (Titian, London, 1910, p.84), while continuing to attribute the figure of Jerome and part of the landscape to Titian himself, had already suggested that the picture was completed by Francesco.

7 C. Wilson, Italian Paintings XIV–XV Centuries in the Museum of Fine Arts, Houston, Houston and London, 1996, pp.323–33.

8 Joannides (2001, p.317, note 13) makes a good case for linking the Glasgow and the Dresden pictures, but attributes them to an unknown assistant of Titian rather than to Francesco.

9 See U. Ruggeri, Valentin Lefèvre (1637–1677), Reggio Emilia, 2001, cat.no.I.9.

10 A number of different families laid claim to this escutcheon: see E. Morando di Custoza, Libro d'Arme di Venezia, Verona, 1979 (Conti); E. Morando di Custoza, Blasonario Veneto, Verona, 1985 (Dauli, Dotti, Ruggiero).

27

1 See, for example, Wethey, 1969, pp.175–6, cat.no.X–23; Mancini, 2001, p.123, cat.no.2. Neither of these writers mention the versions in Bergamo (probably by Francesco; see note 3 below), or in the Szépmúvészeti Múzeum, Budapest. The latter is attributed to Polidoro da Lanciano in the inventory of the collection of the Archduke Wilhelm in 1659 (see Garas, 1967, p.56), and may indeed be by him.

2 Following Crowe and Cavalcaselle, 1877, II, p.468 and Berenson, 1907, p.122.

3 As already suggested by Mancini, 2001, p.34.

4 F. Rossi, Accademia Carrara: catalogo dei Dipinti Sec. XV–XVI, Milan, 1988, p.301, cat.no.1025 (as by Francesco Vecellio).

28

1 Information kindly provided by Vera Moore.

2 It was also engraved for the Theatrum Pictorium of 1660 (no.47) by Petrus Lisebetius (Pieter van Liesbetten): see Brigstocke, 1993, p.120.

3 It was attributed to Polidoro by Berenson, 1907, p.123 and 1957, p.142.

4 For the Descent, see Mancini, 2001, pp.138–9. The author does not, however, mention the Virgin and Sleeping Christ Child, which he presumably does not accept as by Polidoro.

5 Wenley, 2003, p.80.

29

1 Pfäffikon, 1978, p.98, cat.no.58, where it is stated that this picture, now in a private collection in Switzerland, was in the collection of Lord Clinton at Fettercairn from about 1820. In fact, the original Scottish owner in the 1820s would have been Sir William Forbes of Pitsligo, 7th baronet, who was the grandfather of Harriet (died 1869), wife of 20th Baron Clinton.

2 Vasari, 1966–87, VI, pp.170–1.

3 See C. Phillips, 'Paris Bordone', Burlington Magazine, XXVIII, 1915, pp.93–8; Canova, 1964, pp.6–7; Grabski, 1987, pp.206–7; Humfrey, 1990, p.128.

4 This picture, which belonged to Sir George Warrender (1782–1849) of Lochend by 1829, and was lent to the Edinburgh Old Masters exhibition of 1883 (cat.no.313), was acquired by Sir Thomas Barlow, London, in 1946. See Manchester, City Art Gallery, Art Treasures Centenary. European Old Masters, exh. cat., Manchester, 1957, p.16, cat.no.56.

5 Ridolfi, 1914–24, I, p.234 ('Il Signor Paolo del Sera possiede picciol quadro con la Vergine e più Santi di maniera molto delicata').

6 Boschini, 1660, p.402 ('Un singolar, perfeto e bel quadreto / Gh'è de Maria, de Paris da Treviso, / Con Sant' Antonio Abate. In Paradiso / Par che sia fato el Cristo bambineto; / Gh'è l'Eremita Gerolemo santo. / Del Genoa trevisan ghe xe 'l retrato, / Miedego de gran vaglia e de carato. / Pittura veramente de gran vanto!')

7 For Del Sera, see Savini Branca, 1965, pp.58–9, 111–12, 277–9.

8 Ridolfi, 1914–24, I, p.233; Canova, 1964, p.121. With Simon Dickinson Ltd, London, 2003.

9 S. Maschalchi, 'Giovan Carlo de' Medici. An outstanding but neglected collector in seventeenth-century Florence', Apollo, CXX, 1984, pp.268–72. See also the same writer's letter on file at the Glasgow Museum, quoting the cardinal's inventory of 1663: 'Un quadro in tela dipintovi la Madonna, con il nostro Signore che li avverte al collo, con S. Girolamo che accenna al Crocefisso, e due frati, uno inginocchioni, con Paese, alla

Lontana'. The reference to the support as canvas is clearly a mistake.

10 Laird, 1877, p.39.

30

1 Treviso, 1984, pp.56–8, cat.no.3.

2 See Washington, Phillips Collection and National Gallery of Art, Places of Delight: The Pastoral Landscape, exh. cat. by R. Cafritz et al., Washington, 1988, p.39, fig.36.

3 Further arguments for this dating, already implied by Canova, 1964, p.102, are provided by Grabski, 1987, p.207, and M. Lucco, 'Venezia 1500–1540', in Lucco, 1996, I, p.85.

4 Waagen, 1854, III, p.288; McLellan Gallery, 1855, no.106; Glasgow Gallery, 1864, no.391.

5 The catalogue of 1908, for example, is very confused (Paton, 1908, p.23). Besides recording an earlier attribution to Palma Vecchio, the compiler claimed that Waagen, 1854, III, p.289, had attributed the work to Giorgione. But Waagen was referring to a different picture, a Virgin and Child with Saints John and Catherine, which had previously been attributed to Bonifacio, and which was perhaps the one that came from the Riccardi Palace. Waagen's attribution for this latter picture was followed in the McLellan catalogue of 1855 (McLellan Gallery, 1855, no.90, 'Giorgio Barbarelli'), but by the time of the 1864 catalogue the picture is no longer listed, and may have been sold.

31

1 Although of good quality, that picture, previously in the collection of John Graham-Gilbert, is unfortunately in too damaged a condition to be included in the present exhibition.

2 A dating of 1528–30 is plausibly suggested by Cottrell, 2000, p.96.

3 Waagen, 1854, p.315.

4 W. Hanna (ed.), Letters of Thomas Erskine of Linlathen, 2 vols., Edinburgh, 1877, p.100. See also the appendix of principal collectors and dealers.

5 Berenson, 1907, p.87. A. Venturi, Storia dell'Arte Italiana, IX / 3, Milan, 1928, p.1068, lists the picture as by Polidoro da Lanciano.

32

1 For further discussions of the portrait in the context of Lotto's career, see Humfrey, 1997, p.110; Humfrey in Washington, 1997, pp.185–7.

2 Goffen, 1997, pp.192–8; McGrath, 1997, pp.81–2.

3 Jaffé, 1971.

4 L. Syson and D. Thornton, Objects of Virtue. Art in Renaissance Italy, London, 2001, pp.56–8.

5 J. Dunkerton, N. Penny and A. Roy, 'Two paintings by Lorenzo Lotto in

the National Gallery', *National Gallery Technical Bulletin*, XIX, 1998, pp.52–63.

6 Graves, 1913–15, I, p.421.

7 Crowe and Cavalcaselle, 1871, II, pp.159–60, 532.

33

1 A complication with this proposed dating is that there is no record of the portrait in Lotto's meticulously detailed account book, kept from 1538 until his death in 1556/7. See Zampetti, 1969, especially the chronological list of commissions on pp.335–71. This may indicate that the portrait was painted during Lotto's stay in the Marches from 1533 to 1540. However, there do exist a number of other pictures by Lotto datable to the period after 1538 which for some reason he did not record in the *Libro*.

2 For earlier sixteenth-century Venetian portraits of architects and their attributes, see J. Anderson, 'Constructing architectural identity in Renaissance Italy', in Trenerry, 2000, pp.10–13.

3 See Humfrey, 1997, pp.114, 158–60, 174, with references.

4 For the known portraits of Sansovino, see D. Howard, 'Portrait of Sansovino attributed to Titian', in Trenerry, 2000, pp.16–25.

5 Zampetti, 1969, p.361, with further references; Humfrey, 1997, pp.180–2.

6 As first proposed by T. Pignatti, *Lorenzo Lotto*, Milan, 1953, p.146. For a recent detailed discussion of this picture, see R. Contini in Rome, Palazzo Giustiniani and Berlin, Altes Museum, *Caravaggio e i Giustiniani*, exh. cat. ed. by S. Danesi Squarzina, Milan, 2001, pp.238–40. It is usually dated to about 1530–40, but stylistically it seems closer to Lotto's work of the 1540s or even later.

7 Letter from Irvine to Forbes, 27 June 1827; Forbes's record of payment, dated 2 July (both documents in private family papers).

34

1 Apart from the entry in Christie's 1977 auction catalogue, W.R. Rearick was the first to publish the portrait, in an entry on a portrait from the circle of Palma Giovane in Baltimore (in Rosenthal, 1981, pp.131–2, fig.2, and p.144, note 21). Charles Hope's more thorough analysis was published the following year (Hope, 1982).

2 Rearick in Rosenthal, 1981, p.132; and Hope, 1982, pp.158–61.

3 As emphasised by Rearick in Rosenthal, 1981.

4 Vasari, 1966–87, VI, p.168 ('Il nostro Danese scultore ha in Vinezia, in casa sua, un ritratto di man di Tiziano d'un gentiluomo di Ca' Delfini').

5 The official careers of both candidates are surveyed by Hope, 1982.

6 Hope, 1982, followed by P. Conisbee in P. Conisbee, M.L. Levkoff and R. Rand, *The Ahmanson Gifts. European Masterpieces in the Collection of the Los Angeles County Museum of Art*, Los Angeles, 1991, pp.65–7.

7 M. Rossi, *La poesia scolpita. Danese Cataneo nella Venezia del Cinquecento*, Lucca, 1995. An association with Titian is also evident in another bust attributed to Cattaneo, the *Portrait of a Jurist* in the Frick Collection, New York (J. Pope-Hennessy, *The Frick Collection III: Italian Sculpture*, New York, 1970, pp.172–7, with a dating to around 1552). Indeed, the features of this anonymous sitter closely resemble those of Titian's Jacopo Dolfin portrait.

8 As already suggested by Rearick in Rosenthal, 1981, p.144, note 21, but without supporting arguments.

9 Venice, Archivio di Stato, Testamenti Francesco Bianco, Ba. 126 no.487, and Ba. 128.III. ff. 214v–220.

10 B.G. Dolfin, *I Dolfin. Patrizi veneziani nella storia di Venezia*, Milan, 1924, p.287.

11 G. Pavanello, 'La collezione di Antonio Canova: dipinti e disegni del Quattrocento all'Ottocento', in Pavanello, 2000, pp.327–79, especially pp.331, 334, 338. The portrait may be identified with items in two posthumous inventories of Canova's collection (for which see Pavanello, 2000, pp.353–4): 'Tiziano. Ritratto di un Senator Veneto' (measuring 4.1 by 4.9 Roman palms); and 'Tela da non potersi attribuire che a Tiziano. Ritratto di Personaggio Illustre Veneto, con le mani'.

12 These events are recounted in Ewing's privately printed letters addressed to Mr Mathieson of Glasgow, Letter X (May–June 1845), pp.23–4 ('...Morosini, the conqueror of the Morea, whose portrait by Titian – certified by the Podesta of Venice to have been purchased by Canova out of the original palace – I have been so fortunate as to acquire'). I am grateful to Ewing's descendant Alexander Hamilton for bringing this document to my attention. Further evidence of a Morosini connection is provided by the early nineteenth-century label on the back of the picture, which names the sitter as 'Senator Morosini Barbon': Hope, 1982, p.158.

13 Suida, 1933, p.cxcv.

350

1 Pallucchini, 1969, p.90; W.R. Rearick in Venice, Fondazione Cini, *Venezia da stato a mito*, exh. cat. ed. by A. Bettagno, Venice, 1997, pp.335–6. The portrait is omitted from the recent monograph by Valcanover (1999). Critics who support the attribution to Titian

include Wethey, 1971, pp.25–6, 83–4; and Shapley, 1979, pp.485–8.

2 E. Camesasca (ed.), *Lettere sull'arte di Pietro Aretino*, 3 vols., Milan, 1957–60, I, pp.172–7.

3 A. Olivieri in *Dizioario Biografico degli Italiani*, XVIII, Rome, 1975, pp.827–30.

4 These include versions in the Hermitage, St Petersburg, and in the Seminario Vescovile, Padua, as well as those referred to in the following two notes.

5 For the Chrysler picture, see W. Suida, *Tizian*, Leipzig, 1933, p.164; B. Suida Manning, 'Titian, Veronese and Tintoretto in the collection of Walter P. Chrysler, Jr', *Arte Veneta*, XVI, 1962, pp.49–50.

6 Waagen, 1857, p.454 (as Tintoretto). This picture, later in the Allendale collection, was sold at Christie's, 14 December 1990 (lot 406).

7 Shapley, 1979, pp.487–8.

36

1 Jaffé, 1971; M. Jaffé in London, 1983, pp.224–5.

2 Ibid.

3 For the two branches of the Pesaro family and their rivalry, see R. Goffen, *Piety and Patronage in Renaissance Venice: Bellini, Titian and the Franciscans*, New Haven and London, 1986, pp.132–7.

4 The attribution to Titian was enthusiastically endorsed by Wethey, 1975, p.266, but the picture has been silently omitted from subsequent monographs. The attribution to Dente was made by S. Claut, 'All'ombra di Tiziano. Contributo per Girolamo Denti', *Antichità Viva*, XXV, 5–6, 1986, p.19; idem in Lucco, 1996–9, III, pp.1285–6.

5 J. Woods-Marsden, 'Toward a history of art patronage in the Renaissance: the case of Pietro Aretino', *Journal of Medieval and Renaissance Studies*, XXIV, 1994, pp.275–99.

6 Jaffé, 1971, p.702; Brigstocke, 1982, p.505.

7 Edinburgh, 1883, no.328: 'Titian, Two Princes of the Pesaro family'.

37

1 For Gritti as a patron of art, see Tafuri, 1984; and D. Howard in *The Dictionary of Art*, 1996, XIII, p.678, with references.

2 For the iconography of Gritti, see L. Puppi, 'Iconografia di Andrea Gritti', in Tafuri, 1984, pp.216–35; Weber, 1993, pp.49–67.

3 The document of 18 August 1540 was published in W. Bode, G. Gronau and D. von Hadeln (eds.), *Archivalische Beiträge zur Geschichte der venezianischen Kunst aus dem Nachlass Gustav Ludwigs*, Berlin, 1911, p.134.

4 For the so-called 'succession portraits'

of the doges, see Wolters, 1983, pp.84–6.

5 For these two portraits, see Wethey, 1971, pp.109–10; Zeri 1973, pp.76–7; Weber, 1993, pp.122–5. Zeri records another version, once in the collection of Paolo Giovio in Como, and in 1969 in a private collection in Chiasso.

6 Letter from Irvine in Milan to Forbes in Paris, 14 July 1827; Forbes's record of payment, dated 19 July (both documents in private family papers). See also Jaffé, 1971, p.702, note 37.

7 Sale Rainy, London, 2 June 1842 (lot 25; with the incorrect information that the picture was acquired in Venice).

8 Edinburgh, 1883, cat.no.187.

38

1 G. Lorenzi, *Monumenti per servire alla storia del Palazzo Ducale di Venezia*, Venice, 1868, p.259.

2 For Doge Donà, see Da Mosto, 1966, pp.308–13; for his iconography, see Weber, 1993, pp.127–8.

3 Weber, 1993, p.73.

4 This version, currently on display at Schloss Ambras, Innsbruck, is recorded in the Hamilton inventory of 1638 (no.105) as 'One duke of Venice sitting in a chaire with a curtain behinde his heade of ... [no attribution offered]'; Garas, 1967, p.66. It was later engraved by Lucas Vorsterman the Younger for the *Teatrum Pictorum* of 1660 (no.98), and copied on a small scale by Teniers (formerly at Blenheim Palace; acquired in 1991 by the Prado Museum). See G. Heinz and K. Schütz, *Porträtgalerie zur Geschichte Österreichs von 1400 bis 1800*, Vienna, 1976, p.266; Madrid, Museo del Prado, *David Teniers, Jan Brueghel y los Gabinetes de Pinturas* (exh. cat. by M. Díaz Padrón and M. Royo-Villanova, Madrid, 1992, pp.62, 100–1).

5 Russell, 2003, p.25.

6 Copy of the original MS in the library of the National Gallery, London, p.12, no.49.

7 Waagen, 1838, II, p.373; Waagen, 1854, III, p.483; Richter, 1883, p.4 no.10.

39

1 London, Hayward Gallery, *Andrea Palladio: the Portico and the Farmyard*, exh. cat. by H. Burns *et al.*, London, 1975, pp.171–2, with a proposed date of about 1525.

2 For the Berlin portrait, and for Beccaruzzi in general, see G. Fossaluzza, 'Profilo di Francesco Beccaruzzi', *Arte Veneta*, XXXV, 1981, pp.71–83. The author does not mention the *Hunting Scene*, despite the fact that it was attributed to Beccaruzzi by Berenson (1907, p.87). Berenson's catalogue of Beccaruzzi's works in 1907 was greatly over-inflated, and by the time of the 1957 edition of his *Lists* he had reconsidered most of his earlier

attributions to the artist. By then the *Hunting Scene* was unsatisfactorily described as by 'Paris Bordone or Pordenone' (Berenson, 1957, p.206).

3 'Nell'altra facciata accanto sotto al Cornicione un quadro grande con Caccie e Cani con Figure et altro del N. 337 con cornice dorata del Giorgione': P. Della Pergola, 'L'inventario Borghese del 1693', *Arte Antica e Moderna*, 26, 1964, p.223, no.77. Aidan Weston-Lewis kindly drew my attention to this reference and proposed the connection with the Hopetoun picture.

4 Hopetoun archive, NRA(s) 888, Bundles 616 and 620; references kindly provided by Pat Crichton. See also Skinner, 1968, p.372. For Thompson Martin, see cat.no.43, and Forbes, 1996, p.43.

5 Waagen, 1854, III, p.310.

40

1 M. Muraro, *Il Libro Secondo di Francesco e Jacopo dal Ponte*, Bassano, 1992, p.153: 'Un quadro de la instoria como li tre Magi andò a oferire nel Presepio' (A painting of the story of how the three kings went to offer gifts at the Nativity).

2 Venice, Archivio di Stato, Descendenze Patrizie: Testamenti, Buste 1244, no.397 and 164, no.460.

3 As suggested by A. Weston-Lewis in Clarke, 2000, p.36.

4 See the survey of opinions in Brigstocke, 1993, pp.26–8.

5 For Jacopo's pictorial sources, see G. Ericani in Fort Worth, 1993, pp.272–4; Brigstocke, 1993, pp.26–8.

6 Aikema, 1996, pp.27–9.

7 P. Boccardo and L. Magnani, 'La committenza', in *Il Palazzo dell'Università di Genova*, Genoa, 1987, p.84, note 100, no.24: 'Un'Adorazione de Maggi del Titiano'. It is still recorded in the palace of Francesco Maria Balbi by C.G. Ratti, *Instruzione di quanto può vedersi di più bello in Genova*, 2nd ed., Genoa, 1780, p.186.

8 As suggested by P. Boccardo, 'Le 'rotte mediterranee' del collezionismo genovese', *Bolletino dei musei civici genovesi*, X, 28–30, 1988, pp.100–1. The Admiral's inventory of 1647 includes an item described as 'otro Lienço Grande de una navidad de Mano de basan': see M. Burke and P. Cherry, *Collections of Paintings in Madrid 1601–1755*, Los Angeles, 1997, I, p.424 no.390. Representations of the Nativity – whether Adorations of the Kings or of the Shepherds – were admittedly staple products of the Bassano workshop, but the inventory specifies that it was a large canvas, and a number of other important pictures certainly passed from the collection of the Admiral to that of Balbi.

9 Brigstocke, 1982, p.479.

10 Brown, 2003b, p.94.

11 Waagen, 1857, p.429.

12 Crowe and Cavalcaselle, 1871, II, p.291. See also Crowe and Cavalcaselle, 1877, II, p.468.

41

1 The picture was classed as a copy by Gilbert, 1986, pp.473–4, and it was exhibited as such in the Savoldo exhibition in Brescia and Frankfurt in 1990: see R. Stradiotti in Brescia, 1990, p.109. But its status as an autograph variant was rightly affirmed by D. Carritt, 'Pictures from Gosford House', *Burlington Magazine*, XCIX, 1957, pp.343–4, and more recently by Frangi, 1992, pp.125–6.

2 The early dating, argued by R. Longhi (*Saggi e Ricerche 1925–1928*, Florence, 1967, pp.149–55), by Gilbert (1986, pp.169–70) and implicitly accepted by E. Lucchesi Ragni (in Brescia, 1990, pp.174–8), was supported by Cottrell (2000, p.49), with the observation that a shepherd with his face similarly shaded by a hat in Bonifacio's *Virgin and Child with Saints* in the Prado, Madrid, appears to derive from Savoldo's *Shepherd*. More compelling, however, are the stylistic arguments of Frangi (1992, pp.125–6) in favour of a dating to about 1540 for both versions of the *Shepherd*.

3 Frangi, 1992, p.122.

4 C. Gilbert in Brescia, 1990, p.43.

5 Wemyss, 2003, p.74.

6 The picture is almost certainly identical with one labelled as by Giorgione and described by Waagen as 'Portrait of a Man, with a landscape background'. Waagen thought it closer to one Francesco Domenici, who signed a portrait previously seen by him in the collection of Edward Cheney in London (Waagen, 1857, pp.175, 441).

7 Crowe and Cavalcaselle, 1871, II, p.429. See also C. Parisio, 'Girolamo Savoldo nelle interpretazioni di Giovanni Battista Cavalcaselle e Joseph Archer Crowe nella History of Painting in North Italy', in G. Panazza (ed.), *Giovanni Girolamo Savoldo pittore bresciano. Atti del Convegno*, Brescia, 1984, p.145.

42

1 For a dating of these portraits on grounds of costume to *c.*1536–48, see D. Davanzo Poli, 'Abbigliamento veneto attraverso un'iconografia datata: 1517–1571' in Fossaluzza and Manzato, 1987, pp.250–2.

2 Waagen, 1854, III, p.483. Crowe and Cavalcaselle (1877, II, p.462) attributed it to 'Bernardino Pordenone', that is, Licinio.

43

1 For the iconography of David the musician, see V. Scherliess, 'Davide: pastore, re e cantore celeste', in Cremona, Santa Maria della Pietà and Vienna, Kunsthistorisches Museum, Palais Harrach, *Dipingere la Musica. Strumenti in posa nell'arte del Cinque e Seicento*, exh. cat. ed. by S. Ferino-Pagden, Milan, 2000, pp.49–51.

2 By P.V. Begni Redona, *Alessandro Bonvicino, il Moretto da Brescia*, Brescia, 1988, pp.530–31; P.V. Begni Redona in Brescia, 1988, pp.94–5.

3 The picture's authorship was recognised by Mina Gregori: see F. Frangi in Gregori, 1986, p.179.

4 F. Frangi in Gregori, 1986, p.179 (*c.*1525); P.V. Begni Redona in Brescia, 1988, pp.94–5 (*c.*1530).

5 D'Onofrio, 1964, p.205, no.220 ('Un quadro con David che sona la lira, et hà uno inanzi in ginocchione co le mani giunte, di mano di Giorgione'). The connection between this reference and the Southesk picture was first noticed by Aidan Weston-Lewis.

6 It reappears in the Aldobrandini inventories of 1626, before 1665, and 1682: see respectively Della Pergola, 1960, p.432, no.102; D'Onofrio, 1964, p.205, no.220; Della Pergola, 1963, p.66, no.167. These inventories record the support as canvas, and the height as 2¾ Roman palms (c. 66cm).

7 Buchanan, 1824, II, p.6; Fredericksen, 1988–93, I, p.135. The picture exhibited by Day in 1800 has sometimes been thought to be identical with the Giorgionesque *Homage to a Poet* in the National Gallery, London (acc.no.1173): see Gould, 1975, pp.109–10. But when in the Aldobrandini collection this bore an attribution to Raphael, and the inventories correctly describe the support as panel, whereas Moretto's picture is on canvas.

8 Southesk, 1904.

44

1 Copy of original MS in the library of the National Gallery, London, p.13, no.52.

2 Waagen, 1838, II, p.373; Waagen, 1854, III, p.482. The attribution to Bonifacio was rejected by Richter, 1883, pp.66–7.

3 For the latter painting see Lucco, 1996–9, I, p.107, fig.136.

45

1 Very similar pairs of rabbits reappear, for example, in Bonifacio's *Virgin and Child with Saints* pictures in the Walker Art Gallery, Liverpool, and at the Bob Jones University, Greenville, SC.

2 Westphal, 1931, pp.71–2; Simonetti, 1986, p.114; Cottrell, 2000, p.111.

3 Sold in the Napier sale at Christie's, 11 April 1877: see Simonetti, 1986, pp.98–9.

4 In the Campbell of Succoth collection until 1947: see Simonetti, 1986, p.113.

5 Westphal, 1931, p.151, note 235. For a contrary view, see K. Kuczman in *To the Donor in Homage. A Catalogue of Restored Paintings and Family Momentoes from Karolina Lanckorońska's Donation*, Cracow, 1998, pp.50–52.

6 J. Britton, *Catalogue Raisonné of the Pictures belonging to the most honourable the Marquis of Stafford in the Gallery of Cleveland House*, London, 1808, p.107, no.101; Ottley and Tomkins, 1818, II, no.17; Passavant, 1836, p.130.

7 For this picture, see Buchanan, 1824, II, p.67, no.28; Fredericksen, 1988–93, I, p.533. The buyer's name is not recorded, but it is likely to have been the Marquess of Stafford's uncle, the Duke of Bridgewater (died 1803). The picture did not previously belong to the collection of Citizen Robit, but it was probably acquired by the dealer Bryan in Paris at about the same time as the Robit sale (1801).

8 Waagen, 1838, II, p.51.

9 L. Cust and W.L. Bourke, *The Bridgewater Gallery*, London, 1903, no.15.

46

1 For the iconography of this legend, see M.A. Lavin, 'Giovannino Battista: a study in Renaissance religious symbolism', *Art Bulletin*, XXXVII, 1955, pp.85–101.

2 Canova, 1964, p.81.

3 For a recent survey, see B.L. Brown, 'From hell to paradise: landscape and figure in early sixteenth-century Venice', in Venice, 1999, pp.424–31.

4 See G. Fossaluzza in *Pinacoteca di Brera: Scuola Veneta*, Milan, 1990, pp.87–91; Humfrey, 1990, p.170.

5 Boschini, 1660, pp.367–8 ('Certamente de Paris no se vede / In tuta sta Città cosa più pia, / Come in Casa Venier santa Maria, / Che in Paradiso aponto se crede. / Oh che bel colorito! oh che vaghezza! / Gh'è do legiadri e nobili Bambini, / Che è Cristo e San Zuane. Oh che Putini! / No mostra el vivo mai tal tenerezza. Ghe xe un paese, che par che Natura / Ambissa d'abitar dito sì belo; / Sant'Isepo è lontan col so ASenelo, / Che se pasce de morbida verdura.')

6 Savini Branca, 1965, p.286.

7 Canova, 1964, p.77 (mistakenly recording it as on loan to the National Gallery of Scotland); Martinoni, 1983, p.265 (where the provenance is traced back to the Imperiali and Balbi collections in Genoa); G. Mariani Canova in Treviso, 1984, p.88, cat.no.23. Another version of the Edinburgh composition, claimed as an original, was published by V. Sgarbi, 'Note su Paris Bordon', in Fozzaluzza and Manzato, 1987, p.172. But as observed by A. Weston-Lewis in Memphis, 2001, p.16, this appears to be at best a workshop replica, and it may simply be a copy.

8 Ridolfi, 1914–24, I, p.233 (as in the collection of Leopoldo de' Medici, Florence); Grant, 1828, p.19; Canova, 1964, p.121.

47

1 See the letter of 22 March 1827 from Buchanan to James Skene quoted in the introductory essay. Buchanan states that the 'Titian' was from the Palazzo Borghese in Rome.

2 Waagen, 1857, p.63, called the picture *Venus Reposing*, while Berenson, 1957, p.46, and Canova, 1964, pp.102–3, called the figure a courtesan.

3 Canova, 1964, similarly placed the picture close to works that she dated to around 1540.

4 Graves, 1913–15, I, p.81; Waagen, 1957, p.63. The picture was also exhibited at the Royal Academy in 1886.

48

1 Rylands, 1988, p.89.

2 C. Santore, 'The tools of Venus', *Renaissance Studies*, XI, 1997, pp.191–2.

3 The allegorical aspect of the picture is emphasised by G. Mariani Canova in Treviso, 1984, p.78; Grabski, 1987, p.209; A. Weston-Lewis in Tokyo, 1993, pp.145–6; A. Weston-Lewis in Clarke, 2000, p.38.

4 Canova, 1964, pp.77–8; Canova in Treviso, 1984, p.78; Canova in Fossaluzza and Manzato, 1987, p.146; Brigstocke, 1993, pp.36–7.

5 Canova, 1964, p.75.

6 Ridolfi, 1914–24, II, p.234 ('una femina con seno scoperto che si mira in uno specchio tenutole da una vecchia con una bella giovane a canto').

7 F. Magani, 'Il collezionismo e la committenza artistica della famiglia Widmann, patrizi veneziani, dal Seicento al Ottocento', *Memorie dell'Istituto Veneto di Scienze, Lettere ed Arti*, XLI, 3, 1989, p.34.

8 As kindly pointed out to me by Piero Boccardo, Durazzo bought four pictures from the collection of Cardinal Widmann in 1661. The subjects are not specified, but given the later presence of the *Venetian Women* in Genoa, it seems probable that it was one of the four.

9 Brusco, 1781, p.37.

10 H. Brigstocke in Thompson, 1972, pp.29–32.

11 Waagen, 1854, III, p.269.

49

1 For this picture (110 × 220cm), see P. della Pergola, *Galleria Borghese: I Dipinti*, Rome, 1955, I, p.123; N. Ivanoff, 'Antonio Palma', in *I Pittori Bergamaschi dal XIII al XIX Secolo*, III, Bergamo, 1979, p.391. A related composition in the Muzeul de Arta, Bucharest was attributed to Giulio Licinio by L. Vertova, 'Giulio Licinio'

in *I Pittori Bergamaschi: Il Cinquecento*, II, Bergamo, 1976, p.554, and considered to derive from the Borghese picture. But the attribution is unconvincing, and the Bucharest painting seems in fact to precede both the Borghese and the present pictures.

2 Ridolfi, 1648, 1914–24, I, p.289 ('In casa degli eredi del Serenissimo Doge Erizzo vi è l'historia del Figliuol Prodigo, & il Signor Vicenzo Zeno hà in gran quadro gli avvenimenti del medesimo, e come vien raccolto dal Padre').

3 For the identification of Vincenzo Zen as Vincenzo di Zuane, see Savini Branca, 1965, pp.291–2.

4 Cottrell, 2000, pp.313, 352–64.

5 Berenson, 1907, p.98.

6 Waagen, 1838, III, p.252; Waagen, 1854, III, p.383.

7 Redford, 1888, I, p.154.

8 Wenley, 2003, pp.77–8.

9 Edinburgh, 1883, no.347 (as 'Veneziano Bonifacio').

50

1 For the dating and provenance of Veronese's picture (192 × 297cm), see Pignatti and Pedrocco, 1995, pp.282–3.

2 For a discussion of these pictures and of Bordon's style in the 1550s, see Canova, 1964, pp.52–8; Treviso, 1984, cat.nos.28–33; G. Mariani Canova in Fossaluzza and Manzato, 1987, pp.154–7. Another work close in style and date is the *St Andrew with Daniel and Habakkuk* from the church of Santa Marina in Venice, now in the Ca' Rezzonico (see F. Pedrocco, *The Egidio Martini Collection at Ca' Rezzonico*, Venice, 2001, p.17.

3 Russell, 2003, p.24.

4 Copy of original Luton House MS inventory in the library of the National Gallery, London, p.12, no.44.

5 Waagen, 1838, III, p.373; Waagen, 1854, III, p.483.

6 Richter, 1883, p.3, no.8. The compiler of the catalogue records a curious downgrading of the picture: 'Style of Paris Bordone, and formerly attributed to him'.

51

1 In the original, two-shilling exhibition catalogue the picture was still described as the story of Salome; but in the luxurious *Commemorative Catalogue* by Lord Balniel and K. Clark of 1931 (p.153, cat.no.445) it was changed to that of Tuccia. See also Constable, 1930, p.752.

2 McGrath, 1997, II, p.274.

3 As pointed out in Dunkerton, Foister and Penny, 1999, p.129.

4 Waagen, 1857, p.460, and successive editions of the Glasgow Gallery catalogue.

5 De Vecchi, 1970, p.89; Pallucchini and Rossi, 1982, p.147. Constable (1930, p.752) rejected the attribution to Schiavone, but did not wholeheartedly accept Tintoretto as an alternative.

6 R. Echols, 'Giovanni Galizzi and the problem of the young Tintoretto', *Artibus et Historiae*, XVI, 31, 1995, pp.94–5.

7 R. Echols, 'Tintoretto, *Christ at the Sea of Galilee*, and the unknown later career of Lambert Sustris', *Venezia Cinquecento*, VI, 12, 1996, p.132.

8 McLellan Gallery, 1855, no.104. See also Waagen, 1857, p.460.

9 'Donna Romana che porta aqua alla Crivia (sic)'. See Mary L. Cox, 'Inventory of the pictures in the collection of Alethea, Countess of Arundel, at the time of her death in Amsterdam in 1654', *Burlington Magazine*, XIX, 1911, p.283. The connection with the Glasgow picture was suggested by P. Rossi in Pallucchini and Rossi, 1982, p.149.

52

1 Brigstocke, 1993, p.163.

2 Rossi, 1974, pp.104–5

53

1 Rossi, 1974, p.105, dates the portrait to *c*.1549–50.

2 Brigstocke, 1993, pp.162–3.

54 & 55

1 Crowe and Cavalcaselle, 1877, II, pp.275, 512–13.

2 Crowe and Cavalcaselle, 1877, II, p.278, 515–16.

3 Wethey, 1975, p.139; M. Mancini, *Tiziano e le corti d'Asburgo nei documenti degli archivi spagnoli*, Venice, 1998, p.64.

4 Recent surveys of the series include Hope, 1980, pp.125–37; J. C. Nash, *Veiled Images. Titian's Mythologies for Philip II*, Philadelphia, 1985; Gentili, 1988, pp.162–216; Fehl, 1992, pp.115–29. See also Brigstocke, 1993, pp.178–86.

5 H. Kamen, *Philip of Spain*, New Haven and London, 1997, pp.178–86.

6 Wethey, 1975, pp.139–40.

7 Ibid.

8 F. Haskell, 'Introduction' in London, British Museum, *The Paper Museum of Cassiano dal Pozzo*, exh. cat. ed. by N. Turner *et al.*, Milan, 1993, pp.3–4. I am grateful to Aidan Weston-Lewis for this reference.

9 S. Kennedy North, 'The Bridgewater Titians II', *Burlington Magazine*, LXII, 1933, pp.10–16.

10 S. Kennedy North, *Report on the Conservation of the two pictures 'Diana and Actaeon' and 'Diana and Callisto' by Titian in the Bridgewater House Collection done by S. Kennedy North, December 1932*, in the National Gallery of Scotland Archives.

11 A. Martindale, *The Triumphs of Caesar by Mantegna in the Collection of Her Majesty the Queen at Hampton Court*, London, 1979.

12 *Diana and Actaeon*: 14 threads per cm weft: 11 threads per cm weave. *Diana and Callisto*: 17 threads per cm weft: 17 threads per cm weave.

13 J. Plesters, '*Bacchus and Ariadne*. The materials and technique', *National Gallery Technical Bulletin*, II, 1978, p.37.

56

1 For the dating of the *Midas*, and for a convincing account of Schiavone's stylistic development, see Richardson, 1980, especially pp.163–4, cat.no.263.

2 Richardson, 1980, pp.59–60, 190–1, cat.no.327.

3 Richardson, 1980, p.181, cat.no.306.

4 Graves, 1913–15, III, p.1206. The picture is described in the catalogue of the Mulgrave sale in May 1832 as 'a grand Gallery Picture, in the highest state of preservation'.

5 Waagen, 1857, p.63. Lord Elcho, lent it to the British Institution exhibition in 1855, cat.no.23. The picture is listed by Berenson in 1907 (p.131), but no longer in 1957.

57

1 F. Russell in Washington DC, National Gallery of Art, *Treasure Houses of Britain: Five Hundred Years of Private Patronage and Art Collecting*, exh. cat. ed. by G. Jackson-Stops, New Haven and London, 1985, p.326. Russell's proposed dating to *c*.1560/5 seems slightly too late. The attribution of the picture by Rearick (in Washington, 1988, p.34) to Zelotti is unconvincing.

2 For these two works, see Washington, 1988, p.34; Pignatti and Pedrocco, 1995, pp.45–6; Priever, 2000, pp.18–19. A related composition is in the Hermitage, St Petersburg: see Pignatti and Pedrocco, 1995, pp.53–4, with a dating to the early 1550s.

3 Washington, 1988, p.34; Priever, 2000, pp.18–19. Pignatti and Pedrocco, 1995, p.46, attribute the picture to Veronese, with a date of about 1547.

4 Pignatti and Pedrocco, 1995, pp.110–12.

5 Copy of original Luton House MS inventory in the library of the National Gallery, London, p.10, no.37. The inventory records 'on each side two paintings of Faith and Hope in chiaroscuro' also by Veronese; these pictures remain in the Bute collection.

6 Russell, 2003, pp.24–5.

7 Waagen, 1838, III, p.374.

8 Richter, 1883, p.5, no.14.

58

1 S. Sponza, 'Sul ciclo già a Santa Maria dell'Umiltà', *Quaderni della Sprintendenza dei Beni Artistici e Storici di*

Venezia, XX, 1996, pp.119–26.

2 A. Ballarin, 'Aggiunte al catalogo di Paolo Veronese e di Jacopo Bassano', *Arte Veneta*, XII, 1968, pp.42–3; W.R. Rearick in Venice, Fondazione Cini, *Paolo Veronese: Disegni e dipinti*, exh. cat. ed. by A. Bettagno, Vicenza, 1988, pp.97–8; V. Romani in Fort Worth, 1993, pp.347–8.

3 P. Michel, *Mazarin, Prince des collectioneurs: Les collections e l'ameublement du Cardinal Mazarin (1602–1661)*, Paris, 1999, pp.107, 319, 341, 383, 576. For the engaving by Jacob, see P.J. Mariette, *Receuil d'Estampes d'après plus beaux Tableaux*, Paris, 1729–42, II, p.68, no.XXX (inscribed: 'Du Cabinet de Mr Fagon, Conseiller d'Etat').

4 Graves, 1913–15, IV, p.1575.

59

1 The reconstruction, drawn by Linda Murray, was first published by P. Murray, *Dulwich Picture Gallery: a Catalogue*, London, 1980, pp.134–5, cat.no.270. For the Dulwich fragment see also R. Beresford, *The Dulwich Picture Gallery*, London, 1998, p.251.

2 The provenance of the work was convincingly traced to San Francesco, Lendinara, by D. von Hadeln, *Paolo Veronese*, Florence, 1978, pp.161–2. The MSS of Masatto and Bartoli, both in the Accademia dei Concordi, Rovigo, were published for the first time in Brandolese, 1795. For the church of San Francesco, see Luisetto, 1986, pp.891–915; P. Pizzamano in Bagatin, Pizzamano and Rigobello, 1992, pp.209–15.

3 'Nell'altro Altare in fondo alla chiesa in tavola con il morto Redentore in alto sostenuto dagli Angeli, e sotto S. Michele Arcangelo in atto di calpestare Lucifero in mezzo a varj santi, con alcuni ritratti, ec. è opera grandiosa fatta nel 1565 da Paolo Veronese': see Brandolese, 1795, p.247.

4 ANTONIVS ET HIERONYMVS / DE PETROBELLIS. SIBI. AC. HEREDI / BVS. VIVENTES. SARCOPHAGVM HVNC / POSVERE. ANNO DNI. MDLXIII. Recorded in a MS by Antonio Campagnella, and quoted in Luisetto, 1986, p.915; Bagatin, Pizzamano and Rigobello, 1992, pp.212–13.

5 'L'insigne tavola, che si vedea nel grandioso, e magnifico altare della Nobile Famiglia Pietrobelli, formava l'ammirazione degli intelligenti. Il Signor Bartoli è di fermo parere, che fosse opera di Paolo Veronese, ed aggiunge che fu fatta l'anno 1565, congetturandolo forse dalla data che si legge nel fregio del soprao[r]nato dell'altare.' Brandolese, 1795, p.39.

6 A. Cappellini, *I Petrobelli*, Genoa, 1950 (unpaginated).

7 Biblioteca Comunale di Lendinara, Archivio Petrobelli, A-7-3-5.

8 Ibid.

9 R. Pallucchini, *Veronese*, Milan, 1984, pp.150–1, 184; Pignatti and Pedrocco, 1995, p.402.

10 Scholars who have accepted the date of 1563–5 implied by the sources include W.R. Rearick in Washington, 1988, p.140; Cocke, 2001, p.192.

11 An attempt to attribute the picture to Carletto by L. Crosato Larcher, 'L'Opera completa del Veronese', *Arte Veneta*, XXII, 1968, p.222, was rightly rejected by Pignatti and Pedrocco, 1995, p.402.

12 Callegari, 2000, p.102 ('Così fu venduta a quarti come si fa della carne da macello').

13 Fredericksen, 1993, III / 2, p.1087.

14 Passavant, 1836, p.142; Waagen, 1838, II, p.243; Waagen, 1854, II, p.61.

60

1 The other example is the *Prospero Alessandri* in a private collection: see P. Humfrey in Fort Worth, 2000, pp.63–6.

2 See N. Raponi in *Dizionario Biografico degli Italiani*, II, Rome, 1960, pp.59–60; Gregori, 1979, pp.241–2; M. Gregori in Bergamo, 1979, pp.129–30; Rossi, 1991, p.80.

3 Gregori, 1979, pp.241–2; E. Schleier in *Gemäldegalerie Berlin: 200 Meisterwerke*, Berlin, 1998, p.382; M. Gregori in Fort Worth, 2000, p.21.

4 R. Gironi, *Pinacoteca del Palazzo Reale di Scienze e delle Arti di Milano*, 3 vols., Milan, 1812–33, no.LII; P. Brignoli, *Nuova Guida per la Città di Brescia*, Brescia, 1826, p.209; S. Ticozzi, *Dizionario degli Architetti, Scultori, Pittori*, 4 vols., Milan, 1830–3, III, p.13; F. Lechi, *I Quadri della Collezione Lechi in Brescia*, Florence, 1968, p.183.

5 C.J. Nieuwenhuys, *Description de la Galerie des Tableaux de S. M. le Roi des Pays Bas*, Brussels, 1843, pp.199–200.

6 Letters in private family archive.

7 Rainy, London, 2 June 1842 (lots 5 and 24).

8 The picture was lent by the Earls of Warwick to the exhibitions at the British Institution in 1861 (cat.no.28) and the Royal Academy in 1871 (cat.no.10): Graves, 1913–15, II, p.823; and to the exhibition of *Italian Art* at the Royal Academy in 1930 (cat.no.446).

61

1 Dunkerton, Foister and Penny, 1999, p.142.

2 Waagen, 1854, III, p.302. According to documents now preserved at Hamilton Central Library, the portrait is already recorded in inventories of the Palace dating from 1825 and 1835. I am indebted to Godfrey Evans for this information.

3 K. Madsen *et al.*, *Catalogue of a Collection of Paintings exhibited in the Danish Museum of Fine Art*, Copenhagen, 1920.

4 The succession of owners between *c.*1920 and 1979 was traced by Gregori, 1979, p.279. I am grateful to Eckart Lingenauber for kindly clarifying some details of the provenance.

62

1 Tassi, 1793, I, p.169. Although not published until 1793, Tassi's account was composed in the 1750s.

2 Gregori, 1979, pp.256–8; M. Gregori in Bergamo, 1979, pp.154–7, cat.no.39. Gregori's identification superseded an earlier, tentative suggestion that the sitter was G.C. Zanchi's brother Basilio.

3 G. Ballistreri in *Dizionario Biografico degli Italiani*, XIV, 1972, pp.195–6; Gregori, 1979, pp.256–8; Gregori in Bergamo, 1979, pp.154–7; F. Rossi in Bergamo, 1979, pp.326–7; Rossi, 1991, p.84.

4 Respectively in the Count Moroni collection, Bergamo, and the National Gallery, London, and datable to *c.*1552 and *c.*1557–60. See Gregori, 1979, pp.237–8, 274–5.

5 For Arsensio's medal, see G. Toderi and F. Vannel, *Le Medaglie Italiane del XVI Secolo*, I, Florence, 2000, p.217 no.587; P. Attwood, *Italian Medals c.1530–1600 in British Public Collections*, 2 vols., London, 2003, I, p.228.

6 This picture belonged to the Dukes of Sutherland for most of the nineteenth century, but it hung in their London residence of Stafford House, and was never brought to Scotland.

7 D. Thornton, *The Scholar in his Study. Ownership and Experience in Renaissance Italy*, New Haven and London, 1997, p.156.

8 See also London, National Gallery, *Giovanni Battista Moroni. 400th Anniversary Exhibition*, exh. cat. by A. Braham, London, 1978, p.35; Brigstocke, 1993, p.105.

9 According to the MS annotations to Tassi, 1793, by Antonio Piccinelli (writing *c.*1863–5). See R. Bassi Rathgeb, 'Le postille di Antonio Piccinelli alle *Vite* di Francesco Maria Tassi', *L'Arte*, LVIII, 1959, p.127.

10 See Brigstocke, 1993, p.104.

63

1 Arslan (1960, p.328) rejected the attribution to any member of the Bassano family, and suggested instead that the portrait might be Lombard.

2 The style of the transparent partlet, rising to a high collar above a square neckline, is similar to that in the Titianesque *Portrait of Irene di Spilimbergo* (Washington DC, National Gallery of Art) of about 1560, but the tucks in the ruff suggest a slightly later date, around 1570. For a survey of

female costume in the Veneto in this period, see J. Bridgeman, 'Dress in Moroni's portraits' in Fort Worth, 2000, pp.44–52.

3 Compare, for example, the family portrait by Fasolo of 1558 in the Fine Art Museums of San Francisco, or his Gualdo family portraits in the Museo Civico, Vicenza.

4 For this painter, see L. Attardi, 'Un contributo alla ritrattistica di Francesco Apollodoro di Porcia', *Bolletino dei Musei Civici di Padova*, LXXVII, 1989, pp.37–42.

64

1 This translation is taken from Panofsky, 1957, pp.146–68.

2 This paraphrase is taken from Gould, 1975, pp.290–2.

3 M. Kahr, 'Titian, the *Hypnerotomachia* woodcuts and antiquity', *Gazette des Beaux-Arts*, LXVII, 1966, pp.119–27.

4 The emblem was later adopted by Cesare Ripa for the image of 'Good Counsel' in his *Iconologia* of 1593: see L. Freund, '"Good Counsel": an adaptation from Ripa', *Journal of the Warburg and Courtauld Institutes*, II, 1938–9, pp.81–2. It appears in the form of a three-dimensional statuette in a painting by the seventeenth-century Venetian painter Marco Liberi representing an *Allegory of Wise Counsel* (Dresden, Gemäldegalerie).

5 N. Penny in London, 2003, p.160. Although Bruno's dialogue was composed after Titian's death, his explanation of the three animals is likely to have followed an existing line of interpretation.

6 N. Penny in London, 2003, p.160.

7 Panofsky, 1957, pp.146–68.

8 As kindly pointed out to me by Charles Hope, Orazio is almost certainly the figure shown kneeling in profile behind his father in the *Madonna of the Misericordia* (Florence, Palazzo Pitti, Galleria Palatina), commissioned from Titian by the Duke or Urbino in 1573. For the alternative view that the two younger men in the *Allegory of Prudence* may be friends of Titian rather than relatives, see J. Fletcher in *Burlington Magazine*, CXXXII, 1990, p.742.

9 N. Penny in London, 2003, p.160.

10 J. Cranstoun, *The Poetics of Portraiture in the Italian Renaissance*, Cambridge, 2000, pp.119–24.

11 As first suggested by D. von Hadeln, 'Some little-known works by Titian', *Burlington Magazine*, XLV, 1924, pp.179–80. See also A. Dülberg, *Privatporträts. Geschichte und Ikonologie einer Gattung im 15. und 16. Jahrhundert*, Berlin, 1990, pp.45–58.

12 *Catalogue Raisonné des Tableaux, Sculptures … qui composent le Cabinet du feu Monsieur le Duc de Tallard*, Paris, 1756, pp.48–9, no.84. For a full account

of the provenance, see Gould, 1975, pp.290–2.

13 Graves, 1913–15, III, p.1317.

14 Buchanan, 1824, II, pp.277–8; Edinburgh, 1883, no.335.

65

1 Aidan Weston-Lewis undertook the research on the provenance of this picture, and was kindly assisted by Christopher Lloyd, Lucy Whitaker, and Francis Russell.

2 Currently with Richard Feigen, New York. Published as an autograph Titian by A. Morassi, 'Una Salomè di Tiziano riscoperta', *Pantheon*, XXVI, 1968, pp.456–66. The author proposes to identify this version of the compostition with one formerly in the collections of Bartolomeo della Nave, the 1st Duke of Hamilton, Archduke Leopold Wilhelm in Brussels, and the Austrian imperial collections; he was certainly incorrect, however, to claim that it once belonged to Charles I.

3 See M. Falomir in Madrid, 2003, pp.208, 378. The X-radiograph is p.106, fig.77.

4 It may be questioned, however, how far the big-boned, almost Rubensian fleshiness of the figure revealed by the X-radiograph is consistent with Titian's work of the 1540s. An alternative interpretation of the evidence is that the Prado *Empress Isabella* might not, after all, be one of the two posthumous portraits of her that Titian is known to have painted for her husband Charles V in the 1540s, but is perhaps a studio replica, painted for her son Philip II in the 1560s. At the very least, the reuse of an existing canvas suggests that the Prado picture was painted in Titian's studio in Venice, and not, as is usually thought, in Augsburg in 1548.

5 In the inventory of Charles II, the dimensions of the picture are recorded as 2 feet 11 inches by 2 feet 9 inches (89 × 83.5cm).

6 O. Millar, 'The Inventories and Valuations of the King's Goods 1649–1651', *The Walpole Society*, XLIII, 1972, p.190, no.78. This is very likely also to be the picture recorded in a French list of pictures for sale at Somerset House in May 1650: 'Hérodes avec la teste de saint Jean, par Tissian': see G.-J. Cosnac, *Les Richesses du Palais Mazarin*, Paris, 1885, p.416. In the past, this latter item has been identified instead with another *Salome* composition by Titian in the Prado, which was acquired around this time by the Marqués de Leganés and entered the Spanish royal collection in 1655. As kindly confirmed by Miguel Falomir, however, the Prado picture is almost certainly identical with one already recorded in Spain in 1607 in the collection of the Duke of Lerma (for which see S. Schroth, *The Private Picture Collection of the Duke of*

Lerma, PhD dissertation, New York, Institute of Fine Arts, 1990, p.83), and was probably acquired by Leganés from Lerma's heirs after 1637.

7 British Library, Add. MSS 17916, no.55. No attribution is given, however, and the present work may alternatively be identifiable with no.37: 'A herodias wth ye: St John Bapt: Head in a platter being an Italian peace'.

8 The various manuscript inventories of the Royal Collection from 1660/1 to 1736 are listed by O. Millar, *Pictures in the Royal Collection: Tudor, Stuart and Early Georgian Pictures*, London, 1963, pp.37–9. The present painting appears as follows: Inventory of Charles II's pictures etc at Whitehall and Hampton Court, c.1666–7 (p.43: '470 Herodias with St John Baptists head, 2'11" × 2'9", listed as in store at Whitehall); Inventory of James II's pictures at Whitehall, Windsor, Hampton Court, and in the custody of the Queen Dowager, Catherine of Braganza, at Somerset House, 1688 (At Whitehall: '358 By Titian. Herodias with St John Baptist's head in a charger'); Inventory of William III's pictures etc at Kensington, 1697 and 1700 (In the Gallery: 'Titian. Herodias with St John Baptist's head'); Inventory of Queen Anne's Pictures at Kensington, Hampton Court, Windsor, St. James's and Somerset House, c.1705–10 (In the Queen's Gallery at Kensington: '97. Titian, Herodias wth St John Baptist's head in a Charger'); Inventory of pictures at Kensington, 1732 and 1736 (p.2, 'In the Great Drawing Room': 'Ditto [Titian]: Judith with Holoferness's head over the Door').

66

1 Vasari, 1568, ed. 1966–87, V, p.471; Sansovino, 1581, p.48.

2 C. Ridolfi, *The Life of Tintoretto* (1642), translated by C. and R. Enggass, University Park, 1984, pp.44–5. The same information is reported by Martinioni in Sansovino, 1581, p.52.

3 Boschini, 1664, p.199. Boschini names the painter of the altarpiece of St Pascal as the Dominican friar Giovanni Laudis (1583–1631), and from this it has been deduced that Tintoretto's painting must have been stolen and the new altarpiece installed before 1631. But if Laudis's picture (now lost or unrecognised) co-existed with Tintoretto's fragmentary lunette in 1642, it is unlikely to have been painted specifically for the altar, and it may simply have been an existing, iconographically appropriate image pressed into service as an altarpiece. In that case, Tintoretto's painting could have been removed at any date between 1603 (when it was engraved by Kilian) and 1642 (when Ridolfi reported it missing).

4 For San Francesco and its chapels see

Howard, 1975, pp.64–74; A. Foscari and M. Tafuri, *L'armonia e i conflitti. La chiesa di San Francesco della Vigna nella Venezia del '500*, Turin, 1983, especially pp.83ff; D. Howard in Macandrew, 1985, pp.505–11; P. Humfrey, 'Co-ordinated altarpieces in Renaissance Venice: the progress of an ideal', in P. Humfrey and M. Kemp (eds.), *The Altarpiece in the Renaissance*, Cambridge, 1990, pp.196–9.

5 M.E. Massini, 'Jacopo Tintoretto e i confratelli della Scuola Grande di San Rocco', *Venezia Cinquecento*, V, 9, 1995, p.114.

6 See F. Corner, *Ecclesiae Venetae et Torcellanae*, Venice, 1749, VII, pp.75–6.

7 See H. Hamburgh, 'The problem of *lo spasimo* of the Virgin in Cinquecento paintings of the *Descent from the Cross*', *Sixteenth Century Journal*, XII, 4, 1981, pp.45–75.

8 The photomontage, prepared by Joe Rock, was first published in Macandrew, 1985, fig.3.

9 H. Tietze, *Tintoretto: Paintings and Drawings*, London, 1948, p.353; De Vecchi, 1970, p.107; Pallucchini and Rossi, 1982, pp.191–2.

10 Macandrew, 1985, pp.505, 508, 516.

11 H. Tietze, *Tintoretto: Paintings and Drawings*, London, 1948, p.352; De Vecchi, 1970, p.110; Pallucchini and Rossi, 1982, pp.187–8.

12 This argument is convincingly made by Nichols, 1999, pp.126–7.

13 A. Vannugli, 'Collezionismo spagnolo nello Stato di Milano: la quadreria del marchese di Caracena', *Arte Lombarda*, 1996, 2, pp.20–1. The picture is described in the inventory of the marquess's pictures of 1668 as follows: 'Otra del Yntierro de Cristo Señor Nuesto de mano de Iacome Tintoretto con su moldura tallada y dorada tasada y tres mil reales' (p.33, no.82).

67

1 Venice, Palazzo Ducale, *Jacopo Bassano*, exh. cat. by P. Zampetti, Venice, 1957, p.230.

2 Brigstocke, 1993, pp.28–9; A. Weston-Lewis in Athens, 1995, pp.248–51, cat.no.32 (English translation p.483).

3 Rossi, 1974, pp.109, 107.

4 These two comparisons were made by A. Weston-Lewis in Athens, 1995, p.483.

5 Rossi, 1974, p.146. This handsome portrait, previously in the Orléans collection and at Bridgewater House, was sold from the Sutherland collection at Christie's, 2 July 1976 (lot 90).

6 H. Brigstocke in Thompson, 1972, pp.29–32.

7 Brusco, 1781, p.37; see Brigstocke, 1993, pp.28–9. The latter is duly cautious in making this identification, but it is supported by the fact that Paris

Bordon's *Venetian Women at their Toilet* (cat.no.48), which was also inherited by the Marchesa Pallavicini, is recorded by Brusco on the same page in the same Palazzo Grimaldi.

68

1 S.M. Newton, *The Dress of the Venetians, 1495–1525*, Aldershot, 1988, p.12.

2 Rossi, 1974, pp.131–2, suggests a date of c.1572; Shapley, 1979, pp.467–8, suggests c.1575–85.

3 Graves, 1913–15, III, p.1314.

69

1 British Museum inv.no.1951-11-10-79. The relationship with the Edinburgh picture is discussed by Cocke, 1984, pp.250–1; Rearick in Washington, 1988, pp.136–7.

2 Brigstocke, 1993, p.196 and fig.62.

3 As emphasised by A. Weston-Lewis in Tokyo, 1993, p.146, and in Memphis, 2001, p.18; in contrast to Rearick in Washington, 1988, p.137, who attributes the picture in its entirety to Veronese's son Carletto Caliari, and Priever, 2000, p.131, who calls it a workshop piece produced under the master's supervision.

4 In the Städel, Frankfurt; Residenz, Munich; Musée Condé, Chantilly. Rearick in Washington, 1988, p.137, attributes the last to Gabriele Caliari.

5 R. Pallucchini, *Veronese*, Milan, 1984, p.130; Pignatti and Pedrocco, 1995, pp.381–2.

6 S.W. Schroth, 'Charles I, the duque de Lerma and Veronese's Edinburgh *Mars and Venus*', *Burlington Magazine*, CXXXIX, 1997, pp.548–50. See also Madrid, Museo Nacional del Prado, *La Almoneda del Siglo: Relaciones Artísticas entre España y Gran Bretaña 1604–1655* exh. cat. (eds.) J. Brown and J. Elliott, Madrid, 2000, cat.no.23.

7 For Lerma's taste and patronage, see J. Brown, *The Golden Age of Painting in Spain*, New Haven and London, 1991, pp.89–90.

8 'Marte, Vener con un Amorino a piedi e un cagnolo, il Marte armato, Venere nuda, con drappo attorno lavorato con fogliami e paese, di mano di Paolo Veronese': see Brigstocke, 1993, p.197; Pignatti and Pedrocco, 1995, p.381.

9 R. Dodsley, *London and its Environs*, London, 1761, I, p.274. See Brigstocke, 1993, p.197.

70

1 The various representations of the Baptism painted by Veronese during the course of his career are surveyed by Goldner, 1981.

2 As stressed by Rearick in Washington, 1988, pp.151–2.

3 For a survey of opinions, see Pignatti and Pedrocco, 1995, pp.398–9.

4 Goldner, 1981, pp.111, 121.

5 Waagen, 1857, p.451. See also J.M. Gray, *Notes on the Art Treasures at Keir, Perthshire*, privately printed, 1887, p.17.

6 See Ridolfi, 1648, p.320; Campori, 1870, p.186; Goldner, 1981, pp.114–15.

7 Campori, 1870, pp.175–8.

8 Goldner, 1981, pp.114–15, pointed out that the Hibbert sale of 1829 included two *Baptisms* by Veronese (lots 39 and 49), and convincingly connected the present picture with the former. The writer was mistaken, however, in supposing that it subsequently belonged to the painter Andrew Geddes. For Charles Stirling as a collector, see the catalogue of the Stirling of Keir sale, Sotheby's, 3 July 1963, and here in the appendix of principal collectors and dealers.

7 1

1 B.L. Brown, 'Paolo Veronese's *The Martyrdom and Last Communion of Saint Lucy*', *Venezia Arti*, 1988, pp.61–8; Washington, 1988, pp.188–9; Cocke, 2001, p.109.

2 See the survey of opinions in Pignatti and Pedrocco, 1995, pp.489–91.

3 P. Humfrey, 'The provenance of Veronese's *Martyrdom of St Lucy* in Washington', *Arte Veneta*, XLIII, 1989–90, pp.89–90. It was recorded in the church by Ridolfi (1648, p.317), by a pastoral visitation of 1723, and by the local Bellunese historian Doglioni in 1780.

4 Letters of 10 July and 24 October 1827 from Irvine to Forbes (private family papers).

5 Brigstocke, 1982, pp.29–30.

6 Brigstocke, 1982, pp.29–30.

7 2

1 For these two works, see V. Romani in Fort Worth, 1993, pp.354–6; and Aikema, 1996, pp.87–8, 93–4, with further references.

2 Nodari, 1994, pp.55–6, fig.35b.

3 Nodari, 1994, p.55, fig.35a.

4 Arslan, 1960, p.287, attributed the picture to Gerolamo Bassano, presumably on the basis of a photograph.

5 Aikema, 1996, pp.87–8.

6 Information from the present owner.

7 30

1 For a convenient and authoritative account of the *Four Elements* cycles, see Rearick in Fort Worth, 1993, pp.432–6. A workshop version of the *Four Seasons* cycle formed part of the McLellan bequest to Glasgow Art Gallery, but these pictures are in too poor a condition to be included in the present exhibition.

2 As argued by Aikema, 1996, pp.138–40.

3 See A. and R. Cohen, *Trafalgar Galleries XII*, dealer catalogue, London, 1994,

pp.8–13, where it is argued that the picture, subsequently acquired by the Minneapolis Institute of Arts, is datable to about 1576–7, somewhat earlier than the Sarasota version of about 1585.

7 4

1 See Arslan, 1960, I, p.203; Belluno, Museo Civico, *Capolavori della pittura veneta dal Castello di Praga*, exh. cat. by E. Fucíková, Milan, 1994, p.70; Nodari, 1994, p.67. Francesco's composition is based in turn on that of the *Circumcision* of 1577 (Bassano, Museo Civico), which he executed in collaboration with his father Jacopo.

2 Arslan, 1960, I, p.222 (not illustrated); Paris, Musée du Louvre, *Bassano et ses fils dans les musées français*, exh. cat. by J. Habert and C. Loisel Legrand, 1998, p.106 (not exhibited or illustrated).

3 As suggested by H. Brigstocke in Edinburgh, 2000, p.110.

4 For example, by Berenson, 1957, p.21. However, Arslan, 1960, p.328, called it 'close to Gerolamo' Bassano.

5 See, for example, a *Presentation of the Virgin* (Sotheby's, London, 21 April 1993, lot 34); a *Queen of Sheba before Solomon* (Sotheby's, London, 12 December 2002, lot 114); and a *Flagellation of Christ* (Dorotheum, Vienna, 27 March 2003, lot 45).

7 5

1 R. Pallucchini, *La pittura veneziana del Seicento*, Milan, 1981, p.28. Arslan (1960, p.257) dated the picture to around 1590, but a slightly later date need not be excluded. The attribution to Leandro is uncontested.

2 See further Edinburgh, 2000, p.112.

7 6

1 For Torriani's biography, see D.A. Mortier, *Histoire des Maîtres Généraux de l'Ordre des Frères Prêcheurs*, 8 vols., 1903–20, V, pp.1–65; L. Gargan, *Lo Studio teologico e la Biblioteca dei Domenicani a Padova nel Tre e Quattrocento*, Padua, 1971, pp.104–6. I am grateful to Father Michael Tavuzzi O.P. for the reference to the latter work, and for his help with the present entry in general.

2 See G.F. Hill, *A Corpus of Italian Medals of the Renaissance*, 2 vols., London, 1930, I, p.280; II, no.108, attributed to the circle of Niccolò Fiorentino.

3 F. Zava Bocazzi, *La Basilica dei Santi Giovanni e Paolo in Venezia*, Venice, 1965, pp.246, 287, 315–16.

4 Boschini, 1674, Sestier di Castello, pp.65–6; Moschini Marconi, 1962, p.18.

7 7

1 The attribution was rejected by Arslan, 1960, p.344.

2 See B.W. Meijer, 'Paolo Fiammingo

reconsidered', *Mededelingen van het Nederlands Instituut te Rome*, NS, 11, 1975, pp.129–30, note 67); Mason Rinaldi, 1978, pp.54, 60. The latter plausibly dates the picture to around 1590.

3 As pointed out to me by Mauro Lucco.

7 8

1 See Pignatti and Pedrocco, 1995, pp.525–6, with an attribution to Benedetto Caliari. The picture is clearly visible on the left in one of Teniers's views of the gallery of the Archduke Leopold Wilhelm (fig.57).

2 For these works, see Vicenza, 1980, pp.110–17.

3 My thanks to Giovanni C.F. Villa for kindly undertaking a search of the collection of heraldic manuscripts in the Biblioteca Bertoliana in Vicenza for me.

4 For this acquisition, see Evans, 2003, p.58.

5 For Sasso and Della Lena, see F. Haskell, *Patrons and Painters*, London, 1971, pp.373–5.

7 9

1 Information kindly provided by the Countess of Wemyss.

2 Waagen, 1854, II, p.83.

3 Rossi, 1974, pp.109–10, 117–19.

4 Berenson, 1907, p.28.

5 As kindly suggested to me by Roberto Contini. For Bassetti, see U. Ruggeri in *The Dictionary of Art*, London, 1996, III, pp.353–4, with further references.

6 As kindly suggested by Sergio Marinelli, who proposed a date of about 1600–5 and a comparison with a *Portrait of a Prelate*, also on slate, which he has tentatively attributed to Ridolfi: see Milan, Palazzo Reale, *Pietra dipinta: Tesori nascosti del '500 e del '600 da una collezione privata milanese*, exh. cat. ed. by M. Bona Castellotti, Milan, 2000, pp.28, 30.

8 0

1 Ridolfi, 1914–24, II, p.168.

2 117 × 98cm. See Moschini Marconi, 1962, p.20.

3 Hopetoun archive, NRA(s) 888, Bundle 620. Reference kindly provided by Pat Crichton.

4 Waagen, 1854, III, p.309. Berenson, 1907, p.85, attributed the picture to Jacopo Bassano.

8 1

1 Da Mosto, 1966, pp.407–13.

2 Mason Rinaldi, 1984, p.143.

3 For this picture, see R. Simon in New York, Piero Corsini Inc., *Important Old Master Paintings*, dealer catalogue, 1988, pp.21–6. Another version is in the Kunsthistorisches Museum, Vienna.

4 See Arslan, 1960, p.266 (as Leandro Bassano); W.R. Rearick in Padua, Palazzo della Ragione, *Dopo Mantegna: Arte a Padova e nel Territorio nei Secoli XV e XVI*, exh. cat., Milan, 1976, p.112; W.R. Rearick in Rosenthal, 1981, pp.131–47; L. Attardi in A. Ballarin and D. Banzato (eds.), *Da Bellini a Tintoretto: Dipinti dei Musei Civici di Padova dalla metà del Quattrocento ai primi del Seicento*, Rome, 1991, p.220. Rearick retained the traditional attribution to Leandro, but Attardi more accurately attributed it to an anonymous Venetian painter, close to Palma Giovane. This version was once in the Palazzo del Podestà in Padua, where Memmo had been provincial governor.

5 C.M. Kauffmann, *Catalogue of Paintings in the Wellington Museum*, London, 1982, pp.29–30.

6 J. Sander and B. Brinkmann, *Italian, French and Spanish Paintings before 1800 at the Städel*, Frankfurt, 1997, p.21 (as a copy after Leandro). W. Suida, 'Studien zu Bassano', *Belvedere*, XII, 1934–7, p.198, mentions but does not illustrate another version, then in the Lazzaroni collection in Rome, which he claims to be of the highest quality and by Palma.

7 See respectively Campori, 1870, p.340, and Dubois de Saint Gelais, 1727, p.210. The picture is described in Queen Christina's posthumous inventory of 1689 as follows: 'Un quadro ritratto di un Doge Venetiano con veste dogale con cappa d'armellino e sotto veste di broccato bianco col suo corno in testa a sedere, quale è poco più di mezza figura al naturale, del *Palma Vecchio*, di tela in piedi, alta p^mi quattro e un terzo e larga p^mi tre e tre quarti con cornice dorata liscia alla romana.' The picture is listed in Bryan's sale catalogue of the Orléans collection, 88 Pall Mall, 1798, p.8, no.24, as 'Giacomo Palma. Portrait of a Doge of Venice'.

8 Ottley and Tomkins, 1818, pp.42–3; Buchanan, 1824, I, p.137; Passavant, 1836, I, p.129; Waagen, 1838, II, p.51.

DRAWINGS
Introduction

1 Vasari, 1906, VII, pp.427–8. This translation adapted from that of G. Bull in Vasari, 1965, pp.443–4.

2 Vasari, 1906, VII, p.447; translation taken from Vasari, 1965, p.455.

3 F. Ames-Lewis, *Drawing in Early Renaissance Italy*, New Haven and London, 1981, p.vi.

4 'Quasi che non si possano porre in più modi diferenti su la tavola, e da quella cassarle e rifarle, come su la carta, ma mi manca il loco di provar la coglioneria di questo goffo del Vasari': see G. Perini (ed.), *Gli scritti dei*

Carracci, Bologna, 1990, p.161.

5 Humfrey, 1997, pp.89, 181.

6 For the latter see London, 1996.

82

The present entry is a reprint, with minor changes, of the one that appeared in the exhibition catalogue Edinburgh, 1999, cat.no.2.

1 Previously incorrectly identified as in the hand of Francesco Maria Nicolò Gabburri (1676-1742), Nicholas Turner has pointed out that this inscription is in the same hand (which has been erroneously identified as that of Carlo Ridolfi) as those on a large group of old master drawings in Lisbon (see the numerous illustrations in Lisbon, Museu Nacional de Arte Antiga, *Dessin: La collection du MNAA*, exh. cat. by J.L. Porfírio and A. Reis Gomes, Lisbon, 1994).

2 For the drawing and the inscription, see Rowlands, 1966; Rylands, 1992, pp.120-2, 251-2, cat.no.D4.

3 For the Serina polyptychs, see Rylands, 1992, pp.162-3, cat.no.19; and pp.194-6, cat.no.52.

4 In favour of identifying it as a *Self-portrait* were Rowlands, 1966, pp.373-4 (with reservations); Andrews (Edinburgh, Merchant's Hall, *Sixteenth Century Italian Drawings from British Private Collections*, exh. cat. by K. Andrews, Edinburgh, 1969, cat.no.50) and Stock (in Venice, Fondazione Giorgio Cini, *Disegni veneti di collezioni inglesi*, exh. cat. by J. Stock, Vicenza, 1980, cat.no.11); against were G. Mariacher, *Palma il Vecchio*, Milan, 1968, pp.116-17, and Rylands, 1992, pp.251-2.

5 For these paintings see Rylands, 1992, p.167, cat.no.24 and pp.223-4, cat.no.81.

6 See F. Rossi's entry in *Pinacoteca di Brera: Scuola Veneta*, Milan, 1990, pp.444-5. The suggestion that the woodcut portrait of Palma Vecchio in the 1568 edition of Vasari's *Lives* was based on this head seems untenable.

7 I am grateful to Mariolina Olivari for supplying the photograph reproduced here and for confirming that she in no doubt that the painted and drawn heads represent one and the same person.

8 Rylands, 1992, pp.173-5, cat.no.32.

9 See, most recently, Rylands, 1992, p.251; Paris, 1993, cat.no.119.

10 For the Rovigo painting, see Rylands, 1992, p.150. Rylands pointed our that the Louvre study corresponds most closely to the head of the adulteress in the *Christ and the Adulteress* in St Petersburg (p.197, cat.no.54, where it is dated to 1520-2).

83

1 See B Berenson, *Lorenzo Lotto*, 4th revised ed., London, 1956, p.107,

pl.300b; P. Pouncey, *Lotto disegnatore*, Vicenza, 1965, p.14, fig.13; Andrews, 1968, I, p.68, Washington, 1990 (2), pp.28-9, cat.no.4.

2 London, 1983, p.180, cat.no.52; Humfrey, 1997, pp.124-6.

3 J. Bonnet, *Lorenzo Lotto*, Paris, 1996, pp.156-7.

4 For the Vienna portrait see Humfrey, 1997, pp.110-11; Washington, 1997, cat.no.33.

5 For a summary of what we know of Lotto's friendship with the brothers Carpan, see Humfrey, 1997, pp.110, 153, 179-81.

84

I am grateful to Arnold Nesselrath, Charlotte Schreiter, Elizabeth McGrath, Graeme Gollan and Lesley Stevenson for their help in the preparation of this entry.

1 A. Nesselrath, 'Lorenzo Lotto in the Stanza della Segnatura', *Burlington Magazine*, CLXII, 2000, pp.4-12.

2 The evidence for Lotto's involvement in the Stanza d'Eliodoro was presented by Arnold Nesselrath in a paper entitled 'From Peruzzi to Lotto in Raphael's Stanze' delivered at a Raphael symposium at the National Gallery, London, on 9 November 2002. His findings will be published more fully in a forthcoming article in the November 2004 issue of the *Burlington Magazine*.

3 Conservation of the drawing was undertaken by Graeme Gollan. The infrared images were captured by Lesley Stevenson.

4 See J.J. Norwich, *A History of Venice*, New York, 1982, pl.34. Timothy Clifford kindly pointed out this comparison.

5 See G.A. Mansuelli, *Galleria degli Uffizi: Le Sculture*, 2 vols., Rome, 1958-61, I, pp.217-18, cat.no.226, figs.224 a-c. I am indebted to Charlotte Schreiter of the Census of Antique Sculpture known in the Renaissance for providing the reference to this and other similar funerary altars, and for suggesting the identification of the portrait as the Emperor Domitian.

6 See A. Nesselrath, 'Il Cortile delle Statue: luogo e storia' in M. Winner, B. Andreae and C. Pietrangeli (eds.), *Il Cortile delle Statue: Der Statuenhof des Belvedere im Vatikan (Akten des internationalen Kongresses zu Ehren von Richard Krautheimer, Rom, 21-3 Oktober 1992)*, Mainz, 1998, pp.7-8, fig.9.

85

1 The sheet was catalogued by Keith Andrews (1968, I, p.150) as sixteenth-century North Italian, but he noted that it might be by a follower of Romanino. The attribution to Romanino himself was advanced by Alessandro Nova in 1986 (note on the mount).

2 For Romanino as a draughtsman, see Nova, 1995. His fig.35, p.166, perhaps offers the best comparison for the careful parallel hatching on the recto of the Edinburgh drawing.

3 Letter from Alessandro Nova dated 3 August 1986 in the Gallery files; Nova, 1994, p.222, under cat.no.10.

4 Nova, 1994, p.222.

86

1 Marcello Aldega and Margot Gordon, *Old Master Drawings*, dealer catalogue, New York, 1992, cat.no.3. The present owner of the drawing has suggested an alternative attribution to Pordenone.

2 For Romanino's drawings, see Brescia, Duomo Vecchio, *Mostra di Girolamo Romanino*, exh. cat. ed. by G. Panazza, Brescia, 1965, cat.nos.110-33; and Nova, 1995

3 Romanino's thematically related *Lamentation over the Body of Christ* formerly in Berlin, for example, was painted for the Sacrament Chapel in the Brescian church of Santi Faustino and Giovita (see Nova, 1994, pp.226-7, pl.116).

87

1 Cohen, 1980, pp.16-24; 70-1, fig.104. The drawing was first published by K. Andrews in Edinburgh, 1976, cat.no.63.

2 That Pordenone may actually have painted a composition like this is supported by the observation that it seems to have influenced Domenico Brusasorci's fresco of the same subject painted in 1551 for the façade of the Casa Voltollina in Trento, and now removed to the city's Municipio (for Brusasorci's composition, see Stefani Mantovanelli, 1979, pp.37-9, fig.9; Stefani Mantovanelli, 2000, p.108, fig.4). Alternatively, both compositions may share a common source, perhaps in a print.

3 Cohen, 1980, pp.77-8, fig.118.

4 Cohen, 1980, pp.61-2, 117-18, figs.105-7.

88

1 See E. Sharp *et al.*, *The Collections of the Detroit Institute of Arts: Italian, French, English and Spanish Drawings and Watercolors, Sixteenth through Eighteenth Centuries*, New York, 1992, pp.38-9, cat.no.6 (entry by G. Smith). The connection with the Edinburgh sheet was noted by Andrews (1968, I, p.27) but was inexplicably denied by Oberhuber (in Venice, 1976, pp.132-3, cat.no.78), followed by Macandrew (in Washington, 1990 (2), p.38, cat.no.9).

2 Sale, Christie's, New York, 28 January 2000 (lot 2). Pen and ink, 35.9 × 48.5cm.

3 Andrews, 1968, I, p.27; G. Smith concurred with this later dating.

4 K. Oberhuber (in Venice, 1976,

pp.132-3, cat.no.78) was the first to argue for an earlier dating.

5 Washington, 1976, pp.158-65, cat.nos.26-9.

6 Washington, 1976, pp.138-9; A. Santagiustina Poniz, 'Notizie su alcuni disegni di Domenico Campagnola della Collezione Mantova Banavides', *Arte Veneta*, XXXIV, 1980, pp.47-50.

89

1 Andrews, 1968, I, p.83.

2 Luca Baroni was the first to reassert this attribution (note in Gallery files dated 1988).

3 Popham and Wilde, 1949, pp.202-3, cat. nos 161-82; E. Saccomani, 'Padova: 1540-1570', in Lucco, 1996-9, II, pp.592, 597, fig.668.

4 See, for example, Florence, 1976, pp.118-20, cat. nos 76-8; Saccomani, 1980, pp.72-4.

5 Saccomani, 1980, pp.71-2, fig.12; Jaffé, 1994, p.72, cat.no.777.

90

1 Andrews, 1968, I, p.147 (not illustrated).

2 For Bordon as a draughtsman, see W.R. Rearick, 'The Drawings of Paris Bordon' in Fossaluzza and Manzato, 1987, pp.47-63.

3 Canova, 1964, p.90, fig.58.

91

1 Dreyer, 1979, pp.365-75; the Edinburgh sheet is discussed on pp.366-7. It was first published by Andrews, 1968, I, p.147, as Venetian School, sixteenth century. J. Scholz (Review of Andrews, 1968 in *Art Bulletin*, LIII, 1971, p.257) argued that it was by Titian himself, a view endorsed emphatically by Meijer, 1974, pp.78-83, who was the first to discuss the connection with the *St Jerome in the Wilderness* woodcut; by K. Oberhuber (in Venice, 1976, pp.91-2, cat.no.37); by Muraro and Rosand (in Washington, 1976, pp.146-9, cat.no.22) and, at that time, by Dreyer himself (1980, p.510).

2 Among those who accepted Dreyer's thesis were J. Byam Shaw, 'Titian's Drawings: A Summing-up', *Apollo*, CXII, 226, pp.386-91; Wethey, 1987, pp.242-3, cat.no.X41. His conclusions have been challenged by, among others, D. Rosand, 'Titian Drawings: A Crisis of Connoisseurship?', *Master Drawings*, XIX, 3, 1981, pp.303-8; K. Oberhuber in Paris, 1993, pp.460, cat.no.103; and most recently by Van der Sman, in Maastricht, 2003, pp.102-3, cat.no.III.1.

3 See Washington, 1976, pp.146-8, cat.no.22.

4 An alternative, if less likely, scenario is that the offset was made much later, after the woodblock had come to the end of its useful life. The block could have been unbolted and dismantled

into its component parts, which were often surprisingly irregular. Two of these would then have been brought together to form a new composition, which was then printed and the resulting print offset to produce the basis of the Edinburgh landscape.

5 Dreyer, 1979, pp.373–5.

6 Wethey, 1987, p.243, who considered it to be no earlier than the seventeenth century. Previously Meijer (1974, pp.82–3), who was the first to publish the verso, had argued that it was by Titian himself.

92

1 See Ballarin, 1971, pp.106–10, 117, note 20 and fig.146. The sheet was previously ascribed more generally to the 'School of Verona': see Andrews, 1968, I, p.149.

2 Most relevant in the present context is the fact that the important altarpiece of *Christ Carrying the Cross with Eight Saints* (Verona, Santo Stefano) was commissioned in 1546 and completed in 1547, with a final payment made jointly to Brusasorci and his father in April 1548: see P.C. Brownell, 'La figura di committente del Vescovo Gianmatteo Giberti' in Verona, 1988, pp.74–6. A series of mythological scenes by Brusasorci frescoed on a vault in the Palazzo Bissari in Vicenza are also datable to 1547: see M. Binotto, 'Vicenza 1540–1600' in Lucco, 1996–9, II, pp.742–5, 789, note 23.

3 As emphasised by Ballarin, 1971, pp.105–10.

4 See Ballarin, 1971, pp.106–9; Stefani Mantovanelli, 1979, pp.57–8; Vicenza, 1980, pp.45–6; Verona, 1994, pp.82–4, under cat.no.13.

5 Ward-Jackson, 1979, I, p.227, cat.no.511 (as School of Verona, late sixteenth century).

93

I would like to thank Giorgio Marini and Daniela Sogliani for their help – several years ago – in obtaining photographic and bibliographic material used in this entry.

1 See Sotheby's, London, 3 July 1996 (lot 53); Colnaghi, New York and London, *Master Drawings*, dealer catalogue by S. Ongpin, 1997, cat.no.8.

2 For the drawing see Venice, 1971, pp.39–40, cat.no.30; Ballarin, 1971, pp.106–7, fig.145; Jaffé, 1994, pp.46–7, cat.no.745.

3 See Ballarin, 1971, pp.106–7 (who, however, argued that there was a hiatus between the execution of the drawing, which he dated to about 1546–7, and the painting, which he placed around 1551–2); Stefani Mantovanelli, 1979, pp.58–61 (c.1554); N. Zanolli Gemi, *Sant'Eufemia: Storia di una chiesa e del suo convento a Verona*, Verona, 1991, pp.96–7; S. Marinelli in Lucco,

1996–9, II, pp.830–2, fig.888.

4 For this drawing see Verona, 1994, pp.87–8, cat.no.15.

5 The connection was spotted by the present writer in 1999, shortly before the drawing was purchased by the Gallery, and was noted in the entry written for the National Art Collections Fund, *1999 Review*, p.104, and in the brief entry in Edinburgh, National Gallery of Scotland, *From the Madonna to the Moulin Rouge: Drawings Recently Acquired for the National Gallery of Scotland*, exh. cat., Edinburgh, 2001, pp.25–6, cat.no.37. This is the first occasion, however, that the drawing and the related fresco have been reproduced together.

6 For the frescoes see C. Perina, 'Pittura' in E. Marani and C. Perina, *Mantova: Le Arti*, Mantua, 1965, pp.370–1, 390, note 56; P. Carpeggiani and C. Tellini Perina, *Sant'Andrea in Mantova: un tempio per la città del Principe*, 1987, pp.103–7, figs.74–5, 77; R. Berzaghi, 'Ippolito Andreasi' in Marinelli, 1998, p.164.

7 For the frescoes in Verona, see Stefani Mantovanelli, 1979, pp.14–21, 62, figs.13–17, 30–1; Stefani Mantovanelli, 2000.

8 The physiognomies of some of the women in this composition are almost identical to those in the *St Ursula* fresco in Santissima Trinità, Verona.

9 Wethey, 1969, p.76, cat.no.15.

10 See Stefani Mantovanelli, 1979, pp.41–4; G. Peretti, 'La pittura a Mantova nell'età di Ercole' in Marinelli, 1998, pp.44–5, pl.8.

11 See Stefani Mantovanelli, 1979, pp.79–81; S. Marinelli, 'La Pittura a Mantova nell'età di Guglielmo' in Marinelli, 1998, pp.72–3.

94

1 See D. Scrase in London, 1983, p.279, cat.no.D52, who, however, retained the previous identification while noting the connection with the statuette. For a full account of Sansovino's sacristy door, see Boucher, 1991, I, pp.65–7; II, pp.331–2, pls.151–60.

2 London, 1983, p.279, cat.no.D52.

3 This was the conclusion of Boucher, 1991, II, p.378, cat.no.133. For figure drawings more convincingly attributed to Sansovino, see Boucher, 1991, II, p.377, cat.nos.129–31, figs.19–20, 25–6.

95

1 It is particularly close in style to drawings in the same combination of media of the *Adoration of the Christ Child* in the Uffizi, Florence, and of *Jupiter and a Nymph* in the Chrysler Museum, Norfolk, Va. (Richardson, 1980, p.114, cat.no.137 and p.130, cat.no.189 respectively).

2 This connection was noted by Andrews, 1968, I, p.113; Richardson,

1980, p.123, cat.no.166. For the painting see Richardson, 1980, pp.165–6, cat.no.272.

3 Zerner, 1979, p.101.

4 See Andrews, 1968, I, p.113.

96

1 McTavish, 1981, pp.210–14, 325–6, fig.201; D. McTavish in London, 1983, cat.no.D51.

2 'Clelia con sue compagne, e quando passa il Tevere, mentre le sentinelle del Rè Porsena dormono'; Ridolfi, 1648, I, p.241.

3 McTavish, 1981, pp.360–1, fig.200.

4 A. Ballarin, 'Jacopo Bassano e lo studio di Raffaello e dei Salviati', *Arte Veneta*, XXI, 1967, pp.96–7, dated the Edinburgh drawing to around 1545.

5 See B.W. Meijer, 'Lambert Sustris in Padua: fresco's en tekeningen', *Oud Holland*, 107, 1993, pp.9–10, fig.12; B.W. Meijer, 'À propos de quelques dessins de Lambert Sustris', in C. Monbeig Goguel, P. Costamagna and M. Hochmann (eds.), *Francesco Salviati e la bella maniera: Actes des colloques de Rome et de Paris (1998)*, Paris, 2001, pp.652–4, fig.4; A. Bristot, 'Dedicato all'amore per l'antico: il camerino di Apollo a palazzo Grimani', *Arte Veneta*, 58, 2001, pp.70, 72, fig.46.

97 & 98

1 For the fullest discussion of the altarpiece and the related drawings, see Lauder, 1997.

2 As pointed out by Lauder, 1997, p.99. For this drawing see also Andrews, 1968, I, p.52; Washington, 1990, pp.36–7, cat.no.8.

3 Lauder, 2003, p.107, fig.5.7.

4 Andrews, 1968, I, p.52. Anne Varick Lauder kindly drew my attention to a drawn copy of the Edinburgh sheet in the Louvre (inv. no.21591), which appears to be considerably later in date.

5 Lauder, 1997, pp.98–9, fig.1.

6 For a thorough analysis of the iconography, see Lauder, 1997, pp.99–103.

99

1 Keith Andrews (in London, 1966, cat.no.9; Andrews, 1968, I, p.52; and Edinburgh, 1981, cat.no.11) connected the drawing with one of the figures on the frescoed vault of the Grimani chapel in San Francesco della Vigna, Venice, executed by Franco around 1560–1 (reproduced in Rearick, 1958, p.124, fig.10e).

2 Unpublished. Inv.no.BnF Est. Ba. 1 (16es). Engraving, 29.4 × 43.7cm. Inscribed at the lower edge, to the right of centre: *.Iachomo Franco. F.* It is not among the prints by Franco listed by Bartsch, XVI, pp.111–60 or Zerner, 1979, pp.156–258.

3 For biographical details of Giacomo see London, 2001, p.226.

4 Berlin, Kupferstichkabinett, inv.no.KdZ 16864. Red chalk over stylus indications, 18.8 × 30.5cm.

5 Compare, for example, the red chalk figure studies in the Metropolitan Museum of Art and in the Royal Library at Windsor Castle for Franco's print of the *Flagellation* (J. Bean with the assistance of L. Turčić, *15th and 16th Century Italian Drawings in the Metropolitan Museum of Art*, New York, 1982, p.95, cat.no.84; and Popham and Wilde, 1949, p.232, cat.no.329, pl.171).

6 Ward-Jackson, 1979, I, p.68, cat.no.137 (inv.no.9091[c]).

7 Published in G. Ludwig, *Archivialische Beiträge zur Geschichte der Venezianischen Kunst aus dem Nachlass Gustav Ludwigs*, IV, Berlin, 1911, p.99.

8 Evidence for this is provided by the fact that, contrary to Battista Franco's usual practice, the drawings in Edinburgh and Berlin are in the same sense as the corresponding figures in the engraving, rather than reversed. Furthermore, comparing the internal dimensions of the figures in the print reveals that all are considerably smaller than their drawn counterparts.

9 For example, the *Flagellation*, *Christ Fallen under the Cross*, the *Raising of Lazarus*, the *Entombment* and the *Adoration of the Magi* (see *The Illustrated Bartsch*, XXXII, 1979, 166–7, 172, 178 and 248).

10 The executioner on the left occurs identically in Franco's signed and dated canvas, *Christ Fallen under the Cross* in the Uffizi of 1552 (Rearick, 1958, p.114, fig.3) as well as the autograph versions in Kassel (B. Schnackenburg, *Gemäldegalerie Alte Meister Gesamtkatalog*, Mainz, 1996, I, p.121, cat.no.GK 54, II, pl.292) and a private collection, New York (sold at Bonhams, London, 9–10 July 2002, lot 376). The kneeling figure on the right is reproduced in one of the rectangular compartments of grotesques painted on the vault above the first flight of the *Scala d'Oro* in the Ducal Palace, Venice, around 1558–9.

11 For discussion of Franco's use of chalk, see G.J. Van der Sman, 'Battista Franco: Studi di figura per dipinti e incisioni', *Prospettiva* 97, 2000, pp.65–71; A.V. Lauder, 'Absorption and interpretation: Michelangelo through the eyes of a Venetian follower, Battista Franco' in F. Ames-Lewis and P. Joannides (eds.), *Reactions to the Master: Michelangelo's Effect on Art and Artist in the Sixteenth Century*, London, 2003, pp.95–7, 103–5.

100

The present entry is a reprint, with very minor changes, of the one that appeared in the exhibition catalogue Edinburgh, 1999, cat.no.8.

1 When it was in Richard Cosway's collection, the drawing was included in Conrad Martin Metz's *Imitations of Drawings* (1798).

2 Bartsch, XVI.18.125; Zerner, 1979, p.174.

3 A similar pose was used independently for Franco's engraving of *St John the Baptist in the Wilderness*: Bartsch, XVI.35.130. For the Vatican fresco, see C. Pietrangeli (et al.), *Raffaello nell'Appartamento di Giulio II e Leone X*, Milan, 1993, especially the plates between pp.168 and 169.

4 For Salviati's fresco, see L. Mortari, *Francesco Salviati*, Rome, 1992, p.118.

5 Very seldom did Franco employ pure etching with the freedom of touch evident in the *Resurrection* print (exceptions are Bartsch, XVI.26.128 and 32.130, both of which, it has now emerged, were originally etched, with seven other roundels, on a single plate: see R. Parma Baudille, 'Disegni di Battista Franco per incisioni', *Arte Documento*, 8, 1994, pp.98–9 and fig.21). For the late dating of these prints, see further Boston, 1989, cat.no.27; Van der Sman, 1994, p.109.

6 For the fresco see A. Coliva, 'Battista Franco e Girolamo Muziano nella Cappella Gabrielli in Santa Maria sopra Minerva: una ipotesi di collaborazione', *Arte Documento*, 6, 1992, p.200 and fig.4. For the related drawings, see R. Parma Baudille, 'L'Ultimo lavoro romano di Battista Franco: la cappella Gabrielli in Santa Maria sopra Minerva', *Arte Documento*, 6, 1992, pp.186–90.

7 For this project see Rearick, 1958, p.127.

101

1 A more clear-cut example of this procedure is provided by a drawing attributed to Leandro Bassano in the Ashmolean Museum, Oxford: see Venice, Fondazione Giorgio Cini, *Disegni veneti di Oxford*, exh. cat. by K.T. Parker, Vicenza, 1958, p.37, cat.no.44.

2 The comparison with a drawing in Munich to which Keith Andrews refers (Andrews, 1968, I, p.14) is not particularly convincing.

102

1 Tietze and Tietze-Conrat, 1944, p.298, no.1777; Rossi, 1975, p.61, where the attribution to Jacopo is rejected.

2 Rossi, 1984, pp.59–60, fig.3.

3 See Macandrew in Washington, 1990 (2), pp.42–3, cat.no.11.

4 Rossi, 1975, pp.45, 54–5, figs.81, 83. The stylistic connection with the former of these was noted by Andrews, 1968, I, p.120.

5 See Tokyo, 1996, pp.132–3, cat.no.48 (English supplement, p.31).

6 Rossi, 1984, pp.57–60, proposed a

connection with the central figure in a painted *Allegory with the Muses* by Domenico (whereabouts unknown) for which a related modello is in the Musei Civici at Trieste (her figs.1–2).

7 Inv.no.1913-3-31-189; Rossi, 1975, p.42, fig.62.

103

1 Andrews, 1968, I, pp.119–20, following Tietze and Tietze-Conrat (1944, p.261, no.1488), catalogued it as by Domenico, but noted the very close resemblance to Jacopo's drawing style. It has to be said that the comparison they cite in support of Domenico's authorship is not particularly compelling. Indeed, no really comparable drawing can be found in recent publications on Domenico's drawings (see P. Rossi, 'Per la grafica di Domenico Tintoretto', *Arte Veneta*, XXIX, 1975, pp.205–11; Rossi, 1984; M. Koshikawa, 'I disegni di Domenico Tintoretto: un contributo', *Arte Veneta*, XLVIII, 1996 / I, pp.56–69). A late drawing by Jacopo in the Victoria and Albert Museum of a figure in a similar pose is arguably closer in style to the Edinburgh study: see Rossi, 1975, p.46, fig.183.

104

1 These and Tintoretto's drawings after them are discussed in Rossi, 1975, pp.2–6.

2 This is recorded, for example, in three drawings by Jacopo at Christ Church, Oxford: Rossi, 1975, figs.10–12.

3 Many of these are cited by Parker, 1927.

4 Byam Shaw, 1976, I, p.205, cat.no.761; II, pls. 427–8; Rossi, 1984, p.50, figs.20–1.

5 Parker, 1927, pl.5. Parker maintained the attribution of the verso to Jacopo, while accepting Domenico's author-ship of the recto; subsequent writers have concurred in giving both sides to Domenico (Tietze and Tietze-Conrat, 1944, p.265; Byam Shaw, 1976, p.205; Rossi, 1984, p.71, note 59).

105

1 For the drawing see Venice, 1971, p.65, cat.no.73; Goldner, 1981, p.123, note 25, and pp.124-5, figs.22–3; Cocke, 1984, pp.292–4, cat.no.126; Washington, 1988, p.201, cat.no.104.

2 For a survey of these see Goldner, 1981.

3 For this drawing see Mongan and Sachs, 1946, I, pp.108–10, cat.no.205; Cocke, 1984, pp.292–4, cat.no.125; Washington, 1988, cat.no.105.

4 As argued by A. Mongan (Mongan and Sachs, 1946, I, p.110); T. Mullaly (in Venice, 1971, p.65, cat.no.73); G. Goldner (1981, p.123, note 25); and W.R. Rearick (in Washington, 1988, p.201, cat.no.104).

5 Cocke, 1984, p.294.

6 Pignatti and Pedrocco, 1995, II, pp.399–400, cat.no.288.

106

1 For the painting see Pignatti and Pedrocco, 1995, II, p.466, cat.no.362.

2 H. Coutts, 'A Veronese Drawing in Edinburgh', *Master Drawings*, XVIII, 1980, pp.142–4, pl.16.

3 As noted by Cocke, 1984, p.346, cat.no.170, who included it among his rejected attributions.

4 See A. Ghirardi, *Passerotti*, Rimini, 1990.

5 Sotheby's, London, 10 July 2003 (lot 162); Jean-Luc Baroni Ltd, New York and London, *Master Drawings and Oil Sketches*, dealer catalogue by S. Ongpin, 2004, cat.no.12.

6 For the series, see Pignatti and Pedrocco, 1995, II, p.466.

7 See B.L. Brown, 'The so-called Duke of Buckingham Series' in Gemin, 1990, pp.231–40; K. Garas, 'Veronese e il collezionismo del nord nel XVI–XVII secolo' in Gemin, 1990, pp.16–24.

107

1 Andrews, 1968, I, p.49 (the date suggested by Terence Mullaly).

108

1 Andrews, 1968, I, p.48, who retained the traditional title despite noting the connection, first pointed out by Terence Mullaly (letter of 21 March 1963 in the Gallery files), with the fresco in the Marogna chapel in San Paolo, Verona.

2 See Verona, 1988, pp.216–18, cat.no.12.

3 For the decoration of the chapel, see G. Baldissin Molli, 'Un fregio poco conosciuto e un quadro inedito di Paolo Farinati', *Arte Veneta*, XLII, 1988, p.102, figs.7–8; Paris, 1993 (2), cat.no.30; Lucco, 1996–9, II, p.818.

4 Paris, 1993 (2), cat.no.30; Verona, 1994, pp.114–16, cat.no.34.

5 Puppi, 1968, pp.xxxvii–xxxviii of the introduction and p.14.

109

1 Andrews, 1968, I, p.48. Andrews nevertheless correctly noted the connection with the Esther and Ahasuerus frieze, which had first been pointed out by Terence Mullaly (letter of 21 March 1963 in the Gallery files).

2 M. Carrara and L. Magagnato, *La storia di Ester affrescata in Casa Sebastiani da Paolo Farinati 1587*, Verona, 1976, pp.23–30.

3 Puppi, 1968, pp.68–72.

4 Puppi, 1968, pp.72–6.

5 A.E. Popham and K.M. Fenwick, *European Drawings (and two Asian drawings) in the Collection of the National Gallery of Canada*, Toronto, 1965, p.26, cat.no.32.

6 H. Sueur in Paris, 1993 (2), pp.100–1, cat.no.38; Verona 1994, pp.128–9, cat.no.44.

7 Puppi, 1968, pp.68–71, note 1 and figs.20–27; B. Meijer in Florence, 1995, pp.137–8, cat.no.51.

110

1 Andrews, 1968, I, p.49.

2 For other drawings of this kind, see Andrews, 1968, I, p.49; Paris, 1993 (2), pp.94–5, cat.no.33; Verona, 1994, pp.120–21, cat.no.38.

3 Puppi, 1968, p.158 note 4.

4 See F.J.B. Watson, 'On the early history of collecting in England, *The Burlington Magazine*, LXXXV, 1944, pp.223–8.

111

1 See T. Mullaly, 'A note on Paolo Farinati's working methods', *Burlington Magazine*, CXXVII, 1985, pp.778–9, figs.60 and 62.

112

1 The attribution of the Edinburgh drawing to Palma Giovane and its connection with the Gesuiti paintings was first made by Alessandro Ballarin. It was previously catalogued as 'Venetian School, 17th century': see Andrews, 1968, I, p.148, who, however, noted the stylistic similarity of the verso to early Palma Giovane.

2 There is no trace of what became of the last two pictures following their removal from the church. The *Presentation of the Virgin* was in the Gemäldegalerie in Dresden until its destruction in 1945. Its composition is known from old photographs and a preparatory study for it survives in the Ratjen Foundation, Vaduz.

3 For full details of this series, see Mason Rinaldi, 1984, pp.91, 94, under cat. nos 91 and 156.

4 In Sotheby's, London, 4 July 1977, *Drawings by Jacopo Palma, il Giovane from the Collection of the late Mr C.R. Rudolf* (lot 5) and Mason Rinaldi, 1984, p.158, cat.no.D102. The subject of the Edinburgh drawing had previously been correctly identified by Andrews, 1968, I, p.148.

5 Two sheets by Palma similar in style were formerly in the Martin Bodmer Foundation (sale, Christie's, New York, 23 January 2002, lots 148 and 149).

6 Similar inscriptions appear on other drawings from his collection: see M. Plomp, *The Dutch Drawings in the Teyler Museum: Volume II, Artists born between 1575 and 1630*, Haarlem, Ghent and Doornspijk, 1997, p.224, cat.no.239 and pp.300–1, cat.no.327, note 2.

113

1 H. Kusáková-Knozová, *Italská renesanční a barokní kresba ze sbírek*

Moravské galerie, Brno, 1969, cat.no.88.

2 Tietze and Tietze-Conrat, 1944, p.202, described it as 'Typical of the end of the 16th century'.

114

1 Andrews, 1968, I, p.137. The correct attribution to Palma was first suggested by Ralph Holland in 1969 (note in Gallery files).

2 For the painting, see Mason Rinaldi, 1984, p.119, cat.no.366. The connection between the Edinburgh drawing and the painting has not previously been noted.

115

1 Tietze and Tietze-Conrat, 1944, p.202, no.891.

2 Boschini, 1664, Sestiere della Croce, p.33.

3 Ridolfi, 1914–24, II, p.156.

4 See A. Loda, 'Un quadro e un disegno per il manierismo bresciano' in *Civiltà Bresciana*, VII, 1, 1998, pp.60–70. At note 14 the author cites previous attributions for the altarpiece, together with a recent proposal that it might be by another Brescian artist, Francesco Giugno, rather than by Rama.

5 Most of these are listed, with bibliographical references, in New York, The Frick Collection, *Italian Drawings from the Ratjen Foundation*, exh. cat. by D. Lachenmann, Bern, 1996, under cat.no.7. To these may be added the Edinburgh sheet, and also the following: a *Christ in Glory with Putti* sold at Christie's, London, 16 May 1978 (lot 23) and subsequently with Mia Weiner, New York (exhibited at Piero Corsini Inc, New York, 1985); a *Coronation of the Virgin with Four Saints* in the Rijksmuseum, Amsterdam (Florence, Istituto Universitario Olandese di Storia dell'Arte, and Amsterdam, Rijksmuseum, *Maestri dell'invenzione: Disegni italiani del Rijksmuseum*, Amsterdam, exh. cat. ed. by B.W. Meijer, 1995–6, cat.no.54); an *Entombment of Christ* in the Museu Nacional de Arte Antiga, Lisbon (Cambridge, Fitzwilliam Museum, Lisbon, Centro Cultural de Belém and Oporto, Museu Nacional Soares dos Reis, *European Master Drawings from Portuguese Collections*, exh. cat. by N. Turner, 2000–1, cat.no.26); a *Flagellation of Christ* in the Museo Nacional de Bellas Artes, Buenos Aires (A.M. Navarro, 'Italian Drawings in Buenos Aires', *Master Drawings*, 39, 1, 2001, pp.48–50; and finally two unpublished sheets in the British Museum: an *Annunciation* (1946–7–13–40) and *Studies of a Standing and a Seated Male Nude* (1991–11–9–21).

6 Mason Rinaldi, 1984, p.120, cat.no.373. Another modello in the Louvre of *The*

Body of Christ supported by Angels, previously connected with an altarpiece of about 1613–14, is in fact directly preparatory for a recently discovered small painting on slate: see Pordenone, ex-Chiesa di San Francesco, *Dal Pordenone a Palma il Giovane: Devozione e pietà nel disegno veneziano del Cinquecento*, exh. cat. ed. by C. Furlan, 2000, pp.190–1, cat.no.54.

7 The British Museum drawing (inv. no. Fawkener 5210–60) is unpublished. For that in the Correr, see Venice, 1990, p.104, cat.no.38a.

116

1 An anonymous note on the verso of a *St Francis Receiving the Stigmata* by Palma Giovane sold at Sotheby – Mak van Waay, Amsterdam, 17 November 1980 (lot 136) reads: 'Palma / St Francis / by / Giac.o Palma the Young. 1544 / 1628 / out of the Sagredo Collection which / was sold by auction at Langfords 1764 / when near three hundred drawings by / this Master were sold: Till then they / were little known in England. / Purchased at Mr. Hudson's sale'. F. Lugt (*Répertoire des catalogues de ventes publiques 1600–1825*, The Hague, 1938, no.1340) lists the vendor as 'Segrado, Venise' and the auctioneer as Prestage rather than Langfords.

2 Zerner, 1979, pp.125–50, nos.2–27; Boston, 1989, pp.251–2, cat.no.132.

3 Zerner, 1979, p.140, no.17.

4 See Mason Rinaldi, 1984, p.186.

5 For these drawings see Mason Rinaldi, 1984, p.160, cat.no.D122, fig.487 and p.157 cat.no.D75, fig.465.

6 Mason Rinaldi, 1984, p.98, cat.no.190, fig.617.

7 Acc. no.1946–7–13–424.

117

1 A related drawing in the Pierpont Morgan Library, New York, is inscribed with the date 1606 and the artist's age, 58. For both painting and drawings see Venice, 1990, pp.212–13, cat.no.91.

2 Mason Rinaldi, 1984, p.146, cat.no.565. A painting in the Uffizi sometimes considered to be a very late self-portrait by Palma in my view certainly portrays a different sitter (see Venice, 1990, pp.236–7, cat.no.103).

118

1 Motta di Livenza, Duomo, *Ornamenta Ecclesiae: Dipinti, oreficeria liturgica e paramenti a Motta di Livenza*, exh. cat. (eds.) A. Argentieri Zanetti and S. Claut, 1988, p.82 (cited by G. Finaldi in London, 2000, p.180).

2 As suggested by Finaldi in London, 2000, p.180.

3 T. Pignatti (ed.), *Disegni antichi del Museo Correr di Venezia*, V, Vicenza, 1996, p.115, cat.no.1303.

119

1 Mason Rinaldi, 1984, p.117, cat.no.341. The connection between the drawing and the painting has not hitherto been noted in print.

120

1 For the altarpiece see Fort Worth, 1993, pp.375–6, cat.no.46.

2 Tietze and Tietze-Conrat, 1944, p.50, no.133 (as Jacopo); Andrews, 1968, I, p.14 (as Leandro), with further references.

3 See Arslan, 1960, I, p.II, pl.340.

4 Acc.no.1895–9–15–858; D. von Hadeln, 'Venezianische Zeichnungen der Spätrenaissance', Berlin, 1926, pl.80 (as Jacopo); W.R. Rearick, 'Maestri veneti del '500' in *Biblioteca dei disegni*, VI, Florence, 1976, p.51, no.28 (as Leandro).

5 Acc.no.1920–11–16; Tietze and Tietze-Conrat, 1944, p.51, no.160 (as Jacopo). It is in fact preparatory for a signed painting by Leandro sold at Sotheby's, London, 21 March 1973 (lot 116).

6 Acc. no. Cracherode F.7.1–72; Tietze and Tietze-Conrat, 1944, p.57, no.222 (as Leandro).

7 See Venice, Fondazione Giorgio Cini, *Da Pisanello a Tiepolo: Disegni veneti dal Fitzwilliam Museum di Cambridge*, exh. cat. by D. Scrase, Milan, 1992, pp.112–13, cat.no.47.

8 See Arslan, 1960, II, pl.190 (as Jacopo).

121

1 For Benedetto as a draughtsman, see W.R. Rearick, 'Black Chalk Drawings by Paolo Veronese', *Master Drawings*, XXX, 2, 1992, pp.161–4; W.R. Rearick, 'More Veronese Drawings from the Sagredo Collection', *Master Drawings*, XXXIII, 2, 1995, pp.133–5; and, for his portrait drawings, F. Nodari, 'Per Benedetto Caliari disegnatore' in Forlani Tempesti, 2002, pp.21–46.

2 See L. Larcher Crosato, 'Note su Benedetto Caliari', *Arte Veneta*, XXIII, 1969, pp.117–18, fig.128.

3 Pignatti and Pedrocco, 1995, pp.383–5, cat.no.271.

122

1 By Terence Mullaly in Venice, 1971, cat.no.82.

2 A technically very different drawing by Malombra in the Metropolitan Museum of Art showing *Pope Alexander III Placing his Foot on the Neck of the Emperor Federico Barbarossa* is almost certainly preparatory for a lost work of this subject described by Ridolfi in San Giacomo di Rialto. See Tietze and Tietze-Conrat, 1944, p.188; Ballarin 1971, p.118, note 39; Palma, 1984, p.73. More recently a large drawing showing the *Coronation of the Virgin with Saints* in an English private collection has been convincingly linked to another lost

painting by Malombra (see A. Piai, 'Proposte per Pietro Malombra disegnatore', *Arte Documento*, 8, 1994, pp.167–70; B.W. Meijer, 'Per Pietro Malombra disegnatore e per Ascanio Spineda', *Arte Veneta*, 49, 1996 / II, pp.30–5.

3 The correct attribution of the drawing and its connection with the Santo altarpiece is due to A. Ballarin (1971, p.118, note 39 and fig.158); see further Palma, 1984, pp.73–4, figs.2–3.

4 Ridolfi, 1648, p.156.

5 Kowalczyk (1967, p.74) and Palma (1984, pp.72, 77, note 7) argue for the earlier date; for the later dating see M. Lucco in Padua, Sala della Ragione and Sale dei Chiostri del Santo, *S. Antonio 1231–1981: Il suo tempo, il suo culto e la sua città*, exh. cat. ed. by G. Gorini, Padua, 1981, pp.50–2, cat.no.30; and A.M. Spiazzi, 'Dipinti del Seicento e del Settecento' in C. Semenzato (ed.), *Le pitture del Santo di Padova*, Vicenza, 1984, pp.217–18.

6 Kowalczyk, 1967, p.73.

7 Without knowledge of the drawing, Kowalczyk (1967, p.76) had already argued that the composition had been narrowed at that time.

8 The precise subject of the altarpiece was clarified by Kowalczyk, 1967, pp.68, 76–8.

9 Ridolfi spells his name 'Ozizouusthi' and describes him as the 'agent' of the 'Polish Nation', that is, the association of Poles resident in Padua, principally those attending the university.

10 Tietze and Tietze-Conrat, 1944, p.189, cat.no.796, pl.CXXXV.2; Palma, 1984, p.75, fig.5.

11 See Pandora Old Masters, New York, *Old Master Drawings and Oil Sketches*, dealer catalogue, 1999, no.4.

123

1 Popham and Wilde, 1949, p.339, cat.no.965.

2 As noted by Andrews, 1968, I, p.128.

3 Ridolfi, 1914–24, II, pp.227–8.

4 For these works see Schulz, 1968, pp.93–4, pls.60–1; Lucco, 1996–9, II, p.767 and pl.825.

5 See Florence, 1976, p.156, cat.no.113 (as Zelotti). The attribution to Tognone was suggested by H. Coutts, 'A Print and two Drawings from the Circle of Zelotti', *Print Quarterly*, 4, 1, 1987, p.50, note 8. That attribution was rejected in Florence, Galleria degli Uffizi, *Cinque secoli di disegno veronese*, exh. cat. by S. Marinelli, Florence, 2000, p.49, cat.no.21.

6 Inv.nos.RL 4816 and 5043. Martin Clayton kindly brought them to my attention and suggested the attribution to Tognone. They are currently catalogued as after Paolo Farinati (Popham and Wilde, 1949, p.218, cat.nos.276–7).

124

1 Andrews, 1968, I, p.150.

2 The attribution to Maganza was first proposed by Alessandro Ballarin in 1977 (note on the mount).

3 For the drawings of the Maganza family, see B.W. Meijer, 'I Maganza e Francesco Maffei disegnatori' in *Scritti di storia dell'arte in onore di Roberto Salvini*, Florence, 1984, pp.473–81; O. Matarrese, 'Appunti sulla formazione di Alessandro Maganza disegnatore e qualche aggiunta al catalogo di Giambattista il Giovane', *Bulletin de l'association des Historiens de l'Art Italien*, 4, 1997–8, pp.23–30; Mason, 1999; and especially O. Matarrese, 'Precisazioni sulla produzione grafica di Alessandro Maganza e della sua bottega' in Forlani Tempesti, 2002, pp.47–90, with further references.

4 See Mason, 1999, pp.212, 214–15, note 10.

5 Byam Shaw, 1976, I, p.225, cat.no.841. Tietze and Tietze-Conrat (1944, p.163, cat.no.676) attributed this drawing to Leonardo Corona.

6 O. Matarrese in Forlani Tempesti, 2002, pp.55, 84, fig.19.

125

1 The drawing was published by G. Robertson, 'A Drawing after Titian's 'Madonna di Ca' Pesaro' by Federico Zuccaro' in *Tiziano e Venezia: Convegno internazionale di studi, Venice, 1976*, Vicenza, 1980, pp.559–61.

2 Acidini Luchinat, 1998–9, I, pp.238–40.

3 See B. Py, *Everhard Jabach collectionneur (1618–1695): Les dessins de l'inventaire de 1695 (Notes et documents des musées de France*, Paris, 2002. A group of ten of these recently appeared on the art market: see Jean-Luc Baroni Ltd, London and New York, *Master Drawings and Oil Sketches*, dealer catalogue by S. Ongpin, 2004, cat.nos.1–10.

4 For Zuccaro's Venetian sojourns and commissions, see Acidini Luchinat, 1998–9, I, pp.227–40; II, pp.132–5.

126

1 Strozzi's authorship of the drawing was first recognised by Hugh Macandrew, who included it in an exhibition of Genoese drawings in the National Gallery of Scotland in 1988 (illustrated and catalogued as no.25 in the accompanying leaflet). It was subsequently published by Piero Boccardo in Genoa, Palazzo Ducale, *Bernardo Strozzi: Genova 1581/82 – Venezia 1644*, exh. cat. ed. by E. Gavazza *et al.*, Milan, 1995, p.306, under cat.no.104.

2 For the painting see Wethey, 1969, pp.136–7, cat.no.109; F. Valcanover in Washington, 1990, pp.240–3,

cat.no.32; D. Jaffé in London, 2003, pp.122–3, cat.no.20; M. Falomir in Madrid, 2003, pp.176–7, cat.no.17.

3 The drawing was sold at Christie's, Monaco, 2 July 1993 (lot 40), where Carletto's altarpiece is also illustrated.

PRINTS
Introduction

I should like to thank Peter Black, Hugo Chapman, Donato Esposito, Allan Hood and Aidan Weston-Lewis for their help.

1 Lane, 1973, pp.304–5.

2 Zorzi, 1996, p.918.

3 Hind, 1935, I, pp.36–7; II, pp.489–97.

4 Kolb dealt in books, among other things, handling for example the Nuremberg *Liber cronicarum* of 1493 (Wilson, 1976, pp.232–35; Schulz, 1978, p.428, note 7). See Washington, 1976, p.35, notes 4–5 for Benalio, 'stampador … exercitante larte impresoria'; note 3, for De Gregoriis; note 6, for Bordon and Giovanni da Brescia; and p.70, for Delle Greche, whose address appeared on a late state of Titian's *Crossing of the Red Sea*.

5 M. McDonald, *The Print Collection of Ferdinand Columbus*, 3 vols., London, 2004.

6 Mauroner, 1943, pp.27–8.

7 Edinburgh, 1990, p.19.

8 Edinburgh, 1990, pp.11 and 43, cat.no.4.

9 Fabbro, 1977, pp.239–41.

10 Vasari, 1906, VII, p.437.

11 Washington, 1976, pp.176 and 191.

12 The inscription on the portrait of Titian reads: 'In Venetia per Gioanni Britto / Intagliatore'. In the case of the portrait of Charles V, Britto's name as publisher appears in connection with a version, admitted to be a rather poor copy, not with the anonymous original; see Washington, 1976, pp.204ff., cat.nos.46–7.

13 Dreyer, 1980, pp.504–5.

14 For the Boldrini, see Washington, 1976, p.243, cat.no.72. It has been argued that the inscription 'Jacobus fecit' on the early sixteenth-century woodcut *The Virgin and Child with Saints Sebastian and Roch* signified Jacob of Strassburg's responsibility for cutting the block: see Massing, 1977, p.43.

15 Amsterdam, 1992, pp.12–15.

16 Borroni Salvadori, 1980, p.lii.

17 Tooley, 1939, cat.no.3; Shirley, 1983, pp.96–7, cat.no.85. This map was actually copied in wood for Pagano around 1550: see Shirley, 1983, p.100, cat.no.89.

18 Woodward, 1997, p.52.

19 For Licinio's *Annunciation*, see M.A. Chiari, 'La fortuna dell'opera pordenoniana attraverso le stampe' in *Il Pordenone: Atti del convegno internazionale di studi*, C. Furlan (ed.), Pordenone, 1985, pp.184–6. The last digit of the date 1544, written on the Virgin's prayer book, is not entirely clear.

20 Mortimer, II, 1974, pp.777–8, cat.no.556; for the frontispiece see Barberi, 1969, I, p.140.

21 Richardson, 1980, pp.74–110.

22 Bury, 2003, p.130.

23 Maastricht, 2003, p.200, cat.no.V.11.

24 London, 2001, p.150, cat.no.102 (a Roman copy); Maastricht, 2003, p.198, cat.no.V.10 and p.194, cat.no.V.7.

25 Carrara and Gregory, 2000, pp.11, 13; Maastricht, 2003, pp.179–81.

26 Maastricht, 2003, pp.176–7.

27 London, 2001, p.187, cat.no.124; Maastricht, 2003, p.176. Van der Sman (2003, p.123) has pointed out that important developments in commercial packaging of prints were made in Venice, in particular the issue of title pages for groups of prints. Bertelli did this for maps too.

28 Borroni Salvadori, 1980, pp.xlii–xliii.

29 Woodward, 1997, p.52. See also Gallo, 1950, p.96.

30 Bagrow, 1948, pp.53–62.

31 London, 2001, p.174.

32 Washington, 1979, pp.495–6.

33 Boston, 1989, pp.248–51.

34 He was the illegitimate son of Battista Franco.

35 Pasero, 1935.

36 Boston, 1989, pp.251–2.

37 Van der Sman, 1999, p.158.

38 Venice, 1999, p.560.

127

1 Bartsch VII.523.16; Hind, 1938–48, V, 153, 14; Levenson, Oberhuber and Sheehan, 1973, p.368, cat.no.141; Zucker, 1999, p.26, cat.no.016; Maastricht, 2003, p.43, cat.no.I.11.

2 For the earlier date see Hind, 1938–48, V, pp.144, 147 and Pignatti, 1973, pp.250–54. For a later date see Landau, 1994, p.77; Zucker, 1999, p.26, cat.no.016 and Venice, 1999, p.320, cat.no.63.

3 London, 2002, p.150, cat.no.85.

128

1 Bartsch XIII.384.10; Hind, 1938–48, V.211.4; Levenson, Oberhuber and Sheehan, 1973, p.428, cat.no.156.

2 Bartsch XIV.317.422.

3 Maastricht, 2003, p.114, cat.no.III.7. Compare, for example, Leonardo's drawing in the Accademia, Venice (Popham, 1946, p.155, cat.no.193B) with the man seen from the back at the lower right of the print.

129

1 Levenson, Oberhuber and Sheehan, 1973, p.432, cat.no.157; Bartsch XIII.381.6; Hind, 1938–48, V.210.2.

2 Hind, 1938–48, V.210.1.

130

1 Bartsch XV.67.3; Wethey, 1969, p.71, cat.no.10; Glasgow, 1994, p.18, cat.no.34.

2 Hope, 1980, p.102.

131

1 Hurt, 1971.

2 Klibansky, Panofsky and Saxl, 1964, pp.212–14.

3 27.5 × 42cm. See Jaffé, 1994, p.115, no.825; Cohen, 1996, I, p.710.

4 Ward-Jackson, 1979, p.124, no.250.

5 Bartsch XII.125.27(1).

6 Johnson, 1982, p.10.

7 D. Landau in London, 1983, p.335, cat.no.P35.

132

1 Wethey, 1969, pp.107–8, cat.no.63.

2 Humfrey, 1993, p.359, cat.no.96.

3 Roskill, 1968, pp.188–91.

4 Vasari, 1906, VII, p.437.

5 Berlin, 1971, p.45, cat.no.9–1; Washington, 1976, p.177, cat.no.35.

6 Baseggio, 1844, p.36, cat.no.19; Passavant, 1860–64, VI.233.53.

133

1 Vasari, 1906, V, p.433; Ridolfi, 1648, p.203.

2 Washington, 1976, p.150, cat.no.23.

3 D. Landau in London, 1983, p.340, cat.no.P42.

4 For the attribution to Boldrini see Baseggio, 1844, p.36, cat.no.20 and Passavant, 1860–64 VI. 235. 59; for Britto see Oberhuber, 1980, p.526.

134

1 Fabbro, 1977, p.238, cat.no.179 and p.244, cat.no.183; Wethey, 1987, pp.26–7.

2 Chiari, 1982, p.44, cat.no.1.

3 Bierens de Haan, 1948, p.151.

4 Mariette, 1969, p.281, note 8.

135

1 Van der Sman, 1994, p.109; Maastricht, 2003, p.164, cat.no.IV.13.

2 Bartsch XVI.122.10; G. Dillon in Venice, 1981, p.316, cat.no.152.

136

1 Bartsch XVI.125.19.

2 Wethey, 1969, p.90, cat.no.37.

137

1 Van der Sman, 1994, pp.108–9.

2 Bartsch XVI.129.29.

138

1 Bartsch XVI.155.4; Kornell, 1989, pp.313–14.

2 Bartsch XVI.141.69.

3 Kornell, 1989, pp.313–14.

4 British Museum, Department of Prints and Drawings, Payne Knight Bequest (acc.no.P.p.1, 50 – P.Anon.60).

5 Van der Sman, 1999, pp.2–3.

139

1 Passavant, 1860–64, VI.105.10; Edinburgh, 1990.

2 Bartsch XIV.200.247.

140

1 Rome, 1976, p.34, cat.no.12.

2 Edinburgh, 1990, p.11, 43, cat.no.4.

141

1 Sellink, 2000, II, cat.no.106.

142

1 Hope, 1980, p.126.

2 Wethey, 1987, pp.50–2, pp.158–9, cat.no.42.

3 Bierens de Haan, 1948, p.205, cat.no.222(1); Sellink, 2000, III, p.85, cat.no.192(1).

143

1 Sellink, 2000, II, pp.160–2, cat.no.120.

2 Fabbro, 1977, pp.239–41.

144

1 Bierens de Haan, 1948, p.174, cat.no.192; Sellink, 2000, III, p.78, cat.no.190(1).

2 Wethey, 1975, III, pp.156–60, cat.no.19A.

145

1 Bierens de Haan, 1948, cat.no.143, copy e; Catelli Isola, 1976, p.54, cat.no.84; Sellink, 2000, II, p.194, cat.no.132, copy c.

2 London, 2001, p.175.

146

1 Wethey, 1969, p.139, cat.no.114.

2 Wethey, 1969, p.140, cat.no.115.

3 For the print, see Bierens de Haan, 1948, pp.144–7, cat.nos.139–40; Sellink, 2000, II, p.176, cat.no.126.

147

1 Wethey, 1969, pp.153–5, cat.no.133.

2 Bartsch XVI.256.20 (second state, not described); Le Blanc, 1854–89, p.367, cat.no.24 (second state), Mauroner, 1943, p.62, cat.no.5.

3 Meilman, 2000, pl.I and p.201, no.6.

148

1 Bartsch XVI.196.33; Schmidt in Meyer, 1872–85, III, p.88, cat.no.53.

149

2 G. Dillon in Verona, 1980, p.267, XI.18; G. Dillon in Venice, 1981, p.320, cat.no.163; Florence, 2000, p.33, cat.no.12.

3 Bury, 2003, p.130.

149

1 Bartsch XVI.165.4; Albricci, 1980, p.20, cat.no.4; G. Dillon in Verona, 1980, p.278, cat.no.XI.42.

2 Respectively Bartsch XVI.166.6, Bartsch XVI.165.3, Bartsch XVI.167.7 and Passavant, 1860–64, VI.179.11.

150

1 Bartsch XVI.169.3 (II); Nagler, 1858–79, III, p.521, cat.no.1317 (2); Albricci, 1980, p.25, cat.no.3 (IV).

2 Respectively, Bartsch XVI.168.1 and Bartsch XVI.169.2.

3 Boston, 1989, p.65.

151

1 Rome, 1978, pp.26–7, cat.no.6; Washington, 1979, p.202, cat.no.104.

2 Bartsch XVIII.90.98; Bohn, 1995, pp.132–6, cat.no.100.

3 London, 2001, p.27.

152

1 Bartsch XVIII.69.63; Washington, 1979, pp.196–7, cat.no.101; Bohn, 1995, p.119, cat.no.096.

2 Another example of reversal is the *Ecce Homo* of 1587 after Correggio: see Washington, 1979, p.246, cat.no.143.

153

1 Wethey, 1971, p.143, cat.no.104, who dates it c.1550; Pedrocco, 2001, p.272, cat.no.234, who dates it to about 1562; D. Jaffé in London, 2003, pp.142–3, cat.no.28, who dates it around 1546–7.

2 London, 2001, p.212.

3 Washington, 1979, p.246, cat.no.143.

4 G. Gaetani, *Domus Caietana*, 3 vols., San Casciano, 1927–33, III, p.171. He was also known to have been very extravagant (see II, p.121).

5 A. Luzio, *La Galleria dei Gonzaga venduta all'Inghilterra nel 1627–8*, Rome, 1974, pp.273–4.

154

1 Mason Rinaldi, 1984, p.85, cat.no.96.

2 British Museum, Department of Prints and Drawings, shelf mark 197*.d.1, f.26v.

3 Bartsch XVI.294.26; Charlottesville, 1991, p.144, cat.no.59.

4 Archivio di Stato, Venezia, Senato Terra, Registri 81 (anno 1611) f.170r (189r new no.), 19 January 1611 (Venetian style).

5 Cicogna, 1824–53, V, 1842, pp.432–4; Pasero, 1935, p.352.

6 Bury, 1985, p.19.

7 Armenini, 1586, pp.53–4.

155

1 Hollstein XXI, 109.182; Bassano, 1992, p.28, cat.no.7.

156

1 Hollstein XXI, 216.14; Bassano, 1992, p.36, cat.no.13.

2 See London, 2001, p.202, cat.no.149.

157

1 Hollstein XL, 10.1(1); Bassano, 1992, p.73, cat.no.57.

158

1 Robertson, 1971, pp.721–6.

2 Hollstein, X, p.46; Chiari, 1982, p.114, cat.no.106; Ruggeri, 2001, p.216, cat.no.I.20.

3 *Notitia dove si ritrovano li originali di Titiano et Veronese intagliati da Valentino le Febre di Bruscellles et publicati da Giacomo van Campen in Venetia 1683*, Venice, 1683, p.6, no.28.

4 The shop is identified as 'in Ruga gagiuffa appresso il Forner'.

159

1 Hollstein, X, p.46; Chiari, 1982, p.101, cat.no.88.

BOOKS & MANUSCRIPTS

160

Standard references: Hain 6924; BMC V: 274 xxii; BM STC Italian 244.

1 *Bibliotheca Smithiana: a catalogue … by S. Baker and G. Leigh … January the 25th, 1773*. Day 5, item 822 or 823; A. Stewart (ed.) *Minute Book of the Faculty of Advocates* III, (1751–1783), Edinburgh, 1999, pp.246–7; Curators' Minutes for 12 February 1773 (Faculty Records, 119, held by the National Library of Scotland).

2 C.F. Bühler, 'The *Fasciculus Temporum* and Morgan Manuscript 801', *Speculum*, XXXVII, 1952, pp.178–83 and note 20.

3 M. Bingham Stillwell, 'The *Fasciculus Temporum*: A Genealogical Survey of Editions Before 1480' in *Bibliographical Essays: A Tribute to Wilberforce Eames*, Cambridge, Mass., 1924, pp.409–40.

4 C.F. Bühler, 'The Laying of a Ghost?: Observations on the 1483 Ratdolt Edition of the *Fasciculus Temporum*', *Studies in Bibliography*, IV, 1951–2, pp.155–9.

161

1 *Standard references:* Hain, *Repertorium* 6694; BM STC V 285–6; GW 9428; BM STC Italian 238; *Elementa Geometriae* sig. A1v.

2 Ratdolt's geometric designs have been described both as woodcuts (for example, in the BMC) and as metal plates (see M. Zorzi (ed.), *La Vita nei Libri: Edizione Illustrata del Quattro e Cinquecento dalla Fondazione Giorgio Cini*, Venice, 2003, p.301).

3 'Maler' is the German for 'painter', and Bernard describes himself as 'pictor' in his will, so the name may well be an epithet rather than a surname. The British Museum catalogue argues that Bernard was the man behind the decoration of Ratdolt's books.

4 This copy is now in the British Library.

162

Standard references: BM STC Italian 80; Brunet, I, 766.

1 John Cuno, cited in M. Lowry, *The World of Aldus Manutius*, Oxford, 1979, p.152.

2 Bembo, 1954, p.2.

3 C.H. Clough, 'Pietro Bembo's *Gli Asolani* of 1505', *MLN*, LXXXIV, 1969, pp.16–45, provides a full investigation of the different states of this edition.

4 Bembo, 1954, p.189.

163

Standard references: Mortimer, 1996, pp.7–87; BM STC Italian 391; Brunet, III, 1143.

1 This may be the Thomas Gaisford (1779–1855) who was Dean of Christ Church, Oxford, and whose collections were sold at auction in 1880 and 1890: see S. de Ricci, *English Collectors of Books & Manuscripts*, Cambridge, 1930, p.165.

2 Fairley was a friend of William Robert Reid (1854–1919), an Edinburgh businessman whose bequest of his collection of books at Lauriston Castle was received by the newly established National Library of Scotland in 1926. Fairley's books were purchased by the Reid Trustees and incorporated into the bequest.

3 B. Richardson, *Printing, Writers and Readers in Renaissance Italy*, Cambridge, 1999, pp.103–4.

164

Standard references: BM STC Italian 530; Brunet, IV, 778.

1 R. Dallington, *The Strife of Love in a Dreame*, was published in 1592.

2 W.A. Chatto, *A Treatise on Wood Engraving*, New York, 1881, p.218.

3 F. Colonna, *Hypnerotomachia Poliphili*, translated by J. Godwin, London, 2003, p.196.

165

Standard references: BM STC Italian 482; Brunet, IV, 294; Mortimer, 1996, p.39.

1 L. Ariosto, *Orlando Furioso*, Venice, 1584.

2 C. Ginsburg discusses Titian's use of Anguillara's translation as a source for *Diana and Actaeon* (cat.no.54) in 'Tiziano, Ovidio, e i codici della figurazione erotica nel '500', *Tiziano e Venezia: Convegno internazionale di studi (Venice, 1976)*, Vicenza, 1980, pp.125–35.

166

Standard references: BM STC Italian 713; Brunet, V, 1104.

167

Standard references: BM STC Italian 644; Brunet, IV, 320.

British Architectural Library, Royal Institute of British Architects, *Early Printed Books 1478–1840. Catalogue of the British Architectural Library Early Imprints Collection*, III, London, 1999, no.2386.

1 W. Lotz, *Architecture in Italy 1500–1600*, revised by D. Howard, New Haven and London, 1995, p.147.

2 J. Ackerman, *Palladio*, Harmondsworth, 1966, p.24.

3 Holberton, 1990, p.123.

4 Holberton, 1990, p.99.

168

1 Hale, 1977, p.37.

2 C. Duffy, *Siege Warfare. The Fortress in the Modern World, 1494–1660*, London, 1979, p.38.

3 Hale, 1977, p.25.

4 N. Adams and L. Nussdorfer, 'The Italian City, 1400–1600', in H.A. Millon (ed.), *Italian Renaissance Architecture from Brunelleschi to Michaelangelo*, London, 1996, p.228.

169

1 J.L. Nevinson, 'Illustrations of Costume in the *Alba Amicorum*', *Archaeologia*, 106, 1979, pp.167–76.

2 This appears opposite p.113.

170

1 For further information on this chart, see G. Tolias, *The Greek portolan charts, 15th–17th centuries: a contribution to the Mediterranean cartography of the modern period*, Athens, 1999, pp.94–5, 182.

2 See London, 2001, pp.171, 174.

SCULPTURE AND DECORATIVE ARTS

171

1 Similar coats of arms can be seen on the façade of the Villa Foscarini at Stra.

2 A. Rizzi, *Vere da Pozzo*, Venezia, 1992, p.139.

172–175

1 Compare, for example, Giovanni Bellini's San Zaccaria altarpiece already mentioned, and works by Marco Basaiti in Vienna (Van Marle, 1923–38, XVII, fig.305) and Cima da Conegliano in Berlin and Milan (Van Marle, 1923–38, XVII, figs.249, 268).

176

1 Pollard, 1984, I, cat.no.118.

2 J.S. Plaut, 'An Unknown Portrait of a Doge by Gentile Bellini', *Burlington Magazine*, LXX, 1937, pp.155–6.

3 Redina, 1984, pp.240–2.

177

1 Carried out by the Research Laboratory for Archaeology and History of Art, Oxford, on 15 July 1996.

2 Venturi, 1901–40, VI, p.455, fig.298.

3 Ibid., p.364, fig.227.

4 L. Planiscig, *Catalogo dei Bronzi Collezione Camillo Castiglione*, privately printed, Vienna, 1923.

5 Venturi, 1901–40, VI, p.449, fig.291; L. Puppi, *La Chiesa degli Eremitani a Padova*, Vicenza, 1970, pp.79–80.

6 See M.A. Michiel, 'Notizie d'opera del disegno' in *Der Anonimo Morelliano*, (ed.) T. Frimmel, Vienna, 1888, p.26.

7 Ibid., p.451, fig.295. Schubring and Bode also favoured this attribution.

8 Venturi, 1901–40, VI, pp.451–2.

9 F. Schottmüller, *Die Italienischen und Spanischen Bildwerke der Renaissance und des Barocks*, Berlin, 1913, IV, pp.109–10, cat.no.268.

10 Venturi, 1901–40, VI, pp.434–48, figs.285–6.

178

1 Robinson, 1865, p.67, cat.no.808.

2 Pope-Hennessy, 1965, pp.133–4, cat.no.491, figs.478–80.

3 Radcliffe, 1992, pp.194–203, cat.no.31.

4 It was first questioned by Wixom in Cleveland, 1975, cat.no.76. The attribution to Severo was upheld in Frankfurt, 1985, pp.522–3, cat.nos.238–9. A magnificent double casket of this form, and also a triangular sandbox with identical relief decoration, are in the Bargello, Florence: see Toderi and Vannel Toderi, 1996, pp.116–17, cat.nos.210–11 (where, however, Radcliffe's arguments were overlooked and the attribution to Severo da Ravenna was retained).

5 Radcliffe, 1992, pp.201–2.

6 The argument proposed by Radcliffe that they originated in Rome does not exclude the contention of Pope-Hennessy, Wixom and the Toderis that many of these caskets were indeed made in Padua.

179

1 For Bellano's relationship with Donatello, see F. Negri Arnoldi, 'Bellano e Bertoldo nella bottega di Donatello', *Prospettiva*, XXXIII–XXXIV, 1983–4, pp.93–101. For an overview of Bellano, see V. Krahn, *Bartolomeo Bellano: Studien zur Paduaner Plastik des Quattrocento*, Munich, 1988.

2 Detroit, 1985, pp.104–6, cat.no.11.

180

1 Robinson, 1865, p.67, cat.no.809 (as 'Florentine quattro-cento bronze').

2 H. Weihrauch, *Europäische Bronzestatuetten: 15–18 Jahrhundert*, Brunswick, 1967, pp.98–100, fig.103;

J.D. Draper in Detroit, 1985, pp.225–6, cat.no.82; Padua, 2001, pp.162–3, cat.no.35 (entry by J. Warren).

3 P.M. de Winter, 'Recent Accessions of Italian Renaissance Decorative Arts, Part 1, incorporating Notes on the Sculptor Severo da Ravenna', *The Bulletin of the Cleveland Museum of Art*, March 1986, pp.121–3, figs.122–4; A. Radcliffe 'Replicas, copies and counterfeits of early Italian Bronzes', *Apollo*, CXXIV, 1986, pp.183–8; V. Krahn, *Bronzetti Veneziani: Die venezianischen Kleinbronzen der Renaissance aus dem Bode-Museum Berlin*, Berlin, 2003, pp.208–10, cat.no.62.

4 C. Avery and A. Radcliffe, 'Severo Calzetta da Ravenna: New Discoveries' in Jörg Rasmussen (ed.), *Studien zum europäischen Kunsthandwerk in Festschrift Yvonne Hackenbroch*, Munich, 1983, pp.107–22.

5 S. Bernicoli, 'Arte e Artisti in Ravenna', *Felix Ravenna*, 1914, p.554 (90). Further notes by Anne Markham Schulz, dated 30 October 1990, in NMS files.

181

1 This form, taken from Antique bronzes, was used by Giulio Romano (*c*.1499–1546) for the design of an elaborate incense burner, or lamp, probably originally intended to be made in precious metal. See M. Jaffé, *The Devonshire Collection of Italian Drawings: Roman and Neapolitan Schools*, London, 1994, p.118, cat.no.233.

2 See Radcliffe, 1992, pp.206–9.

3 Cleveland, 1975, cat.no.94, under which are listed seven similar Severo workshop bronze containers; others are discussed in Avery and Radcliffe, 1983. For another variant supporting a boy carrying a shell, but with a narrower frieze, lion's paw feet and pendant anthemion, see C. Avery, *Renaissance and Baroque Bronzes in the Frick Art Museum*, Pittsburgh, 1993, p.52, fig.7.1.

182

1 Planiscig, 1927, pp.327–68, figs.380–2, 386.

2 M. de Wilde, *Signa Antiquae Museo J. De Wilde*, Amsterdam, 1703.

3 Avery and Radcliffe, 1983, pp.107–11. The signed example was sold at Christie's, London, 8 July 1981 (lot 341).

4 Frankfurt, 1985, pp.449–54, cat.nos.148–55.

5 Frankfurt, 1985, cat.no.150. See further J. Warren in Padua, 2001, cat.no.34.

6 Frankfurt, 1985, pp.455–6, cat.nos.156–7.

183

1 D. Lewis, 'The Plaquettes of Moderno and his Followers' in Luchs, 1989, p.107, fig.2.

184

1 D. Lewis, 'The Plaquettes of Moderno and his Followers' in Luchs, 1989, p.114, fig.10.

2 By Wixom in Cleveland, 1975, under cat.no.45.

185

1 For the Donati medal, see Hill, 1930, cat.no.530.

2 Planiscig, 1927, pp.453–4.

187

1 Pope-Hennessy, 1965, p.65, cat.no.217, fig.114. For a technical examination of the two Washington versions see S. Sturman and B. Berrie, 'Technical Examination of Riccio Plaquettes', in Luchs, 1989, pp.175–88, figs.8, 12a and 12b. Three further examples are in Toderi and Vannel Toderi, 1996, pp.110–11, cat.nos 199–201.

2 As noted by Molinier, 1886, I, p.170. For Mocetto's engraving see Hind, 1938–48, V, p.163, pl.721.

3 Planiscig, 1927, fig.487.

188

1 Pope-Hennessy, 1965, p.69.

2 B. Jestaz, 'Riccio et Ulocrino' in Luchs, 1989, pp.191–202.

189

1 Cleveland, 1975, cat.no.99. Other close parallels are: an inkwell formerly in the J.P. Morgan collection with a triton on the lid, dolphins and a miniature ocean (W. von Bode, *Bronzes in the Collection of J. Pierpont Morgan*, Paris, 1910, I, cat.no.46, pl.XXX); an oil lamp in the Kunsthistorisches Museum, Vienna, designed either to rest on a surface, or be suspended from a chain from above (Frankfurt, 1985, p.501, cat.no.209); and a sand box in the Staatliche Museen, Berlin (Frankfurt, 1985, p.525, cat.no.242).

2 J. Carrington 'A new look at Desiderio da Firenze and the Paduan voting urn', *Bollettino del Museo Civico di Padova*, LXXIII, 1984, pp.105–45.

3 London, Victoria and Albert Museum, *Italian Bronze Statuettes*, exh. cat. by J. Pope-Hennessy *et al.*, 1961, cat.no.74.

190

1 Brigstocke, 1993, pp.195–6, where no attempt was made to discuss the form of inkstand or its maker.

191

1 T. Clifford, 'Mosca's Relief of "Mucius Scaevola"', *National Art Collections Fund Review*, LXXXVI, 1989, pp.144–6; Markham Schulz, 1998, I, pp.234–46, cat.nos.1–7, II, pls.81–106.

2 A. Ballarin, *Il Camerino delle Pitture di Alfonso I*, 5 vols., 2002–4 (last volume forthcoming); C. Hope, 'I Camerini d'alabastro: la collocazione e la

decorazione pittorica', in Ferrara, 2004, pp.83–96.

3 Markham Schulz, 1998, I, pp.237–9, cat.nos.4A–C; Ferrara, 2004, cat.nos.72–4.

4 Markham Schulz, 1998, I, pp.248–52, cat.no.10, II, pls.69–80. The relief is by Mosca and his assistants Pietro Paolo Stella and Giuliano Fiorentino and was carved between July and December 1523.

5 Markham Schulz, I, pp.252–5, cat.no.11, II, pl.33.

6 See Markham Schulz, 1998, II, pls.88–9 for the inscriptions.

192

1 P. Meller, 'Riccio's Satyress Triumphant: Its source and its meaning?', *The Bulletin of the Cleveland Museum of Art*, 63, 1976, pp.324–34. For the Clerk relief, see especially the entry by M. de Vincenti in Padua, 2001, cat.no.65.

2 L. Planiscig, 'Per il quarto centenario della morte di Tullio Lombardo e di Andrea Riccio,' *Dedalo*, 1932, pp.923–4; G. Lorenzetti and L. Planiscig, '*La Collezione dei Conti Donà dalle Rose a Venezia*', Venice, 1934, cat.no.238, pl.XXXVI, fig.71; Cleveland, 1975, cat.no.91; Frankfurt, 1985, pp.456–8, cat.no.158 (as Riccio).

3 Washington, National Gallery of Art, *Renaissance Master Bronzes from the Collections of the Kunsthistorisches Museum, Vienna*, exh. cat. by M Leithe-Jasper, Washington, 1986, pp.132–3, cat.no.27. Adolfo Venturi (1901–40, X.I, p.436, fig.332) had already, in fact, illustrated the Donà dalle Rose *Satyress* and advanced the attribution to Mosca.

193

1 For the iconography of Cleopatra, see Geneva, Musée Rath, *Cléopâtre dans le miroir de l'art occidental*, Musée Rath, exh. cat., 2004. Compare especially Michelangelo's drawing of Cleopatra at the Casa Buonarotti, Florence of *c*.1535 (Inv.2F),

2 L. Planiscig, 'Simone Bianco', *Belvedere*, V, 1924, pp.157–63; U. Schlegel, 'Simone Bianco und die venezianische Malerei,' Mitteilungen des Kunsthistorishen Institutes in Florenz, XXIII, 1979, pp.187–96; I. Favaretto, 'Simone Bianco: Uno scultore del XVI secolo di fronte all'antica', *Numismatica e antichità plastiche. Quaderni ticinesi*, XIV, 1985, pp.405–22; U. Schlegel, 'Eine unbekannte Bust von Simone Bianco', *Antologia di Belle Arti*, 1990, 35–8, pp.148–52.

3 P. Meller, 'Marmi e bronzi di Simone Bianco', *Mitteilungen des Kunsthistorishen Institutes in Florenz*, XXI, 1977, pp.199–210.

4 Pietro Aretino, *Lettere sull'arte*, (eds.) F. Pertile and E. Camesasca, Milan, 1957–60, I, p.120.

5 A. Luchs, *Tullio Lombardo and Ideal Portrait Sculpture in Venice 1490–1530*, Cambridge, 1995, pp.103–14.

196

1 A. Hobson, 'Medals on book bindings', *The Medal*, 27, 1995, pp.3–11.

197

1 Rendina, 1984, pp.285–91.

198

1 Hill and Pollard, 1967, cat.no.416a.

199

1 It was not included in Burns, Collareta and Gasparotto, 2000; nor was it mentioned in Kris, 1929.

2 Burns, Collareta and Gasparotto, 2000, pp.321–2, cat.nos.23–4 (under questionable attributions).

200

1 By G. Pollard in Hill and Pollard, 1967, cat.no.484c. However, the connection with the medal by Bernardi mentioned by Vasari was upheld by V. Donati, *Pietre Dure e Medaglie del Rinascimento: Giovanni da Castel Bolognese*, Ferrara, 1989, pp.62–3, pl.IV.

202

1 Recorded as 'A Raised Portrait of Titian holding a small Portrait in his hand, in Black Wood Frame. 5 in diameter' in the Hamilton Palace inventory of 1876 (see Hamilton, Hamilton Central Library, *Inventory of The Furniture Pictures Articles of Vertu &c &c &c at Hamilton Palace 1876*, p.8.).

2 London, 1981, cat.no.73

3 See Hope, 1990, pp.59–60. In a letter dated 12 March 2004, Charles Hope notes that the lost Titian self-portrait is clearly described in an inventory of Philip's possessions, given to his 'guardjoyas' Gil Sanchez up to 31 December 1553: 'Un retrapto de Ticiano, que tiene delante de sí en las manos un retrapto pequeño de Su Alteza armado con una banda roja' (M. Kushe, 'La antigua galería de retratos del Pardo', *Archivo Español de Arte*, LXIV, 1991, pp.276ff., doc.1). I am most grateful to Professor Hope for this reference.

4 An example of the bronze medal is illustrated in Hope, 1990, fig.4, and in Woods-Marsden, 1998, p.164, pl.104. The bronzed lead specimen in Bowdoin College Museum of Art, Brunswick, Maine, is published in Norris and Weber, 1976, fig.64.

5 G.F. Hill, 'Some Italian Medals of the Sixteenth Century' in *George Habich zum 60. Geburtstag*, Munich, 1928, pp.11–12.

6 An example of the medal of Foscho is illustrated in D. Thornton, *The Scholar in his Study: Ownership and Experience in Renaissance Italy*, New Haven and London, 1997, p.73 (with an incorrect attribution to Alessandro Ardenti).

7 E.J. Pyke in London, 1981, pp.138–9; Pyke, 1981, p.35 and pl.315.

8 By the dealers Kugel's, from whom the wax was purchased by the National Museums.

9 It is worth drawing attention not only to Abondio's work for the Austrian rulers and aristocracy, but to the signed wax of the *Archduke Ferdinand II of Tyrol* by the Paduan sculptor Francesco Segala, which was apparently modelled in Innsbruck around 1580, and the wax of *Leda and the Swan* attributed to Segala. Both are now in the Kunsthistorisches Museum, Vienna, and are illustrated and discussed in W. Seipel (ed.), *Spielwelten der Kunst Kunstkammerspiele*, Milan and Vienna, 1998, pp.78–81.

10 Lennoxlove, Hamilton Archive, bundle 935, letter from Lord Archibald Hamilton to Alexander, Marquess of Douglas (later 10th Duke of Hamilton), undated but probably written in February 1816.

11 One of these cabinets is now on long-term loan from Brooklyn Museum to the Metropolitan Museum of Art, New York. The other, which was also owned by Brooklyn Museum, was sold at Christie's, New York, 26 April 1990 (lot 170) and, again, at Christie's, London, 6 July 2000 (lot 100). There is an excellent illustration of it in F. Lennox-Boyd (ed.), *Masterpieces of English Furniture: The Gerstenfeld Collection*, London, 1998, pp.152–3.

12 I am very much obliged to Charles Hope, Peter Humfrey, Jennifer Fletcher and Jeremy Warren for examining and discussing the wax at a meeting at the Wallace Collection, London, on 23 April 2004.

203

1 See the entry by T. Clifford in Edinburgh, 2000, pp.122–3, cat.no.42.

2 For Sansovino as a sculptor, see Boucher, 1991.

3 See Trent, 1999, pp.16–19. Sadly one arm of this statue has recently been broken off and apparently stolen.

4 Boucher, 1991, II, cat.no.13, pl.v and figs.93–5; Trent, 1999, pp.214–17, cat.no.12.

5 Ibid., figs.451–2; Ibid., p.129, fig.4, pp.352–3, cat.no.78.

204 & 205

1 E. Mandowsky, '"The Origin of the Milky Way' in the National Gallery', *Burlington Magazine*, LXXII, 1938, pp.88–93; Gould, 1975, pp.259–61.

2 E. Weddigen, 'Thomas Philologus Ravennas', *Saggi e Memorie di Storia dell'Arte*, 9, 1974, pp.45–7; Pollard, 1984, III, pp.1289–91, cat.nos.751, 751a and 752.

3 See Trent, 1999, cat.nos.43 (Vittoria), 45–6 (Pagano).

206

1 Kunstkammer, acc. no.5662; L. Planiscig, *Venezianische Bildhauer der Renaissance*, Vienna, 1921, pp.473–5, figs.497, 499 (as Vittoria); Trent, 1999, cat.no.78. Another much poorer cast is in the National Gallery of Prague: see Duisburg, 1994, cat.no.18, where further casts are cited in the Museo d'Arte Antica, Milan and the Museo Correr, Venice.

2 M. Leithe-Jasper, *Alessandro Vittoria, Beiträge zur Analyse seiner figürlichen Plastiken unter Berücksichtigung der Berziehungen zur gleichzeitigen Malerei in Venedig*, unpublished doctoral dissertation, Vienna, 1963. A date rather later in Vittoria's career was proposed by V.J. Avery, *The Early Works of Alessandro Vittoria*, unpublished doctoral dissertation, Cambridge, 1996.

3 Victoria and Albert Museum acc.nos.A.18-1961 and A.19-1961. See P. Motture, 'The Production of Firedogs in Renaissance Venice', in Motture, 2003, pp.294, fig.20, 297, cat.no.6. Another version of this model also belongs to the Victoria and Albert Museum (acc.no.A.104-1956; Motture, 2003, p.297, cat.no.8).

207

1 London, Heim Gallery, *Sculptures of the 15th and 16th Centuries*, dealer catalogue, 1972, cat.no.32.

2 Trent, 1999, cat.no.54. The bust was overlooked by T. Martin, *Alessandro Vittoria and the Portrait Bust in Renaissance Venice*, Oxford, 1998, but was noted in passing in T. Martin, 'New Discoveries and Old Problems in Alessandro Vittoria's Portrait Busts', *Sculpture Journal*, VI, 2001, pp.36–48.

3 Trent, 1999, cat.nos.50, 62.

208

1 Edinburgh, National Gallery of Scotland, *The Exhibition of Industrial and Decorative Art*, 1861, cat.no.504 ('Two very fine Venetian bronze knockers in high relief, one with a figure of Jupiter in the centre, the other with a figure of Neptune. – [lent by] R. Napier, Esq'). It was subsequently catalogued by Robinson, 1865, pp.69–70, cat.no.844.

2 London, Daniel Katz Ltd and Edinburgh, National Gallery of Scotland, *Renaissance Master Bronzes from the Ashmolean Museum, Oxford: The Fortnum Collection*, exh. cat. by J. Warren, London, 1999, pp.78–9, cat.no.23.

3 Trent, 1999, pp.350–1, under cat.no.77.

4 Florence, Museo Nazionale del Bargello, *Bronzetti e anticaglie della guardaroba di Cosimo I*, exh. cat. ed. by A.M. Massinelli, Florence, 1991, pp.70–1, fig.61.

5 F. Cessi, *Alessandro Vittoria, bronzista (1525–1608)*, Trent, 1960, pp.41–2, fig.5; Penny, 1992, I, pp.246–7, cat.no.181; Trent, 1999, cat.no.77 (for the most authoritative recent discussion of this model).

6 Acc. nos.A.1877.20.47, also from the Napier collection, and 1872.5.6.2, bought from T. Chapman, Edinburgh. Similar doorknockers, 40cm high, were sold in the nineteenth-century by J. Michieli e Figli of Venice and were offered for sale in the French version of their catalogue (J. Michieli & Fils, *Collection de bronzes d'art de la fonderie récompenseé*, Venice, n.d., no.82, pl.XXVII): see A.P. Darr (*et al.*), *Catalogue of Italian Sculpture in the Detroit Institute of Arts*, 2 vols., Detroit, 2002, II, cat.no.275.

7 See Planiscig, 1921, pp.475–8, pl.502; Weihrauch, 1967, pp.152–5, fig.183 (the Vienna example); W. von Bode, *The Italian Bronze Statuettes of the Renaissance,* (revised edn. by J.D. Draper), New York, 1980, cat.no 213, pl.CLXXV; J. Balogh, *Katalog der ausländischen Bildwerke des Museums der Bildenden Künste in Budapest*, Budapest 1975, I, p.164–5, cat.no.213; Van Binnebeke, 1994, pp.78–9, cat.no.16. There are two examples of the doorknocker at the Museo Correr, one of them considerably smaller than the other.

8 Weihrauch, 1967, p.155, fig.182.

9 Planiscig, 1921, pp.582, 585, fig.646.

209

1 Edinburgh, National Gallery of Scotland, *The Exhibition of Industrial and Decorative Art*, 1861, cat.no.504 ('Two very fine Venetian bronze knockers in high relief, one with a figure of Jupiter in the centre, the other with a figure of Neptune – [lent by] R. Napier, Esq.'). See also Weihrauch, 1967, pp.152–3, fig.178.

2 Weihrauch, 1967, pp.152, 154, fig.179.

210

1 Paul Petau (or Paulus Petavius) reproduced a cast of this bronze as an antique in his *Antiquariae supellectilis portiuncula* (Paris, 1609 or 10). Petau (1568–1614) was one of Henri IV's ministers, a keen antiquary and numismatist: see: J. Yvon, 'Petau numismate', *Gazette des beaux-arts*, LXVIII, 1966, pp.113–30, no.108.

2 Acc.no.OA 6413; acquired by the Louvre in 1910.

3 Charles Patin (Carolus Patinus) in his *Imperatorum Romanorum: Numismata ex aere mediae et minimae formae*, Paris, 1697, facing p.129, as an antique, and by B. de Montfauçon *Antiquité expliquée*, I (supplément), p.160, pl.61.

4 Penny, 1992, pp.290–2, cat.no.229.

5 W. von Bode, *The Italian Bronze Statuette of the Renaissance*, London, 1908, p.78, fig.94.

211

1 W. Timofiewitsch, *Girolamo Campagna: Studien zur venezianischen Plastik um des Jahr 1600*, Munich, 1972, figs.62–8 and 54–9 respectively.

2 Planiscig, 1921, pp.570, 572, pls.627–8. Commissioned in 1592 and completed by February 1593. See B. Boucher in London, 1983, pp.358–9, cat.nos.S1, S2. The best study of Aspetti's bronzes is C. Kryza-Gersch, 'Original Ideas and their Reproduction in Venetian Foundries: Tiziano Aspetti's *Mars* in the Frick Collection – A Case Study' in Pincus, 2001, pp.142–57. See also C. Kryza-Gersch, *Studien zu Tiziano Aspetti*, unpublished doctoral dissertation, University of Vienna, 1996.

3 Acc.no.NMSk.2260: see L.O. Larsson, *European Bronzes 1450–1700*, Swedish National Art Museums, Stockholm, 1992, pp.24–5, cat.no.3.

212

1 For this plaquette see Molinier, 1886, II, p.118, n. 573; Bange, 1922, p.124, cat.no.94; Middeldorf and Goetz, 1944, cat.no.185; O. Zastrow, *Musei e Gallerie di Milano: Museo d'Arti Applicate: Oreficerie*, Milan, 1993, pp.173–4, cat.no.121 (a magnificent example mounted as a pax, in silvered and gilded back, with a damascened back); Toderi and Vannel Toderi, 1996, cat.no.282.

2 W. von Bode, *Die italienischen Bronzen*, Berlin, 1904, p.122, no.1273.

3 Middeldorf and Goetz, 1944, p.28, no.185. There it is noted that the plaquette could have been by either Vittoria or Campagna, who were both working at Santi Giovanni e Paolo at the same moment.

4 C. Davis, 'Jacopo Sansovino and the Italian Plaquette', in Luchs, 1989, pp.265–89, especially pp.283–4. Curiously, the San Moisè *paliotto* is signed by the founders Jean Chenet and Marin Feron: see Kryza-Gersch, 1998, pp.111–26. For Chenet and Feron, see U. Thieme and F. Becker, *Allgemeines Künstler Lexicon*, VI, Leipzig, 1912, p.457.

213

1 C. Avery, *Studies in European Sculpture*, London, 1981, pp.66, 76–7, pls.9, 11, where related bronzes in Washington, Vienna and Berlin are listed. Another cast, with a seated satyr on the cover, is in Toronto: see K. Corey Keeble, *European Bronzes in the Royal Ontario Museum*, Toronto, 1982, pp.84–5, cat.no.39. Another cast, ascribed to the workshop of Giuseppe de Levis, is in Vicenza: see D. Banzato (*et al.*), *Placchette, bronzetti e cristalli incisi dei Musei Civici di Vicenza: Secoli XV–XVIII*, Vicenza, 1997, pp.109–10, cat.no.130.

2 Planiscig, 1921, pp.602, 612, pl.665;

C. List, *Kleinbronzen Europas vom Mittelalter bis zur Gegenwart*, Munich, 1983, pp.112–13, fig.66.

3 C. Avery, *Renaissance and Baroque Bronzes in the Frick Art Museum*, Pittsburgh, 1993, pp.68–9, cat.no.14.

214

1 Radcliffe, 1992, pp.238–9, cat.no.42 and note 11; Kryza-Gersch, 1998.

2 Pope-Hennessy, 1965, cat.no.486, figs.571–2.

3 Trinity Fine Art Ltd, London, *An Exhibition of Old Master Drawings and European Works of Art*, at Newhouse Galleries, New York, 1994, pp.118–19, cat.no.56.

215

1 F. Russell, *John, 3rd Earl of Bute, Patron and Collector*, London, 2004, p.162.

2 C. Avery, 'Busy and Picturesque: the 3rd Earl of Bute's rediscovered bronze firedogs cast by Andrea di Alessandro Baruzzi, il Bresciano (1530–1569)', *Christie's International Magazine*, July-August 1996, pp.24–5; C. Avery, 'Une Histoire à Transformations', *Connaissance des Arts*, 544, 1997, pp.89–95; 'Recent acquisitions in Edinburgh Museums, 1995–1997', *Burlington Magazine*, CXXXIX, 1997, p.580, fig.IV.

3 P. Motture, 'The Production of Firedogs in Renaissance Venice' in Motture, 2003, pp.276–307. The Bute andiron is discussed on pp.279–83, figs.4–6 and in appendix I, p.296, cat.no.4, with technical discussion of the core. It has not yet been subjected to EDXRF or other quantitative alloy analysis. X-radiographs show that the core is still in place. Fine core-pin holes are apparent in the left breast, upper right arm, lower torso (two places) and left leg of Jupiter.

4 Motture, 2003, pp.282, 284 fig.7, 303 note 22.

5 Motture, 2003, pp.282, 285 fig.8, where it is suggested that the Adonis is taken from a late model by Campagna, observing the similarity to Campagna's marble statue of *St Lawrence* of about 1615–1617 in the church of San Lorenzo, Venice.

6 It has not been noted that the curious short wings of the satyr and satyress, are similar to those of the dragon on Roccatagliata's bronze statuette of *St George* in San Giorgio Maggiore, while St George's awkward pose and tilt of the head remind one of the Victoria and Albert Museum Adonis figure. Indeed, the connections between Campagna and Roccatagliata are at times so close that one wonders whether Campagna may have provided models for Roccatagliata's bronzes.

7 C. Avery, 'Not Quite Sansovino and Not Quite Vittoria: Andrea di Alessandri, called Il Bresciano', with a documentary appendix by V. Avery, *Sculpture Journal*, 9, 2003, pp.46–61.

8 See the entry by P. Motture and N. Penny, in *The Walpole Society*, 60, (*The Ford Collection*), 2 vols., II, p.273, cat.no.RBF588.

9 E. Harris, *The Genius of Robert Adam: His Interiors*, New Haven and London, 2001, pp.251, 253, 359 note 39, fig.372. This gives an excellent idea of the appearance and furnishings of the withdrawing room, but the author confuses the pairs of bronzes.

10 London, 1983, p.238, cat.no.141. The andirons may have come from Palazzo Soranzo di Rio Marino, Venice. This palace is described in Sansovino, 1581, p.393: 'In Rio Marino è degno di memoria quello [palazzo] de Soranzi per costruttura, per marmi, per magnifiche stanze, per ampie Sale, per ricche, e pretiose supellettili, e per gl'ornamenti Specialmente di Eccellenti pitture.'

216

1 G. Rosa, *I mobili nelle Civiche Raccolte Artistiche di Milano*, Milan, 1963, pp.37–8, cat.no.65.

2 A. Feulner, *Kunstgeschicte des Möbels*, Berlin, 1927, p.93, n.84.

3 L. Faenson (*et al.*), *Italian Cassoni in the Hermitage (and other collections in the USSR*), Leningrad, 1983, cat.nos.47–51.

4 Allentown, Art Museum, *Beyond Nobility: Art for the Private Citizen in the Early Renaissance*, exh. cat. ed. by E. Callmann, 1980–81, pp.69–70. Callmann argued for a date of *c*.1520, which is manifestly too early – judging by the style of the cartouche around the lock – and saw a connection with Mantegna. She drew attention to yet another *cassone* of this pattern at Cleveland (*Handbook of Cleveland Museum of Art*, Cleveland, Ohio, 1966, p.99). The front panel of another similar walnut *cassone* decorated with a triumph of Neptune was offered by Sotheby's, London, 7 July 1999 (lot 68), where it was described as Florentine *c*.1560 and incorrectly connected to Buontalenti.

217 & 218

1 Thornton, 1991, pp.168–71.

2 Recorded in the inventory of Hieronimo Pollano, Venice, 1590. An inventory of Zarlino, Chapel Master of St Marco, Venice, 1589, lists twelve 'scagni di nogara' of which six were 'col pozo' and six 'senza pozo' (both inventories cited in Thornton, 1991, p.364).

3 Sale Christie's, South Kensington, 19 April 1996 (lot 11). Pen and brown ink over black chalk, 23.7 × 15.2cm.

4 See Vicenza, 1980, pp.66–73; B. Mazza, 'Bernardino India' in P. Brugnoli (ed.), *Maestri della pittura veronese*, Vicenza, 1974, pp.253–60.

5 Sotheby's, New York, 14 January 1987 (lot 26). Another India drawing in a private collection closely relates to an

allegorical chimneypiece in Palazzo Manuelli-Guarienti, Verona: see L. Attardi, 'Alessandro Vittoria e l'origine dei cimieri ornati nel camino veneto' in L. Finocchi Ghersi (ed.), *Alessandro Vittoria e l'arte veneta della maniera* (Atti del convegno internazionale di studi, Università di Udine, 26–27 Ottobre 2000, pp.41–56, fig.107.

6 This type of knocker, such as the example in the Bode Museum, Berlin (Planiscig, 1921, p.577, pl.635), has been traditionally attributed to Tiziano Aspetti.

7 See Verona, 1980, pp.260–2, cat.no.XI, 7.

219 & 220

1 C. Alberici, *Il Mobile Veneto*, Milan, 1980, p.60, fig.75.

221

1 M.L. Pixley, 'Islamic artefacts and cultural currents in the art of Carpaccio', *Apollo*, CLVII, 2003, pp.9–18, figs.12, 14, 18; Pazzi, 1993, pp.489–90.

2 M-H. Jordan and F. Costantini Lachat, 'Moorish Tracery' in A. Gruber (ed.), *The Renaissance and Mannerism in Europe*, Paris and New York, 1994, pp.275–346; L.A. Mayer, *Islamic Metalworkers and their Works*, Geneva, 1955; A.S. Melikian-Chivrani in *Bulletin d'études orientales*, XXXVII, Damascus, 1974–5, pp.111–26; S. Auld, *Veneto-Saracenic Metalwork: Objects and History*, unpublished doctoral dissertation, University of Edinburgh, 1989; Venice, Palazzo Ducale, *Eredità dell'Islam: Arte islamica in Italia*, exh. cat. ed. by G. Curatola, Venice, 1993–4. However, on its acquisition in 1926 the present candlestick was registered as 'Venetian, 15th century (under Persian influence)'. See also Auld, 2004.

3 Zoppino, *Esemplario di Lavori*, Venice, 1529, reprinted by Christian Egenolff as *Die Modelbuch*, Frankfurt, 1533.

223

1 H. Lavoix, 'Les Azziministes', *Gazette des Beaux Arts*, XII, 1862, pp.64–74. This idea discounted by H. Huth, 'Sarazenen in Venedig' in P. Block and G. Zick (eds.), *Festschrift für Heinz Ladendorf*, Cologne, 1970, pp.58–68. See also: J. W. Allan, 'Venetian-Saracenic Metalwork: the Problems of Provenance' in E. J. Grube (ed.), *Venezia e l'Oriente Vicino. Atti del Primo Congresso Inter-nationale sull'arte Veneziana e l'arte islamica*, Venice, 1989, pp.167-83. See also Auld, 2004.

224

1 U. Krempel, 'Smalti' in *I Quaderni dell'Antiquariato: Smalti, Gioielli, Tabacchiere*, Milan, 1981, pp.11–23; Pazzi, 1993, pp.475–87. One of the most distinguished pieces is a domestic altar encrusted with pearls and with the arms of the Donà dalle Rose family,

which is now in the Scuola Grande di San Rocco (Pazzi, 1993, fig.487).

225

1 Acc.no.S.378; Tait, 1979, cat.no.9, as late fifteenth century.

227

1 Acc.no.73-5-2-109; Tait, 1979, cat.no.63 (as Venetian, second half of the fifteenth century).

2 Venice, 1982, pp.112–13, cat.no.133.

3 Brigstocke, 1993, pp.144–6, where the glass vessels are not discussed. Sarto also painted for Domenico di Jacopo and his wife an altarpiece (now in Palazzo Pitti, Florence) for the castle of Gambassi in Valdelsa (between Volterra and Fiorenza). Gambassi was an important centre for glass-blowers.

4 See G. Taddei, *L'Arte del vetro in Firenze*, Florence, 1954.

229

1 Venice, 1982, pp.105–8, cat.nos.118–22.

2 Acc.no.S.375; Tait, 1979, cat.no.6, as Venetian about 1500.

230

1 Tait, 1979, cat.nos.223–4.

2 B. Klesse, *Kataloge des Kunstgewerbermuseums Köln. I: Glas*, Cologne, 1963, cat.no.169.

3 Hugh Tait in *Masterpieces of Glass*, exh. cat., British Museum, London, 1968, cat.no.230.

232

1 Acc.no.S.644; Tait, 1979, cat.no.102, as late sixteenth century.

235

1 Possibly identical with the Venetian founder and dealer Michelangelo Guggenheim (1837-1914).

2 See further Curnow, 1992, cat.no.48.

3 London, 1987, cat.no.251. See also Conton, 1940; F. Saccardo and S. Gai, *Ceramica veneta dal XIV al XVIII secolo dal Meschio al Livenza*, Venice and Pordenone, 1987.

4 Planiscig, 1927, p.486, cat.no.151 (as Riccio); L. Planiscig (revised by A. Santangelo), *La collezione Auriti*, Rome, Museo di Palazzo Venezia, 1964, p.15, pl.4; Berlin, Staatliche Museen, Bodemuseum, *Italienische Bronzen der Renaissance aus der Sammlung der Ermitage in Leningrad*, exh. cat., Berlin, 1978, cat.nos.10–11; Van Binnebeke, 1994, pp.62–3, cat.no.9; Duisburg, 1994, pp.249–50, cat.no.116.

5 M. Jaffé, *The Devonshire Collection of Italian Drawings: Roman and Neapolitan Schools*, London, 1994, p.116, cat.no.230; U. Bazzotti, 'Disegni per argenterie' in E.H. Gombrich et al., *Giulio Romano*, Milan, 1989, p.458. Bazzotti rightly observed that as the 'tortoise' sits on a bed of shells, Giulio's design was for a salt and not an ink.

236

1 See further Curnow, 1992, cat.no.49.

2 Compare Rackham, 1977, I, cat.nos.1400 and 1406, particularly the handles.

3 Modena, Palazzo dei Musei, *La ceramica graffita in Emilia-Romagna dal secolo XIV al secolo XIX*, exh. cat. by G.L. Reggi, Modena, 1971, cat.no.249.

237

1 See further Curnow, 1992, cat.no.50.

2 Rackham, 1977, I, cat.no.1009. For similar examples see London, 1987, cat.no.252 (a large bowl with *istoriato* scene); and Conton, 1940, pp.182–3, where fragments from the Venetian lagoon are illustrated that were painted with similar landscapes.

238 & 239

1 Such vases were also copied in Sicily, and this may suggest that the pots were made in Venice, filled with conserved fruit in southern Italy or Sicily and then exported in Venetian boats to the Low Countries. See T. Wilson, 'Maiolica in Renaissance Venice,' *Apollo*, CXXV, 1987, pp.184–9.

2 Lessmann, 1979, p.409; Concina, 1975; A. Alverà Bortolotto, *Storia della ceramica a Venezia dagli albori alla fine della Repubblica*, Florence, 1981, pp.16, 88–92; A. Alverà Bortolotto, *Maiolica a Venezia nel Rinascimento*, Bergamo, 1988, p.86, 89, figs.48, 51.

3 Pavone, 1985, pp.49–67.

240

1 See further Curnow, 1992, cat.no.90.

2 Pavone, 1985, pp.49–67, pl.VIIa.

3 For similar examples see Lessmann, 1979, cat.no.691; Concino, 1975, pl.XXXXVI. For a complete list see Lessmann, 1979, p.409.

241

1 See further Curnow, 1992, cat.no.91.

2 For similar examples see Lessmann, 1979, cat.nos.717, 719, 726–7.

242

1 See further Curnow, 1992, cat.no.92.

2 J.E. Poole, *Italian Maiolica and Incised Slipware in the Fitzwilliam Museum, Cambridge*, Cambridge, 1995, pp.419-20, cat.no.450.

3 For similar examples see Lessmann, 1979, cat.nos.696, 717, 720–1.

243

1 See further Curnow, 1992, cat.no.93.

244

1 Ibid., cat.no.89.

2 Lessman (1979, p.335) was responsible for defining the oeuvre of the Zenobia painter, identifying nineteen plates decorated by this distinctive hand.

3 Ibid., cat.no.467.

4 Ibid., cat.nos.468–9. For further examples see Rackham, 1977, cat.no.910 and acc.no.C47–1970; Lessmann, 1979, cat.no.484; R. Gresta, 'Il Pittore Zenobia: aggiunte e considerazioni' in T. Wilson (ed.), *Italian Renaissance Pottery*, London, 1991, pp.74–9.

5 T. Clifford and J.V.G. Mallet, 'Battista Franco as a Designer for Maiolica', *Burlington Magazine*, CXVIII, 1976, especially figs.55–6, 86–7.

245

1 Information kindly provided by Linda Woolley, Curator of Early Textiles at the Victoria and Albert Museum, London. Compare also velvet in Florence described as 'Venetian or Spanish sixteenth century' in G. Cantelli, *Il Museo Stibbert*, Florence, 1974, no.246.

246

1 Venice, Palazzo Ducale, *Il genio della tradizione*, exh. cat. ed. by D. Davanzo Poli, Venice, 2004. E. Zucchetta, 'La Manifattura della Seta Veneziana; I luoghi, I santi patrone, le opere d'arte' in D. Davanzo Poli and S. Moronato, *Le Stoffe dei Veneziani*, Venice, 1994, pp.39–47.

247

1 Information kindly provided by Linda Woolley, Curator of Early Textiles at the Victoria and Albert Museum, London.

248

1 Ibid.

249

1 The Cappella del Sacramento, which adjoins the church, survived the 1583 fire. It originally housed Jacopo Tintoretto's *Christ Washing the Disciples' Feet*, now in the National Gallery, London (fig.35).